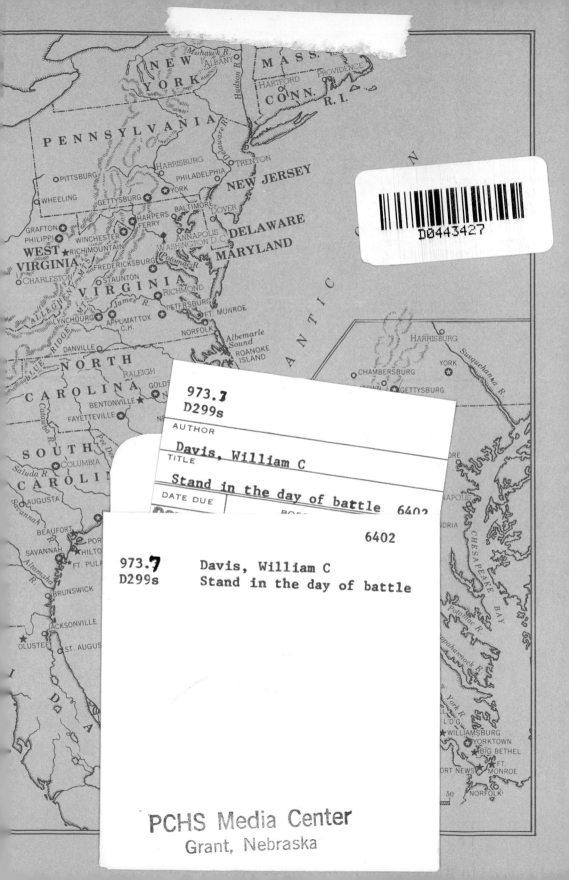

Stand in the Day
of Battle

VOLUME 2
OF
THE IMPERILED UNION:
1861–1865

Stand in the Day of Battle

VOLUME 2
OF
THE IMPERILED UNION:
1861–1865

WILLIAM C. DAVIS

DOUBLEDAY & COMPANY, INC.
Garden City, New York
1983

Library of Congress Cataloging in Publication Data

Davis, William C., 1946–
Stand in the day of battle.

(The Imperiled Union; v. 2)
Includes bibliographical references and index.
1. United States—History—Civil War, 1861–1865.
I. Title.   II. Series: Davis, William C., 1946–   .
The Imperiled Union; v. 2.
E468.D38   1983   973.7
ISBN: 0-385-14895-X
Library of Congress Catalog Card Number 82–45521

6402

CONTENTS

LIST OF PHOTOGRAPHS   vii

AUTHOR'S PREFACE   ix

INTRODUCTION   xi

Chapter 1   "Their Blue-grass and Fat Cattle Are Against Us"   1

Chapter 2   "Shall We Have a Government?"   18

Chapter 3   "It Is Glorious to See Such Courage"   32

Chapter 4   "These Monitors Are Miserable Failures"   49

Chapter 5   "Paper! Paper! Come Get Your Paper!"   68

Chapter 6   "I Am a Damned Sight Better General"   86

Chapter 7   "Hurl Forward Your Howling Lines"   106

Chapter 8   "We Can't Stop to Build Locomotives"   134

Chapter 9   "Go Forward to a Decisive Victory"   150

Chapter 10   "Settle the Fate of Vicksburg"   168

Chapter 11   "All Our Women Are Florence Nightingales"   196

Chapter 12 "The Crowning Stroke of Our Diplomacy"   222

Chapter 13 "No Bed of Roses"   240

Chapter 14 "We Ought Not to Destroy the Seed Corn"   260

Chapter 15 "How Came We to Lose Chattanooga?"   278

Chapter 16 "Nothing Could Be More Magnanimous"   299

Chapter 17 "It Has Proved a Far Better Year"   313

DOCUMENTATION BY CHAPTER   .   328

INDEX   347

LIST OF PHOTOGRAPHS

Following Page 72

1. Braxton Bragg, commanding general of the Confederate Army of Tennessee
2. Major General John Cabell Breckinridge of Kentucky
3. President Abraham Lincoln
4. Clement Laird Vallandigham, leader of the "Copperhead" movement
5. Major General Ambrose Everett Burnside
6. General Robert Edward Lee
7. View of Fredericksburg, Virginia, on the Rappahannock
8. Admiral John Adolphus Bernard Dahlgren
9. A bombproof in Battery Wagner, Charleston, South Carolina
10. A Federal battery on Morris Island aimed at Fort Sumter, South Carolina
11. New York Herald field headquarters for journalists
12. Alfred R. Waud, battlefield artist for one of the illustrated weeklies
13. Mathew B. Brady and some of his photographic assistants
14. Major General Joseph Hooker
15. Lieutenant General Thomas Jonathan "Stonewall" Jackson
16. Wilderness Church and the Melzie Chancellor house, Chancellorsville, Virginia
17. Major General George Gordon Meade's headquarters, behind Cemetery Hill, Gettysburg, Pennsylvania
18. Brigadier General Joseph Reid Anderson

Following Page 168

19. Colonel Josiah Gorgas

20. *Railroads in the South were also casualties*
21. *Major General William Tecumseh Sherman*
22. *Major General John Alexander McClernand*
23. *Major General Earl Van Dorn*
24. *Vicksburg, Mississippi, seen behind Yankee gunboat* Vindicator
25. *Underground bivouac of the 45th Illinois at the Shirley House, Vicksburg, Mississippi*
26. *Admiral David Dixon Porter and officers*
27. *Nurses and officials of the United States Sanitary Commission*
28. *Clara Barton*
29. *A Confederate blockade-runner,* Giraffe, *fitted out in Glasgow, Scotland*
30. *Great Britain built rams for the South like the* Wivern *which eventually were impounded and used by the British*
31. *Major General Theophilus Hunter Holmes*
32. *Lieutenant General Edmund Kirby-Smith*
33. *Jefferson Davis, President of the Confederacy*
34. *John Henninger Reagan, Confederate Postmaster General*
35. *"Parson" William Gannaway Brownlow, Union loyalist in Tennessee*
36. *Alexander Hamilton Stephens, Vice-President of the Confederacy*
37. *Robert Augustus Toombs, once Secretary of State of the Confederacy*
38. *Louis Trezevant Wigfall, once a supporter and later opponent of Davis*
39. *Lee & Gordon's Mills on Chickamauga Creek, northwest Georgia*
40. *Major General William Starke Rosecrans*

Following Page 264

41. *Lieutenant General Leonidas Polk*
42. *Major General George Henry Thomas*
43. *Chattanooga, Tennessee, with Lookout Mountain in the distance*
44. *Major General Benjamin Franklin Butler*
45. *Major General Nathaniel Prentiss Banks*
46. *Major General George Gordon Meade and some of his commanders*
47. *Lieutenant General James "Old Pete" Longstreet*
48. *Fort Sanders, Knoxville, Tennessee*
49. *General Joseph Eggleston Johnston, a postwar photo*
50. *Lieutenant General Ulysses S. Grant*

AUTHOR'S PREFACE

Things happen in the center. Contests, whether wars or games, are more often won in the middle than at the end. So it was with the Civil War, when America at mid-century sought a center ground of its own, a place where North and South could stand together. It took that war to bring them there, though the ground, once found, would remain infirm for a long time to come.

And so it is that there is a lot to happen in the middle volume of a trilogy looking backward at that war. Its predecessor, *Deep Waters of the Proud*, left the divided nation in the wake of the questionable Union victory at Antietam in September 1862, and with the Emancipation Proclamation that was its aftermath. It was not the turning point that so many have sought, but rather a returning point for North and South, when the extremes that drove them to war were softened by the resurgence of consensus. After decades of invective and acrimony, the age-old American impulse of compromise, of leadership from the center, came once more to the fore in 1862. The only problem was that in 1862 it was ruling in two nations, not just one.

In the eighteen months that followed, the months of *Stand in the Day of Battle*, decisions were made, and the war, militarily, politically, economically, and diplomatically, was won and lost. To be sure, there would be more than a year of war left to follow, but the decisions were here in the months of 1863, in the fields of Pennsylvania and Tennessee, in the bayous of Mississippi, and in the drawing rooms of Europe and Richmond and Washington. Making those decisions were a host of men and women, more than any book can recount. And so they figure here in the persons of people representative of their class. U. S. Grant speaks for all of the new warriors who will make war "modern." Wade Hampton of South Carolina acts just as well for those Grant replaced, the warriors of old. Edmund Ruffin, the vitriolic Virginian, gives voice to the frustrations and fulminations of all the rabid secessionists, the men who envisioned a Southern nation. Mary Chesnut, through her wonderful diary, puts life in the stilted picture of all women North and South who fought their own kind of war. Owen Lovejoy, like other Republicans, shows the fire and zeal of the party builders, men with power they were not entirely trained to wield. John C. Breckinridge reveals the heartbreak of all the moderates, men and women torn by both sides, for whom choices were always the most trying. And Charles Francis Adams, cantankerous like all of his tribe, lived every bit of the drama and boredom and exasperation of those who played the delicate game of diplomacy.

These and others stand large in *Stand in the Day of Battle*. It is not intended to make of them heroes or figures beyond their importance. Rather, as in Greek drama of old, they are the chorus, in whose voice we can find some meaning and understanding of a tragedy of another time.

INTRODUCTION

War, like the wheel, moves in circles, yet ever forward as well, its destination unknown, its path uncertain. All that is unmistakable, immutable, is where war has been, and all the more so when people war upon their own kind, upon themselves. No conflict so sears the land, so boils the marrow of a population, as insurrection, rebellion, civil war. It carries more than devastation. It carries contagion, a cultural and emotional pestilence that, like the malarial bite of the mosquito, leaves its poison in the blood to sting again and again long after the infecting insect is dead and dust. Civil war is plague and famine, the unresolved and conflicting aspirations of onetime friends become a death wish. It is warfare gone wrong.

That madness ran high in the 1860s. America at mid-century came to flex the muscles of a burgeoning world power upon itself, making of its own flesh the proving ground for the temper of its steel, the fever of its blood. So many had accepted the coming of the war as inevitable, an "irrepressible conflict" they said, the natural collision of differing values, cultures, economies, the unavoidable clash of urban and rural, industrial and pastoral, the phrenetic and the phlegmatic, the North and the South. Even the great statesman whose brooding presence so dominates the era, Abraham Lincoln, can come to speak almost offhandedly as he says "and the war came."

Everyone blames the other. In the South they are innocent farmers, living out the life their forebears brought to the land two centuries before. Theirs is a distinctive culture, they think. Benjamin Franklin, one "Yankee" they can look to with pride, had declared when a people become distinct from their brethren, they deserve—indeed, require—a distinct national identity as well. So felt the South. They toiled the land, not in factories, they dealt in hospitality, not hard coin. Their interests were distinct to their region, to the crops that supported it, to the system of labor that produced it. They did, after all, buy and sell their workers. But was that any worse than those industrial slaves in the North, underpaid, overworked, unable to live on their wages, or without them? Slavery was, to be sure, a "peculiar institution" to the South, but a benign, paternal, even wholesome means to deal not only with the work to be done, but also with the 3.5 million Negroes who would otherwise be loosed unskilled, uneducated, and perhaps ineducable, upon the country. Surely, with differences such as these, and more, the South deserved to govern itself, to protect its own interests. Self-interest has been and will be the guiding motivation of the American experience since the landing at Jamestown and before, and no one in the newly formed Confederate States of America sought to deny that. All they wanted when they decided to leave the Union in 1860 and 1861 was to be free to pursue that interest. They did not want war. They simply desired, said their new President Jefferson Davis, "to be left alone."

Yet where interests conflict, the only arbiters are compromise or the sword, and in the North, in the old Union, there were those who took a much different view. America was a growing land, soon to be ready to assume its rightful place as a leading member in the family of nations. It could not continue to grow with slavery as its nutriment. The North abandoned slavery decades before the war, and applied ever-increasing pressure on the South to do likewise. It was not only an injustice to the blacks—though free blacks received little enough justice above Mason and Dixon's line—but as well a blight on America's fair name, she the last major civilized nation on earth to permit the bartering of souls. It was an abomination before God. Certainly the workhouses and factories in the North did not swaddle their laborers in riches, but neither did they beat them with whips, mutilate the unruly men, rape the women, and sell the children away from their families. As it happens, neither did the slaveholders in the South by a great measure, but few to the north countenanced the fact. Only recently had the Union gone to war with a foreign "aggressor" and wrested from Mexico a great cache of land to the west. Joined with the territories already claimed but unsettled, the Union could stretch to the Pacific, sprawled over enough acreage for three great nations, let alone one. But it all must be one nation, and the North did not go to war with Mexico and England before it to see all that booty tainted with slavery.

Clad in the righteous armor of truth, so they thought, these gladiators of North and South approached each other, in fact, in the rude and often shabby garb of their own interests, woven in their personal and sectional insecurities, fastened by their fears. They approached the arena as warriors of iron purpose and stern resolve, yet when they met in their circus, the Congress, the legislatures, the public press, the ballot box, the best they could do in battle was to hurl at one another their own frailties.

There was no true compromise. And in the end in the election of 1860, the fickle crowds at the theater turned their thumbs down on the South, or so it seemed. They chose a President—some would call him an emperor in time—to whom the South could not submit. An enemy of slavery, a low-born plebeian from the West, Lincoln and his rude manner seemed hardly fit to rule over and protect the interests of a people who despised him, a people whose crops included indigo, but whose cloaks were purple.

They had no choice in the South, now. As men they must fight for their rights, if necessary. They left the Union in their devotion to a sort of perverted synergism in which the parts are greater than the whole. They left, they hoped, in peace. But they left, as always, with rhetoric, with bravado. "*Morituri te salutant,*" said the gladiators of antiquity before they drew their steel. "We who are about to die salute you."

And the war came. And they died.

What none of them expected, North or South, was that this war would become, in fact, a revolution, not of one side against the other, but of ideology, of society, of economy, of a score of facets of American life that no one could have foreseen would be affected by what everyone did expect would be only a summer's worth of war. The victor in the military struggle was preordained from the firing of the first shot. The infant Confederacy was doomed at birth with premature death. Never in the first year and a half of the war, the eighteen months that saw this war become a revolution, did the South have a clear opportunity to achieve its independence, not so long as the Union and its crafty guiding hand maintained their resolve not to let "the erring sisters" go. The Union will win this war more by will than weapons, yet though the victor might in retrospect be determined from the start, the *outcome* of the Civil War was not.

Certainly that was the lesson of those first eighteen months, if any cared to learn it. The summer's war outlasted the hot weather, to the surprise of most. Indeed, a few like Colonel William Tecumseh Sherman, preparing his brigade for the march into Virginia in July 1861 that would surely end the rebellion, admitted privately that they saw years of fighting ahead. But there had been too much "sooth" already in bringing this war, and too many sayers. Action, swift and decisive action, would count now.[1]

The "action" of those early months, however, demonstrated to North and South that it would not be such a speedy war after all. The Union learned it by suffering two humiliating defeats in a row, first the loss of Fort Sumter to the opening guns of the war in Charleston harbor, and then on July 21 by losing in rout to an enemy arrayed on the fields around Bull Run. Clearly, despite some more heartening successes west of the Mississippi, the Union was not going to prevail this summer of 1861. It would take more men, more material, more organization, more resolve, to fulfill its destiny. But there was an equally lucid message for the South in its victories. The North did not crumble before its invincible foe. Beaten, it retreated not to retire, but to return. There would be no easy victory for the Confederacy. It would be more than a summertime war after all.

The longer it continued, the worse it got for the South as well, though most, North and South, did not see it. In the East, the army that had failed at Bull Run spent the next seven months rebuilding under a self-proclaimed Napoleon who thirsted not only for command of the beaten army, but of all Union armies as well, and for the Presidency itself in time. Major General George Brinton McClellan made himself the measure of the war in Virginia and Maryland for over a year after Bull Run. The cause of the Union failed when he failed, succeeded when he succeeded, moved only when he moved. Even to Lincoln himself, McClellan showed his patrician contempt both for civilian control of the army in a democratic society, and for the motives which animated many of the politicians who sought to use the government to control his army for their own ends. He only wanted the rebellion put down and America returned to the Union of old, with slavery intact and the Federal Government under reins by restricting its powers. The newly risen Republican Party wanted something altogether different, and he and they were destined to conflict. He fought them by refusing to move "their" army until he was ready. They fought him by withholding his troops from him, pressuring the President to find another general, and in the end by removing him from command.

His campaigns were failures. When he moved his army to the peninsula between the York and James rivers in Virginia in the spring of 1862, he had a clear road to Richmond, yet missed the way by his own timidity. He made siege at Yorktown, fought Seven Days of battles, but missed his prize by a few miles. Anxious to command, he feared to lead, and so he failed. Another general, John Pope, led another army into Virginia that summer. With more aggressiveness than McClellan, and less sense, he too failed, a second loss at a Second Bull Run. McClellan's petulant refusal to aid Pope until too late lent major aid to their nemesis, the Confederate General Robert Edward Lee, yet "Little Mac" would take a measure of revenge.

In a bold, but questionable move, Lee invaded Maryland in September 1862, bound for Pennsylvania, and perhaps even Washington. Such an invasion, if successful, might bring the North to its knees, forcing upon it the humiliation and the realization that the South *would* be independent. Yet Lee sought too much with too few, and when there was too little really to gain. But the Confederacy had not learned the lesson of the two Bull Runs. The Union did not yet have the men to win battles, though it did possess a resolve not to lose a war. And McClellan, hesitating, tardy, timorous as always, still managed to meet Lee at last. Despite overwhelming advantages, "Little Mac" barely managed a drawn battle along Antietam Creek in Maryland, but Lee could not weather even a draw. He had to retire into Virginia, and the Union in the East had its first "victory." For McClellan it was his first and last. Despite Lincoln's proddings, he failed to pursue his advantage, and began to let the months slip by while he politicked and, some thought, intentionally allowed the enemy to regroup. Lincoln removed McClellan from command and put him out of the war. Already the revolution was well under way. Lincoln and the Republicans were taking the Commander-in-Chief provision from the Constitution and changing it from a mere statement of intent into a dynamic fact. Uniform or not, Lincoln would be the commanding general in this Union army, and not for another ninety years would a general challenge the civil authority that ruled him.

Greater still was the revolution occurring west of the Alleghenies. Everyone's focus, the eyes of the governments at Washington and Richmond, of the press, and most of the people, were set to view the war as a contest for Virginia. But gradually, beyond their realization at first, the West that had been the guiding motivation throughout the spread across the continent, claimed the major role for itself. In Virginia the first year and a half of the war saw little more than a contest for the hundred miles between the two capitals. To the armies that repeatedly marched and retreated and marched it yet again, surely it seemed the longest hundred miles imaginable. Meanwhile, the armies out West—that West between the Appalachians and the Mississippi—were marching and claiming and losing mileage measured in the thousands. And there the course of the war was being foretold.

It, too, came to be a measure of the rise of one man, Ulysses S. Grant. Starting the conflict as a lowly colonel of volunteers, the recent alumnus of repeated failure, he had a facility—not of his own doing—for being in the right spot at the proper time. Once there, he also showed a disposition—entirely of his own making—for doing the right thing. A political friend from Illinois got him an early promotion to brigadier general, but his own earned successes brought his further ascent. At the war's start the Union strategy called for surrounding the South from all sides and slowly constricting its breath until it expired. Virtually all of the Confederacy lay bounded by water, which made control of the great Mississippi and its tributaries paramount. And Grant and others saw as well that those tributaries, particularly the Cumberland and Tennessee rivers, provided natural pathways to invasion of the heartland of Tennessee, indeed to the very center of the South. He took that control when he captured Forts Henry and Donelson, the Confederate earthworks that commanded entrance to the two rivers, thus opening the interior to Union gunboats, and putting Grant in the rear of the Southern army trying desperately to hold on in Kentucky. The Bluegrass State was abandoned and when the Confederate general Albert Sidney Johnston challenged Grant for control of western Tennessee, and thereby Kentucky, in the Battle of Shiloh in April 1862, Johnston lost his battle, Kentucky, and his life. A general named George Henry Thomas, a Virginian who stayed with the Union, turned the other end of Johnston's line in eastern Kentucky, at Mill Springs. By the spring of 1862 a Confederate Kentucky was only a memory, and a dream.

Grant went into eclipse for a time, but not the Union march in the West. Important island fortresses in the Mississippi fell to advancing Union arms, cities like Memphis and earthworks with names like Fort Pillow soon flew Old Glory, and when Grant once again emerged as a commander that summer, he began his year-long courtship of the fortress city of Vicksburg. West of the great river, small yet important little battles with prosaic names like Prairie Grove captured few headlines in the East, but they saved Missouri for the Union, thereby protecting an otherwise vulnerable flank and rear for the Federals advancing down the Mississippi.

In short, while a year and more of fighting in Virginia and Maryland achieved nothing more than maintenance of the essential status quo prior to First Bull Run, that same span of days had seen demonstrable progress in the West, a clear and steady victorious advance by those rough-hewn Westerners in blue, and the stubborn but equally steady loss of ground for the Confederacy. Kentucky, Missouri, western Tennessee, and New Orleans, all were lost by the South, and once control of the western rivers left the Confederates' hands, so went their best hope of repelling invasion at its start. Indeed, the Lincoln government would have done well to do nothing more than fight a holding action in Virginia while sending its real might crushing into the South from the Mississippi. In fact, a holding action was all that McClellan and his predecessors had accomplished in the East. And there would be more defeats as well before generals brought Lincoln victories in Virginia. But being a politician, and being human, he could do naught else but spend his best efforts on the Washington-Richmond line. A major Rebel army sat less than 100 miles from the capital. Lincoln could hardly weaken the East to strengthen the West. Besides, he like so many others as yet failed to realize that the loss of a capital did not mean either for him or for Jefferson Davis the loss of a war. The Union would only fail to win when it lost the resolve to win; the South would fall only when it finally lost the will and the strength to resist, and that meant not the capture of its capital, but the destruction of its armies, its economy, perhaps even its way of life. This was never a true life-and-death struggle for the North; for the Confederacy it was never anything else.

And so, by September 1862, the war had changed dramatically, the revolution begun but, as always in America, a somewhat conservative revolution. Beginning from extremes, both sides sought the center. Born of rabid localism and states' rights, the Confederacy very quickly gravitated toward a more and more powerful centralized government not so different from the one it had so recently repudiated. So quickly, in fact, that Davis had to contend almost from the start with a vocal and growing opposition within his own government. So intent upon doctrine that they could not see the damage they were inflicting upon their own cause, men like Robert Barnwell Rhett and William Lowndes Yancey, regarding themselves as the fathers of secession, felt betrayed by their own rebellion. Yet, as always in this conflict, the instinct for the general good abandoned the extreme in the quest for the center ground. Davis himself was a compromise, never a fire-eating secessionist, but no ardent Unionist either. Upon him at least, if upon no one else in the South, a majority of Confederates could agree and unite.

Lincoln, too, walked a narrow beat between his own enemies in the extreme. His own party, led by doctrinaire men like Charles Sumner, senator from Massachusetts, wanted a terrible revenge on the South for its affront to the flag. They wanted as well emancipation and even arming of slaves in order to send them into the lists in their own behalf. Intoxicated with their newfound ascendancy in the national government, they wanted the causes of Union and abolition made one. Yet to do so, as Lincoln well knew, would alienate that almost equally large segment of the Northern population that cared little or nothing for the issue of slavery, or even favored it. They were people who would go into this war only for the preservation of the Union, not emancipation, not subjugation. They were people like McClellan. Change dramatically the purpose of the prosecution of the conflict, and many of them would withdraw their support, their purchases of the bonds that were financing the fight, and their enlistments. Indeed, by mid-1862 there was already a vocal and growing minority called Copperheads who openly opposed the war on any grounds, and demanded, as Horace Greeley had said, that the erring sisters be let go. Worse, this sympathy ran particularly high in those states along the border, Maryland, Missouri and, most dangerous of all, Kentucky. Always, North and South, eyes turn toward the Bluegrass State. Lose it to the Confederates, thought Lincoln, and lose the war.

And so Lincoln, like Davis, bridged the extremes, though he managed them better than his Confederate counterpart. He, too, wanted to see emancipation, but he came to it as war policy with agonizing graduality. After all, he could hardly end slavery in states unless the Washington government had the authority to impose and enforce emancipation. Winning the war must take precedence. Yet he would make a start. When McClellan gave him a questionable victory on the Antietam, Lincoln announced a preliminary Emancipation Proclamation. Ironically, it only declared as free the slaves in states then in rebellion against the government, in other words, in areas where he could not yet enforce the decree. But it was a start, it gave promise, and it came only after he and the press and the public gradually accepted abolition as a part of the means of saving the Union, as one more weapon in the arsenal against rebellion.

Neither Lincoln nor Davis did their work alone. Many, many walked with them this dangerous road through a forest of death and madness.

Men like Owen Lovejoy of Illinois, friend of Lincoln's, soldier, congressman, who persuaded the rail-splitter to become a Republican, and who urged him gently but constantly toward emancipation. Men like Charles Francis Adams, who thought Lincoln a fool and caricature at first, but who served him ably as minister to Great Britain, fighting that gentle and courtly battle to keep England neutral despite strong urges in some quarters for John Bull to take open side with the Confederacy. Men like Jay Cooke, entrepreneur, financier, a man with an eye for the main chance, yet one as well with a certain loyalty to the Union, and a genius for selling bonds and notes that could raise the money to arm the armies. Men like David Glasgow Farragut, a Tennessean who remained loyal and, even though seemingly past his prime in years, took a leading role in making the navy an important contributor in the war effort by capturing New Orleans. Now he was working with another contributor, Grant, to pluck the rest of the Mississippi from a tenuous Confederate grasp. And Grant himself, of course, one of the few constants in an ever-changing Union military high command. He was the quintessential Westerner, more competent than brilliant, more fight than talk, unimpressive and indomitable. For four years in the Union army, he would be the measure of success.

But to achieve that success, Lincoln and his friends had to prevail over men of equal variety, of equal conviction, and often of equal or surpassing talent. Davis was becoming an ever better war President, and he had to. His own Vice-President, Alexander Hamilton Stephens of Georgia, was rapidly becoming an opponent. The Yanceys and the Rhetts sniped at him in the press and in the Capitol. Ardent Southern nationalists like the old agriculturalist-turned-soldier Edmund Ruffin would support him, but only so far. Davis did have good soldiers in the field, but they, too, could be troublesome. General Joseph Eggleston Johnston, victor at First Bull Run, quickly became an enemy over matters of rank and promotion. So did Pierre Gustave Toutant Beauregard, the hero of Fort Sumter. But the President did get along with others, competent rising officers like the aristocrat Wade Hampton of South Carolina, who armed and equipped his own small army, Hampton's Legion, for the cause. And he enjoyed excellent relations with a man once the youngest Vice-President of the United States, and now a Confederate major general out in Mississippi, John Cabell Breckinridge of Kentucky. Despite the opponents within his government, Davis also had powerful and able friends. His Postmaster General, admittedly a minor portfolio in a war for survival, was Texan John Henninger Reagan, who could do more with less than any cabinet officer on either side. And his Attorney General, then Secretary of War, and now Secretary of State was Judah Philip Benjamin, a Sephardic Jew from Louisiana who, in addition to unquestioned diplomatic ability, possessed as well that rare facility to avoid infuriating Davis.

All these and more bound their hands with their causes, though for most of them their perceptions of their cause and its goals differed. As always, keeping them together for a common purpose was a matter of constant compromise. Self-interest governed the course of American affairs since its early days, and it was no different now. To win, Lincoln and Davis must both persuade, cajole, threaten, and often mislead, to keep the disparate elements together that they needed to wage their wars, to effect the gradual revolutions that each oversaw. As the second year and a half of the war commenced, so began a new war, a different war. And like so much of the old war of 1861–62, it began in the West, and in the dream of Kentucky.

"The Lord hath appeared for us,
  the Lord hath covered our heads,
  and made us to stand in the day of battle."

From "A Psalm or Hymn of Praise and Thanksgiving after Victory"
in THE BOOK OF COMMON PRAYER

Stand in the Day
of Battle

VOLUME 2
OF
THE IMPERILED UNION:
1861–1865

CHAPTER 1

"THEIR BLUE-GRASS
AND FAT CATTLE
ARE AGAINST US"

On August 14, 1862, an old friend arrived at Major General John C. Breckinridge's headquarters tent near Port Hudson, Louisiana. It was Colonel Josiah Stoddard Johnston, also a Kentuckian, and a relation by marriage, now a member of General Braxton Bragg's staff. He found Breckinridge tired from a busy summer, and anxious about the health of his command in the hot and sickly climate.

The former Vice-President had done a lot since his first taste of battle at Shiloh the previous April. There had been the siege at Corinth, Mississippi, and following that several weeks at Vicksburg, where he and his brigades helped Major General Earl Van Dorn defend the city against the first tentative efforts of Grant and Farragut. Then Van Dorn had sent Breckinridge south late in July with orders to attack and take Baton Rouge. Unhappy with the assignment, as his men dropped in heaps from the heat and malaria, Breckinridge still nearly accomplished the task, failing only when the ersatz ironclad *Arkansas* failed to appear in time to drive Federal gunboats away from Baton Rouge. But then Breckinridge of his own accord moved on to Port Hudson, of more strategic value than his first objective, and there began erecting the earthworks and defenses that would help make it a bastion for nearly a year.

Now came Johnston. He brought a letter from Bragg, and wonderful news. The Confederates were going back into Kentucky. "I should be much better satisfied were you with me on the impending campaign," said Bragg. "Your influence in Kentucky would be equal to an extra division in my army." He had a division waiting for Breckinridge, he wrote, "and I hope to see your eyes beam again at the command 'Forward,' as they did at Shiloh."[1]

Once more the dream of Kentucky. In fact, it had never waned since those sad days in February when Breckinridge and the rest of the army bravely marched out of the state. Kentucky was the Confederacy's natural northern border. More, the state was fruitful, and the South was learning already that it would be hard pressed to produce foodstuffs sufficient to meet the needs of hundreds of thousands of men under arms, not to mention a civil population that would slowly see the produce of increasing amounts of acreage denied it by enemy conquest. And there were men, good men, in Kentucky, and certainly they wanted to join hands with their Southern brethren, but they were prevented from doing so by the Federal yoke then strangling the state. After all, had not three thousand or more already made their way to Tennessee in the early days to take arms and form Breckinridge's 1st Kentucky Brigade? A few thousand men of the Bluegrass served also in the mounted arm, dashing men like John Hunt Morgan. Those Kentuckians all seemed men of daring, men of destiny. The Confederacy needed them and their state.

Even Bragg's wife may have played a part. In the spring of 1862, after the army had retired from Corinth to Tupelo, Mississippi, Elise Bragg wrote to her husband that he must advance at every opportunity "until you are before *Cincinnati*." The Confederates could not win a battle and then rest and wait. "What was done in the heathenish days of Rome, will not answer in the nineteenth century, with R. Roads, rivers, steam navigation." Speedy communications required active armies. "Why not," she posited, "take our army round into Tennessee & thence into Kentucky"? That was precisely what he now intended to do.[2]

In fact, despite whatever influence Mrs. Bragg may have exerted, Bragg's planned campaign was dictated by military and political necessity. Already there existed in his army, and in Richmond, a powerful bloc of Kentuckians whose influence with Davis and the army high command was considerable, and growing. Davis himself was a Kentuckian by birth. He and everyone else, including Breckinridge, greatly misjudged the true feelings of the bulk of Kentuckians. Of Southern rights sympathy, surely there was plenty, but it was a giant leap from sympathy to the taking of arms against the old Union, the Union of Henry Clay. Only the coming campaign would tell.

Early in the summer Bragg executed a brilliant maneuver, moving his army intact by rail from Tupelo south to Mobile, then northeast to Atlanta, then northwest to Chattanooga, Tennessee. It covered nearly 800 miles in barely a week, wonderful considering the chaotic variation in roadbeds and equipment that plagued all Southern railroads. By doing so, Bragg had completely outflanked the enemy in Mississippi and, with the advantage of the unexpectedness of his move, he could look out upon a clear and relatively effortless path through middle Tennessee and into Kentucky. In a plan too ambitious for the practical limits of geography and the Confederate command system, however, Bragg also sought to consolidate his own army at Chattanooga with elements of a half dozen other commands, among them the small army of Edmund Kirby-Smith, who actually commanded the Department of East Tennessee, through which Bragg would pass. And Bragg wanted Breckinridge, and thus began a tale of misunderstanding, jealousy, resentment, and bitterness, that characterized this western Army of Tennessee for the next year and a half, typifying as well the weaknesses in Bragg, the command system, the motivation of many Confederates in uniform, and even the nature of the Confederate experiment.

Breckinridge, in fact, knew of the impending Kentucky move for some time before his friend Johnston appeared with Bragg's letter. Fully a month earlier he wrote to President Davis requesting that he be allowed to accompany the advancing army. Well-timed calls on the President by Kentucky's representatives in the Congress emphasized the perceived importance of having the leading Kentuckian in the South go with Bragg, and Davis confessed to being "moved" by the entreaties. But he could do nothing, he said, with Grant threatening Vicksburg and Van Dorn defending the city with too few men already. Perhaps Breckinridge himself could go, but they could not spare his troops. Yet for the onetime Vice-President, it was essential that his Kentucky soldiers accompany him. The Mississippi and Louisiana climate was killing them, and they, too, would be useful in recruiting in the Bluegrass.[3]

Torn in his frustration, Breckinridge wrote to Bragg that "I would make any sacrifice to join you." But he could not leave his troops. "My heart goes with you," he said. Then Van Dorn began vacillating, thinking he might spare the general, then that he might not. Caught in the middle between two superiors, Breckinridge could only lament that "I groan and obey." At last Bragg peremptorily ordered Van Dorn to release the Kentuckians, and when that produced nothing, the Secretary of War did as well. On September 19, after almost three months of delays, Breckinridge set his command in motion. The men knew where they were going, and sang and danced, and caroused as only they could. They were going home.[4]

Or so they thought. Even before Bragg's troubles in acquiring Breckinridge for his campaign, other problems emerged. The Confederate command system simply did not allow for the sort of thing he had in mind. Kirby-Smith did not feel inclined to see another general come into his department and assume direction of his army. The President declined Bragg's request that the War Department assign Kirby-Smith to him for the time being, and their relations soon broke down. Kirby-Smith decided that, rather than cooperate with Bragg, he would launch his own Kentucky campaign, moving toward Lexington. Bragg, who had hoped first to work with Kirby-Smith to drive the Federals out of middle Tennessee, now changed his own course, fearing that if he did not move his army into eastern Kentucky, Kirby-Smith would be too exposed. Bragg would keep the main Federal army led by Major General Don Carlos Buell, who may have saved Grant at Shiloh, occupied and off Kirby-Smith's flank. If Van Dorn and others would advance as well into western Tennessee, Bragg hoped that "we may all unite in Ohio."[5]

Bragg accomplished something of a reorganization of his army in Chattanooga before launching his campaign. It was an exercise he would engage in repeatedly whenever he thought he smelled malcontents or, worse, enemies in his officer corps. This was to be his first campaign in top command. Before he had responsibility, to be sure, but the ultimate responsibility had rested with Johnston and Beauregard at Shiloh. Now if Bragg won or lost, all the glory or the shame would be his. Something in his makeup made him mortally fearful of failure, and such people, in positions of high authority, inevitably develop a finely tuned paranoia. No exception, Bragg began looking for scapegoats in case of failure even before his army crossed into Kentucky. As always, he would find them in his own camps.

He started the march north on August 28, well before Breckinridge was allowed to leave Louisiana, and while Bragg still entertained a high opinion of him. But the campaign simply did not define its goals well from the start, and despite early successes, its future did not look good. In two weeks the Confederates reached Glasgow, Kentucky, and on September 17 Bragg captured a small Federal garrison at Munfordville. There was an element of almost comic opera in the affair. With barely more than 4,000 men in his command, Federal Colonel John Thomas Wilder found himself surrounded by an army six times his size. He had no real military experience, yet when the demand for surrender came to him, he recoiled at the thought of capitulation. The best thing he could do was to ask advice of a professional. The professional he chose to ask was Confederate General Simon Bolivar Buckner, now released from prison after his capture at Fort Donelson and currently commanding a division in Bragg's army. Under flag of truce, Wilder called on Buckner to ask what he should do! Gallant to the extreme, Buckner declined to advise since it would be a clear conflict of interest, but he did show Wilder around his camps. Seeing the overwhelming strength against him, the Yankee colonel finally conceded that "I believe I'll surrender."

It was the last real success of the campaign. Though in a good spot to cut Buell's line of supply and communications, thus forcing the Federal to attack Bragg on ground of his own choosing, Bragg instead moved on, anxious to reach the central part of the state where the recruits and their foodstuffs should flock to his standards. He then sat his army for ten days at Bardstown, while he went himself to Lexington, where Kirby-Smith had preceded him. On October 4 in Frankfort they installed Richard Hawes as the Confederate "governor" of Kentucky, declaring a Southern administration now in control. That would empower him to conscript soldiers and confiscate supplies, if need be. Yet even while Hawes took his oath, the sounds of a coming battle could be heard in dispatches from Bardstown. Barely had Hawes finished his oath before Bragg abandoned his proclaimed promises to defend the capital against the Yankee invaders, and hastily organized a withdrawal. He would have to do battle.

It came at Perryville four days later. Substantially outnumbered and hampered by his own clumsy misuse of his army, Bragg took heavy losses that totaled nearly one fourth of the men engaged. It was a queer battle, both Bragg and Buell taking occasional advantages, yet both suffering as well from the atmosphere, an unseen enemy that, thanks to a phenomenon called acoustic shadow, at times kept both men from hearing the sounds of major battle close by. Yet at day's end, Bragg could see all too clearly that his Kentucky campaign was done. With Buell in his front in great numbers, he had no choice but to fall back into east Tennessee. Kirby-Smith did as well, and two weeks later the Confederate army passed through Cumberland Gap into the Volunteer State, the great dream failed once more.

But there was one item of great importance to Bragg even before he crossed that state line. Indeed, it had been almost paramount with him for several weeks prior to Perryville. The campaign was not going as planned, and Bragg had to know the reason why. It could not be him. It had to be his enemies in his own command. He had already been sniping at his commanders Leonidas Polk, Van Dorn, Kirby-Smith, and others in letters to Davis in Richmond. But now Kentuckians were failing him. They were not enlisting, and they were not forthcoming with supplies. "Their blue-grass and fat cattle are against us," moaned Kirby-Smith. That had to be the fault of Kentuckians, and none more so than Breckinridge. As early as September 17 Bragg was complaining that he desperately needed the 15,000 arms which Breckinridge was expected to have brought from Knoxville on his way to join the main army. A week later Bragg launched into a defense of himself in case of failure, a defense predicated upon blaming any such reverse on the Kentuckian. "The failure of Genl Breckinridge to carry out his part of my program has seriously embarrassed me, and moreover the whole campaign," he complained to President Davis. The fact that Kentuckians were not recruiting was because Breckinridge was not there to incite them. Bragg apparently saw nothing incongruous about the fact that Breckinridge could not get a majority of Kentuckians to vote for him in 1860, yet was expected to be able to persuade them to enlist for him in 1862. By the end of September, Bragg declared flatly to his top commanders that "Breckinridge has failed." Though fully aware of the obstacles that Van Dorn, Richmond, and even Bragg himself had put in the way of the Kentuckian coming speedily to join him, the commanding general now decided that Breckinridge had simply been guilty of sloth and had cost him the campaign.[6]

Thus Bragg was hardly impressed when Breckinridge, upon overcoming one obstacle after another, finally reached Knoxville on October 3. He had moved his command 1,100 miles in fourteen days, a move that rivaled Bragg's own shift of his army to Tennessee. "I hope you are satisfied with my energy since I was allowed to leave," the Kentuckian wired ahead to Bragg. "I have encountered every difficulty a man could meet." Bragg was not satisfied. And when Tennessee authorities now interfered to delay Breckinridge's movement even more, only the renewed intercession of the War Department in Richmond cleared the Kentuckian to resume the march. It was October 15 before he left Knoxville. The next night he and his command were close to Cumberland Gap, and the next morning's march brought them within sight of the mountains of southeastern Kentucky. But then came a messenger from Bragg. The campaign was over, the army retiring. Breckinridge was to turn his columns around and withdraw to Knoxville. Murmurings ran through the men as they waited at the roadside to find the import of that message. When they were ordered back onto the road, facing south, not north, they knew. In the ranks of the Kentucky Brigade there arose a great spontaneous shout, a single brief cry of frustration, and then off they walked away from their homeland once more. None could know that this was as close as they would come to their native soil for the rest of the war.[7]

Now Bragg commenced almost immediately yet another campaign. Kentucky was lost, for the time being, but middle Tennessee could still be saved. The enemy held Nashville, and to threaten them he ordered Breckinridge to take his command to Murfreesboro. As was often the case, Bragg selected a site with a few advantages, and many more liabilities. Murfreesboro did lie astride two natural routes of march against the capital, but paralleling them sat several more roads by which the enemy could easily advance and outflank the Confederates. Happily, the new Federal commander, William Starke Rosecrans, who replaced Buell shortly after Perryville, seemed in no hurry to move against Bragg. He gave Breckinridge several weeks to rest his men, reorganize his command, and even set up housekeeping in rented quarters in town with his wife, Mary. While Bragg marshaled his forces farther to the southeast at Tullahoma, the Kentuckian made a series of feints with his cavalry designed to create an illusion of greater strength than he possessed. It worked. Rosecrans soon reported that Breckinridge's meager 8,000 men numbered 25,000 or more. That was enough to make the Federals cautious and delay their anticipated advance on Murfreesboro until late December, and it gave Bragg time to enhance his army back to respectable strength, approaching 40,000.

On the surface, things appeared normal in the high command. Breckinridge seems to have been unaware of the growing resentment of Bragg, of the politicking that the commanding general was already doing to discredit his subordinate. Personal relations appear to have been normal. President Davis, sensing the unrest in the command from Bragg's letters, came to visit. John Hunt Morgan, the dashing cavalryman, married a lovely young lady, with all of the generals present and Breckinridge an attentive usher. Mary Breckinridge found herself "in a *transport* of joy" at being reunited with her husband. "My stay in Murfreesboro will always be remembered as the happiest period of my life," she would write just three months later.[8]

Yet within and behind the peaceful façade the army quaked with discontent from the very day on November 30 when Bragg arrived at Murfreesboro to assume command personally. The old wound of Kentucky would not heal quickly, made the worse now by the Kentuckians themselves. The men in the Kentucky brigade objected strenuously to Bragg's using enforced conscription in the Bluegrass to fill his ranks. Worse, he had issued an order that all male refugees from the state found within his lines be drafted. This was intolerable. All Kentuckians in the army were volunteers. Their state had not seceded, Confederate law was not in force in the state. They could hardly be subject to conscript laws. When the one-year enlistments of some of the Kentucky regiments themselves began to expire late that past summer, portions of two of the regiments actually mutinied, refusing to answer roll call and take up their arms when informed that the government intended to hold them in service for three years or the duration of the war. Breckinridge personally persuaded them to reconsider with a mixture of old-time stump-speaking cajolery, honest promises to get them a fair hearing of their grievance, and outright threats. Yet Breckinridge himself, as well as fellow Kentucky officers like Buckner and William Preston, also objected strenuously to the conscription. It was rumored that they talked of resignation in protest.

All this reached the ears of Bragg, and it was not designed to make him forget his anger at Breckinridge and his state. In December a resolution of praise and thanks for Bragg's campaign into the Bluegrass passed the Confederate House of Representatives, failing of unanimity by only two votes, those two inspired by Kentuckians in the capital. Worse, the press gave him a raking over the campaign. Even the governor that he installed so fleetingly in Frankfort, Richard Hawes, came out bitterly in print against Bragg's conduct of the campaign. The effect of it all was that by mid-December 1862, Bragg came to believe that Kentuckians were essentially cowards, not worthy of liberation. Her generals were politicians playing at war, and all of them together were too independent for the good of the army. When a corporal of the 6th Kentucky left ranks without leave on December 4 to go home and help his widowed mother prepare for the winter, hired bounty hunters went after him. They brought him back and Bragg ordered an immediate court-martial on charges of desertion. On December 20 Bragg approved a finding of guilty and a sentence of death. Further, with a nice sense of timing, he ordered that the man be shot by men of his own Kentucky brigade, in the presence of the full command, on the day after Christmas. For five days Breckinridge and the other Kentucky officers pleaded with Bragg to change his mind, or else postpone the execution and refer the case to the President. He refused, asserting that an example was needed to discourage such desertions, regardless of how extenuating the circumstances might be. The very morning of the appointed day Breckinridge made yet another try, but Bragg rebuffed him, allegedly saying that he would shoot every Kentuckian in the army if he had to in order to bend them to his will. Breckinridge shouted back that this was murder and that his men would not be treated like animals. Some companies of Kentuckians apparently ran to their arms, close to mutiny, before Breckinridge controlled them.

Finally the brigade was formed into a three-sided square, with the poor corporal facing it from the open end. Despite repeated refusals to command it, a firing squad was finally composed. Breckinridge spoke a few last words to the condemned, and received from him his personal effects, a pocketbook and a comb. Walking back to his horse, the general mounted as the ceremony of death began. Rain started falling, the squad fired, and the Kentuckian fell dead instantly. At the same moment, Breckinridge "was seized with a deathly sickness, dropped forward on the neck of his horse, and had to be caught by some of his staff." When a lawyer before the war, Breckinridge always declined to act as a prosecutor. It offended his admittedly exaggerated sensitivity of feeling. He would only defend. Yet now he was forced to preside over the military murder of one of his own men. He carried the corporal's effects with him for seven years until he could finally return them to the boy's mother. His loathing of Braxton Bragg he carried for the rest of his life.[9]

The timing could hardly have been less propitious for Bragg to be sowing discontent in his own garden. Even as he baited and prodded Breckinridge and the Kentuckians, so did he sharpen his sword against others in his officer corps. An army busy fighting within itself was hardly ready to meet the enemy, but the enemy was on its way. The very morning that the young corporal died, Rosecrans put his army of 47,000 on the march toward Murfreesboro. He had divined the possibilities available in the roads that flanked the Confederate positions around the town, and saw an opportunity to drive the enemy out of middle Tennessee. When he learned the news, Bragg decided to stand and fight.

Again as at Perryville he would allow the Yankees to attack him on ground of his own choosing, yet not necessarily well chosen. A stream called Stones River wound roughly north to south just west of Murfrees-boro, and along it Bragg arrayed his army. He divided it into two corps, commanded by Generals Leonidas Polk and William Joseph Hardee. Polk, an Episcopal bishop before the war, was ordered to cross the river and form the left of the line, while Hardee—including Breckinridge—remained on the town side of the stream to form the right. Rosecrans' main avenue of advance, the Nashville Pike, came in from the northwest and crossed Stones River just where Polk and Hardee's corps joined. As he awaited the Federal advance, however, Bragg became increasingly worried over reports that some Federals were in fact marching down the Lebanon Pike from directly north. That road would take them behind Hardee's right flank and into the vulnerable rear of the army. To Breckinridge fell the task of guarding the Lebanon route.

Late on December 30, with Rosecrans almost in sight, Bragg received new intelligence that there was no threat on the Lebanon Pike after all, and that the entire Federal army would be facing him west of Stones River. Consequently, he pulled half of Hardee's corps across the stream to prolong Polk's left, leaving Breckinridge and his division the only Confederate command east of the river. The Kentuckian recognized that an elevation in his front called Wayne's Hill was, due to its command of much of the ground across the river, the most important strategic position available. He occupied it with his Kentucky brigade, now led once more by Roger Hanson, released after his captivity from Fort Donelson, and promoted brigadier general. During the day a corps of Federals came into view across the river. Breckinridge probably did not yet know it but their commander was his fellow Kentuckian and childhood playmate, Thomas Leonidas Crittenden, son of the Senator John Jordan Crittenden who sought an unsuccessful last-minute compromise late in 1860, the same Crittenden that Breckinridge so briefly succeeded in the Senate in 1861. It would be Kentuckian against Kentuckian on this part of the line, as it was often throughout the war. The two Presidents, Davis and Lincoln, were both born in Kentucky. Such is the perversity of civil war.

Ironically, both army commanders intended to launch their attacks on December 31 with assaults on their enemy's right. That meant that Bragg would send Hardee and part of Polk forward, leaving Breckinridge entirely out of the action. Yet Rosecrans intended to keep him busy with an attack by Crittenden. Bragg struck first that foggy morning, preempting an immediate move by Crittenden, and so for the first several hours of the day Breckinridge and his division sat idle as the fight raged indecisively west of the river. But information did come in from time to time, and it disturbed the Kentuckian, typifying as well the rather sorry caliber of military intelligence at this stage of the war, and Breckinridge's own inexperience at interpreting it. Renewed word arrived that there might be Federals coming on the Lebanon road after all. If so, that meant that Breckinridge and his division would be there alone to meet

whatever that threat might bring, as well as face the soon-reported crossing of one of Crittenden's divisions in his front. The Federals shortly
recrossed to their own side without a fight, but no one seems to have reported that to Breckinridge. Then more than two hours of confusion
ensued. Bragg ordered the Kentuckian to attack. Breckinridge could not
without exposing the Lebanon road. Ignoring the Lebanon road problem,
Bragg ordered him again to attack. Breckinridge moved forward, engaging
enemy skirmishers remaining on his side of the river, but still unable to
discern that most of the enemy had left his front. He stopped when he
could go no farther without losing a tenuous hold on the Lebanon Pike,
and then Bragg suddenly made an abrupt change and ordered him to fall
back and send one brigade or two if possible across the river to help Polk.
Then Bragg changed his mind again, canceled his order, and instead sent
two brigades to reinforce Breckinridge! The Kentuckian, finally taking
care to ascertain the truth of the reports that had guided his movements
that morning, discovered that there were no enemy on his front or the
Lebanon road after all. By 1 P.M. Bragg ordered him to leave only Hanson
and the Kentucky brigade on Wayne's Hill, and bring the balance of his
division to Polk's aid. All told, three hours had been wasted by bad intelligence, Breckinridge's failure to take pains to check its veracity, and
Bragg's vacillation.[10]

Breckinridge commanded the largest division in the army, as it happened, so leaving Hanson behind still gave him four brigades to bring into
the main fight. Indeed, he sent two ahead and Bragg had already put
them into the fiercest of the fight to be shattered by heavy Federal resistance well before the Kentuckian himself arrived across the river with the
remaining two brigades. It was indicative of the fight all that day, indecisive pounding by Bragg against a Federal line that fluctuated, but did
not break. Still, the Confederates clearly had the initiative as Rosecrans
abandoned all attempts to mount a real offensive of his own. When
Breckinridge arrived at the fight, he led two of his fresh brigades into an
inferno called the Round Forest, but quickly dubbed "Hell's Half Acre."
It had chewed up his first two brigades, and much of Polk's before them,
and now he resumed the assault. He proved more successful than those
before him, soon being joined by part of Hardee's now somewhat unoccu-
pied corps. Together the two generals reconnoitered their front, but still
found their lines too weak to mount another assault, and finally ordered
the attack stopped and the men into bivouac. Though there might have
been a good opportunity for Breckinridge's brigades to deliver a decisive
blow that day, Bragg and Polk had misused them. Had the four attacked
together and at once, the Round Forest must have fallen to them, shatter-
ing the center of the Federal line and forcing Rosecrans to leave the field
or risk overwhelming defeat. This much was conceded even by his own
officers. Yet Polk and Bragg would not wait for the Kentuckian, and sent
in and ruined his first two brigades when they arrived. This was the piece-

meal fashion of attack that time and again in this war destroyed whole corps of soldiers without sense and without benefit, and the foolishness was not to be the exclusive preserve of the nonprofessional alone. Bragg would never learn the lesson. Indeed, his officers complained they could not even find him on the field at times. He commenced battle with no carefully thought-out plan, and then left his subordinates to run the fight. His only real involvement was the bungled effort to bring Breckinridge across Stones River.[11]

Still the Confederates seemed to end the day with the advantage. Indeed, Braxton Bragg was convinced that he had vindicated himself for Perryville—not that failure there was any of his doing—by achieving a resounding success. He wired to Richmond that night that "God has granted us a Happy New Year." He had driven Rosecrans from the field all along the line, he said, and he was certain that the Federals would withdraw during the night toward Nashville. In fact, he had no basis on which to make such a claim, excepting perhaps the probability that, in the Yankee's boots, that is what he would have done. So confident was Bragg that he seems to have made little effort even to examine his own lines or the condition of the troops that he expected to lead in a triumphal pursuit the next day. Victory was certain.[12]

That evening Breckinridge sent his son Clifton into Murfreesboro to tell Mary that he had survived the battle unhurt. The general could not go to see her himself, for he had to move one of his brigades back across the river to join Hanson. It was just as well, for Rosecrans did not oblige Bragg with an easy victory. He stayed to fight again. All day January 1, 1863, the Federals reorganized and consolidated their positions. Part of Crittenden's command crossed again and approached Wayne's Hill, and once again Breckinridge's scouts failed him, and he did not himself go the necessary length to see the real strength in his front. It was a quiet day along most of the line. Early the next morning, before dawn, Mary Breckinridge sent coffee out to her husband. She would have come herself but, expecting a renewal of the fight, the general forbade it. It was well that he did.[13]

Perhaps even as he and Clifton drank their first hot coffee in days, a report came from the scouts that Breckinridge was finally sending out as he should have in the first day's fight. Stealing well ahead of the line, down to the river, a spy saw the signs of a massive concentration of enemy artillery on the heights across the stream, obviously set in snare for any infantry assault that the Kentuckian might send to drive out the Federals who had crossed in his front. Breckinridge himself now rode personally to confirm the news, meeting Hardee and Polk and others along the way. What he saw and heard not only confirmed the report of the artillery buildup, but also gave him a better grasp of the enemy infantry in his front. Then a message from Bragg summoned the general at once to headquarters.

Having learned himself of the division of Federals that crossed Stones River and took position on a summit nearby, Bragg believed them to be a severe threat to his line west of the stream, and further wanted to put his own artillery in their place. Without consulting Breckinridge or either of his corps commanders, and without looking at the ground himself, Bragg resolved to attack. Breckinridge found him at about 1 P.M. standing near a large sycamore beside the river. Bragg told him he would have to lead his division in an attack to take that summit and drive the Federals back across Stones River. No matter that all of his generals opposed the move, or that Breckinridge himself now voiced objections. Bragg said he chose the Kentuckian's division because it had suffered little in the first day's fight, despite the fact that three of his brigades took the highest casualties in the army on December 31. Other critics of Bragg later speculated that, in fact, the general so severely resented the manner in which Breckinridge stood up to him over the recent Kentucky failure and the execution that he now hoped to see the Kentuckian killed in battle and thus be rid of him.

Of course Breckinridge argued. He told of the heavier than expected numbers of Federals in place on the hill in question, and of what awaited him from Rosecrans' artillery as soon as he approached the river. With a stick in hand, he even sketched in the soil a map of the relative positions. Bragg was unmoved. "Sir, my information is different," he said. "I have given the order to attack the enemy in your front and expect it to be obeyed." Breckinridge listened on helplessly, then raced back to prepare his command. Every one of his brigade commanders thought it suicide, and Hanson of the Kentucky brigade termed the order "murderous" and determined to go to headquarters and kill Bragg! The others talked him out of it, but Breckinridge himself was so upset by the impending movement that for the only instance of the war he spoke of his own death before a battle. He told General William Preston that the assault was against his judgment "and by the special orders of General Bragg." They would do their duty, but if he was killed, Breckinridge wanted Preston "to do justice to my memory, and tell the people that I believed this attack to be very unwise, and tried to prevent it." Forty-five minutes later the Kentuckian had perhaps the slim satisfaction of knowing that he had been right, but at the price of a shattered division, with a third of his command, over 1,500 men, lying dead or wounded from what proved to be the most spectacular, and ill-advised, infantry assault of the war in the West.[14]

Bragg helped to doom it from the outset by placing a personal favorite of his, Captain Felix Robertson, one of the most reprehensible characters in the Confederate service, in command of a body of artillery that was to support Breckinridge. But the captain refused to obey the Kentuckian's commands and failed to take any part until at last he helped cover the retreat of the shattered division. To make matters worse, Bragg also at the very last minute replaced one of Breckinridge's brigade commanders with another favorite of fell character, General Gideon Pillow, who had already covered himself with ignominy when he abandoned his command at Fort Donelson. In the advance now, Pillow hid behind a tree rather than accompany the brigade in battle, and Breckinridge had personally to order him out from behind it. There was an initial period of success in the assault, as the Federals fell back before the Confederate onslaught, but then the Union artillery so skillfully placed across the river tore into Breckinridge's ranks and turned the attack into a shambles. Hanson fell mortally wounded, and the fire so cut up the Kentucky brigade that Breckinridge afterward exclaimed in anguish how they had torn his "orphans" to pieces. They would be the Orphan Brigade ever after.[15]

There were too many orphans made that day. It was a pointless attack, and its failure ended the day's fight, and the battle. Bragg at first intended to stay on the field and resume the battle on the morrow, but then vacillated as he had so often, and ordered a withdrawal. This time all of his generals agreed with him. Breckinridge's division covered the retreat as the army leisurely traveled about thirty miles south to the vicinity of Tullahoma. There they would spend the next six months in relative inactivity. But not so Braxton Bragg.

Two failed campaigns in a row gave the commanding general a taste for battle, but only with his subordinates. He opened the fight barely a week after quitting Murfreesboro. In response to press criticism of his retreat, he asked his generals to testify in writing that they had agreed and advised the withdrawal. He promised to resign if his men and officers no longer believed in him. That Bragg would make such a statement to men that he knew loathed him, only reveals the more starkly his detachment from reality. He was an increasingly ill man, physically and mentally. It seemed that he could draw succor only by drawing the blood of his generals.

Every reply proved uniformly unsatisfactory. The generals supported him in the matter of the retreat, though some like Breckinridge pointed out that they had not been consulted until after Bragg made his decision. But in response to Bragg's other statement, all replied that he had lost the confidence of the army. This put Bragg on the defensive, though only temporarily. As the replies came in, the newspaper attacks on him increased, and at least one of the most virulent proved attributable to a member of Breckinridge's staff, done without the Kentuckian's knowledge. This convinced Bragg that Breckinridge was the malcontent who had turned the rest of the generals against him. By mid-February Bragg was certain, and so expressed himself to others, that Breckinridge was his chief enemy. He resolved, therefore, to attack him first.[16]

He started by ignoring army established procedure and hastily sending his own report of the Battle of Stones River into Richmond well before he even received the reports of his subordinates in Hardee's corps.

Thus he put his version of the battle on record first, and it was one in which he was repeatedly failed by his commanders, and chiefly the Kentuckian. Only Breckinridge's delays on December 31 prevented him from destroying Rosecrans in a single day, but that was minor compared to the failures on January 2, and here Bragg assiduously went about building a damning case indeed. He had already seen a report by Captain Robertson of his part in the assault, and in it he said nothing at all critical against Breckinridge. Bragg wrote back to Robertson—and probably spoke personally with him—reminding him that he had held a "special command" that day responsible directly to Bragg, who now ordered him to write another report. It should not be sent to Breckinridge but to Bragg, and clearly implied within the instructions was an order that Robertson was to be highly critical of Breckinridge. The eminently corruptible captain complied by sending a document filled with fabrications throughout. Indeed, years later he would admit that he knowingly wrote a false report at Bragg's direction.[17]

This was only the start for Bragg. He also made a commentary on the strength and losses of his various divisions in the late battle, but singled out only Breckinridge's for detailed analysis, using unqualified statistics to deliberately diminish the percentage of loss in the command, and imply thereby that it had not fought well. Bragg managed to get entirely around the fact that two of Breckinridge's brigades suffered the highest losses in the entire army.

When Bragg's report reached Richmond early in March 1863, its intent became quickly evident, people in the War Department commenting upon the harshness of its attack on Breckinridge. In addition, Bragg had already begun a letter-writing campaign in which he claimed a conspiracy against him among his generals, but naming Breckinridge particularly. The Kentuckian had "failed most *signally* at Murfreesboro," Bragg wrote to General W. W. Mackall, and now tried to lay the blame on him. Bragg expected that his report would clear the matter, and that the scheming Breckinridge "will be beautifully shown up." Yet there were those in the capital who grew increasingly suspicious of what was happening out in Tullahoma. Breckinridge's report had not been received yet. Why was it being held up, asked members of Congress. Kentucky members refused to vote on a resolution of thanks to Bragg for the battle until they got an explanation for the January 2 attack order and why the rest of the army lay idle while Breckinridge was chewed to pieces. Rumors even hit Richmond that Bragg and his foe were to meet in a duel.[18]

In fact, Breckinridge denied that there was any conspiracy either by him or against him. He had written his report and submitted it, and an even-tempered version of the battle it was, at that. No hint of his anger over the January 2 attack could be found. Indeed, when some of his officers reportedly asked him to resign his commission and challenge Bragg to personal combat, he refused. Nor would he engage in army politics. As late as March he still had written to no one in the matter, assuming his report would speak for him. "It is a great mistake to suppose that there is a 'controversy' between Gen. Bragg and myself," he told a friend in Congress. "In a word, [I] *have done nothing* in conflict with strict military propriety." He knew that Bragg had friends working against him in Richmond and elsewhere, but asked that his own supporters be quiet and not attempt to defend him. "If anything is said to my discredit, I hope my friends will be silent," he counseled. "When a man is right there are no remedies equal to silence and time. It is only when he is wrong that it is necessary to preoccupy the public mind by clamor."[19]

Clamor, of course, was what Bragg wanted, but not the kind that he began to see. Far from turning the criticism over the defeat against Breckinridge, he found himself increasingly on the defensive, facing harsh questions about his holdup of the Kentuckian's own report. He had to release it, but in doing so he sought once again to take the offensive, this time by an action unparalleled in his army's history. He sent it to Richmond accompanied by a laboriously compiled "appendix" that constituted a virtual commentary or rebuttal. It sought to charge Breckinridge with deliberately delaying on December 31 sending his brigades into battle, without mentioning that when they halted for that hour it was by Bragg's own order. Then he went on to lodge a palpable touch against the Kentuckian's failure to properly reconnoiter his front on January 2, though Bragg, too, was equally culpable.

Then came an astoundingly manipulated retort to Breckinridge's statement of his numbers engaged and losses. He had reported that he took 4,500 men into the assault on January 2, and lost 1,700. In fact, he had 5,000, and lost just over 1,500. Bragg, however, began to distort the figures at his disposal. He added to Breckinridge's strength men who were not actually part of his command, and at the same time omitted losses from other units that were most certainly a part of the Kentuckian's division. The result was that Bragg showed his nemesis with a true strength of over 6,000, and losses of only 1,300. All this was intended to indicate that the division had not fought well, and that Breckinridge bungled his attack. At no other time in this war would an army commander in the field deliberately falsify information in order to do damage to a subordinate. There could be no better measure of Bragg's imbalance.[20]

When Breckinridge finally learned that his report had been sent in and with such a commentary appended, he asked for a court of inquiry. When he asked Bragg for a copy of his report, Bragg refused, but the ever-obliging Robertson gave the Kentuckian copies of both of his reports, and Breckinridge began to see what was happening. Now he started to gather written testimony of his own, to be used if and when an official inquiry was made. No use was ever made of it all, for no court was forthcoming. Bragg, however, assiduously continued his collecting. Soon he solicited from Pillow yet another perjured report of the January 2 affair.

Besides the fact that Pillow was an unprincipled man—in the Mexican War he had been court-martialed for politicking against Winfield Scott, one of his defense attorneys being a young major of volunteers from Kentucky, John C. Breckinridge—he also had a personal score to settle with Bragg's foe. Breckinridge had caught him in an act of cowardice that day. Breckinridge made no mention of it in his report. A member of his staff did prepare charges and specifications of "conduct unbecoming an officer and a gentleman" against Pillow, but Breckinridge did not ask that it be done, and when presented with the document only consulted Hardee in the matter, and then suppressed it, acting as if "it did not exist." Yet Pillow knew, or feared, that at any time the charge might be made public. Perhaps assuming that his best defense would be to strike first, he, like Robertson, gave Bragg the lie he wanted.[21]

And so it continued well into May 1863. Bragg got his own report published, but when Breckinridge requested through proper channels that his report, too, be placed in print, Bragg forwarded that request along with yet another commentary. The difficulty smoldered on, kept alive by Bragg's hatred, as well as by those who hated him. Breckinridge refused to play the game, remaining silent and awaiting the court which never came. Eventually the whole sordid mess worked to the Kentuckian's advantage. Most of the Confederacy, already disposed against Bragg by his Perryville and Murfreesboro failures, came to regard Breckinridge as largely an innocent victim. Even on Bragg's own staff the view began to take hold, as they saw the way Bragg machinated against him. J. Stoddard Johnston had been fiercely loyal to Bragg all through the heated criticism after the failed Kentucky campaign. When his relative Breckinridge asked Johnston to come on his staff shortly after the Stones River fight, Johnston declined due to his kind feelings for the commanding general. By July 1863, however, after witnessing from the inside what Bragg was doing, Johnston abruptly resigned from his staff. "My relations were too intimate with Breckinridge & my sympathies were with him," he wrote. Nothing could offer a better final word on the discord that Bragg had sown in his own army.[22]

The whole sorry business made of Stones River a battle of great significance, far beyond its simple military import. Of course, the latter was not inconsiderable, for the defeat secured middle Tennessee to the Union for some time to come, and Nashville would not again be threatened for two years. But more important is what the battle did to the Confederate army high command in the West. The controversy that followed left the Army of Tennessee virtually unfitted to fight a battle against its enemies in blue. It was often said of Braxton Bragg that he would sooner win one fight in Richmond than two in the field against the Federals, and there was much truth in the assertion. For six months his army sat near Tullahoma while the only fighting he did was with his generals. During that same half year, Rosecrans' army did little more, content to await events in middle Tennessee. With an opportunity to strike north again, Bragg did nothing. With an opportunity to succor hard-pressed Confederates at Vicksburg, Bragg did nothing more than send small reinforcements, and then he used the occasion to rid himself of an enemy by sending Breckinridge. In short, Bragg's own campaign against his perceived foes in his own ranks incapacitated him and his army. Worse, the echoes of his feud would rebound within the high command for the rest of the war. He attacked Kentuckians as a group. They had strong personal and family ties with a number of powerful Virginia factions, both had strength in the Congress and in the War Department, and each soon developed ties of kinship with elements in the rest of Bragg's officer corps, all of them driven together by the common bond of enmity toward the sick man leading their army.

Such an army, even led by a capable commander, could hardly function successfully in the face of the enemy. It was a situation made for clichés about houses divided and inheriting the wind. And how could Bragg possibly put any trust in battle in men he hated, and who he knew hated him? At Stones River on December 31 he assigned a crucial left flank attack to a general that he regarded as the most incompetent in his army. Two days later his major thrust lay in the hands of a man rumored to have entertained challenging Bragg to a duel. Therein lay the true effect of Perryville and Stones River. By their insidious effects on the mind of Braxton Bragg, they worked a destruction on the principal Confederate army in the West that no mere battle could have achieved, short of absolute annihilation. In the East, Lee was winning—and occasionally losing—battles against great odds with an army that thought and fought as a unit, with a high command that supported its general, and a commander who did not fear the responsibility for risk and for failure. Yet in the East, Lee was fighting ever for the status quo. Out West, where daring stood a chance not only of holding Confederate territory, but also of advancing its borders back into Kentucky, the army occupied itself with little of more consequence than a family feud. Those six months of inactivity by Rosecrans presented a golden opportunity either for a combined effort against Grant in Mississippi, or for a renewed strike to reclaim central and eastern Tennessee. Bragg could conceive combined operations. He had arranged for Sterling Price and Earl Van Dorn to join with him in Kentucky. Their defeats at Iuka and Corinth ended the move. But Bragg could fight only one war at a time, and during the first half of 1863, his war within his own camp took precedence over everything else. When finally, later in the year, he was ready again to take the field against the Yankees, there were battles ahead for winning to be sure, but the war for most of the West was already over, and lost. The guns of Stones River ceased firing on January 2, but the sound of them reverberated louder and longer than any other battle in the troubled Western theater.

CHAPTER 2

"SHALL WE HAVE
A GOVERNMENT?"

Those troubled campaigns out in Kentucky and Tennessee did damage to
more than Braxton Bragg. In no other conflict in American history was
the military course of events so intertwined with political affairs as in this
war, and as the fall campaigns of 1862 approached, so did the first wartime election in decades. As well, it presented a real test of strength for the
Republicans who had so recently seized power in Washington, and the
first expression of support—or lack of it—for the war measures of the Lincoln administration. Here, too, those ubiquitous echoes of Perryville, and
all the successes and failures before it, sounded their knell.

Certainly they sounded for Owen Lovejoy of Illinois. His story up
until 1862 was largely that of the infant Republican Party itself. The
brother of Elijah Lovejoy, the foremost white martyr to the cause of abolition, Owen was one of the organizers of the party back in 1854. Once it
was founded, he became one of the Republicans' leading lights, and a
recruiter as well. He it was who played an instrumental role in the gradual
persuasion of Abraham Lincoln to identify with the new sect. He, too,
though anxious for emancipation and generally a full member of the Radical Republican fraternity, stood by the new President during the difficult
days of 1861 and 1862, when Lincoln set his priorities as Union first, and

emancipation next. He gently yet consistently urged the President toward the proclamation that finally—some thought far too tardily—struck the death blow to slavery and made of this conflict a holy war. "Let Abraham Lincoln make himself, as I trust he will, the emancipator, the liberator, as he has the opportunity of doing," said Lovejoy from his seat in the House of Representatives in April 1862, "and his name shall not only be enrolled in this earthly temple, but it will be traced on the living stones of that temple which rears itself amid the thrones and hierarchies of heaven, whose top stone is to be brought in with shouting of 'Grace, grace unto it.' "[1]

A bit overdone, perhaps, but then the leaders of a newly successful party, of whatever stripe, are always prone to overstatement. But there was more than just showmanship to impel Lovejoy's words in defense of Lincoln and emancipation. The war was not going well for the Union; when the preliminary emancipation announcement came in September many did not receive it well, and Lovejoy and all of his Republican compatriots in the House had to face a fall election. This war could be won on the battlefield eventually, he was certain, but just as surely it could be lost first at the ballot box.

Everything seemed to be running against the administration, and those tied with it, as the summer of 1862 turned thoughts once more to electioneering. McClellan was stalled in Virginia. Would he ever move? Henry Wager Halleck, succeeding Grant for a time out West, did nothing more. Buell and his small army showed no inclination to move in between the two, and the war was not the only problem. The effects that a prolonged conflict must invariably have on a nation were beginning to be felt. Prices rose, supplies of necessary goods dwindled, taxes climbed while incomes, particularly among farmers, did not. There was a surplus of grain this summer, a great market for speculators and shippers, but not for the growers. Increasing numbers of free Negroes and fugitive slaves from the South gave a hint of the social and labor problems that they would pose in the days ahead. And, particularly among the more conservative elements in the North, the increasingly arbitrary—and surely unconstitutional— arrests of suspected Rebel sympathizers and the imposition of enforced conscription boded ill for the survival of constitutional government as they knew it if the Republicans remained in power. All of these ills could be laid at the feet of Lincoln and his Republican majority, and the Democrats were all too happy to put them there and before the voters that fall.[2]

It was only by coalition that Lincoln's party reached power in the first place, and even by mid-1862 it was hardly a cohesive, united body politic of like aims and aspirations. It exercised its will in Congress only via the melding of the policy of its moderates, like Lincoln, with the virulently abolitionist sentiments of the Radicals on the one hand, and the conservative views of the loyal "War Democrats" on the other.

Should Lincoln lose either faction, he lost his majority, and the Republicans would lose their ascendance. More than this, however, out in the provinces, in the states that sent these new Republicans to Washington, policy was no more uniform than in the Capitol. The Republicans of Indiana were not the Republicans of Massachusetts. So fragmented were the values and goals of the various state electorates that Lincoln and his advisers saw from early in the campaign of 1862 that they could give little or no overall leadership. Indeed, members of some wings of the party barely spoke to each other. Secretary of State William Henry Seward and his essentially conservative, Union-first supporters took nothing but scorn from the Radicals like Benjamin Wade and Zachariah Chandler. The latter, with the myopic vision of all zealots, wanted McClellan removed, emancipation immediately, and the former slaves armed to fight for their freedom, oblivious to the irreparable damage such a policy now would do to the cause in the tender border states and among those Democrats supporting the war. The latter were fighting for the preservation of the Union, not to free slaves, and they regarded McClellan—a Democrat—as not only the best champion of their views in the field, but also a potential nominee for a Democratic recovery of the Executive Mansion in 1864. Yet even the Democrats did not agree among themselves. Many like Jesse David Bright of Indiana and Clement Laird Vallandigham of Ohio were against the war and coercion of any form. Let the South go, they said. Called "Copperheads" after the snake, they admitted the right of secession under the Constitution, and their numbers were particularly powerful in the southern regions of Indiana, Illinois, and Ohio. They barely spoke to or were spoken to by the War Democrats. Thus the opposition lay just as fragmented as the party in power. The party system as a whole in 1862 sat in near shambles. The Union and the war were being run by coalition, by compromise, by self-interest and that irresistible tendency toward the center that always characterized American politics. Everyone achieved less than he wanted, but everyone achieved something. As long as that could continue, so would the coalition. Without it, Lincoln's fragile majority in Congress would fade to nothing.

Not only the parties were jumbled. So were the polls. Different states set varying dates for their elections, further hampering any attempt at a coordinated national effort. New Hampshire, Connecticut, and Rhode Island held their Congressional polling in the spring of the year. In October, Pennsylvania, Ohio, and Indiana followed their lead, and the remaining states left their decision until November. While all were electing their congressmen, Massachusetts, New York, and New Jersey, three of the most populous Northern states, were also selecting governors. Early returns from one state can always give added impetus to the cause in another, but which early returns would set the trend? The governorships? The spring New England balloting? It was a political madhouse.

It did not go well for the administration from the start. That spring, with McClellan stalled on the Virginia Peninsula, in those first New England states to cast their ballots, Republican seats were lost, and when the military news of the summer did not improve, Lincoln could well expect that such would be the case in succeeding elections as well. Certainly the message was not lost on Owen Lovejoy. He did not stand for reelection until November, but he began his campaign in August, and at once encountered a heavy obstacle to overcome when General John Pope and his army suffered another defeat at another Bull Run. Would Lincoln never give the nation victories? Worse, Lee crossed into Maryland and Braxton Bragg was moving through Tennessee and into Kentucky in September. Everywhere the war policy of the Republicans seemed to be on the defensive.

All this and more Lovejoy had to meet as he took to the hustings. The racial prejudice against the wave of blacks streaming north ran especially high in Illinois, and in his district. To campaign effectively, he was forced to compromise his abolitionist views, or at least deemphasize them. He opened his campaigning on a platform of suppressing the rebellion and supporting Lincoln in maintaining the Union. Little was said about emancipation. Instead, Lovejoy played upon his genuinely close associations with Lincoln, the trust between the two, and the implied influence that the congressman exerted with the President. When possible he spoke to the best audiences that any pro-Union candidate could address, soldiers home on leave. With them he walked a fine line between advocating severe punishment and confiscation of property for the Rebels, without going so far as to call for the rapine that his Radical friends desired. His first and greatest desire was the restoration of the Union. If abolition of slavery must wait for that greater goal, then so be it. The question in this war—and in this election, he would hint—was not "who shall administer the government, but shall we have a government to be administered."[3]

These were trimming speeches by Lovejoy, echoed by the score in hundreds of other towns around the North that season, compromising the urge of conviction with the necessity of reelection. The support of the war policy was made the harder by Bragg's Kentucky campaign for, even though it ended in his retreat, outrage in the Union still ran high that such a Rebel army could march into the Bluegrass while Buell seemingly did nothing to stop it. This very sentiment, as much as anything, accounts for Buell's being relieved of his command and shelved the remainder of the war, until he resigned his commission. He was a good officer, but not good enough, and not at the right time. His seeming failure was mitigated by McClellan's success at Antietam, but this, too, could be made to work against Lovejoy and his kind. Was it a success for the Lincoln administration, or was it a triumph of McClellan, a Democrat, achieved in spite of the President?

And then hard on the victory in Maryland came the Preliminary

Emancipation Proclamation. It may have transformed the war into a holy cause, but for some aspiring congressmen seeking another term, it only helped their cause become lost. From the time that Lincoln first discussed his proposed proclamation with his cabinet back in July, there were those who feared that it would bring disaster in the fall elections. It was simply too radical a step for much of the nation, for people who did not yet—and might never—equate the cause of the Union with the plight of the slaves. Most of his advisers favored the plan but, of course, wisely decided to withhold it until after a Union victory at arms. That would at least be acting from a position of strength, mitigating somewhat the rather frightening social implications of the act. Yet every one of the President's friends seeking election in October and November, including Lovejoy, would have to contend with the repercussions of a move for which thousands simply were not ready.

While Lovejoy campaigned in his district, trying to make the best of what had gone before, as well as contending with the daily challenges presented by the course of events, the first really significant harbingers of ill tidings were coming from Pennsylvania, Ohio, and Indiana. Their elections, set for October, carried enormous import for the remainder of the November polling, and none of the indications looked good at the outset of the campaign. They did not improve.

All of these states gave Lincoln a majority in 1860. Of course, as always in American politics, elections in non-Presidential years generally tended to run against the party in power, but 1862 seemed a special case. This was not just another election; for the first time in history Americans were voting on the course of a terrible war. Even if every administration candidate were defeated, Lincoln would still be President. This was no parliamentary democracy. But without his majority in Congress, he would be impotent—no appropriations, no draft bills, no loan authorizations, no specially authorized war powers.

The trouble was that all this seemed a distinct possibility, more even than Lincoln appreciated, for never as well was a presiding President so widely and bitterly attacked in the press, on the stump, and even in the counsels of his own party. Some like Charles Sumner of Massachusetts, a leading Radical, were two-faced. He defended Lincoln to some, arguing that the President could not be held to account for the failures of his subordinates. Yet to others he confided that he felt the rail-splitter inept and lethargic. Many accused the President of being but the tool of Seward, and indeed, the Secretary of State had made his bid for precisely such a relationship before Lincoln politely but firmly made it clear that, having been elected President, he would fill the office himself, thank you. Some spoke cynically of Seward holding chloroform to Lincoln's nose to keep him quiet while the New Yorker ran the war, except for "one or two brief spells." "Not a spark of genius has he," complained the divine Henry Ward Beecher, "not an element of leadership; not one particle of heroic enthusiasm." Lesser men became even more vitriolic, and none more than rabid adherents to the Radical creed. Adam Gurowski, a Polish expatriate and constant critic of Lincoln and his policies, declared that he feared the President's incompetence as "an unavoidable evil, an original sin." He declared Lincoln to be good-intentioned, but basically stupid. "You cannot change Lincoln's head," he lamented, "you cannot fill his small but empty skull with brains." Lincoln, he said, was "digging the country's grave."[4]

Attacks of this sort came to sympathetic ears in states like Pennsylvania. The home of James Buchanan, a Democrat who incidentally did as much as many men to bring the country to this pass, the Keystone State clung to its old Democratic traditions. It lay close to the South; Mason and Dixon's line was its southern border. Many in the state kept close personal and political ties with Maryland and Virginia. It was then, as always, a conservative enclave, fearful of the influx of masses of freed slaves in the event of massive emancipation. Indeed, as one of the chief destinations of runaway slaves in the 1850s, Pennsylvania had already experienced the problem of the freed Negro better than many states of the North. The Radicals like Thaddeus Stevens pursued their course, attacking the President—which won some votes here—and championing emancipation and the arming of Negroes, which lost them votes, and in the end the state proved little better than a draw for the administration.

Ohio, too, looked bad for Lincoln. Though the home of Lincoln's most Radical senator, Benjamin Wade, the Buckeye State was no seedbed of abolitionism. Like Pennsylvania, its neighbor to the east, Ohio found thousands of indigent ex-slaves within its borders, and well before the election took steps to curb the influx. The legislature toyed with bans on further settlement by Negroes, and even entertained a measure of expulsion of those already there, a proposal that failed by but three votes, so high did feeling run. In the summer, growing out of fears of lost jobs due to cheap Negro labor, poor white workers in Cincinnati and Toledo mobbed and rioted in their streets. Besides the Negro question, Radicalism itself became a major issue. The legislature at first declined to reelect Wade to his Senate seat, so extreme was he in his views. He only later achieved a return to Washington when no candidate could be put forth against him, the election was postponed, and at the last moment before adjournment the legislators finally gave him another chance. His lack of contrition did not help his, or the party's, cause, as he continued to clamor loudly for emancipation. In October, the Republicans suffered a widespread loss, mitigated only by holding five out of the nineteen House seats, and to do that they had to rely on questionable war "heroes" like Generals Robert Cumming Schenck and James Abram Garfield.[5]

Then came Indiana, an altogether special case. Several days before the election Governor Oliver Perry Morton visited with Secretary of the Treasury Salmon Portland Chase in Washington and predicted disaster at the polls. Indiana would, he said, lose every House seat but two. So dire was the calamity that the two went to see Lincoln to ask that he order Indiana regiments then in the state furloughed briefly so they could go home and vote, the soldiers as a rule supporting the party and the administration. Lincoln promised his help, but it availed little.

Events in Kentucky affected the political course in the Hoosier State more perhaps than in any other Northern area, and the effects all proved negative. Early in the summer Democratic passions were inflamed when General Jeremiah Boyle in Kentucky threatened to arrest anyone there who might seek office in opposition to the President and the War party. This only confirmed what Democrats in Indiana long regarded as a conscious policy of suppressing opposition in border states like Maryland and Missouri, as well as Kentucky. Could it fail to occur in Indiana before long? They thought not. Worse, the Confederate invasion of Kentucky caused consternation in Indiana. Hurriedly raised volunteer regiments rushed across the Ohio, and many of the Federals terribly beaten at Richmond, Kentucky, by Kirby-Smith in August had been Hoosiers. Governor Morton declared martial law in the river counties bordering Kentucky, imposed curfews, and raised the state guard. At the same time Morton and other ranking politicians in the state campaigned vigorously against Buell, who now seemingly held their fate in his hands. Morton regarded the general as "utterly unfit for command of the great army under him." Buell was slow, soft on slavery, and no friend to the Emancipation Proclamation. Morton battled with other generals as well, including Buell's subordinate William Nelson. Morton was actually present when yet a third Federal general shot and killed Nelson over a personal quarrel, and for a time Morton was himself rumored to be involved in some conspiracy.[6]

All in all, a sorry condition of affairs for a party attempting to regain the electorate's confidence for another two years, and not helped in the least by the almost universal bogeymen, the draft and Negro immigration. Yet in addition to all this, Indiana Republicans and War Democrats faced yet another threat almost unknown in Pennsylvania and the Eastern states. Here there flourished a well-organized Democratic opposition, and as well there appeared a fairly well-organized system of secret societies, both among Republicans and Democrats. The latter, though often accused of being treasonous in nature, were in fact motivated far more by genuine rabid opposition to the Lincoln machine, and by not-unfounded fears that military authorities would interfere with the political process if they worked out in the open. Nowhere in the North did rumors of clandestine schemings and paramilitary preparations run more rife than in southern Indiana. The Republican "dark lantern" societies and "Union Clubs" were believed to be hoarding arms sent by Washington for the purpose of controlling the polls and intimidating Democratic voters. Their leaders preached that all members of the opposition were disloyal. The situation became a potential explosion. "Democrats will not calmly wait until their political opponents have made all needful preparations for crushing them under foot," commented an observer. "Preparations of this kind will result in similar action on the other side until the entire North will consist of armed and exasperated men ready but for the tocsin to sound to go to work cutting each other's throats and devastating the country." One organization, the Knights of the Golden Circle, a secret order founded in 1854, achieved far more in rumor than ever it did in fact. Indeed, the group was almost moribund in Indiana in 1862, but the Republican press had it armed and ready to meet Bragg's advancing Confederates with arms open, ready to deliver the state and the North into the hands of treason.[7]

Open and outright lies about the Democrats circulated widely in the press, but Morton outdid all others when a grand jury that he instigated reported during the campaign, in August, that the Knights had some 15,000 members in the state who were actually treasonously inclined, and some claimed membership of over 92,000 in all. "The nest where traitors are hatched," the report called the Knights' meetings. Sixteen men were actually indicted for treason, but not a single case went to court. In fact, the entire grand jury report seems to have done nothing more than adopt every rumor floating through Indianapolis that summer.[8]

This situation was chaotic, and no wonder that Morton predicted defeat. His prescience was marvelous, for the Republicans that October took a heavy loss, and the Democrats achieved perhaps their greatest success at the polls since the debacle of 1860. Democratic majorities were returned to both houses of the legislature, and seven of eleven Congressional seats in Washington went against the administration. Excuses immediately came forth, accusations of treason were renewed, and just as quickly denied. But a few things became evident. Paramount was the declaration by the victorious Democrats that their election was not a repudiation of the cause of the Union. They were not ready and anxious to abet the rebellion. "Armed rebellion must be suppressed by force," they declared in their victory manifesto, but just as "the insane and infuriated faction of Abolitionists must retire before the ballots of a free people." There was some small comfort for Lincoln in that, if he cared to see it. Indiana stood behind him to win the war, they said, but not to win emancipation. They would stand for Union, but not for Republicanism.[9]

Taken all together, the October elections went uniformly against the Republicans, and almost universally the issues related directly or indirectly to the Radicals. By their uncompromising positions, they made of themselves a potent negative issue in the campaign. Abolition, Negro immigration, intimidation, conscription, and a vindictive policy when and if the South were defeated—none of these cries met favor in the ears of the states that bordered the upper South. It did not bode well for what lay ahead in November.

It did not bode well for the President's own Illinois, or for Owen

Lovejoy. As soon as Lincoln announced the preliminary emancipation measure, Lovejoy chose to say little of it, realizing naturally enough that with the voters of his district much like those of Indiana, it was better to let the matter rest. Instead, he concentrated his efforts on defending the administration's war policy, and Lincoln himself. From the middle of September he spent the next six weeks campaigning, speaking at least once daily. His opposition attacked him as a Radical, making that their chief issue, but it did not seem to work. Rather, Lovejoy was able to garner the support even of some influential War Democrats. Still, it never looked good through the state as a whole. The course of the war was not with the Republicans. "If we are beaten in this State two weeks hence," a friend notified Lincoln late in October, "it will be because McClellan and Buell won't fight."

They were beaten. Statewide the Democrats defeated the Republicans by a majority of over 16,000 votes. Of fourteen Congressional seats in the offing, nine went to Democrats. Lovejoy happily held on to his position, but by a margin of barely 600 votes. The only other men who might by some stretch be placed in the Radicals' camp to win reelection were Elihu Washburne—patron of U. S. Grant—and John Farnsworth. Not Lincoln, perhaps, but his party had been repudiated in his home state.[10]

The same lamentable story was enacted elsewhere in November. In New York the opposition took seventeen seats to the Republicans' fourteen. In New Jersey the party captured but one of five seats and lost control of the legislature. The only real victories came in Michigan, Iowa, and California, and a congressman elected from Kansas. Missouri, too, returned a Republican—or at least a Lincoln—majority, but at the cost of disenfranchisement of many opposition voters, and intimidation by armed men at the polls. In New York the Republicans lost the governorship, by many regarded as the most important contest of the election, and they did so in a campaign characterized by increasing polarization of extremes. The Radicals controlled the nomination and gave it to James Wadsworth, while the Democrats put forward Horatio Seymour, once thought of as a compromise candidate for President in 1860 if Douglas, Bell, and Breckinridge could be withdrawn. Expecting at first to be defeated, Seymour promised to employ abuse, extremism, and intolerance in his campaign, as a model. Yet he did stand unswervingly for the restoration of the Union, and that, together with the antipathy that the Radicals' attitude stirred against Wadsworth, gave Seymour the governorship. Massachusetts, on the other hand, was never in question, electing John A. Andrew to the governor's mansion. But New Jersey gave its chief executive office to a Democrat by a majority of three to two.[11]

Putting even the best face on it, the 1862 election proved a disaster for the Republican Party. Two governorships lost in important states, and in the House of Representatives an administration majority reduced to 101 versus 77 anti-Lincolnites. It was still a majority, to be sure, but one that depended more than ever before upon coalition, and it could only be counted certain on very sharply defined issues. With the raising of any special interest or local impact in a measure, that administration majority could melt. It put the President in a dangerous position, calling all the more for that tact and diplomacy that so often characterized his dealings with Congress.

Lincoln himself did not fully appreciate the reasons for the debacle, or its meaning. "We have lost the elections," he told Carl Schurz, and he thought he knew why. First, the Democrats had been left in the majority in many states by the ardent Union men—surely Republicans—having enlisted in much greater numbers. Seeing this, the Democrats made renewed efforts to take advantage of the situation. And finally, the news-paper press, particularly the "friendly" Republican press, "by vilifying and disparaging the administration, furnished them all the weapons to do it with." Then he added, almost as an afterthought, that "Certainly, the ill-success of the war had much to do with this."

That last, in fact, was the nub of the problem. Except for the impor-tant but less-publicized victories out on the Western rivers, Lincoln could point to little but "ill-success." Even the choice of the word showed how sensitive he was to the issue. "Ill-success" could better be called failure. Even the two victories of recent months, Antietam and Perryville, were battles fought on Northern soil against invading armies that had marched with shameful impunity into the Union. Lincoln did not deceive himself for a minute about the dissatisfaction caused by the military situation, or by the unpopular generals who seemed so frequently to achieve high com-mand. Some like Schurz claimed that the administration had "placed the Army, now a great power in this Republic, into the hands of its' enemys." It was a specious charge, and one that Lincoln easily refuted, pointing to the fact that none of the Democratic generals like McClellan and Buell who achieved high position did so without the consistent urging of Re-publicans as well as Democrats. "I have scarcely appointed a democrat to a command, who was not urged by many republicans and opposed by none. It was so with McClellan." And, he pointed out, the Republican generals appointed had not achieved a measurably greater degree of suc-cess in the field. The most successful general to date, Grant, was almost apolitical, though inclined more to the Democracy.[12]

It could hardly be a surprise, then, that the voters of 1862 declared their lack of confidence in Lincoln and his administration, however much they supported in most respects the basic cause that he served. Lincoln, Republican, and Union were not yet synonymous. Loyal men could stand by the last without necessarily supporting the others. The people simply were not satisfied. The dissatisfaction was made the worse by the Republi-cans' introduction of emancipation into the equation, linking it with the cause of Union, and seemingly forcing the country to support both or nei-ther. The Proclamation won Lincoln many votes where he did not already need them, in places like Massachusetts and Michigan. But it cost him dearly where he did need the ballots in the middle Atlantic and Western states. Nothing shows more clearly how closely Lincoln had chosen his time for promulgating the Proclamation. Had he done it earlier, after the Forts Henry and Donelson victories, it might have imperiled those April elections, which went bad enough as it was. Done then or during the summer, the act would have allowed more time for debate and growing sentiment against it, thus imperiling the even more dismal October returns. As it was, the furor caused in the few days between the preliminary proclamation and the October polling cost the administration many votes. And its impact on November is unmistakable. If Lincoln erred at all in his timing, it was in not withholding the explosive announcement until after November. But McClellan gave him a victory in September, and if the President had learned one thing already in this war, it was that he could not count on military successes when he wanted them. Had he let that victory slip past, he might have had to wait a long time for another. As events would prove out, there would have been a long wait for, despite the marginal success at Stones River and Perryville, Lincoln would not again get a major victory in the field for nearly nine months. Thus his instincts served him well.

Others took good service of their instincts as well in this election fall of 1862, for in the growing unrest over the course of the war, the crushed Democrats of 1860 saw their chance to regain their strength. Two years before they had been a party fragmented and destroyed. Even after allowing for the departure of those who went South into the new Confederacy, the Democrats who remained were divided, angry, vindictive, and uncertain. The old party of Jackson was gone. Indeed, what they and their Republican counterparts did not yet realize was that the old party system of Jackson was gone as well. The Democrats, like their opponents, would no longer depend upon simple party loyalty. Diplomacy, compromise, coalition, would be as necessary to them in forging an effective minority as it would be to the Republicans in maintaining their majority.

The pieces of the old party were not easily put back together. The Douglas Democrats, those who stood fastly by the Union in 1860, and who now supported the prosecution of the war, lost their leader when the "Little Giant" died soon after the war's start. No new champion sprang immediately to take his place—if anyone could—and the demands of the war further confused matters because so many potential political leaders went off to the fighting, many of them in hopes of furthering their careers. Prominent Democrats like John Alexander McClernand of Illinois were given significant army commands, not because of any demonstrated military prowess, but because such a move would help cement the support of their Democratic followers to the war policy. McClernand's only military experience prior to being commissioned a brigadier general was two months as a private in 1832! Much the same was the case with John Alexander Logan, again of Illinois, though he at least recruited his own regiment and rose by demonstrated talent.

Gradually many of these ardently loyal men would become Republicans, especially after the war. For the rest, there remained the ticklish business of doing their duty as Americans and standing by the war, and their duty as Democrats by providing a loyal opposition. The choice was made the more difficult by the frequent lures put in their path by Lincoln. He offered the same temptations to Democrats of other stripes as well, and some took the bait. Benjamin Franklin Butler of Massachusetts had voted consistently to give Jefferson Davis the Democratic Presidential nomination in 1860, and when the party split, he just as ardently supported the candidacy of John C. Breckinridge. Many of his fellow Democrats of like views were later branded as Copperheads or outright traitors, but Butler—like many others—charted his course in 1860 by his conviction that only a Democratic victory could avert war. His support for Davis might later seem questionable, but his stand for Breckinridge was based firmly in the latter's sincere commitment to Union. Thus, when the war came, Butler already stood in the Union camp, his past associations forgiven, and he quickly acquired a high commission in the army. His lead brought thousands more Democrats to Lincoln's rallying cry.

Yet there was another Democracy, as radically and vehemently opposed to Butler and the War Democrats as it was to Lincoln and the Republicans. The Peace Democrats, chiefly men in the border states and the Western states bordering the Ohio, regarded the war against the Confederacy as unconstitutional, unholy, and not a war for Union but a campaign of conquest and subjugation. Many of them were, in all but nativity, Southern-minded Democrats, believers in the right of secession or, if not, then convinced that once the South had left the Union there was no constitutional authority for Lincoln to try to force it back in. The only way to reunite the sections was to appease the South. In their eyes it was Radicalism and abolitionism that precipitated this conflict. As Clement Vallandigham of Ohio declared, only "God and the great tribunal of history" had the right to pass judgment on the legitimacy of secession. Certainly Abraham Lincoln did not. In the 1860 campaign he declared that in Congress he would not vote a single dollar "whereby one drop of American blood should be shed in a civil war." Vallandigham was no friend to secession, but better peaceful separation than enforced reconstruction by war. He, like many other Peace Democrats, advised Lincoln to learn "a lesson of wisdom from the secession of the Thirteen Colonies."

Men like Vallandigham took heart at the early 1862 election returns. "There is yet hope," he wrote to former President Franklin Pierce in April. "The Democratic party was not dead; it only slept; but it is now stirring itself as the strong man rousing himself from his slumbers. Its success is our only hope." Vallandigham even attempted to assume the fallen mantle of Douglas, but it proved an ill fit, for he no more represented the sentiments of the Douglas Democrats than did Butler. As a result, he only helped widen the gulf between the Peace and War democrats. Calling for unity on state rights, including the subject of slavery, he helped drive men of the McClernand stamp even closer to the administration. "The Constitution as it is, the Union as it was," he cried to his fellow Democrats in Congress, but such a backward view only alienated most of his peers. The war wing of the party was hardly outdone by the Republicans themselves in condemning Vallandigham's attempt. "Slavery, imperilled by her own treason in the Slave States," cried Horace Greeley, "summons her trusty servitors in the Free States to the rescue." Still Vallandigham fought his cause, denouncing arrests of suspected disloyal persons, the military failures in the field, and the moves toward abolition as a national policy. Even he was not the most conservative of Peace Democrats. Some argued that the Union of old was done, that the Federal armies should be withdrawn and peace be made at once. The War Democrats wanted all issues but the restoration of the full Union and the suppression of the rebellion set aside. Vallandigham stood in between, thinking that the Union could still be mended by peaceful compromise.

Lincoln and his people were no fools. They recognized a strong foe in Vallandigham, and made concerted efforts to see him defeated that fall. They managed to get General Robert C. Schenck, one of the few minor heroes of Second Bull Run, nominated to oppose the Ohioan. In the ensuing election, Schenck defeated his opponent in one of the bitterest and most slanderous canvasses of the season. Accusations of treason and disloyalty repeatedly rested at Vallandigham's door, not tempered in the least by his inflammatory pronouncements and his increasingly militant stand against Lincoln. If Vallandigham was not really a traitor, he looked in every respect like one, and in the high-pitched tenor of this war, the appearance all too often brought more action than the reality.[13]

Vallandigham's defeat was one of the very few causes for dismay among Democrats in 1862. They won impressive gains, but in one vital element they failed. They were still no more united a party than in 1860. Like their Republican opponents, they could not make their whole as great even as the sum of their parts. There still remained no cohesive party platform or policy, only vaguely defined notions that an opposition must be presented. Beyond that, everything went into faction. Indeed, the party would not be rebuilt for decades, and not until after its departed Southern brethren returned to the fold in days of reconstruction. The reasons are simple. Almost since the time of Jefferson, the politics of the Democratic Party had come increasingly to be defined by the South, in part because doctrine originated there in the hands of a generation of dominant Southern statesmen. As well, much other party policy emerged in reaction to Southern needs in the necessity to hold the party together to maintain a shaky hold on the Executive Mansion and a Congressional majority. The epithet "doughface" was not applied to Northern Democrats who catered to the South without good reason, for it was only such a posture that made Pierce and Buchanan Presidents. Thus, when the South left, it took more than just a majority of the membership with it. It took the heart of the party and left only the shell. In peacetime, the Democracy might have been able to reform itself into an effective and united opposition. But in war, with the issue of opposition tied so intimately with treason, where concepts greater than party commanded attention, the Democrats enjoyed scarcely a chance for reformation. At best they could revel in their considerable gains in 1862, and then derive no advantage from them. They could gadfly Lincoln with renewed intensity, but they never had a hope of offering a majority of Northern voters an attractive alternative.

Nevertheless, it is well for Lincoln and his administration, and for the feuding Republicans who made his tenuous majority, that the November elections did not come a few weeks later. The electorate responded mercurially to the tempo of the war, and even the pervasive commitment to the fight for the Union that always guided Northern voters could be swayed by immediate events. Unquestionably the victories, such as they were, at Antietam, Perryville, and Stones River, won the administration votes. Just as certainly, the humiliation of the two invasions of Northern soil and the admittedly lackluster nature of all three successes cost Lincoln votes. A major Union defeat might easily have made the difference in taking from the administration its now narrow margin in the House, especially if it came close to the election.

Such a defeat was coming, as humiliating as any before it, and more senseless. In numbers involved, it would be the greatest battle ever fought in the hemisphere, and it only missed the election by six weeks. The war —always the war.

CHAPTER 3

"IT IS GLORIOUS TO
SEE SUCH COURAGE"

It had been very politic of Lincoln to withhold removing "Little Mac" from command until November 5, 1862. That was just one day after the major elections, when the dismissal of a popular Democratic general could no longer hurt the administration. Lincoln made other changes in the Army of the Potomac that same day, changes with far-reaching impact on the campaigning of the next many months. The court-martialed Fitz-John Porter fell with his beloved McClellan, and the fiery Major General Joseph Hooker replaced him at the head of the V Corps. Lincoln intended that David Hunter take over the III Corps but apparently later changed his mind. And, of course, to fill the shoes so tardily occupied by McClellan, the President selected Major General Ambrose Everett Burnside of Rhode Island.[1]

It seemed on its face to be a good choice. For one thing, Burnside did not aspire to the command, and Lincoln was learning already that these self-important generals with exalted ambitions frequently produced nothing more than ego and problems. Burnside was a young man, just two years older than McClellan and now just a few months beyond thirty-eight. He was born, in fact, a Hoosier, the son of a slave-owning South Carolinian. Like Andrew Johnson of Tennessee, young Burnside learned the tailor's trade and went in business for himself when only nineteen. But then came the opportunity to go to West Point, and he took it. He accepted a commission as second lieutenant of the 2d United States Artillery upon his matriculation in 1847, just in time to go to Mexico, but too late to see real action. Following the war he did garrison and post duty in the Southwest, fighting Apaches and boredom, until he resigned his commission in 1853 and removed to Bristol, Rhode Island. There he went into manufacturing, chiefly a new form of cavalry weapon called the Burnside carbine. He designed the gun himself, but like most breech-loading and relatively rapid-fire weapons, it was still ahead of its time so far as the United States army was concerned. Ironically, some of his carbines were doing service in the present conflict.

He was a large man with a confident air and a winning manner. His high forehead, considerably balding, gave an impression of intelligence. Of course, the dominant feature with him was his grand chin whiskers, two great tufts extending from moustache to ear, teased and trained to stand straight out. They gave him a kindly, jovial look that matched his personality. The people of Rhode Island thought well of him, made him a major general in the state militia, and nominated him to an unsuccessful bid for Congress. Briefly he also worked for the Illinois Central Railroad for his friend and employer, George B. McClellan.

Then came war, and with it Burnside quickly saw his calling. He raised the 1st Rhode Island Volunteer Infantry for three months' service, and led it to the relief of Washington in that frantic spring of 1861. When his regiment went home, he stayed on as a colonel of volunteers to command a brigade under McDowell at First Bull Run. He performed well enough that two weeks later he found himself a brigadier general. Lincoln liked the enthusiastic young officer. He had less of conceit and more of wit than most of the generals the President dealt with. And the Chief Executive sensed something of greatness in the man, enough so that he gave him an independent command to lead an expedition to the North Carolina coast. In October 1861 Burnside proposed to put three brigades aboard ships, support them with navy war vessels, and move against Roanoke Island, New Bern, and parts inland. On February 7, 1862, Burnside began an attack on Roanoke Island that proved successful the next day. Five weeks later he captured New Bern, then besieged Beaufort in April. He achieved unqualified success against light opposition, and gave the Union a firm foothold in the upper Confederacy. When he was called to Fort Monroe that summer to reinforce McClellan, his old friend naturally found a good place for him. Lincoln promoted him to major general. And now, well dissatisfied with McClellan, the President may even have offered Burnside command of the Army of the Potomac. Quartermaster General Montgomery Cunningham Meigs believed that the President made the offer—or at least thought of it—just prior to the ill-fated Seven Days campaign back in the spring. Later, when the Confederate army under Lee marched north into Maryland, Lincoln reportedly again tried to place Burnside in the command rather than have to call on McClellan. But the Rhode Islander apparently declined to replace his friend in the command, and Lincoln was stuck once more with "Little Mac."[2]

All that was different now. Burnside would accept the command, of that Lincoln was assured, particularly when the reluctant general was told that, if he declined, the position would be proffered to the rabidly ambitious and scheming Joe Hooker. Burnside cared little enough for the responsibility of a commanding general, but even less for the thought of serving under Hooker, and that decided the matter.

Though criticized then and later for entrusting such a position to the affable young Burnside, Lincoln in fact exercised his best judgment, based on the best available information. Burnside was, after all, one of the few indisputably successful commanders in the East, no matter that his North Carolina operations came at little or no opposition. Too, Burnside was politically acceptable, an ever-present factor in the military equation. And he seemed to inspire confidence, in all but those who knew him best. His piratical air, achieved by a calculated informality of dress and manner, disarmed those often put off by the fuss and finery of the textbook soldiers.

Yet associates within the army, though they personally liked the man, felt misgivings about his elevation to the high command. Charles A. Dana, a War Department observer, found that when Burnside "first talked with you, you would think he had a great deal more intelligence than he really possessed. You had to know him some time before you really took his measure." Many, however, kept their feelings to themselves. Only after Burnside had been tried and found wanting did they volunteer their convictions held all along that he was incompetent for the army command.[3]

In fact, Burnside himself felt his incapacity, thus his two prior refusals. When actually ordered now to supplant McClellan, he had little choice, but again and again he gave indications of his uncertainty. He refused to accept graciously compliments at his elevation. General George Gordon Meade reported rumors that Burnside "wept like a child" in the days following his assumption, openly asserting that he was unfit for the position. In fact, Burnside became ill in the next few days, ostensibly from overwork, but more likely from anguish. Much of that anxiety came from the certain knowledge that he, a man whose only offensive command until now had been a few brigades marching through unresisting North Carolina coastal communities, was now expected to lead an army of 120,000 in an offensive against an enemy that had chewed up McDowell, Pope, and McClellan before him. And he must do it quickly before the winter ended operations.[4]

Actually, McClellan left Burnside in a good position for a speedy advance, one that he could and should have made himself but for his fears and imaginings. Following the check at Antietam, Lee withdrew his battered army into the Shenandoah to refit, while McClellan remained content to sit north of the Potomac and posture. Both armies needed time to rest after the fury of the bloodiest single day's fighting of the war, but Lee, rarely happy at complete repose, still managed to embarrass "Little Mac" by sending a cavalry raid led by General James Ewell Brown "Jeb" Stuart in a ride completely around the Federal army and into Pennsylvania. It accomplished little but to place even more pressure on McClellan to advance. Finally he did, not getting his army across the Potomac until November 2.

Lee countered McClellan with an army much swelled during the several weeks' inactivity. Stragglers returned to the ranks, new regiments were added, and by early November he numbered more than 80,000. Further, the Confederate Congress finally authorized division of his army into corps, a marked improvement in command structure over the old manner of numerable divisions being grouped informally into "wings." And Lee had two new lieutenant generals promoted to command his two corps, though they were old, familiar names, James Longstreet of Georgia, and Thomas Jonathan Jackson, called "Stonewall" for his stand at First Bull Run.

When McClellan finally moved south, on a line just east of the Blue Ridge, toward Warrenton, he left one corps at Harpers Ferry threatening to advance into the Shenandoah on Lee's left flank, and as well to guard against Lee moving rapidly through the Valley and back into Maryland and McClellan's vulnerable rear. Once again, as in all the Virginia campaigns, the Shenandoah Valley was the trump card. Running north to south on a line between the Blue Ridge and the Alleghenies, the Valley offered a natural pathway for invasion into the North or the South. Better still, it was crossable on the east at only a few gaps, and control of those openings could allow an army to move virtually unseen, to appear suddenly at the worst possible place for an enemy. Already in this war control of the Valley had been the deciding factor during the First Bull Run Campaign, during the Peninsular Campaign of the following spring, in part during Pope's defeat at Second Bull Run, and of course in Lee's advance into Maryland the previous September. No wonder, then, that both Union and Confederate commanders would always seek to start their offensives by a move toward control of the Shenandoah or else, as with McClellan now, by closing off its opening at Harpers Ferry.

Lee took a gamble that, against a better general, would have been daring unto foolishness. He divided his army, sending Jackson and the 40,000 men of his II Corps into the Valley to Winchester, while with Longstreet's 45,000-man I Corps, he fell back slowly before "Little Mac's" even slower advance. Lee was no fool, though. Should McClellan follow him far enough, Jackson might be able to sweep through one of the gaps onto the Federal right flank and deliver a crushing blow. But McClellan, presented with a gilded opportunity, was a fool for doing nothing with it. On the day that Burnside replaced him in command of the Army of the Potomac, he outnumbered Lee and Longstreet in his front at Culpeper by nearly three to one, with Jackson at least a day's march away should he be able to force his way through one of the Federally guarded gaps.

And now this was Burnside's opportunity, and he refused to take it. His main supply line was the Orange & Alexandria Railroad. He learned that the line lay in bad repair and vulnerable. Fearful like so many of his fellow army commanders of losing his communications, he determined that the risks of continuing with McClellan's plan outweighed the benefits. On November 9, then, Burnside outlined his new plan of operations. Even if he did stay and fight Lee at Culpeper, and then move against Jackson, he felt that the defeated enemy would still have several lines of retreat to Richmond, and he would only have to fight yet another battle there. Besides, Lee would probably retire to Richmond without a fight if the entire Federal army advanced directly against him now. What Burnside proposed instead was that he mass his army as though intending a move against Culpeper, meanwhile stockpiling supplies for a surprise movement down the northern bank of the Rappahannock River to Fredericksburg, some thirty miles east. Such a move would always keep him between Lee and Washington, and at the same time put him on the shortest route to Richmond. Like so many before—and after—him, Burnside somehow equated capturing Richmond with ending the rebellion. Taking the Rebel capital, he said, "should be the great object of the campaign, as the fall of that place would tend more to cripple the rebel cause than almost any other military event, except the absolute breaking up of their army." Almost as an afterthought did the general mention the possibility of defeating Lee in the field.

General-in-Chief Henry Halleck did not like the plan. He preferred the much greater advantage already enjoyed by a divided Lee in Burnside's front. The two generals met over the plan, each unyielding, and after Halleck disclaimed any responsibility for the scheme, Lincoln approved it on November 14. "It will succeed if you move very rapidly," advised the President, "otherwise not." Therein lay the crucial test of Burnside's plan. He would have to do more than make a surprise move. By his own admission, the Confederate intelligence was superior to his own. Lee would not be fooled for long, and then he would march his own army to impede Burnside's crossing the Rappahannock at Fredericksburg. The Federals must get there first and be ready virtually without a moment's delay to cross the river.

That is what Burnside expected to do, for as part of his November 9 plan he also called for a great quantity of stores to be brought by canal barge to await his arrival near Fredericksburg. And to precede the cattle herds and supply trains that would come overland, he wanted a sufficient supply of pontoon boats to allow his engineers to build two bridges across the Rappahannock. Once across and joined by the supplies converging from the several routes requested, he would organize his supply trains and equip them with enough provisions for the army for twelve days or more, seemingly thinking that two weeks would be all the time necessary to invest and conquer the enemy capital.

Burnside, like Lee, also sought a reorganization of his army, a further refinement of the corps system. He would divide it into "Grand Divisions," left, right, and center, to be commanded by his senior generals, Joseph Hooker, William Buel Franklin, and Edwin Vose Sumner.[5]

Burnside began his movement the day after Lincoln approved his plan, a good beginning for a scheme that depended upon speed and constant movement. Just two days later Sumner's advance reached Falmouth, across the Rappahannock from Fredericksburg. There they found supplies already starting to arrive, but no pontoon boats. Fredericksburg was almost defenseless before him. Burnside had indeed stolen a march on Lee and the river crossing was his for the taking. But no pontoon boats. Sumner, alive to the danger of delay, asked that he be allowed to ford his command over the river, but Burnside became afraid. The weather turned bad and the threat of rain made it possible that the river would rise, close the fords, and leave Sumner isolated on the other side before the rest of the army could cross. And so Sumner sat and watched. On November 19 Burnside wrote to Washington and urged speed with the boats, but as it later appeared, those in the capital in charge of shipping the bridge building materials failed to share Burnside's sense of urgency, and therefore did nothing to hurry his order.

By November 22 the commanding general was becoming frantic. "Had the pontoon bridge arrived even on the 19th or 20th, the army could have crossed with trifling opposition," he complained. Others in his army fussed as well, chiefly the scheming Joseph Hooker. Admittedly a foe of Burnside's, Hooker thought that he was the better choice for army commander, and was openly condescending of his superior. Burnside played right into his hands when he directed that his corps and grand division commanders correspond directly with the War Department in many routine matters, rather than go through army headquarters. That gave plotters like Hooker the perfect opportunity to manipulate behind Burnside's back. While ostensibly reporting the condition of his command on November 19, Hooker criticized "Burn" to the Secretary of War. "I regret that the major-general commanding did not keep up the show of an advance" against Longstreet, he chided. Conjuring remembrances of the "McClellan delays," Hooker repeatedly hinted that Burnside would not move swiftly enough to maintain his advantage. "I feel more anxious concerning this movement," he wrote, "as I learn, informally, that we are to experience a delay of several days in the erection of bridges over the Rappahannock." In fact, it was that very same day that a captain of New York engineers finally decided to begin forwarding the pontoons from Washington. They would arrive on November 25. Unfortunately, Longstreet got there first.[6]

Lee was genuinely taken unawares by Burnside's rapid shift eastward to Fredericksburg, though the possibility of such a move had occurred to him and even to the Richmond press, which several days before predicted that there would be a battle on the Rappahannock. It was on November 17 that he learned of Sumner's progress toward Falmouth and that Federal transports were moving with supplies up the Rappahannock. "This looked as if Fredericksburg was again to be occupied," he reported some months later. At once he ordered two divisions of infantry and some cavalry on the march to stop the crossing, while Stuart reconnoitered the movements of Burnside north of the river. The cavalryman's probes the next day revealed with certainty that the entire Army of the Potomac was on its way to Fredericksburg, and on the nineteenth Lee ordered the balance of Longstreet's I Corps to start the march. Two days before he had advised Jackson of the probable situation, and now he wrote to "Stonewall" with confidence that Fredericksburg was where the armies would meet. Yet, though less than half the size of Burnside's force, Lee did not immediately direct Jackson to join him, but did order him to come east of the Blue Ridge. On November 23 he directed Jackson to Culpeper, giving him the option of threatening Burnside's right flank or of coming on to Fredericksburg, but the next day decided that Jackson must join him immediately. Four days later "Stonewall" came into the lines on the hills and heights around the city.[7]

Longstreet got there on November 21, four days before the first pontoons, and thus was Burnside's surprise movement gone up in smoke. An attractive opportunity did still remain to him, for Lee's two corps were just now more separated than before. If he could effect an undetected movement once, the Federal might do so again, move the bulk of his army back up the Rappahannock, leaving Lee and Longstreet at Fredericksburg, and strike at the isolated Jackson. But Burnside had come here to cross the river, not march back and forth along it. He came to move on Richmond, not Lee's army, and already one of the faults that some of his officers perceived began to show. He was obstinate. Finding it hard to make up his mind under pressure, he found it even more difficult to change it, even in the face of incontestable arguments to the contrary.

Burnside would cross, that was certain. Where was another matter. The Rappahannock offered several potential spots for laying the pontoon bridges. The Federal's first choice was at Skinker's Neck, some fourteen miles below Fredericksburg, and he had hoped to cross on November 26. But by that time he had only sufficient pontoons for one bridge, which would require twice the allotted time for the army to cross. So he waited. Meanwhile, Lee sent Jubal Anderson Early's division—Early of the stutter and irascible temperament—to Skinker's Neck when evidence of the enemy's preparations for a crossing became obvious. And so once again Burnside had to change his mind. He did so grudgingly, and without careful thought or preparation. "I concluded that the enemy would be more surprised by a crossing at or near Fredericksburg, where we were making no preparations," he wrote. Unfortunately, he came to that conclusion without making a good reconnaissance. He believed that the main body of Lee's army was at Port Royal, another ten miles beyond Skinker's Neck, and that only the enemy left flank confronted him. In fact, all but two divisions of the Army of Northern Virginia awaited him on the heights behind the city. Lee wisely did not display his army to full view, and even the balloons that Burnside sent up for observation could not detect the powerful numbers behind the Confederate defenses. Burnside's own plan helped contribute to the confusion on enemy strength, for he posted a heavy concentration of artillery on Stafford Heights to cover the crossings, and Lee, unwilling to face the terrible fire from those guns, had decided not to contest the crossings at the riverbank, but to let the Federals attack him in place in his earthworks. Thus Burnside's own cannon helped keep Lee out of view of his observers.[8]

It was a terrible place for a battle. With the river crossable only on bridges that might have to be erected under fire, just building the pontoon spans would be a major feat. Then troops crossing in narrow file would be exposed to a terrible fire with no protection whatever, only to alight on the other side to find the enemy posted in the houses in town, and in heavy force behind breastworks on the heights beyond. The Rappahannock ran roughly northwest to southeast in front of Fredericksburg, with the city itself extending for something over a mile along its bank. Once there had been a bridge for wagon and foot traffic, and another bridge for the Richmond, Fredericksburg, & Potomac Railroad, but both spans were now destroyed. Commencing 1,500 yards back from the river, the ground began an increasingly steep rise to an eminence known locally as Marye's Heights and Marye's Hill. It ended behind the lower end of town, and on the other side of its down slope rose another series of heights set farther back from the river, and heavily wooded in places.

By the time that Burnside was ready to launch his "surprise" attack across the river, Lee was well emplaced. Having decided not to contest the crossings for fear of that plunging fire from Stafford Heights, the Confederate commander only sent sharpshooters forward into the streets of Fredericksburg. Three of Longstreet's divisions then went into defenses thrown up along the forward crest of Marye's Heights, those on the right flank greatly enhanced by a waist-high stone wall in front of a sunken road. Longstreet's remaining divisions, led by Generals George Edward Pickett and John Bell Hood, took position just beyond the gap between Marye's and the heights next to it. Meanwhile "Stonewall" Jackson, whom Lee was wont to leave to his own devices in selecting ground, made rather shoddy dispositions on Hood's right. Due to the nature of the ground and the heavy forest, he actually left a gap of 500 yards or more between his left and Hood's right, an Achilles' heel that would be further weakened during the course of the battle, and yet another last opportunity for Burnside to salvage something from the series of bad decisions and unaccountable delays that had brought him to this pass. Stuart's cavalry guarded Jackson's right, assisted by the horse artillery of Major John Pelham. All told, Lee had perhaps 85,000 men on the field.

To meet that, Burnside might have counted nearly 113,000. Never before or after in this war would so many men grapple on a single battlefield. Indeed, never in the course of affairs in the New World would armies of such magnitude do battle. Yet ironically, in few other battles of this war would numbers engaged count for so little. Such is the perversity that dogged this campaign from beginning to end.

Burnside gave his Left Grand Division under Franklin the task, appropriately enough, of holding the left of his line, facing Jackson's corps across the river. Sumner's grand division would constitute the right of the line, making its crossings at Fredericksburg itself and moving through the town and directly up against Marye's Heights. Hooker would stand in reserve behind Sumner, the whole to be supported by artillery fire from the guns massed all along the five-mile length of Stafford Heights.

Burnside sent the pontoons and the engineers from Skinker's Neck to their assigned places in front of Franklin's and Sumner's positions during the night of December 10, and at 3 A.M., December 11 they commenced their task. The work went well in front of Franklin, and by ten-thirty that morning one span sat completed almost without opposition. Soon afterward a second pontoon bridge went up beside it. Upriver, however, there was a different story. By 6 A.M. two of the three bridges planned to cross to Fredericksburg were only two thirds built when the Mississippi riflemen barricaded in the windows and rooftops of the city opened fire. The engineers had no choice but to retreat out of range. Several times later that morning they tried to resume the work, but each time were driven back. The artillery could not support them, thanks to a heavy fog that obscured vision. Brigadier General Daniel Phineas Woodbury personally led a band of eighty volunteers back to the unfinished bridge, but the enemy fire was so great that many were quickly hit and the rest refused to move. Only when the fog cleared at noon could the artillery start to drive the Rebels out of town. Then, at the suggestion of General Henry Jackson Hunt, 120 men of the 7th Michigan loaded themselves into the pontoons, twenty to a boat, and paddled across under a deadly rain of bullets. Several took hits on the crossing, but all boats finally made the other side, where the Michiganders immediately formed and began the work of smoking out the sharpshooters in the buildings along the riverbank. More men followed in other pontoons, and by dusk the two bridges were complete. It had been a marvelously heroic exploit, to which Burnside himself paid tribute. "No more difficult feat has been performed during the war than the throwing of these bridges in the face of the enemy by these brave men," he told Halleck. It is well that the commander did not know that General Woodbury thought him an utter fool.[9]

During that night one of Franklin's divisions crossed over on the left and secured its bridgehead, while Oliver Otis Howard's division of Sumner's corps crossed into Fredericksburg itself. There was still some heavy skirmishing with the Mississippians not yet dislodged, but by dawn of December 12 Burnside held the town. Under cover of a dense fog, the remainder of the two grand divisions made the crossing with light opposition, and took up their appointed line. Hooker remained on the north bank in reserve. That night Burnside himself went over to visit with his several commands, view the terrain as best he could, and revise his plan of attack to suit the changed circumstances. It was well after midnight when he recrossed to his headquarters, and his subsequent attack order makes clear that he once again failed to perceive the true strength of the enemy in his front. He was under the impression that the seizure of two roads leading into town from north and south would force the enemy to withdraw from the heights. He was right, assuming that Lee was not there in force, and apparently Burnside still believed that the main body of the Confederates was somewhere south of him near Port Royal. Indeed, he thought that Sumner only needed to send a division forward to take a road behind Marye's Heights, a position held by more than half of Longstreet's corps. And, in fact, the next morning the divisions of Early and Hill returned to the main army so that virtually no substantive Southern forces were anywhere along the Rappahannock except at Fredericksburg.[10]

It was Franklin who struck first, sending forward the division of George Gordon Meade, a temperamental but consistently competent Pennsylvanian. At 9 A.M. he moved his division forward, running into the skirmishers of General Ambrose Powell Hill's division almost at once. Immediately he reported that a battery was opening fire on him from somewhere along the old Richmond road to the left. Forty minutes later it was reported as two batteries. In fact, it was two pieces of horse artillery of the dashing young Major John Pelham. As the fog lifted that morning, Pelham and Stuart had been treated to the magnificent sight of Meade's division marshaling in the open prior to its advance, a stirring vista to men like Stuart who had been in the Regular army before the war. When Meade reached the Richmond road, Pelham's concealed battery opened up, though at first only one gun fired, and under Pelham's personal direction. Yet that gun was sufficiently effective that Meade mistook it for a full battery and turned one of his brigades aside to counter the threat. Pelham soon moved the piece to a new site, commenced firing again, and thereafter repeatedly moved his guns and fired and moved again. As he rode with the guns from position to position, the red-and-blue necktie wrapped around his hat fluttering in the wind, the young artillerist captured even the attention of Lee. "It is glorious to see such courage in one so young," said the Virginian. He would refer later to the boy as "the gallant Pelham." Only after a peremptory order from Stuart did the major finally take his guns out of the way of Meade's advance, having already stalled it for perhaps three quarters of an hour. There would be few feats of individual heroism in this war that could match it.[11]

With Pelham out of the way, Meade pressed on, first ordering a heavy artillery barrage of Jackson's positions on the wooded height. That done, the Federals pressed on in one of the most successful attacks of the day. Jackson's men were posted behind a railroad embankment and along a road. Meade's brigades steadily drove them back, having struck a fortuitous weak spot right in the center of Jackson's front. Shortly after noon the Federals pushed right into the middle of the enemy position and still advanced, though with increasingly heavy fire on their flanks. John Gibbon's division supported Meade's right, but the division of Abner Doubleday, who fired the first Federal shot at Fort Sumter but who never really invented baseball, had to turn aside to counter a threat from Stuart's cavalry. Thus Meade was almost alone, especially after his division and Gibbon's became separated in the dense wood. Soon the rallying Confederates drove Gibbon back out of the trees and across the railroad once more, and Meade could not hold on much longer. By two-fifteen Meade, too, was pulling back. A furious Meade ranted to his friend and corps commander, John F. Reynolds, "My God, General Reynolds, did they think my division could whip Lee's whole army?" Despite the heavy fighting, Franklin had not sent the reinforcements that might have held the advantage so briefly gained. "We are fortunate it is not worse," a disgruntled Reynolds would write a few days later.[12]

Jackson was fortunate, too. That morning before the fighting, he stood with Lee at headquarters, where there was an unrivaled view of the entire prospective battlefield. Longstreet joined them. "Are you not scared by that file of Yankees you have before you down there?" asked Longstreet.

"Wait till they come a little nearer," said Jackson, "and they shall either scare me or I'll scare them!"

By the time Jackson rode over to his corps, Pelham had already begun the scaring, but soon the general saw Meade's breakthrough and the hurried rushing of reinforcements to plug the gap thus created. It was Early, in part, who recaptured the lost ground, and then the Confederates, as if bent on avenging the insult of their line being pierced, pursued the withdrawing Federals despite repeated orders to halt. Jackson knew what would happen, and it did. As soon as the charging units came under the range of the formidable enemy artillery across the river, they were stopped and driven back with considerable loss. Watching the whole from his eagle's nest high behind Longstreet's line, Lee could not help saying aloud that "It is well that war is so terrible—we should grow too fond of it!" The spectacle had been magnificent.[13]

Lee could equally well say this of the scene in front of Marye's Heights, for there the bravery had been just as grand, and the slaughter even more terrible. Franklin's attack had already been under way for perhaps two hours by the time Sumner's advance began. Burnside wanted the attack on his left well developed, in hopes that Franklin would be pressing Lee's right flank back just as Sumner's attack hit. When "Burn" was under the impression that Meade was doing well, he gave Sumner the order to move, and the attack commenced almost at once. Their orders were to press the Confederates back and follow them right into their works, then to continue on into Lee's rear. The division of General William French led the assault, marching out of a light fog to charge up Marye's slopes right into the fire of Thomas R. R. Cobb's brigade as it sat behind the stone wall. Supported by other elements of Lafayette McLaws' division, Cobb drove French back with terrible losses. Then came the division of General Winfield Scott Hancock, only to meet the same repulse, and after him came Oliver Otis Howard's command. Each division advanced to the slope under a heavy artillery fire, and then climbed the heights through constant rifle fire. So heavy was the leaden sheet before them that many men, though uninjured, could not safely retreat with their brethren, and remained the rest of the day lying on the ground feigning death. Others hid behind the dead and dying, praying for nightfall.

Many huddled in a drainage ditch that had played its own role in the debacle. Crossable only at two points, it forced the advancing columns into narrow file, allowing the Confederates to concentrate their fire on the massed targets. Small wonder it was that by one-thirty that afternoon Sumner's grand division lay badly mauled and in need of help. That left Hooker.[14]

Burnside spent much of the morning pacing back and forth on the opposite side of the river, nervously reading the reports from Franklin that first indicated success, but then became increasingly gloomier. Looking across in his front to where Sumner was being ground to a ruin by Longstreet's corps, Burnside repeatedly grumbled to himself that "That height must be carried this evening." Refusing to admit that the order to assault such a position was foolhardy in the first place, Burnside's obstinate nature took over now and demanded that more good men be sent after those already fallen to prove that he had been right in directing the attack. At one-thirty he sent the order to Hooker to cross the river and advance.[15]

Hooker was a schemer to be sure, but not a fool. He, too, had watched the day's fight so far, and when he got Burnside's order he personally looked over the ground he would have to cross and decided that it could not be done. He went in person to Burnside to protest the order.

Riding up on his white charger, Hooker struck cavalry commander Alfred Pleasonton as "the maddest man he ever saw." Fearing to be present at the coming interview, the cavalryman actually slipped outside the head-quarters building, but still overheard as "Hooker made the air blue with adjectives" over Burnside's mismanagement of the battle thus far. Un-moved—certainly the despised Hooker could never move the stubborn Burnside in any event—the commanding general directed that the attack be made.[16]

Hooker groaned and obeyed, though he later admitted that his heart was not in it. At about three-thirty he sent General Charles Griffin's divi-sion into the inferno, followed by Andrew A. Humphreys', and each met the same fate as Sumner's before them. As darkness approached, the divi-sion of George Getty also made the fateful crossing of the drainage ditch, only to fail as had all before. All told, Burnside sent some sixteen attacks against the line behind that stone wall, and not one got closer than twenty-five yards. But nearly 8,000 Federal soldiers, the equivalent of a medium-sized division, lay dead or bleeding in front of that wall. And Burnside had nothing to show for it except a battered army that was rap-idly coming to despise him. He ordered Franklin to renew the attack over on the left to support Hooker, but Franklin had had enough this day as well. Besides, he ineptly placed his grand division in such a fashion that he had no reserve, and forming units for an attack would require consid-erable shifting of his divisions. There was not time to do so before dark, he told his commander, though more likely Franklin simply did not want to. The sooner this battle was done and forgotten the better.[17]

And so it ended. Burnside crossed into Fredericksburg that night, a thoroughly beaten man. "It was plain that he felt he had led us to a great disaster," said General Darius N. Couch, "and one knowing him so long and well as myself could see that he wished his body was also lying in front of Marye's Heights. I never felt so badly for a man in my life." It was obvious to all that the general was crushed. "Oh! Oh, those men! Oh, those men!" he said, repeatedly pointing across the way to the stone wall, "Those men over there! I am thinking of them all the time." So unnerved was Burnside that he began ranting on about how none of his generals would tell him the truth, and that his only true friend was his ex-slave cook, Robert. The man became almost incoherent, and for at least the next twenty-four hours he seemed unable to keep hold of himself or think clearly.[18]

Composed somewhat during the night, the general consulted with his commanders before dawn the next day and announced that they would renew the attack. "Well, it's all arranged," he said. "We attack at early dawn." He would lead the IX Corps into the thick of the fight personally. "We'll make up for the bad work of today." In fact, his intention of standing at the head of his troops in a renewed fight very probably be-trayed an unconscious death wish, the only way he could be free of the memory of "those men over there." However, his officers would have none of it. Almost to a man they opposed him, led by Hooker and Sumner. While they showed him on maps how impregnable the enemy works were, Burnside lost control once again and ranted that his officers were disobedient, that given reliable and loyal generals he would destroy Lee. Finally he calmed, grudgingly, and never admitting that it was not possible to salvage a victory, at last issued the order for a general withdrawal with tears in his eyes.[19]

That was the end of it. The Army of the Potomac lost over 12,000 in killed, wounded, and missing. The Confederates, who fully expected that Burnside would renew the battle and destroy his army, counted barely one third the losses. On the night of December 14, after arranging a truce that afternoon in order to gather wounded and bury the dead, Burnside carefully removed his army back across the Rappahannock, where it would winter in sight of the terrible town that had cost it so dearly, beside the river of death that so many crossed never to return.[20]

As soon as the battle ended, a new fight began as those in the North started the obligatory hunt for scapegoats. Burnside himself, once restored to his senses, manfully accepted most of the blame. "I am responsible," he told Halleck. "The fact that I decided to move from Warrenton onto this line against the opinion of the President, Secretary [Stanton], and yourself, and that you have left the whole management in my hands, without giving me orders, makes me the more responsible." Still, Burnside perceived genuine enemies in his high command. In a faint echo of Braxton Bragg, himself fighting his own generals at this moment, Burnside toyed with the idea of relieving Sumner of command and actually arresting Hooker. But Burnside was not the man for infighting any more than he was the man to command the Union's principal army. Besides, the Radicals quickly took up the cudgel, and they had their own ideas of who was to blame. They wanted Franklin's head, and found a ready ally in the ever-scheming Hooker. With an unsuccessful Burnside probably not long to remain, Hooker needed only to eliminate Franklin to be in line for the command. Sumner was already unpopular enough to be out of the contest. But Burnside did not play the game, and refused to assign any guilt for the debacle to Franklin. Instead, he went personally to Lincoln and offered even to publish a statement accepting all blame for the humiliating defeat.[21]

Interestingly, the President did not remove the general from command as many expected, perhaps because of the manly way in which Burnside took his responsibility. As a result, with some maneuvering season remaining before the winter freeze, Burnside began planning anew in hopes of redeeming his fortunes. Yet he distrusted virtually all of his ranking generals, and henceforward did not consult with them. Instead, he surprised them on the day after Christmas with an order for a general movement and crossing below Fredericksburg. Lincoln stopped the campaign almost immediately after two of the army's generals informed him of it and of their conviction that such a move would simply bring on another Fredericksburg. On December 31, 1862, the general went himself to Washington to confer with Lincoln, and while there heard confirmation of rumors back in camp that certain of his generals had been feeding the President lies about him. Stating that he did not enjoy the esteem or confidence of his subordinates, Burnside suggested that he be relieved. Going further, as if to force Lincoln to replace him, he accused Halleck and Stanton of having lost the good will of the army and the people and suggested that they, too, should be dismissed. He even repeated the charge and handed it to Lincoln in writing in the presence of the surprised war secretary and general-in-chief. Once again Burnside seemed to have misplaced his senses.[22]

When he returned to his army, the general planned yet another campaign with a river crossing. Lincoln discouraged him. Then in January 1863 he finally moved, taking advantage of a spell of unexpectedly good weather. He intended to march up the Rappahannock to Banks' Ford, and there cross the river while diversions on either of Lee's flanks masked the move. It was a reasonable plan, and given good weather it could have worked. But then the heavens opened and conspired against one of the most luckless generals ever to command an army. With the campaign just beginning, a torrential winter rain commenced and did not let up for days.

Somehow Burnside sensed that this was his last chance. Despite the downpour, he pressed on with his campaign. On January 20 the army began to crawl slowly westward along the upper bank of the Rappahannock. The rain slowed the movement to a virtual crawl. Dirt roads, pounded by tens of thousands of feet, turned into a clinging mire that sucked shoes from feet and so clogged wagon wheels that vehicles simply could not move. Every stream and rivulet swelled so with the water that each became another river crossing in the army's path. Still, Lee seemed oblivious to the movement. Burnside already had a pontoon span nearly across the now-swollen Rappahannock at Banks' Ford, but the artillery that he moved up to protect it made an absolute morass all around the approaches to the crossing. The continued rain on the twenty-first and twenty-second only added to the impassable nature of the ground. Worse, though the army had only about six miles to travel to the ford, it could barely make more than a couple of miles a day. Animals fell dead from exhaustion in the fight to slog through the mud, and the morale of an already dispirited army plunged. Even though Burnside actually got some troops across without resistance except from sharpshooters, it was apparent that the campaign was a failure. Lee had found ample time to get his own people to the opposite shore, and once again the surprise was gone. In more wearying days the army plodded back to Falmouth, while the men openly jeered Burnside in the camps, and derisively dubbed the operation "Burnside's Mud March."[23]

Now his reserve finally cracked. On January 23 he made a move to redress the plotting that he knew was going on behind his back. He prepared his fantastic General Order No. 8. In it he declared that "General Joseph Hooker . . . having been guilty of unjust and unnecessary criticisms of the actions of his superior officers . . . is hereby dismissed the service of the United States as a man unfit to hold an important commission." Hooker had sown discontent, told lies, and politicked shamelessly, all true. But Burnside did not have the authority to evict him from his commission, nor did he have the power to do it to Generals W. T. H. Brooks, John Newton, and John Cochrane. Further, the order relieved from duty with his army Franklin, William F. Smith, Samuel D. Sturgis, Edward Ferrero, and others. In a move obviously revealing Burnside's confused and troubled state of mind, he also relieved Cochrane from duty in article IV of the order, after having already kicked him out of the army in article III.

The general took the order to Washington and gave it to Lincoln on January 24. With it he presented an ultimatum. Either the President would accept and act on General Order No. 8, or else he would have to accept Burnside's resignation from the service. Lincoln stalled at first, then confessed that he had decided to replace the general already, but he would not countenance a resignation. "We need you," said the President, "and I cannot accept your resignation." The next morning, after consultation with Halleck, Lincoln formally relieved Burnside of command of the Army of the Potomac. At the same time, he relieved Sumner and Franklin. That left only Hooker. Now he would have the command that he had schemed for for so long, but thanks only to Lincoln, who already distrusted the man. Stanton and Halleck preferred Rosecrans, but he at least had delivered something of a victory at Stones River and should not be removed.[24]

So ended the troubled seventy-eight-day command of Ambrose Burnside. It was the shortest tenure of any commander of the major eastern army except for McDowell, and surely the most tragic. In its aftermath, Burnside finally shed some of his honorable shouldering of responsibility by testifying before the Committee on the Conduct of the War that Franklin was the cause of the loss at Fredericksburg. Since Burnside had become a Radical himself, the Radicals controlling the committee needed someone else upon whom to fix the blame, and Burnside shamefully played their game. They acquitted him of any guilt for the defeat, but his own conscience never accepted the verdict.

Lincoln had learned a lesson, too. His judgment of men was not as infallible as he might think, and generals who doubted their abilities might be just as disappointing as those with overconfidence. Hooker would get his chance soon to disprove the maxim, as well as to contend with the spirit of dissension and intrigue that he had himself done so much to foster in the army. Perryville and Stones River seemed paltry in the measure with the overwhelming loss at Fredericksburg. The fact was that the situation in Virginia was no better than it had been a year before, and now there was another winter to sit through before new generals and new battles could change the balance. Would no one come forth to bring Lincoln victories?

The night after the battle of December 13, as the soldiers of blue and gray huddled for warmth at their fires, seeking to drive the horrors of the day from their minds, an atmospheric phenomenon seldom seen in that latitude appeared in the western sky. An aurora caused a glowing phantom light to shine in the distance, far up the Rappahannock. The soldiers, as warriors of all times, could look into it for omen and symbol. Was it to mark the great Southern victory? Virginia preserved for another season? Was it the end of Burnside, or the rising star of Hooker, or nothing but a light in the sky?[25]

Or was it a last electric spark of life as the ghosts were given up by the wasted dead of Fredericksburg?

CHAPTER 4

"THESE MONITORS ARE MISERABLE FAILURES"

How elusive those victories seemed, and some would evade Lincoln for years more before they were his. As the spring of 1863 began its bloom, the President could look back on two years of war and see little profit for the cause. Certainly there were the scattered successes, and more certain still—though so many refused to see it—was the fact that just as the boundaries of the Confederacy slowly contracted, just so the cause of the Union gradually advanced to triumph. But to sustain a war for the long term, he needed more than an occasional success. He needed great victories to lift the morale of his people. He needed to redress in the Northern mind and heart the terrible humiliations suffered. One of those bitter memories, the first one suffered and always the most irksome, was the initial insult to the flag when Fort Sumter fell. Charleston was the seedbed of the Rebellion. Could it but fall to Mr. Lincoln's arms, then a great wrong would be avenged, and a dagger thrust deep into the underbelly of the Confederacy. As it proved, his dagger was often too dull, and that underbelly not so soft. The taking of Charleston in the end required a virtual siege that lasted the length of the war.

In the aftershock of the fall of Fort Sumter, Lincoln and his government did not concern themselves with a renewed effort to assert Federal authority in Charleston harbor. A Confederate army in their front at Manassas proved a more immediate worry. Yet certainly they had to turn their eyes to the South Carolina coast soon, for Charleston was more than symbolic. Its harbor was one of the finest on the Southern coastline, and one of the most active shipping centers for the heavy trade abroad that the Confederacy needed to sustain itself. Despite the imposition of the blockade off Charleston, the runners proved quite adept at eluding the Federal vessels. Furthermore, the city offered an important communications and rail center, a major connection with Savannah, Atlanta, and the western Confederacy. And a toehold here would afford Federal invaders an easy route to take Savannah or Wilmington, North Carolina, or a host of other lesser port towns from the undefended land side, at the same time providing the best possible supply base for extended military adventures deeper into the Southern heartland.

The first operation aimed at Charleston was, in fact, an indirect one. In November 1861, Flag Officer Samuel F. I. Du Pont brought a hefty naval squadron to Port Royal Sound, seventy miles below Charleston. He steamed into the bay, right between two enemy forts, Beauregard and Walker, and at once commenced shelling the earthworks into submission. One of them was commanded by Brigadier General Thomas Drayton, who finally evacuated. One of the Federal officers taking part in the bombardment happened to be Commander Percival Drayton of the U.S.S. *Pocahontas*. Brothers. Fearful that Du Pont might think that he hesitated to attack his own sibling, Commander Drayton led his ship into the thickest of the fight against Fort Walker, pounding it mercilessly. As boys, the two South Carolinian brothers had played together not far from there.[1]

Though not much of a military event, the capture of Port Royal proved to be of considerable importance. It was a much-needed victory for Lincoln. Better, it placed Union forces squarely between Charleston and Savannah, and it afforded the blockade fleet an excellent base for coaling and refitting its soon-to-be-overworked vessels. And it threw Charleston into a momentary panic. "There is a great terror prevailing here," wrote a frightened citizen. "I regard the city in hourly peril. I believe it could be taken in six hours." Many left the city taking their best possessions with them, and shortly the military commander asked Richmond for permission to declare martial law. The furor soon subsided as it became obvious that the enemy was not marching on the city nor making any apparent preparation to do so, but for a fleeting moment Charlestonians experienced much the same consternation that they had so gleefully visited upon their Northern brethren seven months before.[2]

With Port Royal taken, Du Pont landed soldiers that, quickly augmented, grew to number 12,000, a small army commanded by Brigadier General Thomas W. Sherman. In fact, had Sherman followed the initial success with a speedy move against either Charleston or Savannah, he stood an excellent chance of succeeding. Instead he remained content with occupying Port Royal and nearby Hilton Head Island, making of them the beginnings of what would become the Union's most important supply base on the Southern seaboard.

In part as a reaction to this Union threat, the Confederate War Department created just two days before the attack a new department containing South Carolina, Georgia, and part of Florida. The man selected for the new command was thus far an unknown quantity in this war, though he achieved a measure of notoriety in the Mexican conflict. General Robert E. Lee served as an adviser to Davis during the Bull Run Campaign, major general in command of Virginia forces, and pursued an unsuccessful fall campaign in western Virginia. Some were not pleased with his assignment to the new position, particularly South Carolina governor Francis W. Pickens. Four months earlier he remarked scathingly that Lee was not "the man his reputation makes him." Pickens concluded that "Lee is not with us at heart, or he is a common man, with good looks, and too cautious for practical Revolution." This reputation for caution led some to call him derisively "Granny Lee."[3]

Lee reached Charleston the very day of Du Pont's attack, and at once reacted to the threat. He had over 300 miles of coastline to protect, and all too few resources for the task. There were barely more than 5,000 soldiers in and immediately around Charleston. Even as he gave orders for the commencement of strengthening existing fortifications along the coast, he visited with Pickens and spoke of enlisting South Carolina militia into the Southern service to protect the city. He personally inspected as much of his defensive works as possible, one of the first stops being Fort Sumter, and there he made a more impressive impression than he had with Governor Pickens. An observer called him "the most striking figure we had ever encountered, . . . with broad shoulders well thrown back, a fine justly-proportioned head posed in unconscious dignity, clear, deep, thoughtful eyes, and the quiet, dauntless step of one every inch the gentleman and soldier."[4]

For the next four months Lee engaged his command almost solely in the work of digging and erecting stronger and more extensive earthworks and defenses. He had been in the Engineers in the old army, and he knew his business when it came to fortifications. His soldiers failed to see the wisdom of it all. "Granny" soon became "Spades" Lee instead, but the work was well done and served in the defense of Charleston for years to come. Lee and Pickens made their peace and the governor provided him with state troops for his small command, and best of all Sherman showed no inclination at all to move against him. Rarely would a Federal commander be more cooperative, but then Lee would be fortunate in facing "cooperative" opponents in blue for all but the final year of the war.

Not until late in December did the Federals finally make a hostile gesture toward Charleston, and a passive one at that. Charleston had just recently suffered a terrible fire that destroyed a number of fine homes and several factories and warehouses, as well as the Carolina Institute Hall, where the original ordinance of secession was signed. The wind whipped the flames from building to building for hours, with no firemen to stop them. Most of them were serving in the army now. All told, over 540 acres of the city lay charred and in rubble, ruins that would not be cleared or rebuilt during the remainder of the war.

Hard on this loss came a menacing Federal fleet, yet one that did not intend to fire a single gun except in self-defense. Since Lincoln imposed the blockade of Southern ports back in April, the Union navy struggled to implement such a policy effectively over thousands of miles of Southern coastline. To Secretary of the Navy Gideon Welles's alert and aggressive assistant secretary, an idea occurred that might materially aid the program, while allowing the blockading fleets to spread themselves a little thinner without harm. Gustavus V. Fox proposed that they sail or steam otherwise useless or condemned ships into the mouths of several harbors and river mouths, and there scuttle them in the main shipping channels. Properly placed, such obstacles would be difficult to remove and a constant menace to blockade-runners. Welles and Lincoln approved, and in October the secretary gave orders for the purchase of twenty-five old vessels of varying description.[5]

Most of them had been whaling ships, and some dated back to the Revolution and before. All were stripped of useful hardware, and each had a long pipe fitted into the bottom of the hull, with a seacock attached. Opening that valve would flood the hull and sink the ship. To make them more of an immovable obstacle once on the bottom, Welles filled the holds with granite. And thus this came to be known as the Stone Fleet.

With that spirit of competition that sailing men seem born to, the captains of the various doomed vessels actually raced to see which might be first to reach their appointment in Charleston harbor. In fact, they were originally intended for Savannah, but the Confederates scuttled some of their own vessels there in such a manner that the Federals could not find their way into the proper channel to do their work. So off they went to Charleston. Entrusted with the oversight of the operation was Captain Charles H. Davis, who openly exhibited the seaman's distaste for willfully sinking his ship. "I had always a special disgust for this business," he complained. It grew in part from his prewar days when he helped with making improvements in Charleston harbor.[6]

It was not a smooth journey to the harbor on December 19, some of the ships, barely more than hulks, being unmanageable, and others so loaded down that they had to be towed across the sandbar outside the harbor. The sinking began that same day, and continued on through the morrow. There was some symbolism in the conclusion of the operation on December 20. As the final ship went down that evening, set ablaze to glow in the darkness until she finally sank at midnight, it was one year to the day from the signing of the ordinance of secession that began it all. The fact was not lost on Lee, who regarded the move with utter contempt and, what was rare, showed it. "This achievement, so unworthy of any nation," he wrote to Richmond, "is the abortive expression of malice and revenge of a people which it wishes to perpetuate by rendering more memorable a day hateful in their calendar."[7]

At first the Federals believed that they had achieved a signal success. The main channel into Charleston was closed, leaving only two others, and they could presumably be closed in the same manner. Shortly Welles went to work buying another "fleet." It proved more difficult this time, yet by mid-January he had another, smaller, flotilla of granite-filled hulks on their way to Charleston. Bad weather drove some off their course, but on January 20, 1862, and in following days, another fourteen sad vessels went to the bottom, this time in Maffitt's Channel, one of the principal routes used by blockade-runners. This presumably left only a northern channel open, and that, too, could be blocked in the same way. Or so they thought. The fact soon became apparent that the mud on the bottom of Charleston's channels simply swallowed the heavy ships. Rather than sitting as obstructions to shipping, they quickly settled deep enough so that shipping passed over them in safety. Before long the granite hulks could not even be found by dredging. And in the passage of months, new channels appeared, thanks to wind and weather. The whole scheme proved a failure, and less than a week after the first fleet went down, authorities in Charleston could report that "From such observation as has been lately made the sunken fleet is gradually disappearing."[8]

In the end, the whole affair proved a considerable embarrassment to the Union navy, and to Lincoln. Besides failing to halt the blockade-running trade—it only delayed it for a few days—the move also caused a howl of protest in several quarters in the North and abroad. Far from the temporary war measure of a blockade justified by the existing conflict, these sinkings struck many as virtually permanent obstructions, thereby not just a measure against the insurrection, but a blow to Charleston for decades after the war's conclusion, however it might end. "Such a cruel plan would seem to imply despair at the restoration of the Union," thought the British foreign office. Both England and France became upset, and it was only a few weeks since the United States had finally ended one diplomatic crisis by releasing from prison the Confederate diplomats James M. Mason and John Slidell, taken rashly by force from a British vessel in international waters. Secretary of State Seward found himself well pressed to explain that the whole affair was simply a misunderstanding. No one intended the permanent closing of Charleston, he said. It was a temporary war measure. Neither he nor Fox nor anyone else suspected just how temporary it would be.[9]

The remainder of the winter passed quietly for Charleston, though busily. Lee never stopped his digging and building, most of it under the direct supervision of Brigadier General Roswell S. Ripley, an Ohioan whose uncle was currently chief of ordnance for the United States army. In March 1862, only shortly after Lee commenced a policy of planting "torpedoes"—floating or slightly submerged contact mines—in the waters of his command, he was ordered to return to Virginia to serve as President Davis' chief adviser. And of course, within a few weeks he assumed command of the Army of Northern Virginia. In his place, Richmond assigned Major General John C. Pemberton. It seemed to be the odd fate of Charleston, the spawning ground of Southern nationalism, that frequently its commanders were to be Yankees like Ripley. Pemberton was a Philadelphian, a man like Ripley who probably derived his Confederate allegiance from his marriage to a Southern lady. Pemberton, as Lee before him, found Ripley to be an abrasive, contentious subordinate, and soon relieved him of command at Charleston.

Pemberton himself soon achieved a considerable measure of unpopularity in his own right. As soon as he took command, unfortunate events began. On May 13, 1862, the black pilot Robert Smalls achieved his headline-making escape from Charleston in the cotton steamer *Planter*. He brought to the blockading forces not only a useful little coastal steamer and a handful of newly freed Negro crewmen, but also useful military information. The blacks received prize money from the captured vessel, and Smalls himself went on to do pilot duty with the Union navy. Altogether it was a terribly embarrassing episode for the Confederates in Charleston. Making matters worse, Pemberton himself approached Charleston's defense with a view that Charlestonians and Governor Pickens found distinctly unpalatable. The city should best be defended by abandoning the forts in and around it, destroying them, and meeting the enemy in the field! Pickens immediately asked that the general be relieved.[10]

But it was the enemy that presented the greatest threat to the besieged city. Repeated withdrawals of troops from Pemberton's command left him in a weakened and vulnerable position, one not ignored entirely by the customarily complacent Federal commanders at Port Royal and Hilton Head. A series of islands lined the coast between Port Royal and Charleston. Edisto, Seabrook, John's, James, all led gradually toward Stono Inlet and the southern door into Charleston itself. The Confederates originally tried to provide defense at every one of them, but the limitations in soldiers and supplies made it impossible. Gradually Pemberton pulled back from each one successively. By mid-June the Federals held a firm foothold on the southern part of James Island, and it was apparent that they would soon attack the Confederate command there vainly trying to keep this last island stronghold. Pemberton had barely 6,500 soldiers there, against an enemy that he estimated at 12,000, and daily growing.[11]

The man in command of that expanding blue horde on James Island was David Hunter, just recently restored to active field operations after being wounded on his birthday in the First Battle of Bull Run. Now he commanded the forces advancing on Charleston along this southern route. His intention was not to hazard an engagement with the enemy dug in on the island until he had considerably augmented his forces and, particularly, the siege artillery of which he was so fond. On June 13 he had gotten onto James Island within five or six miles of Charleston, and expected to make a final assault on the city as soon as more troops arrived.

Unfortunately, when he left Brigadier General Henry W. Benham in command temporarily on James Island, he failed to completely instruct Benham in his intentions, or else the general did not listen. "I gave positive orders to General Benham that no advance should be made until further explicit orders had been received." Hunter himself returned to Hilton Head on June 11, allowing Benham only sufficient discretion to protect his existing camps. At the same time, apparently, Hunter did comment that it would be necessary for them to capture or destroy the enemy positions and batteries at Secessionville, farther up the island. Benham either misinterpreted this as authorization to move in spite of Hunter's orders not to engage the Confederates, or else decided to do so anyhow in the expectation of victory. Soldiers who disobeyed orders and won triumphs were seldom censured.[12]

Benham consulted with the commanders of the three divisions under his control, Horatio G. Wright, Isaac I. Stevens, and Robert Williams, and all joined in unanimously opposing an attack on Secessionville as a violation of orders. Obviously, they as well as Benham knew the intent of Hunter's instructions. Wright and Stevens acted out a little debate before their commander in which Wright asked the other questions. They had already advanced to within attacking distance of the enemy by June 15, in what Benham chose to call a "reconnaissance in force." Hunter had forbidden him to attack, not to feel out the Confederate works. Stevens' artillery had managed to drive the Rebels from their works at times, but they always afterward returned as soon as the fire ceased. When Wright asked Stevens if he thought that the earthworks could be taken on the morrow as Benham planned, Stevens replied that "It is simply a bare possibility to take the work." Benham would not be dissuaded. Overruling all their objections, he ordered an attack the following morning.[13]

It was an absolute failure. Beginning at shortly after 4 A.M., Benham sent three succeeding assaults against the well-dug-in enemy. The first attack found only 500 Confederates to resist it, but that proved enough to turn back the advance. By the time Benham's second charge hit the Secessionville fortifications, the defenders had been augmented by 2,000 reinforcements sent by the commander on James Island, a man with something of a history of successful defense against overwhelming numbers, Brigadier General Nathan G. "Shanks" Evans. Back at First Bull Run it was he who, with half a brigade, held up the advance of two Federal divisions—one of them David Hunter's—until reinforcements came to stabilize the line. He was a braggart, an inebriate, and generally unruly and insubordinate. He would be court-martialed before long, but no Southern general ever took to battle with more spirit or determination.

By 10 A.M. Benham gave up, having been beaten everywhere along his line by a force barely one third his size. Evans lost just over 200 in killed and wounded or missing. For Benham the number ran considerably higher, to 683. And the rash Benham himself would soon be a casualty. Hunter placed him under arrest immediately upon learning of the loss at Secessionville, and sent Benham north to face a possible trial. "This step has cost me much regret," said Hunter, "as previous to this unhappy act of rashness he has been industrious, energetic, and wholly devoted to his duties." More regretful still, the attack stimulated renewed efforts to reinforce Charleston, and the opportunity for a successful assault on the city itself, which Hunter once hoped to make, soon became impractical. On June 27, seeing no further purpose to be served by remaining on James Island, Hunter ordered its abandonment.

It had been a trifling battle, barely more than a skirmish by the standards now being established by the armies in Virginia and Tennessee. Yet it saved Charleston, and not just for the summer of 1862. Brigadier General Johnson Hagood, one of the Confederate commanders immediately involved, claimed years later that Secessionville should be regarded as a pivotal battle of the Civil War. Had Benham won, there was little to stand between him and Charleston. His loss reprieved the city and forced Hunter to retire and look for a new line of approach. It put Benham out of the war for more than a year. The Federals did not make another significant military move against the city for the rest of the year. For the next twelve months, it would be up to the navy to try its steel against the bastion city of South Carolina.[14]

Even the success at Secessionville could not keep Pemberton his command in the face of the political opposition against him. Finally, in September 1862, a familiar face came to relieve him. P. G. T. Beauregard, the hero of Fort Sumter and Bull Run, was back in South Carolina. Pemberton would go west, trading one siege for another as he took a new command in Mississippi, at Vicksburg.

Beauregard was an engineer at heart and went to work at once augmenting the defenses of the city and the forts surrounding. He ringed the harbor with heavy artillery, strengthened the boom that stretched across the channel to obstruct unfriendly traffic, and expanded the mine-laying program. He built new sand and earth fortifications on Morris Island, one soon to be called Battery Wagner, and hurried the work of completing two ersatz ironclad gunboats, the *Chicora* and the *Palmetto State*. There was a sense of urgency about it all, for in October came word from Richmond that Du Pont and his fleet were expected to attack within two weeks. Beauregard's response was a promise to Richmond that "We will endeavor to give Commodore Du Pont as warm a reception as circumstances will permit." Despite his confidence, however, Beauregard confessed that "much has still to be done."[15]

Fortunately, the Federal navy gave the Creole general more time than he could possibly have wished. The intelligence of Du Pont's advance proved incorrect. Furthermore, when Beauregard received another such warning in late November and advised his commander in Charleston to be ready, the enemy fleet was in fact on its way to North Carolina, leaving Charleston safe for the remainder of the season. Indeed, when finally the roar of guns was heard across the choppy waters of Charleston harbor, they heralded the beginning of a Confederate attack. The besieged city, like the bee in a spider's web, though surrounded and ensnared, could still sting.

The people of Charleston shared with others, North and South, much exaggerated notions of the power and potential of the heavy, lumbering ironclads that so captured the American imagination. With two of them abuilding in the harbor, Charleston editors and citizens bitterly speculated over why they were not sent forth to destroy the blockading fleet and free the port once more from the hold that, though not strangling, still certainly constricted the breath of the port. "Why is it that with—gunboats at this port well armed, manned, and officered, and 'spoiling for a fight,' we do not clear the blockade?" complained the Charleston *Courier*. Indeed, even a third ironclad was slowly growing above its keel, financed chiefly by contributions of jewelry and fund-raising functions by the ladies of the city. "The Ladies Iron-Clad Gunboat," as it came to be called, was far from completion as 1863 dawned, but not so the other two. They must attack.[16]

The pressure grew too great for Commodore Duncan Ingraham, now commanding the so-called Charleston Squadron. The ironclads were built solely for harbor defense. They were too heavy and slow and unseaworthy for real maneuver and fighting on the ocean. Nevertheless, aside from the pressures on him, Ingraham could count some positive factors in his favor. He had not one, but two ironclads, a genuine fleet, and nowhere else in the Confederacy did a harbor commander enjoy such a luxury. Better than that, though the ships were untried, he had a surfeit of experienced officers. There were men who had fought at Hampton Roads the previous March when the *Monitor* met the *Virginia*. He had two officers from the formidable though ill-fated *Arkansas*, that the past summer had severely discomfited Farragut's fleet on the Mississippi. Taken in sum, and added to the calm seas of late January, Ingraham could attack the blockading ships off the harbor mouth with something approaching a fair chance. All he needed was a good tide, a dark night, some fog, and a little luck. On January 30, 1863, he got it all.

It was eleven o'clock that night when the small fleet left its moorings and set off toward the mouth of the harbor. The two ironclads were painted a dull grayish color, perhaps in an attempt to make them less visible. Their crews streaked grease on their sloping sides in the hope that the slime would help deflect enemy shot. It had the double purpose as well of protecting the iron sides from the heavy sea spray that could quickly turn the metal into a rusted waste. Three gunboats accompanied the iron monsters, and at about 2 A.M. they all anchored just inside the sandbar at the harbor mouth, awaiting the rising tide that would allow the deep-draught vessels to cross. At about four-forty the depth was right, and over they went. The wooden vessels dropped behind the ironclads, and in the early morning haze they set out blindly toward the as-yet-unseen enemy ships.

The *Palmetto State* struck first. At about 5 A.M. the pilot and Ingraham, who was aboard, made out a ship before them. They aimed straight for it. "What steamer is that?" came a cry from the U.S.S. *Mercedita.* "Drop your anchor; you will be into us!" At the last moment an officer aboard shouted, "This is the Confederate States steamer *Palmetto State!*" Before anything could be done aboard the Federal ship, the ironclad drove its iron ram deep into the wooden ship's hull, and at the same moment an 80-pound rifle in the bow sent a shot through the steam works and out the *Mercedita*'s other side. At once her commander determined that she was sinking and sent an officer to surrender, but already Ingraham was turning his ship to the aid of the *Chicora.*

The other ironclad went into action about twenty minutes after the *Palmetto State,* and some distance farther to sea. As a result, the rest of the blockade fleet was alerted by the firing on the *Mercedita* and were somewhat ready for the attack. Still, the *Chicora* gamely went into battle. Without slowing, she sent several shells into a schooner, then steamed on toward the *Quaker City,* opened fire, and had the pleasure of seeing the enemy side-wheeler turn and run. Next came the *Keystone State,* but one incendiary shell from the *Chicora* set the Federal ablaze and put her out of the action. While another ship began towing the *Keystone State* to safety, the *Palmetto State* kept an eye on the action. The *Mercedita,* as it turned out, proved able to limp away from the scene without sinking, and Ingraham, by seven-thirty, despaired of any further successes. With their steam up, all of the blockading vessels could outdistance the ironclads now and were rapidly running away. He could see the *Chicora* fighting to keep up with five other ships, all pulling away from her and her blazing guns. They had done all they could that day, and now the commodore signaled for the fleet to return to the bar and await the evening tide that would carry them over and back into Charleston harbor.[17]

It was an altogether excellent day for the little navy. Later that same day Ingraham issued a bold proclamation stating that he had "sunk, dispersed, or drove off and out of sight for the time the entire hostile fleet." Therefore he declared the blockade of Charleston to be raised, an important act, for in international maritime law an ineffective blockade was an illegal one. Foreign consuls in Charleston were escorted outside the harbor to see for themselves that no enemy vessels lay in sight, and copies of the proclamation went at once to agents in Nassau, one of the staging ports for blockade-runners readying to run into Charleston. The facts, of course, belied Ingraham's claims in the end. Not a single blockade ship went down, and all those injured reached Port Royal to repair. Furthermore, later that same afternoon some of Du Pont's ships returned to their stations off the city. As a result, not a single merchant ship entered the port during its brief hours of freedom unhampered by the blockade. Thus the blockade was not officially lifted, and such was the view taken by the British Government and others.[18]

For the moment, however, Charleston had a brave band of heroes in its intrepid ironclad seamen, and it feted them royally. The enemy took more than casual notice of their exploit, too. Recognizing the threat that the two gunboats posed to the blockade fleet, Secretary Welles soon sent to station off the harbor the greatest fleet of ironclads in the world. Even the original *Monitor* was to join the flotilla, but as she made her way south, being towed by the U.S.S. *Rhode Island*, the unseaworthy little vessel was caught in a heavy storm off Cape Hatteras, North Carolina, and on December 31, 1862, she sank to a lonely grave in two hundred feet of water. But her progeny remained to press the siege of Charleston.

The weather prevented real active operations by the Federals that year, but everyone knew that an attack must come. Du Pont rapidly built up his formidable fleet until, by spring, it numbered nine great ironclads. The huge *New Ironsides*, one of the most successful armored ships of the war, led a fleet comprised of the monitors *Weehawken*, *Passaic*, *Montauk*, *Patapsco*, *Catskill*, *Nantucket*, *Nahant*, and *Keokuk*. He did not repose great confidence in the abilities of the armored vessels, yet he urgently asked for them after the threat created by the enemy vessels. Du Pont believed the defenses that Beauregard was erecting would not fall to a naval force. Fort Sumter and the several other masonry and earthen works ringing the harbor were simply too strong to be reduced with naval guns, particularly considering that a monitor carried but two cannon in its turret. Worse, though formidable in close quarters, the ironclads were not built for or suited to long-range work in deep waters. Unfortunately, the Navy Department did not appreciate the limitations of the ships, despite Du Pont's fears. Welles and others regarded them as impregnable, and in sending them to the admiral, the secretary expected him to boldly steam into the harbor and "demand the surrender of all its defenses, or suffer the consequences." Du Pont wanted to see Charleston taken by land, by the army. Washington decided that he could as well do it himself.[19]

Du Pont made his move on April 7, 1863, with little or no confidence of his own success. Five days before, he left Port Royal to join the ironclad fleet at North Edisto Island. There he put the monsters under tow for Charleston, for they were too clumsy to contend with the ocean by themselves. On April 5 the *Keokuk* approached the bar outside the harbor and laid buoys to mark the water depth for the attack to come the next day. On the morning of the sixth the balance of the fleet crossed the bar, the *New Ironsides* in the lead, intending to make straight for Fort Sumter and reduce it first before attacking the city proper. The weather shortly turned foul, however, and Du Pont put his ships at anchor for the night, intending to attack on the morrow.[20]

Obviously, if the admiral had any intention of achieving a surprise, his movements betrayed themselves to Beauregard and the Confederate defenders of the city. On April 5 the general ordered noncombatants to leave, and looked to his already extensive preparations to meet an attack from the water. His own ironclads had their steam up ready to enter the defense, and the artillerymen stationed all around the harbor had carefully fired testing shots at different elevations, and measured where their projectiles splashed down, marking the spots with buoys. Thus when an enemy ship approached one of the buoys, the Confederate gunners knew the exact range, elevation, and powder charge to use. More mines went into the channels. Never in the war would the Southern defenders be so ready to repel an attack as at Charleston on April 7. Unless the ironclads were really as tough as Welles thought, it would not go well for them.

It did not. Du Pont formed his fleet in a single "line ahead," the *Weehawken* in the lead, pushing before it a wooden raft expected to catch mines before they could damage the hull. The tide did not allow him to advance until nearly noon, and then almost at once the raft became tangled with the lead ironclad, delaying the procession for more than an hour, all the while under the watchful eyes of hundreds of expectant Confederate cannoneers.

Then the *Weehawken* went ahead. First she came past some buoys whose purpose Du Pont did not entirely divine. He thought them mine markers, especially after a "torpedo" exploded against the mine raft. But the ironclad pressed on. The she signaled to the fleet that there were obstructions in her path—the log booms and rope snares that Beauregard had laid in previous months. They closed the opening of the harbor from Fort Moultrie on the right to Sumter on the left side of the channel. A few minutes later the batteries on Sumter and at Moultrie and on Morris and Sullivan's islands opened up on the fleet, and fired incessantly for the next hour and forty minutes.

Pandemonium broke loose in Du Pont's flotilla. *Weehawken* found that she could not cross the obstruction. That forced her to turn toward Fort Sumter, and likewise the vessels that followed. The sudden change in direction, unplanned, did not go without difficulty, and the *New Ironsides* twice had to anchor briefly to avoid running aground, and still managed a minor collision with two of the monitors. She never did maneuver her batteries to bear against Sumter, but the monitors did. *Keokuk* got within 500 to 600 yards, having taken the lead in the confusion, and there she remained for perhaps thirty minutes. The rain of fire that hit her from the two forts nearly destroyed the ship. She carried two gun turrets, but within minutes both were put almost completely out of action. The ironclad fired only three times. Ninety enemy projectiles struck her in that half hour, some nineteen of them piercing her hull along and below the waterline. "In short," said her commander, "the vessel was completely riddled." He pulled her out of the fight to prevent her sinking, but only to a sufficient distance to be out of range of the Confederate guns. There he fought all night to keep her afloat, but when the water turned rough the next morning she went down to the bottom in a span of minutes.

That was only the beginning. The *Nahant* got within 500 yards of Sumter when it, too, felt the effect of enemy iron. Two shots jammed the turret so that it would not turn. Then solid shot started striking the pilothouse with such force that they knocked loose the heads of the bolts holding the armor to its backing. The boltheads became instantly deadly missiles in their own right, flying about the pilothouse, knocking the pilot unconscious twice and fatally wounding the helmsman. With the steering jammed as well, only superhuman efforts managed to get the crippled ironclad back out of the fight, its armor cracked and dented and peeling from its turret in places. She fired only fifteen times in forty minutes.

The *Passaic*, commanded by Percival Drayton, did little better. She fired four times before her turret machinery jammed. Then her pilothouse was twisted from its mountings, exposing those inside in such a fashion that one more shot would have lifted them and the remainder of the housing right off the ship. Thirty-three times the enemy iron found her sides. The *Patapsco* only fired five times, and the *Nantucket* launched only three shots before enemy fire put her out of the action. The others in the fleet maintained some fire with less damage, but to no effect. Du Pont felt certain that another thirty minutes of action would see the entire fleet disabled.

In the brief time of the fight, the flotilla fired only 139 shot and shell. In the same period the forts sent 2,209 projectiles against them, and 323 found their marks on the six most damaged ironclads. Du Pont regarded the effort as an utter failure, feeling fortunate to have escaped with any fleet at all. At four-thirty he signaled to withdraw from the action, intending to renew it the next day. But when he spoke with his captains and learned the extent of the damage done, he abandoned any such thought. Seeing what barely an hour's action against the heavy guns of the forts had done to his fleet, there was no possibility of relying upon their strength for another effort.[21]

What was more galling yet, the whole affair barely inflicted any damage at all upon their enemies. The majority of the shots fired by the Federal fleet arched across the water toward Sumter, and many found their target. The masonry of the sea-face of the fort was so well constructed and thick, however, that the shells did nothing more than gouge out holes in the brick. A few other shots hit Fort Moultrie, and there inflicted the only Confederate fatality of the day, when a flag staff was cut down and, in falling, struck a gunner. For the people in Charleston itself, most of whom ignored Beauregard's order to leave, the battle proved a lark, reminiscent of a day almost exactly two years before. Intended to be prisoners by Du Pont, they were merely spectators.[22]

"I attempted to take the bull by the horns, but he was too much for us," a disgruntled Du Pont wrote to David Hunter. "These monitors are miserable failures where forts are concerned." He was right. The reduction of a great pile of brick and mortar needed many guns and a long time. The expectation that Du Pont could steam boldly into the harbor and silence two forts that had been constantly strengthened for two years, not to mention the numerous other batteries in the Charleston defenses, was simply absurd. Lincoln and Welles were both culpable, the latter more than the former, though in small measure they can be excused. This was the first real trial of ironclads against forts. The *Monitor* and the *Galena* made a nearly disastrous attempt the year before at Drewry's Bluff on the James River, trying to attack enemy earthworks high above the river. The *Galena* was torn up badly and the *Monitor*, though not materially damaged, proved ineffective. But Welles could not draw much of a lesson from such an encounter, and so had to learn at the expense of Du Pont. The trouble was, the secretary failed to learn the lesson very well, and refused to see its meaning. He and the President were almost immediately critical of Du Pont, not of the monitors. Lincoln ordered the admiral to remain on station off Charleston, and Welles began an unfortunate battle of the pen with Du Pont. The press attacked the seaman viciously, one paper crying, "Oh! that we had a Farragut here to take command at once, and do what has been so weakly attempted by Admiral Du Pont." Even though his officers unanimously supported their commander, Du Pont could not avoid being sacrificed. Welles did not like failure, and made cause to shift whatever of blame rested with him—which was plenty—to the shoulders of a man who had advised against the attack in the first place. When the admiral persisted in declining to sacrifice his fleet by renewing the attack, the secretary finally advised him on June 3 that he would be relieved of command. It was a sad and unjust end to a great naval career.[23]

Now the baton passed once more to the land forces in the constant struggle to wrest Charleston from the arms of secession. General Hunter was supposed to have cooperated with Du Pont in the April 7 attack, but did nothing, there being in fact little to do. He, too, found himself relieved in June, however, to be replaced by Brigadier General Quincy A. Gillmore, a career engineer who had been largely responsible for the capture of Fort Pulaski near Savannah the year before. Here was a man with considerable genius for planning and for preparation, but of a nature contentious, unwilling to shoulder blame for failure, and of a scheming and often dissembling mind. His tenure would be a stormy one, made the more so by Du Pont's replacement, John Adolphus Bernard Dahlgren, developer of the Dahlgren gun used widely on Federal—and Confederate —warships. Both were proud, egotistical men who, though they got on well together for some time, eventually fell into a bickering and argumentative debate that continued for the rest of their lives.

Gillmore had orders to take Charleston, and to do so with the cooperation of the navy. How he did it was left pretty much to him. Looking at a map of Charleston and its environs, he deduced largely what Hunter before him had concluded. The key to taking the city with an army lay in approaching it from the south. The entrance to the harbor was protected on that side by Morris Island. Battery Gregg on Cummings Point covered much of the harbor mouth with its guns, while providing protection for Fort Sumter as well. If Federal siege batteries could be implanted there and at other positions on Morris Island, they could batter Sumter into rubble and thereby clear the path for Federal ships to pass into the harbor and take the city. That would in turn force the evacuation of Sullivan's Island and, with it, Fort Moultrie.

To achieve this, Gillmore had first to take Morris Island and, in particular, Battery Wagner, that formidable earthwork that had been abuilding for nearly a year. He believed that he could do so without great difficulty. He had almost 12,000 troops at hand and nearly 100 pieces of powerful artillery and siege cannon. With Dahlgren's fleet to support him, he could not fail. Late in June he notified General Halleck in Washington that he should own the better part of the island in a week or less.

Dahlgren arrived at his new command early in July, and on July 5 he rushed to confer with Gillmore about the impending movement. Gillmore stated that on the day of attack the fleet should enter the channel abreast of Morris Island early in the morning at the same time that he launched his attack. "My desire [is] that there should be perfect and cordial understanding between us in these combined operations," the general concluded. Dahlgren was anxious to assist. Without there being time for the Navy Department to give him instructions, the seaman on his own responsibility set about cooperating with Gillmore, intending to take the ironclads into the action "to relieve the troops as much as possible." He did not understand that more was expected of him. In the ensuing days Dahlgren worked feverishly to repair and prepare his fleet for the action scheduled to take place on July 10. Seven of the ironclads—six monitors and the *New Ironsides*—were all that he would be able to bring to bear.[24]

Gillmore intended to deceive the Confederates on Morris Island as to his intentions. On July 9 he landed 4,000 soldiers on James Island and threatened to cut off Charleston's rail link over a bridge connecting it with Savannah. The two feints, one north and one south of the city, did indeed scare Beauregard, but did not cause him to materially weaken the garrison at Gillmore's planned point of attack, Battery Wagner. In fact, the Confederates there soon discovered what they took to be the enemy's real plan. In the dark hours of July 8, and early the next morning, Southern scouts found troop barges secreted in some inlets below Charleston. Later they heard the ringing of axes as trees in front of Wagner were being felled. Obviously, the Federals intended an assault and an amphibious landing, while the felled timber cleared the way for an artillery barrage. Thus the Confederate commander on Morris Island put his soldiers on the alert, and just in time.[25]

At dawn on July 10, 1863, Gillmore's guns opened and he began landing his troops on the southern end of Morris Island. The barrage took nearly three hours, shaking the island terribly, and assisted by Dahlgren, who brought four of his monitors close in to the shoreline and bombarded enemy artillery positions with his great naval cannon. By the end of the firing, just before the troops landed, most of the Confederate gun emplacements had been destroyed or disabled, and the remaining Southerners driven back to Wagner. In the ensuing landing, only one barge was put out of action by enemy fire, and the Federals gained their foothold and began to advance up the island with little opposition. Some 2,000 made the landing and steadily pushed less than half their number of defenders back, aided all the while by the advancing fire of Dahlgren's ships. Leading the attack was something of an apparition, Brigadier General George C. Strong, a Vermonter who jumped out of his barge too soon and promptly disappeared under the water. For a minute only his hat could be seen as it floated off to sea, but soon the general surfaced and hauled himself out. His boots soaked, he led the landing assault in his stocking feet, and shortly afterward mounted an errant donkey. From his perch atop this noble steed, he led the remainder of the attack.[26]

When the advancing blue front reached the enemy earthworks, now called Fort Wagner, they stopped. Wagner was a formidable affair that literally crossed the entire width of the island at a narrow point. It mounted several powerful guns, sufficiently so that when they trained their fire on *Catskill*, flying Dahlgren's flag, they hit it some sixty times and inflicted some damage. Still, unlike Du Pont, Dahlgren was pleased with the performance of his monitors. "I was most favorably impressed with the endurance of these ironclads," he said two days later. But at the same time he learned firsthand that they were not suited to warm-weather work. That morning when he arose before four o'clock, he already found the day "warm and oppressive." It got worse steadily, and the worst place anyone could be on a hot, humid, South Carolina summer day was inside several tons of poorly ventilated ironclad. The ships soaked up the heat, transferred it to their interior, and there it mingled with the already high temperatures given off by the engines and boilers. The humidity formed in great drops on the bulkheads, in puddles on the floors, and the men forced to work in the bowels of the monsters experienced temperatures of 130 degrees and more. The comparatively unenergetic work demanded of men other than gunners and engineers still managed to exhaust them in such a climate. "No one can form an idea of the atmosphere of these vessels," wrote Dahlgren at the end of the day.[27]

More astounding than the heat aboard his vessels, however, was what Dahlgren saw ashore. Sometime after noon, with the Confederates hurrying into the works at Wagner, he saw the blue lines halt without attacking the fort. "It was the enemy's weakest moment and *our* opportunity," he lamented five years later, "that would never offer again to us as it did then." With perhaps 8,000 or more troops at hand, Gillmore sent only 2,000 onto Morris Island and then sent no more. The Confederates, weakened, driven back, somewhat confused, and outnumbered, made an easy mark for the combined land and sea forces. Gillmore reported that he halted the advance because of "the heat being intense and the troops exhausted." Certainly that was so but, as Dahlgren would later point out, a few hours of rest must surely have allowed them to renew the attack with fair hopes of success, particularly since, with a clear view for some distance around, the Federals could see that Beauregard was sending no reinforcements to Morris Island. "A most unfortunate conclusion," the admiral called it, and even discounting his later hatred of Gillmore, still he seems more than justified in lamenting that "the best chance for taking Wagner by an off hand assault was lost."[28]

Gillmore would not wait for long to renew his assault, however. Further, he apparently expected that Wagner would easily be his, for he sent only Strong's brigade into the attack, and did not even think to ask Dahlgren for renewed naval support. The result was an attack at daylight that gained the parapet of the fort but could not hold it against the spirited defense of the 1,200 Confederates and their artillery. Though he would report barely 150 casualties from the two days' fighting, in fact the morning attack of July 11 cost him 339, and nothing gained. The Rebels counted but twelve casualties, while one dispirited New Hampshire Federal lamented that "the troops all fell back to their former positions of the day before, with the same accompaniment of hot sun, hot sand, hot shot, and hot shell." Gillmore would have to earn Fort Wagner, and it would take him another three months to do it.[29]

Only a week passed before the next attempt, however, and this time Gillmore exercised more of his muscle. In the days between his attacks he brought siege artillery onto the island and began a steady bombardment of Fort Wagner on July 18. All day long some thirty-six cannon poured a plunging fire into the earthworks, assisted once more by Dahlgren's ironclad fleet. Then at dusk, masked by a furious cannonade, Gillmore massed two of his brigades, led by Brigadier General Truman Seymour, and launched a dimly lit assault. Dahlgren, once again, disapproved, finding that he could not support the attack with his monitors for fear of hitting friendly troops in the darkness. Had the attack been started that morning, he felt confident that he could have pinned the Confederates to their works. Yet Gillmore believed that attacking at dusk would cover the movement from view by the Confederates on James, Sullivan's Island, and Fort Sumter.

Once more Strong's brigade led the assault, his leading regiment being Colonel Robert G. Shaw's 54th Massachusetts. This was a different regiment than all the rest. It was black. Only the officers were Caucasian. For the 650 Negro soldiers and their white commanders, this was their first real action of the war, and only the second assault to involve black troops. They felt the eyes of their brave and committed Colonel Shaw, of Massachusetts, and perhaps of their millions of black brethren, upon them. They must do well.

Alas, Gillmore's ruse did not work, and as his leading column emerged from cover, not only Wagner's, but also the guns from several other Charleston batteries and forts opened fire on them. Once Shaw's men got within reach of the enemy parapet, Dahlgren had to cease fire, and that allowed the 1,200 defenders to line their works and deliver a deadly rifle fire into the black horde before them. "The troops went gallantly on," said Gillmore, but soon the hail of fire proved too much for them and the 54th stalled. Seymour had to send his reserve brigade into the attack. Finally the Federals obtained a lodgment on the parapet which they held in bitter fighting for perhaps three hours in the confused darkness, but at last they were forced to retire. It had been a terrible fight, and costly. General Strong took a mortal wound. Seymour fell, put out of action for six months. Colonel Haldimand Putnam, commanding the second brigade, died on the field. And so did Colonel Robert G. Shaw. One fourth of his regiment, 272 black soldiers, fell with him at the top of the parapet. The next day outraged and vindictive Confederates, incensed that a white man would lead Negro troops against them, buried Shaw in an unmarked grave beneath the bodies of his slain soldiers. It proved to be an unwitting act of enshrinement for the colonel. He became at once a hero in the Union, a symbol to black and white alike, and a rallying point for the enlistment of thousands of blacks. When Federal authorities later made attempts to locate his body, his father asked that they cease. He was where he belonged.[30]

Gillmore could well be stunned by the repulse. His total losses were tenfold greater than those of the Confederates, and his chances of quickly taking Wagner and Charleston by that side door had gone up in smoke. Beauregard would be ready for such attacks in the future. As a fitting admission of the situation, the Federal's first move the day after the battle was to erect a defensive work on the south end of Morris Island. Now he would guard himself against attacks by the Confederates. He knew that he could not take Fort Wagner by a frontal assault, and that called for a considerable modification of his plans for capturing Charleston. He only needed Wagner in order to use the position to reduce Fort Sumter to a point where it could not hinder the passage of Dahlgren's ironclads into the inner harbor. Now he must bypass Wagner and try to bombard Sumter from other ground already in his possession, though Wagner still held considerable military value. Consequently, even as he prepared to begin battering the great fortress in the harbor, Gillmore brought up his siege artillery to do the same thing to Wagner. What he could not accomplish—or was not competent enough to accomplish—with the foot soldier, he now set out to do with engineering and great guns. And thus the Siege of Charleston, so close to success this summer of 1863, would go on, and on, and President Lincoln would wait longer still for a real victory in South Carolina.[31]

But much had been done here, nevertheless. The navy learned of what stuff the monitors were truly made, and their commanders found the harbor a proving ground for the infant science of ironclad tactics. The whole North learned that black soldiers could fight as well as white, and die as well, too. Beauregard discovered what could be achieved by luck and daring, that his own ironclads were a match for the blockading vessels in close quarters, that Sumter and Moultrie could defy the enemy iron vessels without fear, and that the tiny command at his disposal could defend their works against much greater numbers. They were South Carolinians, for the most part, and they would fight for their native soil with unbridled ferocity.

What neither of the opposing commanders discovered, however, and what surely neither expected, was that the experience of the past year and more helped dictate that Charleston's would be the longest siege of the war. Yet somehow it was fitting. If any spot in the beleaguered Confederacy should hold out until the very end, then surely the poets, the historians, even the Confederates themselves would have willed that it be Charleston, the birthplace of the rebellion.

CHAPTER 5

"PAPER! PAPER! COME GET YOUR PAPER!"

The growing discord in the Union's Charleston command did not elude the watchful eyes and ears of a noncombatant corps that followed all the armies everywhere. "There is a want of harmony, a zig-zag conduct of the siege, growing out of bickerings and dissentient efforts on the part of the two branches of the service there brought together." And besides fighting just each other, Gillmore and Dahlgren stood united in their mutual battle with a common enemy, the press. A few weeks after the failed attack on Fort Wagner, when a report of a confidential nature appeared in the Philadelphia papers, Halleck ordered Gillmore to arrest all the war correspondents in his department and send them to Hilton Head, safely away from military secrets that they might divulge. Though no friend to the press, the general simply confined them to quarters on Morris Island. It was not the first time that gentlemen of the fourth estate were to be confined or arrested in their fight for information, nor would it be the last. They, like so many others in those fantastic years, were builders of an industry and an institution whose time was coming in a hurry, and they would not be denied.[1]

In the years prior to the Civil War, the newspaper press in the United States was a rather benign influence in American life. The atti-

tude of all but the few great tabloids was distinctly provincial, and the notion of a concerted effort to gather and disseminate the news of the nation as a whole was an oddity. Though the telegraph bound the country
by some 50,000 miles of wire, the availability of instant communications
was little used by even the major dailies. The wire rates were simply too
high, and the decades since the growth of a widespread newspaper industry had not seen events of such magnitude or interest that a publisher
could readily translate costly "late" news into increased sales. Even the
war with Mexico did not provide a real stimulus for newspaper growth
and innovation.

The average newspaper was a family affair, a small private enterprise
used chiefly to sell advertising and to express the personal views and prejudices of its editor/publisher. Cities of modest size generally had two such
sheets, diametrically opposed to one another on almost every issue of the
day excepting patriotism and civic pride. Since the chief editorials were almost always political, the editorial columns took the place in a way of the
real news from Washington. It came to the readers sifted through the pen
of the publisher. If one paper in town was Democratic, then surely another would spring up Whig or, later, Republican. In Lexington, Kentucky, in 1850, when no Democratic newspaper stood to contest with the
Whig *Observer & Reporter*, several prominent citizens joined in contributing for the formation of such a competitor, even bringing in an editor
to run it. The Lexington *Kentucky Statesman*'s first order of business
upon going into print was to support the Congressional campaign of
Democratic candidate John C. Breckinridge, himself a stockholder in the
enterprise.[2]

It was a paltry living, seldom supporting more than the editor or
owner in any style at all. "Reporters" were an unknown breed, news of
nearby local events being covered by the editor himself or by residents
who contributed without credit, and frequently without pay. Columns
were often filled simply by printing letters sent to the office by townsfolk
traveling abroad or to remote parts of the Union. Most of the newspapers,
particularly in the West and rural East, were weeklies. Only the major
cities could support dailies, and even some of these, like the Cincinnati
Enquirer, in fact did little more one day than rearrange in different format precisely the same type it had printed the day before. There were no
great banner headlines, no "yellow journalism," and few truly noteworthy
"men of the press." What excitement was provided in the columns of
most sheets came from the vitriolic charges and countercharges of the
rival editors. They often became highly personal in nature, despite the
fact that many of the seeming opponents were close friends, and on occasion the battle begun with the pen was finished on the dueling green or
the city streets. It was an interesting and to some degree exciting time for
the publishers themselves, but for few others. The war would change all
that.

Only in New York and a few other cities did there dwell real giants, men whose sheets gave them true national prominence and influence. Horace Greeley and his *Tribune*, Henry Raymond of the *Times*, William Cullen Bryant of the *Evening Post*, and James Gordon Bennett and his *Herald* dominated American newspaper publishing. Greeley was distinctly a crackpot to many of his readers, with peculiar social and political ideas and, when the war came at last, the unpopular notion that the "erring sisters" should simply be let go. Raymond and his Republican *Times* were more moderate, and more temperate, while the other two papers tended toward the sensational, and Bennett proved the true information entrepreneur. He published for the common man, unlike his eclectic compeers, and he had a better grasp of what the common people would pay to read. Scandal and gossip could find their place in his pages, but so did a variety of other subjects not usually regarded as newsworthy. Foreign news, generally neglected, appeared in most of these major dailies, as well as a considerable quantity of national news gathered by the New York Associated Press, a loose cooperative of several city papers' news-gathering operations, to which the major dailies and a number of provincial papers North and South subscribed.[3]

The Southern press on the eve of the war was not much different, though, as befitted the Southern temperament, it did appear rather more combative. Literacy in the South ran much lower than in the North, yet her major newspapers enjoyed wide reputation and influence. Editors like George D. Prentice, George W. Kendall, and John Forsythe exerted a considerable reach via the pages of the Louisville *Journal*, the New Orleans *Picayune*, and the Mobile *Register*. Moreover, and unlike most of the Northern press, Southern papers often printed the latest literature as well as news and tidbits from correspondents. Their editors molded their sheets into much more literary and critical journals, but aimed distinctly at the South's upper classes. Few papers indeed reached to the poor white and the average tradesman, and fewer still really profited from their news enterprises. Most depended for their custom on job printing for local business and hopefully the state legislatures. It is no wonder, then, that with the most lucrative printing business being of a political nature, the Southern press took a more active interest in affairs of state. Being on the right "side" in Richmond or Nashville or Charleston could mean getting some tidy business from the party in power. And thus the Southern newspapers tended to identify themselves very strongly with individual politicians, his rise being theirs, as with Breckinridge and the *Statesman*.

The publishing center of the South was Richmond, even before it became the Confederate capital. It boasted four major daily sheets, the *Enquirer*, the *Examiner*, the *Whig*, and the *Dispatch*. Before the war was well started the *Sentinel* made it five. The founder of the *Whig* had been killed in a duel with a son of the founder of the *Enquirer*—such were the animosities that these editors could arouse in one another. Probably the most able of the Richmond editors was John M. Daniel of the *Examiner*. Certainly he would prove the most colorful, taking as his model the London *Times*, though his own associate, E. A. Pollard, could easily compete with him. Both were cynical, pugnacious, vitriolic, and intolerant to a high degree. The *Dispatch*, under its editor, James Cowardin, was much more modest by comparison, yet it had outstripped its competition in circulation by 1861, and stood as one of the largest dailies in the South. The Richmond press were fiercely independent as a rule, excepting perhaps the *Enquirer*, which played the political game in the Confederate capital better than the others early in the war.[4]

There was yet another kind of publishing in the country as it came to war, and one that perforce introduced a new kind of correspondent when the conflict began. The rest of the press published only the written word, but *Harper's Weekly Illustrated Newspaper* and *Frank Leslie's Illustrated Newspaper* actually subordinated their editorial content to large-spread illustrations of the major events of the previous week. In fact, the illustrations were crude by any standard, woodcut sketches made by a team of engravers, each working on a section of an illustration, the whole then being joined together for printing. The method led to unfortunate differences in style and quality even within a single picture, but it got them engraved quickly. Providing the illustrations themselves were a number of "special artists," men like Alfred R. Waud, Edwin Forbes, Winslow Homer, Theodore Davis, and even men in the army like General David Hunter's adjutant, Colonel David H. Strother. As the war progressed, the artists were often at the very front lines, pad and pencil in hand, capturing the scene for the engravers back home. Within sometimes less than ten days a battle scene could be in the hands of a hungry reading and watching public. It would be, in the cant of a later generation, the first multimedia news reporting, and even the South gave it a try when, in 1862, the *Southern Illustrated News* began to appear in Richmond.[5]

Even though the general nature of newspaper publishing was hardly geared for covering a major conflict when the guns opened on Fort Sumter, still the Northern and Southern press did not entirely meet the crisis unprepared. Several of the Yankee papers, chiefly those in New York, already had correspondents in place in the South when secession came. Some of them wrote under assumed names or *noms de plume* for safety, but others boldly signed their dispatches, and the big four New York dailies had reporters present in almost every major Southern city by the end of 1860. Greeley's *Tribune*, thanks to his abolitionist views, was particularly hated, yet his reporters kept to their posts despite genuine danger to their lives. Their correspondence had to go north in disguise, often in code.[6]

When the guns of Sumter opened, several Yankee reporters were arrested in Charleston and elsewhere, then soon released. When they returned to the Union, they found that their infant industry was exploding. For the first time in American history, there were media events of such importance and interest that speedy reporting by eyewitness writers could make for a sell-out edition, and often several printings in a single day to meet the demand. A big war meant big news, and for those with more pluck and enterprise, big money. At once a keen competition began between the major dailies in the big cities to bring the latest and most sensational news to their subscribers first. New York led the rest, and soon a veritable legion of ill-paid, ill-equipped, and sometimes illiterate reporters fastened themselves to the armies. A correspondent could cost anywhere from $1,000 to $5,000 a year, not including expenses for his outfit and transportation. He might use up six horses in a single year. It required as well a small army of stenographers and typesetters to translate a new dispatch into the next morning's edition, and the telegraph bills soon became enormous, a problem compounded by the nature of the wires themselves. Only one correspondent could send his dispatch at a time and, with a premium set on speed and being "first," the reporters often resorted to stratagems and deception to hold or commandeer the wire. Some reporters got to the telegraph operator well in advance of preparing their dispatches, and had the man simply tap away at passages from the Bible until the news flash was ready. One operator reportedly had worked his weary fingers well into Leviticus before the reporter's copy was ready. In time the telegraph companies ended the abuse by limiting every correspondent to fifteen minutes per use.

The New York *Herald* set about its reporting operations with the organization of an army itself. In time Bennett's paper would have a correspondent stationed and traveling with every division of every corps of every army in the field. They worked out of specially rigged *Herald* wagons that accompanied each corps, and labored under the firm assertion that reward depended upon beating the competition with the stories. In the first year of the conflict Bennett may have spent as much as $100,000 just on this army correspondence, and by war's end some estimates of his investment ran as high as three quarters of a million. The weekly telegraph bill that summer of 1861 ran to $1,000 and more.[7]

Beyond this, Bennett organized a special Southern department in his office for collecting information from the Confederacy. Especially prized by the *Herald* and all other papers were newspapers published in the Confederacy. In the second year of the war the compiler Frank Moore began publishing volumes of his *Rebellion Record*, made up chiefly of official and semi-official documents dealing with military affairs, but incorporating as well a significant digest of newspaper articles from Union and Confederate papers. They might be enemies across the lines now, but there were still friends and relatives as well, and there soon appeared a ravenous hunger in the Union for information on events within the rebellious states.

1. The greatest enemy of the Confederate Army of Tennessee was its own commanding general, Braxton Bragg. (Chicago Historical Society)

2. Bragg's most hated enemy was Major General John Cabell Breckinridge of Kentucky. After Stones River, Tennessee, their quarrel symbolized the army. (Author's collection)

3. *President Abraham Lincoln, troubled ruler of a troubled Union, faced opposition not only from the Democrats, but also from the Radicals within his own party.* (The Kean Archives, Philadelphia)

4. Left, a sworn opponent to all who sought to prosecute the war against the Confederacy was Clement Laird Vallandigham of Ohio who led the "Copperhead" movement. (Library of Congress) 5. Below, the luckless leader of a luckless Army of the Potomac, Major General Ambrose Everett Burnside knew he had been elevated beyond his ability. It cost thousands of lives at Fredericksburg, Virginia, to prove it. (National Archives)

6. *Burnside's opponent never fell short of his nation's trust. This unusual photograph of General Robert Edward Lee was taken in 1863.* (Confederate Museum, New Orleans)

7. *Here on the Rappahannock, at Fredericksburg, Virginia, Burnside and Lee proved the latter's belief that "It is well that war is so terrible."* (National Archives)

8. *Admiral John Adolphus Bernard Dahlgren led the navy in its attempts to take Charleston, South Carolina, and led it as well in contentiousness with his opposite number in the army.* (Library of Congress)

9. *The black 54th Massachusetts was nearly destroyed trying to take a bombproof in the interior of Battery Wagner, the Confederate fort that guarded Charleston's southern approach. Members of the unit pose at left after the fort's final fall.* (U.S. Army Military History Institute)

10. One of the Federal batteries on Morris Island, South Carolina, that slowly battered Fort Sumter. (Library of Congress)

11. Journalists crawled all over the armies to get at the news. Some newspapers, like the New York Herald, *maintained substantial field units.* (National Archives)

12. Artists like Alfred R. Waud were employed by the "illustrated" weeklies to travel with the armies. They sent their battlefield sketches north to be reproduced. (Library of Congress)

13. Photographers jumped into the opportunity afforded by the war and went wherever the armies and the limitations of their equipment would allow. Mathew B. Brady stamped his name on the work of all of them, even though his eyes may not have allowed him to expose a single negative himself. He stands at right with several assistants and their equipment. (The Kean Archives, Philadelphia)

The publishing offices could be a bedlam. "What a busy place the editorial office of *The Times* was," recalled one newsman. "Politicians, office-holders, Colonels, and Government spokesmen came there. We were constantly receiving packages from correspondents at all points of the compass, special dispatches from the front, or from many a front, official documents or advices; covert news from army officers, visits from wire-pullers or pipe layers, information from the departments at Washington, and gratuitous suggestions from men of all sorts and conditions." The scene was much the same elsewhere in New York, and in the other cities that vied with it for domination of war news, chiefly Philadelphia. Almost overnight the once-placid Northern press had become a fiercely, sometimes brutally, competitive enterprise. The transformation changed the nature of news reporting and publishing for a century and more to come.[8]

Very quickly the informal press "associations" like the New York Associated Press became too limited to serve the voracious needs of the nation's newspapers. Western versions emerged quickly out of outrage at the high prices demanded by the Eastern combines and their bad service. Soon the Western Associated Press vied with the New York, Philadelphia, and Southern associated presses. There were other growing pains for the industry to overcome as well. Limitations of press machinery could not keep up with the new demands. Paper became scarce and many sheets had to reduce their page size to conserve. There were many failures, and more mergers as advertising fell off while circulation income could not entirely meet the demands of maintaining the reporters in the field. Even Greeley complained that, though the *Tribune* was not going broke, still "we shall be glad to just live till the War is over." Changes in the frequency and format of the papers came rapidly, giving rise to a large number of new Sunday editions, and sheets that published only on Sunday. The massive headline, spreading across the front page in letters several inches high was born, as were both morning and evening editions of the same newspaper. The voracious appetite for more and more war news pushed the publishers to ever greater investment and expansion, though some wags claimed that the only reason for the evening edition was to correct the lies told in the morning sheet. Most papers printed "extras" when a hot breaking story came over the wires. And still there was not enough news to meet the public's wants.[9]

Though they may not have seen it at the time, the major dailies were going through what the *Times* would years after regard as two fundamental revolutions in their craft: the ascendance of "individual, competitive, triumphant enterprise in getting early and exclusive news," and the potentially huge circulations to be had by those who could supply "prompt and accurate reports of the day-to-day doings of mankind the world over."[10]

Though some of the same influences affected Confederate publishing

as well, their outcome was far different, and yet predictable. The blockade, inflation, scarcity of manpower and materials inevitably gripped the
Confederate press in a slow stranglehold from which there was no escape
but by innovation and enterprise. As everywhere else in the South, the
dominating factor in its press soon came to be ersatz. With fewer miles of
telegraph wire, and that dominated by the military, newspapers could not
long afford the exorbitant rates charged for time on the lines. The associated presses were largely disrupted by loss of personnel to the armies,
and loss of territory to the enemy. The constant threat, and frequent reality, of severed rail and wire communications made getting and printing
speedy news extremely difficult, and often impossible. Then there were
the presses. Like all machinery in the new nation, publishers' presses
found themselves in want of parts and skilled repairmen. Soon those that
could not be repaired were cannibalized to make parts for others. The
type became worn and, by war's end, was almost illegible on some papers.
Smaller printers resorted to wooden type that had not been seen for a century or more, and sheets that once were dailies sometimes became bi-
weeklies or even weeklies.[11]

And there was the ever-present danger of being put out of business
by the enemy. Federal soldiers seemed to like nothing more than destroying the presses of Rebel newspapers, and dumping their type into the
street. Poor editor John Wartmann of the Harrisonburg, Virginia, *Rockingham Register*, found himself repeatedly in the path of the contending
armies. Every time the Yankees went through, there went his type. At
least three times he put himself back in business with his weekly, managing to stay in publication throughout the war, with all-too-frequent interruptions. He had to be reporter and, at times, typesetter as well.[12]

Yet surely no Confederate newspaper lived quite the saga of the
Memphis *Appeal*. Even prior to the war it enjoyed an enviable reputation
in the nation's press circles, and was a considerably profitable enterprise.
That last was especially good, since it allowed its editors Colonel John
McClanahan and Benjamin F. Dill to continue publishing when war
came, despite the increasingly high prices of everything needed. A firmly
Democratic sheet, the *Appeal* naturally joined hands with the new Confederacy and gave it unqualified support. It raised its own army unit, the
Appeal Battery, and filled its ranks with its own employees, sending them
to serve well at Shiloh and Corinth. But even its own printers could not
stay the march of Grant in Tennessee, and soon Memphis fell. On June 6
the city surrendered, and that same day a train left Memphis carrying a
boxcar with the *Appeal*'s press, equipment and type, and staff. They were
off for Grenada, Mississippi, and just three days later the indomitable
sheet published once more. "Sooner would we sink our types, press and establishment into the bottom of the Mississippi River and become wandering exiles from our homes, than continue publication under Union occu-

pation," the paper proclaimed a month before. Wandering exiles is what they became.

The Union march continued, and five months later it was Grenada that was threatened. With the aplomb that characterized McClanahan and Dill, they simply packed and moved again. "So long as two or three states are gathered together in the name of the Confederate States, so long will we be found advocating, as zealously as ever, a continued resistance." They printed a farewell edition, mounted the boxcar once more, and were off for Jackson. Making the best of their Odyssey, McClanahan put a sign saying "Memphis Headquarters" above his room at Jackson's Bowman House, and there continued his enterprise. Inside the colonel could usually be found holding forth eloquently to his followers on the nobility of the press and, of course, of the *Appeal* in particular. A reporter from Knoxville then heard him say that the move to Jackson had nothing at all to do with the Federals. Mimicking McClellan's excuse for his failures on the Peninsula that spring, McClanahan explained that he had simply made a "change of base," planned for months. Out of the laughter that followed, one listener complimented him on demonstrating a truly wonderful example of strategy.

By May 1863 the paper had to move again in the face of a Federal advance toward Vicksburg. The war was showing in the old *Appeal*. Gradually the size of the paper and the number of columns reduced. It ran only two pages now, and had to make its own ink from shoe polish. With the proper fuel to fire its press boilers in short supply, the paper used its own columns to advertise for firewood.

The coming of Grant in May 1863 caused a greater problem than before, but the *Appeal* met the challenge. It made the journey to Atlanta by rail, having to wind its way south to Mobile, then through Montgomery, and on into Georgia. Never in history had a newspaper so repeatedly moved away from its subscribers! Yet many of the sheet's readers moved with it. The *Appeal* proved to have an extremely loyal following in the Army of Tennessee, many of its soldiers contributing to its columns regularly. Their misfortunes were those of McClanahan and Dill as well, their determinations shared with each other. It came as close to being an official army organ as any paper in the country.

Once back in operation in Atlanta—the *Appeal* actually stopped along the way to run a few extras at Meridian, Mississippi—the sheet managed to stay put for fully a year before its next displacement. Indeed, there were two other "refugee" newspapers printing in Atlanta at the same time, the Chattanooga *Daily Rebel* and the Knoxville *Daily Register*. Despite the considerable importance of the Richmond press, Atlanta became now the real center of Confederate journalism. The *Appeal* flourished. Considerable job printing for the army returned a profit, and readership soared. McClanahan and Dill began two editions daily, morning and evening, their combined circulation topping 14,000. The editors became frequent and coveted visitors in social circles, and their sense of humor never failed them. Newsboys, as in the North, hawked the papers from street corners, calling, "Paper! Paper! Come get your paper! Fresh off the press, the Memphis-Grenada-Jackson-Meridian-Atlanta *Appeal!*" Times even became good enough that the typesetters of several Atlanta sheets successfully went on strike for better pay.

The sedentary existence of the *Appeal* could not last, of course. By the summer of 1864 the peripatetic journal had to move yet again as the city came in danger of advancing Federals. While all the other papers of the city were silenced, the *Appeal* kept publishing until the last possible day, despite the opinion of the chief enemy commander who said that "all newspapers have quit Atlanta except the Memphis *Appeal*; that, I suppose, is tired of moving and wants to be let alone." Far from it. McClanahan and Dill took their press south to Montgomery, to resume publishing after an interruption of barely more than two weeks. They stayed with it until literally the end of the war, only ceasing publication when their last home, Columbus, Georgia, fell to the Federals in April 1865. Their presses were destroyed at last, and Dill captured, though McClanahan escaped. When the captured editor was brought before the commanding general of the Federal forces, the general exclaimed, "Have we caught the old fox at last? Well I'll be damned!" He greeted his captive with genuine good cheer, and genuine good whiskey, the best Dill had tasted during the war. And by November 1865, the *Appeal* was back in Memphis and back in business. McClanahan was killed in an accident shortly before, but Dill carried on their work. The paper ceased using the much-traveled Hoe press in 1872, stating in its retirement issue that, when the Civil War's history was written, "there is no weapon of war, or sword, or book that will have greater historical value than this trial-worn piece of mechanism." How right they were, but, alas, Benjamin Dill was not there to bid his old worn-out friend farewell. He, too, died late in 1865, but not until he saw the *Appeal* back in operation. As he lay abed, dying of pleurisy, an employee came to him with the first issue of the resurrected *Appeal*. Dill's response was to look for typographical errors and count the number of advertisements, a publisher to the end.[13]

Not every Confederate could boast of the adventures of the *Appeal*, but all could sympathize with many of its hardships. None so taxed the Confederate press as the shortage of paper. The South had few paper mills before the war, and no new ones were built after Sumter. The drain of men and supplies that affected every other industry hit the papermakers as well. Newsprint became increasingly scarce within months of the outbreak of hostilities. Papers cut back their page size, then the number of pages, then the number of issues. Paper prices skyrocketed as much as 2,000 percent! By war's end, some journals issued a page no greater than ten by fifteen inches. They used writing paper, scrap and packaging, even wallpaper. And for the considerable quantity of writing paper consumed editorially, before the copy reached the printing stage, the journalists were even more frugal, and inventive. "Brown paper, waste paper, backs of old letters, and rejected essays, and unpaid bills (made out to delinquent subscribers), bits of foolscap torn from the copy books of youth, and the ledgers of business men furnish the manuscript of the thunderous 'editorials' and horrible 'locals' of the press of the Confederacy," said the Richmond *Examiner* in June 1863. It even reported one editor who worked on a slate, erasing one day's work to make way for the next.[14]

As a result, hundreds of papers failed. In 1861, fifty of the sixty journals in Texas alone went out of business, and after two years, all but nine of Mississippi's seventy-five sheets continued to publish. Subscription rates, often no more than a penny a day in the North, came to run as high as $100 or more a year, with rates sometimes changing even daily. The editor of the Atlanta *Confederacy* captured the almost nonstop frustration of a Southern editor in a marvelous essay in 1863. Met at the office in the morning by an exorbitant price raise from the paper mill, he then encountered several inches of water on the floor from a bad steam engine on the press. It mixed with an unusually high amount of spoiled paper sitting on the floor as a result of a bad lot that would not go through the press. Meanwhile the writers said they could not function in the cold, the coal supply being gone. The subscription clerk, in addition to shivering, desperately tried to figure out the actual worth of "blotted, torn-up, badly patched shinplasters" sent from Alabama for a subscription with the injunction to "fling him in" the newspaper for a year. With several hundred different national, state, local, and even private business currencies in circulation, knowing what any of it was really worth proved a superhuman task.

Then an hour of dealing with walk-ins from the street, none of them subscribers, but people who asked information without buying the paper. When finally the editor got to his office to compose himself for the day's stirring exhortation, the interruptions continued. A lady wanted to do him a six-column article on love twice a week. The printers demanded copy that was not yet ready, but they must have something, for, as when an iron is hot, the printer had to strike while the press was working. Once out of the editorial chair, and downtown for business, he was accosted repeatedly for news by people who could find it in his paper, but will not pay for it. Then that afternoon came a hundred questions as to when the evening edition will be ready, when for two years it had always appeared at 5 P.M. "These are not half our daily troubles," he concluded, adding that many more serious were not even mentioned. "Now, under these circumstances if our wife should happen to die, and our head become a little frosted over, and we should happen to go out among the girls just for recreation, we hope the dear creatures will remember this recital of our woes and not think we are growing old."[15]

But the Confederate press did grow old, and prematurely. Yet at the same time, it did an incredible job of bringing the news to a population that before 1861 had shown little interest in it, and in many cases an inability even to read it. They used volunteer correspondents, soldiers with the army, for extensive personal, though not always well-informed, war news. Sometimes the same correspondent wrote for more than one paper, a practice that encouraged the already popular trend toward pseudonyms. Names like Sallust, Bohemian, See De Kay, and others appeared below their contributions, masking the names of the writers. In fact, few papers could actually afford to keep paid correspondents with the armies, though some achieved genuine fame as was their worth. Félix G. de Fontaine, a Frenchman, had actually provided the New York *Herald* with an account of the Fort Sumter bombardment, but soon thereafter he began a productive career with the Charleston *Courier*. Peter Alexander worked for no fewer than five major dailies during the war, contributing as well to the London *Times*.[16]

For most of the conflict, predictably, the news center if not the publishing center of the South lay in Richmond. There some of the best talent came to serve the craft, and there most of the major stories emanated. There, too, came some of the experimentation with journalism as a trade that Confederates were able to indulge. Daniel of the *Examiner* proved the chief artisan. "Always particular about every thing that concerned him," wrote an observer, "he was especially so in regard to his paper, with which he would now and then artistically experiment." Daniel tried a special headline on the front page one day, and then no head at all the next. He strove for a particular style, unlike the florid, overblown prose that characterized most of the American press. Simple, readable, "plain Anglo-Saxon" was his ideal. "Write plain English," he admonished all; "it is good enough to convey all that you should have to say." Above all, he sought "style" in the *Examiner*, the intangible that made a journal stand above its peers. By and large, he achieved it, only to die, as perhaps he should, three days before his paper fell to the enemy.[17]

The role of the press in this war proved to be twofold. Even as the conflict exerted an enormous influence upon it as an industry, so did journalism wield a considerable impact on the war. Battles were won and lost on the field, but reputations and careers could be won—and created— almost as quickly in the press. As a presumed expression of the will of the "public," the prejudices and expectations of a few hundred editors could carry as much weight in making military policy as double their number of congressmen. Even Presidents could not avoid having to bow to the power of the press despite their own contrary views. Lincoln enjoyed a varied career with the gentlemen of the craft. He shared with them a natural inquisitiveness, a desire always to know more, and something even of a fascination with gossip of a political sort. One of his closest friends, Noah Brooks of the Sacramento *Union*, virtually had the run of the Executive Mansion, even acting as an informal adviser to the President. And the rest of the press enjoyed generally good relations with the rail-splitter. Some thought them too good. The opinionated Secretary of the Navy, Gideon Welles, complained that Lincoln "permits the little newsmongers to come around him and be intimate." Even the President himself could sometimes complain that a problem with journalists was that they liked to be "ahead of the hounds, outrunning events, and exciting expectations to be later dashed into disappointment." Yet he felt kindly toward reporters for the most part, even allowing them to impose upon him to an embarrassing degree. Often he walked out of cabinet meetings when a journalist sent in his card, only to ask for a piece of news. "You gentlemen of the press seem to be pretty much like soldiers," he said, "you have to go wherever sent, whatever may be the dangers or difficulties in the way. God forbid I should by any rudeness of speech or manner, make your duties any harder than they are . . . If I am not afraid of you, it is because I feel you are trustworthy." He was a friend to the press, he said, ready to acknowledge "its tremendous power for both good and evil." He would feel that power in this war, and in ways that well might make his words seem a bit dissembling.[18]

The Lincoln government and the press managed to antagonize each other almost from the start. The insult to the flag at Fort Sumter put the Northern publishing community into an uproar. It was humiliating, they said. When would Lincoln redress the wrong. Throughout April, May, and June of 1861 the press, particularly that in New York and Washington, repeatedly demanded that the army march on Richmond, put down the rebellion, and imprison or hang its leaders. That outcry centered on Virginia, where Confederates glared across the Potomac at the Union's very capital. Pressure from the press played no small part in forcing Lincoln and McDowell into a hurried campaign to Bull Run before the army was truly ready. Once the failure became known, the same journals then began to crucify McDowell and other generals deemed "unsuccessful."

Yet the government fought back in an equally infuriating manner, by censorship. Bull Run was fought on a Sunday, and the news of the scope of the defeat was certainly known in the War Department that evening. Yet the word that first reached the New York press for that evening's editions told of a smashing victory. The Monday morning editions elaborated upon the triumph, and only later in the day did they finally receive telegraphic word of the true nature of the battle. Seward had begun a limited censorship out of the Washington telegraph office shortly after Fort Sumter, and in varying forms it continued until July 21, when General-in-Chief Winfield Scott learned of McDowell's disaster. He at once issued a ban on any telegraphic messages about it going out of the capital. The Northern press was enraged. They called the censorship "a wanton and reckless trifling with the feelings of the public," and protested vigorously in the editorial columns.

Yet the situation would obtain under varying forms for the rest of the war. The government need not be overly blamed, either. In the enthusiasm of a new industry coming of age, the story, any story, was the paramount concern of reporter and publisher. All too often little or no judgment was exercised in the editorial offices about the validity of a report, or of the advisability of running it. Getting in print before the competition assumed all-importance. As a result, despite the continuing efforts of the War Department to exert some control on the kind of military information that reached publication, the journalists usually found a way to bypass the censors. Reports on troop movements, strengths and organizational changes in the armies, speculations on planned strategy, even confidential documents not yet released to their addressees, all too frequently appeared in the Yankee press. By their own admission, Confederate generals, particularly Lee, prized current Northern newspapers highly for the useful information they gave him on the enemy's doings. More than once, Lee actually had information before his opponents! It is not too much to say that at times the news in the sheets actually brought about engagements that would not have taken place otherwise, and death and destruction not planned.

Because of this, an increasingly strained relationship grew between the reporters and a number of the generals. More than once Halleck ordered correspondents expelled from within army lines, particularly when a battle was imminent. Pope issued an order of this kind during his Second Bull Run campaign. Grant later expelled reporters from his army, and ordered the arrest of at least one correspondent for "publishing false intelligence for a malicious purpose." Sherman loathed the press, and would one day promulgate an order that any newspaperman found with his army on its next campaign was to be tried at once and shot! "I won't have a damned newspaperman on the expedition," he growled, "not one." When Halleck commanded the Western army after Shiloh in 1862, he expelled the reporters there as well, and some of the editors actually supported the move. In fact, it was a somewhat self-serving support, for the real responsibility for the intelligence given away to the enemy in printed columns lay not with the correspondents, but with the editors who decided what and what not to print. Still, the New York *Times* commented acridly on "the writers of this class who are constantly giving the world information as to our strength and our position; who . . . do not hesitate to advise Gen. Halleck, condemn Gen. McClellan, and criticize the operations of the profoundest minds . . . They are particularly severe on West Pointers, and are ardent admirers of men in proportion as their early education unfits them for the vast and intricate responsibilities of Generalship. Invariably the officer who is most free with his table, bottle, horses and information is (to them) the greatest soldier."

By 1863 the censorship system was fairly organized, and particularly effective after defeats, when not only the people at home, but also the enemy, had to be denied the true magnitude of the loss. After Fredericksburg extreme exertions were employed to minimize Burnside's fiasco. But it would never be truly effective, for control seemed to bounce from department to department almost at random, largely leaving what was deemed to be "safe" up to the individual whim of the man who happened to be watching the telegraph at the moment. No real policy of control of public information would be forthcoming, which meant that the haphazard attempts at censorship often proved chaotic, and even self-defeating.[19]

In fact, it was in the Confederacy that censorship achieved a far greater degree not only of success, but also of willing cooperation from its object, the press. And something approaching a basic policy evolved, largely voluntary, but with some guidance from Richmond. It came in part from the fact that a de facto censorship had existed in the Southern press for years, thanks to legal bans on publications that promoted abolition. Consequently, already conditioned to legislative management of information, there was little protest from the public or the press when in May 1861 telegraphic censorship was authorized, or when the next month it was extended to mail and newspapers. Indeed, within a short time the newspapers themselves and their correspondents agreed upon an informal system that worked rather well. The newly established Confederate Press Association even issued instructions to its reporters and agents for determining the difference between legitimate news and information that might be helpful to the enemy or injurious to the cause. Troop movements, reports on ironclads, munitions supplies, and details on the whereabouts and description of defensive works, all were strictly prohibited for discussion. They could publish "all intelligence of our own movements taken from northern papers," however. Some individual newspapers went even further, adopting their own special censorship codes, requiring no mention of troop numbers and movements, no speculation upon future campaign objectives, and no mention of strength of Confederate arms involved in a battle being described.

Southern editors proved considerably more responsible in the matter of cooperation than their Yankee counterparts, and the Confederate military and civil authorities frequently complimented the press on its attitude. Just as in the North, however, the generals in the field rode a rough path with the correspondents. There were arrests and expulsions here, too. Braxton Bragg, who seemed to be a favorite with no one but President Davis, incurred probably more editorial wrath than any other. He feuded continually with some correspondents, and one of the catalysts of his vendetta against Breckinridge after Stones River was a bitterly critical report of his Kentucky campaign written by a journalist who happened to serve on Breckinridge's staff. And the press responded with predictable concern when legislation in the Confederate Congress sought to impose heavier restrictions and penalties for breaches of censorship doctrine. However, the Congress itself stood with the publishers when they opposed the attempts of martinets like Bragg and Van Dorn to make it a punishable offense simply to write in uncomplimentary fashion about a general. The journalistic community responded kindly to this kind of support, which helps explain the surprising length of time that serious censorship endeavors proved successful. The system did not really begin to break down until 1864, as increasing reverses created a heavy demand for more and more information. Yet even as late as 1865, in March, with all crumbling about them, the Richmond *Whig* could cheerfully accept the censorship of military news coming from the new Secretary of War, John C. Breckinridge, saying that "if anything of interest transpires which can be published, we are confident that the intelligent Secretary of War will cause the news to be promptly communicated to the press."[20]

The real press communicants, of course, were the reporters in the field. In time they would come to assume in the public mind, North and South, a romantic aura that surpassed that of the mere soldier. And they showed themselves to be more than a little self-conscious of their special place in things. Few other civilians could stroll with impunity through the quarters of privates and generals alike. Very few were privy to high-level discussions, or enjoyed the convivial board of the generals and high command. Those journalists who managed not to foul the temper of some uniformed lord could come and go at will, discuss anything, and often give and take advice on military matters as though a member of the command. It was a heady feeling. Further, a close-knit camaraderie grew among the correspondents, despite the fact that they were in the business of competing with each other for the same stories. Often told were the stories of the false lead one would leak to another to throw him off the trail, or of the ruses to tie up the telegraph line until a "scoop" was in. Yet the stories were told in gatherings of the very men they were about. An informal organization in the North came to call themselves the "Bohemian Brigade." They lived and celebrated together, numbering in their fold not only newspapermen, but also the battle artists. And the artists of another burgeoning industry were welcome to their gatherings as well, the war photographers.

As the war gathered strength for its explosive beginning, there were over 2,500 "daguerreotypists," "ambrotypists," and photographers of other descriptions practicing their art in the old Union. Their craft was but two decades old, yet had already been to war briefly in Mexico and when Roger Fenton took his camera to the Crimea in the 1850s. By 1861, the photographic artist was firmly entrenched in every city and most secondary towns of the nation. Over four hundred practiced in the states soon to form the Confederacy. Georgia had seventy-seven, and Virginia seventy-two. Florida, on the other hand, could count only five, whereas some of the major Northern states had literally hundreds.

The giant of the industry, even before the war began, was certainly Mathew Brady, a man who combined real artistic ability with an entrepreneurial genius. His eyesight was failing badly by 1861, and he rarely if ever worked behind the cameras in his Washington and New York studios, but he possessed a remarkable ability to find and train brilliant assistants. A "Brady" portrait was a requisite for any public or political figure. Even foreign dignitaries sat for his lens, and he pioneered in the business of mass-producing carte-de-visite—literally "visiting card"—sized photos which were widely traded and collected. In the rage for the new kind of image that swept the country, thousands of people had albums filled with these carte-de-visite portraits of people they had never met.

Not surprisingly, when the war came Brady smelled an opportunity. "A spirit in my feet said 'go,' and I went," he would say later. Perhaps. But that inner voice might as well have spoken from his pocketbook, for enormous commercial possibilities presented themselves. The hungry market in the North would consume war images in huge quantities, he reasoned, and on that assumption he equipped a field wagon, trained and equipped his assistants, and set them off to follow the armies. In all probability, he never exposed a single war view himself. He simply could not see well enough to focus a lens. Yet he so left his stamp upon the endeavor that for a century and more afterward, it would be assumed automatically that a photograph taken by any of the hundreds of men who made exposures during the war must naturally be a "Brady."

Those who did the real work were masters of their craft. Alexander Gardner and his brother James, Timothy O'Sullivan, the Gibson brothers, Samuel A. Cooley, Haas and Peale, McPherson and Oliver, the Bergstresser brothers, George W. Houghton, George Barnard, and a host of others left an unexcelled record of a people at war in their photographs. They worked largely for Brady, or themselves, though some actually did contract work for the army, copying maps, photographing installations, and even, reportedly, attempting to photograph Confederate works from an observation balloon. At least one officer, Captain A. J. Russell, was an official United States army photographer, equipped and assigned his duty by the War Department. And across the lines there were great artists as well. Indeed, the Confederates beat even Brady to the war business. J. D. Edwards of New Orleans, a forgotten artist of great ability, made a magnificent series of views of Braxton Bragg's Confederates and their fortifications at Pensacola, Florida, even before the guns of Sumter. He of all men deserves the title "Photographer of the Confederacy" that went instead to another great chronicler, George S. Cook, whose views of Fort Sumter in 1863 captured the besieged fortress so eloquently. A. C. McIntyre of Montgomery, with a true sense of history, photographed the inauguration of Jefferson Davis in 1861, and the team of Osborn and Durbec made the most complete photographic record of any Civil War engagement when their camera spent two or more days chronicling Fort Sumter and its environs just a day or two after its April 1861 surrender.

The Confederate photographers viewed their craft strictly as a commercial venture throughout the war. Chemicals and other supplies became increasingly scarce. Much was smuggled across the lines from supply houses in New York, and what there was could not be wasted on outdoor views which, however interesting historically, were not all that salable. Osborn and Durbec did manufacture a limited number of their images as stereopticon views, but limitations of raw materials, or the tightness of money, soon smothered the venture. Instead, the Rebel artists used their precious resources on the profitable business of portraiture, men and officers in uniform being anxious to send home and preserve their images in the most momentous event of their lives. After 1862 only two or three artists would again take their cameras outside their studios. And when their region fell to the enemy, more than a few simply continued in business, providing the same service for the Federals. None is known actually to have transported his equipment and followed the armies like Gardner and O'Sullivan.

The photographers to the North, on the other hand, found more than just the mundane to occupy their time. Indeed, the great artists like Barnard and Cooley, the Gardners, and others rarely if ever indulged in portraiture. With unlimited production facilities awaiting their images back home, they were at the front to capture the war itself. None actually made genuine battle photographs showing men in combat. The technology was still too time-consuming, and their apparatus too vulnerable to enemy fire. But they came close, and they did cover virtually everything else. The portrait work was done by a greater host of lesser-known men, artists who set up their tents wherever the armies went, who rarely took outdoor scenes, but simply satisfied the great need of the soldiery for portraits. Sometimes a cameraman, like Houghton, left his home and traveled to the front solely to record local boys at war, and then returned to market his images. Others stayed with the armies throughout the war. And an enterprising few, like R. M. Linn, located themselves in scenic places and let the armies come to them. Linn established his "Gallery Point Lookout" at the summit of spectacular Lookout Mountain beside Chattanooga, and there served the constant stream of customers, great and humble, who wanted a portrait with the grand Tennessee Valley as a backdrop.

Yet they were "newsmen" as well. Besides the wide distribution of stereo views, published in series by Brady, Gardner, E. and H. T. Anthony, and others, these images of the war reached the public in the press itself, after a fashion. The printers, of course, did not yet have the technology to print photographs in newspapers and magazines. But hundreds of these photographs went to *Harper's Weekly*, *Frank Leslie's*, and the New York *Illustrated News* where, just as with the drawings by Waud, they were converted to woodcuts. And so they were true photojournalists, as well as entrepreneurs, and historians. They, too, could make a reputation. Lincoln had often quipped that a single portrait of him made after a famous speech at the Cooper Union in New York was in fact what elected him President, for it achieved a phenomenally wide circulation in 1860. It was easier to vote for a man one could see. And so it was with the generals. Few posed as frequently as McClellan, flooding the North with portraits for the eager market. So, too, did John Charles Frémont, Henry Halleck, and a number of others like Nathaniel Prentiss Banks, with political pretensions. The real fighting generals seemed to have less time for it all.[21]

Everything was ready in place, then, for a revolution in the manner and means of bringing the story of this conflict to the people whose lives it so influenced. The editor, the correspondent, the artist, and the photographer all happily found their industries just ready at just the right time. They found an opportunity and a challenge, a chance to lift their crafts to never-expected heights of professionalism, and at the same time the admonition to do so responsibly and in concord with the best interests of a greater cause, their countries. These men of North and South would in the end give a flawed performance, achieving a great deal, yet falling short of the ultimate goal through ambition, avarice, haste, and simple human frailty. It made them, thus, no different than their fellows on the battlefields and in the Congress halls. They were men of their time.

Their power could not be denied, and it was a might, as Lincoln had said, that could do great good and great evil. Unfortunately, now and then the latter proved the case. As Lincoln soon discovered, the press and its attendant practitioners could occasionally create a man whose image proved to be greater than himself. In a war where public opinion counted for so much, a President sometimes had to make a decision based not upon what he felt best, but upon what the people would accept. In the aftermath of the fiasco at Fredericksburg, with Burnside clearly unable to continue in command, the rail-splitter had to look elsewhere for the general to give him victories. Unfortunately, the people knew already whom they wanted. The press had created a hero, and they must have him. The correspondents called him "Fighting Joe."

CHAPTER 6

"I AM A DAMNED SIGHT BETTER GENERAL"

Abraham Lincoln faced a difficult problem with the fall of Burnside. The man had to be replaced, yet two of his three grand division commanders were relieved just shortly before him. Secretary of War Stanton and General Halleck preferred Major General William S. Rosecrans for the command. He was the only "winning" general they had at the moment, and that on the slim basis of his Stones River fight. Grant, though well regarded, was still enveloped in a campaign along the Mississippi. Of the senior generals with the Army of the Potomac, John F. Reynolds and George G. Meade seemed the best prospects, yet the President finally discarded them all in favor of Burnside's bitterest enemy, Major General Joseph Hooker. Lincoln was not in all ways satisfied with Hooker, as he would soon tell him, but saw no other choice. As a senior general in the Army of the Potomac, he had to be given serious consideration and, thanks to the influence of the press, the President believed that the country was with him more than any other candidate.

Certainly Hooker could be an affable man, and a capable commander. And he was good-looking, a fact that the widespread carte-devisites did not fail to convey. Though forty-eight, he looked younger, with a robust, vigorous appearance, fair hair, blue-gray eyes, and the erect bearing of a soldier. He came out of West Point in 1837 midway in his class, served in Florida, and then fought gallantly in Mexico, winning three citations. There followed that long, dreary garrison duty on the West coast that had almost crushed Grant and greatly bored Halleck, Sherman, and others. He resigned and turned farmer in the lush Valley of the Moon near Sonoma, California, but when the war came he was anxious to get into the fight. Already he enjoyed a reputation for an intemperate mouth, having loudly criticized Winfield Scott's handling of affairs in Mexico, and now old General Scott did not hurry to find him a place back in the service.

Indeed, Hooker was an intemperate man in many ways. "His defects, like evil angels, walked by him always," wrote an early observer. Fellow officers like General Carl Schurz found that he was "a man with no firm moral force but he is a good soldier and in addition has the talent publicly to display his achievements in the most favorable light." Meade privately expressed his doubts that Hooker had sufficient talent to command an army, adding that "I fear he is open to temptation and liable to be seduced by flattery." Hooker flattered himself more than enough for most of those around him, and besides his egotism he showed a strong penchant for drink and ladies of the evening. The widely repeated story that prostitutes came to be called "Hookers," thanks to his frequent liaisons with them, is probably false, yet certainly he showed little selectivity in his feminine company. And he loved to intrigue. That was what distressed Lincoln most, for he had seen it from the inside with poor Burnside. Grant regarded him as "a dangerous man." "He was not subordinate to his superiors. He was ambitious to the extent of caring nothing for the rights of others."

Yet he had some positive qualities and won wide popularity. Besides his good looks, he was frank and outspoken, enthusiastic, confident, polished, dignified, and undeniably very courageous under fire. His men thought much of him, and thus far in the war he seemed to have performed well with them. Commissioned a brigadier on May 17, 1861, he saw the fight at Bull Run only as an observer, then told Lincoln that "it is no vanity in me to say that I am a damned sight better general than you had on that field." Soon McClellan gave him a brigade, and soon thereafter a division. He fought well during the campaign on the Virginia Peninsula, and in the process attracted the attention of the press. Then came a simple typographical error that catapulted him to prominence, showing that the power of the press lay in more than its accurate coverage. A correspondent sent to the New York *Courier and Enquirer* a last-minute report on desperate fighting all along the line. The edition was all in type and locked into forms, ready for the press in just minutes. Then came another dispatch with further information, headed "Fighting—Joe Hooker." It was intended, obviously to the compositor, that this was an addition to what was already in type about Hooker under the heading "Fighting." In the rush to get the edition out, however, the hyphen was inadvertently omitted, and a headline read "Fighting Joe Hooker." A proofreader saw it at the last minute. "I rapidly considered what to do," he said. "Well, I said to myself, it makes a good heading—let it go." Other papers soon picked up the accidental sobriquet, and "Fighting Joe" was loosed on the hero-hungry Northern public. Hooker himself never cared for the name. "It sounds to me like Fighting Fool," he complained. "People will think I am a highwayman or a bandit."[1]

Yet "Fighting Joe" he was to remain, as he went on to fight at Second Bull Run, and lead a corps at Antietam, where he took a bad wound. By the time of Fredericksburg he was a major general commanding a grand division. He showed a penchant for being in the right place at the right time on the battlefield, which only enhanced his very popular image. Beyond that, he was as well highly attuned to the political currents in Washington, and very determinedly made an abrupt about-face in his own political leanings, from conservative Democrat to Radical Republican, in order to curry the favor of the reigning powers. And at intriguing against his superiors, particularly Burnside, he proved genuinely adept. Yet Lincoln saw no option but to give him the command. The press had accidentally created an aura of victory about him, and the President could only hope that the man might grow to fit the image.

But Lincoln did not entirely trust Hooker, and showed the wisdom to let him know it. Hooker assumed his new command on January 26, 1863. That very same day the President wrote him a decidedly unusual letter for a Commander-in-Chief to be giving to his general in the field, and it perfectly expressed the reservations the President felt. "I have placed you at the head of the Army of the Potomac," said Lincoln. "And yet I think it is best for you to know that there are some things in regard to which, I am not quite satisfied with you." Hooker was brave, of course, and confident, which was good. He was ambitious as well, which, "within reasonable bounds, does good rather than harm." Lincoln also thought that the general did not mix politics with his profession, in which he was entirely mistaken but could not then know.

But then Lincoln came to Hooker's conduct under Burnside. "You have taken counsel of your ambition, and thwarted him as much as you could," said the Chief Executive. It greatly wronged a good officer and the country. "I have heard, in such way as to believe it, of your recently saying that both the Army and the Government needed a Dictator." Lincoln was appointing him to the command in spite of such imprudent— indeed, treasonous—remarks. "Only those generals who gain successes, can set up dictators. What I now ask of you is military success, and I will risk the dictatorship." He would have the government's full support, yet the President confessed that he feared the selfsame spirit of dissension and suspicion that Hooker had infused into the high command would now turn against him as well. "I shall assist you as far as I can, to put it down." But for now, Hooker must fight not his own generals, but the enemy's. "Beware of rashness," said the President, "but with energy, and sleepless vigilance, go forward, and give us victories."[2]

It was a brave risk the President took, and Hooker seemed cognizant of it at once. His attitude toward Lincoln turned to one of almost fawning. After the President handed him the letter, and Hooker read it, he told others that "He talks to me like a father. I shall not answer this letter until I have won him a great victory." Unfortunately, many of Hooker's subordinates could not share even Lincoln's guarded confidence in their new commander. The longtime career officers believed that "Mr. Lincoln had committed a grave error in his selection." Only the men in his immediate command at division and corps levels had seen him in action in such fashion as to feel attached to the general, but now that he would be at headquarters, that personal contact would be at a minimum. Even the enemy officers who had known Hooker expressed little fear at his accession. According to his chief of artillery, Lee did not believe that Hooker could handle a command larger than a corps, and Beauregard, who would not have to face him, mused that "If Hooker had two to one against Lee, then I pity the former."[3]

But Hooker had the command now, and in time he would have nearly double Lee's strength. First he had to remold an army nearly shattered by the defeat of Fredericksburg and the disheartening experience of the Mud March. He approached the problem first with the same manner of two-faced statements that characterized him in earlier months. In his first order assuming the command he closed with an utterly hypocritical "cordial good wishes" for Burnside. But after that he showed some genuinely good judgment. In a meeting with Lincoln and Stanton he advised that Burnside's experience demonstrated the inadvisability of a winter campaign. Instead, he would wait until the spring and use the time to good advantage in rebuilding the army's morale and fighting trim. Desertions were running as high as 200 a day, and over 85,000 men and officers were absent and scattered over the country, for various reasons. He quickly cut the desertion and absentee problems, then discovered which officers were "disloyal" and had them dismissed. Leaves were reduced and rigorous training introduced. Hooker believed "idleness to be the great evil of all armies," and whenever the weather allowed he worked the army vigorously at field exercises. He revamped the cavalry, placed now under the command of General George Stoneman, and began a policy of continual harassment of Lee's picket outposts. His artillery he already regarded as in a superb state of readiness. Yet Hooker did confess, and perhaps too loudly, that he still believed the quality of his infantrymen to be less than the Confederates'. "With a rank and file vastly inferior to our own, intellectually and physically," Lee's army still had "by discipline alone, acquired a character for steadiness and efficiency unsurpassed, in my judgment, in ancient or modern times." He would confess to his Radical friends that "We have not been able to rival it," hardly a comforting admission from a man who would have to lead his "inferior" troops into battle shortly.[4]

In time "Fighting Joe" did rebuild substantially the morale and fitness of his command. The Army of the Potomac remained on the north bank of the Rappahannock throughout the winter of 1863, and steadily grew in strength. By April the muster fell just short of 150,000, with another 45,000 in the defenses of Washington, though at Hooker's own request these defenders were not part of his army. The new general did show considerable ability at reorganization, doing away with the clumsy grand divisions and returning to a somewhat more efficient corps system, with seven corps commanders reporting directly to him, or to the army's new chief of staff, General Daniel Butterfield. Indeed, it was Butterfield's hand that effected many of the administrative reforms, though he would later be remembered only for the erroneous supposition that he composed the haunting bugle call "Taps." But neither Hooker nor Butterfield achieved a stellar success when they abandoned the supply wagons that carried the army's sustenance in favor of thousands of pack mules. Camp followers were officially banned from the camps, though many still plied their trade, and some found it more than incongruous that Hooker, so often associated with prostitutes in truth and fable, would banish his presumed companions from his command. To help build a spirit of élan, corps badges were designed by Butterfield, to be worn by each member of each corps. It worked well, for soon enough did the wearers of the Maltese cross or the clover decide that they were infinitely better soldiers than those who wore the triangle or St. Andrew's cross. Healthy competition between commands elevated the morale of all.

Soon enough the new general found himself called "Administrative Joe" in the minds of many, but he never put the coming fight out of his mind. Every reform effected grew out of the single purpose of readying his army to meet the seemingly invincible Lee and his Army of Northern Virginia. His only instructions from Washington had Halleck's injunction that "In regard to the operations of your own army, you can best judge when and where it can move to the greatest advantage." The only special instructions were the omnipresent need to protect Washington, and to keep Harpers Ferry safely out of enemy hands. There must be no more invasions of the North via the Shenandoah Valley. The general's confidence grew even as his army. "If the enemy does not run, God help them," he boasted in March. "I have the finest army the sun ever shone on. I can march this army to New Orleans. My plans are perfect, and when I start to carry them out, may God have mercy on General Lee, for I will have none." Lincoln privately expressed concern that Hooker was boasting too much. Knowing that there was no substitute for actions speaking as loudly as words, Lincoln sat through Hooker's fulminations, but then cautioned him "in your next battle *put in all your men*."[5]

General Robert E. Lee would have to follow that same injunction if he were to avoid needing the Lord's mercy as predicted by Hooker. Even as the Federals spent their winter rebuilding for the coming spring campaigns, so did the Confederates. Lee started with a considerable advantage over Hooker. His had been a winning army since the start, with only the check at Antietam the previous September to dampen its pride. Further, Lee enjoyed a command system that was already in place, his two corps well organized and smoothly functioning except for the occasional outbursts provoked by the sometimes exasperatingly peculiar Jackson. Senior officers had been with the army almost from the start, and men and generals enjoyed a degree of unit pride not yet developed north of the Rappahannock. And already there was a mystique growing about Lee himself, the ever-expanding cult of "Marse Robert," an indefinable quantity that could pull from his men feats that they themselves despaired of achieving.[6]

While Lee was refitting his army, however, he did not lie idle. All through that winter he kept his cavalry, admittedly the best on the continent at that time, in almost constant motion, feinting, feeling out Hooker's positions, looking for the weakness that might be exploited when the good weather came. Riding about the Virginia countryside that winter with Stuart was a hero of First Manassas and the Peninsula, who then transferred to the mounted arm as Stuart's second in command. Brigadier General Wade Hampton of South Carolina had come a long way since his days as one of the most moneyed planters in the Palmetto State. An early supporter of secession, he had no military qualifications other than a large fortune with which he personally recruited and equipped his Hampton Legion, and oftentimes those were all the qualifications a man needed. Yet quickly he showed a natural ability as a leader. At Bull Run he played an important role in the Confederate victory, taking a bad wound in the process, and on the Peninsula he performed equally as well. Handsome, courtly, large and rugged, he seemed a natural for the cavalry when Lee reorganized the army in July 1862, and Stuart seemed happy to have him. Lee steadily acquired an increasing respect for the South Carolinian's "standing and gallantry." As the warmer weather approached, however, Hampton's command ran short of good mounts and was ordered into the Virginia interior to find new ones. As a result, he was to miss the forthcoming campaign, but he would be heard from very shortly thereafter, and in the finest traditions of Southern manhood.[7]

If Hampton was not to be present in the cavalry skirmishing that took place in March and April, however, another hero certainly was. Major John Pelham, so distinguished at Fredericksburg, took part both in the relaxed months of January and February as the army rested and wintered, and in the renewed mounted probes of March. Stuart had become devoted to him, the two camping together and sharing their meals, their jollity, and even their reading. Then on March 17 came word that enemy horse had been seen in Morrisville, near Kelly's Ford on the Rappahannock. What it meant could not be told, but it might indicate an unexpectedly early advance in an attempt to steal across the river. If they were going to cross, then Kelly's Ford would be the place. There was barely an outpost stationed there that morning, and Brigadier General Fitzhugh Lee, nephew of the army commander and one of Stuart's trusted subordinates, hurried what men he could find to the threatened spot. Pelham went with them, as did Stuart, though the major's guns were not yet on the field. In the resulting fighting, as Pelham rode with the cavalry in a charge, a shell fragment tore through the back of his head and left him dying on the field, a boyish smile on his face. Finally the Federals retired, but that evening Stuart wept, and Lee wrote mournfully to Richmond of the "long career of usefulness and honor" thus cut short.[8]

While the cavalrymen were fighting and dying, Lee tried to solve the command problems and fill the vacancies caused by bullets and transfers. Then to counter a threat in North Carolina, Lee had to transfer his I Corps and General James Longstreet away from the Rappahannock. Longstreet, "Old Pete" to his men, could be a troublesome subordinate. He craved independent command, chafing at being always under the thumb of Lee who, though he admired him, seemed nevertheless too conservative and too much bound by the situation in Virginia. Longstreet spent the next two months countering threats on the "south side" of Virginia, at Suffolk and elsewhere, as well as in North Carolina, all with little effect. By the end of April, when events in Lee's front caused him to summon "Old Pete" back toward the Rappahannock, little had been accomplished other than to terribly weaken the Army of Northern Virginia just as Hooker prepared his offensive.

Lee might well be in trouble as May approached. Jackson and his chief subordinate, the talented Ambrose P. Hill, had been feuding, and Stonewall himself sometimes seemed not to be in the best of health. But his wife gave him a baby girl in April, and that charged the old warrior for the coming fight. He would have to be charged, for with Longstreet gone, Lee had only Jackson's II Corps and Stuart's cavalry to meet the enemy, along with two of Longstreet's divisions that had remained. Lee could count barely 60,000 effective troops at hand, and he knew that Hooker numbered better than twice that number. Whenever the Federals moved, it would be a near thing indeed for Lee to prevent their crossing the Rappahannock, much less defeat him once over. On April 29 he summoned Longstreet to return, but no one knew for certain whether "Old Pete" would arrive in time. He would not.[9]

Hooker had work to do if he was to show Lee no mercy, and he set off to a good start. By early April the roads, though still muddy and almost useless for wheeled traffic, could stand the tramp of thousands of feet, and he decided that it was time to launch his offensive to make Lee howl. Further, he had about 40,000 men whose terms of enlistment were about to expire, and he must fight now if he was to get the benefit of them. He intended originally to commence operations on April 13 by sending Stoneman and his cavalry some distance up the Rappahannock where it would cross and then sweep down on Lee's left flank and rear, while the main army crossed at Fredericksburg and attacked. But heavy rains ensued almost as soon as the cavalry left, and Hooker saw no choice but to abandon the plan. He met with a disappointed Lincoln a few days later, promising that an offensive would still be going in a few days, and told a fellow general that he would "destroy Lee's army or his own within a week."[10]

Hooker then conceived a plan with many excellent qualities, not the least of which is that he finally saw, as Lincoln had for some time, that the objective should not be Richmond, but Lee's army itself. On that army he focused his plans. Once again he called for Stoneman to ride around Lee's left and get in his rear, hopefully disrupting communications with Richmond. At the same time, Major General John Sedgwick was to cross his enlarged command, the I, III, and VI Corps, at Fredericksburg to threaten and attack Lee's right. Then the V, XI, and XII Corps would cross in Lee's front, under Hooker's direct command, and position themselves in the vicinity of Chancellorsville. Lee would be caught between Hooker and Sedgwick, with his rear threatened by Stoneman. If successful, the plan was designed not just to defeat Lee, but to virtually destroy his army. The only real flaw was that Hooker depended upon his ability to concert his actions with Sedgwick, an almost impossible expectation given the delays the still-soggy roads would surely cause. Once the movement began, "Fighting Joe" also failed to recognize that the same soaked ground would slow Stoneman. The general was in a hurry, now, and nothing, including weather, would be allowed to slow his campaign.[11]

On the evening of April 26, 1863, Hooker issued his orders for the next day's march. Indeed, he stayed up well after midnight giving instructions for the movement to commence at dawn that morning. Well before full light the blue-clad warriors began their tramp out of the camps around Falmouth. They had rested and refitted for four months now, and they should be ready. They had a new general with a fighting reputation, and numbers that seemed overwhelming. They should be ready. The sky turned dark and cold; rain falling frequently soon drenched the soldiers, who still lightened their loads by discarding, of all things, raincoats. They were carrying up to sixty pounds apiece in their knapsacks, and the forming mud made it seem double that. Still their spirits ran high, and when Hooker himself appeared along the lines, the men sang and cheered. "Joe Hooker is our leader," ran one song, "he takes his whisky strong."[12]

It all went perhaps better than Hooker might reasonably have expected. The weather, though ominous, allowed him to move with reasonable dispatch, and none of his marching columns fell behind schedule.

Only the cavalry suffered that difficulty, but the general ignored Stoneman's difficulties and kept the infantry to its original timetable. By April 28 the Army of the Potomac had begun its crossings of the Rappahannock at Kelly's Ford, some miles above Fredericksburg. Meanwhile, Sedgwick glared across the river at Lee menacingly. Already "Marse Robert" knew that a flank attack was afoot, having in fact predicted such a move some five days before. Yet by the next day Hooker's campaign continued right as planned. Stoneman was finally across the river and approaching the enemy communications, and Hooker with the main body was well crossed and moving into an area known as the Wilderness, toward Chancellorsville, and the vulnerable Confederate left flank. By April 30 Hooker was encamped in and around the village of Chancellorsville, elated with his success so far, and telling his troops that "the operations of the last three days have determined that our enemy must ingloriously fly, or come out from behind their defenses and give us battle on our ground, where certain destruction awaits him." Of course, this was not quite what Lee had in mind.[13]

At the time Hooker began his movement, Lee had actually been considering an offensive movement of his own, despite Longstreet's absence. Instinctively he understood that, outnumbered as he was, his only hope of avoiding being thrown on an unprofitable defensive was by striking boldly where the enemy was not. He was eyeing the Shenandoah, but when reports came in of accelerated Federal movements across the Rappahannock, Lee realized that he no longer faced a slumbering enemy. He had his army thinly spread out on a front nearly twenty miles long, with three divisions some eight miles down the river to cover a crossing by way of Skinker's Neck, Richard H. Anderson's division near Chancellorsville to cover his left, and the rest scattered in between. When Sedgwick crossed the Rappahannock just below Fredericksburg on April 29, Lee's fears were realized, and he knew that Hooker was certainly moving on his left. Stuart and his cavalry were off to the west, and actually cut off from Lee for a time, slowing the flow of information that would be vital to a defense.

The countryside could work to Lee's advantage, however, and he would not fail to use it so. Chancellorsville sat nine miles directly west of Fredericksburg, with a good road leading to the country village. Lee could speedily move troops from one point to the other along a so-called plank road. Further, Chancellorsville lay in the middle of the Wilderness, an area so densely wooded that movements by large numbers were virtually impossible. That alone would nullify much of Hooker's superiority in forces. It was a confusing territory, not well mapped, and better known to the Confederates than to the Federals. Lee would be able to move the bulk of his army from Fredericksburg and south of it to the Chancellorsville region almost undetected. At the same time, he could leave a relatively small force at Fredericksburg itself to try to hold Sedgwick. After all, many of the troops with him had fought there four months before. They would have to assault those same fearful works on Marye's Heights, and that fear alone would give Lee an edge. If all the factors available to him were employed, and if Hooker did not move so quickly that Lee could not move first, then the Confederates stood at least a chance for a good defense. An actual offensive against the Federals seemed out of the question.

Hooker made his first mistake on April 30, as he reached Chancellorsville. He was still in the tangled territory that would hamper his army's maneuvers, and Lee was still at Fredericksburg. Another two hours' march would have gotten him clear of the dense forest and onto more advantageous ground. Yet at 3 P.M. that day he stopped, waiting for his II and III Corps to cross and join him. It would prove a costly mistake, and one not readily understandable in light of Hooker's confidence in his success. But instead of moving, he remained content with writing congratulatory messages, claiming that "the rebel army is now the legitimate property of the Army of the Potomac. They may as well pack up their haversacks and make for Richmond. I shall be after them." Even though some of his subordinates, chiefly Meade, urged that the army press on, Hooker felt that he had achieved enough for that day, and against any other opponent such might have been the case. Even Lee, now, was in desperate trouble, in genuine danger of being overwhelmed if the enemy attacked him in unison and in full force. Only daring would save him.[14]

Of daring Lee had aplenty, even given the very unfavorable situation in which he found himself. Upon Hooker's advance to Chancellorsville, Anderson and his division withdrew about four miles and began throwing up defensive earthworks, while the Confederates at Fredericksburg were themselves preparing for an attack upon their entrenchments. Yet Lee saw his only defense in offense, and studied which of the two threatening bodies of the enemy he should strike. On April 30 he and Jackson carefully looked over Sedgwick's lines before them to see if they offered any promise of a successful attack. Unfortunately, Stafford Heights once more bristled with assembled Federal cannon, and Lee quickly had to abandon any thought of an offensive under the tons of iron that those guns could send into his ranks. That meant that he would have to leave a token force to hold Sedgwick in check, while he moved with the main body of his army to strike at Hooker at Chancellorsville. To face Sedgwick, Lee left the crusty Virginian Jubal A. Early with a precious 10,000 men to withstand four times their number. Early was the man to do it, but all really depended upon how hearty Sedgwick's attack would be if and when it came.

To Jackson, Lee gave the simple order "Move, then, at dawn tomorrow up to Anderson." Stonewall did not delay. At midnight he awakened his corps and put the men on the road toward Chancellorsville. By 8 A.M., May 1, the general himself came to Anderson's position and at once ordered him to stop digging. They would be attacking this day. No need for defenses. Throughout the rest of the morning the Confederate divisions would be arriving in the vicinity of Tabernacle Church on the plank road, just four miles short of Chancellorsville. Undoubtedly the opening of the battle would come in a matter of hours.[15]

Hooker knew fairly well what Lee was doing, for he had observation balloons aloft across the Rappahannock and behind his own lines. He also had divined the pathetically thin Confederate line left at Fredericksburg. Even before receiving this news, Hooker spent several hours of self-congratulation, retiring the night before in a euphoric mood. "The enemy is in my power and God Almighty cannot deprive me of them," he gloated. As a result of his overconfidence, Hooker simply would not be hurried. Not until 11 A.M. on May 1, when the III Corps arrived, did he finally resume the march toward Fredericksburg. Henry Slocum's XII Corps advanced on the plank road, followed by Oliver O. Howard's XI Corps, Howard now recovered from his loss of an arm on the Peninsula. A man of unquestionable bravery, Howard would prove in this war to be one of the least reliable generals in the high command, yet he continued to advance in rank and standing. Hooker would have cause to regret that in the days to come.

While Slocum and Howard followed their route, another smaller column advanced on the Orange Turnpike, parallel and just a few hundred yards north of them in places. Sickles was to remain in reserve at Chancellorsville while two of Meade's V Corps divisions were snaking their way along the south bank of the Rappahannock off to Hooker's left. He entertained every expectation that Lee would at once fall into confusion as soon as he saw the army arrayed against him.[16]

After two hours on the march, the first Federals came out of the Wilderness into more open ground, and there Hooker found a surprise. The Confederates began skirmishing with him, and in the distance could be seen substantial numbers of the enemy near Tabernacle Church, with some defenses thrown up, and the obvious intent of standing their ground. Lee fell back some distance before the advancing Federal skirmishers, then stopped them briefly, counterattacked, and then himself was stopped. It was minor and indecisive fighting by only a few units, yet it clearly revealed Hooker's advantage. He had open ground in which to maneuver and, better yet, Meade's line of unopposed advance had taken him to a position barely one and a half miles from Lee's unprotected right flank, and virtually in position to deliver a quick attack on that flank and his rear, as well as to cut Lee off from reinforcement by Early at Fredericksburg. Never before had the Army of Northern Virginia stood so close to virtual destruction.

And now, for reasons that baffled his subordinates as well as himself, Hooker simply lost his courage. He had sent orders to Sedgwick to begin his assault on Early, yet managed to garble them so that the commander at Fredericksburg could not really divine what Hooker wanted. Sending more orders only served to confuse Sedgwick further. He made a demonstration, though not an attack, and then Hooker later sent him word not to make the demonstration. Thus, Sedgwick's command did almost nothing to seriously threaten Early, leaving Lee free to face Hooker. "Fighting Joe," however, somehow believed that the "threatening attitude" that he ordered Sedgwick to demonstrate would itself be sufficient to force Lee to return to Early. "When I gave the order to General Sedgwick," said Hooker, "I expected that Lee would be whipped by manoeuvre." Instead, the Confederates stood in his front ready for battle. Some days later "Fighting Joe" would confess to Abner Doubleday that "for once I lost confidence in Hooker, and that is all there is to it." Despite the remonstrances of his senior commanders, he ordered them to abandon the advance and fall back to their camps around Chancellorsville. Meade, too, was ordered to withdraw from his position on Lee's flank. Soon thereafter Hooker indicated to Butterfield that he expected Lee to attack him, having abandoned all intention of maintaining his own offensive. General Darius Nash Couch, who saw Hooker that afternoon, believed that he had lost all his balance, overwhelmed by his responsibility and the fact that he could not directly control an army now spread over nearly twelve miles. When Couch left after hearing Hooker's order to retire, he entertained "the belief that my commanding general was a whipped man." In days to come charges of drunkenness would be leveled at Hooker, but there was no truth to them. He was simply scared and beaten by his own fears.[17]

Not so Robert E. Lee. He left the work on this front to Jackson during the morning and early afternoon, while he personally observed what was taking place in Fredericksburg. By about 1 P.M., satisfied that Sedgwick was not going to attack, Lee and his staff rode to join the II Corps as it faced Hooker beyond Tabernacle Church. Even as he arrived, around one-thirty, the Federals were already beginning their slow retirement to Chancellorsville. Jackson had perceived the movement, mistaking it for a retreat in the face of his own advance. He decided to press his advantage, advising his subordinates to "Keep closed on Chancellorsville." And already he looked for good ground that might allow him to break out and maneuver, as he had done in the Shenandoah a year before. When Lee joined him, Stonewall could report that he was steadily pushing Hooker back, and then the two of them rode to their left to look for a route to turn Hooker's flank. Then came word of a rumor that Hooker was in fact abandoning his offensive, and might even abandon Chancellorsville. That was the sort of news that inspired Jackson. Press them, always press them, he told his men. A retreating enemy must be followed and tormented continually to garner the best of the situation. Finally Jackson's men found the Federals barricaded behind breastworks of their own later that afternoon, and Lee decided that Hooker had retired as far as he intended to, and that assaults now would be too costly for him to afford. "Marse Robert" would satisfy himself for the rest of the daylight hours with skirmishing to keep the bluecoats constantly threatened, while he and Jackson looked for their chance to press their advantage. Though still in a tight place, Lee could smell an opportunity here. All he needed was pluck, and Jackson.[18]

Stonewall did not fail him. Obviously Sedgwick was too strong to attack, and now so was Hooker's main body behind the breastworks they had erected. A weak point had to be found, and Jackson, with his longtime penchant for the wide flank march, began to look to the south, around the enemy right. Earlier he had told Lee that he believed Hooker would withdraw entirely on the next day without an attack being necessary. Lee disagreed politely but firmly, stating his own early preference for a move against Hooker's right. Further conversation finally led them to the belief that their only true opportunity lay to their left, and it was confirmed well after dark when Jeb Stuart himself arrived and gleefully announced to them that Fitzhugh Lee had discovered that Hooker's right flank, Howard's XI Corps, was virtually "up in the air." Hooker had concentrated Slocum's corps and Darius Couch's II Corps immediately around Chancellorsville. Extending his line to the left, he placed Meade's V Corps along a creek that ran north into the Rappahannock. Howard extended the line to the right along the Orange Turnpike, and his own right flank sat virtually unprotected, vulnerable to a crushing blow that would curl him up and allow the enemy to drive right into the rear of the army. Howard himself was no great general, but Hooker must share the blame as well. Having sent almost all of his cavalry off under Stoneman, he had only a small division of it left with the main army, and this he placed two miles behind Chancellorsville instead of positioning it in its proper spot, covering his one and only flank not protected by a natural barrier like a river. He may have expected that the denseness of the Wilderness itself would protect his flank, but that was an armor easily pierced by men who knew this country.

Jackson had such men. During the rest of that night he had scouts out surveying the available roads that might lead him to Howard's flank unseen. Men native to the neighborhood came before him to hastily sketch rude maps of the roads and trails. Jackson had promised Lee that he would move at 4 A.M. May 2, but they had not yet settled precisely what troops would go with him and just what they would expect to achieve. All that Jackson settled in his mind as he lay that chilly night, coming down with a cold, thinking of what he might do with this opportunity. Finally, hours before daylight, he arose, sent out more scouts, and when they returned he completed his audacious plan. He sat with his officers at a fire, drinking coffee to fight the cold. Presently they heard the clatter of his sword, which he had propped against a tree, falling to the earth. When Colonel Armistead L. Long picked it up and returned it to

Stonewall, Long thought to himself that it was a bad omen, but said nothing of it.

Presently Lee arrived, and off in the east the first glow of the predawn could be seen. Jackson now outlined to Lee his plan. Confederate troops would move from their positions near the plank road some two miles southwest to Catherine Furnace, then continue another two miles until they hit the Brock Road. There they would turn right and have perhaps five miles to march before they reached the vicinity of the Wilderness Tavern, right in the heart of the forest. That would bring them no more than a mile and a quarter from, and directly across, Howard's exposed right flank. Thus, in a greatly circuitous route, they would march completely around the Federal flank almost unseen. The Wilderness was their friend, not Hooker's.

So far Lee understood, and had probably anticipated Jackson's plan, before he expressed it. But then the commanding general asked what troops Stonewall proposed to take. "My whole Corps," Jackson replied. When Lee asked what that would leave him with to face the bulk of Hooker's army in his front, Stonewall calmly replied that he would leave two divisions! The proposition was startling. Jackson would take 26,000 men on a flank march, leaving Lee with barely 17,000 to face perhaps 50,000 directly in his front. Should Hooker attack him, sheer force of numbers would certainly outbalance generalship. Early and Sedgwick were too far away now to matter. Yet Lee gave his assent. He, like Jackson, would take a risk. It was all they had, but in his decision he carried the responsibility not only for the possible loss of a battle, but also with it the loss of his army and the Confederate cause itself in the East.[19]

It was well after the appointed hour when the Confederate divisions began their march. The refinement of the battle plan had caused considerable delay yet Jackson, a stickler for punctuality, seemed not to mind. He smelled a triumph. The roads were good now, no longer soggy, and he could keep the columns to his preferred two miles per hour, with ten minutes' rest. Still it would take many hours to march the twelve or more miles to the point of attack, but a greater danger lay in portions of the route itself. At several points, the roads the Southerners were to travel passed in distant view of the enemy. As a result, by 9 A.M. Hooker received intelligence of a large column of the enemy moving toward his right. He may have lost his courage, but not his wits, and he suspected at once an attempt to strike at his right flank. To Howard he sent a warning to look to his flank. Looking at a map in his headquarters, and seeing the dust clouds raised by the marching Confederates, "Fighting Joe" repeated to himself that "It can't be a retreat; retreat without a fight? That is not Lee. If not retreat, what is it? Lee is trying to flank me." He repeated his order to Howard to be ready for an attack from the west. Howard, however, did almost nothing, even when later in the day his own signalmen sent forward reported the move as well.

But if Howard and Hooker would remain passive in the face of this threat, not so the commander of the III Corps, Major General Daniel Edgar Sickles. A man of greater vanity and ego would have been hard to find. A lawyer and then a Democratic politician and congressman, he was best known in the country for his murder trial in 1859. Though a well-known philanderer himself, Sickles took mortal offense when he learned that his wife was seeing another man, and upon encountering the offender, Sickles shot him dead in the streets of Washington. The slain was the son of Francis Scott Key, composer of "The Star-Spangled Banner." With lawyer Edwin M. Stanton as his defense counsel, Sickles pleaded an "unwritten law" of the rights of husbands, and won acquittal. Sickles knew not the first thing about matters military, but as a prominent War Democrat, he won an immediate general's star from Lincoln. In the ensuing months of campaigning he demonstrated some ability in command—though a troublesome man at all times—and an unquestioned bravery. Having fought under Hooker, he now commanded "Fighting Joe's" old corps, and chafed at having been left out of the fight so far.

That changed when Sickles, too, began to see Jackson marching across his front. For three hours that morning he watched the Confederates moving toward the west. "The movement indicated a retreat on Gordonsville or an attack upon our right flank," he decided, and notified both Hooker and Howard. It was old news to them, and Hooker was becoming increasingly confused once more. His earlier resolve that Lee was attacking faded in the face of a growing new conviction that the Confederates were in retreat. Still he remained cautious, but in response to Sickles' urgings he allowed the III Corps to feel out the enemy. Sickles sent a battery to shell the column first, driving them into the woods and out of sight. For a time Sickles believed that he had stopped Jackson, but a reconnaissance soon disabused him of that notion. Reporting this to his commander, Sickles soon received orders to move in force to discover what was happening. Sickles sent two divisions forward and struck tentatively at Jackson's column, taking prisoners who informed him that it was the whole Confederate II Corps. The prisoners exaggerated Stonewall's strength into 40,000 or more, and Sickles believed them.

In a short time Sickles saw what he took to be signs of a complete success, which only further confirmed Hooker's conviction now that the enemy was on the run. He sent the one reserve brigade of the exposed XI Corps to assist Sickles in what was in fact nothing more than a pursuit of Jackson's rearward columns as they marched southwest on the path set for them. By detaching that brigade of Howard's, Hooker left the XI Corps completely isolated from the rest of the army, with a great gap between it and the rest of the Federals created by Sickles' advance. By about 4 P.M. Hooker finally gave Sedgwick a firm order to attack at Fredericksburg, telling him that "we know the enemy is flying." Yet even if he believed that Lee was retreating, then Hooker's best move was to attack vigorously rather than let the Confederates escape. Yet still "Fighting Joe" seemed barely functional, his courage not yet returned, nor his good sense. He was a man desperately wanting events to follow their natural course to his benefit, without himself having to make decisions that would alter that course. The responsibility of army command that he had wanted for so long simply was too much for him.[20]

And then Jackson overwhelmed him. By 5 P.M. the Confederates had completed their fatiguing march and stood poised on Howard's right flank. Another general might have halted here to rest the men overnight before attacking with only a bare two hours of light left. But not Stonewall. He knew that he had been seen on his march, and could only surmise that even now the enemy might be prepared to meet him. Delay could be fatal to the assault. It must come now.

As soon as the divisions came up, Jackson formed them in line, watching as he did so the old officers he had served with for so long. Many had been his students at Lexington in years gone by, and now he said to one alumnus, Colonel Thomas T. Munford of Stuart's cavalry, that "the Virginia Military Institute will be heard from today!" So would Jackson. At five-fifteen he looked at his watch. "Are you ready?" he asked one of his generals. Affirmative. "You can go forward then," said Stonewall calmly.[21]

The attack crushed Howard from the first instant. The first brigades encountered a sudden flurry of wild game running through their camps, animals flushed by the as yet unseen Confederate advance. Many of the Federals were actually lounging about, their weapons stacked, when the first shots heralded Jackson's coming. The rout began immediately. Not a single unit made a genuine stand except for the brigade of Colonel Adolphus Buschbeck, which managed to stall the Confederates for several precious minutes while the balance of the corps streamed toward the rear and the Rappahannock in utter confusion. Only when the enemy seemed about to surround it on both flanks did the valiant brigade join in the withdrawal. Howard lost over 2,400 casualties in barely an hour, and not his efforts or those of any other officer could stop the surge of panicked soldiers. Howard would later admit to his complete folly in not heeding the repeated warnings sent him, showing him to be at least a much better man than he was a general.

Jackson pushed the Federals back nearly two miles before a startled Hooker managed to put up a defense. Once again an atmospheric inversion caused the men at headquarters in Chancellorsville not to hear the sounds of the battle nearby. Hooker learned of it only when an aide was looking through his binoculars and saw the horde of retreating Federals rushing toward them. "My God, here they come!" he shouted. Hooker rode to the front at once, and began the mammoth task of halting some of the routed XI Corps and, with aid from other nearby commands, erecting a defensive line. By this time the steam had gone out of Jackson's advance as well, the terrain and fatigue working together with the growing darkness to confuse orders and directions. Around 9 P.M. the advance finally stalled, and the two opposing lines halted for breath.

His associates found Jackson euphoric. Battle stimulated him to a greater degree than anything but his religion, and he regarded his command as but an arm of the Almighty. That arm had more good work yet to do in this battle, of this he felt certain. Thanks to his flank attack and some tentative advances made by the understrength Lee on the rest of Hooker's line, the Federal army was surrounded on three sides in and around Chancellorsville. The rallied remnants of Howard's corps extended Hooker's left flank back to the Rappahannock, while Meade and his V Corps extended his right in the same direction. This left one ford, and one only, by which Hooker could cross his army to the other side—United States Ford. Jackson knew that, and now if he could find a way to cut off the enemy from that crossing, the rout of Howard could be turned into the destruction of Hooker. He would have to hazard a night attack to do so, but the iron was still hot, and he must strike quickly. Stonewall and his escort rode off into the darkness in search of a road that would lead them into Hooker's rear. What they found were confused portions of their own troops, lost in the darkness and in the shadows cast by the moonlight. A. P. Hill was with him, and when they had ridden far enough, Jackson turned back intent upon ordering the attack continued. Then a shot rang out of the darkness, followed by others. Hill ordered the firing to cease, believing that it was friendly fire. Stonewall's horse bolted briefly into the woods. "You are firing into your own men," shouted an officer at the unseen riflemen. Then right in front of him Jackson saw the sheet of flame from a volley. A bullet crippled his arm; another struck his right hand. The horse bolted again, branches and boughs hit him, and then his officers steadied the horse and finally stopped the firing. His arm broken and almost in deep shock, Jackson was hurried to the rear, even as Federal skirmishers and men simply lost hovered in the vicinity. Hill was wounded soon thereafter as he attempted personally to protect the fallen general. Only after a torturous and dangerous trip to the field hospital in the rear did Jackson finally have his wounds examined and anesthetic administered. His left arm was shattered and useless. That same night the doctors amputated it, and yet Jackson was soon conscious enough to give some directions to the new commander of the II Corps, Stuart, the senior general present.[22]

The fall of Jackson and Hill ended further Confederate movement that night, and well it was for Hooker. Yet as the Southern advance faded, so did Federal resistance grow. Soon Hooker had Major General John Fulton Reynolds' I Corps in the line, along with other reinforcements, and late that night "Fighting Joe" even regained enough of his old spirit to order his one and only offensive movement of the battle. Sickles' corps, almost cut off from the army and abandoned by Hooker, moved in an intended attack on Jackson's right flank, but in the dark the whole affair was confused, and finally they had to fall back to the high ground at Hazel Grove just west of Chancellorsville.

Hooker did not know it, but despite his disaster of May 2, when the dawn broke on May 3 he still held the theoretical advantage over Lee, and the Confederate army was in a worse position than the day before. Lee's and Stuart's halves of their army were separated by several hours' march, with more than double their number in between them. Better yet, Hazel Grove, occupied by Sickles during the night, commanded the southern flanks of both halves of the Confederate army. Well-placed artillery there would make the enemy positions untenable, and it provided a perfect launching place for flank attacks on Lee and Stuart. Even the untrained Sickles saw this, but when Hooker came to examine the position he was a beaten man, defeated in spirit and in mind. All he could see was that the enemy stood on both sides of him, and he wanted out. Hooker ordered Sickles to withdraw from his position, even though it would allow Lee to place his own artillery on the summit, and from it bombard the Federals.

Lee and Stuart certainly did not hesitate to take advantage of their opponent's mistake. While attacks were launched on both sides of the Federal perimeter, Stuart began placing his big guns on the abandoned eminence, eventually having fifty cannon in position, each of them sending shells into the flanks of Slocum's and Sickles' commands. The fighting became furious on both sides, and before long the Federals' ammunition began running low. Hooker himself took almost no part in the day's events, but instead merely wandered about, crying over the slain General Hiram Berry, and sending Sedgwick absurd messages that he was driving Lee before him. About 9:30 A.M., as he leaned against a pillar on the porch of the Chancellor house, a Confederate solid shot struck the post and the concussion threw him to the ground, severely stunned. As he arose, the pillar itself then fell and struck him hard on the head and back. Hooker would remain in something of a stupor for days to come, and in later years would finally lose his right side to paralysis. The rest of this day he was often barely coherent, yet he would not turn over the command to the next senior officer. When Meade and Reynolds asked permission to attack Stuart's vulnerable left flank, Hooker declined. All he could think to do was to withdraw farther from the Confederates that constantly plagued him.[23]

Shortly after 10 A.M. the Federals left Chancellorsville, and Lee and Stuart quickly pursued, and once more linked their forces. Now the great danger to the divided Confederate army was past, and Lee wanted to push the attack. But just then came word of Sedgwick, who had finally moved after two days of inactivity thanks to bad orders. Early that morning he had pushed Early out of Fredericksburg, and only after four costly assaults did he finally claim Marye's Heights a fairly won prize. Early withdrew to the south, leaving nothing between Sedgwick and Lee's rear except the brigade of Cadmus Wilcox. Sedgwick pursued at once, forcing him back, and it was news of this that persuaded Lee to withhold his renewed attack on Hooker. Instead, he sent Lafayette McLaws and his division hurrying to Wilcox's aid. McLaws halted when he reached Salem Church, about three miles from Fredericksburg, and here Wilcox soon joined him. Sedgwick had unfortunately delayed his pursuit for an hour, but by 4 P.M. he was ready to attack, thinking naturally enough that there could be few Confederates in front of him since Hooker was surely occupying all of Lee's army at Chancellorsville. Sedgwick sent only one division into his attack, then saw it surprisingly repulsed, then followed up by an attack by McLaws. He stopped the Confederate advance, but the gathering darkness stopped further fighting.

For poor "Fighting Joe" Hooker, this whimper was the last of the battle of Chancellorsville. He was ready to quit. Indeed, he had done so from the moment that Lee first resisted him. All day May 4 he remained idle, leaving Sedgwick to fend for himself as Lee turned his attention from Hooker to the Federals at Salem Church. He reinforced McLaws and himself assumed command of 21,000 Confederates, but Sedgwick was no Hooker, and he skillfully contested their advance. Carefully covering his line of retreat, Sedgwick well repulsed the uncoordinated attack of the by now exhausted Southerners that afternoon, and later under the veil of darkness safely took his command across the Rappahannock. Hooker that day outnumbered Stuart in his front by three to one, yet thought of nothing but retreat. Though he blustered somewhat of attacking the next day, that night, when he convened a council of war, he repeatedly spoke of withdrawal. Even after a majority of his corps commanders voted to stay and fight, he overruled them. Later he spoke with Meade, who could not help but be moved by the general's pathetic aspect. "Poor Hooker himself," wrote Meade, "after he had determined to withdraw, said to me, in the most desponding manner, that he was ready to turn over to me the Army of the Potomac; that he had had enough of it, and almost wished he had never been born." The Federal position was still overwhelmingly in its favor, but even if the only Confederate in their front was old Lee himself armed with a riding crop, Hooker would not have attacked. He had beaten himself better than any general ever defeated by "Marse Robert."[24]

Early on May 5 Hooker began his preparations to withdraw the army north of the Rappahannock, and that evening and through the night the movement was completed. Lee, with a bent for rashness that had cost him dearly at Malvern Hill and again at Antietam, intended to launch a massive attack on May 6 despite the overwhelming numbers against him. He might hope for success, given Hooker's performance so far, but his own army was virtually exhausted, his command system in disarray, and his own ammunition low. It would have been a foolish act, but Hooker preempted him. Early on May 6 Lee's advancing skirmishers found that there were no Federals left in his front. The whole business was over.

What remained now was to count the casualties and make excuses. Hooker could find little to boast about in his campaign. His plan had been good, excepting his misuse of his cavalry, but from the first he mishandled his army and showed a streak of moral cowardice that shocked his officers. It cost him 17,000 casualties out of an army of nearly 134,000. When he first reported to Lincoln he tried to cover his loss, saying that he did not attack Lee and whip him because "I saw no way of giving the enemy a general battle with the prospect of success which I desire." But no amount of "Fighting Joe's" posturing could conceal his folly. As his messages reached Washington, the President saw through them at once. Even before hearing definitely of the defeat, he told his press friend Noah Brooks that Hooker had "been licked." When the confirmation came, Lincoln was distraught. "I shall never forget that picture of despair," said Brooks. Lincoln's face was ashen as he entered the room with a telegram in his hand. He knew instinctively its content, but asked Brooks to read the message that announced the recrossing to the north side of the Rappahannock, the abandonment of the fight. Lincoln was the color of the French gray wallpaper behind him. "Never, as long as I knew him, did he seem to be so broken up, so dispirited, and so ghostlike." Lincoln clasped his hands behind his back and paced back and forth muttering, "My God, my God, what will the country say! What will the country say!" Utterly distracted, he finally paced out of the room.[25]

The gloom would not be solely for the North. Lee's victories were always costly. It was in the nature of things when an outnumbered army had to depend upon daring and aggressiveness to make up for its lack of numbers. His losses totaled nearly 13,000, close to one fourth of his army, and with little really to show for the victory except the psychological destruction of yet another Yankee general. After Chancellorsville the positions of the armies were virtually what they had been prior to Fredericksburg. Two great and costly battles produced nothing more than a maintenance of the status quo. And perhaps even that had shifted against Lee now, for one of those casualties of the fighting in the Wilderness was Stonewall Jackson. His operation went well enough, and for some days he seemed well on the way to recovery. But then the complications attendant to an amputation in these conditions set in. Pneumonia developed, and by May 9 it was apparent that he would not live. His wife came to his side, and throughout May 10 spoke with and comforted him. He was ready to die, though entertaining occasional hope of recovery. Early in the afternoon he declined rapidly. Told it was Sunday, he felt great relief. "I have always desired to die on Sunday." Then, shortly before 2 P.M., lost now in a failing mind's world of images past, he called out clearly: "Let us cross over the river, and rest under the shade of the trees." Then he began his own crossing, to rest eternally.[26]

CHAPTER 7

"HURL FORWARD YOUR HOWLING LINES"

General Wade Hampton regretted that he had missed Chancellorsville. So, for that matter, did some of the residents of the vicinity. "If old Hampton had been there," they said, "the Yankees never would have got across the river." Indeed, he had proved himself more than a competent cavalryman, and with his brigade remounted and refitted for a season's campaigning, he rejoined Stuart in May not long after the conclusion of the fighting along the Rappahannock. Hill had recovered from his wound and assumed command of the slain Jackson's II Corps, which in turn allowed Jeb Stuart to return to his beloved horsemen. By late May other commands also came back to the corps with their new horses, and on June 5, when Stuart reviewed his command at Culpeper, there were almost 10,000 cavalrymen. He put them in camp around Brandy Station nearby, awaiting the part they would play in whatever Lee planned next, not to mention what Hooker might plan.[1]

The outcry in the North after the debacle at Chancellorsville proved predictably hot and acrimonious. Charges of Hooker's presumed drunkenness went into print, along with demands that he be replaced at once by Meade. Lincoln stood by Hooker for awhile yet, perhaps in part because "Fighting Joe" stood so tight with the Radicals. On May 7, after regaining his composure from the previous day's dire news, the President calmly wrote to his general asking, "What next?" He wanted another movement while Lee's communications were somewhat disrupted, but cautioned against "anything done in desperation or rashness." Yet an early advance would go far to assuage the humiliation of the recent defeat. He wanted to know if Hooker had another plan, adding that, if not, then "I, incompetent as I may be," might be able to formulate one. Hooker responded that he did, indeed, have an idea, but that he would only communicate it if Lincoln expressly asked for it. Lincoln summoned the general to Washington a few days later, probably as much to assess the man's personal condition as to learn of his thoughts. By this time the President's anxiety for an advance was cooling as he learned that Lee was once more well established at Fredericksburg and with his communications restored. And now Hooker's officers were beginning to mutter against him, as he had done to Burnside before him, and Lincoln wisely surmised that this was not the time to risk another battle.[2]

Robert E. Lee, on the other hand, took exactly the opposite view. Immediately after Hooker left the field, Lee began the necessary reorganization of his battered army. There were officers to promote to fill the vacant posts of men now dead, and structural realignments that Jackson's death required. The greatest change was the creation of a III Corps, to be commanded by A. P. Hill, while Jackson's old II Corps would go to his lieutenant, General Richard S. Ewell. "Old Baldy," as his men called him, had lost a leg after his wounding at Groveton the previous summer, but now he felt ready, and Lee was willing to take a chance that the loss of a limb would not impair Ewell's fighting spirit. Lee spent nearly a month at the work, and meanwhile Longstreet returned to the fold to reunite the I Corps with the army once more. Daily Lee felt his strength gaining, and with it the necessity of seizing the initiative before Hooker or his successor recovered from Chancellorsville. His charge, as always, was to defend Virginia, yet despite what would be Lee's greatest victory of the war, an enemy army still camped with impunity just across the Rappahannock. Holding him there would not be good enough. With the summer coming and with it months of good marching weather, there was no telling when and where the Yankees might move next. Virginia was being hard pressed to support and feed the Army of Northern Virginia, and the fall crops of the Shenandoah were months away. And even in his enhanced strength, upward of 80,000, Lee realized that an attack upon Hooker would still have all odds against him.

Only in maneuver did there seem to be an opportunity to rid Virginia of the enemy and at the same time take advantage of Confederate strength. The way to force Hooker out of the Old Dominion was to threaten the North. It was a favorite idea of Lee and Jackson's since nearly a year before. The sweep down the Shenandoah and into Maryland at Harpers Ferry, then up into Pennsylvania, and finally a swift march toward Washington. It was what they planned in 1862, and now it was what Lee decided to do once again. Briefly he considered sending part of his army west to reinforce the Confederates now fighting for control of Vicksburg, but that idea was soon abandoned by Lee and Davis. They felt that a victory over Hooker on Union soil might materially aid the growing peace movement in the North. There was ill-advised hope, too, that it might persuade foreign powers to consider again the recognition of the Confederacy that the loss at Antietam seemed to have checked. The Southerners could fill their haversacks and their quartermaster wagons from the crops of the rich Cumberland Valley of Maryland and Pennsylvania, and, of course, Hooker would have no choice but to follow them and leave Virginia. A secondary benefit might also accrue if the invasion put enough fear into Lincoln for him to call reinforcements from the West, thus relieving the pressure on Vicksburg. This much and more set the army in motion on June 3, bound in that swaggering gait of the Confederate soldier, for the fields of Pennsylvania.

While Lee planned his move, Hooker did not remain idle. It took him time to recover from the shock of Chancellorsville, but by late May he was observing the enemy movements, sensing that Lee would soon be sending his columns to the Shenandoah once more. He advised Washington that very probably the Confederates were about to try another invasion into Maryland or beyond. Once again he began to plan, which he did very well, and when he learned on June 5 that the Army of Northern Virginia was in motion, he thought he saw an opportunity. To Lincoln he suggested that he could cross the Rappahannock safely now and then move directly on Lee's rear. Halleck liked the plan at first, but then he and Lincoln decided that Hooker must remain on the north side of the river, where he would always be in a position to keep himself between Lee and Washington. Yet before any firm plan could be decided upon, the armies began to encounter each other, and Wade Hampton finally got into the fighting once again.[3]

On June 9, as part of Lee's campaign, Stuart packed his baggage after giving yet another grand review the day before for Lee himself. Now the commanding general wanted his mounted arm to cross the Rappahannock and move along its northern bank to screen the movements of the main army south of it. Early that morning the Confederate cavalrymen rode toward the fords, not suspecting what they would encounter. Hooker's observation balloons had revealed Lee's marching columns to him, and he sent his own cavalry, under its new chief, Brigadier General Alfred Pleasonton, to ride with his corps to the Brandy Station vicinity and learn what Lee was about. The evening of June 8 Pleasonton had his 11,000 troopers encamped close to the Rappahannock fords, planning to dash across them early the next morning. While one column engaged Stuart at Brandy Station, two other detachments would cross several miles above and below and strike the two Confederate flanks.

The move took Stuart completely by surprise. He had expected to get his brigades across the river without opposition, but suddenly he heard the sound of firing in his front, and all at once came word that the enemy was across the fords and moving toward him. The first Confederates met were barely able to slow the Federal advance, and soon Pleasonton's artillery shells were falling among the main body of their enemy. Stuart was at first stunned by what was happening. Being attacked in his front by a foe he did not expect, he next received word of the crossings on his flanks. He was in deep trouble before he had really gotten into the fight. Hastily he ordered his men forward. Hampton hurriedly collected the men of his brigade in time to receive an order from Stuart to oppose the advance of a bunch of Federals on their right. There the South Carolinian skirmished through much of the rest of the morning while Stuart himself tried to stem the Yankee advance. Slowly the Confederates rebuilt their position, much hampered by the early withdrawal of their major artillery from high ground on Fleetwood Hill, where Stuart himself made his headquarters. From this eminence he watched the progress of the battle, to be shocked about noon when he could see massive columns of blue horsemen advancing, one of Pleasonton's flanking columns, approaching in his rear. He had but a single cannon to try to stem the advance, yet it held the enemy long enough to bring reinforcements from another part of the field.

There followed a series of charges and countercharges in what proved to be the first set-piece cavalry battle of the war, and the last. Slowly Stuart had to give way, until the Federals had gained a position on the very slope of Fleetwood. Finally came more reinforcements. Hampton was returning to the field. He carried a huge two-edged sword, and now he drew it and called to his men to charge uphill against the enemy.

Ahead they raced right into the steel of the Federals above them. Hampton brought a few cannon with him, and as soon as they were on the slope the Rebel guns unlimbered and began sending scatter loads into the enemy. The whole scene fascinated those who watched from afar. "It was like what we read of in the days of chivalry," wrote one of Stuart's staff, "acres and acres of horsemen, sparkling with sabers, and dotted with brilliant bits of color where their flags danced about them, hurled against each other at full speed and meeting with a shock that made the earth tremble." Hampton himself towered over the battle and stood right in the middle of it. "He was seen everywhere, amid the clouds of smoke, the crashing shell, and the whistling balls, fighting like a private soldier, his long sword doing hard work in the melee, and carving its way as did the trenchant weapons of the ancient knights." Finally the Federals broke and retired from the field, leaving Stuart and Hampton once more in possession of Fleetwood Hill.

It had been a great battle, and Stuart was fortunate indeed that he had not been severely defeated. Only Confederate pluck, the gun that delayed the advance of the flanking Federals for a time, and Pleasonton's failure to press his attack vigorously, saved him. He could claim the victory, since he still held Fleetwood Hill, and his own casualties of 500 were less than the enemy's 850 or more. But Pleasonton had accomplished his mission, learning Stuart's strength and capturing information on the enemy's movements. Equally important, the Union cavalry had finally demonstrated that it could stand the equal of the Southern horse in a straight fight. The widely held notion in the North as well as the South that a Confederate cavalryman was almost invincible, no longer obtained. And, though of no moment to Pleasonton, he had also managed in bitter skirmishing near Kelly's Ford to kill Wade Hampton's brother Frank, his face slashed by an enemy saber and his body pierced by a pistol ball. Stoic in his grief, Hampton sent his brother home to South Carolina for burial. For him, as for the Confederacy as a whole, there would not be victories without heartbreaking loss.[4]

While Lee continued on toward the Shenandoah and Hampton remained for a time at Brandy Station to clean up and gather stragglers, Hooker kept watchful eyes on enemy movements. Then he virtually made a fool of himself when he proposed to Lincoln on June 10 that he should simply ignore Lee's move, leave it to Washington to assemble forces to hold "Marse Robert" in check, while he led the Army of the Potomac in a thrust south to take the now unprotected enemy capital at Richmond. Lincoln remained patient with him, though already fairly convinced that Hooker would have to be replaced. "I think *Lee's* Army, and not *Richmond*, is your true objective point," wrote the President. "Fight him when opportunity offers. If he stays where he is, fret him, and fret him."[5]

Not until June 13 did "Fighting Joe" finally begin moving his own army, and then he remained content with keeping himself between Lee and Washington, rather than "fretting" the enemy. As a result, the day before, Ewell and his corps crossed into the Shenandoah almost without opposition, and the next day began battling a Federal garrison at Winchester. The Union commander there, General Robert Huston Milroy, would enjoy an almost universal reputation for incompetence in days ahead, but he did not receive much help from his superiors in the face of Lee's advance. Though Washington knew the Confederates were moving toward the Valley, no one bothered to tell Milroy exactly what was happening. He did receive strong suggestions that he should pull back to Harpers Ferry on June 12, but then his own ineptitude came into play when he refused, saying that he could hold Winchester "against any force" Lee could send. Milroy had about 7,000 against Ewell's 20,000 or more. In the resulting two days of fighting, Milroy lost two thirds of his command captured, and would soon face a board of inquiry over his bumbling mismanagement. The Shenandoah now belonged once more to Lee.[6]

The enormity of Lee's gamble on this campaign rapidly became more and more evident as he spread out his army in the ensuing days. Before

long the advance and rear elements of his command were separated by
more than 100 miles, though his control of the Blue Ridge gaps leading
into the Shenandoah ensured that Hooker would not likely break through
to attack any one of his isolated elements. On June 17, after two weeks on
the march, Ewell and his corps had sidestepped the few remaining Federals huddled at Harpers Ferry by crossing the Potomac a few miles
upriver, and were on the march through Maryland. The cavalry brigade
composing his far-flung advance, under Brigadier General Albert Gallatin
Jenkins, was actually riding well into Pennsylvania. Longstreet was following, though many miles back, and A. P. Hill was just entering the Valley
after having remained at Fredericksburg to face the enemy until Hooker
started his own march. Stuart very successfully kept himself on the east
side of the Blue Ridge to prevent as much as possible Hooker's gaining
any real intelligence, but as soon as the Confederates began crossing into
Maryland, the Confederate cavalry could no longer hide Lee's movements
from Federal sympathizers. Rapidly Hooker received up-to-date and accurate information, while his own cavalry managed much better to keep Lee
unaware of his own doings.

But Hooker was in deep trouble now, and not from Lee. His relations
with Washington were rapidly deteriorating, thanks in large part to the
enmity of Halleck, whose feelings toward Hooker—perhaps growing out
of their acquaintance in California years before—were genuinely malicious and petty. Hooker actually complained of this to Lincoln even as
the campaign was under way, warning that so long as Halleck felt such
animosity toward him, "we may look in vain for success." Rather than
succor, however, Lincoln gave Hooker a terrible blow when he responded
by removing himself from the position of intermediary between the two,
and told Hooker that henceforward he would give orders only to Halleck,
and Halleck would give them to Hooker.

"Fighting Joe" had barely a week left to command when he went to
Washington on June 22 to discuss the military situation. The enemy was
now well into Maryland and Pennsylvania. Hooker was doing his job of
dogging Lee and protecting Washington, but he felt increasing pressure.
The drinking rumors began once more. He and Halleck clashed over what
to do with the garrison at Harpers Ferry. On June 25 he finally crossed
the Potomac with his own army, even though he still preferred to move
against Richmond and let the people of Maryland and Pennsylvania "protect themselves" from Lee's aggression. By the next day he had his army
in and around Frederick, Maryland, and finally formulated a good plan to
deal with the enemy. His crossing of the river surprised Lee, who still
thought Hooker was south of the Potomac, and now he wanted to move
against the Confederate rear and cut Lee's communications. But Washington interfered. Once again it would not let him have the Harpers Ferry
garrison, and then on June 27 came the final blow. Halleck wired to one of
Hooker's subordinates that he was to "pay no attention to General

Hooker's orders." Infuriated, then resigned, Hooker interpreted the message well. "Halleck's dispatch severs my connection with the Army of the Potomac," he said. He was right. Lincoln and his advisers, despite the fact that another great battle might be imminent, decided that they could not risk Hooker losing his nerve a second time. This same day, through some careful maneuvering, they got Hooker to resign rather than be relieved, though "Fighting Joe" may have actually hoped that his tender would not be accepted. It was, and on the next evening an officer reached the army from Washington. After a brief stop at another tent, he proceeded to Hooker's headquarters, and there informed "Fighting Joe" that his resignation was accepted. That same night the heartbroken and dispirited general left the army with an emotional farewell. He would be heard from again in this war, and in better terms than now, but one more humiliation awaited him in a few days when a spiteful Halleck would actually have him arrested briefly. There could be no more sad ending to a sad history of a man flung by powers beyond his control into a responsibility beyond his competence. And now once more Lincoln needed a general.[7]

The stop that officer made before giving Hooker the news was at the tent of Major General George G. Meade of Pennsylvania. The command was to be his, and Meade met the announcement with unfeigned wonder. It had not occurred to him that he should be selected to replace his friend. Indeed, at first he believed it unfair to Reynolds who, he felt, more deserved the command. In fact, several weeks before, Lincoln had indeed offered John Reynolds, another Pennsylvanian, the command, but that general turned it down when he found that he would not have an absolutely free hand. Confronted not with an offer, but with a positive order to assume Hooker's place, Meade as a soldier found himself now with no choice. "Well," he said, "I've been tried and condemned without a hearing, and I suppose I shall have to go to execution."[8]

There were good reasons for giving the Army of the Potomac to Meade. When Lincoln and Stanton conferred on the matter, neither could find anything objectionable in the general's record, and Reynolds having taken himself out of contention, Meade was the next logical choice. Besides, said the President, Meade was a Pennsylvanian, and since the coming battle would probably be fought in the Keystone State, it seemed likely that Meade would fight well "on his own dunghill." Indeed he would.

George Gordon Meade was born, in fact, in Spain, the son of a prosperous international merchant who lost his fortune in the Napoleonic wars. Meade gained appointment to West Point and matriculated in 1835 high in his class. He resigned just one year later and went into engineering, then returned to the service in 1842 never to leave it again. In the Mexican War he fought bravely and won promotions, but thereafter returned to his beloved engineering, working on coastal fortifications, marine breakwaters, and surveys. In the fall of 1861 he found himself promoted to brigadier and commanding a brigade of Pennsylvanians that he subsequently led on the Peninsula. Though he took two wounds in that campaign, he recovered quickly enough to fight at Second Manassas and then lead a division at Antietam in Hooker's corps. His performance at Fredericksburg that winter won him command of the V Corps, and his service at Chancellorsville was more than competent. Indeed, had Hooker listened to Meade's advice, the debacle might instead have been a glorious triumph. He was a cantankerous man, easily aggravated, sometimes pettifogging over details. Yet his associates credited him with a clear head, a commendable lack of ambition and braggadocio, and unquestioned bravery. If the army did not meet his elevation with wild enthusiasm, certainly it did not object. And his fellow corps commanders thought enough of him that Slocum and Sedgwick, actually his seniors, readily agreed to serve under him. And Reynolds seemed genuinely delighted. When he first visited Meade at headquarters, the two exchanged warm assurances of regard and support, Reynolds frankly telling his new commander that he was happy that it was Meade, and not he, who received the peremptory order to supplant Hooker. That done, they began at once to plan how to counter Lee's invasion of the North. At the time he received the command, Meade did not even know where all the components of his army were placed. With the prospect of a battle within a few days, he had much to learn. As events would show, he had just two days to prepare himself for the greatest battle ever fought in North America. Few captains in history have addressed a greater challenge.[9]

The first problem facing the new commander was to determine what his army was doing, and where. Indeed, as Hooker began to inform him of the widely spread divisions, Meade actually expressed surprise, and thus provoked an already sensitive Hooker into a brief outburst. He then outlined to Meade his belief that Lee would not attempt to cross the Susquehanna River to take Harrisburg, Pennsylvania, since the Confederates were not believed to have bridging equipment. Rather, he suspected that the Army of Northern Virginia would reach the Susquehanna, then turn south to threaten Baltimore and Washington. Meade privately thought that Lee would, in fact, try to cross. There was a good bridge in place at Harrisburg, and the river itself was often low enough to wade in places during the summer. Lee intended just that. Once having learned the condition of the army, Meade retired to write to Halleck. "I must move toward the Susquehanna, keeping Washington and Baltimore well covered," he wrote. If Lee should turn toward either place, then Meade would "give him battle."[10]

Even as Meade penned his dispatch to Washington, he was unknowingly starting to gain an advantage over his adversary, for that same day Lee decided to stop his northward march and concentrate his own scattered army. Certainly Ewell was enjoying success after success. Following his victory at Winchester, he had continued north into Maryland, his movement screened by Stuart, who achieved three small triumphs in engagements at Aldie, Middleburg, and Upperville, Virginia. On June 24 Longstreet and Hill finally crossed the Potomac with their corps, and the next day Ewell skirmished in Pennsylvania itself. Then he sent Early and his division marching east through Gettysburg toward York. There he would be able to cut off the rail link between Harrisburg and Baltimore, while Ewell's own line of march increasingly threatened to isolate the Pennsylvania capital from aid from the west. Early, in turn, would send one of his brigades east from York to the bank of the Susquehanna at Wrightsville, threatening to cross. By June 28 the Confederates were in position to attempt a crossing, faced only by some Pennsylvania militia standing between them and Lancaster, Harrisburg's last link with Washington.

The balance of Ewell's corps was threatening Harrisburg itself. Having taken Carlisle, and the United States army post at Carlisle Barracks, Ewell sent Jenkins forward again. He occupied Mechanicsburg on the morning of June 28, and while his men consolidated their capture, Jenkins himself sat down in a local hotel with a pitcher of water and a stack of the latest Yankee papers, looking for intelligence. After his men had impressed from the citizens a goodly supply of rations and forage for their mounts, the Confederates moved on toward Harrisburg. They got as far as Oyster's Point, a bare three miles from the Susquehanna, skirmishing there the next day while Jenkins himself scouted routes by which he could launch a crossing. Seeing what he wanted, Jenkins sent the news to Ewell in Carlisle, and he in turn ordered General Robert Emmett Rodes to have his division ready to attack and take Harrisburg the next day, June 29.[11]

They would never make the attack. Once the army crossed the Potomac, Stuart's usefulness in screening Lee's movements came to an end and, realizing this, Lee sought a more profitable endeavor for his cavalry. On June 22 he gave Stuart orders to move north and take a position to guard Ewell's right flank. In ensuing correspondence and discussion, however, a situation arose in which Stuart had an option of just how to get there. Still sensitive to the criticism he received for being surprised by Pleasonton at Brandy Station, and remembering the glowing encomiums of the year before when he rode around McClellan's army, the daring horseman decided now that rather than take Lee's suggestion—an order some called it—to move straight north between the armies, he would instead take Hampton's and two other brigades and abandon Lee while he rode south and east, and finally entirely around Hooker. It would not prove to be a wise decision, and for Lee it left him almost completely without the valuable intelligence of enemy movements that was vital to his risky invasion.

Despite Stuart's absence, Lee's had been an easy march so far. By

June 28, with Ewell on the verge of taking Harrisburg, the work of gathering supplies was going well, and Early had even threatened $28,000 in cash from the people of York. Spirits in the scattered corps of the army ran high, and as Hill and Longstreet reached the vicinity of Chambersburg, it looked like fair campaigning lay ahead of them. But Lee, with Stuart no longer sending him information of Federal movements, still operated under the belief that the Army of the Potomac had stayed below the Potomac. As a result, on the evening of June 28 he was issuing orders for Ewell to take Harrisburg while Longstreet assisted him and Hill moved toward York and crossed the Susquehanna nearby.

Then at 10 P.M. arrived one of Longstreet's best scouts, James Harrison, with the news that Meade now commanded, not Hooker, and that the Federals had crossed the Potomac and were headquartered at Frederick, Maryland, with cavalry moving north toward Emmitsburg and Gettysburg. In one stroke, the northward invasion came to an end. At once Lee found himself in trouble. North of the Potomac, the Federals were within easy striking distance of the Confederates' only line of supply, and would not have to contend with the barrier of the Blue Ridge to take it. Should Meade close the Shenandoah at Harpers Ferry and blockade the Potomac fords above it, Lee would be trapped. He needed that route to send south the supplies his men gleefully gathered, and without it he would run short of ammunition constantly being brought to him. He had no choice now but to call Ewell back and try to divert Meade's attention from his own rear. Thus the plan first suggested of working against Lee's communications had worked exactly as he said it would. A simple river crossing by the Army of the Potomac effectively ended an invasion by an army more than forty miles away.[12]

The only way to keep Meade away from his rear was for Lee to threaten Baltimore or Washington. Ewell and Longstreet were called back from the anticipated attempt on Harrisburg, and the Pennsylvania capital was saved. Hill and Early were ordered back from the York area, and all were to move toward Cashtown or nearby Gettysburg. The orders went out on June 29, but Jenkins and his command seem not to have received them for some time, for the next day, in the vicinity of Sporting Hill, they finally fought a small battle with hastily assembled defenders of Harrisburg. Inconsequential in itself, it would be the northernmost meeting of blue and gray in the East. Then Jenkins, too, began to withdraw. Lee may not have had a firm idea of exactly what he wanted to do next. Certainly some of his orders were garbled, some of them transposing Cashtown and Gettysburg, to the confusion of Early and others. Further, he seemingly had become so accustomed to Stuart's silence the last several days that he almost ignored the four brigades still available to him, including Jenkins. Not until June 29 did he finally order them to him where they might do some good. Still, he certainly recognized that Cashtown

offered him a few advantages. If Meade advanced from Frederick, Cashtown would be on his left flank, offering Lee a chance of attack, while the
ground at Cashtown itself seemed good should he assume the defensive.

Meade, like his adversary, also seemed somewhat uncertain. Indeed,
some around him thought that the enormous weight of assuming command of a major army and having to face a seemingly invincible opponent all in the course of less than a week was proving too much for him.
He lost sleep, his appetite, and frequently his patience. The day he assumed the command he lamented to his wife, "Oh, what I would give for
one hour by your side to talk to you, to see my dear children and be
quiet." But he would have to wait for any quiet. Now he must stop Lee.
His first choice was to assume a defensive line along Big Pipe Creek, just
south of the Pennsylvania border and squarely between Lee and Baltimore. With Lee still at least two days away, Meade could choose his positions well and be more than ready for the enemy. By June 30 he had his
army in the vicinity and ready to prepare its defenses, but then he began
to vacillate. Gettysburg, just twelve miles north, looked like a good spot as
well, and one where he could choose his ground. Keeping his options
open, Meade finally decided to send Reynolds forward with the I, III, and
XI Corps to Emmitsburg and Gettysburg to meet or delay Lee, and look
for a better place to give battle. Reynolds was to move on July 1, but
meanwhile cavalry led by Brigadier General John Buford was sent ahead
on June 30 to see what the enemy was doing. Buford rode through Gettysburg toward Cashtown, and shortly came upon the leading elements of
Hill's corps, marching toward Gettysburg to commandeer a supply of
shoes reportedly stored there as well as to occupy the town. Gettysburg
served as the hub of a wheel that converged no fewer than ten major
roads leading from Baltimore, York, Hanover, Emmitsburg, Harrisburg,
and other points. Control of the town would give Lee a great advantage
in his intention of threatening Washington and at the same time preventing Meade from moving against his own communications. When Buford
encountered the Confederates, he skirmished with them briefly and the
Rebels fell back to Cashtown. Hill, however, believed that the main body
of the Federals had not reached Gettysburg yet, and he asked Lee to let
him take it first. Lee agreed, still blind as to enemy movements thanks to
Stuart's absence. Neither expected to find any substantial body of the
enemy in the little town, and Lee obliged Hill's request. Lee in fact
believed that Meade was still many miles south at Middleburg. Buford,
meanwhile, bivouacked his men just outside the town and sent patrols out
in several directions. He believed that this was the place to fight and stop
Lee, and send word back to Reynolds and Meade. He expected that he
would engage the enemy again on the morrow.[13]

The next day, July 1, 1863, just before noon, a courier from Buford
rode frantically into Meade's headquarters. The Confederates were advancing against him in heavy numbers, driving him back. Happily Reyn-

olds and his leading divisions were near and would soon be on the field, and now Meade paused before taking action, knowing that when Reynolds arrived and took in the situation, he would decide more than adequately whether this was the place to engage. After all, Meade himself did not even have a good map of the Gettysburg area until this very morning, whereas Reynolds was on the scene. Still, Meade alerted his corps commanders to be ready to march in any direction on an instant's advice. Then came another courier, this time from Reynolds. The enemy was advancing in force and would take the high ground beyond the town before he could. "I will fight them inch by inch, and if driven into the town, I will barricade the streets and hold them back as long as possible," said the corps commander. Meade was pleased. "That is just like Reynolds," he said, "he will hold on to the bitter end." Howard's and Slocum's XI and III Corps would join him soon, and after that Reynolds would decide whether to fight or retreat. Then at 1 P.M. came yet one message more. Reynolds was dead. Meade showed visibly the shock that he felt. "Reynolds dead?" he moaned. "Reynolds!" And the battle was going against them. At once Meade gave Major General Winfield Scott Hancock a map and told him to assume Reynolds' command. It looked more and more certain that Gettysburg was where the armies would clash decisively.[14]

Certainly no one in Gettysburg, Pennsylvania, had ever expected two great armies to come and fight over its tilled fields. It was a typical country farming town of its time, perhaps 2,000 people, stores, a small square, a courthouse. It took importance only in its position astride all those roads that fanned out like wheel spokes to every point of the compass. It was a market and trading town, before the war largely Democratic, with a lot of support for Breckinridge in the election of 1860. Lincoln was not popular here, even now, but with the war come, most Gettysburgers gave it their qualified encouragement.

A series of hills and ridges gave the vicinity its surpassing interest to the military just now. Immediately north of town sat Oak Hill, an eminence of sufficient height that it commanded a view of much of the surrounding countryside. From its southern slopes extended directly south for almost two miles a lesser summit called Seminary Ridge after the Lutheran seminary located on its slope. Behind and west of that ridge ran another spur of Oak Hill called McPherson's Ridge, dotted with woods wherein Reynolds had met with the bullet that killed him. Immediately below Gettysburg sat Cemetery Hill and, extending south from it, Cemetery Ridge. It and Seminary Ridge ran directly parallel to each other, rarely separated by more than 1,000 yards. Two miles below town Cemetery Ridge terminated in rugged underbrush and two commanding hills called Big and Little Round Top. Big Round Top, the southernmost, was absolutely impassable, but Little Round Top's summit was reachable, and bare enough to support artillery that would be able to command the whole of Cemetery Ridge. Between the Round Tops and the southern end of Seminary Ridge, a distance of something more than a mile, sat wheat fields, peach orchards, and a dense granite outcropping to be called the Devil's Den.

The mix of these ridges and hills afforded opportunity for an engagement of almost classic character, with natural obstacles and advantages aplenty for those ready to confront them. A. P. Hill was anxious to try.

Early on July 1 Hill moved his two divisions under Generals Henry Heth and William Dorsey Pender out of Cashtown and onto the road toward Gettysburg. By 8 A.M. they met with Buford's advance pickets, and soon thereafter with Buford's two brigades of cavalry themselves, now posted on the slopes of McPherson's Ridge and Oak Hill. Buford was heavily outnumbered, and knew it, but the new breech-loading Spencer carbines carried by his men gave them a considerable advantage over the muzzle-loading single-shot rifles of the Confederates, and one Yankee could deal out as many bullets as half a dozen Rebels in less than a minute. Aided by a single battery, Buford managed to hold Hill's advance for more than an hour and a half, while Reynolds himself arrived to survey the situation. The general ordered Buford to hold his ground until the first Federal divisions arrived, and an hour later, around 11 A.M., General James S. Wadsworth brought his division onto Seminary Ridge and finally relieved the daring cavalrymen. At once he delivered a smashing charge into the Confederate lines that stunned Heth and shattered two of his brigades. "Forward men, forward for God's sake and drive those fellows out," said Reynolds as Wadsworth went into the fight. Reynolds rode with them, to his death.

When the general fell, Abner Doubleday automatically succeeded to the immediate command on the field and began erecting a defensive line on McPherson's and Seminary ridges. Meanwhile, Buford had gone to the north side of town where Ewell's corps was advancing in great strength. Once again Buford sought to fight a delaying action until more Federals could arrive. Should Ewell manage to take the town itself, he would be in Doubleday's rear and a disaster could well ensue before the battle was fairly started.[15]

The fighting calmed for about an hour shortly after Reynolds' death. Finally around noon Oliver O. Howard arrived on the field, bringing his XI Corps with him and, being senior to Doubleday, he assumed command. Two things became immediately evident to him. First, reinforcements were still needed. They were facing probably Lee's entire army. Second, as he passed through Gettysburg, Howard noted the excellent defensive position offered by Cemetery Hill, and as a safeguard he left one of his divisions there while he took the other two toward Oak Hill and the fighting. Then came word, as well as visual evidence, of the threat from Ewell's corps advancing from the north, and Howard had to turn his two divisions—now commanded by Major General Carl Schurz— to meet the challenge. Schurz shortly took position immediately on

Doubleday's right flank, the Federals making at least a fairly steady and continuous, if outnumbered, line. Consulting with Doubleday, Howard urged him and his commanders to hold their position as long as possible and then retire. Cemetery Hill would offer an excellent position to regroup. Shortly afterward, having informed Sickles and Slocum of the fighting going on, Howard apparently remembered that he had forgotten to ask them to come and reinforce him. Now he corrected the oversight, but too late.[16]

Lee was much in the dark about what was happening at Gettysburg this morning. He was riding almost leisurely along the Cashtown road when he first heard the sound of the guns some distance ahead, and immediately his mood turned to impatience. He had not ordered Hill to engage the enemy, and did not wish to until all his corps were once again consolidated. The risk of being defeated in detail was simply too great, and everything was made worse by Stuart's absence. "I cannot think what has become of Stuart," the general said almost inaudibly. "In the absence of reports from him, I am in ignorance as to what we have in front of us here." It might be just a detachment, or it might be Meade's whole command. "If it is the whole Federal force we must fight a battle here."[17]

Hill and Ewell were already fighting that battle, and quickly Lee began to apprise himself of what they were doing. After the hour's lull in the battle, Hill began to renew his attack on Doubleday along the ridges, while Ewell sent his first division on the scene into what proved to be an ill-fated attack on Schurz. Providentially, Early arrived with his division after marching from York, and came on the field at the right place and the right time. He struck Schurz's exposed right flank, and once again, for the second time in two months, the XI Corps went into a near rout. This left the remainder of the Federal line no alternative but to withdraw. The Yankees gave way slowly and deliberately at first, but then the inevitable confusion set in, though no panicked retreat as at Chancellorsville. While large numbers of stragglers from the XI Corps did flee the field, the rest joined with the I Corps in reestablishing themselves on Cemetery Hill and on Culp's Hill just east of it. By now it was close to four-thirty in the afternoon, and the retreating Federals could take heart as they approached Cemetery Hill, seeing fresh troops there to support them, Federal batteries covering their withdrawal, and General Winfield Scott Hancock waiting to take over.

He had arrived some time earlier, joining Howard on the hill and relieving him of command. Howard was senior to him, but Meade's order for Hancock to take over could not be argued, though Howard felt humiliated. Doubleday, when he arrived, seemed less inclined to cooperate, but Hancock quickly began giving orders directly to Doubleday's generals and that settled the difference. Both Doubleday and Howard thereafter gave their full cooperation to the younger yet more talented Hancock. It was thanks to the new commander that one of Doubleday's divisions went to

Culp's Hill, which would prove to be a major asset to the Federals. Within the next two hours the first elements of Sickles' and Slocum's corps began to arrive. Lee was on the field, now, and wanted to press his advantage.[18]

"Marse Robert" actually arrived after 2 P.M., in time to watch the renewed fighting that finally forced the Federals back through Gettysburg. Hill, who believed that the enemy was thoroughly whipped and "entirely routed," showed no interest in pursuing them, and halted his command on Seminary Ridge, where Lee joined him. Ewell, however, pressed his advantage and followed the enemy right through the streets of the town itself, cutting off and capturing hundreds. One not captured was Brigadier General Alexander Schimmelfennig, who found himself isolated from his command and forced to take refuge in a hog shed where he would hide for three days before escaping. The nearby residents would smuggle food out to him by hiding it under the pig slops. In later years wags referred derisively to the diminutive shed as "Schimmelfennig's headquarters."

Lee knew better than Hill that the Federals were far from routed. Looking out from Seminary Ridge, he took in the natural strength of the position on Cemetery Hill, and could well see the preparations for a stand being made there. Hancock showed no inclination to continue the retreat. Obviously he expected to fight until reinforced, and that could only mean that major elements of Meade's army were nearby. Faced with this realization, Lee felt that he had to exploit his temporary numerical advantage on the field while he could. Half of his own army had yet to show on the field, but with four hours of daylight left he should be able to drive the enemy from his front. He had not wanted to fight here, but with the battle started, he had no option but to fight it through and hopefully beat Meade's army in pieces. Hill's men he could see for himself were exhausted after the day's fight so far. Of Ewell's condition, Lee knew little. Thus, having decided that Cemetery Hill must be taken, he gave the task to "Old Baldy." Yet once again Lee showed his unfortunate penchant for making himself the slave, rather than the master, of his generals. Time and again in this war he will give an order, and then qualify it with the words "if practicable." Stuart had seized upon just such an ambiguity in his orders, and now Lee was hurting by his absence. In his orders to Ewell to take Cemetery Hill, Lee now only suggested that the attack be made, "if practicable." That left a hesitant general an escape from the possibility of repulse, and Ewell seized it now. His troops were tired and he did not like the look of the Federal artillery massing on top of the hill. Even when his third division arrived, with an hour of light still left, Ewell preferred not to risk the attack, and Lee's repeated suggestions did not sway him, nor did the urgings of his own generals. A considerable opportunity thus was lost. There was no guarantee of success, but that the effort was not made is difficult to excuse, in both Ewell and Lee.[19]

It was almost midnight when Meade himself finally reached the field.

He, like Lee, passed an uncertain day. He still teetered between fighting at Gettysburg and falling back to the Pipe Creek line. All day he kept himself in Taneytown where several roads brought couriers in constantly with news. He knew that the losses were heavy, and that most of Lee's army seemed to be gathering at Gettysburg. He kept his other corps commanders in constant readiness, and chafed for word from Hancock. At 6 P.M. the first message arrived. Hancock could hold his Cemetery Hill position at least until dark. That would give Meade time to settle his mind, but the word that the Cemetery Hill spot was a good one helped make Meade's decision for him. "It seems to me," Meade wrote back to Hancock, "that we have so concentrated that a battle at Gettysburg is now forced on us." If he got the whole army there on the morrow, he ought to beat Lee.[20]

Later messages from Hancock confirmed the decision, and at once all of the Federal corps were ordered to march with haste to Gettysburg. Meade left himself sometime after 10 P.M., having been joined by Hancock who gave him a firsthand assessment of the situation. It was a moonlit ride north to Gettysburg, the path marked all along the way by the increasingly evident signs of men moving toward battle. Soon Meade came within his own lines on Cemetery Hill, and immediately called a war council with his ranking commanders present. All agreed that this was the place to fight Lee, and Meade thanked them for their views, especially since he had already made the same decision himself. Then he set off on a tour of his lines, marking in the bright night illumination the geographical features, the glow of campfires in the distance that gave a bare idea of the enemy's numbers and positions, and the condition of his own men. He formulated in his mind a determination to attack the next day, but some time after daylight on July 2, having passed a sleepless night, he learned from a reconnaissance that Lee's position was as good as his own. That changed matters, and Meade and his generals decided that they would let the enemy bring the battle to them. Indeed, it was the best decision he could make, for Lee had no option but to attack, else risk trying to retreat when Meade was actually closer to the Potomac fords than he was. His only route back to Virginia was through Gettysburg, and Meade.[21]

By noon on July 2 virtually all of both armies, excepting Sedgwick's VI Corps, were on or near the field. Lee planned that on this day he would attack Meade's left flank by sending Longstreet's recently arrived corps in a turning movement that he hoped would eventually find "Old Pete" crumbling the enemy left and marching straight up into the Federal rear. Once that was happening, one of Hill's divisions would attack from its position on Seminary Ridge and then Ewell would strike at the enemy right. Longstreet did not like this, and said so. He advised the evening before that the Confederates not pursue the battle here. Meade's position on Cemetery Hill looked too strong. He wanted to sidestep the whole affair and head south, trying to get between Meade and Washington. That would force Meade to attack them on ground of their preference. Here Lee would have to fight Meade's battle. Lee listened politely, but replied that "we must attack him."

Lee was considerably disoriented. His health plagued him, and all during the battle he reportedly suffered the discomfort of diarrhea. Stuart's absence nagged at him. He could not read Meade as he had been able to predict what McClellan and others would do. It was strange country and events seemed, for a change, to be out of his control. Where was Jackson, he might well have wondered. Lee had drawn strength from him. Now with Stonewall dead he missed that rapport, despite cordial relations with all his corps commanders. Nothing seemed right, and during the day of July 2 Lee repeatedly paced and rode and showed his agitation. Despite Longstreet's objections, he ordered that the attack be made, yet it was well through the morning before the order went out, and Lee had intended that the assault begin at dawn, further evidence of "Marse Robert's" discomfiture.[22]

Despite his displeasure, "Old Pete" moved his corps slowly south along the back slope of Seminary Ridge until he was almost directly opposite the two Round Tops, trying as he went to keep from being seen by the enemy signalmen whom he could see on Little Round Top's summit. As he moved forward, however, he encountered something he did not suspect. Instead of being on Cemetery Ridge as expected, he found a large body of the enemy right in his front. It proved a surprise both to him and to those bluecoats' commander, Meade.

Meade had formed his lines during the night and early morning into something of a fishhook shape, the barbed end of it on Culp's Hill curving around to the left along the crest of Cemetery Hill, and then the shank of it running due south along Cemetery Ridge to the Round Tops. Slocum and the XII Corps composed the right of the line on Culp's Hill, while Howard's XI Corps held Cemetery Hill. Then in succession the I Corps, Hancock's II Corps, and Sickles' III Corps extended the line down to the vicinity of the Round Tops, though Meade failed to actually occupy Little Round Top itself with more than observers. He did order Sickles to be sure to hold the eminence, but Sickles was in a mood this day to be insubordinate, and repeatedly ignored directives from headquarters. He took his time about going into the line on Hancock's left, and once there decided that he saw better ground some distance in his front, around a wheat field, peach orchard, and down to the Devil's Den. He sent skirmishers forward just in time for them to clash with Longstreet's belated advance. Both generals were surprised at the encounter.

Then error seemed to compound error. Meade sent Buford back to his supply base and failed to replace him with other cavalry out on the left so that Sickles' left flank was in fact unprotected. One of Longstreet's division commanders, Major General John Bell Hood, detected both this and the unprotected Little Round Top, and asked that he be allowed to attack. He could curl up Sickles' flank and at the same time place artillery atop the hill from which it would command the entire Cemetery Ridge line, forcing Meade to abandon his position. Longstreet, perhaps angry still at his orders from Lee, refused, insisting upon adhering to the orders to the letter, and they said nothing of Little Round Top.[23]

But now Sickles almost forced Longstreet to take advantage of the situation. Despite Meade's refusal to allow him to move to the ground in his front, which Meade's chief of artillery Henry J. Hunt had pronounced untenable, Sickles now moved his corps forward, casually leaving a great gap between himself and Hancock on his right, and leaving the Round Tops perfectly exposed. He chose a place that required more troops to defend than he had, and one that required that he form his corps into a salient-shaped formation, two wings extending backward from an advanced point in a wheat field. This gave the Confederates a perfect chance to catch Sickles in a fire from two directions. Hancock was incensed when he saw what Sickles was doing, and well predicted the result. "Those troops will be coming back very soon," he muttered.

Indeed they would. A courier brought Meade word of what Sickles had done, but by the time the commanding general raced to the III Corps position it was too late to retract the move. Sickles began to argue with him even as Longstreet's attack began, saying that he held higher ground than before. Meade could be cruelly sarcastic when provoked, and now responded that "there is still higher ground in front of you, and if you keep on advancing you will find constantly higher ground all the way to the mountains." Indeed, Meade probably wished right then that Sickles was perched off on some Allegheny peak rather than here jeopardizing his army by his foolishness.

It was too late to withdraw, and while Sickles and his men began a fruitless defense of their position, Meade rode to the rear to learn that Little Round Top still had not been strengthened. Word came from Gouverneur Kemble Warren, his chief engineer, that Confederates were even then moving around to outflank Sickles and take the hill. He urgently asked for reinforcements, and in one of the closest calls of the war Warren commandeered a V Corps brigade and with it held the hill against attack until artillery could be manhandled to the summit. With the big guns there, Little Round Top would not again be threatened.

Now the full force of Longstreet's attack on Sickles struck. Almost at once Hood crushed Sickles' left flank and captured Devil's Den. It was after this that Hood raced on toward Little Round Top to be stopped by Warren's timely arrival. Meanwhile the III Corps center and right held on longer, torn by a merciless crossfire. Soon Sickles felt a piece of enemy shell rip through his leg, almost completely severing it but for a small slip of flesh that held the dangling limb. The whole scene became a command jumble. Before his wounding Sickles had been commandeering every reinforcement unit that came to his vicinity, regardless of where Meade had intended them to go. The commanding general was trying to fill the gap left when Sickles moved out of the line before Longstreet struck Cemetery Ridge as well, and finally had to give generals of reinforcing units directions to report to no one but the intended commander, no matter what Sickles ordered them to do. Sickles' wounding gave Meade a providential opportunity, and he called on Hancock to take command of the III Corps and see it successfully back in the main line.

Meanwhile the gap between the II and III Corps was still there and men ordered from Slocum's corps on Culp's Hill were not arriving as quickly as hoped. At one point, only Meade himself and four of his staff occupied the hole in the Federal line. The aides watched their general anxiously, wondering if he really intended that they should stand their ground there with the enemy advancing. A Confederate regiment could be seen several hundred yards away, coming toward them. Meade only sat more erect, then stood in his stirrups. He drew his sword and so did they. The image of a general commanding a major army about to lead himself and four frightened young aides in a charge against five or six hundred enemy soldiers was a scene straight from medieval romance, yet seemingly that is what Meade intended. It was that or forfeit the gap in his line to the Confederates and risk losing the whole show. With visible relief one of his aides then shouted that reinforcements were finally on their way, and two I Corps divisions shortly came into line to fill the void. General John Newton rode to Meade and offered him a stimulant from a handy flask, and Meade took a deep draught despite being just then covered in a spray of dirt by a cannon shot that struck the ground just in front of him. Then, his blood still up, Meade himself led the Federals in a charge that halted the enemy advance, and at last the near calamity on the Federal left was set aright. The III Corps came back into line after terrible losses, Little Round Top stood secured, and the gap on Sickles' right existed no more. One of Hancock's officers exulted in his diary that "Now Sickles' blunder is repaired. Now, Rebel chief, hurl forward your howling lines and columns." Meade himself showed his relief at his success. "It is all right now," he yelled to the men. "It is all right now!"[24]

It was nearly dark when the left of the Federal line stabilized, but the day's fight was hardly over. Ewell, ordered to launch his own attack on the Culp's Hill vicinity, began an artillery barrage as a preliminary to his advance, but answering Union guns soon silenced the Confederate batteries. Ewell dallied for much of the day, fretful over not finding emplacements for his artillery that were to his liking, and without this he hesitated to make the full attack that Lee wanted "if practicable." His artillery finally opened around 4 P.M. from such positions as it had, and during the ensuing two hours of shelling before his guns were silenced, "Old Baldy" finally decided that he could attack. He probably did not know that at that time Longstreet's assault against Sickles was being generally successful, nor could he have known of the confusion behind Federal lines, with the very troops holding the Culp's line being weakened to support Sickles and Hancock. Then bad orders and jumbled command further delayed the actual order to advance, so that it was actually after dark when only two of Ewell's divisions, rather than his whole corps as intended, began their attack. The division of General "Allegheny Ed" Johnson attacked on the left, gaining a foothold on Culp's forward slopes in some entrenchments left unguarded by the Federals. After that, though, the hill was too rugged and too well defended. Johnson went no farther. On his right, however, the cranky old Jubal A. Early led his division against the northern tip of Cemetery Hill in a crushing attack that carried straight to the crest against Howard's XI Corps. Howard and Schurz managed their defense well, aided by reinforcements rushed them by Hancock, who had foreseen an assault at that place. The fighting proved desperate and bloody, and finally Early was forced to abandon the prize so briefly gained.[25]

Twice in the same day Meade had been saved by being able to shift reinforcements back and forth inside his interior lines, and twice Hancock had played a leading role, which Meade would never forget. Though the skirmishing continued in some spots well after 10 P.M., the day's fighting was finally over, and the two exhausted armies retired to their fires to eat and rest. Meade himself went to his little headquarters in a tiny house just behind Cemetery Hill. Someone lit a candle, dropped a few splashings of hot wax onto a table, and stuck the tiny taper into it. Soon the generals gathered. Water and a single cup were brought in, the chairs and a bed were soon filled with occupants, and cigars began to fill the room with smoke. It could hardly seem out of place. These men had been looking at each other through smoke all day.

While an exhausted and slightly injured Warren unintentionally fell asleep on the bed, Meade began to address the assembled commanders. It was time to decide what to do on the morrow. One by one the generals detailed the condition of their corps. Losses were counted, deserters and stragglers tallied, and the final number of men in the infantry actually present and fit for another fight put at about 58,000. Should they stay or retire, asked Meade. All but one or two allowed that they held a good position where they were, and should remain. Should they attack, or let Lee attack them? All seemed to agree that they should not hurry to assault the enemy, at least not until the next afternoon. That would give them time to consolidate the army and see what Lee intended. If he should attack them before then, they should be able to hold their position. Meade did not think Gettysburg a good place to fight a battle, particularly an offensive one, and so this wait-and-see approach suited him perfectly.

Shortly after the meeting adjourned, Meade took young General John Gibbon aside. With Hancock in charge of the III Corps, Gibbon succeeded to the management of the II Corps, which held the very center of the line on Cemetery Ridge. "If Lee attacks tomorrow," the older general advised, "it will be in *your front*." Lee had attempted to assail the Federal left and failed that day, and that evening tried the right with the same result. If he attacked again at all, it would be in the center.[26]

Lee was fighting his worst battle of the war, and for a change it was he who was doing what his opponent expected. Meade read Lee now just as "Marse Robert" had read McClellan before him. All day on July 2 Lee had failed to exert real command over his army or to concert its actions. He believed that he had some gains from the day's fighting, yet the enemy still held every bit of significant ground in their position. During much of the afternoon and evening he sat by himself on a stump on Seminary Ridge watching the battle through his glasses without directing it. Accustomed in the past to giving orders and then leaving his corps commanders Longstreet and Jackson to fulfill them without interference, Lee was now trying to work that way with two new men who never fought a corps in battle before, Ewell and Hill, and neither proved too energetic this day.

Now Lee had to plan for another day's fighting. Finally he heard from Stuart on the afternoon of the second, the cavalryman arriving with Hampton's and two other brigades. Lee also had one fresh division not yet sent into the inferno of Federal fire, Major General George Pickett's. Around them Lee would build his hopes for July 3. He and Ewell consulted long into the midnight hours, and Lee finally ordered that the II Corps attack again and take the Culp's Hill position from Slocum, thinking erroneously that Johnson's division had gained a significant advantage on the Federal right flank. Hopefully that would enable the Rebels to turn Meade's right and curl it back on his center. Meanwhile, Longstreet was ordered to frontally attack the Cemetery Ridge line. The two generals did not meet personally this night, and so the orders, like so many of Lee's instructions here, came to "Old Pete" in less than a concise and unmistakable form. He was to augment his command with Pickett's division and attack at first light, simultaneously with Ewell. And Stuart, finally with the army once more, would ride south around Meade's left flank, and then drive straight into the Federal rear just as Longstreet struck. The combined move would be devastating if all worked well.

But Longstreet clearly objected to his orders. He had seen on July 2 the strength of Meade's position, even when held by an incompetent like Sickles. The Federals had perhaps hundreds of pieces of artillery on that ridge, and to attack it the Confederates would have to rush across nearly a mile of open ground, all the time under the fire of those cannon. "Old Pete" did not like frontal assaults. Lee, unfortunately, would resort to them on occasion when nothing else had worked. Longstreet perhaps understood just a little better the fact that the rifled gun was simply too accurate and quickly fired to make the old-time infantry charge sensible against a well-defended position.

Unhappy with the orders, Longstreet managed to delay obeying them. Thus when Ewell started his assault early on July 3, the Confederate I Corps was not yet in position, and when Lee rode to Longstreet he found his subordinate actually moving the command toward Meade's left flank once more. Lee was certainly angered, for Longstreet's move forced him to abandon his plans and start anew. Perhaps "Old Pete's" remonstrances about the strength of the enemy line gave him pause as well, for now he went back with his general and others to the edge of the woods on the center of Seminary Ridge. There he took out his glasses once more and surveyed Meade's line. He found what looked to be the best spot to attack, a medium-high section of Cemetery Ridge where there was little natural cover for Federal infantry or artillery. It would be the hardest to defend, he reasoned. Further, the ground his troops would have to cover to reach it looked easily traversable. And there was a clump—some called it a copse—of trees in the center of the goal that his regiments could use as their aiming point. It would help keep them on target in what would be an admittedly difficult assault. To prevent Longstreet's fear of heavy losses to Union artillery during the assault, Lee decided to mass almost every gun in his army and bombard this section of Meade's line, pulverizing enemy artillery and defenses alike. To make the assault, Lee would send 15,000 men, the largest single infantry attack yet made in the East. Longstreet would command.[27]

Again "Old Pete" objected. Citing his years of experience in the army, including the war in Mexico, Longstreet pointed across the fields before them and declared that "I think I can safely say there never was a body of fifteen thousand men who could make that attack successfully." Lee listened politely to his general's objections, but ordered that the plan proceed unchanged except for attaching one of Hill's divisions to Longstreet, and part of another. "Old Pete" would attack with Pickett's and Heth's divisions, assisted by half of Dorsey Pender's division, 13,500 all told. They would also direct the fire from 159 cannon spread all along Seminary Ridge to converge on that clump of trees. The cannonade would commence at 1 P.M., and the infantry assault as soon thereafter as the artillery had done their work. Pickett would move on the right, Heth on the left, with the remaining commands behind them. It was a last desperate gamble by a noble chieftain who simply did not know what else to do.[28]

Meade knew what to do that day, and did it well. He carefully surveyed almost his entire line, suffering hesitation only early in the morning when Johnson's attack on Slocum at Culp's Hill commenced. But in an hour's fighting the Confederates were driven back and the Federal line remained intact. He seemed to know all morning what was coming. "The enemy intends to try and pierce our center," he advised Sedgwick that morning. He moved reinforcements from place to place, keeping his corps ready to move at quick notice should the Confederates pierce his defenses. Somehow Gibbon forced Meade to eat a hasty morning meal of an unfortunate chicken and some commandeered vegetables, but shortly after noon Meade left to return to his headquarters behind the center.

He arrived at just about 1 P.M., and only minutes later the Confederate barrage began. Meade waited a time before asking his batteries to reply, and then ensued a two-hour duel between the big guns. Meade himself stood much of the time in the doorway of his little headquarters building, and while there one enemy shot actually grazed his side slightly before burying itself in a box on the porch. The obvious concentration of the fire on his center only further evidenced Lee's intention as Meade had guessed it, and now he began ordering his corps commanders to detach available troops to come and form a reserve for his center. When the enemy guns stopped, he knew the attack would begin. Soon he ordered his own artillery to cease firing. They would need to conserve their ammunition to help repel the assault, and their doing so might also fool Lee into thinking that he had silenced the Federal guns and thus would not face them as he charged toward Cemetery Ridge.[29]

Indeed, Meade did deceive Lee. The great bulk of the Southern artillery fire actually overshot the ridge and buried itself harmlessly in the fields beyond. Yet when the Federal return fire stopped, many Confederates believed that they had driven the Yankee guns from the field, particularly when they actually saw some batteries retire from Cemetery Ridge in the vicinity of the clump of trees. It was about time, for the Rebel cannon were nearly out of ammunition and would have barely enough left to support the charge. Back to Longstreet went the message, "For God's sake come quick." Pickett read the note first and asked Longstreet if he should advance. "Old Pete" was silent, extremely disturbed over what he feared was about to happen. Finally he simply nodded his head and Pickett was off to lead his division forward. Shortly Longstreet rode to the edge of the woods lining Seminary Ridge to watch.[30]

The initial sight that greeted the men in the Federal line was staggering, a vision none ever forgot. Where a moment before there had been just a line of trees with cannon belching forth smoke and fire, now there appeared gaily colored flags and banners by the score, and regiment after regiment of Confederate soldiers in a front a mile wide. The rising breeze shook out the folds of their banners and fluttered them gently, clearing as well the smoke from the field, as if the Almighty wanted those there assembled to have an unfettered view of the business to follow. They seemed for a moment to halt and redress their ranks in front of those woods, and then with measured step the flower of Lee's army began its advance while regimental bands played them on. The ghosts of a thousand times a thousand long-dead heroes of old might well have looked on to see the final great charge in a tradition that spanned the millennia from the time men first mixed their war with ceremony. In the last desperate act of a great general who simply was not himself, the most glorious drama of battle for centuries past came to its final act. Called Pickett's Charge by most, Longstreet's Assault by others, it is entirely Lee's attack.

And it is doomed to failure from its start. Almost as soon as the Confederates began their crossing of the fields between the ridges, the silent Union artillery opened once more, pouring fire from all along its line into the tight lines advancing. Bursting shells at longer range gave way to canister, scatter loads, as the Rebels came ever closer to Cemetery Ridge. Despite growing gaps in their ranks as their fellows fell killed and wounded, the Confederates closed up and kept coming. Even the Federals pouring a lead and iron bath over them could not help but be moved by the courage and determination of the foe. In the confusion, and thanks in part to some unexpectedly rough ground that Lee had not seen, the line of advance shifted for some brigades and the wings of the two divisions began to wander. Then Meade's own troops moved out, brigades surging forward to strike the exposed flanks of the coming line. Yet still the Confederates came on until their vanguard reached the very clump of trees, their target. Led by General Lewis Addison Armistead, holding his hat aloft on his saber so his men could see him, they flew into the Union line and penetrated it. The fighting became hand to hand, and furious. Armistead fell mortally wounded, Gibbon and Hancock both took serious wounds, and hundreds were killed or captured. Quickly Meade's lines reformed and reinforcements providentially arrived at the right place and time. The breakthrough was closed as quickly as it had opened, and the Southerners now had to face a gauntlet for their lives as they retired back across those fields of death to Seminary Ridge.

Lee watched the entire affair from a point directly opposite the clump of trees, his heart sinking as he saw the inevitable slowing of the advance, the hesitation as the breakthrough was made then stopped, and finally the determined and unpanicked withdrawal. As the weary and bloodied men streamed back past him to their old lines, he comforted them, repeatedly absolving them of any blame. "It's all my fault," he said time after time. Yet at once he and Longstreet set about rallying the shattered divisions to meet the expected counterattack. Surely with this advantage, Meade would press forward and try himself to split the now terribly weakened Rebel center. Yet the attack did not come. Meade's own command was in a bad way with Gibbon and Hancock out of action, and his center corps was much disorganized. He did order an attack made on Lee's right, an excellent move since Lee would have been expected to have weakened his flank to support the great assault. The orders were not well carried out, however, and fatigue and darkness finally settled on two exhausted, battered, and bleeding armies that welcomed the respite. "We had quite saved the country for the time," said General Warren; "we had done enough."[31]

The battle was done. Neither army moved the next day. Lee spent his time digging his army in, still fearing that he would have to face an assault, yet daring Meade to try. The better side of his old determination controlled him once more. Unwillingness to admit defeat had cost him 7,000 of the 13,500 who charged the day before, but now he showed a different resolution, and his army, after suffering its worst field defeat of the war, showed of what it was made. That night, in a hard-driving rain that taunted them, the beaten Confederates began their withdrawal toward the Potomac, toward Virginia. If they saw no more of this plagued Pennsylvania and its hills named for churches and graveyards, it would suit them well.

Meade passed July 4, 1863, in reorganizing his army and watching Lee. Perhaps with a bold attack he could have destroyed the remnant of Lee's army, but Meade was smart enough to know that he had already capitalized on several of Marse Robert's mistakes, and he could not count on their continuing indefinitely. So long as Lee had even a corporal's guard at his side, he could sting mightily. He had won enough. When on July 5 he sent out a reconnaissance to feel the enemy position, the enemy was gone.

It had been the costliest battle of the entire war, before or after. Of perhaps 80,000 men engaged, Lee lost over one third, among them many of his finest generals and officers like Armistead and Hood, though the latter would recover. The command of the Army of Northern Virginia was almost wrecked, and would never fully recover. Meade, too, suffered badly, losing 23,000 out of perhaps 90,000 present, and he too lamented the loss, temporarily, of able subordinates like Hancock and Gibbon. It is doubtful that he missed Sickles, whose lost leg finally put him where he belonged, out of the war. And in time even the Confederates would admit that Meade had fought a great battle. "There was not during the war a finer example of efficient military command than that displayed by Meade," wrote General Edward Porter Alexander, and even Lee later declared that he would not have attacked had he suspected that Meade would show such skill in concentrating his corps. The Union commander himself showed little inclination for brag on his exploit. "I would rather understate our success than claim greater results than I have accomplished," he said when an officer complained that his victory message to Washington was too modest. It was hard to exult with the relentless July sun already starting its work on nearly 7,000 bodies strewn all across the field. The smell would remain for weeks, and relief efforts were sent from all over the North to tend the wounded and bury the dead. And finally poor General Schimmelfennig was able to emerge from his "headquarters," when once again Gettysburg itself came into friendly hands.[32]

There was another battle of Gettysburg on July 2 and 3, though the contending armies knew little of it until later. As he had throughout the campaign, Jeb Stuart continued to disappoint Lee's expectations during the great battle. After leaving Lee on June 24, he swung east and crossed the Potomac headed toward Washington. He got as close as Rockville,

Maryland, where he captured a Federal supply train of 125 wagons, with which he proceeded to encumber his progress. Though certainly a great catch, the wagons slowed Stuart more than his generally good judgment should have allowed, and he then further complicated his expedition by resting the men more than time warranted, and by not maintaining some contact with Lee. Stuart had to learn of his commander's whereabouts by reading Yankee newspapers. He skirmished with Federal cavalry at Hanover on June 30, then headed for Carlisle, hoping that he would find Lee there. He did not, but finally learned that the army had gone on to Gettysburg. It was well into the afternoon of July 2 when finally the Confederate horse came to the battlefield. While Stuart conferred with Lee, Hampton remained with the three fagged brigades behind the left of the Southern line. There, as so often on this field, he came to a passage at arms that sprang almost from the pages of mythology.

Hampton sat astride his great charger while his men rested from their all-night ride. He was somewhat in advance of his brigade, soaking up the welcome sunshine, when a bullet sailed through the air nearby. Without thinking what might be the foe in his front, Hampton alone went forward to discover the source of the fire. He stopped at a fence and looked to a wood beyond. There, perhaps 125 yards away, he saw a nineteen-year-old boy from Michigan, Frank Pearson, standing on a stump with his cavalry carbine in his hand, readying another shot. Hampton pulled his cavalry revolver and both men fired almost at once, each missing. They passed a second fire in the same manner, this time the Federal bullet singeing the general's chest. Then Pearson's weapon refused to fire, the barrel fouled with spent powder. In a gesture of unbelievable naïveté, the boy held up his hand for Hampton to hold his fire. In a gesture equally unexpected, the general raised his pistol into the air, then pointed it heavenward, awaiting his adversary's pleasure. He watched while Pearson went through the business of swabbing the bore of his carbine and reloading. Then they fired again, and this time Hampton put the boy out of the fight with a badly damaged wrist.

Only moments later, even as Pearson retired, more Federal cavalrymen appeared on the scene. One rode directly for Hampton, raised his sword, and gave him an ugly gash on the side of the head before riding off. Hampton tried to shoot him but at that moment his pistol began to misfire, and would do so repeatedly until the frustrated general finally threw it at his fleeing enemy. In later years Hampton would come to know as friends and correspondents both Pearson and the lieutenant who nearly cleaved his skull. It was certainly a peculiar war.[33]

Lee gave Stuart a somewhat chilly reception, though there was no time for recriminations, and that was not Lee's way in any case. He now wanted the cavalryman to protect his left flank and rear from Meade's cavalry, and later that day they did clash in a minor engagement at Hunterstown, where the Confederates drove the foe from the field, thanks largely to a charge by Hampton, his bandaged head throbbing with pain. Then that night, while the armies rested, Lee ordered Stuart to ride around Meade and strike his rear even as Longstreet hit his center. But when Stuart tried to carry out the order the next afternoon, he got no closer to Meade's rear than two miles before Federal brigades, one of them led by a dashing boy general, George Armstrong Custer, stopped his advance. It proved a confused and mistaken affair, Hampton's brigade charging when he really wanted them not to, men and animals getting lost and wandering into friend and foe alike. It was a harsher fight than Brandy Station, but not so well organized. It became in places nothing more than a series of personal encounters between single men and small groups of riders. Men simultaneously drove their sabers into one another, and then died together, clenched in death so that later they could hardly be separated. Even the generals fought hand to hand, and Hampton was naturally to be found in the midst of it. He nearly lost his life. A squad of Federals rode toward the isolated South Carolinian and soon nearly surrounded him. He dispatched at least three of them with a revolver that worked better than the one thrown away the day before. Friends rode to help him but were dropped from their saddles. Soon Hampton found himself backed up against a fence, a bewildering number of sabers flashing in his eyes as his attackers aimed and sometimes delivered blows at him. His wound opened, his vision began to blur, then somehow he rode out of it to assist another Confederate. Soon more Rebels appeared and briefly drove the Federals back. "General, general," one cried, "they are too many for us." Urged to escape, Hampton leaped his horse over the fence, but just as they reached the apex of their jump, a piece of a Federal shell struck him in the side. He kept the saddle and rode off to safety, to be out of action for four months. Behind him, Stuart finally stopped, far short of Meade's rear, and the battle was finally done.[34]

The exultation in the North after news of Meade's victory could hardly be contained. At last the seemingly invincible Army of Northern Virginia and Lee had been defeated in a real stand-up battle, not just by default as at Antietam. The Army of the Potomac had come of age, and all on the eve of Independence Day. The omen could not be ignored. Yet there were those who found disappointment in the aftermath of the battle, and few more so than Abraham Lincoln. His chagrin began on that very July 4 when a message came that Meade had issued an order of congratulation to his army in which he said they must still drive the Confederates from Northern soil. Lincoln slapped his knees in frustration when he read that. "Drive the invader from our soil! My God! Is that all?" He wanted the enemy army pursued relentlessly and destroyed. That was the only way to win this war, not simply expel Lee to come back and fight again. When Meade did begin to pursue Lee, it was a leisurely and hesitating affair. He feared Lee's reorganized strength, but more likely was simply overcome by nervous anxiety after only a week in command and a terrible battle as well. In fact, Lee was weakened to perhaps only 35,000 effective troops by the time he reached the Potomac on July 6. There he found that rains had swollen it so that the fords could not be used. There was no bridge at hand, and he prepared to stand for one last battle, the river at his back. Should Meade attack with his 80,000 and more, the Confederates would die or drown. Yet Meade remained cautious, and Lincoln began to fear that he actually wanted to see Lee escape. Meade did not have that killing instinct that so characterized Jackson and even Lee.

Washington repeatedly urged an attack on Lee, but still Meade moved slowly onward, ignoring all attempts to prod him. He may have been wise, for Lee erected a potently powerful defensive position on the Potomac while he began preparations to build an ersatz bridge. Indeed, on July 12, when Meade finally decided to attack, five of his six corps commanders demurred after viewing the enemy lines. Still he persisted, deciding that he would attack on July 14. But that morning Lee was gone. He quietly crossed the river in the night and headed once more on the long road to Virginia.

"We had them within our grasp," moaned a dejected Lincoln. "We had only to stretch forth our hands and they were ours, and nothing I could say or do could make the army move." So morose did the President become that at one point he even intimated that there was treachery involved, but quickly his reason returned. When Meade learned of the attitude prevalent in Washington, he immediately asked to be relieved of his command. To his wife he confided that he had expected this from the moment he took over from Hooker. "Unless I did impracticable things, fault would be found with me." Lincoln actually almost sent a letter to Meade in which he stated flatly that Meade could have ended the war, but that now it would continue indefinitely. He thought better of it, and soon would be defending Meade as "a brave and skillful officer and a true man," to whom he would finally confide that he was "profoundly grateful for what was done without criticism for what was not done." Meade would keep his command.[35]

And Lincoln, who had a victory that he needed, would keep looking for the victory that he wanted.

CHAPTER 8

"WE CAN'T STOP
TO BUILD LOCOMOTIVES"

It was more than the rashness—perhaps desperation—of Robert E. Lee that gave Meade his victory. It proved a triumph as well for the tenor of Northern economy and industry. It is axiomatic that an industrialized nation, with uninterrupted access to its raw materials, begins any armed conflict against an agrarian opponent with a considerable upper hand. A society with a firm industrial base can go to war in strength almost from the first. If it lacks at the moment the necessary agricultural base to feed its armies, it needs only a single planting season and reasonable cooperation from the elements to fill the gap. A society whose primary economic base is in the soil, however, may well be able to feed its armies for a time, but it needs much more than spring rains and summer sun to plant and nurture the industrial plants that feed a war. The appointment of the armies at Gettysburg in the summer of 1863 illustrates the point far more than those who toiled over those fields for three July days ever understood. Even with its widespread pastoral commitment, the Confederacy after just two years of war found itself hard pressed to feed Lee's army. Until its own crops were ready for harvest, Lee had to resort to supplying his legions by raiding Pennsylvania. The increasing breakdown and scarcity of farm machinery, the worn-out equipment that milled and refined the grain, the inadequate facilities for packaging and preserving perishables, and the rapidly deteriorating condition of the transportation facilities necessary to bring foodstuffs to the armies, all contributed to the discomfiture of the men in the field, and affected military policy. Without the necessary industrial framework, the South could not even rely upon its time-honored agriculture to see it through. Though the Confederacy took its first great battlefield defeat in July 1863, it had in fact been losing battles in the factory since the days of Bull Run.

Southern industry before the war reflected as well as anywhere else the peculiar turn of mind in the Old South. Most men of wealth and influence genuinely disdained manufacture and trade as undignified means of investment, preferring the Jeffersonian ideal of planting. So entrenched did this notion become that it played an integral role in antebellum politics and, of course, a prominent part in feeding the incipient feeling of distinct and separate nationalism in the South. To engage in manufacturing would make a Southerner more like a Northerner when, in fact, the goal of most was to remain as different as possible.

As a result, only two industries really began to flourish in the decades before the war, and both grew directly from the pastoral motivation of the Southern planter, and from his "peculiar" labor system of slavery. In Southern industry, as in economy, cotton was king. It expanded the railroad and textile industries, but served only to retard most other areas of manufacturing which would have served the Confederacy well in the days following Fort Sumter. By 1860, with nearly one third of the population of the United States, the South produced barely one tenth of its manufactures.

Cotton overrode all. Planters and those with big money kept almost all of it tied up in the land necessary to grow the soil-exhausting crop, and in the considerable slave labor force necessary to harvest. As a result, there was little real capital left over for building plants and buying machinery. Further, the slave was not viewed as being skilled or intelligent enough to work with machinery, and the partially skilled poor whites immigrating from Europe who could operate the factories went almost exclusively to the North. On top of all, the political ideology of Southerners, particularly the nationalists, declared that industrialization would impair the slave system and thereby threaten the solid opposition to a protective tariff that was a hallmark of Southern policy.

Only where cotton was concerned did the system open up. Cotton mills grew up through the South at almost the same time that factories were abuilding in the North, and with some distinct advantages over their Yankee counterparts. Southern mills enjoyed excellent water power sources, cheap labor, and a direct source of the raw material right from Southern gins. As a result, some of the mills built in the 1840s and '50s proved to be models of their kind, and none more so than the Graniteville, South Carolina, textile mill built by William Gregg. It was a virtually paternalistic factory community much like those that would spring up in the North at Pullman, Corning, Lowell, and other places after the war. Gregg built not only the factory, but also the workers' housing, landscaped his grounds and provided each cottage with a garden. Indeed, he intruded himself into the workers' lives away from the factory, banning alcohol, enforcing schooling, and prohibiting dancing. Graniteville may have been the exception rather than the rule, but it showed that where cotton was concerned, manufacturing was quite all right, and even conducive to the kind of entrepreneurial and social experimentation that Southerners so derided in their Yankee brethren. In North Carolina alone some thirty-two mills came "on line" in the 1840s. Even at this, the North still outproduced the South in textiles before the war by three to one, but the degree of industrialization below Mason and Dixon's line where cotton was concerned aptly signifies the essentially agrarian commitment to King Cotton.[1]

Some other smaller industries arose, still connected with the land. Tobacco factories turned the leafy produce into plugs and twists. Hemp growers sold their crops to rope-making plants. Brick kilns were numerous, as were cottonseed oil mills and, of course, cotton gin manufacturers. Yet still did all of these endeavors draw their impetus from the agricultural values of the region, as did the only major genuinely industrial activity, iron-making. A number of small iron furnaces had operated in the South going back to the days before the Revolution, but for the most part their output was small and for local use in smithies. A real industry based on iron manufacture and milling did not arise until well into the nineteenth century, and then it centered almost exclusively in Richmond, and in just two companies, the Old Dominion Nail Works, and the Tredegar Iron Works. The former, as its name implied, manufactured almost nothing but "cut" nails for the Southern building trade. Tredegar, on the other hand, diversified considerably, and would become in time the leading industrial manufacturer of the Confederacy.

And it was Tredegar, chiefly, that supplied the other major industry that began to burgeon in the South in the 1850s, railroading. Yet once again, the primary reason for the iron rails' spread was not expansionism, as in the North, or trade with the West, or settlement, or the enhancement of yet more industry. Rather, the Southern rail system grew almost solely in order to feed the cotton gins and mills, and some coastal trade with the interior. As a result, though there were 8,700 miles of track in the South by 1861, it was often in a bewildering array of track gauges, junctions, and regulations. In Georgia, South Carolina, Mississippi, and elsewhere, the rail routes were designed almost exclusively to get the cotton to the gins, and the baled fiber to the wharves for shipment to Europe or the North. Thus, with always the intent of sending freight toward the coast, little thought went toward the efficacy of shipping between interior points. Four different rail lines served New Orleans, yet not one of them could send its cars on the rails of any of the others, for each built in a different gauge. The same situation, though not so extreme, obtained through much of the rest of the South. The result was that, with the exception of the route from Richmond to New Orleans via Knoxville and Chattanooga, it was nearly impossible for a load of freight to originate at one point of the South and travel undisturbed more than a couple of hundred miles. Time after time freight cars reaching the terminus of one road had to be unloaded, drayed across town by wagons and teams, then reloaded onto new cars to continue their journey. Indeed, for some towns a major source of revenue was such hauling, leading to stiff opposition against a uniform rail width. Even within themselves some lines chose absurd differences in gauge. The Roanoke Valley Railroad of southern Virginia began building from its two ends working toward the middle, yet each end commenced in a different gauge. Unfortunately, the war interrupted its construction so that its builders were saved the interesting problem they would have faced when finally the two sections came together and did not match! Unquestionably, the rail system—if it could really be called a system—of the South was not at all suited to the demands of a nationwide armed conflict. Though useful to be sure, it, like the rest of Southern industry, was more than a decade behind its Yankee competitors and, like the rest of manufacturing in the section, the victim of the bent for localism and self-interest that dominated Southern politics and brought the South to war.[2]

In 1861, when war came, Southern manufacturing as a whole was on the rise despite the insular attitudes of men of capital and politics. The value of its industrially produced goods had trebled in the past two decades. Cotton manufacture increased threefold in the same period, and several cities, despite their prejudices, were becoming increasingly identified as industrial centers. Richmond dominated the scene, but in Virginia Petersburg as well enjoyed some prominence, as did Lynchburg. In South Carolina, Charleston boasted some heavy manufacturing, even having the South's only steam locomotive works. Georgia, rich both in raw materials and centrally located by rail for shipment of ores from other states, dominated Deep South industry. Augusta, Griswoldville, Macon, and other cities all had their plants. In Alabama, Florence and Selma had light industry, as did even a few towns in Mississippi.[3]

Yet there was no way for this meager base to cope with the demands made by the war. In the first months of the conflict, as thousands of sunshine soldiers and summer patriots flocked to the banners to get in the fun before it all passed, the demands upon Southern industry were not so very burdensome. Many units equipped themselves with arms and manufactured goods already in hand, and the substantial captures made when armories in the Confederate states were taken over from the United States provided a substantial supply of ordnance, small arms, and equipments. There were enough spare parts in stock to keep the railroads running and the steam presses and rolling mills in operation, and the blockade was not sufficiently effective to keep a fair flow of parts and raw materials from arriving from Europe. For a time, even Northern suppliers shipped materials South until Federals quickly and harshly descended on trade with the rebellious states.

The first real effects of the war on Confederate industry were felt, as in most wars, in consumer goods. The only difference is that in the South those effects were felt much sooner, as virtually all of Confederate manufacturing turned in whole or part into war industry. At the outset, the new Confederate Government naturally assumed control of existing shipyards and arsenals and turned them immediately to their own war purposes. As time went on, necessity dictated that both army and navy begin the active administration of the industries that supported their endeavors, formally organizing departments within themselves to oversee their manufacturing. In the War Department, Colonel Josiah Gorgas, a Pennsylvanian by birth, took appointment as the head of the Ordnance Office and meticulously applied his manifest skills throughout the war, winning promotion to brigadier in 1864. Joseph E. Johnston credited him with creating the Ordnance Department "out of nothing," and indeed he almost did. He took whatever manufacturing capabilities had been captured and began to refit them, enhancing and frequently moving the precious machinery to new locations, closer to the raw materials, and farther from the advancing Federals. In the first year of the war Gorgas even purchased and outfitted five blockade-runners to supply him with necessities not available in the South.

As the war progressed, however, Gorgas soon realized that the blockade could not be relied upon to provide the flow of arms and ammunition required, nor could the frequent bonanza of abandoned weapons that victorious Confederates found on the battlefield meet their needs. Credit abroad was no longer readily accepted; the blockade was getting too tight. The Confederacy had to begin manufacturing its own weapons and by 1863 was well on its way to doing so in surprising quantities. President Davis himself set the tone of the endeavor with his January 1863 message to Congress. "Dependence on foreign supplies is to be deplored," he said, "and should, as far as practicable, be obviated by development and employment of internal resources."[4]

Considering the obstacles in their path, Gorgas and his associates achieved something of a miracle of organization and administration. From the first they so completely occupied and controlled military-related industry that no significant group of entrepreneurial industrialists arose in the Confederacy as they did in the North. While outright nationalization of industry would have enraged states' rights proponents, the War Department achieved it de facto by the enormity of its demands, its control of the routes of supply of raw materials, and the undenied commitment of private industry in the South to the war effort.

By 1863 Gorgas could boast in his diary that his department, from being the worst supplied in the War office, "is now the best." He had organized large arsenals at Richmond, Fayetteville, Augusta, Charleston, Columbus, Macon, Atlanta, and Selma, with smaller ones scattered throughout the country. In Augusta, Georgia, with the help of the brilliant George W. Rains, he established a magnificent powder works. At Petersburg, Virginia, he placed a lead smelting plant. Cannon foundries were located in Macon and Columbus, Georgia. Shot and shell came out of a plant at Salisbury, North Carolina. Leatherwork needed to equip men and machines came from a shop at Clarksville, Virginia. A factory in Asheville made rifles, one in Macon made pistols, and so did another in Columbus. "Where three years ago we were not making a gun, pistol nor a sabre, no shot nor shell—a pound of powder—we now make all these in quantities to meet the demands of our large armies." So Gorgas could boast, and with justifiable pride. But this was in early 1863, with the industrial and raw material potential of the Confederacy strained to its very limits.[5]

Further, the army had to compete with the navy and other departments for time on the machines of the South. When it became evident to Secretary of the Navy Stephen Russell Mallory that he would not be able to buy a navy sufficient to arm the new nation, he turned to the challenge of building one, and particularly a fleet of ironclads, powered by steam. No class of vessel could put a greater strain on the industrial plant of the South, or put him more in conflict with Gorgas. The same mills and foundries would have to cast and roll iron for his ships as made cannon for Gorgas. Mallory, in fact, would have in time to resort to recycling railroad iron into the armor plating needed for his warships, and cannibalizing old stationary engines to provide motive power for the vessels.

But there was much more needed besides guns and ships. The mining of the raw materials even came to be managed by the military, or at least considerably interfered with by them. Coal, iron, copper, lead, and niter were all produced by the War Department's Niter and Mining Bureau, while the Quartermaster's office looked to the production of the staples of its service, particularly salt mining for meat preservative. The Quartermaster also established virtual cottage industries throughout the Confederacy to manufacture blankets, uniforms, shoes, and boots. Even the stirring red battle flags carried by each regiment came in time to be mass-produced to a single pattern. Substantial numbers of civilians exempted from the military service found employment in these various industries. By 1863, in Selma alone some 10,000 workers toiled at war manufacturing.[6]

Yet despite the predominant role of the Confederate Government in industry, some few private enterprises stood out, and none more so than Richmond's Tredegar Iron Works. Indeed, by war's end it would be the leading manufacturer in the entire dying nation, and one symbolic of the voluntary wedding of private with public manufacturing. The firm went into business formally in 1837, and four years later, after hard times in the financial crisis of 1837, its management went into the hands of young Joseph R. Anderson. A Virginian, just twenty-eight in 1841, he had gone to West Point and come out in 1836, then resigned to go into civil engineering. That pursuit brought him to the attention of the Tredegar managers. For the next several decades, the fortunes of Anderson and the ironworks were to be one.

When war came in 1861, the Confederate War Department found Tredegar to be the only heavy industry in the South that was ready instantly to convert to war production. Its machinery had already produced heavy siege cannon, and in the first months of the war virtually all of the government's orders for big guns went to Anderson. As soon as Sumter was fired upon, Anderson and the plant managers offered its services to the government, and for the rest of the war Tredegar would be the South's primary manufacturer of ordnance, its output alone more than equaling that of all other Confederate foundries combined. Here, too, lay one of only two rolling mills in the South that had ever produced rails for the railroads. And at Tredegar Mallory would find the only capability for rolling the two-inch plates of wrought iron necessary for cladding his ironbound vessels for coastal and river defense. When the U.S.S. *Merrimack* fell to Confederate hands and the work of converting her into the ironclad C.S.S. *Virginia* began, it was to Tredegar that Mallory sent his orders for armor. To accommodate the navy, Anderson had to alter the actual machinery, yet did so obligingly. Further, since Tredegar was still a private firm only dealing with the Confederate Government on contract, Anderson had to set priorities on whose work should be done first within the limitations of time and raw materials. He never failed to put the war work first. "We are now pressed almost beyond endurance for the heavy iron work to complete one of the war vessels," wrote a manager of the works to a disappointed customer who had to wait. "It is a most fortunate thing that we could render this assistance to our little Navy—It could not have been done elsewhere in the Confederacy."

Despite the continuing private enterprise nature of Tredegar's operations, its relationship with the government became more and more intimate. Confederate authorities controlled the rail shipments of raw materials and gave priorities to the shipment of Tredegar's orders. Indeed, it was a particular complaint of railroad operators that they could not get Tredegar to tool up to replace their worn-out engines and rails for all the priority work being done for the government. Anderson converted much of his specialized machinery to war needs in such a fashion that it could not readily be used for nonmilitary purposes. "We can't stop to build locomotives," said the operators in 1862, being too busy at manufacturing cannon. "We are so much engaged in defending the country," complained a partner in the firm, that they could do little else. Later that year one of the partners would moan that they were "overwhelmed with business, all for the Government." Only a little work could be done for the railroads, thus virtually forcing the major transportation industry into a supply competition with the War Department.

Soon Richmond had to get even more deeply involved with Tredegar, using its authority over the railroads to guarantee access to the pig iron that kept the mills going, and later actually getting involved in the procurement of the pig iron itself. Thus Gorgas and his associates helped turn the War Department–Tredegar partnership into a virtually vertical business organization, controlling in whole or part the manufacturing process from the mining of raw materials, to the shipping to furnaces, provision of the pig iron to Tredegar, and then buying the finished products. Before long the Confederate Congress itself would become a partner in the enterprise, passing repeated special legislation to encourage and supply Tredegar's needs, even to advancing money on contracts. Yet despite the extremely intimate relationship, when Anderson and his partners repeatedly offered to transfer ownership of Tredegar to the government itself, they were politely refused and, instead, rewarded with higher prices paid for their manufactures. Formal nationalization of a major industry would have touched off a howling outcry.[4]

By 1863 the enforced partnership between the government and private industry had achieved considerable gains for the war effort. Indeed, at this time some like Gorgas could claim that the South was now self-sufficient in its military industrial needs. Private manufacturers had been encouraged by government contracts and preferential legislation, government-owned shops expanded, thousands of men exempted from military duty so they could work the machines and mills, and enormous amounts of money—admittedly increasingly inflated Confederate notes—infused into the industrial economy. Congress passed legislation fixing maximum profits from government work at 33.3 percent, yet when public funds went into the building or expansion of a manufacturing plant, the government reserved the right to command two thirds of its output. Control of the railroads virtually put Richmond in command of industry everywhere.

The result was an amazingly complex and, on the face of it, liberal revolution of the Southern industrial base and economy. In 1861 the South was by all measures still a backward region barely worthy of a standing in a world well into the Industrial Revolution. By 1863 the Confederate Government had turned it completely around. Admittedly, the industrial plant was wearing badly by the second year of the war. Managers resorted to increasingly ersatz measures to keep their machinery operating, and the quality of the raw materials suffered, as did the means of transporting them to the factories. And of course it was a critically restricted industrial revolution, its sole produce war materials. New plants for consumer goods, for farm machinery, rolling stock, paper mills, even the traditional textiles, did not get built.

In fact, however, revolutionary though it was, the industrial turn-around of the South between 1861 and 1863 was uniquely Southern, con-servative, for the government did not nationalize industries or the rail-roads. Instead, it offered encouragement, inducement, legislation, and sometimes threats to be sure, to engage Southern manufacturers in a part-nership in the war. In so doing, however, it also declined the centralized leadership and control necessary for a nation to make the best and most productive use of its industrial base. For a nation like the Confederacy, where that base was small and overworked at the outset, such control was absolutely vital. Inevitably, government and private enterprise came to work at times at cross purposes, and the lack of a central authority, partic-ularly with the railroads, led even to the various government departments working against and competing with each other. Therein lay the critical weakness, not only of Confederate industrialization, but of the Confed-eracy itself. And despite the seeming miracles wrought in Southern manu-facturing for the war, by 1863, and particularly by the summer of the year, it was becoming increasingly evident that even at its best, Confederate in-dustry was unequal to the task before it. Transportation was being increas-ingly disrupted. Shortage of pig iron was beginning to tell. Rolling mill production was falling off from an 1862 production high, as was railroad rail. Ordnance production at Tredegar alone fell by 20 percent. Pig iron production would increase in 1863, but the wear to the plants and the shortage of other materials would continue the decline in manufactures. Prices were beginning to soar. Iron items that sold for three and four cents per pound in 1861 were up to thirty-five cents a pound when the guns hurled tons of iron at Gettysburg. Another year would see the pound price at one dollar, and over two dollars by war's end. In short, the won-der is not that the remarkable Confederate industrial revolution failed in the end, but rather that it succeeded to the degree that it did, and for as long.[8]

The men at whom Lee's army fired so much of Tredegar's iron in July 1863 suffered from no such dearth of plant or produce. The North came to war with a virtual industrial empire intact, its machinery ready for the challenge, and its operators fired by the entrepreneurism to readily exploit the profits to be made from supplying the needs of the hungry Washington government. Almost all of New England, and particularly Massachusetts, burgeoned with the clicking and whirring sounds of ma-chines making products for men. Already Pittsburgh heard the hissing and saw the flying sparks of the steel industry that would make it a world leader. Coal mines throughout Pennsylvania disgorged tons of burning black rock to fuel the furnaces and boil the steam that turned the engines of Yankee progress. Textiles in Massachusetts. Lumber in Maine. Clocks in Connecticut. Locomotives in Pennsylvania. Farming plows and tools in Illinois. Great cities spawned by manufacturing populated virtually every state in the North. There was a revolution in communications, with East and West linked by telegraph and the railroads, of almost universally uniform gauge, linking the Atlantic with the trans-Mississippi. Great entrepreneurs were already making fortunes by their pluck and invention and craft. Samuel Colt dominated the market for personal small arms. Cyrus McCormick was reaping profits as his invention reaped crops for farmers. Isaac Singer's sewing machines made clothes in thousands of private homes. Steel, iron, coal, oil, and a hundred other one-day giants were well along in their adolescence when Fort Sumter made the whole country grow up in a hurry.

While men would argue then and later over whether or not the war boosted or retarded industrialization in the North, none could contend that some major change was needed by 1861 if the rapid growth in plants and production were to break out of the grip of government diffidence and interference. Industrialization was yet too new for a consistent policy to have been adopted by any of the ruling parties in Washington. The Democrats, of course, showed little interest as a group. Their concern lay in minimizing, not emphasizing, the elements that made North different from South. The Whigs had established a far more industrial-minded approach during their heyday with their stand for tariffs to protect domestic goods from foreign imports. But the Whigs were gone by 1861, and a new party in power, the Republicans, showed themselves the spiritual descendants of the Whigs of old. Their tariffs would be more stringent yet, their energies for industrial expansion more pronounced. All things came together at precisely the same moment, it seemed. Northern industry needed a government in power that would provide it the legislative incentives for expansion and remove the irksome stumbling blocks in local restrictions that hampered further development. The Republicans took power with a war on their hands that would place heavier demands on the nation's industrial plant than it had yet experienced. Each was ready for the other, and it was the war that took them to the altar. Their offspring would be legion.

In the first days following secession and the fall of Fort Sumter, Yankee industry in fact suffered a momentary collapse. Banks and businesses with large investments in the South, or those that held large Southern debts, were forced into bankruptcy. Perhaps as much as $150 million in Confederate debts were repudiated, leaving the Yankee business climate in a state of shock. Particularly fearful was the enormous New England textile business. Confederates had suspected that one of King Cotton's subjects was, in fact, the Yankee milling industry, for textiles made from Southern cotton were perhaps the largest staple of the Northern industrial economy. In New England some 200,000 people found employment in the mills, and a major share of the United States' foreign trade took form in its textile manufactures. Unfortunately for Confederate expectations, however, Yankee mills had a surplus of ginned cotton on hand when the war broke out, thanks to a heavy crop in 1860. Still, with the outbreak of hostilities, most Northern mills closed down for a time, and during the first year of the war a near depression shook the trade. The mills operated at barely half their prewar output, but by mid-1862 the trade began to pick up again. With hundreds of thousands of men in uniform, the domestic demand for textiles regrouped and soon charged ahead, fed by cotton captured in the South and new sources developed abroad. Those that could not get cotton converted their looms to woolen manufactures.[9]

Naturally the needs of the military came quickly to play the single major role in bringing Yankee industry out of the post-Sumter collapse. A good harvest that summer found abundant markets with the armies growing across the country. The flurry of war contracts from Washington stimulated many businesses to reopen their doors and, with often minimal expense, convert their plants to military products. And the tariff acts sponsored by Congressman Justin Smith Morrill in 1861 and 1862 gave a sharp advantage to domestic goods over imports. First iron and wool, and then other industries benefited from the heavy increase in importation duties. The spirit of entrepreneurism, challenged by the needs that the war would bring, brought many capitalists back into the industrial investment business, and the wealth of newly developed technological inventions fairly begged men of vision, and avarice, to tool up for the duration.

The major industries, of course, would naturally be those of most importance to fighting the war, and this war was fought by iron and rails. The Morrill acts particularly stimulated the iron industry, its inducements magnified a thousandfold by the enormous demands made by the War Department. Old furnaces and rolling mills were hastily put back on line as bids for government contracts jammed the mails to the capital. Pennsylvania, the old Keystone State, was already prepared to be the cornerstone of the Union's iron needs. New rolling mills and foundries went up, production soared, and the coal industry needed to fire the furnaces burgeoned along with it. Big guns that dwarfed those of Tredegar started to roll toward the arsenals. And while the railroad building industry in the South came to a grinding halt as soon as the war opened, that of the North expanded phenomenally. Some rail shops doubled their prewar production, and the Pennsylvania Railroad alone put more than 50 locomotives and 3,000 new cars into service.[10]

Undeniably, the substantial and continuing orders from the War and Navy departments put many manufacturers back in business after the summer 1861 slump, and many more businesses started just to take advantage of the contract business. Whole industrial cities found themselves lifted back into production and prosperity by the military's needs. Providence, Rhode Island, surged out of the collapse with contracts for clothing, cannon, rifles, bayonets, including Ambrose Burnside's carbine. Before the close of 1861 her manufacturers could boast of "plenty of work, good prices, and general contentment." Cincinnati's clothiers had contracts for over six million uniforms by the time Braxton Bragg's Kentucky invasion threatened to reach the Ohio River city. Pittsburgh built steamboats and began the work of converting snag and dredge boats and barges into armor-clad warships like the *Benton* and the *Essex*, and at Mound City, Illinois, and elsewhere, important navy yards constructed from nothing the mighty gunboats designed by James Buchanan Eads and others to wrest the Mississippi from the enemy. Leather shops and wagoners and coopers and boxmakers and printers and meat-packers and a thousand other varieties of commercial and industrial manufacturers found in the war with the Confederacy a bonanza to lift them from the depression that same war had briefly cast them into.[11]

The windfall hit the shoe business in particular like a godsend. There was little difference between a civilian and a military shoe or boot at the time, and thus the industry was ripe for speedy and effective conversion for war production. Further, newly invented machinery happened along at just the right time to take the manufacturing process out of the hands of the individual worker who could make perhaps three pairs a day by hand and enable the same worker to produce seven and eight pairs a day by machine. Further, the war encouraged the further invention and refinement of existing and new machinery, for the contracts for shoes and other items demanded that certain specifications of durability be met. While many, of course, provided shabby goods anyhow and took a hopefully quick profit, responsible manufacturers installed the latest developments in their trade technology, which in turn encouraged not only their own industry, but also the machinery manufacturers as well. The advances in one sector of industry thus enhanced and advanced progress in others. And the advent of mass production methods and machinery meant that skilled handworkers were far less essential. That freed thousands of men for the armed services, began to bring women into the working force in the factories, and allowed the industries to spread outside the New England and middle Atlantic states into the West, where unskilled labor was plentiful.

The same transformation took place in the woolen business, the demand for millions of uniforms and the limited supply of cotton making the animal fiber virtually a textile king during the war. The flocks of the North could not come near supplying the ever-increasing demands of the looms and the military supply bureaus. Soon South America, Africa, and several British Empire countries like Canada and Australia, were adding their fleece to that of New England and the Midwest, and still the looms demanded more. Prices soared and fortunes were made, many firms literally doubling their capital investments. The factories ran twenty-four hours a day, seven days every week, rivaling the production even of the British leaders in the industry, and placing heavy demands upon the machinery manufacturers.

And so it went. War contracts, the Morrill tariffs, and simple good timing wrought virtual wonders in revitalizing and expanding Yankee industry. Indeed, in a very brief time these same manufacturers came to regard war contracts as their right. It was an American war, being fought by American armies, and their needs and the nation's should be supplied by American manufacturers. Arms makers in particular came to view very dimly importation of arms from Great Britain, and lobbied extensively, and effectively, against it. The clothiers took the same approach, and their outcry was sufficient to wrest from Quartermaster General Montgomery C. Meigs a promise not to place orders abroad so long as Yankee looms and mills could supply army demands.

The business of food processing and packing, already in its infancy when the conflict began, took giant leaps. The tin can was to be a common sight, its contents varying from preserved blackberries to condensed milk to boiled meats. The art of home canning was simply adapted to galvanized—often crudely—tin and copper cans, the container filled and topped, the contents then heated to kill bacteria and expel air in order to form a vacuum seal. The seal, of course, was what they were after; the dead bacteria were practically unknown to packers as yet, an unexpected and unappreciated benefit. Still, thousands of soldiers would sicken, and many die, from botulism. Millions of others were fed quickly and easily by preserved edibles that a few decades before could not have reached the front at all. Meat, too, was preserved not only in containers, but in the old salted and dried manner as well. And vegetables were heat dried and packaged to be boiled for consumption perhaps many months later. The dehydrated produce, often called derisively "desiccated vegetables" by the soldiery, were still a far better and more reliable source of nutrition than the dependence upon foraging the countryside would have allowed, and it helped relieve the commissaries in the field from buying fresh vegetables at inflated prices from local vendors.

Fledgling giants like the oil industry partook of the boom, though even their energetic managers could hardly foresee the much greater future for them in the years beyond the conflict. The industry came into being at Titusville, Pennsylvania, barely two years before First Bull Run, and a boom was already under way when the armies first clashed. Natural and animal oils had been necessary for illumination for centuries, but this "black gold" from the ground was even more adaptable for lighting and lubricating needs, and easier to process. By 1861 towns like Oil City, Pennsylvania, were already filled with the clamor of wells and drills and the blighted landscape that would characterize the whole history of the oil industry. By the time of Gettysburg, the oil fields yielded over 10 million barrels a year, much of it being exported abroad, and all of it bringing an attendant boom in the ancillary services of transportation, refining, and burning the precious stuff. And it helped put the whaling industry out of business. Pennsylvania alone boasted more than a hundred refineries. By the end of the war, oil had become one of the Union's principal mediums of exchange in Europe.[12]

And it was all accomplished in a much different fashion than in the Confederacy. For one thing, Northern industry was never completely occupied by its war-related business as was manufacturing in the South. Even while the shops and factories were turning out guns and uniforms and shoes, they made mass-produced clothing in standard sizes, farm implements, books, medicines, toys, games. While every firearm manufactured in the Confederacy after 1861 was contracted for or intended for sale to the government, in the old Union the brisk trade in personal and sporting firearms flourished, and even expanded under the management of men like Samuel Colt into foreign markets. Yankee industry, though undeniably heavily committed to the war, met its military commitments with only one hand. The other continued to produce the consumer goods and discretionary items that citizens and soldiers alike demanded. Even such peripheral businesses as the clock and watch industry flourished anew with the heavy demand for cheap but reliable pocket timepieces at home and in the field.

And all this came at a much lesser price of government interference and control than in the South. To be sure, the tariffs and contract stipulations on quality of merchandise both assisted and regulated much of the factory output, but only in a very few cases did Federal contracts so dominate a manufacturer that he could not entertain civil business as well. Washington did not manipulate the railroads so as to favor one vital war industry over private enterprise, nor did the government in fact exercise anywhere near the general control of the roads that existed south of the border. Advances to industries deemed necessary to the war effort were not made from the common treasury, for there was more than enough capital in the Union to fund new buildings and machinery, and in the operation of the system the capitalists could readily see lucrative rewards for their risks. Inventiveness and entrepreneurism found more than ample encouragement in the contract system, and the extensive trials and tests conducted by the authorities tended to ensure greater rather than lesser quality. In the case of field cannon alone, virtually scores of new designs and varieties were devised and proposed to the War Department during the war, and for most of them working models were submitted to the testing laboratory at the Washington Arsenal. There meticulous examinations and trial firings produced decisions on which would be put into production, which would win contracts. In the Confederacy, it was often the Richmond offices that created a design, and then looked to a manufacturer to make it.

Herein lay the greatest boost to Yankee industry, as well as to the industrial war effort. The lure to the entrepreneurs unleashed a wave of inventiveness, of risk-taking, of imagination. It was the capitalist free enterprise system personified, and it worked. Great fortunes began to characterize future great men. Andrew Carnegie began to achieve his future domination of the iron and steel industry. John Davison Rockefeller flourished in his small Cleveland, Ohio, oil business which, in 1870, he would incorporate as the Standard Oil Company of Ohio. Charles Alfred Pillsbury made a fortune in flour milling and founded a future empire. Jay Gould went into railroading as did competitors Collis Potter Huntington and Cornelius Vanderbilt. Philip Danforth Armour learned the grocery and meat business, only to pioneer in meat packing in years to come.

But the cost was no small price, for this rapid shift in industry during the war proved, some thought, to be a mixed blessing. The rapid growth of plant and production was undeniable. However, much of that plant had been built specifically to meet the needs of war industry, and when once the war ended, as surely it must, would those factories and their machines be readily adaptable to undertake or resume the manufacturing of nonmilitary consumer goods? The question seems not to have occurred to many in the euphoric days of greater and greater production, more and more investments, and rapidly rising profits. Without doubt, the conflict bred a generation of entrepreneurs, men willing to dream big and take chances. They were, as well, fiercely competitive, sometimes at the expense of traditional business ethics. Indeed, the war redefined some of those ethics. The avarice and shady dealings of the later Gilded Era could oftentimes be traced to the scramble over contracts in the 1860s. And the war also encouraged government to remove many of the state and Federal restrictions that impaired business expansion, thanks chiefly to the active encouragement of the Republican Party.

If the war did have a negative impact upon industry, it came in its failure to encourage new industries, for the lion's share of expansion and innovation came in the existing trades. Even though the Bessemer steel process was known, and even being practiced in a limited way in Kentucky and Confederate Georgia, the dominant metal industry remained iron. Certainly the oil boom came at the same time as the war, but still its expansion was primarily in the private economy and not war-related. The textile and clothing businesses experienced rapid growth during the conflict, yet their methods and technology remained largely the same as before the war. In short, then, what the conflict did was to accelerate the spread and acceptance of methods and machines already known and in use before the firing of the guns. In the decades following the war, no great incremental increase in production was evident over the decades previous to the conflict; no new processes developed as a result of the war gave a significant boost to new manufacturing.

But it would be misleading to suggest, and to the industrialists of the 1860s it would have seemed preposterous, that the overall impact of the war upon Northern industry was negative. It created the mood, the climate, the experience, the capital, and freed much of the labor force that would commingle in the decades to follow to thrust the United States into world industrial importance. And, more important, in the early 1860s it gave Lincoln the tools of war necessary to sustain the greatest and best-equipped armies in the hemisphere through the most technologically costly and destructive war in history, to that time. Meade and other generals would not suffer for want of arms or food or means of transporting them to points needed. They would not be forced to invade their enemy's territory in order to supply their needs, and their own industrial base was so widespread that no enemy invasion could seriously disrupt or threaten the continued production and flow of necessities to the armies. When Meade and Lee clashed at Gettysburg, the Union soldiers were better fed, better clothed, better armed and equipped than their adversaries. And behind them, in a million homes and factories, the soldiers had families and friends whose daily needs of life were not severely compromised by the preoccupation of industry with making war. There was no want of food or of clothing, very little resort to the ersatz and crude innovation that forced Southern civilians into knitting hats and shoes, charring corn for coffee, or making their whiskey from the tops of pine trees. By the days of Gettysburg, the people and the industrial plants of the Confederacy had reached the limit of their productivity and resources. They could do no more and could hardly hope to sustain even that level of output indefinitely. But as Meade took his leisurely path to follow Lee to the Potomac, he had behind him a rapidly burgeoning Northern industrial might that had not yet begun to fully flex its muscle. At last the Union had a great victory in the field, but in the factory and workshop Mr. Lincoln's army of manufacturers had been on the glory road for nearly two years, with more and more to come.[13]

CHAPTER 9

"GO FORWARD TO A DECISIVE VICTORY"

The benefits of the North's industrial supremacy accrued not just to the armies in the East, but to those in the West as well. Yet it was a different war out there in many respects, one of rugged, hard-bitten men, men of lean aspect and fierce tenacity, men who had known loss and defeat and who, therefore, strove all the more for victory. There was a sense out there that the war was being won or lost in their bailiwick, despite the preoccupation in Washington and Richmond with the fighting in Virginia. Perhaps it was this feeling that made them all the more tenacious, more determined. These were no brahmins and planter aristocrats fighting this hardscrabble war in Tennessee and Mississippi and Louisiana. There were no frills and few affectations. They played their game of war for keeps. It was the only way they knew.

Certainly it was the only way known to Ulysses S. Grant. He was already a phenomenon by the fall of 1862 when he addressed his greatest challenge to date. He was a man who had sunk from mediocrity to the bottom, and he was well acquainted with the points in between. Soldier, storekeeper, leather tanner, customs clerk, land salesman, he succeeded consistently only in failure. More than any other officer in a responsible position by this second year of the war, Grant had touched the cellar of his life with nowhere to look but up. After he resigned under a cloud from the army in 1854, he spent the next seven years simply looking for something that he could do at all well. In 1861 he found the war, and in its destruction and carnage he found his salvation. No man genuinely hated the war more than he, or wished it ended sooner, yet no one in all the continent would in the end gain more from it. If predestination truly governs the affairs of men, then at the dawn of time it was decreed that this man and this conflict would be wedded one to another irrevocably.

At first, of course, it seemed not to be much of a match. When Grant offered his services to the government shortly after Fort Sumter, he received not even the courtesy of a response. Finally that summer the state of Illinois entrusted him with a volunteer commission as colonel of the 21st Illinois. In August, thanks to the friendly influence of a congressman, he donned a brigadier's star, which must already have seemed a heady success. Yet his first efforts seemed dogged by that old enemy, failure. His first military endeavor, a minor expedition to root out enemy bushwhackers at Belmont, Missouri, barely escaped being a disaster. Yet Grant did learn there that he did not fear the enemy any more than they feared him, and that alone was a small victory. Never again would he be afraid of his adversaries, be they guerrillas or great armies.

From that little engagement, Grant soon leaped into national prominence when he organized and led the joint army-navy expedition that took Forts Henry and Donelson on the Cumberland and Tennessee rivers. The move pierced the very heart of the Confederate hold on Kentucky, forcing them to abandon the state and much of Tennessee with it. Two months later, on April 6–7, 1862, he survived a surprise attack at Shiloh and turned the near rout into a stubborn and successful defense that in the end cost the enemy much more than it cost him. Success came at a price, for his national acclaim incurred for him the jealousy of his department commander, Henry W. Halleck, and soon afterward Grant found himself removed from active command. Only after "Old Woodenhead" Halleck's incompetence in the field was fully demonstrated did Washington call him to the War Department and return Grant to his command. That fall troops under Grant's command managed to defeat attacks by Sterling Price and Earl Van Dorn at Corinth and Iuka, Mississippi, thereby denying those reinforcements to Braxton Bragg in his invasion of Kentucky. Grant held firmly the upper hand in western Tennessee and northern Mississippi. His reward was command of the Department of the Tennessee, including all that territory between the Mississippi and Tennessee rivers, and from Cairo, Illinois, as far south as he could go. The Mississippi itself had been cleared of Confederates at its mouth at New Orleans, and Rebel bastions along its banks at Memphis and elsewhere had already fallen. Almost all that remained to make the Father of Waters a Union highway was the capture of two enemy strongholds at Vicksburg, Mississippi, and Port Hudson, Louisiana.

Grant had long believed that Vicksburg provided a key to the collapse of the western Confederacy. Admiral David G. Farragut's gunboats had managed to pass the formidable batteries on the bluffs surrounding the city more than once, but those guns had to be silenced permanently in order to open the great river to steady Federal traffic. Further, as long as Vicksburg denied control of the stretch of river between it and Port Hudson, the enemy could continue its communications and flow of supplies from its westernmost territory in Arkansas, Texas, and western Louisiana. Take Vicksburg, and one third of the territory of the Confederacy would be severed.

Grant assumed his new departmental command on October 25, 1862, and already a plan coursed through his mind. He had spent the two preceding months in inactive garrison duty with his army spread over four states. Now he chafed for action. This was one general that Lincoln would never have to urge to celerity. Primal instincts within the general compelled him toward constant movement, incessant pressure on the enemy. Like a pit bulldog, his teeth once clenched on his enemy's hide, he never turned loose.

There was a new Confederate commander in Mississippi, and Grant wanted to smite him. General John Clifford Pemberton, so unpopular at Charleston earlier that year, found himself sent west by Richmond in October. He relieved Van Dorn of overall command, reducing the latter to direction of the cavalry operating in Mississippi. Pemberton knew that an attempt on Vicksburg was inevitable. He took command of a small army demoralized by its defeat under Van Dorn, and facing a considerably more numerous foe. Like so many other successful Confederate commanders, then, Pemberton knew that he would have to rely upon his cavalry to operate against Grant's communications and supply lines in order to slow the Federal advance. Slowing it was perhaps all he could expect, but it would give him time to garner reinforcements and erect formidable defenses in and around Vicksburg.[1]

This was precisely what Grant feared, exactly the sort of knowledge that made him so insistent upon speedy movement. One week after taking his new command, Grant told Halleck, now in Washington, that he intended to move against Grand Junction, Tennessee, just across the Mississippi line. If possible he would push on to Holly Springs and even Grenada. Once started, he would not stop if he could help it. He was going to move south on the line of the Mississippi Central Railroad, and each of these points along the way led toward Jackson, the state capital, and just forty miles east of Vicksburg. He had importuned Halleck for weeks to allow such a movement to begin, and finally the new general-in-chief told him that he could "Fight the enemy when you please." On November 2, 1862, Grant began his move.[2]

He launched his move with perhaps 30,000 men, estimating that his opponent's strength matched his own. In six days he took Grand Junction and La Grange, Tennessee, and sent a large body of soldiers forward into northern Mississippi to reconnoiter. Here at once he began to collect as much forage for his animals and stockpile supplies for the men as possible. He would be moving deep into enemy territory when he crossed into Mississippi, with Van Dorn in his front and the cavalry of General Nathan Bedford Forrest on his right flank. His supply lines would be vulnerable some distance behind him, and that meant that he would have to establish a major supply base as close to his own front as possible. It did not yet occur to Grant that he might be able to make his army subsist on the very territory they were invading. Holly Springs, twenty-five miles south of Grand Junction, would make an excellent base. When Van Dorn obligingly fell back before the Federal advance without resistance, Grant took possession of his new base on November 20 and promptly began building it into the cornerstone of his campaign to take Vicksburg.[3]

So far the campaign went as planned, and Grant could even find time for a little mirthful amusement at the expense of a considerably overweight member of Halleck's Washington staff. In a deserted house in Mississippi, his soldiers found a mammoth "pair of unmentionables," no doubt underdrawers. Grant sent them to Halleck, twitting him that since the garment was "entirely unsuited in dimentions for any member of this Army, and thinking that so much material should not be lost in these times," he would give them to Halleck's assistant. Hidden within the jestful presentation, no doubt, lay a biting gibe at the ample backsides of deskbound Washington soldiers. Yet at the same time that this strange general could twit his superior, so also did he continue, as all his life, in the vain pursuit of winning from his overbearing father the simple approval that every son seeks of his parent. Jesse Root Grant rarely concealed his own feeling that his son was a failure, and even now, as one of the leading captains of a great army, still Ulysses tried almost pathetically to win the old man's favor. From the war's start he proudly wrote of his accomplishments, of the movements of his commands and, as far as security would allow, of his plans. He tried vainly to get his father to soften in his critical attitude toward Grant's wife, Julia, and now in the midst of his campaign he wrote once more, not reprovingly as man to man, but in the tentative manner of the son still fearful of offending the father. Old Jesse reproached Julia repeatedly in terms condescending, and Ulysses intimated that his father must be "so prejudiced against her that she could not please you." The closest that the general could come to castigating his father was to say that "This is not pleasing to me." And then he closed with the news that he would be moving again soon. "I feel every confidance of success," he said. He always said it to Jesse Grant. But the old man had heard that from his boy many times before and still he had failed. And that is why U. S. Grant knew with all the more determination that in this war he must succeed. It might be his last chance.[4]

As he marshaled his supplies at Holly Springs, Grant called to his most trusted lieutenant, General William T. Sherman, to leave Memphis and move south with two divisions to join in the march toward Jackson. Sherman, ever trusty, brought three divisions for good measure, and was ready for the campaign to commence before the end of November. But by now the rumblings of other enemies could be heard in the East, and Grant began rightfully to fear that his plans were about to be upset. Politics would, as always, begin to interfere. Major General John A. McClernand was politicking mightily in Washington for an independent command in the West, and unfortunately he carried a lot of prestige. A prominent Illinois Democrat before the war, he remained loyal and Lincoln rewarded him with a commission. McClernand proved a blatant egotist, claiming for himself repeatedly the glory for others' accomplishments, and in the process engaging in shameful intrigues against his superiors. He tried to engineer himself into replacing McClellan in the East and, when that failed, started turning his insidious influence toward winning an independent command in the Mississippi theater. The simpleton Grant could hardly be a threat to him, and before long he would undoubtedly be winning the war for the Union, and soon thereafter the Presidency.

Grant had no use for McClernand. "I doubted McClernand's fitness," he said later. Even by the time he left on his campaign, Grant already felt upset over rumors conveyed to him and reports in the press that somehow McClernand would be entrusted with a separate command, within Grant's department, with the task of moving by water down the Mississippi to take Vicksburg. "Two commanders on the same field are always one too many," he said, "and in this case I did not think the general selected had either the experience or the qualifications to fit him for so important a position." Grant actually feared for the welfare of the soldiers who would be entrusted to the politico. On November 10 he finally put the question plainly to Halleck, asking, "Am I to understand that I lay still here while an Expedition is fitted out from Memphis?" The next day the general-in-chief reassured him that there would be no independent commands within his department. "You have command of all troops sent to your Dept, and have permission to fight the enemy when you please."[5]

Given that encouragement, Grant had proceeded south, yet all the while the rumors of a move down the river continued. By December 3 he was suggesting that he halt his own progress at Grenada, on the Yalobusha River, holding Pemberton's main body there while the now almost assured campaign down the river took Vicksburg, and two days later he reiterated the proposal, suggesting that Sherman be entrusted with the command and his force augmented by Federals then stationed at Helena, Arkansas. That same day Halleck wired that the country south of Oxford need not be held, but that 25,000 troops should be gathered at Memphis for the move against Vicksburg. Grant immediately sent Sherman and his divisions back to Memphis, and quickly his intent became evident. Years later he admitted that "my action in sending Sherman back was expedited by a desire to get him in command of the forces separated from my direct supervision. I feared that delay might bring McClernand." It did. Despite Halleck's assurance that Grant could entrust the command of the Vicksburg expedition to whomever he wished, orders reached him on December 18 that the President directed him to divide his army into four corps, giving one of them to McClernand, and to him as well the chief command of the Vicksburg expedition. The only saving feature of the order was that McClernand's command would not be entirely independent. He must still answer to Grant. It was to be only a part of a very bad week.[6]

Just the day before Halleck's instructions arrived, Grant issued General Orders No. 11, probably the most controversial single administrative act of his wartime career. Typical of his innocence in social and political matters, he seems not to have suspected in the least the outcry it would bring. On that day he ordered all Jews "as a class" expelled from the limits of his department. That Grant felt a considerable prejudice against Jews, going back probably to childhood, is undeniable. He probably learned it from his intolerant father, who only shared a widely held disdain felt toward Jews in the Western states, and particularly among men like Jesse Grant who competed with Jews in trade. The same prejudice enjoyed considerable support in the army, much enhanced by the number of Jews engaged in buying captured cotton and reselling it, often illicitly. Grant had tried repeatedly to control the trade in cotton in his department in order to benefit his army, and some traders, many of them Jews, had circumvented his efforts in order to sell the staple themselves farther north. And shortly after arriving at Holly Springs, Grant's father, his instincts toward profit aroused, came to his son's headquarters intent upon doing some cotton trading himself. Anxious as always to win his parent's favor, Grant may have tried to expel the Jews to lessen the competition.

Whatever his motives, the general's order sparked an immediate controversy. In the next few weeks it proved difficult to implement, and on January 4, 1863, Halleck responded to the order by saying that it must immediately be revoked. Halleck and Lincoln both found it objectionable because "It excluded a whole class, instead of certain obnoxious individuals. Had the word 'pedler' been inserted after Jew I do not suppose any exception would have been taken to the order." Lincoln expressed his feelings with equal clarity. He did not object to expulsion of traders, even if they be Jewish, and supposed that to be the real intent of Grant's order, "but as it in terms prescribed an entire religious class, some of whom are fighting in our ranks," he had to revoke the edict. The order caused some embarrassment in Grant's own officer corps, which numbered a few Jews, and the governor of one of the Western states that provided several regiments in Grant's army was as well of the faith. Both houses of Congress toyed briefly with condemnatory resolutions but finally rejected them. And Grant himself, looking back on the episode, later believed that he deserved the reprimand, as he "had no right to make an order against any special sect." After a time the issue died away, though it was never entirely forgotten. Six years later, when Grant would seek the White House, his enemies would revive the matter and open anew old wounds.[7]

Then came December 20. Sherman was back in Memphis, even then starting the move down the Mississippi, with McClernand on the way. The Jews in the Department of the Tennessee were wondering just what had happened. And Earl Van Dorn had stopped falling back before the Federal advance. With Grant at Oxford, he led his cavalry in a ride around the Federal right flank toward Holly Springs, twenty-five miles behind Oxford. Should Van Dorn take or destroy that base, Grant's move would be aborted perhaps for an entire season, with winter coming on. That same day Julia and the Grants' son Jesse rode south on the Mississippi Central to join him in Oxford. He did not meet them at the depot as usual, but when they arrived at his headquarters he seemed cheerful enough. "I have only time to kiss you," he said, then cuffed his son playfully and returned to his office. Reports of Van Dorn's movements had reached him just minutes before and, though he did not show it—as he never revealed anxiety—the general was certainly glad to see his family arrived safely. Van Dorn was striking over the same railroad they had just traveled, and probably only chance prevented Julia and Jesse from falling into enemy hands.

Then, despite Grant's orders to be vigilant, the garrison of 2,000 at Holly Springs was surprised and overwhelmed by Van Dorn, the supply base destroyed, and even Julia's carriage, which had been left there, burned. Some Confederates even came to the house where she had stayed and asked for her. Van Dorn then moved on up the track toward Grand Junction, while on December 19, Forrest and his cavalry struck Grant's rail communications in Tennessee, at Jackson. The raids were a brilliant stroke, and devastatingly effective against Grant, who actually suspected treachery on the part of his subordinate commanding at Holly Springs, but that hardly mattered now. On December 21 Grant began to withdraw north toward the Tennessee border. For the next two weeks he and his army had to live from their current stock of provisions and what they could take from the land, for no rail communications opened to him until after the New Year. "I determined, therefore, to abandon my campaign," he lamented.

But Grant never really quit. Holly Springs did not alter his basic aim, but only showed him a better way to accomplish the goal. He learned that it was not possible to maintain such a long and tenuous supply line deep into the enemy's territory. However, he did control the Mississippi from Cairo to Vicksburg, the great river providing a magnificent route for supply that the enemy might try to interrupt but which, with no fleet, they could hardly accomplish. Then too, with McClernand on his way to take command of a corps leading the attack on Vicksburg, Grant saw the advantage in himself being present and taking immediate command of the whole operation down the river. All these things decided his mind within twenty-four hours of the Holly Springs disaster. On December 21 he wrote Halleck that he intended to go to Memphis himself, and from there take two divisions to join Sherman, who was already on his way to Vicksburg.[8]

In the next three weeks, however, events moved beyond Grant's control, and largely outside his knowledge, for the Confederate raids isolated him not only from supplies, but also from information. As a result, the last news he had was that Sherman was leaving Memphis and McClernand, presumably, was on his way to join the expedition. In fact, however, Sherman departed on December 20 before McClernand arrived in Memphis. Admiral David Dixon Porter gathered a large fleet of steam transports and ironclads to take the army down the river. "The preparations were necessarily hasty in the extreme," said Sherman, "but this was the essence of the whole plan." He must reach Vicksburg while Grant still had Pemberton's main body tied down near Grenada. Five days of steaming brought the expedition to Milliken's Bend on Christmas, with less than ten miles to cross to Vicksburg. The next day Sherman pressed on to the mouth of the Yazoo River, which empties into the Mississippi just a few miles above Vicksburg. The Federals went up the Yazoo about thirteen miles to the vicinity of Chickasaw Bayou and there found a road that led directly to Vicksburg. It took Sherman two days to move his divisions through the dense bayous and forests that led toward the city, and precious little ground was covered. He encountered some light resistance from skirmishing Confederates, but nowhere did they make a concerted stand. An advance of about four miles finally brought the Federals to Chickasaw Bluffs, and there Sherman learned why the resistance had been so light. When he looked at the enemy position atop the bluffs, he found it to be "strong by nature and by art, and seemingly well defended." His estimate of the numbers facing him was 15,000, less than his own command of 25,000. In fact, Pemberton had barely 11,000 in the line on the bluffs, but they were more than enough. Just a week before, he had barely 6,000, but Van Dorn's bold stroke, in forcing Grant to withdraw north, allowed Pemberton rapidly to concentrate at Vicksburg the majority of his army from Grenada. It all happened in time to hand "Billy" Sherman an upsetting defeat. When his divisions attacked on December 29, the Confederates repulsed them everywhere along the line, and with ease. "We had accomplished nothing," lamented Sherman, and an attempt two nights later to renew the attack by moving up the Yazoo to Haynes' Bluff fared no better. "I became convinced that the part of wisdom was to withdraw," said Sherman sadly, and so he did. He took his command back to Milliken's Bend, and there on January 2, 1863, McClernand finally arrived to assume overall command.[9]

When he met with McClernand, Sherman told of his failure, but read into it a harbinger of success. Pemberton had faced him with much greater numbers than were supposed to be near Vicksburg. Of course, nothing had been heard from the isolated Grant for almost two weeks, but the fact that Pemberton had such a force at Vicksburg must surely mean that Grant had forced him to retreat to the city, and must therefore be nearby. McClernand quickly disabused the general of his misconception, and told the full story of Holly Springs. Two days later, January 4, McClernand formally relieved Sherman, who would now command one of two corps of the expeditionary force. Very quickly Sherman discovered that McClernand had very little idea of what he would do with his new command. He spoke only in general terms of "cutting his way to the sea," and the like, but his subordinate could not wring from him a real plan of action.

Finally Sherman suggested one of his own. Eighty miles above Vicksburg, the Arkansas River emptied into the Mississippi, and thirty miles up the Arkansas sat Confederate fortifications at Arkansas Post. Thanks to the enemy's lodgment there, Federal shipping passing the mouth of the river was subject to frequent attack, and as a result many Union warships that would be needed for the assault on Vicksburg were diverted to do convoy duty. Sherman called on McClernand on his headquarters boat, the *Tigress*—it had been Grant's after Shiloh—and suggested that they not stand idle but reduce and capture Arkansas Post. McClernand did not care for the idea, but he and his subordinate made a midnight call on Porter on his flagship, *Black Hawk*. In his nightclothes, the admiral listened, scarcely concealing his animosity toward McClernand. Indeed, during the meeting Sherman took him aside and asked what was bothering him. Porter confessed candidly that he "did not like" McClernand and had disliked him ever since the two were introduced by Lincoln more than a year before. Of course, Porter may have feared that McClernand might eclipse his own rising popularity, for the ambitious admiral had intrigued even against his own stepbrother, Farragut, to promote his career. No matter now, Porter would cooperate, himself commanding the naval part of the expedition. Then, as both Sherman and Porter feared, McClernand announced that he would command the expedition personally.

It was entirely successful, despite a genuinely bitter fight, and on January 11 Arkansas Post fell to the Federals. Sherman and Porter had almost exclusively directed the fight, but McClernand immediately began a campaign to usurp the credit to himself. "Glorious! glorious! my star is ever in the ascendant!" he exulted to Sherman. "I'll make a splendid report." Then he began what would be a campaign to minimize the role played by the navy. Obviously, Porter's curt attitude had not gone unnoticed. Just as clearly, McClernand's ambition, fueled by a demonstrated inability as a general, bid fair not only to jeopardize the harmonious workings of the combined Western forces, but also to threaten even Grant in time.[10]

Grant, indeed, heartily disapproved of the whole Arkansas Post expedition when finally restored communications told him what was happening. He thought it a diversion of his troops for no really useful purpose. Yet once he learned the full extent of the campaign's success, Grant relented and eventually came to regard it as a positive step. That change in attitude may also owe something to a first impression that McClernand hatched the idea, and then the later discovery that it came from Grant's favorite, Sherman. Grant could play favorites, and did. Men once trusted who did not let him down would be trusted again and again. Those who failed him once, or criticized, or intrigued against him personally, were not forgiven. It was part of the difference between being a great general, which Grant surely was, and being a great man. Lincoln was that. So was Lee. Grant would not always stand the measure.

But even if he did approve the capture of Arkansas Post, Grant could not overlook McClernand. He ordered the general and his troops back to Milliken's Bend, but well before then he knew that McClernand could not stay in command. Immediately after the Arkansas fight Porter sent Grant a message stating that he "anticipated no good results from McClernand's commanding the army." "I was certain McClernand and myself could never co-operate harmoniously." Grant visited with McClernand, Porter, and Sherman personally on January 17, and during their discussions on the next moves against Vicksburg, the latter two made quite evident to their commander that "both the army and navy were so distrustful of McClernand's fitness to command that, while they would do all they could to ensure success, this distrust was an element of weakness." Three days later Grant informed Halleck of the interview, revealing that he had already decided to assume command of the expedition against the Rebel citadel in person. He had finally received authority from Washington to relieve McClernand if he wished, and now he would. "I felt great embarrassment about McClernand," he said later. His preference would have been to put Sherman in command, but Sherman was junior to McClernand in seniority of rank. Indeed, McClernand stood senior to every general in the department except Grant himself. Thus the only way to avoid an embarrassing scene in relieving the politico was for Grant himself to assume command. Grant joined the army on January 29, and the next day assumed the direction of the campaign. "General McClernand took exception in a most characteristic way—for him," said Grant. The ousted general, now reverting simply to command of the XIII Corps, protested in letters to his commander that were almost insubordinate, more reprimands than complaints. When McClernand asserted that he had held his command by order of the President, Grant finally told him that he had relieved him by order of the President, adding with unfeigned satisfaction that "I regard the President as the Commander-in-Chief of the Army and will obey every order of his." McClernand's complaints would not stop with Grant, as he loudly voiced his hurt to the War Department and to Lincoln. Later a member of his staff would start anew the old rumors of Grant's drinking, if not at McClernand's urging, then certainly in the knowledge that it would not displease him. Yet Grant won out for the time, and now there was another campaign to plan.[11]

The challenge, as the general saw it, was to establish a base on good, dry ground, not the swampy bayous that slowed Sherman, somewhere on the Vicksburg side of the river. From such a place he could move against Pemberton. The only alternative would be to take the whole army back to Memphis, refit and marshal as much strength and supply as possible, and commence once more on the Mississippi Central line. But this was just days after Fredericksburg. The North was much discouraged. A move back to Memphis, even as prelude to an advance, would be interpreted as yet another retreat. As he said later, Grant decided then that "There was nothing left to be done but to *go forward to a decisive victory.*" From the date of his January 17 meeting, he began working on the way to accomplish that decisive victory.

It would not come quickly, or easily. The winter rains in 1862–63 kept the Mississippi and tributaries unusually high. As a result, the kind of high dry ground needed for Grant's move on Vicksburg proved indeed hard to find, and when he could find dry land, it frequently came in the form of thin strips miles long, sometimes right atop the levees built to hold back the waters. James Birdseye McPherson's XVII Corps could find no dry ground closer to Vicksburg than Lake Providence, seventy miles distant. The situation simply did not allow the kind of movement that he wanted to make, and yet there was increasing pressure from the North for him to do something. "There seemed no possibility of a land movement before the end of March or later, and it would not do to lie idle all this time." He lamented at times the failure of the Union to seemingly control the pressure of the press as well as did the Confederates. That pressure forced him into taking steps in which he felt little genuine confidence but, as he said, it would not do to sit idle. He commenced "a series of experiments to consume time, and to divert the attention of the enemy, of my troops and of the public generally."[12]

Several months before, during the first unsuccessful attempt to take Vicksburg, General Thomas Williams had set his small command to digging a canal or ditch. Vicksburg sat on the point of a sharp bend in the Mississippi. Williams had intended to cut a canal connecting the two sides of the bend about four miles west of the city. So doing would bypass the bend, and Vicksburg, entirely, allowing Federal troops to be moved above or below the city at will. Williams did not succeed, however. He thought that simply making a small cut across the mile-wide point of land would allow the river erosion to do the rest, but the stream refused to change its flow.

On the same day that he reported the lack of confidence in McClernand, Grant informed Halleck that he would try Williams' scheme again, but this time with more gusto. The general put 4,000 men to work on the job, augmenting their numbers at times with several hundred contrabands, runaway slaves that flocked to his lines for safety and freedom. The fact that Lincoln himself, a man much acquainted with this river, had confidence in the plan, surely spurred on Grant's efforts, though he never expected much from it in his own mind. Later in February Grant added two dredge boats to the work force, and by March 4, despite the unfavorable weather, he believed that the canal would be navigable within a very few days. "Or at least I hope so." Three days later, thanks to rains and high water, the dam at the upper end of the ditch gave way, ruining the work of weeks before and setting the whole operation back. "Even if the canal had proven a success," said Grant, "it could not have been of much advantage to us." It ran perpendicular to the line of gun-studded bluffs at Vicksburg, and within long-range fire. Indeed, when Pemberton discovered what the Federals were about, he had a battery planted solely to torment the dredge boats, finally driving them out. But at least, failure though it was, the digging kept the men at work and the Northern press satisfied that something was being done.[13]

Indeed, much more was being done. While the men and freed slaves sweated over their toil in the great ditch, their general looked for other ways to get his army onto high dry land behind Vicksburg. On January 30 he learned of perhaps the most novel and imaginative route of all, and one of the least practical. He had stationed Major General James B. McPherson and his XVII Corps at Lake Providence, Louisiana, seventy miles upriver from Vicksburg. The lake was itself the remnant of an old bend in the river left isolated by a change of bed in the Mississippi many years before. From it flowed Bayou Macon. That, in turn, flowed into the Tensas River, and it then emptied into the Washita River. The Washita terminated in the Red River, and that flowed southeast another twenty miles to empty into the Mississippi between Port Hudson and Natchez. In effect, this provided a route parallel to the Mississippi and west of it, by which Grant could move gunboats south without passing Vicksburg's batteries. All the bayous and rivers were more than deep enough for traffic, excepting Macon, which was narrow and filled with fallen timber, and Bayou Baxter, which had considerable trees growing in what would have to be the main channel. Those would have to be cut off underwater near the bottom, no easy task.

All that was necessary to set this scheme in motion was for a canal to be cut from Lake Providence to the Mississippi, to allow Porter's ships into the lake to start the long descent. He gave the order to McClernand for one of his brigades to do the work, and it went rapidly. On February 5 Grant himself went to the lake to see how it was progressing. The water in Providence sat some eight feet below the level of the river, and certainly when the channel was opened, the influx of water would swell both the lake and the bayous leading out of it quite enough for Porter's craft.

That same day, anticipating a speedy movement, he ordered McPherson to bring one of his divisions to him, to join the troops already there. "This bids fair to be the most practicable route for turning Vicksburg," Grant advised his trusted lieutenant. Yet soon that, too, came to nothing. The work was not done quickly enough, or so Grant thought, and the trees and debris in the bayous proved much more difficult to remove than imagined. The continued high water everywhere made it difficult to get the working parties and dredge boats to the work site. By the first week of March, Grant's optimism faded rapidly. He reported to Halleck that now there "is but little possibility" of accomplishing his hopes. Even though the canal into the lake was not yet opened, a small steamer had been dragged overland, and aboard it Grant and McPherson surveyed the work left before them. "I saw then that there was scarcely a chance of this ever becoming a practicable route for moving troops through an enemy's country." Even if Porter's transports could make the passage, they would be subject to Confederate sniping all along the way. Nevertheless, "I let the work go on, believing employment was better than idleness for the men." Some time later, when finally the Lake Providence canal was opened, it proved a failure.[14]

Even while working on the Lake Providence route to outflank Vicksburg, Grant put more of his men to work on yet another water highway, this time on the east side of the Mississippi. High above Vicksburg, 160 miles upriver, sat Helena, Arkansas. Just across from it, on the Mississippi side, flowed what had long been called the Yazoo Pass. Many years before, steamboats trading with the rich cotton plantations in the interior of the state had steamed into the pass, then into Mook Lake a mile from the river. From there they could pass on into the Coldwater River and follow its flow south into the Tallahatchie. Fifty miles farther south the Tallahatchie helped form the Yazoo. By taking this route, Grant would be able to place his troops ashore above or behind Vicksburg, as Sherman had tried to do at Chickasaw Bluffs, but with a much greater prospect of success. All that was necessary to get started was to cut through a levee built across the mouth of Yazoo Pass some years before. On February 2 they made the cut. The river was eight feet higher than the water in the pass, and as soon as the cut was opened, the rush of water quickly washed away all trace of the levee. That same day two small steamers passed into the pass, turned around, and came out again, demonstrating its navigability. However, with a continuing influx of water as the pass and the lake and tributaries continued to rise, Grant's people determined that it would not be safe to move forward for another four or five days. Indeed, the river soon overflowed miles of the countryside around before the rising water reached its own level.

On February 7 Lieutenant Colonel James Harrison Wilson of Grant's staff reconnoitered aboard a small gunboat, and found that he could get into the Coldwater all right. However, he soon learned from local people that the Confederates had suspected Grant's intentions when they saw the water rising, and even then were busy at the work of felling trees into the Coldwater and Tallahatchie at five-mile intervals. Their removal would not be a simple exercise, and many had been cut just below the waterline, leaving submerged stumps that could rip out the bottom of a steamboat. Still, by February 24 Grant was ready to order Brigadier Leonard Ross to take his 4,500-man brigade aboard transports and begin the trip through the Yazoo Pass. It took the expedition two weeks to clear its way through the obstructions and narrow channels to the point where the Tallahatchie joined with another stream to create the Yazoo. And there they found a low-lying island on which the Confederates had built an earthwork called Fort Pemberton. The ground in the vicinity was such that Ross's troops could in no way take part in an assault on the fort. The best they could do was to establish a battery to shell it, while the two gunboats accompanying the expedition, the *Chillicothe* and the *Baron De Kalb*, used their heavy guns to attack the work. In two attacks, the Federals failed, the *Chillicothe* was temporarily disabled, and the soldiers were not able to support with an assault. Ross did not renew his movement, and now once more the engineers resorted to the spade. Seeing that Fort Pemberton barely sat above the water, the Federals tried another cut in the Mississippi levee in the hope that the additional water would raise the Tallahatchie another two feet. That would submerge the Confederate works, but the attempt failed, and Ross and his small expeditionary force began to withdraw. On their way back they met with Brigadier General Isaac Ferdinand Quinby, whom Grant had sent with another brigade and orders to assume command of the movement. Quinby himself returned to reconnoiter Fort Pemberton, saw that it could not be taken and that the water had failed to rise, and decided to return to the Mississippi and abandon the enterprise.[15]

No fewer than three attempts to get around behind Vicksburg had come to failure, all in the month of March 1863. Yet Grant could not quit. Indeed, in the absence of certain knowledge of what Ross and Quinby were doing, he felt some unease over their isolated position. He wanted to make certain that they could be reinforced speedily, and the best way seemed to be to have troops ready to meet them below Fort Pemberton. Here, then, would come his fourth and last effort. On March 14 he sent Porter to explore the possibility of getting ships from the Mississippi into the lower Yazoo without having to pass the Confederate batteries planted on Haynes' Bluff. Here, happily, the heavy winter rains served to their advantage. Three separate streams flowed south into the Yazoo near and above Haynes' Bluff. Steele's Bayou emptied into the river immediately below the bluff, while just above it came Deer Creek. Farther along, the Sunflower River passed into the Yazoo, and some distance up the Sunflower a tributary called Rolling Fork connected it with the upper reaches of Deer Creek. Somehow, these streams and the generally flooded landscape might offer what Grant and Porter needed.

In some places the water level had risen seventeen feet. "Great forests had become channels admitting the passage of large steamers between the trees," Porter discovered, "and now and then wide lanes were met with where a frigate might have passed." After sending a little tugboat to scout a possible route, Porter himself, joined by Grant, set out to see for himself. With a leadsman on the bow bawling out the depth as they went, the Federals slowly moved up the Yazoo toward Steele's Bayou. Shortly before coming to Haynes' Bluff they found an opening in the woods on their left almost concealed from view. Yet as they steamed slowly into it they found fifteen feet of good water beneath them. For five miles beyond they traveled, floating above what Porter took to be an old road. Then they found that they could pass through the forest, the opening being wide enough for one of the ironclad gunboats to fit through. The forest finally led them to Deer Creek, and that is as far as they went. They knew that they could proceed from that point without difficulty, and stopped for fear of alerting the enemy of their intentions. Now Grant had another campaign to set in motion.[16]

On March 16 Grant began issuing his orders. He had scanty reports now that Ross had engaged at Fort Pemberton, but knew nothing of the outcome. He must get soldiers onto the upper Yazoo quickly if they were to support Ross and Quinby. To Sherman he sent instructions to send engineers and workmen to start at once the work of clearing a secure path through to Deer Creek. Sherman moved at once, as Grant knew he would. In that subordinate, the commander believed that "I have a host," a man "worth more than a full Brigade."

Porter did not find his way entirely unimpeded. He went in with five of the large old "Pook Turtle" gunboats, *Louisville, Cincinnati, Carondelet, Mound City,* and *Pittsburgh.* These vessels had little difficulty, but the troop transports that were to follow had such high smokestacks that they repeatedly fouled and tangled in the forest branches overhead. Porter was somewhat taken by the oddity of the situation. "It was a curious sight to see a line of ironclads and mortar-boats, tugs and transports, pushing their way through the long, wide lane in the woods without touching on either side," he wrote. "It all looked as though the world had suddenly got topsy-turvy, or that there was a great camp meeting in the woods on board ironclads and transports." The rising waters had driven thousands of animals into the trees, and frequently now the sailors aboard a chugging ironclad would find coons and squirrels bounding across their decks.

Pressing on, Porter began to experiment with using the mighty ironclads to ram and pull out trees that stood in the way of his passage. For the most part, their roots loosened by the water, the timbers gave way, and by the time that Sherman finally reached Porter, the fleet had come just to the point of crossing into Deer Creek. The two commanders went on up the creek for a few miles, Porter confidently believing that he had passed the worst of it, with nothing ahead but smooth steaming. Sherman went back to oversee the clearing of a path for the transports to follow, thinking that no problems lay before them. Then on March 19, while his men were working, he began to hear the muffled boom of naval cannon off to the north. Clearly Porter was engaging someone, and a considerable fight it seemed to be. That night a Negro came into his camp and handed him a piece of tobacco. Inside the plug, written on fragile tissue, was a message from Porter, in a distinctly unmilitary cast. "Dear Sherman: Hurry up, for Heaven's sake. I never knew how helpless an ironclad could be steaming around through the woods without an army to back her."

Porter had really hit a snag. Just at the point of entering the Rolling Fork to cross into the Sunflower River, Confederates had placed several cannon and a number of riflemen. They felled trees to halt Porter's further progress, and then almost without warning opened fire. At once the admiral had a real problem. The banks were so close and so high that his big broadside guns on the ironclads could not be elevated to fire over them at the Confederates. Only the relatively small deck guns could do that, but the rifle fire from the shore rapidly picked off the crews, who had to stand fully exposed in order to work the cannon. Finally he managed to put his mortars into the fight, and then ably lobbed shells amid the Confederate guns and silenced them. During the brief but welcome reprieve Porter found the black man, named "Tub," and sent him with the message to Sherman. The man charged a half dollar for his service, but bravely corrected the admiral when Porter called him "Sambo."[17]

Then the enemy fire commenced anew, and a further threat appeared. Logs began flowing out of the Rolling Fork into the Deer Creek channel, jumbling together effectively into a barricade. Ironically, the same high water from the Yazoo Pass cut that enabled Ross and Quinby to make their advance, now worked against Porter by bringing down with it tons of flotsam. And then word came from his rear that the Confederates had gotten behind him and were felling trees into the creek. Obviously the enemy intended to bottle the ironclads in Deer Creek and force their surrender or destruction. Then the firing started to build. The ironclads, trapped in a channel too narrow for them to turn around, were sitting targets. "The Confederates had completely checkmated us," Porter said later. After some time he still managed to drive off the enemy artillery, and then began the laborious process of getting out of the trap. A tug took a line from the *Cincinnati*, while the ironclad in the gunboat's rear took another line, and so on back through the fleet. After an hour they managed to pull the *Cincinnati* free from a tangle of willows holding it, and then the fleet shipped their rudders and drifted with the current downstream. The Confederates pursued, opening fire frequently until darkness fell, when Porter tied up his fleet to the bank, loaded the deck guns with grapeshot, and spread grease over the sides of the ironclads to deflect shot. He was still in a desperate fix, and he knew it. Already a determination took hold in his mind. He would not surrender. If he could not fight his way out, or if Sherman did not arrive in time, he would blow up every ship.[18]

Sherman hurried as best he could to relieve the navy. As soon as he read the message in the tobacco, he sent 800 men on their way by land. That left the general almost alone, and he then put himself into a canoe and paddled down the stream to the nearest gunboat, the *General Price*. Ironically, this was a vessel captured from the enemy the year before, but from it Sherman now organized a hasty relief expedition. He put some working parties into an empty coal barge, commandeered a tugboat nearby, and with it towed the barge back toward the fight. It was well after dark, but that did not stop them. "Crashing through the trees, carrying away pilot-house, smoke-stacks, and every thing above-deck," Sherman and the little tug plowed on into the darkness. Finally the night stopped them, and they disembarked and marched on by foot, carrying burning candles in their hands to light the way. The next day, all still afoot including "Uncle Billy," they forged ahead, barely stopping to rest, all the while the sound of Porter's guns in the distance urging them onward. The men in the ranks were much impressed to find that their general could set a pace that took them over twenty miles that day, much of it in fact wading through waist-deep water. Finally they came up on the rear of the Confederates who were felling trees to prevent the ironclads' escape, and easily drove them away. It was with considerable relief that Sherman a few minutes later looked up the creek and saw the gunboats blazing away at the enemy on the banks. Almost instantly with Sherman's appearance, the Confederates melted away into the canebrakes and cotton fields, and the fleet was saved. An officer found a horse for the general, who mounted it bareback and rode along the bank to see Porter, all to the cheers of the sailors. Sherman found Porter standing on the deck of the *Cincinnati*, protecting himself behind a makeshift shield of iron taken from a section of ruined smokestack. "Halloo, Porter, what did you get into such an ugly scrape for?" the admiral remembered Sherman shouting. "So much for you navy fellows getting out of your element; better send for the soldiers always." Porter complained that "This is the most infernal expedition I was ever on; who in thunder proposed such a mad scheme?" He had helped propose it himself! Obviously the enemy was now well alerted to their intentions in this direction, and there was nothing left to do but retire back to the mouth of the Yazoo, yet even that took another three days, and rarely did those Western sailors feel again such relief as when their flat-bottomed ships glided once more into the open water of the Mississippi. They had had more than enough of forest sailing.[19]

And U. S. Grant had yet another failed attempt to get behind Vicksburg. Even though he admitted not expecting much from any of his four attempts, still the frustration of none of them succeeding, and all in fact failing within a week, clearly disturbed him. "I am very well but much perplexed," he wrote to Julia the same day that Porter's fleet returned from the disastrous expedition. "Heretofore I have had nothing to do but fight the enemy. This time I have to overcome obstacles to reach him. Foot once upon dry land on the other side of the river [and] I think the balance would be of but short duration." Now he must find another way. Though he felt well, indeed better than he had in a long time, still the frustration fatigued him greatly. "It would be a great holiday for me to have one month to myself," he confessed. Being a great general was not all glory. And particularly not when the prize of all his longing, the fortress city of Vicksburg, still sat insolently on its bluff challenging him to come and take it. Five times now, since the days of Holly Springs, it had eluded his grasp. But never, never did the man contemplate defeat. Often as not in this—and any—war, the general who lost was the general who quit. Grant had quit too many times in his life before this war. It was his vocation now, he did it well, and he knew it. He could never quit, and that meant, as he confidently believed, that he could never fail.[20]

CHAPTER 10

"SETTLE THE FATE OF VICKSBURG"

Not far from where Grant kept his headquarters, within the sound of a cannon's thunder, sat a city, a people, an army, and a general, all of whom waited with an uncommon resolution the coming of the enemy horde. Vicksburg was a typical river city and had been for some years since its founding by the Reverend Newitt Vick. Its chief market was river trade and cotton shipment, its population rather prosperous merchants and tradesmen, almost all of them in some way deriving their livelihoods from the Mississippi. Immediately at the war's outset, the Confederacy saw that this city, sitting as it did on the point of that bend, controlled a vital spot on the river. Traffic was its most vulnerable when slowing to round such a bend, and from the high bluffs all along the Mississippi side of the stream, both above and below Vicksburg, the city could virtually dictate who should or should not pass up or down the river. Its fortification began early, and continued during the summer of 1862 when Van Dorn was first sent there. A powerful ironclad, the C.S.S. *Arkansas*, had been built up the Yazoo to protect the city, and did good service before its destruction at Baton Rouge in August. Yet so long as the Federals failed to advance beyond Baton Rouge from the south, or Helena from the north, the real work of fortifying the city waited until

14. *Above, Major General Joseph "Fighting Joe" Hooker. His bluster and brag got him Burnside's command, but he lost his nerve in his one battle. (Library of Congress)* 15. *Left, it was men like Lieutenant General Thomas Jonathan "Stonewall" Jackson that put the scare into Hooker. But Jackson, alas, fought his last battle at Chancellorsville, Virginia. (Library of Congress)*

16. A postwar view of Wilderness Church, at left, and the Melzie Chancellor house, and the fields around Chancellorsville, Virginia. (Chicago Historical Society)

17. Major General George Gordon Meade, the first Yankee to inflict a real defeat in the field on Lee, did so at Gettysburg, Pennsylvania, in July 1863. Here, behind Cemetery Hill, Meade made his headquarters. Dead horses and the debris of battle are scattered over the ground. (Library of Congress)

18. *Defeat in the field severely strained the already crippled Southern industry. Men like Brigadier General Joseph Reid Anderson of the Tredegar Iron Works bent every effort to keep producing the weapons of war so desperately needed.* (Courtesy of William A. Albaugh)

19. *In the Confederate War Department capable bureau chiefs like Colonel Josiah Gorgas managed virtual miracles of manufacturing and supply with dwindling resources.* (Library of Congress)

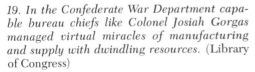

20. *All across the South the ravages of war laid waste its industry, and its railroads.* (Library of Congress)

21. *Major General William Tecumseh Sherman knew about waste, and deplored it. As Grant slowly closed his grip on Vicksburg, Mississippi, Sherman sustained a terrible waste of life as he tried to find a door into the enemy citadel.* (The New-York Historical Society)

22. *Almost a complete waste was Major General John Alexander McClernand. He politicked himself into and out of an important command on the Mississippi. No one grieved to see him leave the army.* (National Archives)

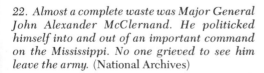

23. *Major General Earl Van Dorn would have done better to spend more time at defending the Mississippi and less at romancing other men's wives. In the end, he died in a battle of the sexes.* (Valentine Museum, Richmond)

24. *In this 1864 view of Vicksburg, the Confederate citadel on the Mississippi, the city is seen behind the Yankee gunboat* Vindicator. (U.S. Army Military History Institute)

25. *The bivouac of the 45th Illinois at the Shirley House during the siege of Vicksburg, Mississippi, 1863. People on both sides went underground for safety.* (U.S. Army Military History Institute)

26. *Standing at center on the U.S.S.* Malvern *is Admiral David Dixon Porter, the egotistical and scheming navy commander who played an important role in Grant's success on the Mississippi.* (Library of Congress)

27. *To relieve the hardships of soldiers and civilians, philanthropy flourished in the war. Nurses and officials of the United States Sanitary Commission traveled with the armies.* (Library of Congress)

28. *Women entered the society in new ways, chiefly as nurses, led by able organizers like Clarissa Harlowe (better known as Clara) Barton.* (American Red Cross)

29. *Unable to meet its needs from within, the Confederacy came increasingly to depend upon blockade-runners fitted out abroad. Here at right is the runner* Giraffe *at Glasgow, Scotland, in 1862, preparing to run into the Confederacy.* (Naval Photographic Center)

30. A greater diplomatic issue than the blockade-runners were the fearful rams—like H.M.S. Wivern—being built in Great Britain for the South. Some thought that England and the Union nearly came to war over ships like this one. England impounded them eventually, and put them in her own service. (U.S. Naval Historical Center)

31. *Major General Theophilus Hunter Holmes,
the tired and infirm commander of the Confederate trans-Mississippi department, yielded
gracefully to . . .* (The Museum of the Confederacy, Richmond)

32. *Lieutenant General Edmund Kirby-Smith.
In time, cut off from the rest of the Confederacy,
his department came to be called "Kirby-
Smithdom," a kingdom in itself.* (The Kean
Archives, Philadelphia)

33. *President Jefferson Davis found himself fighting two wars by 1862, one with the Union, and one with the dissidents in his own country.* (The National Archives) 34. *To be sure, Davis had his supporters, men like the very competent Postmaster General, John Henninger Reagan of Texas.* (Civil War Times Illustrated Collection)

35. *Yet Union loyalists virtually controlled some portions of the Confederacy. "Parson" William Gannaway Brownlow dominated the press in east Tennessee with his Knoxville Whig until the Confederate authorities suppressed the journal.* (The Kean Archives, Philadelphia)

36. *Left, leader of the opponents of Davis within the Confederacy was his own diminutive Vice-President, Alexander Hamilton Stephens.* (Civil War Times Illustrated Collection) 37. *Bottom left, Robert Augustus Toombs of Georgia, once Davis' Secretary of State and an aspirant for the Confederate Presidency, uttered attacks on the administration that approached treason.* (Library of Congress) 38. *Bottom right, Louis Trezevant Wigfall of Texas began as a supporter of Davis, but quickly became an ardent enemy over personal matters. He, like so many others, simply could not compromise.* (The National Archives)

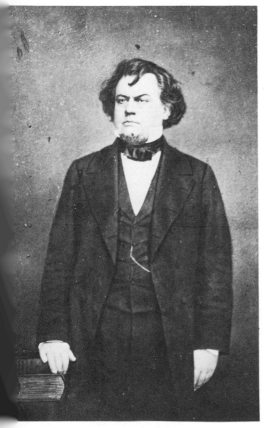

39. *Lee & Gordon's Mills on Chickamauga Creek, northwest Georgia, where Bragg won the greatest Confederate victory.* (The National Archives)

40. *Major General William Starke Rosecrans fled with his panicked army after the Confederates defeated him at Chickamauga. His action humiliated the North, and virtually ended his career.* (Library of Congress)

the press of emergency. Its new commander, John C. Pemberton, simply had too little in men and material to both slow Grant's advance from Grand Junction and build earthworks.

But once Grant's overland move had been checked by the Holly Springs coup, the Confederates began to gather more of the men needed, while the failure of repeated waterborne attempts by the Federals gave Pemberton time. Immediately upon taking his command, Pemberton had surveyed his department and begun artillery emplacements when he could. There was much confusion, for Van Dorn, though a dashing fellow, was no administrator, preferring more the gay life. Indeed, in May 1863 an irate husband would murder Van Dorn for violating "the sanctity" of his home and his wife. Not so Pemberton. He had a city, 5,000 people, and, he felt, the future of the Confederacy to protect. He speedily reorganized the administrative offices of his army, husbanded supplies, relocated scattered outposts, and all the while strove to baffle Grant's repeated attempts on his prize. In this, thanks in large measure to the weather, Pemberton had succeeded. By the end of March 1863 the Federals were no closer to taking the city than they had been a year before.

Yet Grant had already begun to give Pemberton a serious problem. All told, the Confederates had perhaps 32,000 men in their ranks, most of them stationed in Jackson and Vicksburg, with another 6,000 downriver at Port Hudson. Supplying them, even with the efficiencies achieved by the new general, presented a considerable challenge. He could only draw succor from the interior of Mississippi itself, along the railroad through Jackson, from the Yazoo River, or from across the great river in Louisiana. But Grant's advance to the mouth of the Yazoo cut off that route for the most part, as well as making supply from across the Mississippi difficult, and the railroad was unreliable at any time. By March Pemberton had to look to hauling his supplies overland in wagons, and there the soggy roads conspired against him. Still, despite his handicaps, Pemberton managed to keep his army fed, and even to stockpile some supplies. As the spring of 1863 came to being, he could count perhaps four weeks' provisions in his commissary storehouses, more if he played the miser.[1]

Nor was Pemberton the only Confederate commander with a river bastion to guard. Back in August 1862, after his failure to capture Baton Rouge, John C. Breckinridge spied the natural strength of the high bluffs on the river at Port Hudson, Louisiana, and began fortifying the place. He was ordered toward Kentucky before the work could be completed, but others followed him, and as early as the end of that month batteries placed on the bluffs began to stop Federal traffic that tried to pass up the river. By October there were fourteen heavy guns in place, and more coming in the months to follow. It proved a miserable place, uncomfortable, wet and humid, with yellow fever a common companion in camp in the warm months. The monotony was broken only by the occasional enemy sortie up the river, which was always turned back.

But then in December, just as Grant started to move south, a new Federal commander began to move north. Benjamin F. Butler had been replaced in command at New Orleans by an equally inexperienced political general, Nathaniel Prentiss Banks, a Massachusetts-born congressman and former governor, with no military experience or ability whatsoever. Jackson had humiliated him in the Shenandoah in 1862, and later that year at Cedar Mountain, yet Lincoln sufficiently valued the usefulness of Banks's prestige in raising recruits that he kept him in important commands. Banks immediately reoccupied Baton Rouge, and with his command of 11,000 could probably have pressed on and overwhelmed the garrison at Port Hudson. He did not, even when ordered to make a demonstration against the bastion in order to relieve some of the pressure facing Grant as he advanced on Vicksburg. Port Hudson was the vulnerable left flank of Pemberton's Mississippi River position, but not until March did Banks begin to make tentative moves against the place. That left Grant on his own.[2]

Within days after the failure of the Steele's Bayou expedition, Grant had another campaign under way. There indeed lay part of his strength as a commander. He was incredibly flexible. Whereas the generals who had commanded and failed in the East went into campaign with a single plan, and turned back when that plan went wrong, Grant saw in a single military situation a variety of options. Indeed, the plan he now set in motion had been in his mind even while he was still testing the other now-defunct movements. The only option that he did not consider was retreat.

By now no one argued the feasibility of moving against Vicksburg by the Yazoo, or by trying to divert the Mississippi to their use. Sherman was all for going back to Grand Junction and recommencing the movement that had been under way the previous December. There, he thought, lay their best avenue of approach. Grant, however, in that peculiar streak of stubbornness, would not retrace his steps. It was a trait he had since youth. If lost on a road, he would not backtrack, but instead continue forging ahead until he found his way out. So would he now. To go back would enrage the North, embarrass the administration, and perhaps result in his removal. McClernand was blatantly politicking against him again, and there must be no reasons volunteered for Washington to remove Grant from his command. To Julia he continued to express his confidence that he would find the right way. "It is hard to tell when the final strike will be made at Vicksburg. I am doing all I can and expect to be successful."[3]

On April 4 he divulged to Halleck his new plan. Running south from Milliken's Bend, on the west side of the river, there sat a series of bayous, most of them navigable to barges and small steamers. Roundaway Bayou led into Bayou Vidal and that to Lake St. Joseph. From the latter a very short overland march would put troops on the Mississippi shore opposite Grand Gulf about fifteen miles south of Vicksburg. His dredges could cut for him a canal from Milliken's Bend into the bayous, and his light-draft vessels could then pass safely via a circuitous route to any of several points below Vicksburg. There they could load soldiers aboard and ferry them across the Mississippi to the east side. For the soldiers themselves, Grant believed he had found a good wagon road that ran along the bayous, one that could support both wagons and artillery. All that was needed was a little dry weather to let the water level recede. Indeed, Grant had suggested somewhat this same route to Halleck two months before, but the rains came, and the opportunity went. Now the chance was coming again. It also required Porter and his fleet, and for them a dangerous part indeed. The coal barges and other craft that would ferry the troops across would need to be towed and would need the cover of heavy gunboats. Ships big enough for this work could not pass by the bayou route. Porter would then have to run his ships past almost fourteen miles of enemy batteries lining the east bank in order to get below Vicksburg. He had done the same the year before when Grant first moved against Vicksburg. Certainly he could do it again, and Porter never for a moment hesitated to promise his full cooperation. Grant had no authority over the navy here at all, and yet he and Porter seemed never to quibble or disagree, and almost always the sailor had the wisdom to defer to the general. The admiral, like Sherman, preferred the Grand Junction route, but having once voiced his thought, he thereafter entered wholeheartedly into the new plan. So did McClernand. Indeed, Sherman believed, as did others, that the politico was scheming more than ever to get Grant's command, yet without any plan of his own. He set afoot a plot to flush out McClernand's lack of a strategic concept, but Grant refused to play the game. He knew, perhaps, that McClernand would hang himself on his own sooner or later.[4]

Finally the waters went down and the grand expedition could begin. On April 16 Grant and Porter were ready. The admiral got steam up in his fleet late in the evening, noting with amusement that the men aboard the gunboats were delighted to be getting away from the infernal Yazoo River, even if they did have to run a gauntlet of enemy batteries. Pets like dogs and crowing hens and roosters were left behind, to prevent their sounding off at the wrong moment. The night was dark enough that Porter hoped much of the fleet could get past at least some of the batteries before their presence was discovered. The sailors piled cotton bales on the sides of the transports so vital to Grant's plan, expecting that the fiber would absorb cannon shot that might otherwise hole their bottoms. Porter carried his flag aboard the *Benton*, the mightiest ironclad on the river. Behind him at few-minute intervals, followed the ironclad *Lafayette*, the *General Price*, the *Louisville*, *Mound City*, *Pittsburgh*, and *Carondelet*. Then came the transports towing coal barges filled with fuel. Porter looked back in the darkness when the *Benton* began her passage. "As I looked back at the long line I could compare them only to so many phantom vessels."

As the *Benton* approached the first bend in the river crowned by Rebel batteries, Porter felt confident that they would pass unnoticed. "The rebels seem to keep a very poor watch," he told the ship's captain. Just then a blazing light appeared along the shore, illuminating the batteries, the city beyond, and the Yankee fleet. Porter thought that an accidental fire—its timing terrible—had just broken out. Grant believed that vigilant Confederates simply discovered the move. Certainly it was almost impossible to keep the chugging engines from sending sparks out their stacks, and sometimes even plumes of flame. Regardless, now the Southerners knew what was up and opened fire immediately. To Sherman, who had taken some men and shallow boats around through the bayous to a point below the city, ready to aid survivors of wrecked ships, "the scene was truly sublime." Grant himself watched from a steamer upstream, and echoed Sherman's words. "The sight was magnificent, but terrible."

"Every fort and hill-top vomited forth shot and shell," said Porter. The men inside the ironclads casually heard the iron hail strike their sides and bounce harmlessly off the armor. Soon, however, the transport *Henry Clay* came aflame. Rebel shells knocked overboard the blazing cotton bales, making the ship all the more vulnerable, and giving the river itself the satanic appearance of water aflame. At last the crew abandoned the ship before she burned away and sank. Another transport was lost in like fashion, but the rest of the fleet came through safely. A few men were wounded, chiefly by rifle fire aimed at the gunports, but enemy shot and shell did not kill a single Federal, much to Grant's great relief. Soon after the *Benton* passed the final battery, Porter saw a small boat ahead and heard his ship hailed. It was Sherman. "Are you all right, old fellow?" yelled the general. Porter happily allowed that he had come through unscathed. Sherman could hardly resist another gibe at the admiral, adding that "You are more at home here than you were in the ditches grounding on willow-trees. Stick to this, old fellow." Then Porter had time to look back and watch the rest of his fleet coming through the trial. "It might have answered for a picture of the infernal regions."[5]

The whole passage took an hour and a half, since the boats drifted with the current, fearful of using their paddle wheels for power except in emergency. One ship moving faster than another might soon have caused a jumble, or accident. Finally Porter anchored around a bend that ended the line of enemy batteries, and one by one the other vessels anchored in line off his stern. During much of the night the bits of blazing cotton gently floated past them, reminders of the inferno they had just passed through.

Grant felt well pleased. And now he was ready to begin the next phase of his plan. As soon as he had found the good wagon road that ran along the Roundaway and Vidal bayous, he had ordered McClernand on March 29 to march his corps south to New Carthage, a small town on the Mississippi that connected with Vidal by a small channel. From that point, McClernand should be able to move against and take Grand Gulf, some fifteen miles farther south. The latter town was the ideal place for ferrying the troops across, and it offered access by several good roads for a movement deep into the interior below Vicksburg. Unfortunately, the water still sat high enough that McClernand's men made slow progress. Though some of his corps arrived at New Carthage on April 6, it was eleven days later when Grant arrived in person to see that McClernand still was not ready. Further, McClernand decided finally that New Carthage was not the place to cross the river. Instead, he took the march once more toward Hard Times, a hamlet almost directly across from Grand Gulf. He reached the place, joined by McPherson's corps, and both were ready to cross on April 29. Porter, meanwhile, brought his transports and gunboats downriver, augmented by another six steamers towing barges loaded with supplies that had run the batteries on April 22. Grant abandoned his hope of supplying the soldiers by the bayou route, and had to risk instead sending rations downriver past the batteries.[6]

Pemberton remained unaware of Grant's expedition for several days after it commenced. About April 17 he finally discovered that McClernand was marching south, and of course the passage of the gunboats certainly told him that something was planned for his left flank. That flank was protected only by 4,000 Confederates under Brigadier General John Stevens Bowen at Grand Gulf, yet Pemberton failed to reinforce Bowen for several precious days, and feebly when at last he did so. He kept all of his cavalry busy on another venture, and maintained the bulk of his command in Vicksburg proper where it faced only Sherman's corps in front of the Yazoo bluffs. A concentration at Grand Gulf was his best move, and he did not make it. In his defense, however, Pemberton was under terrible pressure from Richmond to hold every point in his department. Able to yield nothing, he was not able to prevent losing by using his army to best advantage. Once Grant got across the Mississippi, an overland campaign against Vicksburg was inevitable, and unstoppable, barring massive Confederate reinforcement. Pemberton's only hope of success throughout the entire campaign was to keep the enemy from crossing, and faced with that necessity his wisest course would have been to risk official disapproval and mass everything he could at Grand Gulf.

But he did not, and on April 29 the attack began. Porter's gunboats found the batteries too strong to silence, and so Grant simply moved his operation downstream a few miles to Bruinsburg, and there crossed on April 30 with no opposition at all. At the same time, by Grant's orders, Sherman made a demonstration at Haynes' Bluff in order to prevent Pemberton sending reinforcements south to Bowen. Then Sherman, too, began marching along the route taken by McClernand and McPherson, and by May 7 he had his XV Corps across the Mississippi. Now Grant's entire army, over 40,000 strong, lay on the east side of the Mississippi. Only small detachments remained behind to cover crossings and maintain communications. Bowen evacuated Grand Gulf on May 2, after having fought a brief encounter at Port Gibson four miles south. McClernand delayed repeatedly in performing this part of his assignment, and only defeated Bowen when McPherson arrived to reinforce him. Bowen had but 9,000 men to face McClernand's full army corps, and resisted bravely until simply forced to abandon the field. On May 3 Grant himself established his headquarters in Grand Gulf, and wrote gleefully to Sherman that "the road to Vicksburg is open." His son Fred was with him, greatly entertained by the sounds of the guns, and the general himself felt elated. It had been, as he put it, a victory of "management," saving him a great loss of life while gaining "all the results of a hard fight."[6]

Yet there had been some fighting, and when Grant took Port Gibson he received some reassuring news, and from a captured Southern newspaper. On April 17, as a diversion to distract Pemberton from the main movement about to commence, Grant had ordered Colonel Benjamin Henry Grierson with 1,700 troopers of his brigade of cavalry to ride out of their camps at La Grange, Tennessee. For two months Grant had matured in his mind a plan to have the trusty cavalryman strike into the heart of Mississippi, cut the railroad at Jackson that helped supply Vicksburg, and then sweep on south, burning and destroying as he went, finally making his way to Banks at New Orleans or Baton Rouge. No great damage would actually be done by the raid, other than disrupting, at least temporarily, Pemberton's communications. But the threat of a large force of Federals driving in his rear could well force the Confederate commander to spread himself thin rather than concentrate against Grant. And it might lure his attention away from the real movement of importance, the sweep to Grand Gulf.

It proved to be one of the most brilliant cavalry raids of the war, in every way as spectacular as any of Stuart's rides in the East, and militarily more important than all of them. Grierson encountered the enemy on April 18, the very day after leaving La Grange, and thereafter skirmished frequently in the course of his ride. Two days later, after discovering several men in the command who simply would not be physically up to the rigors of the raid, Grierson created a diversion of his own by ostentatiously sending them back north in such a manner that many Confederates thought that the entire command was withdrawing. Other feinting parties went out as well, while the main body rode south through the very midst of substantial numbers of the enemy. On April 24 they reached Newton Station, on the railroad to Jackson and Vicksburg. Effortlessly they occupied the town, just in time to capture a train from the east loaded with supplies, and soon thereafter they took another. Immediately Grierson destroyed the engines, and sent parties to dismantle or burn bridges and trestles and take down telegraph poles and lines.

That same day, the raiders rode out of Newton Station, and now the Confederates were after them. Pemberton had news of their exact position and began concentrating forces to meet and stop the horsemen. Cavalry went into place north of Grierson to cut off a retreat. Infantry placed itself between him and Vicksburg, and part of the small command at Port Hudson was ordered out to catch the raiders if they tried to join Banks. Grierson baffled all of them by riding due west where, on April 27, he crossed and cut the Mississippi Central about thirty miles below Jackson. That done, he began the race south toward Baton Rouge. By now the Confederates were converging on him from several directions, and reports of his movements made it obvious that he would try to move along the line of the Mississippi Central to reach Banks. A powerful trap was laid for the raiders near Union Church, Mississippi, but Grierson had scouts out dressed in Confederate butternut, and they discovered it in time for him to turn about and ride around the peril. Finally, however, just before they reached the Louisiana border, the jaded men and horses met with three companies of enemy cavalry at Wall's Bridge. It was May 1, the fifteenth day of the raid, and the Federals had been in the saddle in constant motion for all of them. The enemy confronted them from the other side of the bridge they had to cross to reach safety. In a brief but bloody fight, Grierson pushed his way through, and then raced on toward a crossing of the Amite River. There, at Williams' Bridge, the Confederates might well have cut off any hope of his retreat, but they did not want to burn the bridge, and took their time about reinforcing it. As a result, after passing over Wall's Bridge, Grierson made it safely across the Amite as well, and then began a tense dash for the safety of Bank's lines at Baton Rouge. Riding seventy-six miles in the final twenty-eight hours, the battered and wearied troopers came once more in sight of friendly faces.

The gains of the spectacular raid were considerable. Over 600 enemy soldiers were put out of the war, along with fifty miles or more of railroad track and more telegraph wire. By the colonel's estimate, he had captured and destroyed more than 10,000 Rebel weapons, untold stores and supplies, and captured perhaps 1,000 animals. His own total casualties in killed, wounded, and missing, came to twenty-five. Even better, he had succeeded in diverting substantial numbers of the enemy, including all of Pemberton's cavalry, thus denying to Grand Gulf the reinforcements so desperately needed. On May 1, the day before Grierson reached safety, Grant could already tell Porter that "Grierson of the cavalry, has taken the heart out of Mississippi." To Halleck he exulted two days later that the raid "has been the most successful thing of a kind since the breaking out of the rebellion."[7]

For all the success he had enjoyed thus far in the campaign, Grant now had to pay with bad news that upset his plans somewhat. He and Halleck had agreed that once he got his army across the river below Vicksburg, he would send one of his corps down to join Banks in taking Port Hudson. Then the two armies would unite for the final thrust on

Vicksburg. It had been Grant's plan to send McClernand on the errand, thus getting him out of the way, and putting both of the two political generals on their own. Perhaps a secret inner desire to see them shown up for their incompetence in a situation where neither could shift blame to professional officers in part animated Grant. But he would not now get the chance. When he reached Grand Gulf he heard from Banks. The Massachusetts general had gone on an unauthorized and pointless expedition up the Red River instead of moving directly against Port Hudson, and now advised that he would not be able to approach the river bastion until May 10 at the earliest. To Grant this meant that his own program would be delayed by at least a month, a month in which Pemberton would steadily be fortifying and reinforcing Vicksburg, a month Grant could not afford. He had no choice, then, but to considerably alter his plan. He would move independently of Banks, leaving that general to do his best against Port Hudson. But what was most dangerous, and bold, he would move away from his supply base at Grand Gulf. His supply line was already too long, and he had discovered the previous December what could happen when communications lines were too lengthy in the enemy's country. If he moved now on Vicksburg, it would only lengthen the line more, making it all the more liable to enemy raids. Thus, though he would not cut his own supply line, he would take with him what he could, live off the land, and trust to large, heavily guarded supply trains to subsist his march toward Vicksburg. Even the bold Sherman objected to the idea, and Grant did not even inform Halleck, knowing that he would not approve. It was a decision to be made on the spot and the instant, an opportunity and a risk to weigh. To Sherman he confessed that "I do not calculate upon the possibility of supplying the Army with full rations from Grand Gulf." He only expected to get from there as much basic necessity as he could "and make the country furnish the balance." In the march from the Bruinsburg crossing, McClernand and McPherson had traveled seven days on two days' rations, augmenting their rations with what the countryside could provide. On this same basis, now, he would continue his campaign. On May 9 he sent a last letter to Julia. He would move on the morrow. Two days, a week at most, would bring on "the fight which will settle the fate of Vicksburg." He did not contemplate the possibility of failure.[8]

Shortly after the seizure of Grand Gulf, Grant sent McPherson and McClernand on massive reconnaissances along the south shore of the Big Black River, which paralleled the Mississippi about ten miles east of Vicksburg, and emptied at Grand Gulf. The results were what Grant had feared. McPherson discovered that Pemberton was not massing all his available forces around the city itself. It was also learned that a small force of the enemy was in Jackson. At first Grant believed that if McPherson had pushed hard he might have taken Vicksburg under siege at once, but later he doubted that it would have been successful. Instead, he decided now that he would move against the railroad between Vicksburg and Jackson, thus at one stroke preventing the Jackson Confederates from reinforcing Pemberton, and at the same time putting the Federals in position to march along the railroad directly to Vicksburg.

It was difficult ground the bluecoats had to cover, and they moved slowly at first. McClernand and the XIII Corps formed the left flank, Sherman and his XV in the center, and McPherson's XVII on the right. Grant knew that he outnumbered Pemberton, and that the enemy would not dare come out of Vicksburg and attack him. Therefore, he decided to move for the railroad and then take Jackson first. Thus he could defeat the enemy in detail. He erred gravely in his estimate of enemy numbers, however. By the time his corps got astride the Vicksburg & Jackson Railroad, Pemberton's 32,000 in his rear and the 6,000 in his front very nearly equaled the 44,000 Grant had at hand. A daring Pemberton might well have sortied from his works and delivered a devastating blow to the Federals. But he did not.

But the Confederate commander did go partway to Jackson. It was because the man commanding the small body of troops in the state capital was his own superior, an old face from the Virginia campaigns, General Joseph E. Johnston. No other general except Pemberton himself would be as important to the fate of Vicksburg, and yet Johnston would never see the city. He was an annoying man, filled with talent, and more contention. He was the true architect of the Confederate victory at Bull Run back in 1861, and performed well in resisting McClellan's drive up the Virginia Peninsula in the spring of 1862 until a wound put him out of action for many months. Already his argumentativeness, combined with the President's, had put him and Jefferson Davis seriously at odds, and the two men would never again make their peace. When finally he recovered, Johnston received orders from Davis to go to the West as commander overseeing all of the Confederate armies there: Bragg's, Kirby-Smith's, and Pemberton's. He had been sent there as well to investigate the discontent within Bragg's high command and, if necessary, to relieve him, but Johnston seems to have known better than to submit an uncomplimentary report on one of the President's favorites.

Now Johnston had come to Jackson with just two brigades, all he could immediately muster, with orders from Davis to relieve Vicksburg. Pemberton had the same orders from the President, but was as well getting instructions from Johnston to leave his works and attack Grant. The two appeared contradictory, and left Pemberton in something of a quandary, until he decided to do a little of both. As Grant marched northeast along the Big Black, Pemberton left just one brigade in the city itself, and spread the rest of his army along the Big Black where the railroad crossed it. Farther he would not go, and that left Johnston on his own in Jackson.

The Federal march proceeded unimpeded until May 12, when McPherson ran into a small body of Confederates at Raymond, a few

miles west of Jackson. He pushed them aside after a hot little engagement, and the next day he and Sherman came close to the capital. Johnston himself only arrived in Jackson that same night, and the following
day was barely in place before the Federals attacked. Of course, there was
never a question of the outcome, with two brigades trying to resist two
corps. Late that afternoon, May 14, Johnston evacuated the town and retired twenty-five miles north to hover on Grant's flank and desperately try
to marshal reinforcements. He would be heard from again before the campaign was done.[9]

Grant indulged himself a bit by spending that night in the same
room occupied by Johnston just the night before. The next afternoon he
called together his corps commanders for a conference. He had captured a
message from Johnston to Pemberton that indicated the latter would attempt to move around their northern flank to reach the Vicksburg garrison, and thus combine against them. To prevent this, Grant ordered
McPherson to march immediately toward Vicksburg to the nearest road
junction which Johnston could use. He directed McClernand toward the
same vicinity, and detailed Sherman for the work of destroying the rail
and manufacturing facilities. After the orders were given, Grant himself
accompanied Sherman on an incredible tour into a factory that had not
ceased its production even during the battle, nor when the Federals took
the town. "Our presence did not seem to attract the attention of either
the manager or the operatives, most of whom were girls," said Grant.
They watched the workers making what was obviously cloth for military
tents, and on inspecting one bolt found the letters "C.S.A." woven into
the fabric. Right before the eyes of the conquering Federals, the factory
blithely continued making goods for the Confederate army! The generals
watched a bit longer, then Grant calmly told Sherman that he thought
the people had worked enough for one day. The workers were allowed to
go home with as much of the cloth as they might want for themselves,
and then the factory went to the torch.[10]

As the Union army corps took their route of march toward the Big
Black, Pemberton, too, finally moved again. He was getting conflicting information now, and orders from Johnston that he could not follow. He
actually thought to strike south at Grant's communications and supply
lines, not realizing that such lines did not exist. On the evening of May
14 he called a council of war of his senior generals. Johnston's message
about combining against Grant was just received. Pemberton expressed
his own view that Vicksburg stood paramount and that he should not
move forward at the peril of losing the city or being defeated. The others
concurred, but then a suggestion came forward that they go ahead and
move on Grant's communications. Discussion produced a consensus in
time, and on the next day the move was to begin. By late on May 15
Pemberton had gotten as far as Champion's Hill, a considerable eminence
just four miles west of Bolton, the junction toward which Grant's corps

were converging. That night the two opposing armies stood at the hill
and the junction, not knowing of each other's presence. That same night
Grant wrote a message to Halleck telling him where he was and what he
was doing. He informed "Old Brains" that he was not cooperating with
Banks after all. "I could not lose the time," he said simply. The next
morning he directed one of his divisions to start on the road toward the
Big Black, adding that "I think you will encounter no enemy by the
way."[11]

It was about dawn when the first indications that Pemberton was
near his front reached Grant. At once he began ordering all his corps forward to concentrate on the Champion's Hill position. "The fight may be
brought on at any moment—we should have every man on the field."
Grant began to expect that this might be the decisive fight of the whole
campaign. By seven-thirty Grant himself was on the road riding toward
the front. At almost the same moment, the first picket firing broke out between the Confederates and the Federal advance. As Grant reached
Champion's Hill, the skirmishing had almost reached the peak of a battle,
with still more and more troops on both sides coming into the fight. Even
Grant had to admit that Champion's was an excellent position, higher
than any ground for some distance around, and commanding all approaches. Pemberton had one division on the hill itself and two others on
a ridge extending south of it. There was absolutely no way of going
around him. Grant would have to go through. By 11 A.M. the battle had
grown in intensity, with McPherson attacking on the right, against the
hill itself, while McClernand moved against the center and left. In time
one of McPherson's divisions gained a hold on Champion's but could not
maintain it because McClernand failed to keep up enough of a demonstration to prevent Pemberton from reinforcing the hill from the ridge.
The Federals were driven back off the hill, forcing Grant to recall his
right-most brigade from an advanced position to assist. What Grant
would not know until later was that this brigade, part of the division of
Major General John Alexander Logan—one politico who made a brilliant
general—had gotten behind Pemberton and was actually in possession of
the only road the Confederates could use to retreat. In calling that brigade to assist McPherson, Grant gave up an unknowing chance to destroy
Pemberton there and then. Instead, by 4 P.M., when Pemberton decided
that he had done as much as he could, the Confederates were able to
evacuate and retire toward Vicksburg. Grant lost about 2,500 men in the
battle, but Pemberton's casualties totaled over 3,800. Only McClernand's
reluctance to obey his orders to attack the ridge prevented the Federals
from overwhelming the Rebels.

That night the Confederates withdrew to the Big Black and there
manned earthworks to contest a Federal crossing. Pemberton and 5,000 of
his men remained there, while the rest of the beaten army continued on
its way to the defenses at Vicksburg itself. That same evening McCler-

nand and McPherson advanced to within seven or eight miles of the river, and Grant and his staff rode in advance of them. Indeed, that night, hours after dark, they found they had gone beyond even their pickets, and had to ride back a mile to find their own lines. The general spent the night in a house by the road. The Confederates had used it as a hospital during the battle, and the wounded and dying still filled the building. Instead of sleeping that night, the general commanding the army that had visited suffering upon these pitiful bleeding men spent the hours tending to their wounds and attempting "to do as much to alleviate the suffering of an enemy as a friend." To any but those who fought it, this war would often simply baffle description.[12]

"I am of the opinion that the battle of Vicksburg has been fought," Grant boasted to Sherman. His army sat squarely between Pemberton and Johnston. There would be no junction of the two, but just to make certain Grant ordered his favorite subordinate to take his XV Corps over the Big Black a few miles upstream and cross. That would keep him between the two Confederate forces and might also allow him to cut off once more Pemberton's route of retreat should the Southern commander decide to stand on the Big Black for a few hours. But Pemberton did not. He had already sent most of his army back to Vicksburg, and as McPherson and McClernand approached the river and moved against the trenches on the east side of the crossing, Pemberton burned the bridge and retreated, leaving those in the trenches no way of escape but surrender. Grant was becoming overconfident now in the face of repeated success. His orders to Sherman indicated that he believed "Billy" could march into Vicksburg itself with little opposition. Ironically, at the moment that Grant was pushing the Confederates across the Big Black, a week-old message from Halleck arrived ordering him to return to Grand Gulf and cooperate with Banks as originally planned. Then they could take Vicksburg. Grant announced that the order was no longer pertinent, and that he would ignore it. Just as the message bearer remonstrated with him that it must be obeyed, they heard the sounds of the final successful charge that carried the Confederate trenches at the bridge, and Grant mounted and rode away without another thought to his technical insubordination.[13]

The destroyed bridge halted the Federals' progress as the Confederate army could not. Grant had to set his engineers to building makeshift bridges from materials at hand or with the army. One structure was simply a raft. McPherson personally oversaw using bales of cotton as pontoons to make another, while a third bridge was built from materials on the spot. Pioneers felled the trees on either side of the river into the stream itself, so that as they fell the upper branches of timbers from one side entwined with those of trees from the other. He then used that as a base for a roadway. Within twenty-four hours, by 8 A.M., May 18, all three bridges could stand traffic and the army could move again.

That day Grant rode off to find Sherman, and together they watched as the XV Corps advanced toward Haynes' Bluffs from the rear. Most of the enemy works were abandoned, but some resistance was still going on, and a man standing right next to the two generals was killed before their eyes by an enemy bullet. Soon the remaining Confederates departed, and Grant watched as Sherman now began to feel the euphoria, to smell a great success on the way. "Uncle Billy" confessed that he had never until that moment felt they would succeed. Now he could look upon the place where the previous December he had sat helpless. The bluff was theirs now, and with it access to the Yazoo and the Mississippi above Vicksburg. Thus the supply line broken eighteen days before could now be reestablished. Grant had achieved a genuinely remarkable feat. Sherman told him to his face that it must be one of the greatest campaigns in all military history.[14]

By the next morning, May 19, the entire Federal army was in line facing Vicksburg. What they faced was a line of earthworks and parapets, reenforced with wooden obstructions and planted with batteries, that stretched from Fort Hill, on the Mississippi, around the north side of the city and then south until it linked again with the river. In all, the works covered nearly seven miles, and Pemberton now had but 20,000 to man them. One of his divisions had been cut off from him at Champion's Hill, and could not get through the lines to rejoin the army. That left him with roughly one man for every two feet of defenses, very little considering that many of his troops were artillerymen, and that a good defense needed depth as well as width.

As Grant approached, McClernand formed the left of his line, McPherson the center, and Sherman the right. Grant believed that a siege was not necessary. The enemy seemed sufficiently weakened that one hearty assault ought to break through. He ordered his corps commanders to get as close as they could during the morning hours of May 19. At 2 P.M. three volleys would be fired from the artillery, signaling a general charge all along the line. At the appointed hour the assaulting troops advanced against the guns of the Rebel fortifications, and in some places took a lodging in the parapets. "The enemy fought hard and well," said Sherman, and what was taken could not be held. The Federals fell back, though in some spots remaining under cover within fifty yards of the enemy works. That night they began to dig in themselves, and to many bluecoats it looked like a siege was coming. Grant did not want it. He did not have enough men present for a real siege, only about 35,000 effectives being with him in the assault. A siege would require time, more men, and a great risk of disease and exhaustion in the coming summer. On May 20 he called his corps commanders together. In discussion, they agreed that the attack the day before failed chiefly because they had been forced by the ground to attack at the enemy's strongest points. If Porter could bring his gunboats down to aid by shelling—he had started the night before— and if they could select weaker places in the defenses to strike, another assault ought to break through. Grant ordered an attack at 10 A.M., May 22.[15]

The attack went off exactly on time, after an hour's bombardment by Porter's gunboats. The Federals gamely charged up to the enemy works, and in several places gained lodgments. Then Grant received word from McClernand that his corps had penetrated the enemy line and he needed reinforcements to exploit the success. Grant's own observation post was so placed that he could see McClernand's corps, and he saw no such breakthroughs, but when repeated requests for support came, he saw no choice but to comply, believing that the commander on the spot could usually assess the immediate situation in front of him better than an observer—even if his superior—at some distance. Grant sent reinforcements, and ordered Sherman and McPherson to renew their efforts to create enough pressure on the Confederates to prevent Pemberton from massing resistance to McClernand. "I don't believe a word of it," Grant had said to Sherman when he received McClernand's note proclaiming his success, but Sherman, too, urged that the note had to be credited. It cost them dearly, for the renewed assaults proved expensive in casualties and productive of nothing. Further, when Grant went in person to McClernand's front, he saw that nothing at all had been gained but a few outer trenches, and that the main line of Confederate defenses had never been pierced. "This last attack only served to increase our casualties without giving any benefit whatever," lamented Grant.

Yet there was a secondary benefit from the attack, though one that no one at the moment would have expected. There was enormous ill will created against McClernand in the high command as a result of the needless losses that resulted from his error. Of course, he already enjoyed little enough respect among his peers. But then a few weeks later he issued to his corps and had published in the Northern press a congratulatory order. In it he complimented his men for taking a real lodgment in the defenses of the city—which they had not—and added that they would certainly have captured the citadel itself but for the failure of Sherman and McPherson to do their part. When Grant learned of it he was furious. He called on McClernand for a copy of the order, and when he received it he immediately relieved the troublesome politico from his command. To Halleck, Grant confided that "I should have relieved him long since for general unfitness for his position," but McClernand had clearly done it to himself now. In addition, McClernand was still the next senior general in the army. Should Grant fall or be disabled, the politician would then be in command, and Sherman and McPherson clearly could not—or would not—work with him. McClernand would of course protest, and even toyed with ignoring the order of removal, since he believed his appointment to the command by the President took precedent over any order of Grant's. But in the end he lost and left, to be replaced by a favorite of Grant's, Major General Edward Otho Cresap Ord. A few weeks later, one of Grant's staff encountered McClernand in a St. Louis hotel. "He looked very abject," said the officer. "I never saw a man so cut down." He would return to the field for a time in a minor command a year from now, but he was out of Grant's hair at last, and that in itself counted for a small victory.[16]

And now Grant had once again to alter his plan, yet flexible as always, he was ready. Hours after the assault failed, he wrote to Halleck that "The nature of the ground about Vicksburg is such that it can only be taken by siege." This was the eventuality he had long hoped to avoid, but there seemed now no choice. And a siege was assured of success. He controlled all land routes into the city, and Porter controlled the river. Not a morsel of food or military supplies could reach the city, and he suspected that provisions already in Pemberton's storehouses were low. He estimated that the city would have to fall "within one week." To Porter he was less optimistic. "There is no doubt of the fall of this place ultimately," he wrote, "but how long it will take is a matter of doubt." One thing was certain: he intended to lose no more men by attacks. He put Sherman and others to work digging tunnels under the enemy works. They would try to place blasting powder there and blow holes in Pemberton's fortifications, as well as taking limited objectives with minimal losses. And a continual artillery bombardment began, as much to exhaust the garrison in Vicksburg as to destroy Pemberton's works. In the siege to come, Grant would be fighting not just the Confederates' metal, but their state of mind. Days after the failure of the last attack, the Federals turned mole. "All was now ready for the pick and spade," said Grant, and soon the Union earthworks rivaled those of the enemy. They might not yet be able to get into Vicksburg, but Pemberton would never get out. The only real threat to the besieging army was Joseph E. Johnston. He was still in Mississippi, and feverishly trying to build an army with which to strike Grant's rear. "I knew Johnston was receiving reinforcements from Bragg," said Grant, and to guard against that he placed his cavalry along the Big Black to hold the fords Johnston would have to use. Sherman, too, from his position on the north side of the city, would be a safeguard against attack by Johnston. And then, for the next forty-seven days, it was a game of dig and dodge and wait. Sooner or later the city would have to fall.[17]

So feared the Confederates, though in the first days of the siege they put up a brave face. In the Virginia press, far removed from the scene, editorials proclaimed that "We are pretty sure that General Pemberton will hold the place in spite of all Grant can do against it." The same determination flowed through the dirty, tired men in butternut and gray who lined the trenches around the city. Indeed, long into the night after the failed May 22 attack, the Confederate soldiers repaired their works. It was no easy task for them—exhausted from a day's fighting in the hot sun—to drop rifle and wield pick and spade all through the dark hours. Still, rations were plentiful in this first day and the few following. Cooks prepared hot meals for the soldiers, and everyone expected relief from Johnston within a few days. Indeed, when the men saw some of Grant's wagons and men moving to the rear, on their way to strengthen supply lines, the Confederates interpreted it to mean that Johnston had already moved against the Big Black crossings and would be in Vicksburg at any time.

May 24, the end of the first week since the Federals reached the environs of Vicksburg, dawned hot. It was Sunday, yet the houses of worship were deserted, for the inhabitants of the city huddled for shelter from the enemy shelling, as they would do for the next six weeks. Already many residents had made crude dugouts into earth embankments in the city. Any hillside, particularly one facing away from the river where the gunboats lay, quickly sprouted a honeycomb of tunnels and caves where the citizens of the beleaguered city carried on much of their daily lives. For those who refused to live underground and remained in their homes, there existed the constant danger of being hit by enemy fire. Just the previous Saturday some of Porter's shells fell into at least three of the city's homes, including the residence of one of Pemberton's division commanders, Major General Carter Littlepage Stevenson.

Life in the caves produced some remarkable instances of heroism, and a lesson in communal living. Yet the distinctions between class and race were not entirely eradicated. The slaves still prepared the meals as a rule, and did so outside the caves, while their masters within maintained some semblance of the old way of life. "It would have been an amusing sight to witness the domestic scenes presented," wrote one cave dweller. The mealtimes were, of necessity, irregular, for the servants could only venture outside during lulls in the shelling, and since those occurred generally when the Yankee gunners themselves were dining, the besiegers and the besieged finally wound up sharing the same dining hours. They ate corn bread and bacon for the most part, and three times a day at first. They brought their beds and chairs, even carpets and bookcases, into their subterranean homes. Mary Loughborough, daughter of an officer now in the fortifications, tried to make the best of it. "I went regularly to work, keeping house under ground." She lived in a cave that had been dug straight into a hillside for six feet, then branched perpendicularly into wings on either side. In one wing she placed her bed and "the other I used as a kind of a dressing room." The latter was as well the only place in the cave where she could stand erect; in the rest of the dugout she had to stoop or sit. Standing upright soon became a luxury much appreciated. The servants meanwhile did their cooking at the mouth of the dwelling, and in the evenings, should there be a reprieve from the shelling, the mouth became a front porch where the tenants sat to visit with friends and gather the latest news from passersby. The most feared news was of cave-ins, for there were many, with people often buried alive for hours, and more often dead when finally found. It remained a constant terror throughout the siege, and after a few weeks the fear of enemy shells became less than that of being buried alive. Scores of those who moved into the caves in late May chose to risk life on the surface.

The scene that presented itself to the people of the city could be awesome at times, despite the horror. One evening Mary Loughborough sat at the entrance of her cave with her servants all around her and watched the beautiful fireworks as shells from Porter's mortar boats flew in high sparkling arches above the city, and then fell. She marveled at "the passage of the shell, as it travelled through the heavens, looking like a swiftly moving star." When they fell they seemed to leave behind a trail of fire, and the incendiary projectiles, often bursting in the air prematurely, scattered their fragments "like large, clear blue-and-amber stars." Still there was fear, always fear. "Miss," one of her servants asked, "do they want to kill us all dead? Will they keep doing this until we all die?" She could only answer, "I hope not."[18]

However bad it was for the citizens of Vicksburg, the trial of the siege rested even heavier on the soldiers along the front. For some days the dead from the May 22 fight could not be buried. "The effluvia from the putrefying bodies had become almost unbearable to friend and foe," wrote Sergeant Willie Tunnard of the 3d Louisiana. Finally a truce was arranged to bury the fallen, and during that truce came "a strange spectacle in this thrilling drama of war." The soldiers from both sides thronged together, "gaily chatting with each other, discussing the issues of the war, disputing over differences of opinion, losses in the fight, etc." Many Federals invited Confederates into their lines for a meal and some good coffee, and an occasional glass of "Oh, Be Joyful" or "Who Hit John." The Federals seemed exultant in their impending victory, the Confederates equally defiant and determined. Men of some regiments, like Tunnard's 3d Louisiana, found old friends and even relatives among some of the Yankee western units. Many were the scenes of sad parting when the truce ended. "I trust we shall meet soon again in the Union of old," one Federal officer said in farewell to his guest. "The only union which you and I will enjoy, I hope," came the reply, "will be in kingdom come."

The plentiful supplies of the first days soon dried up in the face of increasing uncertainty over Johnston's relief of the besieged garrison. Stringent measures were enforced, both to conserve supplies and keep as many men as possible in the trenches. Minor offenders were released from arrest in order to stand their duty. There was to be no firing of any sort without specific orders, in order to conserve ammunition. Even chewing tobacco came to be confiscated for rationing. Animals could not be fed entirely from stockpiles of forage, and Pemberton toyed with driving all the wagon and artillery mounts outside the lines rather than see them starve. Soon improvisation took over, and the Confederates began to augment their meager supply of war materiel from what came to hand. Couriers

who stole through the lines with messages from Johnston also brought
what they could carry, like 18,000 musket caps brought by one man.
When Federal shells fell inside the lines but failed to explode, Pemberton's ordnance people set about rearming them to send them back to
their owners.

As the supply of the most necessary staple, meat, began to dwindle,
Pemberton started to increased the soldiers' allowance of sugar, rice, and
beans. But soon the meat ration fell by half. Then came the genius of his
impressment of tobacco, for now he distributed plugs to the men, and
chewing the leaf tended to assuage hunger. Yet by the first week of June
it became increasingly evident to Pemberton that Johnston would be slow
in coming, if he ever came, and the stamina of his command was declining. The general himself became increasingly morose. The shelling caused
him constant casualties, while he could inflict few if any in return. The
newspapers in the city did their best to maintain civilian morale, yet the
pressure on him from the city fathers was unflagging, and the anger of civilians at being forced to share this trial unceasing. Soon large factions
arose among the populace who began suggesting to Pemberton how he
should conduct his defense, and all the while he could hear nothing from
Johnston. After May 25 he went two weeks without word. "I shall endeavor to hold out as long as we have anything to eat," he wrote to his
commander. By June 12 the army's provisions had almost given out, with
no meat left. Pemberton ordered his commissaries to impress cattle from
citizens in the city. At the same time, with flour dwindling, rice was sub-
stituted in part, and soon thereafter they tried grinding peas together with
corn meal and baking a bread of it. "It made a nauseous composition,"
said one soldier. It was almost impossible to thoroughly bake the mixture
so that both pea flour and meal would be fit for consumption. Yet they
ate it, and called the mess "cush-cush." Some maintained that "it had the
properties of India-rubber." By June 15, with a variety of expedients, Pemberton estimated that he could hold out for another twenty days. That
meant that by July 5 he would have nothing to feed his men.[19]

That morale in the beleaguered army remained as high as it did is a
tribute to the undaunted spirit of the Confederate soldier. The men filled
their time with pranks directed at the enemy, sinking counter mines of
their own to interrupt Grant's tunnels. When they could they met with
their foes between the lines for trade and talk. They read newspapers,
now the Vicksburg *Citizen* calling itself an "illustrated" sheet thanks to
its being printed on wallpaper. As the Federals constantly pushed their
works closer, in places to within twenty yards of the Confederate lines,
gibes and hand-thrown projectiles could be lobbed back and forth. One
Yankee threw a piece of hardtack across with the word "starvation"
written thereon, only to have it hurled back at him with a defiant "Forty
days rations, and no thanks to you" scrawled in return. Late in June even
the supply of impressed meat ran out, and Pemberton had to order army

horses and mules slaughtered. "We assure the ignorant reader that the food was consumed with a keen relish worthy the appetite of a gourmand, or an epicure over the most dainty repast," said Tunnard. Still, many could not bring themselves to taste of the flesh, and certainly they would not have sampled the other new staple of soldier diet, trapped rats. "Hunger will demoralize the most fastidious tastes," Willie Tunnard concluded, "and quantity, not quality of food, becomes the great desideratum." Before the siege ended, rats were almost entirely exterminated from the city. Tunnard preferred them for breakfast, fried.

The city was almost a ghost town, now. The stores were virtually stripped, and some looted, if not destroyed in the shelling. Signs had fallen down, houses fallen to ruin, trees down, the streets barricaded for a last defense. Starving soldiers wandered the streets looking for anything edible, sometimes paying exorbitant prices for ginger beer and other beverages of very uncertain origin. Gardens were torn up by the shelling and hungry people, the sidewalks shattered, the shrubbery neglected. Much of what was combustible had been torn down for firewood, and even the cemeteries had been vandalized. Dogs and cats roamed at will, and even the remaining rats, banded together for survival, raced about in broad daylight, scurrying even between the feet of the soldiers as they, too, scavenged for food. "Lice and filth covered the bodies of the soldiers. Delicate women and little children, with pale, care-worn and hunger-pinched features, peered at the passer-by with wistful eyes, from the caves in the hill-sides." And all this to the accompaniment of the almost constant bombardment, aimed not at the town, but at the fortifications. Yet despite the best aim possible, shells must inevitably hit the city as well. Worse, every few days came the sound of a greater explosion as another mine was detonated. On July 1 an enormous detonation beneath the works of Tunnard's 3d Louisiana sent tons of earth and scores of soldiers flying into the air. "It seemed as if all hell had suddenly yawned upon the devoted band, and vomited forth its sulphurous fire and smoke upon them." Nearly 100 took serious or mortal injuries. At first, as the seeming mountain of displaced earth hovered in the air before falling, the men raced away to avoid being buried. Then they raced back to fill the gap in their line before the enemy assaulted. But the Federals, mindful of Grant's intention not to lose any more men, did not attack. They remained content with the disruption. Besides, their explosions frequently sent the Confederates over to them. Grant told of one explosion that lifted a black man out of the Confederate works and hurled him across the thirty or forty feet between the lines, dumping him hurt and frightened among the Federals. How high had he gone, someone asked? "Dun no, massa, but t'ink 'bout t'ree mile."[20]

It had to end soon. Grant, with Halleck's anxious cooperation, continually built up his forces and strengthened his position. Soon he had 71,000 men in his army. His works became ever more formidable, and ever closer to the enemy's. The work of mining, haphazard at first, he finally coordinated, determining after the July 1 explosion to set off no more but, instead, to wait until several were ready and light them all at once and assault immediately afterward. Yet the opportunity would not come. The siege would not last long enough.[21]

By late June the opposing trenches and works were close enough that Yanks and Rebs could freely talk with one another without leaving their fortifications, and in some cases the pickets could actually meet for friendly conversation. One Confederate openly confessed to a Federal in this manner that Pemberton was in such a bad way that he would attempt to break out, not by attacking, but by building rafts to take the army across the river to Louisiana under cover of darkness. On June 29 Tunnard and his comrades saw the skiffs and rafts under construction, and soon speculation broke out in the army over their purpose. "It would have been an insane enterprise," the sergeant confessed, for the crossing would have been made under the guns of Porter's fleet and could not well be concealed. Apparently Pemberton agreed, for the attempt was not to be made, and perhaps he never intended that it should be made, devising the boats only as something to keep hands and minds occupied and hope alive.

But by that July 1 all hope had died in Pemberton. He addressed a circular letter to his divisional commanders. Unless Johnston should arrive, attack, and raise the siege, or else somehow manage to get supplies into the city, evacuation would be unavoidable. Even evacuating seemed very improbable, but now he asked for a statement of the condition of the troops and a frank assessment of their ability to withstand the rigor of such a movement. At best it would mean hard marches without rest, and most probably a bitter fight to get into open ground first. The responses came quickly, and uniformly. It could not be done. The men would cheerfully continue the siege, but their exhausted and emaciated bodies simply could not stand an evacuation. They suffered from constant exposure to the elements. Their limbs were often swollen and cramped from want of exercise, their nerves shattered by lack of sleep and the constant bombardment. When the Yankees attacked, they always repelled them. But their bodies could take no more. Even with unlimited provisions, Pemberton rightly believed that his command could not hold out more than a few days. It was time to end it.[22]

It was perhaps ten o'clock the morning of July 3 when a flag of truce appeared on the Confederate works. Across the continent Lee and Meade were preparing for the afternoon's assault that would decide the battle at Gettysburg. Here now another decision, bloodless, began its course. General John Stevens Bowen, whom Pemberton had left defenseless at Grand Gulf some two months before, now appeared with a message for Grant. Pemberton asked for an armistice for a few hours in order that he and Grant could discuss terms for the surrender of Vicksburg. "I make this proposition to save the further effusion of blood, which must otherwise be shed to a frightful extent."

Grant saw immediately the import of the truce when the flags first showed. "It was a glorious sight to officers and soldiers," he said. Many saw in this the certain salvation of the Union. When Grant met with Bowen, he found in him an old friend. They had been neighbors in Missouri years before. Now, however, after an amicable greeting, Grant refused Bowen's mission. He would not arrange terms, he would dictate them. Bowen was a man of good and honest judgment, and undoubted humanity. Anxious to see the whole business ended, he would not let the door so slightly opened be closed. On his own responsibility, he suggested that the two commanding generals should at least meet. It could do no harm, and to this Grant agreed. With his reply he also sent Pemberton a letter. All the Confederate need do to stop the effusion of blood was agree to an "unconditional surrender of the city and garrison." "I have no terms other than those," he added, and any who remembered Grant's capture of Fort Donelson the year before knew that to be true. But, as always, Grant softened the moment he sensed that an enemy was soon to cease being a threat. "Men who have shown so much endurance and courage as those now in Vicksburg," he said, "will always challenge the respect of an adversary, and I can assure you will be treated with all the respect due to prisoners of war."

At 3 P.M. that afternoon the two generals met. They had known one another well in the war in Mexico, and greeted each other with some warmth. But when Pemberton asked once more what terms Grant offered, and received the same reply, he snapped that "The conference might as well end." He turned away, but then Bowen intervened once more. Might not he and one of Grant's generals speak in the matter? Grant did not object, and he and Pemberton resumed conversation, speaking perhaps of pleasanter things, while Bowen and Major General Andrew Jackson Smith conferred. When Bowen proposed that the surrender of the city might be enough, and that the Confederates be allowed to march out with their arms, Grant ended the interview. He would send a letter that night with his final terms. Meanwhile, hostilities would not resume until the correspondence between Grant and Pemberton ceased.

That night Grant conferred with his commanders. They favored insisting upon unconditional terms, but Grant was beginning to think of something else. If he took the Confederates as prisoners of war, he would have to ship some 20,000 or more of them to the North, where they would be imprisoned and shipped about at great inconvenience until they might be exchanged for Union prisoners held in the South. All this would tie up much of his own army for awhile. Further, most of these Confederates came from states in the region. Grant thought them tired of the war. If he should, therefore, parole Pemberton's army on the spot and send them to their homes, many would undoubtedly stay there for the duration. He would thus deprive the Confederacy of manpower, and at the same time leave the burden of feeding and supporting the paroled men with the South. That night he proposed this to Pemberton. Officers could keep their side arms and one horse per man; enlisted men could take their clothing, rations, and cooking utensils. All they need do first was sign their paroles.

Shortly after midnight came Pemberton's reply, accepting but asking in addition that "in justice both to the honor and spirit of my troops" they be allowed to march out of their works with their colors and arms, stack them in front of the Federal lines, and then Grant might occupy the city. In substance, Grant agreed.

The next day was July 4. Pemberton had hoped not to surrender on that day of all days, but it could not be helped, and in the end he hoped that it might get him more magnanimous terms. At 10 A.M. his army formed ranks and marched out of their fortifications and laid down their arms. Then in sullen silence they returned to their camps to await parole and give vent at last to the anguish of defeat. Two hours later they were taunted by Fourth of July salvos fire from Porter's gunboats. But the Federal soldiers who quickly poured into the city offered not an insult, not a gibe or word of gloating. Tunnard found that "no word of exultation was uttered to irritate the feelings of the prisoners." Instead, when individual soldiers and sentinels came into their camps, they frequently brought with them haversacks filled with food and silently gave them to the famished Southerners. The next day Grant opened his own commissary to the vanquished. Bacon, hominy, peas, coffee, sugar, bread, soap, and candles, all went out to the Confederates, and with it went the hearts and sympathy of the victors. For several days there followed a camaraderie not soon forgotten.[23]

Grant himself rode into the city with his troops, his first call being at the waterfront to congratulate Porter. After touring the fallen citadel, he returned to his headquarters and sent a simple message to Halleck. "The Enemy surrendered this morning," he said. Within a week all of the prisoners, 30,000 of them as it turned out, were paroled and released and, as Grant had hoped, relatively few of them returned to the war. As Grant watched the relations between the Confederates and his own soldiers, he was struck by the cordiality and delicacy of the victors toward the defeated. "Really," he would say, "I believe there was a feeling of sadness just then in the breasts of most of the Union soldiers at seeing the dejection of their late antagonists." Certainly no one could be more dejected than Lieutenant General John C. Pemberton, however. Just the day after the surrender came a message from Johnston that he would finally attack Grant's rear on July 7. The news taunted Pemberton as no gloating Federal could. He had been largely a victim. Certainly he suffered from his own errors, and they were many. Yet some had been forced upon him by Johnston, and more by Richmond. The War Department sent him orders which conflicted with the orders from Johnston, and Pemberton often did not know which to obey. The government interfered with Johnston, too, so that he did not have a free hand in gathering an army to relieve Vicksburg. Given finally the choice between saving his army and saving Vicksburg, he had bravely tried to do both and failed, just as those sworn to support him failed. Yet he had accomplished something. For forty-seven days Grant had been tied to Vicksburg, unable to help Banks at Port Hudson, unable to prevent Johnston's halting attempts to raise another army, unable to combine with Rosecrans against Bragg in middle Tennessee. What might have been if Pemberton had abandoned the city in May and saved his army, none can say. But for now he knew what was coming. The press in the South would crucify him, and not the least for surrendering on July 4. He still held the confidence of President Davis and of most of the army's high command that knew the circumstances of the surrender, but the soldiers and the people blamed him. Soon rumors of treason, hearkening back to his Northern nativity, would circulate. No command would be found for him, and ten months later he would resign his commission as lieutenant general. Davis, unwilling to let him leave the service, made him instead a lieutenant colonel of artillery. He served out the war, almost forgotten. But now, given his parole, he left Vicksburg to find Johnston and report to his superior officer. He found him in a day or two, and after dark one night Pemberton walked out of the shadows and up to Johnston. The latter jumped up with delight and extended his hand to the old friend. "I am certainly glad to see you," he said. Pemberton lifted his own hand, not to clasp Johnston's, but to give a stiff salute. With no word of greeting, but in the measured tone of a man raging with anger and disappointment and betrayal, he said: "General Johnston, according to the terms of parole prescribed by General Grant, I was directed to report to you, sir!" A tense moment of silence, then Pemberton saluted once more and walked away. The two would never speak again.[24]

Somehow, now, the victories that eluded the Union for so long seemed to come in abundance. Gettysburg on July 3, Vicksburg on July 4, and yet one more in just a few days. Finally Banks had moved against Port Hudson. There could hardly be an excuse for his dallying and his wasted campaign on the Red River. In fact, he did not approach the position until late in May, and on the twenty-seventh he finally began his attack with a heavy bombardment. There followed an unsuccessful assault, characterized chiefly by the overly celebrated fighting of two Louisiana-raised black regiments, who fought well, but not half so well as the Northern press would proclaim. The fight lasted twelve hours. Banks had boasted that he would occupy Port Hudson that evening, but when his assault failed he began to whine that his troops were too few and, with the old song so popular with all the good politicians turned incompetent generals, he began blaming his subordinates. Now he, too, had no choice but a siege.

For the next eighteen days the Federals dug in around the enemy works, and the bombardment began. It was Vicksburg on a smaller scale, yet Banks would not learn the lesson Grant took on May 22. Banks would attack again, and on June 14 he launched costly assaults that netted him nothing but casualties of almost 2,000. Surfeited on blood, he settled into a siege, relying on the artillery to pound the enemy into submission. The 7,200 Confederates, commanded by Major General Franklin Gardner—a native of New York—soon found the little town of Port Hudson blown to pieces. Shattered glass became mixed with rations in several of the commissary storehouses, and soldiers soon found themselves spitting slivers of windowpanes out of their bread. By the end of June the food almost completely gave out. Here, too, they would eat mules and horses. The men at first were hesitant, so the very first mule meal was eaten by "Daddy Long Legs," as they called him, General Gardner. Soon, with the gallows humor of all soldiers, the men in Port Hudson began braying, saying that their diet was affecting their dispositions. In time even the mules gave out, and Gardner himself could be seen dining on "broiled rats, sugar and weevily peas."

Late in June, Banks began preparations for renewed attacks, knowing that the enemy was starving and should be weakening. Yet those assaults, like the ones before, were repulsed at high cost. Banks decided to renew his preparations and launch a major attack on July 7 that would surely drive Gardner into the river. His hold on his own army was weakening in the face of desertions, mutiny in at least one regiment, and flagging confidence in him among his officers. Indeed, when the news of Vicksburg's surrender arrived on July 7 it may have been as much Banks's salvation as Gardner's doom, for another bungled assault like those before could only have resulted in Grant assuming control of the affairs at Port Hudson, and Banks, like McClernand, might soon have met his eclipse.

The news of Vicksburg came late in the morning, and at once the troops were informed. Cheers ran from regiment to regiment, and quickly the rumor crossed the lines to the Confederates. At first the Rebs thought it a lie, but Banks soon sent an official copy of the dispatch from Grant. Gardner was sitting on the porch of his headquarters, patiently acquiescing in the shortage of tobacco by smoking a pipeful of magnolia blossoms. When he read Banks's message he immediately showed his concern and called a conference of his officers for that evening. The consensus was obvious. They could accomplish nothing further by holding out. They must sue for terms, and the next day they agreed to surrender. Even then Gardner, who showed more daring in his defense than had Pemberton, managed another small victory over Banks. He managed to postpone the formal ceremonies of surrender and parole, so that as many of his men as wished might use the night to escape.

The next day, July 9, Gardner formally surrendered. There was far less of the camaraderie here than at Vicksburg. The Confederates, far from being as dispirited as their comrades to the north, remained defiant. "Damn you!" they said. "You couldn't take us by fighting! You had to starve us out." Even in victory Banks blundered, by paroling the Confederates in an irregular manner. Soon thereafter Richmond would quite rightly declare the paroles null, and by fall the men of Port Hudson were back in the ranks fighting the Union. It was a great victory for occupation of Southern territory, but a sorry comment on Banks. Gardner gave up with barely 6,000 men left, less than half of them actually fit or detailed for duty; his losses during the siege amounted to 871 all told. Banks, on the other hand, employed in his siege as many as 40,000 men at one period, and at the time of the surrender had almost 30,000 in his command; his losses tallied 8,400, almost 5,000 of them in combat. Gardner and his brave command had outdone Banks in casualties inflicted by sixfold. No accusations of perfidy ever attached themselves to Franklin Gardner. Despite his New York nativity, and the fact that he had a brother in the Union army and his father was serving in the Treasury Department in Washington, Gardner's loyalty to the Confederacy remained unquestioned. He would not be himself exchanged until the fall of 1864, but then he would return to the army in the West to continue his admirable service. Of course, there was more to be heard from Banks as well, and in much the same tenor as before.[25]

And yet one victory more remained to close this Vicksburg campaign —for it was all one campaign really—and to close the string of heady successes that July brought for the Union. Grant stood secure in Vicksburg, now, with two Confederate armies wiped from the face of Mississippi and Louisiana. Yet a third remained, tardy perhaps, but still present, and still a potential threat. Joe Johnston took his time in moving against Grant. Now Grant would move against him. Oddly enough, it was all playing a part in another war as well. The threat to Vicksburg gave Braxton Bragg a chance to move against an enemy in his war with his army.

On May 23, with the news that Vicksburg had been invested, Bragg received appeals from Davis and Pemberton alike for reinforcements to go to Johnston. While he disliked to weaken his army, still he could not deny Johnston, now his superior. However, he could use the occasion to rid himself of troublesome individuals. At once he chose to send Breckinridge and his division, and should the aggravating Kentuckian be killed or captured in the coming campaign, then all the better. Reluctant to lead his beloved Kentuckians of the 1st Kentucky "Orphan" Brigade back to the hell of Mississippi, where they had suffered so terribly in the heat of the year before, he asked Bragg if he might leave them and take a brigade of Mississippians in their place. For such men, it would be a homecoming. Bragg left the matter to Breckinridge, and he in turn assembled the Orphans and put the matter to them. Immediately these men of the Bluegrass interpreted the question as a simple choice between their commander and the hated Bragg. That settled it quickly. Unanimously they elected to face the heat and fevers of another summer in Mississippi.

The division moved quickly, and by June 1 Breckinridge was in Jackson, where Johnston welcomed him and put him at once in command of the area. The state capital was almost defenseless, and feverishly the Kentuckian began the work of erecting earthworks. He called out local militia to do post duty so his veterans would be on the front, and cajoled 200 Negro slaves from the governor to assist in the digging. Jackson must be made defensible, and a base for an attack against Grant as well. "Time is blood now," he said. Johnston, meanwhile, sat at Canton some twenty-five miles north, gathering troops and awaiting his chance to swoop down on Grant's rear. Then by July 1, with the situation looking increasingly desperate, Johnston linked his forces with Breckinridge at Jackson and assumed personal command. Now they had an army of about 28,000, no match for Grant, but in a combined attack with Pemberton there might be hope for success. This same July 1 he sent Breckinridge and his division out in advance along the Vicksburg & Jackson Railroad, and by July 4 the Kentuckian and his men camped beside Champion's Hill. The sun was killing men from heatstroke in alarming numbers, but while Breckinridge considered the problem in the welcome relief of the evening, a Federal prisoner just captured was brought into his headquarters. It was 11 P.M., and the Yankee had news. Vicksburg had fallen.

The disaster changed everything. Breckinridge notified Johnston at once, and early the next morning Johnston ordered him to retreat with all speed to Jackson. Two days later the Kentuckian was back in the trenches at the capital, and Johnston prepared his army for an attack he knew must come soon. It would, for as soon as Grant had ridden into Vicksburg for his first look at the conquered city, he sent Sherman orders to move against Jackson. "I want you to drive Johnston out in your own way," he said, "and inflict on the enemy all the punishment you can." He gave his trusted general the IX and XIII Corps, in addition to his own XV Corps, and Sherman moved with them at once. By July 10 he had his army in place facing Johnston's works, and began an artillery shelling that continued for several days. Attacks and probes were made here and there, one against Breckinridge's division being smartly repulsed on July 12. It was a petty little victory, but just now any success seemed a great one, and Johnston complimented the Kentuckian and his "fine division" on their triumph.

But the Confederates could not stay. Daily Sherman extended his lines around the Southern flanks. In the heat that continued killing men every day, the Federal commander did not care to expose his men to battle as well. He learned from Grant that an enemy could be defeated without costly attacks. And Johnston had learned from Pemberton that a man who waited too long might be bottled up. On July 16 he decided that he had stood as long as possible. That night he gave orders for an evacuation, and the next day they were gone. When Sherman entered the city, he found it deserted. A Federal division followed in pursuit for a few miles, but Breckinridge was covering the retreat as he had at Shiloh and Stones River, and he was good at it. Finally the pursuit halted. "Pursuit in that hot weather would have been fatal to my command," said Sherman, and he was right. By the time he reached Morton, where the army halted, Breckinridge counted 500 men lost to the heat during the retreat.[26]

And there, at last, was an end to it. A campaign that traced its roots as far back as the days just after the fall of Corinth could finally be called done, and fairly won. The eastern and western Confederacies were split. A major army no longer existed to fight in the Rebellion. The "Father of Waters," as Lincoln put it, flowed "unvexed" to the sea. Yankee commerce could ply the Mississippi once again, and Federal armies and gunboats could make unrestricted use of it and its tributaries to pursue their enemy into the heartland of the Deep South and the Trans-Mississippi West. Here lay a gateway into the backyard of the Confederacy, and one that could not again be closed. Spectacular though it was, the victory at Gettysburg ended only a campaign and severely damaged Lee's high command. The triumph along the Mississippi took a major step in ending the war. Lee would fight and win again; Pemberton would not. Virginia still remained a Confederate state and well defended; Mississippi and much of Louisiana would not.

A few days after the victory, President Lincoln wrote in his self-effacing way to congratulate Grant. "I do not remember that you and I ever met personally," said the President. Now he thanked him for "the almost inestimable service you have done the country." In passing, Lincoln expressed his own misgivings about Grant's conduct of the campaign after the taking of Grand Gulf. He would have preferred that Grant move to join Banks rather than move first against Vicksburg. "I feared it was a mistake." Now, said the rail-splitter, he wanted to "make the personal acknowledgment that you were right, and I was wrong."

Nice words, to be sure, and Grant of course appreciated them. Yet he never found time to answer the compliment, even when Lincoln asked if he had received it. There were more important matters. He sent for his family to join him. And on July 6 he wrote to his father: "Vicksburg has at last surrendered after a siege of over forty days . . . Remember me to all at home." Only Halleck was notified of the victory before Jesse Grant. Perhaps someday the father would approve of Ulysses.[27]

CHAPTER 11

"ALL OUR WOMEN ARE FLORENCE NIGHTINGALES"

The news of the triumphs of July came to the two peoples at war like thunderbolts, their effects, though opposite, almost equally electric. When confirmation of the news of Gettysburg reached New York, the rejoicing seemed boundless. One man in the city delighted that "the charm of Robert Lee's invincibility" was broken at last, and at last the Army of the Potomac had "a general that can handle it." Everywhere on the streets people met and cheered that "This ends the Rebellion." Those of more reflection realized, though, that "there must be battles by the score before that outbreak from the depths of original sin is 'ended.'" Well, Grant gave them another victory, and Banks yet one more, and Sherman another to begin the tally of that score.[1]

Yet there were many, once the cheering stopped, who could not help looking at the still-prospering Union and ask themselves and their leaders why it had all happened, and why it continued to happen. Here in the North, as in the Confederacy, the euphoria of the first bright days of war gave way rapidly, first in the face of repeated defeat, and then in the seeming endlessness of the conflict. The people of the Union knew that they outstripped their foes in every class of war activity—production, men, weapons, finance. Certainly the war was not a spare-time affair for them, yet they fought it almost with one hand behind their backs, reserved for the business of expanding their trade and society and industry. Why in the face of all this, had the war gone on so long? There was a skepticism, a cynicism, in the land that had not been there in 1861. The North was suffering from the only malady, in fact, that could possibly cost it the ultimate victory. It was tired of the war.[2]

Divisions came between people of the North, as should be expected. Though united in the war, Republicans and Democrats, capital and labor, and the hundred other unmatched pairs that make up societies would naturally continue the low-keyed conflict that marked their heritage for millennia past. But somehow this war was having an accelerating effect, and magnifying the gaps between the classes into gulfs. The enormous profits to be made from war production and industry did not go to the people who did the work; they went to the owners and capitalists. Those with money simply made more. The laborer might have more work, but sometimes actually received less for it. The well-brushed blue uniforms with the glimmering buttons of officers covered many a son of well-born families, but the farmers and the laborers who went into the army served the dirty and bloody war at the front. The benefits, and there were many, seemed all to be going to one class, while the work and the bleeding was left for another. The wealthy could afford to buy "substitutes," men who for a sum would go into the army in another's place, thereby relieving him from his obligation for service under the draft. The laborer could hardly afford to buy his way out of the army. It is no accident that, both North and South, the cry soon became widespread of its being a "rich man's war, and a poor man's fight."

That resentment and a hundred others engendered by the turmoil into which the war threw society remained subordinated by the greater evil of the conflict itself for the first two years of fighting. In the face of defeat and humiliation, the people of the North showed a heroic determination, a resilience that their foes never expected to encounter. And in the first years, that determination and seeming single-mindedness made them also intolerant of dissenters. Those who questioned the administration were quickly branded as disloyal unless their other overt acts showed them to be behind the war. Only strong support for the war and the Union prevented many a Democrat from being castigated. Those who opposed the conflict soon learned the old lesson that dissenters in a time of national peril, however pure their motives, are walking a perilous path. Thus was Breckinridge forced to flee from his home into the Confederacy in September 1861, when his only crime was opposing the war. Thus were other members of Congress, like Jesse Bright of Indiana, expelled from the Senate for supposed disloyalty. In towns and villages across the country, the pressure of community disapproval and alienation proved powerful inducements for the faint-hearted to enlist. This was not just a war against the South. It was a national time of testing, and those who did not answer the call with gusto quickly found themselves *personae non gratae*.

In the 1862 elections the same held true, and men like Vallandigham were repudiated at the polls. Yet after a year of war none could dispute that unrest did grow in the North. Vallandigham and those like him still commanded a significant number of votes, even in defeat, and the Democrats did gain slightly in Congressional seats and governorships. Most of those elected differed with Lincoln on policy, not on the war itself, but the ranks were growing of those who wanted peace at any cost, who stood rigidly by the old constitutional guarantees and resisted coercion of any sort, whether of states or individuals. That they were a clear threat, or regarded as such, is evident in the Lincoln administration's increasing moves to stop them. Newspapers were closed or suppressed on occasion, and extreme measures were taken in rare instances. When Vallandigham, no longer in office, continued to speak publicly of the "wicked and cruel" war, and accused Lincoln of using it as a pretext to establish a Republican dictatorship, the military authorities in Dayton, Ohio, arrested him. Not coincidentally, they did so the day after the defeat at Chancellorsville. In the face of such a humiliating defeat, this gadfly was not to be tolerated. On May 6 a military commission tried him and found him guilty of uttering treasonous statements. On May 19, the day of Grant's first assault on Vicksburg, Lincoln ordered him banished from the United States and sent beyond military lines. Ironically, the Confederates did not want him any more than the Union, and soon he was in Canada, planning a return to the North in defiance of Lincoln's order. The outcry against Lincoln's order was immediate and greater than he expected, ample evidence of the increasing temper of the people. Lincoln, said some, was nothing more than "a weak imitation of the besotted tyrant Nero."

There was much more than Vallandigham causing the people to question the management of the war. The long string of military failures, of course, gave considerable fuel to the fire of unrest. Then there was the Emancipation Proclamation. To many it looked like an attempt to divert the true purpose of the war from Union to social revolution or worse. It could mean a rapid influx of very cheap labor in freed slaves, and at a time when white workers were hard put to earn a living. Despite the high profits of industry, the laborers' wages lagged greatly behind the rise of inflation due to the war and the increasing quantity of paper money printed by the government to meet its debts. When Grant took Vicksburg, consumer prices were up by 43 percent from their 1860 level, yet wages had risen only 12 percent. Strikes broke out in almost every manufacturing town, and even the most recent members of the work force, women, walked off their jobs in protest for higher pay. Certainly, on the face of it, the North presented a generally united front in commitment to prosecuting the war and restoring the Union, but beneath that veneer seethed multiple currents of unrest that even the news of the twin victories of Gettysburg and Vicksburg could not calm. By the summer of 1863 that unrest in some places—like New York City—needed only a catalyst to touch off violence. The time could hardly have been less propitious, then, for the implementation of what many regarded as the most discriminatory bit of class legislation yet, the draft.[3]

The Union needed conscription, of that Lincoln was certain. The volunteer system had worked for the first many months of the war, yet the conflict's voracious appetite quickly devoured all the fodder of the first patriotic enthusiasm, and more men had to be found. In part it was the administration's fault, for in the early expectations of a speedy victory, many regiments were enlisted for only eighteen, or nine, or even three months. By the end of 1862, when most of those enlistments were long expired, the combined Federal armies counted just over a half million men. There were nearly 100,000 desertions already. "We must see to it that the ranks of our armies, broken by toil, disease, and death, are again filled with the health and vigor of life," said one senator. The debate in Congress and Lincoln's approval soon produced the first Federal conscription act in the nation's history. On March 3, 1863, the President signed it into law.[4]

In the order of such things, it was a mild law, like so much of what came from Lincoln's hand, a restrained approach to a radical idea. It decreed that all males aged twenty to forty-five should be liable for conscription, but in two distinct classes. Those first to be called would be all single men within the age category, and those married men aged twenty to thirty-five. Should this category be exhausted, then the government would call up the married men over thirty-five. The act provided for a generous number of exemptions, ranging from mental and physical infirmity, to the draftee's being the sole means of support for his parents or children. If a man already had two brothers in the army, he stood exempt. Without doubt, the Union needed the draft, just as the Confederacy soon discovered that it needed conscription as well. Yet the very idea of forcible enlistment struck a nerve in the American personality. It violated all notions of individual rights and liberty. "This law converts the Republic into one grand military dictatorship," complained a New York weekly, and a member of Congress from Ohio complained that "this is a part and parcel of a grand scheme for the overthrow of the Union and for the purpose of building upon its ruins a new government based on new ideas—the idea of territorial unity and consolidated power."[5]

Yet what rankled most were two provisions of the bill in particular. One provided that a man might escape his obligation when drafted if he could persuade—which meant pay—another to go in his place. The government did not care who its soldiers were, just so the requisite number

filled the ranks. The other obnoxious clause allowed a man to purchase
his way out of the draft for $300. However, when a man purchased his
way out of one conscription list, it was no guarantee that his name might
not appear again on a later draft call, when of course he could buy his
way out again.

The outcry against these provisions, particularly among the poor and
laboring classes, ran bitter and hot. For many, $300 was a full year's in-
come. A man within the age limits who had children and a wife might
have no alternative but to leave them to their own devices while he went
off to war. Exemption was not available to fathers who had wives, for the
women should be able to support their children somehow. Only fathers
of motherless children could escape. And if a poor man somehow found
the $300 to pay his commutation, he could wind up on a later list just like
the capitalist and sons of wealth. The act created a clear distinction between rich and poor, making it probable that the one class could remain
at home and profit even more from the conflict, while the other, those
who stood to profit nothing from victory or defeat, would pay the price of
both with their blood. Soon those who opposed the draft measure were
singing a song with their own words put to a popular war tune:

> We're coming, Father Abraham, three hundred thousand more.
> We leave our homes and firesides with bleeding hearts and sore.
> Since poverty has been our crime, we bow to the decree;
> We are the poor who have no wealth to purchase liberty.[6]

The enrollment took longer than expected to begin, and once started,
late in May, it did not run smoothly. In all, some 3,115,000 males were
enrolled eventually, though nearly one third were exempted quickly for
physical disability. And almost as quickly as the enrollment began, so did
the resistance. Violent outbursts came in Ohio and Indiana, Copperhead
country to be sure, and in all the border states. But in Wisconsin and
even Pennsylvania, too, the opposition took a bitter turn. Yet if anyone
had been disposed to predict the place most likely to erupt in violence
over the draft, they would have to have signified New York City.[7]

It was a city with a history of civil violence. For New Yorkers it was
release, protest, even entertainment. In the four decades following 1834
the city suffered sixteen major mob riots with loss of life and property,
and innumerable lesser outbursts. Elections, holidays, holy days, labor dis-
putes, racism, and ethnic hostility toward immigrant groups, almost any
occasion could end in fighting. The city teemed with rival gangs of
workers, street toughs, volunteer fire companies, militia, Irish nationals,
Germans and Hungarians, and poor free blacks. They formed loose associations like the Bowery Boys and the Dead Rabbits. Sometimes the combative blood of the fire companies in particular rose so high that they ignored a blazing building in order to beat each other senseless. It was a
city filled with rival groups with nothing better to do than resent and sus-

pect each other. Their one common bond, however, was poverty. The overwhelming majority of these people lived on the low edge of the wage and subsistence scale. The draft would take them first.[8]

Many expected violence in the city as July dawned and the enrollment and draft were ready to take their first conscripts. The welcome news of Gettysburg and Vicksburg, thought some, would calm the anger of the opposition, however, and the date for the drawing of names from the lists would start on July 11. The governor and the mayor as well as other Democratic politicians spoke out against conscription, but still some observers seemed sanguine. When a blindfolded clerk drew several hundred cards with names out of a bin that day, there was no demonstration, and a diarist in the city wrote that the people took it "good-naturedly thus far." He believed that "this draft will be the *experimentum crucis* to decide whether we have a government among us," but then tempered his calm by saying that "we shall have trouble before we are through."

Some 1,236 names came out of the bin that day. Crowds gathered around to hear the names read, and when a friend's name came forth, his chums goaded him with "Goodbye, Patrick!" and "Goodbye, James!" The crowd dispersed quietly when the draft office closed. But many of the men gathered again in the bars and taverns that evening, and the grumbling began. Those who complained most were some members of the Black Joke Engine Company Number 33. The state militia held volunteer firemen exempt from militia duty, and these men felt the Federal draft should do the same, yet several of their number heard their names called that day. The draft office would be closed on Sunday, July 12, but they decided that on Monday morning the fire company would attack the office and destroy its lists and all records of the conscriptions of men of the Black Joke. Quickly the word spread, and several other groups of men and workers decided that they would go along to watch the fun. All the elements for the spontaneous combustion of mob riot thus went into place.[9]

Reinforcements came to protect the draft office when it opened that Monday. Sixty policemen stood guard as the names once more came out of the bin. Fifty-six were announced when a cry was heard that the mob was coming. Soon the Black Joke boys pulled up in a wagon, threw stones and brickbats, someone fired a pistol, and in they charged. Nothing could stop them. They ransacked the office and set it afire, a blaze that soon spread to neighboring buildings. The scores of onlookers quickly caught the contagion and began looting the surrounding houses, breaking windows and carrying away anything of value. The New York Draft Riots had begun and would not cease until much bloody work had been done.

The atmosphere had already been charged by the morning press, which announced that the Irish laborers were threatening an uprising. Rumors swept through the city, bringing hundreds and hundreds out of their offices and workhouses, away from the factories and docks, to see, and

later participate. The heat of the summer, the frustration of two years of war, the high prices and low wages, and the damned draft all conspired to turn the city into a bedlam. Most of the state militia regiments were away, called out weeks before to go to the defense of Pennsylvania. There were a few regiments of Federal soldiers stationed in the city, and now they must be brought forward to protect it from itself.

All that day the rioting grew in intensity and spread from block to block. At the Second Street Armory the militia placed cannon in the street to prevent the looters breaking in and seizing the arms stored there. The cannon might deter the rioters, but nothing else did. Policemen by the score were battered and overrun. When some squads of Federal soldiers tried to fight their way through the mob at Forty-second Street, they were severely repulsed. An orphan asylum went up in flames, as did scores of other buildings, the fires spreading rapidly. The fires, in turn, called forth more of the fire companies, many of them abandoning their hoses and ladders to take up paving stones and clubs. A witness, whose entry in his diary betrayed the very class distinction that helped ignite this inferno, observed that "The crowd seemed just what one commonly sees at any fire." It had at its fringes a seeming layer of decent curiosity seekers, but soon the central core of "the lowest Irish day laborers" broke out and charged off toward Lexington Avenue. "The rabble was perfectly homogeneous. Every brute in the drove was pure Celtic." Beside them marched their "low Irish women," most of them seeming "stalwart young vixens and withered old hags." The telegraph lines were being cut and street railway track torn up, and those more prone toward paranoiac speculation decided that Jefferson Davis lay at the root of it all. Telegrams were sent by the lines still up, calling on Lincoln and Washington for assistance. Before they could respond, Providence acted in the guise of heavy rain to quell the rioting for the moment. "Mobs have no taste for the effusion of cold water," said the smug diarist. But before the mob retired to the drinking halls and alleys for the night, its taste for blood had already begun to appear. It was a white mob. It hated the police, the draft officials, the soldiers in its way, and all blacks. Most of the first three escaped its grasp, but too many of the last did not. The rain that fell that night cleansed the lifeless bodies of several Negroes that dangled from ropes or lay sprawled in the streets, beaten beyond recognition.[10]

Alas, the rain did not last long enough, and during that night the confusion between civil and military authorities over who should take charge only added to the certainty that the carnage and destruction would continue on the morrow. It did, with greater intensity, opening with the senseless beating murder of a Negro seaman early in the morning. For the rest of the day blacks in the city were the particular targets of the rioters. Many whites, particularly storekeepers, actually did what they could to prevent the beatings, some taking goods to the black homes so that their occupants would not have to venture onto the streets. But still the killing went on, as did the burning. The sub-Treasury and customs house had to be barricaded. Police stations fortified themselves. All city transportation came to a halt, and of course hundreds of storefronts were looted. The mob carried away anything that came to hand, from luxuries to useless articles. Precisely what day laborers expected to do with top hats from Brooks Brothers no one could say, but the clothiers was ransacked just the same.

That morning the police began to attack, though not successfully at first. Soon 150 men of the 11th New York joined them, under the command of Colonel Henry O'Brien, and then 150 more, and volleys fired above the heads of the mob drove them away from one block. They would not forget O'Brien. Both east and west sides of the city blazed with burning buildings and unrestrained rioting. Some police were besieged in their own precinct houses, and others simply left the city rather than face the mobs. Governor Horatio Seymour made an attempt to quell the mobs by coming to City Hall and delivering a speech. "I beg you to disperse," he said, deploring the violence. "There is no occasion for resisting the draft, for it has not yet been enforced." He proclaimed his own opposition to the conscription and promised to fight it "to see that there shall be no inequality between the rich and the poor." Indeed, he would even try to raise money to help those who could not afford to buy exemption. Though the speech was certainly not intended to stir the mob to further action, neither was it the sort of oration that loyal men wanted to hear, and Seymour would ever after be charged with abetting the violence by promising his own opposition to the draft.[11]

That afternoon volunteer companies began forming to resist the mobs, and some old nine-months regiments now mustered out of service saw the majority of their members come together once more for the emergency. Some 1,200 men volunteered for special police duty as well, and the government clerks at the customs house and other Federal buildings armed themselves and drilled for action. A gunboat anchored off the Battery, ready to shell the Wall Street area if necessary. By now all semblance of pretext was abandoned. The draft was hardly mentioned by the rioters. They were out for loot, destruction, revenge of a hundred old scores, and simple entertainment. Thugs from New Jersey even crossed the river to take part in the revelry. That afternoon they tried to take a large store of arms from the Union Steam Works, failed, and then began robbing gun stores instead. Only the rifles of the soldiers, firing into the air, had been able to disperse the crowds, and now the mob leaders wanted to fight back. For the rest of the afternoon solitary shots foretold that some Negro or lone policemen, or a man of apparent wealth was being attacked. The essential nature of this uprising as one of poor against rich became increasingly evident. Men in well-tailored clothes dared not enter the streets. "Down with the rich men," came the cries. "There goes a $300 man." A well-to-do lawyer was gunned down on Thirty-sixth Street for no reason other than his prosperity.

And soon the mob revenged itself against O'Brien. He found his home looted, and as he came to salvage what he could a mob formed quickly and attacked. He was clubbed from behind, got away briefly, and then was attacked again. They knocked him senseless, and then everyone took a turn at kicking him, even children. They lit fires under his limbs, dragged him back and forth across the street, and attacked any who tried to help him. It took the colonel hours to die.[12]

"The people are waking up," said George T. Strong as he watched the course of the rioting, "and by tomorrow there will be adequate organization to protect property and life." Yet when July 15 came, the rioting continued, now more systematic, and directed at the blacks. Their homes were sought out and looted, then destroyed. The Negroes themselves became hunted creatures. "Everywhere throughout the city they are driven about like sheep, and numbers are killed of whom no account will ever be learned," said the press. This was the critical day for the riots. The authorities were exhausted. Some of the ardent anti-administration newspapers were clearly urging the rioters on in their depredations. The attacks on blacks continued and murders mounted. More troops arrived, and bayonet charges and salvos from cannon drove the mob back. The 7th New York was on its way, and the 65th New York as well, with more guns and more artillery. Though the fighting was almost constant throughout the afternoon, it was apparent by nightfall that at last the law was gaining the upper hand. The next day there were over 4,000 trained soldiers in the city, and the rioters were outclassed and outgunned. Sporadic outbreaks occurred in isolated places during the day, but clearly the violence had spent itself. Stores began to open once more and home guards and vigilance committees joined the police in safely patrolling the recent battlefield. Still men were killed, buildings burned and looted, but the hours were numbered for the rioters, and the next day the mayor could announce that the New York Draft Riots were done.[13]

The aftermath, however, continued to influence the city and the nation for some time to come. Over $1.5 million in damages was done in the four days, and at first enormously exaggerated estimates of the dead circulated, being accepted for years afterward. Some put the tally at over 1,000, others claimed 1,400 and more. Yet the best reckoning available from the official records of the uprising shows only slightly over 100 deaths directly attributable to the riots, and some of those were from peripheral causes. A few ill people died because their doctors were afraid to leave home to bring them their medicine. One black man, overcome by fear of the rioters, hanged himself. The verifiable total of deaths comes to 119, the worst cost of civil uprising in the country's history. Of the rioters themselves, only some 400 were actually arrested, and half released without charges. Just eighty-one went to court, and most were convicted, but of lesser crimes than charged. The worst sentence any received was ten years in prison. Some went back home after nothing worse than paying fines, one as low as six cents.[14]

It was an ugly page, coming as it did right on the euphoria of the Union's great string of victories. The draft had only been the catalyst to set off an explosion of class and race hatred that festered in the city for years even before the war. The Negro population of New York City went into a decline, as thousands moved away in fear. In time the conscription act would be enforced, and without further substantial demonstration. But for four days the city burned with the fire of hatred and prejudice. Through it all a poet, Herman Melville, watched and listened, and wrote of "Red Arson glaring balefully," of the "Athiest roar of riot," of how "the town is taken by its rats."[15]

This was the second battle upon Northern soil that summer; Gettysburg had been the other. But when the excitement of both had quieted, the people of Lincoln's land continued in the way they had for two years, living with a war that seemed always to be there. They might not accept it, but they got used to it. Like the seasons, it was always there. Familiarily bred their fears out of them, though not their determination. They farmed and toiled, and most simply tried to live around the higher prices, the lower wages, the few shortages of goods, and the many losses of friends and loved ones. At the same time, however, they came to accept, too, the beginnings of some fundamental changes in the old order of things. Like most of the changes in this era of war, they were not rapid and revolutionary, but more along the order of a sudden impetus to gradual shifts already underway. Certainly nowhere could this be seen better than in the changing role of women.

Contrary to popular notion, women had already entered the economic and industrial sphere by the time the war came. In 1860 there were over a quarter million ladies employed in some trade or industry, most of them working in the textile and shoe factories of New England, where they made better than half of the region's industrial labor force. In order to get a job, any job, they worked longer hours for less pay than the men. By 1863 their incomes were shocking. Some women who worked eighteen hours a day, six days a week, took home a weekly earning of $3 and less. A seamstress in New York City could make as little as seventeen cents a day.

Women had made their first inroads into private enterprise as well, though on an equally limited scale, and with mixed success. Some manufactured china and porcelain, others kept hotels and saloons, and some managed farms and even plantations. They broke into the traditional men's professions of office work, and by 1861 a few even worked in some of the United States Government departments in Washington. The men did not always care for the idea. Secretary of the Interior Robert

McClelland declared in the late 1850s that "There is such an obvious impropriety in the mixing of the sexes within the walls of a public office, that I am determined to arrest the practice." Fellow male workers did their best to discourage it, too. When Clara Barton worked in the Patent Office, the men in the concern stared at her, blew cigar smoke toward her, spat tobacco juice near her, and "gave cat-calls or made obnoxious remarks."

Of course, Elizabeth Blackwell had broken into the medical profession in 1849, and numbers of women, some 400 of them, held jobs as postmistresses. But still there were no lawyers wearing skirts, few in clerical robes, and none in the military. They might be teachers, though men were preferred, and female schools and "seminaries" flourished in the North during the 1850s. The education was not wasted on them, and several turned to one avenue that lay open without much prejudice—writing. Harriet Beecher Stowe led their ranks when her *Uncle Tom's Cabin* became one of the major best-selling books of the century. Yet even here the men were not always tolerant. "D_____d scribbling women," Nathaniel Hawthorne called them. It was only "if the Devil was in her," he said, that "a woman ever writes anything worth reading." To be sure, most of their produce were lurid romances and glib travel narratives, but some women of the pen turned to more spirited and significant fare. They assumed front-rank positions in some of the abolitionist press, and quickly spread from that to leadership in a variety of reform and public welfare areas. And by the 1850s the women were banding together in the cause of their own rights. Susan Brownell Anthony was already a name known and vilified among conservative men, and feared even by most women. Lydia Child, the Grimke sisters, Lucretia Mott, and black women like Sojourner Truth and Harriet Tubman were all enjoying greater and greater publicity in their twin crusades for abolition of slavery and emancipation of women. Certainly, the old order was already under serious challenge by feminine society when the war came, with some small economic and social gains. But more important is the fact that the prewar decades had trained them in organization and management, developing the skills that needed only some great opportunity for employment, and fulfillment. The war came at exactly the right time.[16]

For every man who answered the call in 1861, there seemed to be a woman—often more than one—who gave her heart to the cause as much as her gentleman. Indeed, in their invective and patriotic expressions, the women frequently achieved heights of spirit and venom hardly approached by their men. Perhaps it was because words were the only weapons they could hurl against the Rebellion. Certainly they could not don uniform and fight—they were not supposed to. A British observer found that the women of the North were "the bitterest, most vengeful" of the populace. At once they cast about to find what they could do to defeat the enemy. First, of course, they encouraged their husbands and sons to enlist in what must certainly be a speedy march to victory. In years after, however, the encouragement often waned as a mother who already had one or two graves to tend tried to keep her last son at home. These women supported the draft, resenting those who stayed at home while their men went and fought and died.

At first, too, they took a prominent role in outfitting their men for the war. A flurry of home seamstressing never before or after seen in America accompanied the first wave of enlistments. Stockings, shirts, "draws" as the men called their underdrawers, scarves, and even long woolen underwear came from the looms and needles of tens of thousands of women. In the rush there often came a pair of trousers with two left legs, or the gloves that Quaker ladies knitted with only four fingers on the right hand—no trigger finger. Almost uncountable aid and relief societies appeared everywhere, 20,000 by one reckoning. They furnished clothing and food for the men raising in their towns, sent them succor in their training camps, met them at railroad stops on the way to the front with cakes and pies and letters from home. They wrote letters for the illiterate, and read them to those too tired or ill to read for themselves. And scores of regiments would go into battle following gay banners sewn by the ladies at home, often from articles of special meaning like wedding dresses.[17]

All this individual effort soon fell naturally together under the impetus to organize. As in so many other regions of this conflict, administration and management would bring greater success than simple enterprise. Grant saw it in the campaign to Vicksburg, and the women of the North saw it in their relief and welfare efforts. Before long several of the diverse bodies began to come together in larger units with common goals. The first formed was the United States Sanitary Commission, which began operations in June 1861, one of its first officers being the stuffy New Yorker George Templeton Strong. Its leadership did not include women, but its functional purpose in advising the government and the people of what was needed by the soldiers put thousands of women to work supplying those needs. It brought system to their endeavors in producing relief for the wounded and some sanitation in camp and field. Women gave food and made clothing, and as well engaged in fund-raising, charity bazaars, and benefits, even soliciting donations, in order to fund the Commission's work. In all, during the war, some $15 million came forth for the Commission's purposes, most of it raised by the loyal ladies of the North. And when tired soldiers came home on furlough, there were refreshment saloons for them in most of the major cities, all maintained and funded by the Sanitary Commission.

So successful did this organization become that rival bodies soon formed, begetting a genuine competition to see which philanthropic women's organization could do the most. In November 1861 the United States Christian Commission took form, and quickly competed with the

Sanitary for public attention and good works. One of its commissioners was Jay Cooke, the foremost financier in the Union. The two groups had similar methods, but with differing goals, the one to relieve the bodies of the soldiers, and the other to uplift their spiritual being. In both, the role of women in the rank and file proved vital.[18]

They did more than raise money and make bandages. Hundreds, if not thousands, of women put both to active use. The European and American world was still enthralled with the romantic image of Florence Nightingale and her nursing mission to the wounded and diseased during the Crimean War just a few years before. As soon as the new war erupted, the women of the North and South turned out in surprising numbers. "All our women are Florence Nightingales," said the New York *Herald*, and there was much of truth in it, yet here again the role of the woman suffered a change. For two centuries the mother and wife had been expected to be nurse to the family, but as a professional the female nurse remained an oddity. And social convention seriously questioned the acceptability of a woman working in an army hospital filled with men. The war changed all that. It was a means by which ladies could actively express their patriotism, their support for the war. For those who had sons or husbands or fathers in the army and away from home, it gave them occupation, and in tending to the men of other women, a vicarious connection with their own distant loved ones. It was exhausting work, demanding, dirty, and sometimes dangerous. Few could tolerate it for the length of the war, yet when the conflict ended no one would again question the employment of women as military nurses. Some women, most notably Clara Barton and Dorothea Dix, launched brilliant careers as organizers of the nursing corps, and scores of others attained considerable notoriety, and authority. Mary Bickerdyke, called "Mother" by the men she tended, brought system and organization to hospitals in the West, and did not hesitate to order about even men of considerable rank. A surgeon thus buffeted complained to Grant, without avail. "My God, man," replied the general, "Mother Bickerdyke outranks everybody, even Lincoln." In all, perhaps 2,000 other mothers like Mrs. Bickerdyke made careers as army nurses for Lincoln. Most of them encountered the prejudice of the male doctors, who still regarded all aspects of the medical profession as distinctly the province of their gender. Almost all suffered from the rigors of the job, 10 percent or more breaking under the strain, and several died in the field from disease or overwork. One who perished was Margaret Breckinridge, cousin to the general on the other side. Yet a few did achieve a particular notoriety, and even military status. In 1864 Mary A. Walker received a commission as an assistant surgeon, and with it the right to wear the Federal uniform. When she was captured late in the year, she offered the Confederates a sight truly amazing, "a *thing* that nothing but the debased and depraved Yankee nation could produce." The Rebels found her "dressed in the full uniform of a Federal Surgeon," adding that she was "not good-looking and of course had tongue enough for a regiment of men." A beauty she was not, nor was she a particularly effective surgeon, but she knew how to sell herself. For years after the war she wore that uniform and the Medal of Honor awarded her after the surrender, earning a living as a professional oddity.

Once the war was done, many forgot the services of the nurses, and some who knew better actually claimed that women's "best service was rendered in connection with extra diets, the linen-room and the laundry." Yet it simply was not so, nor were many women content to remain noncombatant spectators. In a romantic society like that of the early Victorian age, heroic figures of the past acquire a powerful influence over young men and women, attracting both admiration and emulation. So with Florence Nightingale. So, too, with Joan of Arc. However exaggerated Joan's real adventures, to the young women of the 1860s they were all too real, and crying for repetition.

Of course Washington never entertained for a moment the notion of arming women for the fight, yet many ladies themselves, particularly the young, felt trapped by their sex and denied the really important and glorious opportunities offered only to men. They wanted more. The first and most generally approved attempts at paramilitary service came from women's groups in New York and elsewhere. Assuming the possibility that there might be an enemy invasion, some ladies organized to study drill and tactics, even practicing with weapons, and donned "nice little uniforms" for the occasion. The community made much over them, and home guard units sprang up all across the North, and the South. None ever went into battle, and most withered after the first year of the war. Yet it was a start. Equally celebrated, and somewhat longer lasting, were the *vivandières*, women who, like drummer boys, wore uniforms and marched and trained with the regiments. They were more mascots than soldiers, sometimes carrying the banners on ceremonial occasions, but when the men left for the front, the women in uniform stayed behind, sometimes as a liaison between the regiment and the home community.[19]

For some few women, however, even this was not enough. They wanted to be with the armies and in the fighting. All told, about 400 women North and South actually donned uniforms and took up arms, of course without the knowledge or detection of the authorities. The physical examinations of the time often proved cursory, and it was not impossible that a woman with a boyish figure and bobbed hair might escape the examiner's scrutiny. More difficult, of course, was avoiding being discovered by her mess and tent mates. The soldiers bathed together in streams and ponds when the opportunity appeared, and there more than anywhere else lay the danger of discovery for these latter-day Joans. The other likelihood of exposure came when a woman took a wound. In hospital, no amount of disguise could prevent a doctor or nurse's encounter with some anatomy that should not be there.

Some girls, like a mysterious woman known only as Emily, actually became obsessed with the idea that they truly were Joan of Arc. She was found out when mortally wounded late in 1863, and sent her parents a final message that she had "expected to deliver her country, but the fates would not have it so." An unidentified girl was found dead on the field after Shiloh, killed in action. Several women, with their husbands' or brothers', or fiancés' approval, enlisted with them in their regiments and fought through the war. Mary Owens saw her husband killed in the same battle where she took a wound that put her out of the war.

The list of those who served and fought is not long, for many who preserved their secret during the war kept it in the years after. Only those who were discovered make up the bulk of the tally. While Grant invested Vicksburg, Fanny Wilson of New Jersey found her charade exposed. She tried to reenlist in another regiment a few months later, only to be discovered yet again. Some, of course, never even got to the front, their feminine traits and actions betraying them. A Wisconsin girl's disguise lasted only long enough for her bunkmates to see the distinctly unmasculine way that she put on her shoes and stockings.

Some did make it through the war, however, and none more successfully than Jennie Hodgers. Little is known of her except her Irish nativity, but in 1862, aged just nineteen, she enlisted in the 95th Illinois and served a full three-year term. Her fellow soldiers found her to be quiet and secretive, but "Albert Cashier" was a good-enough soldier in the fighting at Vicksburg and elsewhere. After the war she continued her masquerade, and in 1899 even managed to fool the surgeons who examined her when she successfully applied for a pension. Only an automobile accident in 1911 revealed to her physicians what she had kept secret from the army for so long. Her old comrades were shocked, though remembering how discreet Cashier had always been. Sarah Seelye, too, made good her disguise. She served as Franklin Thompson in the 2d Michigan Infantry for two years, fighting at the First Bull Run and in the Seven Days battles. Only when taken with malaria did she finally reveal her sex, and then she continued to serve as a nurse.[20]

Despite the romance that a few attached to these women soldiers, most men and women of the North regarded them as somewhat less than wholesome. Indeed, it cannot be denied that the majority of women who made the masquerade did it for business purposes as prostitutes. Indeed, the greatest contingent of women at the front was usually that of the camp followers. The commanders repeatedly tried to control their movements and ban them from the lines, but always the men and women found a means for supply and demand to meet. Yet surely the most enterprising were those who risked battle in uniform, whatever their motive. Occasionally nature's natural course revealed them, as when a sergeant in Rosecrans' army suddenly gave birth to a baby "in violation of all military law and of the army regulations."

However they served, as nurses, soldiers, spies—spying was popular and acceptable—couriers, fund-raisers, or whores, the women of the North took part in this war as their kind had never done before. Further, they broke out of the conventional mold that society had built around them, even if only for a time. Women took up smoking, they began to philander just as their men always had now that husbands were gone, their language changed, divorces rose in number, they drank and adventured. Much of their accused decline of moral standard owed its impetus to poverty, the low wages paid them, and the necessity of staying alive while the menfolk of the family played at war. But much also resulted from the newfound sense of independence and self-reliance that came from running the farms and stores, and even businesses, on their own. In the crushingly oppressive social restrictions coming for women in the next two decades, much of this independence would go underground once more. But the women of America had savored a taste of something better. Some made much of it, more did little or nothing, and a few simply wallowed. Yet that taste would linger in their mouths for years to come, and they would not again be entirely as they were before.[21]

All this came years before the cries of reform would become common in the political arena, yet thanks to the demands of the war and largely through the efforts of these women and the like-minded men of conscience, a social revolt in the realm of public welfare was aborning as well. They came in response to the immediate needs of the armies at first, of course, but shortly after the formation of the Sanitary and Christian commissions, the American tradition of poor relief and welfare began to alter in its treatment of the civilian population.

Even before the war, observers inclined to be critical of the United States still had to admit that Americans seemed unusually concerned over the poor and disabled, and more generous in their charities than would be supposed. Despite the avaricious nature of the Yankee merchant and the luxurious indulgence of the wealthy planter, both seemed equally inclined to share at least a small part of their windfall with the disadvantaged, particularly under the aegis of the church. Indeed, the greatest of the benevolent associations in the 1850s were the Protestant Bible societies and missionary enterprises. As the war approached, the combined contributions to these societies alone totaled over $1 million, and that did not include donations to the poor and almshouses, the private schools, the anti-slave organizations like the American Colonization Society, and the many local churches, lodges, Young Men's Christian Associations, and other bodies. Beyond this, Americans North and South responded quickly and generously to disaster relief endeavors, whether for a yellow fever outbreak in New Orleans or to the hard-pressed settlers of frontier Kansas. The tradition of the helping hand went back to the days when all Americans lived on a frontier, when each gave and took the assistance of the other out of mutual necessity. Of course, the rise of capital and planter economies had tempered that by 1860, yet still giving was deeply engrained in the American mind. It was also entertainment of a sort, with its charity balls and bazaars. And it was the undisputed arena in which women could break out of their home lives and become managers and organizers.[22]

With the coming of the war, these people stood ready to undertake even greater responsibilities and challenges. The first addressed was soldier relief, chiefly by the two great commissions that dominated the field. But other modes of public welfare burgeoned as well, many of them merely expanding existing charitable agencies. A soldier received eleven dollars a month in pay, barely enough to support modest entertainments and necessities in the field, much less being sufficient for him to send money home to support a family. All across the North societies for the relief of soldiers' wives and children, and widows and orphans, doled out money and food to the unfortunate. State hospitals for the insane, the deaf and dumb, and the blind managed not only to stay in operation despite the drain on capital but, by the last years of the war, actually began to flourish. Even state appropriations went on the rise. Orphanages in particular benefited, chiefly because battlefield death created so many orphans, and the states of the Union almost uniformly took the position that the fatherless children were the responsibility of the people for whom the parent had died. Many orphanages began solely to care for these children in particular, to the exclusion of others, and out of it came the Children's Aid Society, which placed these children in new foster homes, generally in the West.[23]

In a separate category came the enormous welfare efforts made in behalf of the Negro. One of the old arguments of the planters against emancipation was that, once freed, the black would be a burden on society, unable to care for himself. Since many of the slaves were untrained and unskilled, and wholly unaccustomed to absolute responsibility for their lives, the protest carried a shade of truth. Sensing this, or fearing it, aid societies for the freedmen and runaway slaves commenced almost as soon as the frightened escaped blacks began to find their way into Federal lines. At first Yankee generals like Benjamin F. Butler simply provided for the "contrabands," as he called them, by seizing or taxing the wealth of Southerners in rebellion. Then Northern groups like the Gideonites began raising money and teachers to go to the South and begin the education of the freedmen. Barely was Port Royal taken in South Carolina before the first experiments began in bringing the slaves out of illiteracy, and as the war went on, military commanders themselves sometimes set aside portions of land for settlement by the former slaves. The armies found work for the contrabands, paying them in food and shelter, and sometimes with a meager wage. Self-help and education were the goal, and for the latter a score of Northern associations sent their teachers to the occupied territories. And toward the end of the war moves began to establish a sound economic base for the blacks. The Freedmen's Savings Bank took as its sole task the holding of deposits from Negroes, their investment, and the payment of interest.[24]

Philanthropy, public and private, went further, with more generosity, than any in the Union might have expected. It came out of conscience, enterprise, abundant opportunity, conviction, sometimes even speculation, and largely because there was so much money available in the booming economy after 1862. Whatever the motives impelling the charity, it created a legacy that lasted for long after the guns themselves stopped making widows and orphans. Yet much of the philanthropy that continued came as the direct result of the war. Tens of thousands came back from the field maimed for life and unable to work. More, drugged heavily because of the pain from their wounds, became addicted to the opiates. The displaced, the damaged, the disadvantaged all looked to their brothers to keep them, and in a large way they did.

This is, they did in the North, for though all of the influences that so tended to change, even revolutionize, society in Yankeedom exerted themselves as well in Dixie, the response was necessarily much different. Cursed as everywhere with too little of too much, the Confederacy proved simply unable to cope with the massive strains placed upon its crumbling social structure.

If anything, Southern society before the war lay closer to the tension of class versus class than did the North, though chiefly on a regional basis. The very poor and the very wealthy formed equally minute portions of the body politic. There was, in fact, a considerable middle class of Jefferson's beloved yeoman farmers, people who owned neither slaves nor great estates, but who subsisted on their own, on their own land. Yet their interests as well as those of the poor were essentially governed by the ruling minority of aristocrats and the politicians and editors dominated by them. As a result, here, too, the cry came forth of rich men making the war so that the poor men would have to fight it. The difference was that for generations in the South the poorer classes paid heed to their conditioning to show deference to their betters. In the North they did not. But the coming of the conflict, and the social and economic tensions it created, proved a considerable leveler, for now the aristocrats not only made common cause with the middle and lower classes, but also came to be dependent upon them.[25]

Once the halo of the glorious cause began to tarnish, as the war appeared likely to last more than a single glorious summer, the hardships began in the Confederacy, and the distinctions of class became more pronounced. The much more rapid rate of inflation, the greater shortages, and the virtual halt of much enterprise created a far more pervasive and insidious strain on the people than in the Union. In 1863 in North Carolina and Virginia women rioted over food, and in Richmond their protest over bread soon followed the pattern of the draft rioting in New York by degenerating into simple vandalism and destruction, the venting of the eternal frustration of the poor.

The draft did not produce in the Confederacy an explosion such as in New York, but the opposition and resentment over conscription was no less widespread, and no less based on feelings of class discrimination. The first Confederate conscription act did not provide for a man actually buying his way out of his obligation, but it did allow the paying of substitutes, and that was just as good. Further, the law established a bewildering variety of exempted professions and classifications of workers: teachers, miners, river and harbor pilots, nurses, ironworkers, druggists, railroad men, and almost all officeholders in state and Confederate governments. Even other classes of exemptions lay at the whim of the War Department, and very quickly it became evident that a man with any influence could manage an exemption if, barring any other means, he simply took a part-time government job. This alone created resentment, not to mention the affront that any national draft presented to the whole notion of states' rights upon which the rebellion was seemingly based. Several state governors, most notably Joseph Emerson Brown of Georgia, actually refused to honor the law, or circumvented it by claiming an inordinate number of men as government workers.

It did not help that the War Department's Conscription Bureau, charged with enforcing the draft, frequently showed little interest in how or with whom it filled its quotas. Then the Congress made even sharper the class consciousness of the measure when it extended exemptions in 1862 to anyone who owned twenty or more slaves. Clearly the aristocrats were preserving themselves and their own sons from the fighting, leaving it to the middle-class farmer and the poor white who did not have the luxury of an exempt occupation. The abuses within the system, and the widespread evasion, prevented the Confederate conscription from ever approaching the effectiveness that Davis designed for it.[26]

What also did not help with conscription, nor the twin evil of impressment—forcible seizure of crops or livestock for the army in return for often valueless scrip—was the fact that the Confederacy, too, had its "copperheads." The support for secession lurked chiefly along the tidewater regions of Virginia and North Carolina, in the lowlands of Georgia, and along the meanderings of the Mississippi and its Deep South tributaries. Yet cutting right through the heart of the Confederacy ran the Appalachian Mountain range, and the people of the hills and mountains in great numbers stood by the old Union. They felt little in common with the secessionists. Tidewater and piedmont had rarely mixed, either in family or in society. These were people whose parents had come from the North, largely of Scots and British descent, the so-called Scots-Irish, and their views stood much in common with those of their cousins and uncles

in Pennsylvania and New York. Indeed, in time every single state now in
the Confederate constellation except South Carolina would raise one or
more regiments to go and fight with the Union. To these people, the
Confederate draft presented nothing but despotism. They evaded it, they
refused to sell their provisions to the pressmen, or else concealed them,
and they made the tax collectors squeal before they paid levies to support
the war.

The same perceptions of the difference between who made the war
and who had to fight it could be seen in the cities as well as in the mountains. Labor in Southern industry, just as in the North, found itself working more and making less. There were not the hearty band of capitalists
profiting from the conflict that New York or Massachusetts could boast,
but still small fortunes came into a few hands, and not those of the
workers. Strikes brought men and machines to a halt here, too. They seldom succeeded, for management usually had nothing more to give, but
the important issue is that they occurred at all. Before the war Southern
labor stayed almost as docile as the slaves, and largely because of them.
No strike could be very threatening to an employer when the white
workers who walked off the job could be replaced quickly by blacks.[27]

Yet if slave laborers could prove to be the undoing of strikes and
work stoppages, they did, nevertheless, prove to be the very salvation of
the army. It was only the presence of a huge captive work force that allowed so many white Southerners to take arms. Indeed, at the high point
of the war, the summer of 1863, there were probably as many able-bodied
black men living and working behind the lines as white, and perhaps
more. As a result, the ever-present Southern fear of slave uprisings took a
considerable leap, and rumors of plots flew wildly across the country. Only
after the first two years of the war passed without a revolt did the fear
calm somewhat, in the face of an obvious disinclination toward rebellion
on the part of the blacks. Instead, they continued at their tasks, often
with little or no awareness of the great conflict raging. Many, fed with
wild stories of Yankee barbarity, actually feared the coming of Federal armies, while others, accustomed to white domination by generations of experience, remained quite loyal to their masters, or if not, then showing little interest in what happened or who won. Even though some 180,000
Confederate blacks escaped their bonds and came to fight in the Union
army, far more of their brethren apparently took the attitude that, whoever won, the lot of the black man would remain the same. Bond slave or
wage slave made little difference.[28]

Ironically, the slave system still had the effect during the war of
uplifting many Negroes. With the white men away, the black men had
to fill their places and, in many instances, take their responsibilities.
Training, education, authority, experiences all foreign to most slaves now
inevitably came into the hands of several. And in other cases, when the
white master left, the slaves refused to answer to his wife. They became

independent, if disorganized, thinking for themselves for a change and doing what suited them, and when. As the enemy armies advanced into the Confederate interior, many slaveholders fled with their blacks, and large numbers of Negroes ended up living and working in the ever-more-crowded cities, chiefly Richmond and Atlanta. As they became more vital to keeping the industry of war running, so it became more difficult to handle them in the old ways of the master and overseer.[29]

The changes brought about in the status of women in the South proved much more substantial, and the blow that the war delivered to the largely mythical Southern belle was not easily overcome. Far more than in the North, the woman in the South had been placed by writers, editors, romance, and her own men, upon a considerable pedestal. Or rather, that is where her image resided, for the real Confederate woman differed little from her sisters outside Dixie. Her frustrations and aspirations stood much the same, and to her, too, the war offered a meager opportunity to break out of her conventional role.

In much there was little to distinguish the Yankee from the Rebel woman. They equaled each other in their vituperation of the enemy, their exhortations to their men to go and fight, their disdain of the malingered and the $300 men. They knitted and sewed, sent food and luxuries to the mustering camps, met the trains at the stations with pies and drinks and bright smiles. They, too, proved effective fund-raisers by their bazaars and fairs and the sale of their handmade goods, yet more frequently they set more limited goals for their money, like uniforms for a particular regiment, or tents for men in winter camp. The ladies of Charleston even partially funded the ironclad *Palmetto State*, and other "Ladies' Gunboat" funds appeared elsewhere in the Confederacy. They, too, filled the places in the schoolrooms and colleges vacated by men taking arms. Even the counting houses and factories saw crinolines instead of denims on their workers. When Grant and Sherman entered the tent-cloth factory in Jackson that summer of 1863, the bulk of the workers were local women. They took over the farms and managed the plantations, and to them fell a burden not visited upon many Northern women. They had to maintain their agrarian economy in the face of increasing shortages in almost every necessity. Tools and implements broke down. Preservatives and flavorings, dyes and formulae, had to be created increasingly by innovation, and the task did not find the women wanting. From seed to market they managed their crops, raising much of the food that fed the armies, and making almost all of the fabric that clothed and sheltered the soldiers.[30]

Just as the offices of the government in Washington opened to women under the manpower shortage, so did those in Richmond. And everywhere across the South, the hospitals opened their doors. Perhaps 1,000 or more women held paying jobs as nurses, their tasks made the more difficult because of the lack of medicines and pain-killers, which were available to nurses in the Union. Even black women sometimes found employment in the wards, and at least one white woman, Sally Tompkins, was actually commissioned a captain in the Confederate army for her services. The Confederate nurses faced special problems, often being left with absolute administrative authority over a hospital, and more often having to move it and patients both in the threat of an enemy advance. Here, more than anywhere else, the image of the pale, delicate, fluttering butterfly of a woman came into crashing conflict with a new reality of Southern life. Many of the women, themselves accepting the myth of Southern womanhood, were repelled by what they did, and put it from their minds when the war ended. But more looked back with pride on what they accomplished, despite their husbands' treasured picture of them as helpless—and often brainless—creatures.[31]

In the Confederacy, too, the women sometimes came to the front. Many wives followed their husbands from camp to camp, and many wives of officers became beloved of whole brigades. Breckinridge's wife, Mary, joined him in camp whenever possible. She became a particular favorite with the Kentuckians of his Orphan Brigade, and for one special regimental competition she made a Confederate flag from her own wedding dress as a prize. The Kentuckians named their cannon after the wives of their officers. When Roger Hanson lay dying after the senseless charge at Stones River, it was Mary Breckinridge and other wives, including his own, who tended his last hours.[32]

And certainly many enterprising women fought in the ranks posing as men. Just as in the North, most of them had—by Southern standards—less than noble motives, prostitution, even transvestism. But many still served just to be with their husbands and sweethearts, and some solely out of patriotic fervor. When a recruiter came to enlist Keith Blalock in the 26th North Carolina, he refused to go unless wife Malinda could come too. The recruiter agreed to conceal her identity, and for two months she fooled all until Keith was discharged for medical reasons. She then revealed her sham to the colonel, and left with her husband. Oddly enough, in some cases this distinctly masculine pursuit could seemingly work to the advantage of a young woman. Far from being shunned as peculiar, some women who fought in the ranks were later lionized, enough so that one enterprising woman spent some time after the war writing a lurid, and completely fictional, account of her wartime pose as Captain Harry Buford. She called herself Loretta Velazquez, though her real name may be lost to history, and chances are excellent that her only real service to the Confederate cause was as a prostitute in Richmond, and later a paid informant manufacturing perjured testimony *against* the Confederate Government.[33]

Going hand-in-hand with the advanced status of women in the Confederacy was the rise of public welfare, just as in the North, yet with many distinctive features that would be peculiar to the South. Here, too, the work began with individual efforts at sewing and baking. Soon soldiers' aid societies began to appear, and already established groups like the YMCA took part in collecting clothing and supplies for the benefit of the armies. No great nationwide commissions arose as in the North. The concept ran against that devotion to localism that helped establish the Confederacy in the first place, and such a lack of widespread organization and system naturally made less effective the random efforts. Some Confederates actually lamented this. "We had no Sanitary Commission in the South," complained one soldier. "We were too poor; we had no line of rich and populous cities closely connected by rail, all combined in the good work of collecting and forwarding supplies and maintaining costly and thoroughly equipped charities. With us, every house was a hospital."

When the government issued an appeal for needed items, it was a special call for a particular emergency. Once filled, no effort continued to stockpile the benefits of philanthropy. Some states did organize their own agencies, like the Georgia Relief and Hospital Association. Even Kentucky, not really a Confederate state and isolated from Southern armies after Bragg's failed campaign in 1862, still managed to fund and collect supplies for the Kentucky Relief Association, the benefits going almost exclusively to the Orphan Brigade, and having to be smuggled through the lines. Each state, as well, tended to establish its own hospitals solely for the wounded of its nativity, an inefficient system that also saw wide variation in the treatment accorded to different soldiers.[34]

A problem unique to the Confederacy, and that placed an enormous strain upon the generosity of the people, were the tens of thousands of refugees. As the Federal armies advanced into the South, farmers and displaced laborers, their factories gone up in smoke, fled to the interior looking for a place to live and subsist. Many simply could not accept living under Yankee domination and abandoned their homes. "Half the world is refugeeing," complained one Confederate. Most were women and children, the aged or infirm, looking for security. In the early days of the war, the entire South turned a sympathetic eye on the unfortunates. They were, said one editor, "objects of the tenderest . . . sympathy." And the refugeeing exodus knew no social bounds, throwing mighty and lowly together on the crowded roads toward Richmond or Atlanta. The wife of General Lee was herself one of the very first refugees when she fled their home in Arlington, Virginia, in 1861, and Mrs. Jefferson Davis refugeed briefly in the spring of 1862 when it looked as if McClellan might take Richmond. Indeed, the families of a majority of the prominent high command in the Confederacy left their homes to take the road at some time during the war, and the movement went right on down the social scale, including even bankers and banks, and businessmen. The peripatetic Memphis *Appeal* came to take great pride in its refugee status.

Yet not all refugees met with sympathy in their plight, and as the war marched on and shortages of food and shelter increased, the great bulk of the displaced people came to be regarded with suspicion, even

scorn. Those who fled from the border states that did not secede, for instance, often found chilly receptions, despite the fact that their men
might be in the Confederate army. "We Kentuckians think ourselves as
much Southerners as anybody," complained Elodie Todd of Lexington,
"but the inhabitants of this little town think that because Kentucky is *not*
on a *Cotton Plantation* . . . there is no difference between me and a
Northerner." Certainly it did not help that her sister Mary was the wife
of Abraham Lincoln. Then there were the mountain people, Unionists
fleeing not the Yankees, but their own vindictive neighbors. Even once escaped, they often found themselves victimized on the road by ardent
Confederates.

In time the procession would seem endless: officers in bright uniforms, clerks, planters, wagoners and workmen, women and children with
precious belongings loaded to overflowing on carts and wagons, and increasing numbers of deserters. One observer thought the sight deserved a
great painter, thinking that Hogarth would find much in it to challenge
his brush. Within this constant exodus there rode the beginnings of a distinct new class in the South, a blending of planter and laborer, into the
simple body politic of the displaced. After the first year of the war the
rich could hardly be distinguished from the lowly. All wore dirty tatters,
all perspired, all drank at the same troughs, and all shared the same fear
of the enemy and uncertainty. They found common union in discomfort
and misery.[35]

And they placed an insurmountable burden upon the charity of those
Confederates not on the road. The Confederate Government itself simply
never effectively addressed the problem. The first attempts, as with army
relief, came in the form of emergency calls in response to isolated events.
When New Orleans fell or Fredericksburg was threatened, widespread appeals went out for the displaced citizens, but once the immediate problem
seemed alleviated—or forgotten—the efforts died away. Only the press
consistently supported the welfare of the refugees, sometimes themselves
supporting fund-raising drives and bazaars. It was the press that finally
proposed the organization of civilian relief agencies like those for the soldiers, but the call fell on disinterested ears. Even President Davis chose to
ignore the problem, doing nothing officially and even privately saying little more than that he supposed "the refugees and exiles would be well
provided for." The several states did provide modest assistance for the
families of soldiers, and in time certain classes of refugees. State legislatures also passed some tax relief measures, sparing the refugees having to
pay levies on property they had abandoned, and some states also raised
tax monies for the aid of "the transient poor." Attempts were made to
prevent foreclosures on the homes and lands abandoned. But all of this
barely benefited a small fraction of the refugee population. The only real
assistance received by the wanderers and exiles came on an individual
basis from friends or family, or the open heart of some citizen. The only

systematic distribution of charity came in the major cities, which thus attracted more and more of the refugees to Richmond and Atlanta, placing
ever greater burdens on hard-pressed cities and causing increasing resentment among the permanent residents. Indeed, the only truly national relief policy for the refugees came at the end of the war, from the conquering Federals. And nothing, except disenchantment with the war, proved
to be so great a cause of desertion from the Confederate ranks as the
plight of those refugees back in the South.[36]

Most of those who thus suffered were women, and most who contributed to their scanty relief were women. Combined with the effects of the
war on the status of those who did not have to flee—those who worked
and farmed and nursed—the refugee problem contributed to an enormous
alteration in the image of the Southern woman. The pale Southern belle
became a new sort of Confederate woman, hard-working, staunch in the
face of adversity, perhaps a bit less fastidious, but a great deal more self-
reliant. The war prepared her well for the work she would soon share with
her menfolk in rebuilding the South, yet it came at the price of bitterness
and an admitted loss of much of the gentility that the antebellum woman
so coveted. After a few years of war, no Confederate soldier could hate a
Yankee with more venom than his wife or sweetheart. When the advancing Federals came within Southern territory, the women met them with
contempt, even violence. In Nashville, the women often kicked passing
bluecoats, struck them in the stomachs, spat on them, or held handker-
chiefs to their noses when a Northerner passed. In New Orleans the
women pulled aside their skirts when a Yankee passed, that the fabric
might not accidentally touch the despised vandal. "God forgive me if I
hate too much," said one Confederate woman. They sometimes taught
their children and their slaves to hate the Federals, too, and so vehement
was their conduct that even some Southerners had to admit that the in-
sults and indignities sometimes visited upon the women by brutish Federal soldiers may have been invited by their own provocation.[37]

Society North and South, it seemed, was turned upside down in the
war. Whole new areas of opportunity opened for women, and even a few
blacks. For the poor, the only opportunity seemed to be to stay at home
and remain poor, or go and die in a rich man's war, yet even there the revolution in the civil population was not small. Class barriers, particularly in
the Confederacy, did not disappear, but the fences were lowered. In the
Union the growing industry needed more and more labor, even if it did
not pay a living wage. More and more people acquired skills, and know-
how, and the entrepreneurial spark. In the Confederacy the classes found
that they needed each other in ways they never had before, and they
would soon need each other even more to rebuild their dying South. In
both of the warring sections, the high and the low came to be a little less
high and a little less low. Both were drawn by degrees toward the center,

toward what the war was producing, an ever larger and more vigorous and independent middle class. The fruits of that shift did not ripen immediately, but in the decades to follow this war its harvest would be undeniable.

CHAPTER 12

"THE CROWNING STROKE
OF OUR DIPLOMACY"

Harvesting seemed to be the order of business for the Union this summer of 1863. Despite setbacks in some smaller campaigns, and the continued resistance of Charleston, Union arms were victorious in every major theater. And Lincoln was winning victories overseas, in a battlefield on which the Union held the upper hand from the outbreak of hostilities. It came largely thanks to able leaders like Charles Francis Adams, minister to Great Britain, and William Lewis Dayton, minister to France. Adams in particular proved a man of remarkable ability in the delicate business of keeping a onetime enemy, and now an arm's-length neutral, from turning into a Confederate ally. His proved to be the most difficult harvest of all the diplomatic fields plowed, but this summer of 1863 he came ever closer to the bumper crop he and Lincoln so desperately wanted.

Adams was an exasperating man, with all the vanities and prejudices and irascibilities of his illustrious clan. His grandfather was John Adams, and his father John Quincy Adams, two Presidents of the United States not noted for their patience with opposition. Each had tried a hand at diplomacy, and each with a fair measure of success, yet the work did not come naturally to their intolerant minds. Bookish they were, and conceited, and brilliant in their way, and so was Charles Francis. He thought very little of Lincoln. He seemed at first not to trust him, and admitted depression when Lincoln was elected. He felt even worse when brought to Washington by William H. Seward to take his portfolio as minister to the Court of St. James's. Seward brought him in to meet personally with the new President, and Adams thanked the rail-splitter for the confidence that his appointment implied.

"Very kind of you to say so, Mr. Adams," said Lincoln, "but you were not my choice. You are Seward's man." With that uncharacteristic abruptness, Lincoln then turned away to talk with Seward about the patronage appointment of a postmaster for Chicago. It was an incident that Adams never forgot, yet in time he came to understand this strange President, and to accord him more than a grudging respect.[1]

And Adams in turn earned Lincoln's regard, for he proved immediately adept at his task. If he did not succeed in every endeavor, still he failed entirely in none. His first immediate goal was to persuade Great Britain not to proclaim neutrality in the coming conflict, but the Confederate diplomatic corps stole a considerable march on the Union. On the very day that Adams arrived in England, Queen Victoria proclaimed her nation neutral in the American war, thus according to the Confederacy rights as a belligerent. This declared that the Confederacy was indeed a separate nation functioning under its own government, and able to make war. Adams' contention was to have been, and would be, that the rebellion was a purely domestic matter. Without belligerent rights, the South could not look under international law to support from other nations, nor would they be within the law to sell arms and munitions to the Rebels. The queen's proclamation, imitated speedily by other European powers, changed that. Worse, it appeared to be a considerable step toward formal recognition of Confederate independence. Should that happen, treaties of alliance might be made that would bring Europeans into the war against the Union. To many in the South, this early "victory" in statecraft seemed to ensure their triumph, and to Adams it was a dark time indeed when he took lodgings in London with already a major setback confronting him.

Worse news came soon thereafter when Secretary of State Seward virtually hamstrung his efforts with his Dispatch No. 10, which forbade Adams to carry on diplomatic discussions with the British ministers so long as Great Britain continued to have relations with the Confederacy. But with the deftness that soon characterized all his dealings as a diplomat, Adams managed to sidestep the order and at the same time persuade Lord John Russell, British Foreign Secretary, not to engage in further talks with the Confederate commissioners then in London. As a result, though it seemed to begin with such fair prospects, the first Rebel mission to England outlived its usefulness, and its members fell into dispute among themselves.

Davis replaced them in January 1862 with James Murray Mason and

John Slidell, two much more adept statesmen, whose greatest contribution to Confederate statecraft, however, lay in their having been unlawfully seized by Union naval officers while on their way to England. Commander Charles Wilkes took them by force from the British steamer *Trent* on November 8, 1861, thereby causing an international scandal, and an enormous embarrassment for the Lincoln government. So outraged was Great Britain that troops and supplies were dispatched for Canada in case of war with the United States. Adams' son Henry wrote from England that "This nation means to make war," and there was some speculation that Mason and Slidell actually encouraged their capture in order to foment just such a crisis. Cool heads in Washington and London prevailed, however, and in the end the affair ended short of war, with a qualified apology and the release of the prisoners. By the end of January 1862, the whole business blew away as quickly as it had come, and once again Confederate hopes suffered a setback.[2]

Interestingly, both North and South missed the true import of the amicable settlement of the *Trent* affair. Despite incredibly heated passions, the British suffered the affront, accepted at best a lukewarm apology, and returned at once to amicable relations with the United States. The simple fact, which neither side in the American war would appreciate, was that England did not want a war with anyone, and would go to great lengths to avoid one. The South counted heavily on the dependence of British textile mills on Confederate cotton in order to bring John Bull into the war on its side, but English mills were already getting cotton from other sources in nearly sufficient supply, with still a great stock from the huge 1860 crop left over. They would feel the pinch in time, but not enough to endanger their economy, and certainly not enough to go to war against the North. In short, England had nothing to gain from entering the lists with Jefferson Davis. She would have to support a large army abroad at great expense, and she knew that the Lincoln government, though seemingly behind in the military contest, still commanded enormous war resources not yet tapped. An unfavorable result in such a war—and Great Britain could look back on two costly unfavorable results in that continent within the last century—could cost the empire Canada. Lord Russell's protest over the *Trent* business was not that Mason and Slidell were imprisoned, but only that they had been taken from a British ship, and there lay the heart of the matter. The whole episode strained relations between the Union and Great Britain, but at no time did it improve chances of Confederate recognition.[3]

Those relations, once strained, continued to be taut, thanks to the energetic efforts of James Dunwody Bulloch and other Confederate purchasing agents abroad. Early in the conflict the Davis government decided that, while it could not compete with Union might on the high seas, it could strike at the Northern economy by raiding Yankee commerce. This called for a fleet of privateers, usually vessels converted and fitted out for fast steaming, and armed heavily enough to stop any merchant ship. The first successful commerce raider had been the C.S.S. *Sumter*, commanded by Raphael Semmes, soon to be a figure of legend in the South. His ship took eighteen Yankee prizes, and began a diplomatic problem for the British when she docked several times in neutral British ports for supply and refitting. The problem ended itself when Federal vessels blockaded the *Sumter* at Gibraltar, and Semmes had to abandon the ship. But even then the enterprising Captain Bulloch was at work on a miniature fleet of other commerce raiders.

Secretary of the Navy Stephen Russell Mallory sent Bulloch abroad early in 1861 to manage Confederate purchasing operations. The South did not have the facilities to build her raiders, but she could buy them. A Georgian with many years of experience in the United States Navy, Bulloch brought considerable qualifications to the job, not the least of which was a keen understanding of international maritime law. That would be helpful in managing to circumvent British fussiness about maintaining its neutrality while warships were purchased or built in her ports. Mallory gave him a twofold mission. He must immediately get the commerce raiders on the waters, where their depredations would hopefully draw away from the Union blockade enough vessels that the blockade itself would prove to be ineffective. That would serve a considerable diplomatic purpose, Mallory and Davis hoped, for an ineffective blockade by the law of the sea, was illegitimate, and therefore not to be honored by neutral nations. British and French shipping could thus come into Southern ports. Second, Bulloch was to design and commission a new class of warship, an ironclad, seagoing, with a dreadful ram at its bow and heavy guns in broadside. Such a ship could fight with the Yankee frigates and sloops on an advantageous footing, and perhaps lift the blockade without foreign aid.[4]

Barely was the embarrassing episode of the *Trent* out of the way before the fruits of Bulloch's indefatigable efforts created yet another diplomatic crisis. Back in August 1861 he closed a contract with the shipbuilders for the ship *Oreto*. By March 1862 she was ready to go to sea for final outfitting. Already the ship lay in danger, for Adams' agents in the country carefully sifted dockside gossip and rumors within the shipbuilding industry to seek out cases of warships being built. Should they be discovered, the British authorities would have no option but to impound them so long as neutrality was maintained. While Bulloch tried to settle on a captain for the *Oreto*, the Federal spies came perilously close, and finally Adams lodged a complaint with Russell. Bulloch had been careful, however. The law specified that to be a warship, such a vessel must be armed. Thus he built his ships without arming them. That he would do elsewhere, either on the open sea or in a safe port. Russell had to let the *Oreto* go, and on March 22, flying a British flag and manned with a British crew, she steamed out of Liverpool bound for Nassau. There many of the crew would enlist for service aboard, but there the difficulties of the vessel only began. Once more Union officials tried to impound her, and British Admiralty officials finally seized the ship in June and held it until August while a court adjudicated the matter. Finally the vessel was released, with her new captain, John Newland Maffitt, and off she sailed for her rendezvous with a supply ship carrying her armaments. Yet even this came to a bad pass, and finally Maffitt had to run the ship through the blockade with useless guns to safety at Mobile. There, during the remainder of 1862, he finally outfitted the ship properly. In January 1863 the *Oreto* left Mobile, but now she was the C.S.S. *Florida,* and soon to be one of the most dreaded vessels afloat. In the next twenty months she would capture or destroy thirty-eight Yankee merchant ships, and some of those captured she armed and turned into second-generation raiders. They accounted for another twenty-two captures, and all told over $4 million in Northern shipping losses were inflicted. Insurance rates for Northern shipping began to rise, and Mallory began to believe that his program was proving successful. Bulloch was delighted, spurred on to even greater efforts with a second vessel he had under construction. He called it the 290.[5]

Bulloch placed the contract for the second vessel back in August 1861, this time with the Laird brothers firm. Her tentative name came from the fact that she was to be the 290th ship built by the company, and her career was threatened with even greater danger than that of the *Florida.* In the wake of the *Trent* affair, Confederate agents began to detect a shift in sympathies among Britons. "The whole British nation were so frightened in their late quarrel with the Yankees, and have been so delighted to get out of it without a war, that I am afraid we shall have to bring them up to the mark again," wrote Semmes from Gibraltar as he awaited the fate of the *Sumter.* The anticipated result was that there would be even closer scrutiny of shipbuilding activity. That put the 290 in some peril.[6]

Bulloch quickly made the new vessel his favorite, redoubling his efforts to make certain not to violate the neutrality law. He soon discovered that enemy agents carefully watched the progress of the construction, and no one could disguise the rakish design that characterized a commerce raider. He hastened the construction as much as possible, taking increasing pride in his offspring. She would be "superior to any vessel of her date in fitness for the purposes of a sea rover," he believed, "the most perfect cruiser of any nation." On May 15 she was launched, sliding down the ways into the Mersey, ready for trails before setting off to sea.[7]

Already the 290 was the center of a flurry of diplomatic activity. Adams did, indeed, have constant and timely advice of the progress of the ship, and none could contest her designed purpose. Details of her construction came into the American ministry, even down to the selection of her oak planking. Gradually affidavits were gathered, along with other evidence and statements, from dock workers. Rumors were reported to the Yankees of conversations among Confederate naval officers, talking about a new cruiser being built. And anyone could see the ports in her bulwarks for running out cannon. Finally on June 23, 1862, Adams believed that he had enough evidence to take the matter directly to Lord Russell. He found substance in what Adams told and gave him, but when he referred the matter to the Lords of the Treasury, they quoted a report by their agent in Liverpool, a man who had been denying all along that the 290 was in the least suspicious. For the next month Adams and his agent worked with the implacable port authority, who steadfastly refused to countenance their suspicions about the ship. However, Adams showed the good sense to employ independently an extremely prominent barrister, and with his aid they finally got the attention of Russell once more. What followed was a fatal delay that seemed almost drawn from a farce. The issue was sent to the Queen's Counsel for adjudication, and that man had just gone insane! For several days a complete dossier on the 290 sat unexamined in his home, unexamined but not unknown. By some means never revealed, Bulloch learned what was in that envelope, and that once examined it would mean the certain impounding of his ship. Now he must get her to sea at once.[8]

Bulloch told the Lairds that he wanted a thorough all-day trial of the vessel, and on July 28 they took her out. Now he called her the *Enrica* for a time, and while she steamed about along the coast, a whole succession of Bulloch's orders were preceding her. He sent a supply ship toward the Azores, advised another to be ready to deliver his crew, and arranged for a tugboat to accompany the ship on a continuation of her trial, which he decided must be made the next day. On July 29, laden with sightseers and minor dignitaries, the *Enrica* set out once more, accompanied by the tug. But that night he declared that he would not be able to complete the trial, and asked that the guests accompany him back to Liverpool aboard the tug so conveniently present. As soon as they departed, the remaining crew put out to open sea. Two days later the British Government finally acted and sent to Liverpool orders to impound the vessel. By that time, the C.S.S. *Alabama* was on her way. By August 24 she had taken on supplies, guns, and new crew. She also boasted a new captain, Raphael Semmes. "Let me once see you proficient in the use of your weapons," he told the crew, "and trust me for very soon giving you an opportunity to show the world of what metal you are made." They would show the world, and in the doing they would considerably aggravate the relations between two continents of that world.[9]

To say that Adams was angered and disappointed by the escape of the 290 would be an understatement. Both he and his government at home clearly suspected intentional connivance on the part of the British authorities. Later Adams modified his charge, admitting that the escape of the ship came more from a bad set of circumstances and coincidence.

Certainly the port authority at Liverpool, a heavy cotton speculator, had something to gain from aiding the Confederacy, but Russell and his government were certainly clear. As before, they stood to profit nothing from abetting a certain diplomatic crisis. Indeed, when in October William Gladstone made intemperate remarks about Confederate success, saying "they have made a nation," both Russell and Adams were visibly dismayed. The question of Confederate recognition had almost come up for discussion—only discussion—in a cabinet session the month previous, but news of the victory at Antietam put an end to it, and Adams actually felt peaceful, "as calm as a summer's night." Gladstone's remarks took him by surprise, and there followed a period of severe strain as both sides sought to quell the tempest thus aroused. Russell did use the furor as a pretext to propose again a favorite idea of his, that there be an immediate cease-fire. That was not anything close to what the Confederates wanted. It implied no recognition, nor even the third-party mediation that had been proposed earlier in the year. Indeed, the matter of recognition had been dead for some time, and now further reports of Northern determination to win buried it forever, almost. Britain simply had nothing to gain from intervening in the war. Russell, in absolute good faith, continued to hope that Britain might somehow intercede to put an end to the war, but the majority of Her Majesty's government believed that any insertion of John Bull's nose would inevitably get it bloodied.[10]

Then the French complicated matters by coming hard on the settlement of Gladstone's little crisis by offering their own proposal of intervention. All of a sudden Emperor Louis Napoleon had decided that his government would like to see the war in America come to an end. Early in the conflict the Confederates began cultivating the court at Paris as well as that in London. Yet all European powers, France, Spain, even Russia at times, seemed united in determination to take their lead from Great Britain. France, too, stood much to lose by getting into a war with the Union which she might not win. France was adventuring in Mexico, with an out-of-work Austrian archduke, Maximilian, placed upon a puppet throne, in clear defiance of the vaunted Monroe Doctrine. War with the North might give Lincoln a perfect pretext to invade Mexico as well as the South. Besides, the French felt a genuine fear for the breakup of the Union. A powerful and united America stood as some guarantee against British domination of the seas, as a potential ally, as in the Revolution, should the European powers come again to arms. And to Napoleon, himself a man of no little forward vision, the economic interdependence of the two sides of the Atlantic dictated that the Union should be preserved or that, if not, then the conflict must be ended quickly so that the business of business could continue.

Thus his new proposal to Russell for joint effort by Britain, France, and Russia, to obtain a six months' armistice and, more significantly for Louis' motives, a suspension of the Southern blockade. Nothing came of the proposal, for the British cabinet rejected it politely, showing once more the determination not to interfere. It was Russell who conveyed the news to Napoleon, and when Adams learned of it he thanked the Foreign Secretary personally. By now these two difficult men had become friends, an odd relationship for two individuals who both enjoyed a peculiar facility for irascibility. It was this friendship, in fact, which perhaps as much as anything helped accomplish Adams' goals in London. In winning Russell to himself, Adams in a small way won him to the Union as well.[11]

Of course, there were other less subtle inducements. Lincoln could be quite a diplomat, with equal shares of finesse and brute threat. Even while the 290 sat on the ways being readied for the sea, and the diplomatic wrangle that it would foment, so too did other ships being built in the Laird yards. In the spring of 1862 Bulloch began his work on the formidable rams that Mallory wanted him to construct and arm. He spent some time looking for the best construction firm for the job and, at the same time, began to sense a shift in British opinion that in the end might endanger their being delivered to the Confederacy. Nevertheless, he went ahead and gave the contract to the Laird brothers, though suggesting that as a safeguard the ships be built in pieces by several different makers, then assembled in the Confederacy. It was an advanced idea, for which the South was not ready. Laird must do the whole job. That summer they began construction of ships 294 and 295. In time they came to be known on both sides of the Atlantic as the Laird Rams.[12]

They were to be formidable vessels, as befitted ships that would cause anew strained relations between Great Britain and the Lincoln government. At the bow of each ship, about four feet beneath the waterline, a great iron spear jutted forward perhaps seven feet. The experience of the C.S.S. *Virginia* in March 1862, when the ram at her bow sank a Federal warship in Hampton Roads, gave evidence that this ancient dread weapon could enjoy renewed utility when the power of steam engines lay behind it. While using one of the oldest weapons in naval history, the rams were to incorporate one of the newest as well. Their guns would be placed in revolving turrets, like those of the monitors now in the Union navy.

These and other features had but one goal, to be able to break the blockade and play havoc with wooden-sided Union warships. To operate in the shallow coastal waters and river harbors, the rams drew relatively little, could turn on a short radius, and cruise at the rather considerable speed of ten knots or better. The ships did not require large crews, and carried sufficient armor of their own to be proof against most of the iron that Lincoln's seamen could throw against them.

Bulloch was just as canny about the construction of these ships as he had been with his previous vessels. He entered the contract with Laird as a private citizen. The name of the Confederate States of America appeared nowhere in the documents commissioning the ships. In constant consultation with his barrister, Bulloch made certain not to contract for

materials that might be construed to be armaments. A hazy area seemed
to be the matter of the armor sheathing, yet the attorney assured Bulloch
that only actual arms and ammunition were proscribed, and that armor
plating could, therefore, be included without endangering the vessels' de-
livery. To Secretary of the Navy Mallory he confided his belief that if
only he could get the ships safely to the Confederacy, then "these vessels
may yet have important and perhaps conclusive work in the question of
the blockade."[13]

But then Bulloch's problems began, as Lincoln and Adams commenced applying pressure on Russell and his government. Adams and his
agents were hardly oblivious to the work going on at the Laird yard. The
American foreign minister had almost every shipyard in the country under
surveillance to catch signs of warships being built for the South, and there
were more than enough Union sympathizers in the country for a great
deal of information to come in unsolicited. As a result, Bulloch did little
that was not known soon thereafter to Adams and his delegation, and
therefore to Lincoln and Seward. At the same time, the North was already coming to be enraged by the depredations of the Confederate
cruisers already outfitted and at sea, and Adams lodged regular complaints
with Russell over the losses in Yankee shipping to ships outfitted or built
in Great Britain. Soon Adams hinted to Russell that the Union might be
forced to strike back, arming its own fleet of privateers, ships which almost certainly would take a heavy toll on the British carrying trade that
ran the blockade. Indeed, on March 3, 1863, Congress passed such a privateering bill and, though the Union never put it into practice, still it served
as a potent warning to a nation whose life depended upon her carrying
trade.[14]

At the same time that news of the Privateering Act reached England,
so did two new informal agents of Seward's, armed with money and a
novel plan. John M. Forbes, a Boston shipping millionaire, proposed to
the Lincoln government that money be used as a weapon against the
Confederate shipbuilding. If the British Government would not live up to
its responsibility, then why not circumvent them by simply buying the
ships abuilding away from the Confederates. The Lairds and others were
businessmen. Offer them more than Bulloch could pay, and the whole
problem could be solved. Forbes and another millionaire, William Henry
Aspinwall, met with Navy Secretary Gideon Welles and Secretary of the
Treasury Salmon P. Chase, and among them they agreed that the two
would go on a secret mission to Britain armed with treasury bonds worth
$10 million. Their task was simply to buy the ships out from under
Bulloch, and even Adams was to have nothing to do with them, nor
would they work through him.[15]

The two agents reached England in one of the hottest diplomatic
months of activity yet. That same month the Confederate Congress approval of highly speculative bond issue reached Europe, one that tied

some $15 million in loans to Southern cotton. At first the demand proved so great that the price of the bonds skyrocketed on the foreign market, and diplomat James M. Mason wrote exultingly that "cotton is king at last." It did not hold, however, and soon the prices began falling. Even as Forbes and Aspinwall arrived, the Erlanger banking company of France, the original promoter of the loan scheme, applied pressure on Confederate agents to start buying up the bonds themselves, in order to keep the market prices high. They did so, and in the end wound up holding almost half of their own bonds. After Erlanger's percentage was taken out, the whole scheme realized Confederate interests only about $2.5 million, and constituted a failure for all parties involved except the Erlangers.[16]

Yet the failure lay in the future. For the moment, the bond activity seemed to bode well for the South. Worse, Adams' continuing efforts to have other cruisers being outfitted for Mallory impounded did not seem to be working. The *Alexandra* was outfitting at Liverpool, and another ship, called variously the *Japan*, *Virginia*, and *Georgia*, was on the ways at Greenock. And then John Laird of the shipping company, a Member of Parliament, spoke on March 27 in rebuttal to a pro-Union speech by John Bright. With no little animation from self-interest, Laird declared that the North had bought millions of pounds' worth of arms from Great Britain, yet raised this great outcry when the South bought only "two ships, unarmed [and] unfit for any purpose of warfare." Trimming words, to be sure, but Laird did not equivocate when he said that the notion of freedom in the North "is an absurdity." He would much rather be known as "the builder of a dozen *Alabamas*" than as one such as those now warring on their Southern brethren. The favorable response Laird received, followed by a defense by Lord Palmerston in the matter of the *Alabama*, only further spurred the Federals' anger and determination.[17]

Forbes and Aspinwall arrived at the same time that rumors of their mission reached England. The unfortunate turn immediately made them suspect, and subordinates had to do most of the real work while they remained in London. Other agents soon joined them from the United States so that, as the spring wore on, the mission had a considerable body of influential men. They sold their Treasury bonds very successfully, and used the proceeds along with their other funds to augment Adams' network of spies at British shipyards. Bulloch noticed an immediate increase in the number of men hanging about the Laird yards asking questions, and redoubled his fears for the safety of the ships. Nevertheless, the Forbes-Aspinwall mission failed to acquire the vessels, thanks to the early leaks about their intentions. Forbes returned to New York in July with a trunk full of unused bonds, and arrived just in time to have to hide in his hotel while the draft riots raged outside.[18]

And still the Lairds continued their work on the rams. It progressed slowly. Bulloch had expected them to be ready by March or April, yet as the summer approached he found that engine problems and other delays constantly set back the launch date. Then finally the British Government interfered. On April 5, Lord Russell acceded to Adams' imploring and seized the *Alexandra*. The little ship itself was of no importance. Far more significant is that the American minister had finally persuaded Her Majesty's government that a Confederate warship was incontestably being fitted out and "apparently intended for the Confederacy." For the first time Russell took a step to confirm Britain's neutrality, and Adams was delighted. He had complained to Russell about the blind eye Britain turned toward Confederate money-raising abroad, and the foreign secretary responded by saying that his government would not interfere in "commercial dealings between the British subjects and the so-styled Confederate States," whether in matters of money or "even ships adapted for warlike purposes." But Adams and his agents bombarded Russell with evidence of the intent of the *Alexandra*, and in the end it was the interpretation of intent that sealed the ship's fate. The British were uneasy about the North. The rumors of Yankee privateering and the fear of a further degeneration of Anglo-American relations moved Russell to act against the *Alexandra* where he had not against the *Oreto* or *290*. The move set a precedent that frightened Bulloch, for the British had strongly reaffirmed their intention to remain neutral. Now his beloved rams might be next.[19]

Seward and Adams did their best to realize Bulloch's fears. Just days after the seizure, Seward informed Adams that he should tell Russell that further fitting out of vessels intended for the Confederacy would so muddy relations between their nations that they might not be able to "preserve friendship between them." It was a veiled hint of war. But as the summer came on, Russell did not appear to be moving in the matter of the Laird rams, despite the information being sent him. If he did not act, however, Bulloch did. The *Alexandra* case gave him to understand that he had to act quickly. He decided that it would be necessary for him to transfer ownership of the vessels from himself to someone with no traceable connection with the Confederacy. Minister John Slidell had for some time been investigating French interest in building rams for the Confederacy, and now Bulloch turned first to France to find a suitable "buyer." He found a firm that he would have preferred not to do business with, Bravay and Company of Paris, but he had little choice. Bravay said he was even then building two rams for the Egyptians, and his thus buying two rams from Laird and Bulloch would hardly seem suspect. "For a nominal sum" Bulloch closed the deal, and then to further the illusion absented himself from any further appearances at the Laird yards. He hoped now that the rams could go to sea in October. Once outside British waters, Bravay would then transfer ownership to the Confederacy for a modest commission. It might work.[20]

Despite the fact that the tide of British opinion seemed to turn slightly against the Confederate cause after the *Alexandra* affair, Bulloch and other Confederates abroad did not relax their efforts to win over the English and the French people. With the support of the mass, and particularly of the influential upper classes, the governments would have to follow suit. Perhaps one of the most energetic Confederates in the enterprise, then, was the diminutive Henry Hotze. Born in Switzerland, he came to Mobile, Alabama, in 1855, and worked for a time as a journalist before the war. A few months as a soldier bored him in 1861, and late that year Secretary of State Judah Philip Benjamin sent him to Europe to organize the Confederacy's propaganda efforts abroad. In fact, it would be the only public relations activity fielded by either side, and it was aggressively prosecuted by Hotze in the pages of the newspaper he established in London, the *Index*. On May 1, 1862, over the heading "A weekly journal of politics, literature, and news," the *Index* began its career as the only foreign newspaper devoted solely to publicizing the cause of the Confederacy. Every week Southern victories in the field were applauded and exaggerated, Yankee depredations decried—and sometimes invented. Benjamin sent funds from Richmond to support the sheet, for the expenses of maintaining the *Index* could not be offset solely by its sales. Hotze included the writings of Englishmen sympathetic to the Southern cause in his pages, as well as correspondence from America. Hotze even engaged a reporter in New York to send Yankee news.

The whole object of the *Index* was to support the efforts of Confederate diplomats to obtain recognition. As a result, the illegality of the blockade became a favorite topic. Hotze published detailed lists of vessels that penetrated the Union fleets, even quoting tonnages at times, to support his contention that the blockade was ineffective, and therefore invalid. At the same time the *Index* tried to play on the shortage of cotton—which by 1863 was being felt in Britain—and the abundance of the staple that awaited only recognition of the Confederacy. Hotze emphasized the old—and largely mythical—ties of blood between Southern and British aristocracy, their social and cultural similarities. He even recited past instances of British recognition granted to colonies that had revolted, and asked why the same should be withheld now. As the summer of 1863 wore on, Hotze redoubled his efforts, though being careful never to mention Bulloch or the Laird rams.[21]

Other forces worked in tandem with Hotze and Bulloch. The Confederacy employed, in fact, several operatives in Europe engaged in both diplomacy and purchasing. All seemed in these summer months to turn around the issue of the rams, and the decision in that matter might well affect Confederate success in other fields, most of all arms procurement. The Richmond government had sent Major Caleb Huse to England to buy arms and ammunition and cannon for shipment aboard blockade-runners. He proved to be eminently successful, declaring at one point that he intended to "secure the London Armory as a Confederate States arms factory." Soon after arriving in London he engaged several contractors in manufacturing the weapons he sought, drawing his money for payment from Fraser, Trenholm & Co., the Confederacy's foreign bankers. George A. Trenholm served for a time as Secretary of the Treasury in Davis' cabinet, so the firm had something of a preferential standing with the Confederacy. So well did Huse perform his task that years later he would express admiration for the Federal soldiers who could stand for four years of war in the face of the iron he shipped to the Confederacy.[22]

The activities of Huse, Hotze, Bulloch, and other agents, while centered on England, did not of course occur there exclusively. The Confederacy sent diplomatic missions to France, Russia, Italy, even to the Vatican. Yet it was only in France that Southern activity came close to matching that in Great Britain, yet there as elsewhere almost all affairs took their lead from what happened in England. After Mason and Slidell finally finished their interrupted trip across the Atlantic, Mason remained in London while Slidell went on to Paris. The whole episode of the Confederates in Paris stood in stark contrast to what took place in London. To the French mission gravitated a host of peculiar and often troublesome characters, animated indeed by lofty motives, but skilled chiefly in quarrelsomeness and bickering. The first diplomat there was Pierre Adolphe Rost, whose tenure was characterized chiefly by inactivity, since he preferred to enjoy the pleasures of Paris. Shortly to enhance this delegation came one Paul Pecquet du Bellet, a man with no official standing whatever, but simply a New Orleanian stranded in France during the war. He took it to be his task to advise Confederate diplomats on how to conduct the affairs of their portfolio, and became such a nuisance that Secretary of State Benjamin finally refused to answer his correspondence personally. He attempted to establish a French counterpart to the *Index*, but failed, and in the offing managed to offend Hotze. Then he told Caleb Huse how he should proceed in buying arms, in passing, perhaps, letting the major know that he was incensed that the agent was a native of Connecticut. When Du Bellet tried to persuade Huse to buy a lot of inferior rifles—on which Du Bellet might have received a commission—Huse declined and eventually became so exasperated that he left the room. The meddlesome man had the same effect on Edwin de Leon, the one agent that Richmond sent to publicize the cause in France.[23]

Wisely, John Slidell managed to avoid the interfering Du Bellet, but he could not avoid the difficult and frequently exasperating maze of French politics and protocol. The government, it seemed, repeatedly changed its position. It early recognized a state of belligerency in the war abroad, and seemed fair to formally recognize the Confederacy. Yet slavery did not find a sympathetic audience, as in England, and despite a widespread desire to see the United States disunited, French interests dictated that she remain neutral. She had to follow Great Britain, else risk war with her, and at the same time only neutrality could be certain to keep the North from taking action against her Mexican adventure. The shift in French attitude came after the Federal victories at Fort Donelson and Shiloh and, combined with a widespread support for the Union, it doomed any Confederate hopes of success. The Erlanger loan fiasco did not help. Even when Slidell obtained personal interviews with Emperor Napoleon, he did not receive perfectly straight answers. The French, who many thought invented the cat-and-mouse game of diplomacy, kept the Confederates off balance throughout the war, waiting not upon the best interests or rights of the Confederacy, but upon what would best benefit France. It never happened that the two came together.[24]

Yet in the summer of 1863, Bulloch believed that the time had come for him to join his efforts with those sympathizers in France, and his contract with Bravay seemed to be a good beginning. Now the rams dominated all diplomacy, and they seemingly held captive the attention of Seward and the State Department in Washington. The Alexandra's case went before a British court in June, and that court overruled the seizure and rejected Russell's action. The Foreign Office was surprised, and Adams and his legation incensed. Then a few days later, on June 30, John Roebuck, called "the smallest man in the House," arose in the Commons to offer a motion that Great Britain begin negotiations with the other European powers to bring about formal recognition of the Confederacy. That was bad enough, but if it represented a shift in the official British position, then all Adams' work to stop the rams might be lost, and the ships allowed to leave the country after all. It looked just as dismal for the Union as July dawned as it had looked rosy a scant few weeks before.[25]

Adams sensed that this was the time for renewed pressure. Even before he knew of the great victories at Gettysburg and Vicksburg, he began his campaign against the rams. On July 7 the American consul at Liverpool suggested that the vessels be retained because of their warlike intent. "If these ships go," said the consul, "nothing will prevent a war between the two countries." On July 11 Adams sent the consul's evidence and request to Russell, who routinely promised to look into the matter.

Then came the news of Gettysburg and Vicksburg. An exultant Seward wrote to Adams that the army and navy were now stronger than ever, and the fall of the Mississippi citadels freed Grant's forces and much of the navy for other purposes. In his communication lay the intimation that the Union stood ready to offer war to Great Britain if that nation did not start honoring its international obligations. Then he referred to the Laird rams, and declared that such powerful vessels must certainly be intended for attacks on the Northern ports like Boston and New York as well as the blockade. Hereafter events began to escalate.[26]

In Commons, speakers talked openly of the rams, and of how their being allowed to depart would certainly result in war with the Union. In the North every new capture by the Florida and the Alabama renewed the cries for war. Russell declared that he needed real evidence that the rams would go to the Confederacy, and when Adams furnished what he could, a crown court declared that it was insufficient.

Adams stepped up the work of his spies in Liverpool and Birkenhead, where the rams were being built. Money changed hands to buy information from Laird employees, and soon British customs officials made repeated visits and asked pointed questions about the destination of the ships. What everyone knew through rumor, officialdom could not countenance except by direct proof. It did not help that now the *Florida*, badly in need of refitting, came into British waters and there took two American prizes. Many speculated that the raider had come to convoy the rams to the Confederacy. The first ram was launched on July 4, and was almost ready for sea trials.[27]

August, traditionally, was a leisure month in Britain. Russell left London for a vacation, most of the cabinet left the city, and even Adams packed his bags and took a train for a rest in Scotland. But while these leaders rested from the tension of their daily work, others began to unravel not only the tightly wound international situation, but also the true story of the Laird rams. It began with the Lairds themselves. They became increasingly annoyed with the repeated inspections of the ships and the questioning of their workers. In the hope that a show of candor would relieve them, and at the same time not compromise Bulloch, the Lairds obtained permission to reveal to the government that the rams were the property of Bravay. British officials then called on Bravay in Paris to question him, and he admitted that he was acting as agent for the Egyptian Government in the building of the rams. Obviously in an attempt to diffuse the threat posed by the rams, whoever they were for, a British naval agent offered to buy the ships from Bravay, but he declined.

But the Bravay admission had opened the door to another route. British agents in Cairo now approached that government to confirm Bravay's story that he acted as its agent in building and buying the vessels. The story did not check, and then Russell, back from vacation, asked Paris if France owned or intended to buy the ships. No. Russell immediately began investigating the Bravay firm, and at the same time learned that the first of the rams was ready for its first trial in open water. Would it be allowed to escape as had the *Alabama?*

On September 1, Russell issued a statement that on the basis of existing evidence, his government could not detain the rams. Despite the flaws in the Bravay story, the essential point remained undeniable that the ships legally belonged to the French company. Just two days later Adams returned to London from his vacation. He had not yet received Russell's decision, but he was already tired and worn, even after several days' attempt at relaxation. The Adamses never relaxed well. On his return the minister found a letter from Seward dated some five weeks before, but making it emphatic that "we are drifting," he said, "towards a war with

Great Britain." Immediately upon reaching his lodging Adams had sent another in the long series of notes about the rams to Russell. Then on September 4 he sent another one. That same day he finally got Russell's statement of three days before.

Adams had had enough. He and Russell thought much alike in the matter of the rams, of that Adams felt certain. The *Alexandra* affair had given ample evidence of Russell's good intent in that direction. Yet the Foreign Secretary's own government seemed not to stand completely behind him, and Adams feared that the stand taken in April had been abandoned. Besides this, Adams was still tired, fed up with the "moral pettiness" he saw in English diplomacy, and unprepared for further equivocation. He lay awake much of that night, deciding what course to take. Clearly it was time for stronger language. Should those rams leave port and not return, the impact on the blockade, Union merchant shipping, Northern ports, the war itself, seemed incalculable. Part of statecraft was knowing when to drop all semblance of tact and threaten. Clearly the time was now.

The next day Adams sent to Russell a single letter, for which, if for nothing else in his life, the American minister would be long remembered. He acknowledged the Foreign Secretary's recent note. "I trust I need not express how profound is my regret at the conclusion to which Her Majesty's Government have arrived," said Adams. "I can regard it no other wise than as practically opening to the insurgents full liberty in this kingdom." The issue seemed clear, he wrote. "It would be superfluous in me to point out to your Lordship that this is war." Rarely if ever in American statecraft did a diplomat so completely abandon the niceties of his art. Blunt, threatening, remonstrative, the letter almost entirely closed the door on further discussion. It represented a near-ultimatum. If the rams did not suffer impoundment, hostilities must ensue.[28]

Yet more would be made of the letter than it deserved. For one thing, Adams did not really threaten war. He was trying to prevent that. His "this is war" statement actually meant that if Britain did not interfere with the rams, then such negligence would be in violation of her declared neutrality. In short, Britain would be committing an act of "war" by aiding the belligerent Confederacy. Russell obviously thought much the same as Adams. Indeed, it is unfortunate that the two men were not able to meet some days prior to their correspondence, for in private discourse they would certainly have settled the dispute. Both wanted the same thing. But if they had met personally, then Adams' immortal passage, misinterpreted considerably by later generations, might never have come to be written.

The fact is that Russell had begun to move on the rams even before he got Adams' note. On September 3, just two days after announcing the result of his first investigation, Russell directed the port official at Birkenhead to stop the rams from leaving port and "detain them until further orders." He did so entirely on his own responsibility, and on the expectation that given enough time his government would eventually find satisfactory evidence of the real purpose of the ships. "It is of the utmost importance and urgency that the ironclads building at Birkenhead should not go to America to break the blockade," Russell wrote a few days later. He tried to buy them from Bravay, meanwhile keeping the ships under surveillance. Then the sham of Bravay's ownership was revealed, as well as the mythical Egyptian purchase. Confronted with this, Bravay later claimed that the rams really belonged to Turkey, Italy, Austria, and finally Denmark. His veracity sank lower and lower with each new prospective owner.

Adams and Russell continued their correspondence all during the next several weeks, and the frayed tempers of both became clearly evident as the American repeatedly lectured on the violations of neutrality Britain was committing, and Russell just as heatedly protested Adams' intemperate language. Meanwhile the investigation of the rams continued, and a frustrated Bulloch had to sit idly by as more and more agents snooped about the vessels. By September 21 the foreign office established with certainty that France had nothing to do with the ships, that Bravay was a blind, that Egypt knew nothing of them, and that the South would almost certainly be their destination. After five weeks of holding the rams in port under watch, Russell finally decided on October 8 that they should be seized. On October 26 Her Majesty's government officially took complete possession of the ships. Bulloch was crushed. He and Slidell conferred in Paris, and the only remaining recourse seemed to be the Bravay title. Since the ships legally belonged to a French firm, if the Emperor would lodge a formal protest and demand that the ships be released to Bravay, Russell would have to give in or else risk a major confrontation with France. But Napoleon delayed until February 1864, and then decided not to act at all. That left Bulloch with nothing to do but pursue through Bravay the legal means of recourse. In the end he profited, for the British Government paid some £30,000 more than Bulloch, Bravay, and the Lairds had invested, but it was a hollow compensation by that time. The action by Russell, with the approbation of his government, clearly spelled the end of Bulloch's enterprises in Great Britain. Her Majesty had sided with the North, so it seemed, though in fact John Bull merely chose to enforce neutrality with more will than before. If the Confederacy was to continue its shipbuilding program, it would have to be elsewhere. Reluctantly, Bulloch moved to that morass of intrigue and half-truth, France. Perhaps he would fare better there.[29]

Even while Bulloch lamented that the action of Russell left him in the "condition of a disabled ship taken possession of by a current she has no power to stem," the Adams family in the American legation found cause for great rejoicing. "This is a second Vicksburg," Henry Adams wrote to his brother, "the crowning stroke of our diplomacy." It came to the Adamses that at last Union statecraft held firmly the upper hand in the contest for British—and thereby European—neutrality. Queen Victoria herself seemed to take her stand with them when on July 29 she repudiated Roebuck's recognition move in the House of Commons by declaring to Parliament that she saw no reason to "depart from the strict neutrality" observed since the beginning of the war. The cumulative effects of Northern successes on the battlefield, the widespread approval abroad of the Emancipation Proclamation, and Adams' constant and irritating dangling of the laws of neutrality finally made themselves evident. The seizure of the rams settled the case. Great Britain was safe for the Union. While Adams appreciated the risks taken by Russell, he appreciated even more the outcome. The two remained friends, despite the strains of their mutual bad tempers and crustiness. So, too, did the United States and Great Britain remain friends, and hopefully they could so continue. "Thus far we have always harmonized," Adams once wrote of the two nations, "and I trust we may to the end of the chapter."[30]

CHAPTER 13

"NO BED OF ROSES"

John Donne had declared that no man is an island, and so might another poet in a later time have said much the same of the events and individuals in this war in America. Vicksburg and Birkenhead and Paris all stood thousands of miles from one another, yet they all influenced affairs in even the most remote places. The very day after Lord Russell announced, on September 1, that he could do nothing about the Laird rams, a Confederate general in faraway Shreveport, Louisiana, wrote to John Slidell in Paris about the intertwined affairs of France, Mexico, and the Confederacy, and all centered on Texas.

The general was Edmund Kirby-Smith, commanding the Confederate Department of the Trans-Mississippi, and in his letter he revealed much of the frustration of his command. "The action of the French in Mexico," he wrote, "makes the establishment of the Confederacy the policy of the French Government." He urged Slidell to make Napoleon aware of the vast preparations being made by the Federals to subjugate Kirby-Smith's territory. Should the Yankees overrun his department, then the Mexican puppet government would soon find "a grasping, haughty, and imperious neighbor" on its northern border. If the Emperor wanted to avoid the threat of a Northern invasion of Mexico itself, he must first aid the Confederacy in establishing its primacy in the region, and its independence. "This succor must come speedily," Kirby-Smith implored, "or it will be too late." Without foreign assistance "or an extraordinary inter-position of Providence, less than twelve months will see this fair country irretrievably lost, and the French protectorate in Mexico will find a hos-tile power established on their frontier of exhaustless resources and great military strength impelled by revenge and the traditional policy of its Government to overthrow all foreign influence on the American Conti-nent." The Monroe Doctrine was a Yankee policy, not Confederate.

But if Napoleon decided to act, he must do so at once. "If the policy of the Emperor looks to an intervention," he continued, "he should take immediate military possession of the East bank of the Rio Grande." That would give Kirby-Smith his only route since the loss of Vicksburg and the Mississippi, for obtaining supplies and munitions. Then dangling the old carrot of cotton, he assured Napoleon that the staple trade west of the great river "will thus be secured to the French Market." "I have not writ-ten for diplomatic effect," said Kirby-Smith coyly, "but have stated truths which should have weight." Yet in one brief letter he had invoked diplo-macy, economics, foreign trade, military intervention, the foreign policy of his enemy, and a neat summation of the change in the military situation thanks to Grant's success on the Mississippi. Indeed, there were no islands in this war. Every act cast its shadow over every other, and the dark shape could extend even to the remote Trans-Mississippi.

Indeed, Kirby-Smith felt as though he commanded an island at times, one isolated even from its own capital in Richmond, and not just by the loss of the great river. He felt genuine neglect. He even com-plained to Slidell of how "The country West of the Mississippi has been exhausted of its fighting population to swell up the ranks of our Armies in Virginia, Tennessee and Mississippi." He had few left to man his ranks and replace his losses but "the aged, the infirm, and the lukewarm." Ev-erything ran in short supply, and what his department could produce was often as not taken from him for the benefit of Lee and Bragg. Well might Kirby-Smith complain, and he was not the first out in this Western terri-tory to fear that no one heard him.[1]

By the time that Kirby-Smith wrote to Slidell, he commanded a de-partment which, in theory, contained more real territory than all of the Confederacy east of the Mississippi combined: Missouri, Arkansas, west-ern Louisiana, Texas, the Indian Territory that would one day be Okla-homa, and the Arizona Territory stretching to the California border. It contained perhaps 600,000 square miles, a virtual empire.

It was a wild and often turbulent region. Only months before the outbreak of war the frontier army was still battling Indians, Comanches, Kiowas, Apaches, and others. A combination of Federal troopers and local regulators like the Texas Rangers and militia groups preserved what peace there was on the border. Men in Missouri still sat bitterly divided over the issue of slavery, with the memory of the days of "Bleeding Kansas" fresh. Issues were completely different in the territory along the border with

Mexico, the largely Spanish population uninterested in this Anglo war, and many still carrying resentments over the last war when the United States forcibly took this land from their native country. A variety of motives and impulses coursed through this enormous territory, just as in a major nation, and anyone trying to cope with it administratively invited a nightmare. Anyone trying to cope with it militarily asked the near-impossible.

It was a territorial command that evolved considerably, both for Federals and Confederates, with no little confusion and overlapping of authority. Even before the outbreak of actual fighting in 1861, the Davis government recognized immediately that an attempt must be made to hold as much of the West as possible. Arkansas and Texas, as well as Louisiana, had seceded to make common cause with the Confederacy. That was fine. They also entertained high expectations that a pro-Southern majority in Missouri would bring that state into the pale as well. Some sort of formal organization of all this would be necessary, and in April Davis created the District of Texas, with Earl Van Dorn in command. On July 22, 1861, the District of Arkansas, including most of western Louisiana, came into being with Major General William J. Hardee in charge. The Indian Territory would not be officially organized into a department until November, and no formal departmental organization ever included the New Mexico and Arizona lands. Unfortunately, when Davis created all these separate commands, he failed to authorize one central governing command to coordinate all of them, just as he failed to do so east of the Mississippi until the last months of the war. As a result, any gains in these far-flung commands would depend upon cooperation and mutual understanding, the one quality that most Confederate department commanders in this war lacked. Indeed, much of the time the several commanders of these districts seemed not to be entirely certain themselves of who commanded what.

Difficulties set in almost at once. In the beginning, 1861 looked like a good year for the Confederates in the West. They enjoyed repeated success in Missouri. Nathaniel Lyon and his Federal forces gained a minor victory at Boonville in June, but the next month a reverse at Carthage evened the score, and then at Wilson's Creek in August Lyon was killed and his small army defeated. The next month the Confederate advance had reached Lexington on the Missouri River, besieged the Federal garrison, and forced its capitulation. It looked as though the state was fairly won, and on August 19 the Confederate Congress "admitted" Missouri into the new nation. Unfortunately, the state legislature itself never voted for secession. Instead it split, with two legislatures and two governors. Even at this early date, however, General Sterling Price was already complaining to Richmond of the apparent neglect of the West. President Davis tried to reassure him that "the welfare of Missouri is as dear to me as that of other States of the Confederacy," but to most who commanded out here these and future words of comfort from Richmond sounded hollow when not accompanied by more men and materiel.

Yet the interest of Davis in the far West could not entirely be denied. Indeed, one of the first Confederate offensive campaigns of the war came to play this stage, its principal actor himself being a native of the area. Henry Hopkins Sibley was born in Natchitoches, Louisiana, forty-five years before the outbreak of the war, and brought to it a wide experience in the military. He fought in the Seminole War in 1838, served in the military campaign against the Mormons in Utah in the 1840s, and fought well in Mexico. But when Louisiana left the Union, he resigned his commission and took an appointment as a brigadier in the new Confederate service on June 17. He was widely known in both armies, thanks to his invention of the Sibley tent, a standard shelter used in this war. Within a lesser circle of acquaintances he also achieved a reputation as a heavy and intemperate drinker. The frontier service did that to men.

Sibley's commission met him while he traveled the long road from the West to Richmond. There he met with President Davis to present a plan for the conquest of the territory west of Texas, the New Mexico and Arizona territories. From the time that Texas seceded, men in the region looked to the New Mexico residents to follow in kind. Agents went to Santa Fe to muster support for the cause and found considerable evidence of Southern sympathy. So did agents in the Arizona region, where a convention of residents of the Mesilla Valley voted overwhelmingly to invite Confederate annexation. Tucson did the same. There was slim Federal strength in the area, for most of the army regulars had been pulled out in the panic after Fort Sumter, and many installations, like the forts named for the recent ex-President Buchanan and his Vice-President Breckinridge, had to be abandoned altogether. The frontier lay almost defenseless, though the new Yankee commander, Colonel Edward Richard Sprigg Canby, worked diligently to maintain a semblance of Union control. It was obvious to Sibley that the people of the region wanted the Confederacy, and just as obvious that Canby posed little obstacle. Davis agreed, and when Sibley proposed that he could lead a small army of invasion, living off the fertile land entirely and resupplying military needs from captured goods, Davis gave him authorization to mount the campaign. On July 8, 1861, Sibley got his orders. He did not confide to Davis, apparently, that his dream of conquest went considerably beyond his orders. Given his preference, the new general hoped to push clear to the Pacific, take southern California for the cause, and then annex the western sections of Mexico. There was a dream of empire.[2]

Much depended upon speed, and Sibley returned to San Antonio, Texas, at once. There he began recruiting for his "Army of New Mexico," a grandiose appellation for what would be, in fact, a brigade. While he was gone, some minor operations had already taken place, chiefly being the surrender without a fight of several hundred Federals near Fort Fillmore. On August 1 the victorious Confederates declared the establishment of the Confederate Territory of Arizona, headquarters at Mesilla. There they would await the arrival of Sibley for the real work of conquest ahead.

But Sibley met with agonizing delays. Not until December did he finally have his brigade near ready, and at 3,700 it mustered less strength than he had wanted. On December 20 he finally inaugurated his campaign by publishing a proclamation to the people of New Mexico and Arizona. He was coming to bring the territory into the Confederate fold, he said. It was their right, for the future of the Southwest lay with the South. He would relieve them of the tyrant's yoke and establish a new government, and he implored the people to be ready to assist his army with their food and forage. This coming victory, after all, was for them.[3]

Alas, the Confederates did not move quickly. When he issued his proclamation, Sibley had most—but not all—of his army at Fort Bliss, near El Paso, at the very western tip of Texas. "We could go anywhere and do any thing," he boasted, but when he launched his advance along the Rio Grande it proved to be agonizingly slow. A month of marching moved the army less than 100 miles, and it was another month before finally he made contact with the enemy. At Fort Craig, right on the thirty-fourth parallel that separated the New Mexico and Arizona territories, Sibley found a small Federal garrison. By this time the Confederate army had dwindled to about 1,750, but Canby and his Yankees at the fort counted a strength of 3,800 or more. Sibley intended to cut off the fort and force its surrender by taking a vital ford on the Rio Grande and cutting the Federals' lines of communications, but Canby came out and contested the crossing. On February 21 the two armies met at Valverde and, despite his superior numbers, Canby lost. Local troops did not perform well, some even refusing to obey orders. But on the Confederate side, Sibley's men were so tired from the marching that they could not follow up their advantages. They did capture several Yankee cannon and achieved significant success with, of all things, an attack with lances by some Texas cavalry, but when the battle ended they simply could not go on to wrest Fort Craig from Canby. Facing that, Sibley decided to sidestep the fort, believing that it could not hold out long without a steady flow of supplies. The Confederates gathered the battlefield booty left for them and moved on. Sibley had to move quickly now, for the food he expected was not forthcoming, and his command began showing signs of severe unrest. He had to take Santa Fe or Albuquerque quickly in order to supply his tiring army.[4]

Alas, when the Confederates approached Albuquerque on March 2, they saw in the distance columns of smoke rising into the desert sky. The Federals were burning their stores to prevent their capture, but shortly after Sibley established his headquarters in the city, a wagon train of twenty-three wagons fell into his hands, and he breathed easy for a change, confident of having three months' provisions in hand. On March 23 he went on to take Santa Fe. His goal now was the Federal garrison at Fort Union, some miles above the New Mexican capital. Its fall would leave the Confederacy in control of virtually all of the territory east of the Rio Grande and south of Colorado.

On March 26 the two enemies met once more. The Federals were marching south toward Santa Fe and encountered the Confederates moving north. They met in an area called Apache Canyon, the Federals numbering just 418 men, half of them cavalry and the rest members of the Colorado volunteers. They encountered about 250 Texas cavalrymen and a hot skirmish immediately ensued. "How our hearts beat!" recalled one of the Colorado volunteers. "That tremendous event, the burden of history and song, a *battle*, burst on our hitherto peaceful lives like an avalanche on a Swiss village." Well, it was not quite that much of a battle. By standards in Virginia, it was barely a skirmish, but out West such things could decide campaigns, and this one began to stem the Confederate advance. Major John Milton Chivington, commanding the Federal detachment, managed his men well and sufficiently attracted the attention of the enemy so that one officer emptied his pistol three times toward him and then directed a company volley, all of which missed the charmed major. When his men warned him that the Confederate had a cannon shooting at him, Chivington bowed as a shot passed over his head.[5]

The Confederates retired, and two days later in another skirmish the Federals bested them once again. Federal troops were beginning to converge on Sibley, as at last the threat to the territory became apparent. Sibley got word that Canby was marching toward Albuquerque and the small Confederate garrison there. The general at once ordered his "army" to withdraw to the south to protect the garrison and his supply base. Thus Sibley abandoned Santa Fe, and when he finally had his command in Albuquerque he learned that two Federal forces now faced him from opposite directions. When the two united, the Confederates would be outnumbered. All he could do was evacuate the territory to save his army. He withdrew slowly, however, and Canby, though outnumbering him considerably by now, did not pursue vigorously. He had 2,400 soldiers at his command, and finally began a pursuit in mid-April. When they finally came close to Sibley's command, they found the Confederates holding a *fandango* in celebration of leaving the detested New Mexico. Instead of attacking Sibley, however, Canby attacked and captured part of his wagon train the next day, and then skirmished only weakly at a Rio Grande crossing. The Confederates crossed safely, and that was that. By May, Sibley was back near El Paso, safely within the Confederate state of Texas once more, yet even here the retreat did not stop. Now California got into the war, in a passive sort of fashion. Word of the Confederate invasion reached southern California in August. There was little standing between

Sibley and the golden state, so in September a column of 2,000 infantry led by Colonel James Henry Carleton was ordered to go to Canby's aid. Yet it took a long time to build such an expedition in an area with virtually no Federal troops available, so that the winter came and went and it was April 1862 before the column marched away. A month later elements reached Tucson just two days after the Confederates evacuated the town, and finally the Californians saw the Rio Grande on July 4. They stood just 100 miles north of El Paso, and their appearance would have severely disturbed Sibley. A hard drive by the Federals could cut him off from his supply line to the Texas interior. It would have, but it did not, for by this time Sibley found his army so demoralized and under strength, and his own spirits so low, that he had taken all but a garrison back to San Antonio. With the appearance of the California columns, that garrison now withdrew as well, and the whole campaign was ended.[6]

Sibley and his army lay shattered by the experience. Of the 2,500 he led into the territories, only 1,500 came back. They lost all but seven of their wagons of equipment, and all of the cannon they took with them, bringing back only a battery captured from the enemy at Valverde. Sibley himself lost all his fight. He never directed his troops personally in any of the skirmishes, and once back in Texas he actually discouraged the sending of reinforcements, not wanting to be presented with an opportunity to fight again. He had lost what was certainly an impractical gamble to start with, and now he simply wanted the loss over and done. When the news reached the Confederacy, most blamed Sibley himself, and certainly he had not conducted a wise campaign. His own men loathed the New Mexico region, resenting the judgment that had sent them to take it, and most pundits agreed that the whole expedition had been simply "chasing a shadow." Such a vast area could not be taken and held by so small a force, and certainly no army could subsist on its own in the barren wilderness. Sibley would always blame lack of supplies for his failure, yet his own timidity cost him much as well. He would have a long time to try to clear his name of the defeat, for he never again held a significant command in this war. His career, like the Confederate hope for Arizona and New Mexico and the Southwestern empire that might have been, ended in the heat and mesquite and cactus.[7]

By the time Sibley got back to San Antonio, there was at last a new center of command in the region, which showed that Richmond began to realize the import of coordinated control of the vast territory. In January 1862 the War Department created the Trans-Mississippi District, to combine the two commands of Sterling Price and his Missouri state troops with the Arkansas and Louisiana regiments of General Ben McCulloch. The two generals had been feuding over just who could command who, and now Richmond sent Earl Van Dorn to command both of them. Van Dorn seemed to get around in these early days of the war and, as evidenced by his later being shot by an irate husband, he did not limit his circulation to the military. He started the war as a brigadier in Texas, then went to Virginia in September, only to be sent back to the West the following January. Before he could join his new command, a campaign was already under way that, combined with Sibley's failure, would lose the Confederacy more territory in a single season than any other time until the last year of the war.

Price wintered in Missouri in 1861, while McCulloch stayed farther south, in Arkansas. They feuded constantly, but toward the end of January Price's scouts began reporting a Federal buildup in eastern Missouri under General Samuel Ryan Curtis. Soon the 12,000 Federals moved out, their obvious goal being to drive Price out of Missouri, and with barely over 5,000 men of his own, the Confederate had no choice but to withdraw. He hoped that McCulloch would answer his pleas and come to reinforce, but McCulloch appeared to despise Price more than he hated the enemy. As a result, on February 12, 1862, with Curtis only a handful of miles away, the Confederates began pulling out of Missouri. They marched nonstop for five days, the cold freezing the water in canteens and turning beards white with frozen breath. Men could not fall out to sleep for fear of freezing to death.[8]

By February 21 Price finally found McCulloch, and the two joined forces. Together they outnumbered Curtis by about 14,000 to 12,000, and when Van Dorn arrived to take personal command on March 1 he already had an offensive in mind. Indeed, he had big plans. "I must have St. Louis—then huzza!" he declared a few weeks before. Now he christened his command the Army of the West and told his soldiers, "Behold your leader! He comes to show you the way to glory and immortal renown." Suiting action to word, Van Dorn launched his campaign just three days later, intending to attack Curtis with superior numbers while the Federal lay dispersed in Arkansas trying to subsist his army on the countryside and a much attenuated supply line. Just two days later, on March 6, the two armies collided. Only skirmishing took place the first day. Van Dorn did not want to attack the four divisions that Curtis had well placed along Sugar Creek. Instead, the next day the Confederates launched an attack around and behind Curtis' flank at Pea Ridge and began driving the enemy before them. But the Yankees began to hold stubbornly, and soon one of the toughest fights on this side of the Mississippi was in full swing. Van Dorn's attack stopped. McCulloch was killed. Then the command of Indians that had enlisted with the South stopped their fighting and began to plunder enemy camps and, some said, started scalping the dead. Curtis picked a good moment to launch his own counterattack, and the Confederates broke and retired.

That night Van Dorn looked on rather a shambles compared to his great expectations of just a week before. Most of his army was exhausted and fought out, and his ammunition ran low. With several other commanders besides McCulloch killed or captured, his command was in a mess. Yet he decided to risk it for another day. It was a mistake, for that night the remainder of Curtis' army rejoined him, and he now had thousands of fresh troops ready for battle. He attacked at dawn and pushed steadily, until Van Dorn's artillery was silenced and the infantry too low on ammunition to continue the fight. Van Dorn and Price gave the orders to retreat. The fiercest battle to be fought in the Trans-Mississippi was done, and it was a Federal victory. The Confederates retreated one hundred miles south to Van Buren. Missouri was undisputedly saved for the Union for the present, and perhaps for good.[9]

Then came changes. Forts Henry and Donelson fell and the Confederates were preparing to attack Grant at Shiloh. Orders came for Van Dorn to bring his army across the Mississippi to aid in the new campaign, and when he complied, any further threat to Missouri ended at once. Protests came from Arkansans immediately, for Van Dorn would be virtually abandoning the state to Curtis. There seemed no choice, but the gesture also showed how Richmond viewed the Trans-Mississippi. Clearly it was a backwater of the war, not important enough to hold when its troops could be used effectively elsewhere. That the same did not, and would not, hold true of other departments was demonstrated by the failure in future campaigns to weaken the army in Virginia for the benefit of other theaters of the conflict. It happened only twice. To the Trans-Mississippi it happened repeatedly.[10]

As if to compensate for taking away its principal army, Richmond now actually expanded the limits of the command and redubbed it the Department of the Trans-Mississippi. On May 26, 1862, the War Department redefined its borders to include Texas, Arkansas, Missouri, western Louisiana, and the Indian Territory. The following week, with Van Dorn now in command in Mississippi, a new general arrived, determined "to drive out the enemy or to perish in the attempt." Major General Thomas Carmichael Hindman was no stranger to this countryside. Though born in Tennessee, he moved to Arkansas in the late 1850s, and twice won election to Congress, afterward helping to bring about the state's secession. Thanks to his political influence and an excellent record as an officer in the Mexican War, he rose rapidly in the Confederate service, but in this new command he would need more than just skill. He found barely 1,000 soldiers in all of Arkansas, and scattered and badly supplied commands in the rest of the department. Obviously his most pressing problem was manpower, and he ruthlessly set out to remedy it. Using the Confederate conscription acts to raise new troops, he consolidated into Arkansas soldiers from elsewhere in the department, then declared martial law in the state to help in enlisting reluctant men. His methods outraged the state, and some of his superiors. Deserters found themselves summarily shot. Regiments passing through the department bound elsewhere were held up without orders, and Hindman's conscript officers acted as little better than press gangs. Yet for all the unsavory character of his tactics, Hindman built an army. By July he had about 18,000 men under arms, and several thousand more awaiting induction. It was something of a miracle, though few of those literally forced at gunpoint into the army would have thanked Hindman for the feat. Curtis certainly did not. Thoroughly impressed with the enemy in Arkansas, and convinced that Hindman commanded almost double his real strength, Curtis abandoned his position at Pea Ridge in northwestern Arkansas and marched across the state to Helena, now in Federal hands, in order to be near support. Hindman held his army in and about Little Rock, and even when the outnumbered Curtis marched within a very few miles, Hindman did nothing more than send 5,000 ill-armed draftees out to harass his progress. It was a wonderful opportunity to strike a crushing blow against a by now exhausted and underfed enemy, but Hindman did nothing. In his defense, he probably did not entirely trust his "army." Most knew nothing of the military, had never been in a fight, and might run at the first fire. Still, he was considerably embarrassed by Curtis' march, the more so when on July 30 he had to turn over command of the department to yet another general, Major General Theophilus Hunter Holmes. If the people of the department regarded Hindman as a "military tyrant," they would come in time to think of Holmes as "granny Holmes," a man suffering from "softening of the brain."[11]

Holmes was a North Carolinian, almost fifty-seven, a veteran without distinction of First Manassas and the Seven Days fighting earlier in 1862. His appointment to the new command came chiefly thanks to his friendship with Davis, the expectation that he and Price could cooperate in retaking Missouri, and because there was nothing else to do with him. More than once a shelved general would be sent west of the Mississippi to get him out of the way. But Holmes was a real mistake. Ill, almost deaf, unable to make a decision, and tired, he was a kindly man who wanted nothing more than to be left alone. And as subordinates, the policy of sending unwanted officers out West left him with Gustavus Woodson Smith, who froze when briefly in command of the Army of Northern Virginia before Lee took over, and John Bankhead Magruder, under a cloud because of his bad performance on the Peninsula. Hindman, too, was no perfect officer, but for now Holmes left him in command in Arkansas with orders to raise another army, and amazingly he did so. By the fall there were another 10,000 Confederates under arms in northern Arkansas and Hindman chaffed to lead them against the enemy.

Among those in his new army were some 3,500 Indian cavalry led by Colonel Douglas Hancock Cooper. The story of the Confederate Indians went back to the beginning of the war, and their service with the Western army had already proved to be a clouded blessing. The Creeks, Cherokees, Choctaws, Chickasaws, and Seminoles inhabited the Indian Territory ever since their removal by President Jackson in the 1830s. In general, they held strong pro-slavery sympathies, and at the outbreak of the war signed treaties with the Confederacy, but their real loyalties always rested more on individual and personal feelings rather than tribal commitment. It was, after all, a white man's war, and the majority of the Indians bent with the wind. When the South seemed ascendant, as after Wilson's Creek, enlistments among the Cherokee and other tribes ran high. Sensing the potential, Richmond engaged a strange man, Albert Pike of Boston, now a Rebel brigadier, to conclude treaties with the Indians and raise two regiments of cavalry. Eventually Hindman would arrest Pike and others would question both his loyalty and his sanity, but he did manage to enlist as many as 4,000 warriors for the cause. They were a good deal of trouble, even to their Confederate allies. Their commanders forced them to fight fellow Indians in their first battle, and when the pro-Union Indians tried to escape to Kansas, one of the Confederate Indian regiments even switched sides for a day and fought with them. They fought well in the first stages of battle at Pea Ridge, but then fell out and would not answer their officers, some even killing and reportedly scalping fellow white Confederates. If that were not bad enough, Hindman soon accused Pike of embezzlement of government funds, Pike resigned, and Cooper replaced him, and then in September the Federals attacked the Indian cavalry at Newtonia, Missouri, and routed the whole command. By the end of the year the Indian regiments were badly disorganized. Though they remained in the service, commanded in time by one of their own, Brigadier General Stand Watie, the Five Nations soldiers devoted the best part of their war to fighting for themselves. Many looked on this war just as the blacks in the South viewed it. No matter who won, the Indian would not likely fare any better after than before the fight. Best to do what they could for themselves.[12]

Such was the material that made Hindman's army. Though he hesitated to attack Curtis in July, in October 1862 he felt an unstoppable desire to attack. A Federal army led by Major General John McAllister Schofield had invaded northern Arkansas, clearing the state of Confederates down to the Arkansas River. Then he left for Missouri and the winter, leaving behind only about 10,000 troops commanded by Brigadier General James G. Blunt. Hindman determined to attack. When orders came from Richmond that another 10,000 men were needed in Mississippi, Holmes directed Hindman to stop his advance toward Blunt. Hindman simply refused, and instead sent two brigades of cavalry to attack Blunt. The Federals repulsed them and, goaded by the failure, Hindman continued to defy his orders and moved his whole army north. He met Blunt at Prairie Grove on December 7 in one of the most confused smaller battles of the war. Blunt had only 7,000 men on the field at first, and when Hindman attacked he enjoyed an early advantage. But then in one of the best-timed reinforcements of the war, General Francis Jay Herron arrived with another 6,000 Federals and won the day. The weather turned bitter cold and during the night Hindman had to withdraw with

1,300 casualties. The men left wounded on the battlefield either froze to death or were sometimes burned by the fires started during the battle. One of Hindman's regiments actually deserted to Blunt, and some of his new draftees, rather than fight against Old Glory, charged without loading their rifles. During the night scores of wild pigs roamed the battlefield, eating the dead.[13]

In the pursuit that followed, Hindman's army almost disappeared. By the time that the Federals forced him back to Little Rock, the Confederate general commanded only a shadow. Still unwilling entirely to abandon northern Arkansas, he launched a bold cavalry raid led by General John Sappington Marmaduke. The twenty-nine-year-old Missourian led 2,300 Missouri cavalry north into their natal state. By January 8 they reached Springfield, then turned back toward Arkansas and began burning bridges and cutting telegraph wires as they rode. So successfully did Marmaduke accomplish his task that the Federals pulled back almost all of their troops in Arkansas to the security of Missouri and the protection of their communications. For the rest of the winter, northern Arkansas lay almost abandoned by both sides.

That was the northern border of the department. Along its southern line, the Trans-Mississippi saw action as well, and its own share of second-rate generals. The blockade touched the department, for Texas measured 700 miles of coastline from the mouth of the Rio Grande to the Louisiana border. The Confederates made early attempts to fortify the better ports at Galveston, Sabine Pass, and other river outlets, but no one could defend the entire line. Indeed, at one time Galveston's defenses consisted only of a battalion of city militia and several "Quaker guns," wooden trunks mounted on wheels in hopes that distant blockaders would take them for real cannon. By October 1862 the Federals readied an attempt to take the city and sent in a demand for its surrender. When the Confederates all but evacuated, the bluecoats took Galveston without a scratch. "Galveston is very quiet and very dull," complained a correspondent who had hoped for a better story to file. He got it that winter when Magruder arrived to command the District of Texas and marshaled the remnant of Sibley's command, some new militia, and scattered Confederate units into a small army. He made two river steamers into makeshift gunboats and on January 1, 1863, he attacked. The fight lasted four hours. Magruder captured the Yankee gunboat *Harriet Lane*, destroyed two other enemy ships, and drove the Federals out of Galveston and back into the sea. Just three weeks later, at Sabine Pass on the eastern end of the coastline, two more Confederate steamers, their sides protected with bales of cotton, attacked and defeated two blockading ships. The Federals, who had captured Sabine City some time before, evacuated, and Magruder could claim yet another triumph in driving "the Abolition Hordes" from his shores. Though the blockade redoubled its vigilance, both Galveston and Sabine Pass continued to receive a steady flow of traffic in runners who managed to evade the Federals. By the time of Vicksburg, this would be the only route of supply and communication left for the department.[14]

And now came Kirby-Smith. His had been a mixed career thus far in this war. He commanded a brigade under Joe Johnston in the First Manassas campaign, yet just as his command reached the battlefield he fell with a serious wound before his brigade even entered the fight. Still, by 1862 he was a major general, recuperated, and commanding in eastern Tennessee when Braxton Bragg began his Kentucky campaign. Though he declined to cooperate with Bragg entirely, still he had won the battle at Richmond on August 30, and largely in reward Davis made him a lieutenant general when the campaign ended. On January 14, even while Magruder cleared the Texas coastline, Kirby-Smith took a new command, western Louisiana, and a month later Richmond extended that command to include the entire Trans-Mississippi. Holmes and Hindman no longer inspired confidence. "It requires some energetic genius to restore affairs in that quarter," said Colonel Josiah Gorgas, and since Davis liked Kirby-Smith, and the Arkansas delegates in Congress wanted him, the young lieutenant general got the job. "My troubles will soon commence," he lamented. He knew that everyone would find fault with him, that no commander could successfully administer the largest department in the Confederacy with the smallest army. "I shall be happy and cheerfully and manfully discharge my duty," he said.

When he assumed the new command on March 7, Kirby-Smith began an inspection tour, his first destination Little Rock. Even as Richmond assigned him, it warned of unrest due to the mismanagement of Holmes and Hindman, and that must be Kirby-Smith's first priority. As he made his way to Little Rock, the general could see evidence enough by the numbers of deserters strolling the highways. When he reached the capital, he found Holmes positively delighted at being relieved. He told Kirby-Smith that he "gives up the charge of the 'elephant' to us with great satisfaction." In no time at all Kirby-Smith would come to know the weight of that elephant.[15]

Actually, the new general found Arkansas, desertions to the contrary, not to be as bad as he had heard, but still he saw immediately the cause of the disaffection and confusion in the department. "There was no general system, no common head," Kirby-Smith reported to Davis; "each district was acting independently." Attention seemed to be focused only on the point most immediately threatened—or of most immediate interest to the commander involved. Thus while both Holmes and Hindman wanted Kirby-Smith to make his headquarters at Little Rock, he opted instead for Shreveport, a more central location from which he could more manageably rule his department. By April 24 Kirby-Smith was in place, and began to make what few changes in his command he thought advisable. Magruder, though difficult, had successfully defended Texas so far, and he could stay in command of that district. Major General Richard Taylor, son of President Zachary Taylor and onetime brother-in-law of Jefferson Davis, commanded now in western Louisiana. Hindman was transferred to Mississippi, where he would be troublesome on the other side of the river for a change, and Holmes succeeded him in the Arkansas district. The tour of his command, and the return of muster rolls that spring, told Kirby-Smith that on paper he commanded almost 46,000 men. Half sat in Arkansas, 11,000 in Magruder's domain, and the rest with Dick Taylor. In fact, however, sickness and lethargy and incompetence pared down those numbers so that the actual total of effectives came barely to half the official tally, and the men in the ranks were hardly of the best. The cream of the Western soldiery had been drained away to the East, and Kirby-Smith soon complained to Richmond that "the male population remaining are old men, or have furnished substitutes, are lukewarm, or are wrapped up in speculations and money-making."[16]

Nevertheless, Davis and the War Department expected that Kirby-Smith would use this army, such as it was, in the great task, not of defending the department, but of supporting in the struggle to save Vicksburg and preserve the Mississippi. As always, they looked on the Trans-Mississippi as a secondary theater of the war. Indeed, Kirby-Smith was actually directed not to pay much attention to his threatened northern border in Arkansas. Rather, he was to throw troops across the Mississippi whenever and wherever possible in order to create a diversion to pull Grant away from Pemberton. As for the Trans-Mississippi department itself, Secretary of War James A. Seddon himself put into eloquent words the absolute lack of understanding of its problems in Richmond. "From the nature of the country," he told Kirby-Smith of the command, "I am satisfied that the whole country is among the most defensible in the world, and that comparatively few resolute, experienced men could repel hosts of invaders."[17]

Kirby-Smith got the chance to see how his department could so easily repel "hosts of invaders" sooner than he expected. All through March and April he found himself unable to move in support of Pemberton, despite repeated urgings from Richmond. He simply had too few men to cover too much territory, and then Nathaniel Banks took the initiative for his own right. Of course, it was not the initiative that Grant and Washington expected of him. Banks was to take Port Hudson, but first he decided that he must clear the west side of the Mississippi. He may also have been lured to the Red River vicinity by reports of extensive stockpiles of cotton sitting on the wharves at Alexandria, Louisiana, and elsewhere. Indeed, even some of Kirby-Smith's officers had been engaged in illegally trading cotton with the Federals, and Banks—himself an alumnus of the textile industry—certainly saw great potential in capturing the staple.

Richard Taylor well divined Banks's intentions as far back as March, but had too little with which to oppose him. He marshaled what forces he could at Fort Bisland, near Brashear City along the Louisiana coast, and there hoped that he could retard Banks's advance westward from New

Orleans. On April 12 Banks finally sent his 12,000-man army off on his campaign, moving toward Taylor's little command. That same night Federal artillery began shelling the fort, and the next day Banks launched an attack. Yet the Rebel fire proved devastating as the bluecoats charged across open ground, and in the evening Banks's attack stalled, then stopped. But it was only a tactical victory for Taylor, for Banks had also sent 4,000 other Federals to cut off the Confederate retreat, and when Taylor learned of it, he had no choice but to evacuate Fort Bisland that same night. The retreat thus begun, continued in the face of heavy odds, as Taylor finally withdrew fully fifty miles north to Opelousas. Kirby-Smith believed that Banks and Grant were going to cooperate together to destroy Taylor, then seize the Red River. Though mistaken, he still acted with energy and at once ordered all available troops in the department to march to Taylor's aid. Kirby-Smith even appealed to Pemberton for reinforcements, but the Vicksburg commander responded in kind by asking that Kirby-Smith aid him instead.

By April 24, Taylor had fallen back farther, to Alexandria on the Red. There he and Kirby-Smith conferred, only to be caught up in a virtual panic as the Confederate army readied once more to withdraw upon Banks's approach. Kirby-Smith had to commandeer a steamboat to take him upriver to Shreveport once more, and there, too, he found the beginnings of panic in the civil and military population. Nevertheless, even as Alexandria fell to Banks, Kirby-Smith expressed the intention of commencing his own counteroffensive from Shreveport "with strong hopes of recovering the country when the waters fall." Supported by ironclads under David Porter, Banks finally took Alexandria on May 7 with almost no opposition. But then, even as Kirby-Smith feverishly tried to put together a force to drive the enemy from his department, Banks began planing to leave of his own accord. Finally he decided to cooperate with Grant and invest Port Hudson, which he had been supposed to do months before. As the Yankees began their withdrawal, after having laid waste a great deal of the Red River Valley and southern Louisiana, Kirby-Smith appeared almost sorry to see him go. He knew that the fate of Vicksburg depended on the coming battle in Mississippi, and believed that "the fate of the Trans-Mississippi Department in a great measure depends on it." By holding Banks in the department, Kirby-Smith felt that he contributed mightily to the defense of Vicksburg. Alas, it was not enough.[18]

Kirby-Smith felt mixed feelings of relief and anger at the result of the campaign. His department lay territorially as intact after the affair as before, though now destitute of cotton, crops, and even thousands of Negroes who had flocked to Banks's army. Worse, many citizens of Louisiana had actually given assistance to the Federals, and even taken oaths of allegiance to the Union. Clearly, disloyalty ran rife within the Trans-Mississippi, yet one more of the plague of problems that beset this entirely unhomogeneous command. And with Banks now gone, there would be no rest for Kirby-Smith, for at once he had to move to give what assistance he could in relieving Vicksburg. "Public opinion would condemn us if we did not *try to do something*," he said to Taylor. He ordered the general to move north and attempt to cut Grant's supply and communications line in the bayous on the west side of the Mississippi opposite Vicksburg. Taylor objected but went anyhow, arriving just in time to see Grant reestablish his communications via the Yazoo, and thus making the whole expedition a wasted effort. Nothing better came from Kirby-Smith's instructions to Holmes to take his Arkansas command and try to threaten Grant on the west bank of the river. On July 4, even as Pemberton was surrendering Vicksburg, Holmes made a bungled attack on Helena and suffered a repulse. About the only real success, and a small one at that, came when Taylor marched back south after his aborted expedition against Grant, and cleverly captured the Federal garrison at Brashear City. On June 23 he struck and won easily, capturing 1,700 prisoners and a considerable quantity of supplies and arms. "For the first time since I reached western Louisiana," he said, "I had supplies." But his success did nothing to relieve the pressure on Port Hudson as he had hoped, and when Banks captured the citadel, he then turned once more on Taylor. The Confederate had no choice but to abandon Brashear and retire once more into the Louisiana interior.[19]

In all, Kirby-Smith could take little pleasure from his first season of campaigning in the department. He could not help Vicksburg or Port Hudson, he could hardly defend Louisiana, the enemy still held much of northern Arkansas, and now he sat utterly isolated from Richmond and the eastern Confederacy except through the uncertain fortunes of blockade-runners and an occasional scout stealing across the Mississippi. He faced an enormous problem now, and one not offered to other departmental commanders in the South. President Davis managed to state it for him very nicely on July 14 when he wrote that "You now have not merely a military, but also a political problem involved in your command." The Confederate civil government could no longer maintain control over the region. Now Kirby-Smith would have to exercise that control, in tandem with the governors of the states in his command. He would have to be general-in-chief, and "exercise powers of civil administration." Kirby-Smith would be War Department, Legislative, and Executive branches all in one. Davis did not actually specify this, but it was a natural effect of the loss of the Mississippi. There must be a central authority, with the authority to maintain itself, and that could only be the general. Kirby-Smith recognized this without being told. The day before Davis wrote to him he had already convened his first meeting with the governors and the state supreme court justices. When they met in August, it seemed clear that the general regarded his own authority as superior to theirs. And soon thereafter he turned to affairs of state, when he wrote to Slidell over the matter of French recognition and aid. By the end of 1863, people were already beginning to refer to the Trans-Mississippi as "Kirby-Smithdom." In time, though lacking most of the negative connotations of the title, Edmund Kirby-Smith became the closest thing to a military dictator ever to rule in North America.[20]

The same month that Kirby-Smith convened his civil convention, men of his command achieved one of the deepest penetrations of Federal territory thus far, though Kirby-Smith might have wished that it had not happened. With supplies and arms too limited for the raising and moving of great armies, he found himself forced to rely upon a mode of warfare that he disliked in order to maintain some semblance of military activity —guerrillas. "It only entails additional persecution and distress upon our friends," he said, "without advancing our cause." From the very beginning of the war this Western region found ample numbers of men who gravitated toward the life of the partisan, the guerrilla. They were rugged men, and all too often unsavory in character. Ruffians and bushwhackers had been flourishing, after all, since the days of Bleeding Kansas, when rival parties raided and plundered and killed in the name of a cause, but just as often purely for the wanton entertainment and gain of it. Kansas and Missouri both blazed with their violence, and when the war came it merely presented a likely opportunity for many of these men to continue in their adopted profession of blood and booty. Most preferred the Confederate service, in part out of sympathy with slavery, in part as a means of settling old scores against abolitionist enemies, and in significant measure out of the need felt by many backward poor whites to associate themselves somehow with the nobility of the cause. They might not live on plantations and own slaves, but by fighting with and for those who did, many hoped that some of the patricians' social standing would attach itself to them.

However, in time the guerrillas proved to be an embarrassment to the Confederacy, for they proved to be just as hostile and unmanageable to their authorities as they were hostile and brutal to the enemy—further testimony that in this war these men were really fighting for themselves, not a cause. Nowhere in the Civil War would the guerrillas wield such power and terror as in Kirby-Smithdom. There were many who achieved their measure of notoriety, George Todd, William C. "Bloody Bill" Anderson, and more. Others also fought for the Union, and often with equal disregard for the regular laws of warfare, but it was the Confederates who captured the imagination, and fears, of loyal people in the region.

In 1861, Halleck and his successors in Missouri had been unable to control the bushwhackers, many of whom wore no uniforms but simply left their homes for a night raid and then melted back into the citizenry. All "Old Brains" could do was enforce immediate execution for irregulars who fought without the Confederate uniform, and that policy—as old as war itself—brought with it the obvious and equally deadly response from the guerrillas. Soon no quarter was given on either side. "War to the knife," became the cry, "and the knife to the hilt." None of them managed to realize that dread motto better than a diminutive native of Ohio, a man just twenty-five in 1862, onetime schoolteacher, farmer, prospector, and in 1860 a man who switched allegiance to fight on both sides in the war between the anti-slave Jayhawkers and the pro-slave Border Ruffians. William Clarke Quantrill, despite his slight stature, made the archetypal guerrilla. Cold, brutal, a man who had failed in civilian life and who nurtured innumerable grudges against those whom he blamed for his own shortcomings, his was the perfect repressed personality for a would-be leader of brutes and thugs.

Late in 1861, in Jackson County, Missouri, Quantrill formed a small band of like-minded men into a guard to protect the area from raids by Jayhawkers. His undoubted courage and ability with his pistols won him leadership, though it would prove hard to hold. Soon he went beyond fighting Jayhawkers and began raiding Federal scouts, assassinating prominent Unionists, robbing mail and freight carriers, and even skirmishing with Yankee soldiers. As his fame grew, so did the numbers in his band, which included future toughs like Cole Younger and Frank and Jesse James. The service attracted men without scruples or conscience. Finally Quantrill became major news when, on March 7, 1862, he raided Aubry, Kansas, and after looting the town senselessly murdered five defenseless citizens.[21]

During 1862 General Hindman encouraged partisans. He felt no timidity about using guerrillas, and their methods were at times not so different from his own. He sent several officers into Missouri to recruit partisans, and on August 15, 1862, after Quantrill's bushwhackers had captured Independence, he mustered his command into the Confederate service after almost a year of fighting the war on his own hook. Now Captain Quantrill continued his raiding until the winter came when, tasting power and prestige and liking it, he went to Richmond to ask for a commission as a colonel. He did not get it, but he called himself colonel thereafter just the same.

The year 1863 was to be Quantrill's, and the bloodiest in all the guerrilla warfare in the West. He and his men returned to Missouri in the spring and renewed their policy of ambush and raid. By summer they so terrorized western Missouri that a Kansas City journal complained that "Quantrill & Co. do rule in this section of the state." Brigadier General Thomas Ewing, Jr., Federal commander in the area and a brother-in-law to General Sherman, decided to take drastic means to stop the guerrillas. Most of them came from this area, and hundreds of disloyal homes opened up to swallow them from sight after each raid. On August 14, therefore, Ewing issued his infamous General Orders No. 10—later to be followed by No. 11—that virtually depopulated the western counties of all who could not prove their Federal allegiance. Worse, he imprisoned several wives, sisters, and other relatives of prominent guerrillas like Anderson in Kansas City. The building collapsed, killing five and bringing vows of eternal vengeance from the bereaved. Indeed, vengeance was already on the way, personal vengeance for Quantrill, who organized a mass raid on Lawrence, Kansas, the town that had evicted him before the war. He promised his men and the other bushwhacker bands that joined him that they would get "more revenge and more money there than anywhere else."

At dawn on August 21 they struck quickly and brutally. The hellions raced up the streets firing wildly. First they killed virtually all of the two squads of Negro Federals, the only troops in town, and then the men separated and commenced looting the stores and killing any man met in the streets. "Kill! Kill! Lawrence must be thoroughly cleansed," yelled Quantrill, "and the only way to cleanse it is to kill! Kill!" When the guerrillas left at 9 A.M. upon word of approaching Yankee troops, some 150 men lay dead in the streets. He repeated his bloody work in October when he attacked a wagon train carrying General Blunt and his baggage, and killed all but eleven of the 100 soldiers. The dead were later found mangled and desecrated. Some of Quantrill's men began to display scalps on their bridles. He and they had tasted blood, and they liked it.

By this time, Kirby-Smith could point to no other "victories" except those of Quantrill and his kind. Despite his earlier declaration against guerrillas, he now began to defend Quantrill from attacks by other Confederate officers. General Henry McCulloch, brother of Ben, declared that the partisan was "but little, if at all removed from . . . the wildest savage." "I regard them as but one shade better than highwaymen." Yet Kirby-Smith tried to calm his subordinates, men outraged by the style of warfare waged by Quantrill, by asserting that the guerrillas were "bold, fearless men . . . composed, I understand, in a measure of the very best class of Missourians." If so, they spoke of a sorry state of affairs in Missouri manhood.[22]

Such, then, was the pitiful state of the Trans-Mississippi. Often forgotten, and sometimes scorned by Davis and Richmond, used as a graveyard for incompetents and a recruiting place for the Eastern armies, stripped of its produce, and now cut off from the Confederacy, the department and its semi-dictator could look only to murderers and cutthroats for its successes. There would be successes to be proud of in time, armies fighting honorably once more, but in 1863, as before, nearly one half of the Confederacy was left to fight a singular, solitary war, largely with its own devices. No wonder that in September, when Kirby-Smith appealed for help, the appeal went to Paris and not Richmond. No wonder that as 1864 dawned, Kirby-Smith felt in a mood to complain. "The Government must not send me any more cast-off material," he said. "I shall protest against the sending of any more supernumerary brigadier-generals to this department." He already had too many officers exiled here from the East, men without commands that stayed "shelved away somewhere in the interior of Texas, comfortably drawing their pay in retirement." Given his preference, he would hand them all muskets and put them in the ranks. "The means and resources of the Government will be centered with the Armies of Tennessee and Virginia," he would lament. "We here will be left to struggle against immense odds, as best we may, with the feeble resources at our command."

"The commander of this department," he sadly declared, "has no bed of roses."[23]

CHAPTER 14

"WE OUGHT NOT
TO DESTROY
THE SEED CORN"

In time General Kirby-Smith may well have wondered if there even was a Confederate Government somewhere there off to the east. Indeed there was. Makeshift, disorganized, repeatedly disrupted by enemy invasion and friendly incompetence, somehow the Confederate States of America managed to continue operating in fact as well as name, a genuine national government. It reflected by 1863 every attribute of a sovereign nation but one, independence. Yet by 1863 as well, and even before, the telling signs of wear and exhaustion appeared. The North possessed the manpower and resources to make war almost indefinitely if need be. The South did not. Already more and more boys who had not yet shaved their first stubble carried rifles as soldiers. One day President Jefferson Davis rode with his Postmaster General, John H. Reagan, to inspect some troops. They passed one small boy in a uniform, and the two stopped.

"My boy, are you a soldier?" asked the President.

"I am, sir."

"How old are you?"

"Fourteen."

Davis sent at once for the captain of the youth's company. "I think you should send that boy home," said the President. "We ought not to destroy the seed corn." But as 1863 passed on toward 1864, Davis and Reagan and the government would find increasingly that the "seed corn" was all they had left.[1]

In fact, during its first two years of life, the new nation seemed to enjoy an abundant harvest of good fortune, despite the odds against it. From its beginnings in February 1861 at Montgomery, Alabama, the Confederate Government had moved to Richmond to be near the seat of the war, and for a considerable period of time seemed to encounter nothing but success. Fort Sumter, First Bull Run, Wilson's Creek, the Seven Days battles, Second Bull Run, Cedar Mountain, Fredericksburg, Chancellorsville, the repulse of assaults on Charleston—there came one success after another in the field. If most of those triumphs came in the East, it only served to focus more of the government's attention in that theater. There were losses, and important ones, but they all seemed to fall west of the Appalachians, at Forts Henry and Donelson, Shiloh, Perryville, Pea Ridge, Stones River, and somehow, bad as they were, those defeats lay far enough removed from the center of Confederate civil power that the government seemed not to discover their true import. As for the Trans-Mississippi, of course, Kirby-Smith wondered if the rulers in Richmond even discovered its existence.

Thus, before the triple tragedies of Gettysburg, Vicksburg, and Port Hudson, the Confederacy rode high on a wave of military success that really only took blots from the troublesome Grant. It was well for Davis and his government that they enjoyed so many early victories, for the public enthusiasm they generated helped in large measure to compensate for the rapidly deteriorating civil condition of the nation. But once the defeats began, the unrest, discontent, and shortage in the South became the harder to bear, and the people and their leaders less inclined to patiently accept the burden. Rarely in history has so much of a nation's well-being on the home front reflected the varied fortunes of its armies.

Of course, it reflected as well the peculiar abilities and disabilities of the men and women running the infant nation. Davis had formed his government in an attempt to satisfy everyone, and naturally managed only to give offense to many. His cabinet appointments went not to the most talented in every case, but frequently to a faction that needed to be rewarded for its support of secession, or to a state that did not yet have a cabinet member. The old radical Southern nationalists, the "fire-eaters" who more than any others fomented the secession crisis, found themselves almost forgotten in the first appointments. From the very first, Davis like Lincoln began displaying the tendency to seek the middle. Doctrinaire ideologists could make rebellion, but they could not administer it. They held too rigidly to abstract ideas, unable to make the compromises necessary to turn intellectual revolution into practical rebellion. Only

William Lowndes Yancey received a prominent appointment, and, unbelievably, Davis made the intemperate and uncompromising Alabamian a diplomat!

Still, with good men and bad, Davis built a government as 1861 moved on from victory to victory, and none of his ministers proved more successful than the Texan John H. Reagan. He simply stole his Post Office Department from the United States! He had his agents purloin Yankee forms and manuals of operation, and then sent a form letter of invitation to join the Confederacy to the several bureau heads in the department at Washington. Several accepted, and when they came South they brought with them postal route maps, record books for the new department, even some stamps that were used and honored for a time until Washington outlawed passage of mail from the South into the North. Reagan, in fact, achieved more in less time and with fewer resources than any other cabinet official on either side of the Potomac. And in the ensuing months, by carefully watching his mail routes, eliminating those that did not pay for themselves, and rerouting others, he actually managed to achieve the only profitable postal operation in the history of the continent. He even managed to make—or attempted to make—his operations enhance public morale and patriotism. The department designed its own postage stamps, importing perforating machines, presses, and even printed stamps themselves at first. The postage stamps carried portraits of Confederate—and Union—heroes like Washington and Jackson, and images of distinctly Southern patriots, John Caldwell Calhoun for instance. But they carried the visage of Jefferson Davis more than anyone else, the only living American President to appear on stamps in his lifetime. There were suggestions for other likenesses of Confederate heroes, most notably Stonewall Jackson. Licking a small stamp now and then was a small matter, to be sure, but undeniably the stern visage of Jefferson Davis on the other side provided in some measure a reinforcement of feeling for the cause.[2]

It was feeling for the cause that the Confederate Government found hard to sustain as 1863 progressed. "After the battle of Gettysburg and the fall of Vicksburg," said Postmaster Reagan, "there was more or less despondency among public men. And as other misfortunes occurred this increased." When 1863 dawned, Davis had actually declared to the Congress that "we have every reason to expect that this will be the closing year of the War." Defeats in the field changed all that, and accelerated a gradual but insidious deterioration within the Confederacy that began almost as it uttered its first cries of infancy.[3]

There are certain experiences common almost to every revolutionary state in its early days, and the new Southern nation fell heir to most of them. One of the first, as always, was plain old politics. Such movements begin in a high state of unanimity. The South must secede, it must be—and had a right to be—an independent nation. The next step, unfortunately, comes after the separation is made and then the onetime unanimous patriots fall to fighting among themselves. Now that they had their nation, who was to decide what sort of country it should be? A revolution always springs from a single party or coalition of interested groups. Once in motion, however, revolutions also almost always split into factions. With the traditional American system of political parties, the naturally disputative nature of Southern statesmen, and the wide range of interests in the South, the rise of parties in the Confederacy was as inevitable as it was unfortunate.

Indeed, Davis and his cabinet addressed the subject in one of their very first sessions. "What consideration," they asked, "should be given the partisan political divisions which had existed in the South?" Like all revolutionary leaders, Davis and his ministers believed that the war now entered involved the rights and benefit of all people of all parties, and that therefore "the former partisan lines should not be recognized." Appointments to office should go only on merit, a system which in itself virtually guaranteed the rise of party. Davis decided that the test of a public official should be "Is the person true to the Confederate cause?" It was a goodenough policy. The trouble was that Davis would interpret loyalty to the cause as loyalty to himself, and those whom he offended—and they were many—would band together out of mutual necessity. Thus political parties formed in the Confederacy, not along lines of Democrat or Whig, but as pro-Davis and anti-Davis.[4]

The dissent began almost from the first days, and high within the President's own government. He and his Vice-President, Alexander H. Stephens of Georgia, became estranged quickly after Davis showed less and less inclination to consult with the Georgian. Yet Stephens entertained serious fears for Confederate survival, even in the days of May 1861 when all looked bright. Increasingly he came to oppose Davis' measures as they grasped more and more power to the Richmond government. A champion of states' rights, he like so many of the other original secessionists saw their cause being lost to an increasingly nationalistic President. By 1862 Davis and Stephens hardly spoke, and the Vice-President found himself a supernumerary in the capital. Stephens finally returned to Georgia, where he stayed for most of the rest of the war. There he made common cause with Governor Joseph Emerson Brown and several other governors who sought to stem the usurpation of their prerogatives by Richmond. When Davis suspended the writ of habeas corpus and when Confederate commanders in the field declared martial law, he lashed out at them in the press. Soon his adherents, largely men who had been disappointed by Davis, seconded his sentiments. Robert Augustus Toombs, who wanted to be President but lost out, declared to Stephens that "Davis and his Janissaries . . . conspire for the destruction of all who will not bend to them, and avail themselves of the public danger to aid them in their selfish and infamous schemes." Indeed, Toombs would soon become as outspoken as Stephens. "Real control of our affairs is narrowing down constantly into the hands of Davis," he complained. This Georgia group, headed by Stephens and Toombs and Brown, would be the most powerful and influential single center of opposition to Davis in the Confederacy, and those in other states came largely to be satellites of the disaffected Georgia group. North Carolina, too, would give him trouble in time, a trouble he could ill afford, for Tarheels came to the army in greater numbers than men of any other state.[5]

The opposition did not develop just in the several states. Before 1861 was done, the beginnings of an anti-Davis faction appeared in the Congress in Richmond as well, and Davis simply could never tolerate criticism or opposition. Perhaps it came in part from the general unanimity within his cabinet. "The Cabinet of Mr. Davis was so much of one view as to the necessities of our situation," said Reagan, "that, while there were occasional differences of opinion among them, as was to be expected of thinking men, there was no passion nor strife." Indeed, when Reagan himself realized that he was more consistently disagreeing with the President than any of the other ministers, he offered to resign, but Davis, so he said, urged him to remain, saying that "the free interchange of opinions was the way of arriving at correct conclusions." Davis might have said it, but how much he meant it is moot, for when people disagreed with him, he showed an increasing tendency to omit them from his consultations. Indeed, when his second Secretary of War, George Wythe Randolph, proved too independent, Davis sternly rebuked him and Randolph resigned. Davis then consulted with his cabinet and expressed his preference for James A. Seddon of Virginia, Joseph E. Johnston, and Gustavus W. Smith, in that order, as possible replacements. Even there Davis played coy, for he despised Johnston, and Smith had crumbled under the pressure of his brief command of the Army of Northern Virginia. Though he raised the names for discussion, the President had already decreed that it would be Seddon. Then Davis offered the post to him, but the next evening when he conferred with Senator Louis T. Wigfall of Texas, and the senator spent some time advising the President about who ought to replace Randolph, Davis never told him that he had already filled the position. When Wigfall learned of Davis' duplicity, he bitterly denounced him in the Senate, and from that time turned from an ardent supporter into an equally vitriolic opponent. In time, besides questioning every military and domestic move of the President's, Wigfall would even doubt his sanity.[6]

This is often the way it went with other opponents of Davis, explaining as well why the considerable anti-Davis forces never really united into a homogeneous opposition party. Their motives were too personal. Many like Wigfall resented personal slights, others like Brown disliked interference in state matters, and yet others objected to some—but not all—of the administration measures. Almost everyone changed his attitude when-

41. *Lieutenant General Leonidas Polk, onetime bishop, failed Bragg repeatedly at Chickamauga, and then tried to shift blame to others, finally becoming himself embroiled in Bragg's war on his generals.* (The Kean Archives, Philadelphia)

42. *As bad as Rosecrans behaved, just as good did Major General George Henry Thomas perform at Chickamauga. They will call him the "Rock" in days to come, and at Missionary Ridge his command will put Bragg completely to rout.* (Library of Congress)

43. *Chattanooga, Tennessee, and, looming over it, Lookout Mountain. Here Bragg's field career ended, along with the Confederate hold in east Tennessee and north Georgia.* (National Archives)

44. As Lincoln's generals captured more Confederate soil, men like Major General Benjamin Franklin Butler were charged with bringing "reconstructed" Southern governments back into being. Butler tried in Louisiana and, when he failed, was replaced by... (National Archives)

45. Another politician turned general, Nathaniel Prentiss Banks, victor at Port Hudson, Louisiana. (National Archives)

46. *In the months after Gettysburg, George Gordon Meade, seated at left center, tried twice to meet and defeat Lee. Both times Major General William Henry French, standing at left, failed him. Gouverneur Kemble Warren, seated left, and Major General John Sedgwick, seated far right, proved to be Meade's most reliable commanders. The other generals are Henry Jackson Hunt (standing) and Andrew Atkinson Humphreys.* (Library of Congress)

47. *Poor Lieutenant General James "Old Pete" Longstreet, one of Lee's most dependable commanders, feuded with Bragg and then failed in his great opportunity to take Knoxville, Tennessee, from Burnside.* (National Archives)

48. Longstreet's attack here at Fort Sanders, Knoxville, Tennessee, proved absolutely pointless, and days too late. It ended his campaign and his dream of independent command. (U.S. Army Military History Institute)

49. *As 1863 ends and the spring of 1864 is on the way, it is a time for change. The Army of Tennessee, resolute despite its year and more under Bragg, can rise with enthusiasm as General Joseph Eggleston Johnston takes command.* (Library of Congress)

50. *And in the Union, wearing the three stars of the newly revived rank of lieutenant general, Ulysses S. Grant gives great promise of the final victory for which Lincoln and the North have waited so long.* (Library of Congress)

ever advancing Federal forces threatened his home region. It was an opposition born of myriad personal and local interests, an opposition that never had any cohesive policy to offer as an alternative. They united only in loathing of Jefferson Davis.

Even before First Bull Run, talk passed in Richmond that there was disunity in the government. Soon after the battle members of the cabinet began detecting a growing opposition in the Congress. And when the reverses of the spring of 1862 in Tennessee fell upon the ears of Richmond, the opponents really became vocal. To envy and ambition they could now add demonstrated failure in the field, and the combination of all gave impetus to the anti-Davis forces. It did not help that the President maintained a considerable distance from Congress, largely because he distrusted the motives of many of its members. They came to feel that he expected the body simply to blindly approve his acts, and in a measure he did. Thus Thomas R. R. Cobb declared that he would fight mightily to override one of the President's vetoes solely because "it will do my very soul good to *rebuke* him." Davis' aloof and formal manner did not help him either, even with friends. He could not be comfortable, cajoling. Often troubled with physical discomfort, he could not make others comfortable. Richmond editor Edward A. Pollard declared that Davis granted interviews to Congressional delegations "with such a well-bred grace, with a politeness so studied as to be almost sarcastic, with a manner that so plainly gave the idea that his company talked to a post."[7]

For the first eighteen months of the war, in fact, it was Davis himself who provided the chief point of opposition, for his legislative program excited but little controversy. Thus in November 1861, when it was time for regular elections to replace the Provisional Government formed at Montgomery with a permanent body, Davis and Stephens and the Provisional Congress won reelection handily, with no real sign of an organized opposition to the President's continuing in office. But then the shortages of men and materials began. What had come voluntarily and easily before, now had to be raised by conscription, impressment, taxation, and the hated habeas corpus suspension and martial law. Worse, as enemy invasions gradually reduced the territory of the Confederacy, so did the base for taxation and supply constrict. That meant that those remaining unmolested in the Confederacy had to pay and provide more to make up for what was lost. The defeats in the field further took the willingness to compromise out of men in Congress, and by 1863's elections, hostility to Davis, as the presumed author of all the nation's ills, resulted in a marked change in the complexion of the legislature. Out of 106 members who took seats in the Second Congress that year, forty-one could be counted among his opposition. Worse, the reverses in the field now afforded Davis' personal enemies a wonderful opportunity. When the South had been successful in 1861 and 1862, it was hardly politic to attack Davis personally, and his war measures, apparently successful, could hardly be challenged. But now, with the war going badly, his foes could stand behind the shield of fighting his war legislation while really attacking the President. They still failed to form a unified opposition party, but they brought Davis and the country to grief. Indeed, if some utterances be believed, they even thought of bringing the Confederacy to revolution.[8]

Wigfall, as always, would be one of the leaders, and, typical of them in many ways, his hatred of Davis stemmed purely from personal resentments and disappointed ambitions. "Wigfall is strong as you know," wrote an observer, "but erratic." When once he got an idea in his head "he pursues that alone, to the neglect of everything else, no matter how important." All seemed to agree that he completely lacked self-control. In his opposition to Davis, he displayed more than anywhere else his bulldog single-mindedness, and his ungoverned temper. Davis, meanwhile, lost all confidence in the Texan, thanks to his frequent drunkenness. The gulf that opened between them over the Seddon appointment widened rapidly, and irreparably. For the rest of the war Wigfall tried to interfere in army matters, and chiefly by repeatedly championing the cause of Joseph E. Johnston for high command. Indeed, Wigfall felt little confidence in Lee and actually wanted Johnston placed in command of all Confederate armies. By linking himself so closely with Davis' bitterest enemy among the generals, Wigfall firmly and publicly declared his hostility to the President.[9]

Much of the press in the South took up the cries against the President that were first voiced in Congress, and they soon became even more vehement. Once again, the editorial opinions often traced their true lineage back to old personal grudges against Davis, or to ambitions unfulfilled. Robert Barnwell Rhett, one of the fathers of secession, found himself virtually left out of the government when it was formed. As a result, he took the lead of the anti-administration journals early in 1862, and those who worked and wrote for him had to do the same. "Cold, haughty, peevish, narrow-minded, pig-headed, *malignant,*" wrote a Rhett correspondent of Davis. "While he lives, there is no hope for us. God alone can save us."[10]

Indeed, almost from the first, a small but vocal element in Congress and the state governments wished to bring about Davis' removal from office, by constitutional means if possible, by force if necessary. As early as March 1862, James Hammond of South Carolina advised Congressman W. W. Boyce to "Impeach Jeff Davis for incompetency & call a convention of the States. Ad interim make Floyd or Price or Toombs Dictator. West Point is death to us & sick Presidents & Generals are equally fatal." From the first, President Davis showed a preference for appointing and promoting West Point–trained officers to important commands. Whereas Lincoln placed a score and more of politicians in generals' stars, and several like Sigel, Butler, Banks, and McClernand, rose to important commands, Davis had been very sparing in such appointments, and wisely so.

A few like Toombs and Wigfall became generals, but they never achieved important positions. Only two politicians became major generals, and only one, Breckinridge, actually rose to high command, and that thanks to ability. The disappointed hopes of the others, and the reverses suffered by Bragg and Albert S. Johnston, and even Lee, helped to breed a considerable hostility toward professional "Old Army" soldiers and Davis' fondness for them. Nothing else could entirely account for a suggestion that a man like Toombs would be a better general than Lee, or a better "dictator" than the President.[11]

Congress did try to restrain Davis' ability to appoint West Pointers. Early in 1862 it passed a bill creating the position of general commanding all Confederate armies everywhere, an obvious blow aimed at himself as Commander-in-Chief. He vetoed it. Thomas R. R. Cobb of Georgia complained that Davis *would be deposed* if the Congress had any more confidence in Stephens than in him." Davis himself began to believe that there was a conspiracy, a "cabal" that plotted against him. To his turn of mind, that only called for more secrecy and less cooperation with Congress, and thus he only exaggerated the situation. Still, much as they despised him, most of the President's opponents stopped short of the notion of removing him from office. Yancey believed him to be a "conceited, wrong-headed, wranglesome, obstinate" man, perhaps even a traitor to states' rights. But, he said, "a crew might not like their captain, but if they were mad enough to mutiny while a storm was raging, all hands were 'bound to go to the bottom." Yet there were those willing to risk the plunge.[12]

One who at first led the pack was Henry S. Foote of Tennessee, a genuinely remarkable man. Born in Virginia, he practiced law in Alabama, edited a newspaper in Mississippi, defeated Davis for the governorship in 1851, moved to California, then came to Tennessee in 1859 an ardent opponent of secession. As intemperate as Wigfall in his speech and manner, he repeatedly got involved in duels and fistfights, even on the floor of the Confederate House. When he called Edmund Dargan of Alabama a "damned rascal" on the floor, Dargan attacked him with a bowie knife. As other members disarmed Dargan, Foote postured for the galleries, declaring, "I defy the steel of the assassin!" He had at least two other recorded battles, and those unknown may be innumerable. He also hated Davis. By the end of 1863 he declared that Davis was a usurper, adding that if the nation must be run by a dictator, then let it be Lee. It proved to be an idea that would revive from time to time through the rest of the war, and a rumor gained limited currency that Congressman William Cabell Rives of Virginia actually presented the subject to Lee, who refused. It is perhaps an apocryphal story, but displays still the degree of hatred growing toward the President.[13]

Some did not rumor. They attempted to act, and predictably the center lay in troublesome Georgia. At the head of the possible treason lay

Toombs, to be sure, and as well the Vice-President himself! Toward the end of the war Toombs would declare privately that "Nothing can save us but the overthrow of Davis & that must come quickly to be of any service." Early in 1864 he spoke publicly in vicious attack of Davis and his policies, hinting openly that the liberty of Confederate citizens depended upon open resistance. His motto in the months that followed became "begone Davis."[14]

Less blustering and more insidious was Alexander H. Stephens. What incensed Stephens most of all of Davis' presumed usurpations of civil liberties was his suspension of the habeas corpus in cases of suspected treason or conspiracy. It was aimed at those pro-Union civilians who gave aid or comfort to the enemy, but to the governors it smacked of despotism. Governor Zebulon Baird Vance of North Carolina, a state full of disloyal people, said the suspension shocked "all worshippers of the common law . . . by hurling freemen into sheriffless dungeons for opinion's sake." Stephens reacted even more strongly, and immediately planned to oust Davis from office when the winter of 1863–64 saw yet another more stringent suspension announced.[15]

It was a true conspiracy, involving Stephens, his brother Linton, Toombs, Governor Joseph Brown, and others. They met together repeatedly in the early months of 1864, when the new habeas corpus law seemed imminent, to "compare notes on the subject." At the same time they all collaborated on the annual message that Brown would deliver in the Georgia legislature in March. "I confess I contemplate with horror the suspension of the habeas corpus," said Brown. "Every state in the Confederacy should denounce and condemn the wicked act." When finally Brown made his address, most insightful listeners quickly recognized that it was the handiwork of the Vice-President himself, and Stephens confessed that he had "advised it from stem to stern." Brown's speech fumed with venomous condemnation of the administration and the President, and particularly of the writ suspension, yet this was not the only route of attack by the constitutional conspirators. Stephens' brother Linton, with the Vice-President's "consultation," authored a set of resolutions condemning the suspension and actually advocating a negotiated peace with the North. Brown's address had been on March 10. Linton Stephens' resolutions came just a few days later, and on March 16 Stephens himself addressed the legislature in what was a well-timed follow-up to the two previous acts. Though he did not question the power of Congress to withdraw the habeas corpus in emergency, he did protest this latest act on the grounds that it made the President himself arbiter of guilt, giving him virtually dictatorial powers of "illegal and unconstitutional arrests." Under Davis' suspension, suspected persons might be held in confinement indefinitely. In tandem, Stephens condemned as well the latest conscription law, calling all men between seventeen and fifty. This put virtually the entire able-bodied male population of the South under his control. "Could the whole country be more completely under the power and control of one man?" he asked. "Could dictatorial power be more complete?" Stephens reminded his listeners of some of the recent appeals by the leading press in favor of a dictator. "Coming events often cast their shadows before. Could art or ingenuity have devised a shorter or surer cut to that end than the whole policy adopted by the last Congress?"[16]

Stephens and his friends spoke for more than just a Georgia audience. They hoped and expected that their efforts would be broadcast over the Confederacy. "I had but little hope, when this measure first passed," wrote Stephens of the suspension, "that we should ever again have constitutional liberty upon this continent." That he really expected his efforts now to produce a reversal would have been foolishly optimistic, yet he achieved a high measure of success just the same. Governor Brown sent copies of the resolutions and of his message to every company of Georgia troops in the army, and copies as well to every county courthouse in the Confederacy. At his own expense, Brown printed and distributed thousands of copies of Stephens' speech to all Georgia units, and to the county clerks as well, directing them to different persons that received the other materials so that, should one fall into hands unsympathetic to their cause, then probably the other would still be read before the troops and assorted state legislators and politicians. It proved to be, in fact, the only nationwide propaganda effort ever made by any of the several factions forming the "loyal opposition."[17]

Its effectiveness proved surprising. Governors of the states east of the Mississippi met later in the year and formally condemned the suspension, and in Georgia itself a Richmond agent reported that the opposition of Stephens, Brown, and others made enforcement of the suspension impossible. When the February 1864 law expired in August, the Congress reacted to the widespread discontent organized by Stephens and others and refused to authorize another suspension. Stephens and his friends did not engineer the removal of Davis himself, though Toombs would continue to bluster, "Begone, Davis," for the rest of the war, but in this habeas corpus fight, a portion at least of the widespread anti-Davis faction achieved a significant victory over the President. In so doing, though they did not see it, they achieved something of a victory over themselves, for in beating Davis they helped to hinder the Confederacy.[18]

The opposition to the Davis government did not abide solely in Congress and the state houses. Indeed, the hated suspension laws, and particularly the February 1864 measure that set Stephens and his cabal in motion, reflected Davis' efforts to control the much more widespread disaffection in his beleaguered nation. For if legislators and governors devoted much of their time to denouncing the President and his policy, thousands of citizens spent their free hours in the more demonstrative pursuits of conspiracy, sabotage, and outright treason. The Confederacy seethed with disloyalty, and it threatened to break down the system of law and order and thoroughly disrupt the military. It even sought in places to foment secession from secession.

Of course, thousands of Southerners opposed secession from the first. Union sentiment ran strong in the mountain regions. Virtually all of western Virginia, the region that in 1863 withdrew from the Confederacy to become West Virginia, stood by the Union. So, too, did the southwestern spur of the state. Joining it geographically and politically were western North Carolina and east Tennessee, hotbeds of Unionism, along with northern Alabama and Georgia. The Stars and Stripes continued to fly over some courthouses for weeks after secession in defiance of the new Confederates. Even in faraway Texas and other sections of the Trans-Mississippi, Union sentiments drove significant groups to oppose Davis. Many malcontents came from recent immigrant groups, particularly Germans in Texas, and Irish in Arkansas. What most everywhere had in common was little or no involvement with slavery or with the cotton economy, and a shared antipathy for the planter aristocrat class that predated the war by a generation or more.

And there was a genuine sympathy for the old Union, for the days of Jackson when a poor man could be—or thought he could be—the equal of the rich. All this inherent opposition to the new Confederacy only increased as the war measures necessary to sustain the new nation came increasingly to burden the common folk. Conscription angered them more than anything else, for it struck the poor disproportionately. Indeed, it was in Unionist north Alabama that the cry of a "rich man's war and a poor man's fight" first became audible. Brown and others, of course, opposed conscription officially, hampering enlistments and interfering with the movement of their state's troops when possible, but in time the common men found other, more overt ways of opposition. Impressment of their farm and livestock produce only aggravated the situation. As Confederate government notes inflated astronomically, growers became increasingly reluctant to sell to the authorities, and when the military forced them to sell and paid them with worthless scrip, the outcry rose ever greater. The tax-in-kind measures that took the tenth portion of a farmer's produce made matters worse, and the habeas corpus suspension finished the case. Ironically, men who had been the bitterest of enemies in 1860—the most rabid states' rights secessionists and the ardent Unionists—now found themselves informal allies of a sort. All stood bound by the common cause of animosity and opposition to Davis, his government, his armies, and even in places his new nation. Soon in isolated places in the South came the rallying call, "The Constitution as it is and the Union as it was." As deprivation increased for the many while profiteering continued for the few, as the advancing Federal armies brought the promise of relief ever nearer, and as the Confederate authorities resorted to increasingly harsh measures to maintain itself, that early cry spread throughout much of the country. By 1863 there was not a state without a significant disloyal organization, and in some portions of the Confederacy they formed enclaves that even the Confederate authorities could not penetrate or discipline.[19]

The opposition took several forms, but largely the so-called "peace societies" scattered through rural sections of the South. In Arkansas the Peace and Constitutional Society was organized in late 1861. It did not last long, many of its members being arrested in October and November. The society's aims were simply to encourage desertion from the Confederate forces and to be ready to aid the Federals whenever they advanced into the state. East of the Mississippi there flourished a far more organized and successful group, the Peace Society. It spread its tentacles into Alabama, east Tennessee, Georgia, Mississippi, and probably Florida, and so successfully did it maintain its secrecy that little was known of its activities until 1863. It, too, encouraged desertions, as well as promoting within its membership enlistment in Federal regiments being raised in the occupied South. The members communicated with each other by an intricate system of hand signs and code words which, put into practice, resembled nothing so much as a bizarre native dance, or perhaps an infestation of fleas. Upon meeting, one member jerked his right thumb over his right shoulder, to which the other, as a sign of recognition, grabbed his right hand with his left in a prescribed fashion. Both then stared into each other's eyes while they tapped their right feet three times with sticks. Then they broke the sticks and tossed the pieces over their left shoulders. If the Peace Society members did not recognize each other after all this, it is probable that the Confederate authorities did.

The real center of the Peace Society resided in Georgia and Alabama, and in those regions did considerable damage to the Confederate cause. Farther to the east, in southwestern Virginia and North Carolina and east Tennessee, there flourished the Order of the Heroes of America, probably the most ambitious of the three main peace societies, and also the most difficult for Confederate agents to penetrate. It had appeared in one form or another from the beginning of the war until 1864, when it was finally discovered. Indeed, more than the other groups, the Heroes of America operated with active Yankee encouragement. As a premium for joining the society, the Federals promised members that they would not be drafted when the Union took control of the area, that their persons and property would be free from molestation by Union armies, and that they would share in the division of property confiscated from Confederates after the war. It was reputed that even Lincoln and Grant were members of the organization. The Heroes had their own hand grips, code words, signs, and oaths. It was an era when such things fascinated all Americans, a holdover from the 1850s when the Know-Nothings, a rabidly anti-Catholic and anti-immigrant political movement, flourished among the poor whites with its own set of secret signs and sayings. Fittingly, one of the Heroes' passwords was the aptly descriptive declaration "These are gloomy times."[20]

As always, the problems that beset the East seemed worse in the West. Kirby-Smith, commanding the Trans-Mississippi, soon found the disloyal element so potent that "the question is whether they or we shall control." Indeed, in some quarters the only military power lay with the deserters and adherents of the peace groups. Conscription proved a failure in the region, particularly among the immigrant Germans and Irish, and when the Federal armies marched into Arkansas, the disloyal came into Yankee lines in great numbers. Soon the 1st Arkansas Cavalry was formed of these Unionists, and even the governor, Henry Massey Rector, unintentionally encouraged the disaffected when he complained publicly that the Confederacy had abandoned Arkansas. In this atmosphere, the Peace and Constitutional Society grew substantially, but even more healthy were the numerous formal and informal resistance groups. In Texas the Germans stood out boldly and publicly in their opposition. They refused to enlist or be conscripted, openly opposing the Confederacy. Worse, they comprised a majority of the male population in some of the central state counties, and in June 1861 their representatives formed the Union Loyal League. Confederate authorities found them so formidable that General Paul Octave Hébert sent troops to the region and declared the state under martial law in May 1862. That only enraged the Germans, and soon 500 or more of them banded into three companies. Yet they soon dispersed, except for about sixty-five men who determined to leave the state and join the Federals. Confederates followed the Germans until August 10, 1862, when they attacked them as they were camped. The foreigners were defeated soon enough and forced to disperse. Nineteen lay dead, and the nine prisoners and wounded who were captured were murdered a few hours later, each one shot in the back of the head. Only three years to the day later were they buried. Of those who escaped, seventeen were hunted out and killed, and only about eleven of the original band finally were able to join the Federal 1st Texas Cavalry. In all, during the war, as many as 150 of the Germans may have been lynched or murdered in retribution for their "treason."[21]

Despite the attempts at suppression of civilian opposition to the Confederacy and Jefferson Davis, by 1863 it stood forth with impunity in several places. When one regiment was ordered to go to Galveston, so many of its soldiers rebelled that there were not enough left to arrest the mutineers. Near Bonham, Texas, several hundred deserters virtually controlled access to the region, and on the upper reaches of the Red River as many as 2,000 fugitives from the army defied the authorities for nearly a year.[22]

As open as the opposition to the Confederacy was west of the great river, it took even more strident forms on the other side, and presented yet a greater challenge to the reigning powers. All of these states sooner or later enlisted enough men in the Federal service to be represented in the Union army. Alabama raised five regiments of black troops and the 1st Alabama Cavalry, which would see active service throughout the South. Georgia would raise a battalion of white volunteers later in 1864, and Florida would field two regiments of Union cavalry. Louisiana proved far more ambitious, with twelve regiments of black infantry and four white, two white cavalry regiments, and four black artillery units, many of whom fought with Banks in the investment of Port Hudson. Mississippi gave nine colored units and one white regiment of cavalry. Tennessee proved to be the most disloyal of all to the Confederacy, with fourteen regiments of cavalry and several assorted battalions, nine infantry regiments and eight regiments of mounted infantry, and a few artillery units. Whereas most of the Confederate states raised more Negro troops than white for the Union, Tennessee counted just two infantry regiments and three batteries of sable volunteers. Clearly, in the Volunteer State disloyalty to the Confederacy was a white man's affair. Only South Carolina failed to enlist any white troops for Lincoln's army, yet still she manned four black regiments of infantry. North Carolina raised four units each of black and white soldiers, and the Old Dominion Virginia put one battalion of rangers into the Union blue. Such an outpouring of enlistments among the Negro population of the South was only natural. It was their chance to fight for their own freedom, to get back perhaps at those who kept them in bonds for so long. In all, almost 100,000 Confederate blacks took arms in the Yankee service. What is surprising is the number of white Southerners who took the field in defense of the Union, even at the expense of fighting against their own townsmen. Over 54,000 of them took Mr. Lincoln's oath, virtually a small army by Confederate standards, and 12,600 of them died for a Union that they would not live to see restored. In fact, they died in a percentage greater by half than the deaths of troops from the Northern states. If this number of men had been with Pemberton or Lee, Vicksburg and Gettysburg might not have been lost. Such Yankee service by Confederate citizens did not materially aid the North in gaining the upper hand in the war, but it certainly made an already improbable task for the Confederacy that much closer to impossible.[23]

What hurt the Southern cause more than the men who wore the Union blue were those who stayed at home and fought the Confederacy from within. Every time a Yankee army came near, the depredations performed on Rebel communications, telegraph lines cut, bridges burned, increased in tempo. Fugitive Yankee soldiers found succor in disloyal homes. Information on the strength and movements of Southern forces sifted constantly through the lines to the enemy. When Colonel Abel D. Streight led a Federal raid deep into northern Alabama in April 1863, he encountered two organized companies of Unionists who guided his raiders through the countryside. In Alabama the Peace Society even managed to field political candidates for the legislature and the Richmond Congress. Jabez Lamar Monroe Curry, an influential friend of Davis' and of the war, found his Congressional seat taken from him by a peace candidate, and William L. Yancey, one of the fathers of secession, lost his Senate position to an avowed supporter of conciliation. In all, some seven men won election to Richmond as a result of their anti-secessionist views, and in open elections. Military officials in Alabama feared that the elections had been tampered with by men of "a secret sworn organization known to exist," its purposes being "the encouragement of desertion, the protection of deserters from arrest, resistance to conscription, and perhaps other designs of a still more dangerous character." By the dawn of 1863, the generals in the field discovered that the disloyal sentiments from home had reached the army. The Army of Tennessee, in particular, had hundreds of men who had sworn membership in the Peace Society and other disloyal groups and were waiting for the opportunity to desert.[24]

By 1864 as many as 6,000 deserters and Unionists almost ruled northern Alabama, becoming so bold as to burn the Coffee County courthouse and ambush prominent local Confederates. In some counties they prevented the local courts from convening for over two years. The story proved much the same all across the Deep South. In Jasper, Georgia, a Union flag flew despite common knowledge by the authorities of its presence. Governor Brown refused to cut it down, not because he favored the Union, but because he realized that any such act would only further encourage the disloyal. "Let it float," he said. "It floated over our fathers, and we all love the flag now. We have only been compelled to lay it aside by the injustice that has been practiced under its folds." By early 1864 men from the Confederate army stationed in Georgia told their Federal friends that enlistments were dwindling and that men already in service reenlisted solely to get a furlough, and then deserted. The homes of disloyal men were often plundered or burned by Confederate authorities, but the acts of retaliation only made their opponents the more determined. One Unionist leading a band of his kind in Florida, wrote to the Confederate commander in the area that "I cannot control my men since they saw you fire our house." "I ain't accountable for what they do now."[25]

In a few places the disaffected even tried to establish their own local self-government. For years, during the war and after, the story gained currency that Jones County, Mississippi, seceded from the state to form its own government, the "Jones County Confederacy." In fact it did not, but the band of pro-Union men and Confederate deserters there eventually numbered 150 or more, and made repeated raids on Confederate sympathizers in the region, even attacking and capturing a military wagon train. They did not control the county government, but Jones County did become no-man's-land for Mississippi Confederates, the Rebel authorities doing little to attempt its subjugation.[26]

But if Jones and a few other counties in the South did not actually withdraw from the Confederacy, still a few areas became virtual nations unto themselves, their only government that of the opponents of Davis and his war policies. Nowhere was this more apparent than in southwest Virginia, where the real rulers were the Order of the Heroes of America. This group enjoyed considerable numbers and popularity in east Tennessee and North Carolina. In the latter state they even attacked and looted a courthouse, and actively encouraged desertions among the Tarheel regiments with Lee. Retaliation became swift and brutal when men of the Heroes and other disloyal bands were captured, yet in some counties the Unionists were so plentiful that the local militia groups did not dare challenge them. Lee himself began to feel the influence of the Heroes' efforts as the desertions from his North Carolina regiments mounted during the summer of 1863. Many of the soldiers read copies of the Raleigh *Standard* in which editor W. W. Holden advised the people to "cast about and see if negotiations could not be set on foot for an honorable peace." Holden's editorials became so potent that President Davis himself took a hand in trying to suppress the journal. As the peace meetings began, wives and friends at home sent the soldiers in the field letters begging them to return. "The people is all turning to Union here since the Yankees has got Vicksburg," wrote one woman. "I want you to come home as soon as you can after you git this letter." Others declared to the soldiers that "I am never going in the service any more, for I am for the Union for ever and ever, amen." By late 1863, with this sort of sentiment running higher than ever in North Carolina, Governor Zebulon B. Vance felt forced to tell the President that only a hearty attempt at peace negotiations with the North would combat the unrest.[27]

But in southwest Virginia nothing could combat it. Here all of the same influences that brought about the peace societies elsewhere operated. Here, too, all of the manifestations of Unionism were to be seen. But here a genuine disloyal government of sorts came into being, with its own officials and even its own shadow army. It was to be, they said, the "New State of Southwest Virginia." Secession sentiment in the region never ran high. Less than a fourth of its population stood forward for leaving the Union in 1861, and thereafter resistance to Richmond was constant. By the time of Davis' first conscription law in early 1862, some form of organization of Heroes was already working at feeding information to the Federals. Whole judicial districts in Wise County were said to be in the hands of Unionists, and in Russell County the disloyal men marched to aid Federal raiders. In Lee County they marched openly in the streets with their Federal flags. Men worked ardently against conscription, so much so that one commander in the region threatened to shoot as deserters all those who did not step forward. It did him no good.

By 1863 a number of elected and appointed officials in the several counties were, in fact, members of the Heroes of America, and they worked to elect others of their kind. After July 1863 and the reverses, many of those who had given the Confederacy lukewarm support became "completely demoralized," thus swelling the numbers of the disloyal. As 1864 came on, six of the southwestern counties lay securely in the hands of the Heroes with almost all the people therein members. Almost all the public officials knew and used the secret signs and passwords of the society. Justices of the peace in Pulaski County, a sheriff in Washington County, the sheriff and several policemen in Montgomery County, all were Heroes. Toward the end of the year the "New State" was organized out of two of the counties. The Heroes elected a governor and a lieutenant governor and reportedly organized an army of deserters under an appointed "general." They boasted of controlling a majority of the men in at least two Virginia regiments, and claimed that their adherents were spreading the word through Lee's army with great success. No Confederate commander would ever control southwest Virginia. The one who would come closest would be John C. Breckinridge, but that was in the future as the summer of 1863 wore on toward autumn. So desperate would the situation become that the Confederates in the area would ask President Davis to suspend the writ of habeas corpus that they might handle the disloyal summarily. Chiefly as a result of the work of the Heroes of America and other "tory" opposition to the Confederate Government, Davis would do just that in February 1864, and the act in turn put him squarely at odds with the even more potent opposition in his own Congress and legislatures.[28]

Thus, though from differing motivation, the ardently pro-Union and disaffected elements in the civilian population made unintentional common cause with the equally rabid states' rights and ultra-secessionist factions in their local and national governments. There was only one common enemy: Jefferson Davis, with his seemingly ravenous central authority. When a small army of citizens openly rejected the cause, and even took arms against it, when Confederate law and order could not be maintained in whole regions of the nation, and when legislators, governors, congressmen, and even the Vice-President, conspired against the President and his measures, the odds against Davis seemed insurmountable. Davis himself felt this, and at one point apparently spoke of resigning his office for the good of the country. Yet he could only do so, he said, if Stephens resigned as well. Otherwise he would be leaving the Confederacy in the hands of a man whom he firmly believed would give it to the Federals for the asking. Reluctantly, John H. Reagan agreed. "I always regarded him as an upright, honorable man," he wrote of the Vice-President. Indeed, most of the opposition were honorable men, though motivated by a heady portion of self-interest. Yet "I fear," said the Postmaster General, "he allowed his great name and influence to give too much encouragement to malcontents, who caused embarrassment to the Confederate Government, and who endeavored to cast unjust reflections on the policy, actions and services of President Davis." They would continue to cast those aspersions for the rest of the war, making life increasingly difficult, and government increasingly impossible, for the beleaguered man in Richmond who had taken office in 1861 to the words of his now-enemy Toombs, "The man and the hour have met." Davis was having his hour, but it seemed endless, and populated only with enemies and traitors. As he drew deeper and deeper within himself, he found fewer the number of friends to whom he could look. One of them, a man fighting his own long battle against disloyalty, would now offer the paradox of perhaps the worst general in the Confederate service winning the most complete victory ever achieved over the enemy. Braxton Bragg might never stop fighting his generals, but as the fall of 1863 approached, he finally turned his attention to the Yankees for a time.[29]

CHAPTER 15

"HOW CAME WE TO LOSE CHATTANOOGA?"

If there was one general, a political one at that, who stood with President Davis, it was Major General John C. Breckinridge. To be sure, he never believed from the start that the Confederacy could win its independence. As early as February 1862 he confided to a fellow Kentucky officer that "if the South did not fully arouse herself all hope of the Confederacy was gone." By 1863 the South was as fully aroused as it could be, and yet it had not been enough. As Breckinridge summered with his command in northern Mississippi, that truth was all too evident as Federal traffic now passed up and down the Mississippi without interruption. He and Johnston had been too late to save Vicksburg.[1]

He passed the time in resting and refitting his men, and in trying to get a brief leave that he might visit his wife Mary in Chattanooga. She wrote often, sending him rose petals in her envelopes so that "as you open it the perfume will rise like incense, emblematic of my love for you." On August 23 the general applied for twenty days' leave to visit her, but the army interfered instead, ironically ordering him to move toward her nevertheless. Bragg was on another campaign and, hate the Kentuckian though he did, he had to have him in the coming battle.[2]

That summer William S. Rosecrans, commanding the Federal Army of the Cumberland, moved in a well-executed maneuver to feint Bragg's army out of middle Tennessee and back to Chattanooga. That kept him safely out of the temptation to send strong support to Vicksburg. Then in July Rosecrans halted for several weeks. But on August 16 he started to move once again, and Bragg had to move to defend himself. Just why Rosecrans halted for over a month mystified his superiors, and it infuriated them as well. On August 4 he received an incontestable order to advance, and twelve days later he "hurried" to obey. Bragg had his army safely south of the Tennessee River, with Leonidas Polk's corps guarding and fortifying Chattanooga, Hardee's corps on Polk's right, and a new corps under Lieutenant General Simon B. Buckner some sixty miles up the river near Loudon and Knoxville. The Confederate cavalry led by Major General Joseph Wheeler fanned out to the south of Chattanooga watching the Tennessee crossings. When Bragg divined that the Federals were advancing against him, almost certainly intent upon severing his communications with Atlanta and taking Chattanooga, he called hurriedly for all the reinforcements he could get. From the east, Lee sent James Longstreet and his corps. "Old Pete" had been crying for an independent command, or one out from under Lee's thumb, and soon he would have it. Buckner started to move toward Chattanooga. And from Mississippi came Breckinridge with the pitiful 4,500 men left in his division.

It took the Kentuckian just eight days to move his command to Tyner's Station, near Chattanooga, and when he arrived he found some changes in the army. Hardee was gone for awhile, and Daniel Harvey Hill had come from the Virginia army to replace him. Hill it was who inadvertently lost or misplaced a copy of Lee's orders relative to the Antietam battle, orders that fell into Federal hands and almost spelled disaster for Lee. A contentious general, like so many who served out here, still Hill would prove to be the most cordial corps commander Breckinridge would serve. He also despised Braxton Bragg.[3]

By August 20, before Breckinridge arrived, Rosecrans began crossing his army over the Tennessee, at a spot unsuspected and unguarded by Bragg. Thanks to a skillful demonstration in front of Chattanooga, Rosecrans deceived Bragg as to his true crossing place for several days. By September 1, when Bragg finally discovered what was happening, Rosecrans had his entire army south of the Tennessee and threatening to cut off the Confederates from the Western & Atlantic Railroad, their supply line from Atlanta. Bragg had no option but to evacuate Chattanooga.

But then things began to move badly for Rosecrans, and he did not help himself. The terrain south of the Tennessee proved difficult. Instead of affording an easy route of march, the hills and mountainous ridges ran directly perpendicular to the Federal advance. Of good roads they found few, their maps uncertain, and for a change the loyal east Tennesseans were not there to help them, having been driven out or fled when the

Confederate army came. The enemy knew the ground, he did not. Then Rosecrans made a terrible mistake which, under the circumstances, he may have had no choice but to make. He must sever Bragg's communications. To do so he had to march his corps east, and only three roads led across those mountains and ridges. Leaving one of his corps, Gordon Granger's, back at the Tennessee to guard his rear, Rosecrans set his three remaining corps in motion, one to each of the roads. Thomas L. Crittenden, childhood playmate of Breckinridge and his fellow officer in Mexico, led his XXI Corps on the road to Chattanooga itself. In the center Major General George H. Thomas, victor at Mill Springs, Kentucky, back in January 1862, led his XIV Corps directly from its crossing place along the road to Resaca, the most direct route of all to the railroad. And on the Federal right the XX Corps faced the longest march of all as its commander Major General Alexander McDowell McCook marched it along a winding road that at times kept it separated from Thomas by as much as twenty miles. McCook was not an exceptional general, but he sprang of an exceptional family. His father Daniel died in the service this past July trying to capture Rebel raiders. His brother Robert, a brigadier general, had been killed and probably murdered by guerrillas in 1862. His brother Charles fell killed in action at First Bull Run. His brother Daniel commanded a brigade in this same XIV Corps, would become a brigadier in a few months, and would be killed in action nine months from now. Brother Edwin was a colonel in this same army, and would be a general one day. Brother George had declined a general's star, but raised troops back home in Ohio, and four other brothers served now in the Union army. Two cousins would become generals as well, and both of them with this army. The war, it seemed, had become a McCook family enterprise.

And it was Alexander McCook who now most worried Rosecrans. Far out on the right of the widely separated corps, McCook seemed vulnerable to enemy attack from the south, west, and east. To protect him as much as possible, "Old Rosey" assigned almost all of his cavalry as a screen for McCook. That left Thomas in the center with virtually no cavalry in his front to reconnoiter enemy movements. Unfortunately for the Federals, that particular front was just the point at which Braxton Bragg decided once more to test his army, and himself.

Reports of enemy movements came garbled and mixed to the Confederate commander in Chattanooga those first days of September. Bragg failed to keep enough of his own cavalry in his front to provide him with accurate intelligence, and it was September 2 before he knew for certain that Rosecrans was crossing his main army some miles south of Chattanooga instead of north of the city, as Bragg had expected. Yet still Bragg wavered. It took him three days to decide to order Wheeler and his cavalry to begin slowing the enemy advance. Meanwhile, he could not settle on a plan. All he could do was complain to his subordinates that "we must do something and that soon."[4]

In another three days Bragg finally realized the threat to him and began the evacuation of Chattanooga. He intended to fall back some forty-five miles south to Rome, Georgia, and there await Rosecrans' attack. But even as he retreated, Bragg began to receive small bits of information that gradually gave him a better picture of the position of the Yankee corps advancing against him. Now he learned that Thomas was barely more than five miles west of him, approaching McLemore's Cove, a valley between Missionary Ridge and Pigeon Mountain, on a road easily commanded by a gap in both eminences. Crittenden seemed to be moving very slowly from Chattanooga, and McCook was some distance to the south. Sensing perhaps some opportunity to halt the enemy advance long enough to ensure his safe withdrawal to Rome, Bragg ordered two of his divisions to entrap the Federals reported approaching McLemore's. One division belonged to Major General Patrick Ronayne Cleburne, an Irishman, called by some the "Stonewall of the West," and a fellow Arkansan with the other division commander accompanying him, Major General Thomas Hindman, late of the Trans-Mississippi.

The movement did not work well thanks to Hindman's timidity, the equally poor performance of D. H. Hill, and Bragg's own insufficiently explicit orders. Yet that evening Bragg ordered them to attack again the next day, more and more certain that he had a chance of defeating a significant portion of the Army of the Cumberland. If he did so, then he could turn on Crittenden, do the same, and gobble up McCook later. "Old Rosey" offered him an opportunity to destroy a Yankee army in pieces, and Bragg, despite his insufficiencies as a man, was more than general enough to see the possibilities in that.

But the planned attack of September 11 did not come either. Hindman dallied for thirteen hours, and only moved when the enemy in his front themselves retreated a little. Bragg failed to give a peremptory attack order, and that gave Hindman and Hill a perfect escape. They did not like the plan, they did not like the ground or the uncertainty of enemy strength, and they did not like Bragg. Why take the risk? Bragg, though furious, reacted by turning his attention to a new potential. Reports came to him now that Thomas and McCook were too close to each other to safely be attacked, but that Crittenden lay isolated north of him. As a result, he ordered two of his corps, Leonidas Polk and William Henry Talbot Walker with his Reserve Corps, to move north and attack. Once again Bragg failed to give good orders, and the confusion within his command system only made matters worse. No one moved, and those who did moved too slowly. Bragg demanded that Polk attack Crittenden on September 13, but that morning the bishop general complained again that he could not, despite the fact that the Confederates heavily outnumbered the single enemy corps. When Bragg himself came in person, only then did Polk begin a timid advance, only to discover that Crittenden had escaped. Bragg was furious. For the second time in just a few days he had missed a chance to catch isolated portions of Rosecrans' army and defeat them. Now Bragg himself allowed Crittenden to escape yet again, for the XXI Corps lay just five miles away. Instead of himself leading Polk and Walker in an attack, Bragg withdrew his army from the field and began a withdrawal toward Lafayette, fifteen miles south, and just below Pigeon Mountain on the road that Thomas was using. For the next three days he would wait there and do nothing. Bragg, like his generals it seemed, could not sustain his offensive mood. He wavered constantly, could not set his mind, made commitments and just as quickly withdrew them. This was the example he had set for his commanders, and because of it they felt no confidence in his orders, no surety that if they should obey and attack, Bragg would not soon pull them back out or abandon their efforts as wasted. Given the shambles of a command system within the Army of Tennessee, it is a miracle that it could move at all.[5]

Rosecrans, too, had been uncertain of his enemy's whereabouts. Information came to him on September 10 that Bragg might be marshaling his forces, that attack rather than retreat was in his mind, but "Old Rosey" refused to believe the rumor without further intelligence. The near-miss with Thomas at McLemore's Cove and the later close call with Crittenden finally convinced the Federal commander that Bragg intended a battle and was trying to catch his isolated corps. At once Rosecrans ordered McCook to move north to link with Thomas, and by September 17, while Bragg lay idle, the Union army closed up to within reasonable supporting distance between the corps.

The ground over which the armies would fight stretched for seven miles along the west side of Chickamauga Creek, from Glass's Mill on the south to Dyer's Ford on the north. As it happened, the creek—actually more of a river, though fordable at several spots—formed the hypotenuse of a triangle in which the battle would take place. From Lee and Gordon's Mills, just above Glass's, the fighting line would run due north along the road to Lafayette, terminating after about four miles on the rise of Snodgrass Hill. As the Federals approached the field, Crittenden took first position, his line extending north from Lee and Gordon's. There he faced Bragg across the Chickamauga on September 18, awaiting the reinforcements that hurried toward him. Thomas brought his corps up during the night and McCook was on the way in haste. Granger, too, was moving toward the field, though still several miles off. With the three corps immediately along the Chickamauga, or close to it, Rosecrans would have about 50,000 troops available for battle. Facing him across Chickamauga Creek stood or would stand 47,000 Confederates.

Among those Confederates there were some new faces for the army in this theater. On September 18 Longstreet and his corps began to arrive from Virginia. Theirs had been a harrowing and frustrating trip from Lee's command. Also here was the small ersatz division of Major General Bushrod Rust Johnson, a native of Ohio who fought for the South.

Buckner was here now, for his first real battle since the loss at Fort Donelson. Bragg did not trust him because of the surrender to Grant in February 1862, but then Bragg distrusted all of his commanders it seemed. W. H. T. Walker and his Reserve Corps were here, so was Polk, and Hill as well. And also approaching the field was John C. Breckinridge, already perhaps the most traveled general in the Confederacy. He had gone from Kentucky to Mississippi to Tennessee, back to Mississippi, then Louisiana, then off into middle Tennessee during 1862. In 1863 he went back to Mississippi, and now returned once more to Georgia. By the morning of September 18, just arrived from his rigorous passage from Mississippi, he and his division stood poised at Glass's Mill, holding the extreme left of Bragg's line. It was the first glimpse that Hill and his officers would have of their new division commander. "There stands John C. Breckinridge," wrote one of Hill's staff, a man he believed "the most perfect I have ever seen." Others, blue and gray, would see a lot of him before this coming battle was done.[6]

The next morning the battle began. Bragg had still hoped to cut off Thomas from reinforcing Crittenden, but failed the day before. During the night he crossed all of the army but Cleburne's division, Hindman's, and Breckinridge's, to the west side of the creek. Those left behind were to cover the fords on his left and prevent an enemy crossing. Bragg wanted Walker, Cheatham's division of Polk's Corps, John B. Hood commanding that part of Longstreet's Corps that had arrived, and Buckner, all to attack Crittenden this morning. He did not know that Thomas had arrived and, conversely, the Federals seemed unaware that the entire Rebel army sat in their front and were across the creek. The fighting began in the center of the line when Thomas sent a division to Alexander's Bridge to dislodge Confederates reported there. They ran into cavalry led by General Nathan B. Forrest, and soon thereafter into Walker's corps. What followed for the rest of the day was a confused mass of fighting as units on both sides gravitated toward the sound of the guns with little or no overall coordination. Bragg failed to give specific instructions to his generals, and once the fighting began he still refused to believe the Federal strength in his front. When finally he was forced to realize that Thomas had joined Crittenden, he responded with half-hearted piecemeal assaults and a failure to send sufficient reinforcements in good time to the places needed. As a result, he achieved nothing, but Rosecrans was able to learn with fair accuracy just where Bragg's army lay and in what strength. Meanwhile on the far left, Breckinridge passed the day with no orders. When he heard the firing north of him, he sent the Orphan Brigade across Chickamauga Creek to feel out the enemy in his front. As the Federal strength grew, more evidence that Rosecrans was bringing his entire army to the field, General Ben Hardin Helm and the Kentuckians were gradually forced back. Then at last came an order from Hill. Breckinridge was to move at once to Lee and Gordon's Mills, two miles up the Chickamauga. Bragg was toying with the notion of attacking there where he believed the Federal center to be.[7]

But the situation continued to change throughout the day, as Bragg continually failed to make up his mind, and failed to use his cavalry effectively enough to gain the information he needed to make a sound plan. By the time Breckinridge reached Lee and Gordon's late that afternoon, the day's fighting was nearly done, and neither side had much to show for it. Bragg had almost his entire army across the creek, and Rosecrans had all but Granger's corps on the field or in the vicinity. All the attempts at feint and strategy had failed. Both armies would have to meet in a stand-up battle, matched almost man for man. Alas, neither general would manage it well.

As the evening of September 19 came on, Bragg began one of those inexplicable shifts in his command system that characterized his handling of his army in a crisis. Faced with the certainty of a major battle to come on September 20, he imposed an impractical and self-destructive new organization upon the army. Old corps designations would not matter. Polk, whom Bragg thought barely competent, would command the right half of the army, to include one of his own divisions—Walker's—and Hill's corps, while Longstreet, not yet arrived personally on the field, would command the left wing, comprising Buckner, the balance of Polk's Corps, and his own command from Virginia. The utter stupidity of the move was readily apparent to many, but not to Bragg. Longstreet would not arrive until midnight, yet he was to command the left wing in the morrow's attack. Units like Breckinridge's had to be shifted about in order to get them to the proper wings, thus needlessly tiring the men. And several commanders were not even notified of the change. As a result, some generals did not know just who commanded them, and others like Hill, though a lieutenant general, was made subordinate to Polk without being informed. It is apparent that the last year and a half of failure and tension was working on Bragg's mind. He had been sick in body for months. That sickness now lodged in his brain as well. Under any sort of heavy pressure, he could no longer think. Orders for the next day's fight went out verbally to some, in writing to others, and very imprecisely to all. Bragg intended that Polk should launch his attack first in the morning, first with his rightmost division, and then successively by each division in turn until Longstreet's leftmost division should be in the fray. He hoped thereby to turn Rosecrans' left and force him away from his communications with Chattanooga. Yet Bragg left it to Polk to verbally transmit the orders to his several corps and division commanders in the dark and did nothing further to ensure that his army knew what it was supposed to do the next morning. As so often in the past, Bragg could come close to making a bold plan and taking the responsibility for it, but then he stopped just short of commitment, unconsciously leaving everything sufficiently vague so that if something went wrong—as it always did—he could pass the blame to his subordinates.[8]

Certainly Breckinridge knew how that business had worked in the past, but if he wondered about it when he reached Lee and Gordon's only to find himself ordered on the march yet again, he did not say so. As part of Bragg's reorganization, Breckinridge had now to march to the extreme right wing of the army to join Polk's command, for the bishop general intended that the Kentuckian and his division would launch the attack the next morning. It was 10 P.M. when Breckinridge got his men to Alexander's Bridge to cross the Chickamauga. There he met Polk, who informed him for the first time of the new command arrangement. There, too, he asked and received permission to bivouac his command, for they were exhausted from the day's marching. He could get them to the right in time for the attack if they left before daylight. He could, that is, if Polk had bothered to tell him that his division was supposed to attack. Incredibly, Leonidas Polk told Breckinridge nothing of the plan for him to lead off the army's assault the next day, or of any planned attack at all. Neither did Polk tell Hill of the proposed assault, and when a messenger from Hill appeared and ordered Breckinridge to continue on to his assigned place on the right, Polk said to disregard the instructions since Hill was now junior to him. Thus the Kentuckian and his division began to spend the night more than a mile and a half from the spot where they were supposed to be the next morning, and Polk then proceeded to invite Breckinridge to his headquarters for dinner. There the bishop's incredible memory, or lack of it, continued to keep his subordinates in the dark. They ate a quiet supper, talked pleasantly, and Polk did take a few minutes out to write an order to Hill for the morrow's assault. But while writing it, with Hill's senior division commander in the same tent, Polk still told Breckinridge nothing, and then gave the order to one of his men to deliver instead of sending it via several of Hill's own staff who had come and gone during the evening. Hill never received the message.[9]

Breckinridge slept for about three hours in the comfort of Polk's tent. When he awoke at 3:30 A.M., September 20, he left to take his division on to the right. Only now did Polk even hint at what was to come. He hoped, he said, that "the attack" would be made as soon as possible. Yet he did not say what attack, and Breckinridge could only assume that Polk spoke in general terms of an attack by the army as a whole. Thus just two hours before he was supposed to be in place to begin the battle that might well decide the fate of northern Georgia and with it the central heartland of the Confederacy, the general from Kentucky had not the slightest idea of what was expected from him. Thus were battles fought in Braxton Bragg's army.

It was 6 A.M. when the division found its place at the extreme right of the Confederate line, perhaps two miles northeast of Snodgrass Hill.

Breckinridge positioned his three brigades, sent skirmishers to his front, and then rode to his left to visit with General Cleburne, commanding the next division. About 7 A.M. Daniel H. Hill joined them, all still ignorant of the impending attack, and as they compared views they agreed that the Federal line in their front was too strong for them to attack should they be asked to do so. Thomas occupied an area called Kelly Field and had built log and earth breastworks during the night, as well as emplacing cannon. It would be like attacking a fortress. Hill still placed two of Breckinridge's brigades a little farther to the right in a flanking position, then left and allowed the two divisions to cook rations for their breakfast.

As the three generals sat by their campfire, finally came a message from Polk, not for Hill—for the bishop apparently gave up looking for him after a half-hearted effort—but directed to Cleburne and Breckinridge. Still he said nothing of the attack that they were supposed to have begun more than an hour before. He merely told them to attack Thomas as soon as possible. Hill decided that, there being no sense of urgency in the order, the men could finish their breakfasts just the same, and attack in about an hour. After a time Bragg himself finally appeared and demanded to know why he did not see his divisions driving back the Yankee horde before them. Informed of the utter ignorance of the plan by the right wing commanders, Bragg cursed Polk repeatedly and finally gave Hill a peremptory order to attack at once. At nine-thirty, four hours late, Breckinridge sent his division into battle.[10]

He felt some misgivings about this fight. Hood had seen it the night before when he met the Kentuckian briefly and found him moody and gloomy. Hood tried to cheer him, and perhaps he succeeded. Yet some of the men in the ranks, too, felt uneasy over what might happen on the morrow. After all, Breckinridge was once again to hold the right of a line commanded by Braxton Bragg, and the painful memory of Stones River lingered with them all. What folly might their leader commit them to this time?[11]

At last the fight began. Rosecrans had his army spread roughly along the Lafayette road, his right at a place called the Widow Glenn's and his left on some high ground at Kelly Field, in front of Snodgrass Hill. Thomas and his corps, with a division each from McCook and Crittenden, held the left and left center of "Old Rosey's" line. Crittenden with his remaining two divisions made the right center, and the other two divisions of McCook's held the right. Facing them Bragg had Breckinridge and Cleburne opposite Thomas, with Walker's corps in reserve, and Longstreet lined up to oppose the remainder of the Federals. "Old Pete" himself arrived at about midnight the night before, to be met with no formal reception or welcome at all, but merely Bragg's cold formality. The two took an instant dislike to each other.

Forward went Breckinridge and his division. As he soon discovered, he was attacking almost alone, for Polk failed to provide any reserve to back him up, nor did he give him cavalry cover on his right. And Cleburne was late in readying his own following attack, with the result that the Kentuckian and his one division of barely 3,700 men was advancing against more than double his numbers on the extreme left of Thomas' position, and those men faced him from behind defenses. Still they went forward, and at first met with little resistance. Indeed, his two right brigades actually got around Thomas' flank, passing beyond the Lafayette road as they began to press back the Federals. However, Helm and the Orphan Brigade struck squarely into the enemy earthworks. Two regiments stopped immediately when they encountered the log defenses, while the rest of the brigade continued to advance. The two units facing the fortifications attacked and were repulsed three times. Worse, with Cleburne's failure to attack on schedule, the Federals on Thomas' right now concentrated their fire on the Orphans as well. In less than an hour the brigade suffered 30 percent casualties, one of them mortally wounded General Ben Hardin Helm.[12]

"Helm has been killed," cried a shocked Breckinridge when he got the news. But there was no time now for sorrow. He ordered Colonel Joseph Lewis to take the brigade command, then rode to look at his two brigades on the right. He saw the immense possibilities offered by their position. They had cut off one Federal line of retreat along the Lafayette road, and even then stood poised to cut off yet another that led directly to the rear from Kelly Field. They had turned Thomas' flank, well beyond the line of defenses he had built, and now stood ready to curl up the enemy left. All that he needed was support. Still Cleburne did not attack, and when Hill learned of the situation, he appealed in vain to Polk for Walker to be sent into the attack. Should they assail Thomas in his front in force, Breckinridge's flank and rear attack could decide the battle.

But the support did not come, and Breckinridge continued his attack on Thomas' flank alone. As his brigades assailed the Union line, the Kentuckian himself sat atop his bay mare just a little behind the battle line, affecting a studied air of calm to reassure his men. Casually he stroked his moustache, and even from across the raging battle line one of the Federal commanders, John Beatty, could see him and marveled. Years later, when complimented on being a handsome figure when mounted, Beatty replied by thinking back to Chickamauga: "You certainly never saw the Confederate General John C. Breckinridge on a horse." Soon the Kentuckian moved over to steady the wavering Orphan Brigade, where he joined Polk and others. They watched Cleburne lead his attack at last, and then heard the sound of battle toward their center, toward Longstreet. Sensing that somehow Bragg's battle plan was still operating despite his own ineptitude, Polk ordered Breckinridge and others to redouble their attacks on Thomas. It was 11 A.M. now, and as Breckinridge sent his division catapulting once more into Thomas, those sounds of fighting off toward the center heralded the approaching fruits of his finest performance as a division commander.[13]

From the moment that Breckinridge first attacked Kelly Field and its entrenchments, Thomas called repeatedly upon Rosecrans for more and more reinforcements. In the first hour of fighting an additional five brigades came to join him. By ten forty-five Rosecrans sent another four brigades to the threatened flank and, as they marched toward the fight, still another message came from Thomas calling for more. In those early assaults Breckinridge sent barely more than 3,700 Confederates against at least 10,000 Federals, yet so ferocious were his attacks that Thomas felt unable to stop him without continual reinforcement. Finally, to meet his subordinate's demand, Rosecrans had several units in motion in his center and left, with the result that he accidentally created a half-mile-wide gap in the right center of his line just as Longstreet happened to be launching his own attack. The gap opened as the divisions of Johnson and Hood and others advanced, and they had but to shift their charge slightly to the left to march straight through the Federal line. The effect proved electric. The right wing of the Yankee army retreated at once, as did one of Thomas' divisions and most of Crittenden's corps. The flight soon became a precipitate panic, and one that swept up in its fury Rosecrans, Crittenden, and McCook. By 1 P.M. the battle was already a great Confederate victory, and one due more than anything else to the confusion caused by the frantic demands of Thomas in response to Breckinridge's attacks. In time the Kentuckian's friends would credit him solely for creating that gaping hole in the enemy line, but Breckinridge himself remained content to comment that his pressure on Thomas "compelled him to weaken other parts of his line to hold his vital point."[14]

But the battle was not yet done. However unsteady Thomas may have been that morning, he now faced his isolation on the field with iron resolve. He found himself alone with three of his divisions, and one each from McCook and Crittenden, along with a little cavalry and other portions of scattered commands. Longstreet's drive curled up the Federals so that, with the divisions of Polk, the Confederates hemmed him from three sides. The Yankees were in a desperate fix, but Thomas determined to hold his ground to prevent a rout of the entire army. He even won back some of the ground taken earlier by Breckinridge's division, and finally Polk sent Walker into the fight and pulled out the three brigades that had started the battle, exhausted. As Breckinridge, Hill, and Polk conversed behind the lines, they soon saw a new threat appear. Coming from the north, down the Lafayette road, the advance elements of Gordon Granger's corps marched toward Thomas' relief. They were coming straight for Breckinridge's flank. The vacillating Bishop Polk told Hill to fall back, advice which Breckinridge believed would have forfeited the victory just gained, and Hill agreed. He ignored Polk's order, and the coming reinforcements, a full division, sidestepped the Confederates and rushed to Thomas' right flank where Longstreet pressed him sorely. Indeed, Longstreet was doing most of the fighting now, until three-thirty when Polk finally decided to take part once more. He ordered Hill to attack. Hill could see that Breckinridge and his division were badly mauled by the fury of the morning and asked another division to join with Cleburne in the attack. When that commander declined, Hill asked Breckinridge if he could stand one more assault. Yes, he could, and with that the Kentuckian rode to his brigades and told them to fix bayonets. "We have got them in a bad fix," he said, "and must finish them this time."[15]

It was nearing dark when the brigades moved forward once again. Cleburne broke through Thomas' center and Breckinridge, supported by Walker, pushed around the Federal left once more and captured part of the enemy earthworks. As the nightfall made operations increasingly difficult, Hill finally ordered his commanders to stop the attack, but not before they convinced Thomas that it was time for him, too, to leave the field. After a heroic defense, the man who would come to be called the "Rock of Chickamauga" organized a skillful withdrawal. Rosecrans ordered him to do so several hours before, but Thomas was intent upon stalling any Confederate pursuit, and he did it.[16]

Well might Braxton Bragg be elated. His army had won the most complete victory ever achieved by any Confederate army. Not even Lee's success at Chancellorsville rivaled the absolute nature of the triumph. Rosecrans suffered 16,000 casualties and untold losses in valuable material and supplies. To be sure, Confederate losses were even higher, 18,000 and more, including serious wounds to Hood and Hindman, and death for Helm. But despite the terrible losses, cheers swept the army's camps from end to end, and went on well through the night. Bragg himself probably felt vindicated against the attacks of his opponents. If so, he hardly had the right, for he neither commanded nor fought his army that day. Rather, almost by accident did the piecemeal attacks happen to coincide at the right place and time. Only Hill really commanded on the right, and only Longstreet on the left. Bragg and Polk might as well have stayed behind the lines and prayed. After all, it was a Sunday.

For Breckinridge, the tithing that holy day proved terrible. Fully one third of his division, 1,240 out of 3,769, lay dead or wounded. Besides the personal loss of his friend Helm, there was his beloved young chief of artillery, Rice E. Graves, mortally wounded. This evening the general rode to the hospital to see him, and the two visited briefly before the Kentuckian had to leave. As he walked out of the hospital, onlookers saw tears streaming from his eyes. Then he rode out over the battlefield, counting the dead. It was a moonlit, macabre scene that met him. The faces of the dead stared up at him with a gaze that he never forgot. Months later, haunted by the sight, he repeatedly asked himself, "Are you the same man who stood gazing down on the faces of the dead on that awful battlefield?

The soldiers lying there—they stare at you with their eyes wide open. Is this the same world?"

Yet there was a bit of humor to be found as well. After his ghostly ride, Breckinridge returned to the rear where some Yankee prisoners had asked to see him. "Well, gentlemen," he said, "this is what is left of me." Quickly came the answer, "Yes, and a damn fine specimen of humanity you are, too! There is not another such hunk of humanity in our land! I voted for you once, and I want this cursed war over with so that I may vote for you again for President." It continued to be a very peculiar war, and one which Breckinridge himself never felt he really understood. Perhaps none of them did. Perhaps that is why they fought.[17]

Rosecrans did not have time to wonder about the nature of the war. He was too busy hastening back to Chattanooga. By September 21 he had almost his entire army in the city, and in defenses that Bragg had himself erected just shortly before. That "Old Rosey" no longer believed in himself or his army is clear. He made no attempt to hold the strategic ground on Missionary Ridge and Lookout Mountain that completely dominated Chattanooga. Rather, he hung back in the city, almost like a whimpering dog expecting to be beaten, unable to run away and unwilling to fight back. Had Bragg offered a resolute pursuit, which would admittedly be difficult given the heavy losses in the Confederate army, Rosecrans would certainly have abandoned southeastern Tennessee entirely and pulled back to Murfreesboro or Nashville.

But Bragg, as always, did not pursue. He absorbed himself in trivialities during the day after the battle, avoiding making another of those decisions he so dreaded. Accustomed to defeat, he seemed unsure of how to handle a victory. One thing is certain, he was not ready to put his mind to another battle. He brought his army onto the heights at Missionary and Lookout, and then spent a week watching the Federals without acting. Finally, and probably with good reason, considering his own condition, Bragg decided that he would besiege Chattanooga. But with that decision made, he barely informed his commanders, and then for several days did nothing to cut Rosecrans' supply lines, even though he knew that the Federals had only a few days' rations left. It was well into October before the army commander began actively to invest Chattanooga. The reason is that he could not fight two enemies at once, and even as he stood on Missionary Ridge looking at the beaten Federals before, he had already declared war once more upon his generals. This time, he intended a fight to the finish.[18]

Just two days after the fight at Chickamauga, Bragg began his campaign against the enemies he perceived in his own ranks. He saw them as a united body, though in fact they stood divided into several factions, and some did not align themselves with any. Those who dreamed of returning to Kentucky made one group, led by Buckner, those who favored the strategic ideas of the now out of favor P. G. T. Beauregard made another.

Some simply despised Bragg personally, and others banded together by family ties to defend members attacked by him. Breckinridge joined with none of them, yet could be a member of all, and Bragg so regarded him.[19]

Bragg struck first where it was deserved, at Polk. He charged him with the delay of the vital morning attack in September, and when the bishop unjustly tried to shift the blame to Hill, Bragg relieved him of his command, at the same time relieving Hindman as well. Breckinridge, by now a firm friend to D. H. Hill, sympathized entirely with the commander's actions. But he did not take part in Polk's own campaign against Bragg. Three days before his removal, Polk met with Longstreet, Hill, and Buckner, laying plans to engineer Bragg's removal from command, and probably to replace him with Joseph E. Johnston. They began a letter-writing campaign to achieve their aims, culminating in a meeting on October 4 at which Breckinridge, Cleburne, and several other generals were present. All but Breckinridge signed a letter to President Davis, the Kentuckian demurring because he still had his request for a court of inquiry over the Stones River controversy before the War Department. To sign this letter would appear, then, to be an act of self-interest. Bragg himself soon knew of this meeting. He called them "the conspirators" and believed that Buckner engineered it to put himself in command of the army.[20]

The situation so deteriorated that President Davis himself came to the vicinity. He arrived in Atlanta on October 8, to be met by a host of the anti-Bragg men, including Breckinridge and Longstreet. The following day, as the President rode to Bragg's headquarters, each of the generals with him seems to have expressed his case against Bragg, each except Breckinridge that is. The wife of a man accompanying the President would write that there was "Nothing narrow, nothing self-seeking about Breckinridge. He has not mounted a pair of green spectacles made of prejudices, so that he sees no good except in his own red-hot partisans." In the days that followed, the Kentuckian certainly expressed his views to the President, but he confined himself chiefly to a defense of Hill, whom Bragg now began to blame both for the delay at Chickamauga and for the leadership in the October 4 meeting of "the conspirators." Bragg and Davis actually wanted to replace Hill with the disgraced John C. Pemberton, who came with the President, but Hill's division commanders strongly advised against it. Nevertheless, when Davis left to return to Richmond on October 14, Bragg's first act was the removal of Daniel H. Hill from his command. That meant that, as senior major general, Breckinridge now rose to leadership of the corps.[21]

He found little time to exult over his elevation. Despite the rumors that he would be promoted to lieutenant general, as befitted a corps commander, Breckinridge probably doubted that it would happen or that he would hold his post for long. Even as Bragg relieved Hill, he began another reorganization of his army designed solely to break up and eliminate the opposition. He shifted about or dispersed whole divisions, including Breckinridge's old command. Polk and Hindman were gone already, and after Bragg had a flare-up with cavalryman Nathan B. Forrest in which the irascible horseman threatened to kill Bragg if he interfered with his command, Bragg backed down and allowed Forrest to be transferred. By November, only two of the Chickamauga corps and wing commanders were left in place, Walker and Longstreet. William Joseph Hardee came back to the army to replace Polk at I Corps. Breckinridge took the II Corps, with his own, Alexander Peter Stewart's, and Hindman's old divisions. Longstreet commanded the III Corps. So thoroughly did Bragg reorganize the army that, in Breckinridge's division for instance, not a single brigade that had been a part of it in the spring remained. As for Buckner, he was reduced to command of a division.[22]

Now it was left for Bragg to settle his feud with Longstreet, the newest and perhaps most bitter of his critics. All during the month of October and most of November, Bragg so occupied himself with battling his generals that he did little or no strategic planning on how he would deal with the Federals in Chattanooga. Indeed, this was one of the many complaints lodged in the letters sent to Richmond by Hill and the others. All through the month the Confederates groped for a plan, coming up with nothing better than an attack on Rosecrans in Chattanooga while they also assaulted his supply base at Bridgeport on the Tennessee River. On October 28 Longstreet finally launched a feeble attempt to cut that supply route, but failed for lack of real effort. On the same day he and Bragg watched as two Federal corps marched below their position on Lookout Mountain. Washington had sent "Fighting Joe" Hooker from Virginia with the XI and XII Corps to reinforce Rosecrans. Sherman was on the way to Chattanooga with the XV and XVII Corps. On October 19 Thomas had relieved Rosecrans of command in Chattanooga, and four days later another new general arrived to assume overall command. Lincoln had empowered Ulysses S. Grant with command of all Union armies west of the Alleghenies and east of the Mississippi. By the end of October, as the two armies faced each other, it seemed almost a reunion for Shiloh veterans. They had all met before.

On October 31 Bragg could see that his siege was not working. He had not prevented supplies from reaching the Federals, particularly as Grant successfully opened a combination water and land route that brought the Yankees back almost to full rations. The enemy strength was visibly growing, for the Confederates could see the march of division after division as they came into Chattanooga. If Bragg was to avoid being himself put on the defensive by overwhelming numbers, he had to drop the siege and attack. This day Breckinridge, Longstreet, and Hardee rode to Lookout's summit to inspect the possibility of launching an attack on Hooker's command, now placed on the south side of the Tennessee facing them. They unanimously decided against such an attack, and so did

Bragg. Indeed, even before they made their reconnaissance the commanding general had come to another conclusion. He would send two of his
divisions north to Knoxville, where a small Federal command under another general from the east, Ambrose Burnside, held the important east
Tennessee town. Bragg hoped that such a move would force Grant to
weaken his forces at Chattanooga to support Burnside. But after that
what could he do? With virtually a whole corps of his own gone, he
would still face Grant's reported 80,000 with barely 36,000 of his own. He
could hardly hope to attack and succeed. More probable is that Bragg
found in the Knoxville adventure an opportunity to rid himself of more of
his malcontents. His first choice to command the expedition was none
other than Breckinridge, but he soon agreed with Davis that Longstreet
should be given the command, and that effectively removed the troublesome "Old Pete" from Bragg's way. His last major vocal enemy disposed
of, the general could now think about Grant.[23]

Now Bragg's army had but two corps, Hardee and his 20,000 men
and Breckinridge with 16,000. Longstreet left on November 5, and those
who remained faced the impossible task of holding the entire line around
Chattanooga. Breckinridge had six miles of it in his charge, from Lookout
Mountain on the left, across the Chattanooga Valley, and onto Missionary Ridge. Hardee extended the line for several miles along the ridge
until it terminated at Tunnel Hill. For his part, Breckinridge did not feel
entirely sanguine about their position. On the face of it, Missionary Ridge
appeared formidable indeed against any attack. Its steep, rocky slopes
could not easily be approached or climbed. And Federals attacking would
have to do so in full view of the Confederate batteries placed all along the
crest. Bragg thought the position impregnable, and so did the Kentuckian,
but his thinly spread forces worried him. He had but one man for every
two feet of front, with no one as a reserve in the rear. It was too much.
Fearing a possible reverse, on November 19 Breckinridge ordered his division commanders to be ready for a withdrawal, just in case.[24]

He had not long to wait, for Grant was no Rosecrans. On November
15 Sherman finally arrived, and by November 23 the Federals stood ready
to break out from their siege. Hooker held the right of the line, with three
divisions now, and his task would be to attack and take Lookout Mountain. Sherman marched around behind Chattanooga, to put his two corps
across the river and attack Bragg's right at Tunnel Hill. Meanwhile
Thomas commanded the three corps in the center, in front of the city.
Grant wanted him to advance against Missionary Ridge itself, linking
with Sherman after he took Tunnel Hill, and then the two would sweep
down Missionary's crest from north to south. Delays of weather prevented
the Yankees from starting their plan in motion until November 23. Then
they were ready.

So were the Confederates, in a fashion. Late on November 22 Bragg
discovered the threat to Tunnel Hill and began shifting troops to his right

to support Hardee. Breckinridge was left for a time with a gaping hole in his line that he could fill only with campfires, hoping it would fool the enemy into thinking there were still troops present. All night and the next day he shifted his men about, bringing in his meager reserves, in order to make a stable line. The Kentuckian was merely a spectator that day when Grant ordered Thomas to move forward somewhat to occupy an eminence called Orchard Knob, midway between Chattanooga and Missionary Ridge. That was on Hardee's front, and though the Confederates offered some resistance, Thomas took the position without difficulty. Obviously Grant was about to attack. Breckinridge could well expect that the Yankees would move against him next.[25]

So they did. Early on November 24 Hooker launched an attack against the small level area where Lookout's base met the Tennessee. It was the most vulnerable part of the Confederate left, and Breckinridge had barely a division to defend all of Lookout. A dense fog on the heights prevented the Rebel artillery from supporting the men facing Hooker, and steadily the Yankees pushed them back. Breckinridge sent an order that Lookout must be held at all hazards, and he himself began to lead an additional brigade to its defense. Because of the distance and the fog, he did not reach Lookout's base until seven-thirty that evening, in time to find that all he could do was organize and cover a withdrawal. With barely 5,000 men, the Confederates on the slopes could simply not resist Hooker and his 15,000 or more. Still, it was a loss that deeply angered Breckinridge.[26]

That evening the Confederate commanders met in council of war. With Lookout gone, the whole army was threatened. Should Sherman take Tunnel Hill, the two wings of the Federal army could pinch the Missionary Ridge line between them. Hardee advised withdrawal of the army. Breckinridge, however, felt there was not sufficient time. Besides, the ground at Missionary was the best defensive position he had ever seen. If they could not stand there, they could not stand anywhere. Bragg agreed. They would accept Grant's attack on Missionary Ridge. When the meeting concluded at ten o'clock that evening, Breckinridge told a fellow officer that "I never felt more like fighting than when I saw those people shelling my troops off of Lookout today, and I mean to get even with them."

But revenge would have to wait for another field, for both Breckinridge and Bragg were deluded about the ridge's defensibility. In fact, there were numerous places where advancing troops would be concealed from their fire. Worse, the steepness meant that after the Federals got sufficiently close to the crest, the Confederate cannon could not be depressed enough to fire at them. The works on the crest were hastily built and incomplete and, to make matters worse, Bragg had divided every one of Breckinridge's regiments, sending one portion to rifle pits at the base of the ridge, and the other half into the works at the top. Those at the bottom were to fire a single volley when Grant attacked, and then retreat up the ridge. What effect Bragg expected this foolish enterprise to have, he never said, but in practice it would make half a corps crawl up the ridge under enemy fire, and send them bouncing into the line at the top, disrupting for a time their return fire. Worse, Bragg failed to tell the men at the top of what those at the bottom were supposed to do. Seeing their comrades clambering up the hill, the men in the defenses might well think a rout had begun and join them in the retreat.[27]

Later that night Breckinridge rearranged his entire corps onto Missionary's crest. Because Bragg devoted the bulk of Hardee's command to the defense of Tunnel Hill, the Kentuckian found himself defending two thirds of the entire Confederate line on Missionary with considerably less than half the army. Then just before dawn, November 25, Bragg ordered another of his brigades, the Orphan Brigade, off to the right. Shortly after, the general could see Hooker leading his divisions south from Lookout toward the southern end of Missionary Ridge at Rossville. He would certainly be attacked soon. Breckinridge heard the sound of guns to the north. Sherman was attacking Hardee. About 1 P.M. increased activity could be seen within Thomas' lines directly in front of Missionary, and Breckinridge began readying his thin line to meet an attack in its center. Word came from Rossville. Hooker was attacking. Bragg assumed personal command of the center of the line while Breckinridge rushed to his left. He rode three miles, arriving at shortly after 3 P.M. to find Hooker steadily pushing the Confederates up the southern slope of the ridge. Half an hour later Hooker launched his main attack and drove Breckinridge back to the top of the ridge, then began steadily pushing him back farther. In the confusion, his son was captured, and his adjutant. The general himself barely escaped. Outnumbered six to one, Breckenridge's line melted back toward the center though putting up a stiff resistance. Even the Federal commanders facing him later testified that the paltry Confederate forces were handled with skill.[28]

What Breckinridge found when he reached the center of the line defied description. Grant had become worried when Sherman's attack at Tunnel Hill failed to break through in time, and when he did not hear from Hooker of how the move against Rossville proceeded. Believing that it would be necessary to support his two flanking attacks, he ordered Thomas to send his command forward to take the forward rifle pits at the foot of Missionary Ridge. That might distract the enemy away from Hooker and Sherman. Thomas coolly paraded his three corps in full view of the Rebels atop the ridge, sending chills down their spines as they saw endless thousands of blue-coated Yankees preparing to advance against them. The effect of the sight alone proved demoralizing. Then, when Thomas attacked, his men took the pits easily but found that they could not hold them under the fire from the crest. They must fall back, or continue the attack. Authorities would disagree for the next century and more over whether or not Thomas or Grant actually ordered them on to the crest, but on they went just the same. The flaw in Bragg's defenses became immediately apparent. Already spooked by the sight of Thomas' army, the Confederates on the crest became considerably disorganized when the men from the rifle pits retired up the slope. Confusion ensued, and those retiring continued to retire, joined by increasing numbers of other Confederates. As the Federals pressed on up the slope, the scene at the top became a bedlam. Just as Breckinridge arrived at Bragg's headquarters, two Federal divisions broke through the line at the top and the whole Confederate army broke into a panicked retreat. Bragg and Breckinridge tried to stop the rout, but found it hopeless. Finally the Kentuckian simply advised his men, "Boys, get away the best you can!"[29]

One of Breckinridge's divisions failed to panic and set up a line of resistance some one thousand yards back of the crest. There they stood for two hours or more resisting attacks from the Federals, while they covered the retreat of the rest of the corps. Hardee had held at first off to the north, but with the collapse of the center and left of the line, he, too, had to retreat, and this same division aided in protecting his retirement. Breckinridge himself probably went off to try to find and rally the shambles of his corps that had fought Hooker. It was after dark when he rejoined the lone division and ordered them at last to join the retreat. Then he rode off toward Chickamauga Station, six or seven miles to the rear. There Bragg established his headquarters and sought to reform the shattered army.

The next morning, November 26, Breckinridge collected what he could of his corps and began the retreat to Ringgold, Georgia. He kept himself all day with the rear guard as it covered the retreat. Indeed, he started fighting the advancing Federals at 2:30 A.M., and continued sporadically all through the day. By nightfall, the enemy still close on his rear, Breckinridge camped his men on the summit of Pigeon Mountain, huddling around a campfire with the rest of them. In the midst of the worst disaster in the army's history, he suddenly recognized a private whom he had unjustly reprimanded the day before, and now apologized to him in front of his friends. Then he rode off to find Bragg.

The next day the army finally reached Dalton, about twelve miles beyond Ringgold, and Breckinridge himself came in with the rear guard late that evening, after he and Cleburne had spent five hours of continual fighting to stop the Federal advance. Breckinridge even personally took a hand in placing the troops, some of whom even threw rocks at the enemy and rolled boulders down the slopes at them. Finally they burned the bridges over the Chickamauga, and thereby effectively ended what had been a lukewarm Yankee pursuit in the first place.[30]

As Breckinridge arrived in Dalton, he found changes in the wind, as well as the denouement of his long controversy with the commanding general. On November 28, in utter shame after the defeat at Missionary

Ridge, Bragg finally did on his own what so many others had wanted for so long: he resigned. Davis in Richmond would have no choice but to accept the resignation, and on November 30 the President ordered him to turn the army command over to Hardee temporarily. Two days later, lamented by no one, Bragg left the army never to see it again. But in his passing, as in the aftermath of all his battles, he left a final legacy of bitterness and shame. He tried now to blame the defeat almost entirely upon Breckinridge.

On December 1, in a dispatch to Davis, Bragg declared that John C. Breckinridge had failed in his duty, and was unfit for command, all during November 23–27. The reason—drunkenness. In fact, the Kentuckian liked his bourbon when he could get it, though no one ever recalled seeing him under its influence. Indeed, the only liquor he is known to have obtained all through the war was the occasional bottle sent him by Mary. Yet Bragg made the charge. He claimed that on the night of November 25, at Chickamauga Station, Breckinridge actually sank down on the floor of his headquarters "dead drunk," and was still there in the morning. Later he claimed that he put the intoxicated Breckinridge under the charge of Brigadier General States Rights Gist with instructions that Gist was not to obey the Kentuckian's orders. When finally they reached Dalton, on November 27, he said that he relieved Breckinridge of his command, and that the general admitted the justice of it, though it was "the deepest mortification of his life."[31]

Indeed, Bragg began something of a letter-writing campaign of his own to support his charge. Besides his communications to President Davis, he also sent slim accounts to other generals who were close to him. It was all calculated to reveal that the loss of Chattanooga was Breckinridge's fault, not his. "No man, whatever his power, can command an army successfully made up as ours are," he complained, "without the support of his generals." When officers "high in rank . . . can get drunk & stay drunk for several days during such a disaster as we sustained," no one could manage affairs successfully. "I candidly confess my inability to command an army where its senior Generals can with impunity remain drunk for five successive days, as did Cheatham & Breckenridge [sic] about the time of our retreat at Missionary Ridge." Thus, in like vein, did Bragg continue his accusations, not just in the months to follow, but repeatedly for the next ten years.[32]

Certainly Breckinridge shared the shame of the panicked flight from Missionary Ridge. Few were the Confederates who could take pride in any episode of that terrible day. But that the Kentuckian was unfit for duty was a pure fabrication. On the twenty-third he was frequently seen repositioning his line, and the next day personally led part of the resistance on Lookout Mountain. He was not so drunk on November 25 that he could not command the resistance to Hooker, at one point resisting two Federal brigades with just two regiments, and then successfully cover the withdrawal of the army. Instead of being asleep, drunk, on the head-quarters floor that night, he was off giving orders for the next day's re-treat, and at 2:30 A.M. was personally commanding the rearguard fighting with the pursuing Federals. The business about Gist guarding him was a complete falsehood, for the two generals never even saw each other during the retreat, and all day on November 27 Breckinridge was fighting with Cleburne along the Chickamauga.[33]

The affair reveals something far more important than a simple unjust charge against a general. The entire allegation was an invention of Brax-ton Bragg's mind. On the surface, to his friends, Bragg appeared to be a sane and reasonable, if terribly tired, man. He suffered something of a ner-vous breakdown earlier in the year, and admitted two weeks after leaving the army that his resignation was prompted by the fact that his health "was very much impaired." But as this episode clearly reveals, he had lost touch with rationality. The weight of defeat unhinged him. Not content with trying to dump the responsibility on Breckinridge for the defeat, he even delved a year into the past and now produced the completely new charge that the loss at Stones River was also due to the Kentuckian's being drunk. Where his army and his generals and his own failures were concerned, Braxton Bragg was insane.

And he did not, as he claimed, relieve Breckinridge on the spot at Dalton. In fact, the Kentuckian retained his corps command for two weeks after Bragg left the army. But then General Hindman was finally released from his arrest and rejoined his division. That made him senior general in the corps, and automatically he replaced Breckinridge. Yet Breckinridge could hardly argue that he, too, could no longer command out there. The loss of Missionary Ridge was not his fault. However foolhardy Bragg's intent to remain on the summit had been, in the fighting of November 25 even he could not be blamed for what hap-pened. But in the aftermath of such a catastrophe, and following as it did the greatest Confederate victory of the war, the responsibility had to touch everyone. Breckinridge's corps had collapsed, and with it his usefulness in the Army of Tennessee as a corps commander. He felt the justice of his replacement, but still it hurt. When a civilian unwisely goaded him later, asking, "Well, sir! How came we to lose Chattanooga?" Breckinridge responded coolly, "It is a long story," and turned his back.[34]

Many men turned their backs that dreadful December, and many left Dalton never to see this army again. More than that, the Confederacy now had to look over its shoulder to see Tennessee, once a part of its heartland. And President Abraham Lincoln could look forward to adding another Southern star to the Union constellation.

CHAPTER 16

"NOTHING COULD BE MORE MAGNANIMOUS"

In Washington the news of the victory at Chattanooga produced great delight. For Abraham Lincoln it offered yet another challenge in a great work he undertook almost from the beginning of the conflict. To the military governor of Tennessee, Andrew Johnson, he wrote that the civil government of the state must be restored to the hands of sound Union men as soon as possible. "Exclude all others," said Lincoln, "and trust that your government, so organized, will be recognized here." It was time to bring Tennessee back into the Union, time for its "reconstruction."[1]

Since the first guns of the war sounded, Lincoln and Northern leaders debated not whether or not the rebelling states would be defeated, but what was to be done with them *when* they were defeated. And from the first it proved to be a hot debate, indeed. Just how, on what footing, should the Southern states be allowed back into the national government? And what of the attendant problems of individuals? How should the matters of pardon or amnesty for former Confederate officers and men and sympathizers be handled? Should their property be confiscated? Should there be reprisals against their leaders? Should there be rejoicing or should there be revenge?

Back in 1861, before the tempo and anger of the war rose, many felt that the South should simply be allowed to reenter the Union mainstream without reproach. Secretary of State William Henry Seward adhered to this notion, but he stood almost alone among the more radical Republicans on the issue. More typical of their views were the declarations of the Harrisburg, Pennsylvania, press, when it cried out that harsh penalties must be visited upon the South once conquered. In particular, since Southern land belonged "equally" to the slaves as well as their masters, that land should be divided up between them. Other journals and politicians took up the cry. "There is no longer a State of South Carolina, a State of Georgia, etc.," said a Washington editor. By revolting against the government, the seceded states had forfeited all political rights, reducing themselves to the status of "the unorganized public domain." Clearly the old Southern states could not reenter the Union as the states they had been, not until "they have been reorganized and reofficered in all their departments." They must frame new state constitutions and apply for admission to statehood just like any other territory, and then await the pleasure of Congress while it decided to "receive them or continue to hold them in the condition of Territories until satisfactory assurance shall be given that the people have returned to a sentiment of loyalty."[2]

The abolitionists, the men like Charles Sumner and Thaddeus Stevens, perhaps even Owen Lovejoy, echoed those words repeatedly. They wanted blood as the penalty for rebellion. Yet within their party there were other voices that argued for a different sort of reconstruction, and at their head sat Lincoln. He stated his position clearly in his inaugural and in subsequent declarations. By denying the right of secession, he thus denied that the Southern states ever really left the Union. Their actions in legislatures of passing ordinances of secession were meaningless. All that was happening was that certain leaders in those states were in rebellion and leading other people in that rebellion. As soon as their revolt should be put down, they would automatically be subject to the same laws and rights as before. This was a civil disturbance which had no effect at all upon the basic relationship of the states to the Federal Government. "We deny that any State can go out of the Union," declared an administration newspaper, "and therefore there can be no necessity in any event of providing for her 'readmission.' " All any state need do was, upon being freed of Confederate domination, reelect a new state government on the basis of the existing state constitution, and send its representatives to Washington.[3]

It did not take long for the debate to become a virtual battle between Lincoln and the moderates, and the extremists on the other. Soon those who favored lenient treatment of the conquered states—as they would surely be conquered—were derisively called Copperheads for their sympathetic attitude. Those anxious to confiscate land and give it to freed blacks became in the same breath "Niggerheads," and so were the lines drawn. Soon the one side began calling for "grape for the rebel masses, and hemp for their leaders." All property of whatever description should be confiscated, the men disenfranchised, or even exterminated. Horace Greeley suggested that the South be colonized all over again with loyal men from the North, and in Congress Stevens declared that it was better to "lay the whole country waste." He and Sumner and others wanted to bring about not just a restoration of the Union, but a complete social and intellectual upheaval in the South. Beneath it all lay a simple difference of opinion. Lincoln and his friends felt certain that the great and long-held attachment for the Union still dwelt in the South, submerged only temporarily by passion. Indeed, some thought that the rebellion only outlasted 1861 because Lincoln gave the Confederacy a cause to live for when he sought to put down the rebellion. Had he let them alone, the Southern states would have returned to the Union on their own after a brief spell. But others who thought they knew the South declared that the Rebels would never freely return and that not even defeat would make them fit citizens for the Union. The people of the South must be reeducated to think in the proper way, and the teacher should be Congress.[4]

Even before the debate gained full headway, President Lincoln already began garnering experience and experimentation in reconstruction. Long before the Confederate states were invaded and commenced to fall to Northern arms, the border states, particularly Maryland, Kentucky, and Missouri, offered fields for learning the art of bringing Rebels back into the fold. The first lesson was that it would take more than a Unionist majority to keep peace and loyalty prevailing. In Missouri, after the secessionist government went over to the Confederates, Yankee commanders had to use their military influence to assemble a new state convention to declare all state offices vacant and then refill them with loyal men. In Maryland, Lincoln and Winfield Scott had to virtually imprison the legislature to prevent its attempting to consider a secession ordinance, and afterward it was only the presence of Union arms that allowed the loyal state government to function. The experience in those border states taught Lincoln his first principle of reconstruction policy. He would use the military to enforce the installation of a new loyal civil governor, and then go to work trying to bring the citizenry to support him. Nowhere did this policy present a greater challenge than in Kentucky. The Bluegrass State never left the Union, to be sure, but the anti-Lincoln turmoil that ran through it from top to bottom was such that Kentucky might just as well have been a sister with the states in rebellion.

From the beginning of the war Kentucky's position looked precarious. The Senate regarded her two senators, Lazarus W. Powell and John C. Breckinridge, as probable traitors, and finally expelled the latter. Her governor, Beriah Magoffin, had refused to cooperate with Lincoln in the raising of volunteers to put down the uprising, and consistently thereafter presented an obstacle to the continuing fight of the Union men in the state to keep the Bluegrass closely aligned with Washington. Gradually the legislature, safely in the hands of loyal men, eroded away his powers as governor. By the fall of 1862 he was ready to resign, turning the office over to James F. Robinson, and thus leaving the state government in sound Union hands. But Kentucky suffered special problems. Bragg's 1862 invasion alighted anew the Southern sympathies of many—if not to the degree that he had hoped—and Lincoln's Emancipation Proclamation soon thereafter incensed even many of the loyal men in the commonwealth. Robinson himself protested the measure, and the legislature, heartily anti-Lincoln, lodged a formal protest. However loyal these statesmen were to the Union, they did not necessarily equate that with loyalty to the administration then in power. So great was the outcry that Major General Horatio Gouverneur Wright, then commanding Federal troops stationed in Kentucky, believed the legislature stood on the brink of seceding. He wanted to arrest all legislators who uttered secessionist sentiments—or what he interpreted as disloyal views—and do the same to judges and other functionaries. He would place a brigade or more in Frankfort to guard the capital. President Lincoln actually approved of the plan, except for the arrests, so great did he perceive the danger. Federal officers from Kentucky began to resign their commissions in protest, and it was clearly evident that if the Union had not had a substantial military presence, the Bluegrass could very well have gone sour.[5]

The careful balance between military support of a Unionist government and simple military domination of a state proved difficult to maintain. The Union party in the legislature at Frankfort clearly felt that the proximity of force in its behalf gave them carte blanche in the fight with their opponents. When the Southern rights party in the state tried to reorganize itself to present a slate of candidates to oppose the Unionists in coming elections, the legislature refused to allow them use of the hall in the Capitol for their convention. When they tried to convene elsewhere, a Yankee colonel drew up his regiment with fixed bayonets outside and then informed the participants that he would not allow them to express disloyal sentiments. Further, if they should nominate and attempt to run candidates, he would prevent their campaigning. If they should somehow be elected, he would see that they never served. "Such meetings as this you shall not hold within the limits of my command," he said. "Disperse to your homes, and in future desist from all such attempts to precipitate civil war upon your State." His commander, General Quincy Adams Gillmore, then in charge in central Kentucky, supported the officer. "The political status of Kentucky is by no means secure," he said, "and I deem it sounder policy to arrest at once the organization of this rebel element, before it attained such impetus, strength, and character as would demand, six months hence, the exercise of force to retain the State in constitutional obedience."[6]

The action almost united the Union and Southern rights men in shared indignation that a political meeting, of whatever sort, could be disrupted by the military. Nevertheless, the Union men continued to make full use of the military at their backs. In March 1863, when they convened to nominate their own candidate for governor, they toyed with giving the nod to General Jeremiah T. Boyle, then a member of the military occupying forces. Instead it went to Joshua Bell, but he was so disturbed by the army's apparent domination of state affairs that he later declined, and Thomas Bramlette took his place. Bramlette was only recently resigned from the Federal army, and it had been he who was instrumental in the days after neutrality in 1861 in trying to arrest Breckinridge and other men merely suspected of disloyalty. A faction of the Union party broke away in protest to the military rule and provided the only real opposition in the election, but the army interfered so consistently and so pervasively that the outcome hardly resembled a free and democratic election. The military intimidated voters, tried to suppress opposition candidates, imposed an oath upon those who sought to vote, and declared martial law in July in order to prevent the disloyal from voting. Boyle issued a confiscation order, threatening the seizure of property belonging to those who were proven Confederate sympathizers, and then hinted strongly that such proof would be found in voting against the Union party. Not surprisingly, Bramlette and his party swept the polls on a voting day when thousands of intimidated and disgusted citizens simply stayed at home.[7]

So would go the course of "reconstruction" in Kentucky for the rest of the war. The state stood by the Union, but only barely, and it did not necessarily stand by Lincoln, its native son. Only the army kept the Bluegrass from falling into chaos, and this lesson Lincoln would soon apply to his other attempts at bringing the erring states back into the national government. His first real opportunity came in May 1862 when Farragut took New Orleans and a Yankee army under Benjamin F. Butler occupied the Crescent City. Much of Louisiana now lay under Union domination, and more would follow in the months to come. Ardently the President began exerting pressure on his generals in the state to get a new government established and elect representatives to the Congress.

The first problem that faced any general in Louisiana or anywhere else who wanted to start state government anew was to determine just who was and was not "loyal." All too many who had been secessionists when the war began became rapid Unionists when the Yankee armies came. Butler could do nothing more than prescribe an oath of allegiance for all who wished to vote or take part in civil government, but even that proved suspect. Several thousand former Confederate soldiers were captured with the city, yet all but three hundred took the oath. Before long some 61,000 people took the oath in the New Orleans vicinity, and those who did not, along with the 4,000 brave souls who registered themselves as enemies, saw their property subject to confiscation.

Now Butler had to arrange an election. He could only send men to Congress from the districts then under his control, for in all the conquered Southern states the Congressionally apportioned districts would initially remain the same. "In all available ways," said Lincoln, "give the people a chance to express their wishes at these elections." Emphatically he desired the participation of as many citizens as possible, for numbers would give an enhanced prestige to the restored state governments. "At all events get the expression of the largest number of the people possible." Butler encouraged the formation of citizens' Union groups as a start, all of them renouncing secession and proposing absolute yielding to Federal will. In December 1862 the general arranged for an election to fill the Congressional seats from the two districts then under his control, and Lincoln hastened to quell the fears of many Louisianians that Yankee officers from the North might try to run for the posts. Not so, said the President. He had installed George F. Shepley as military governor in Louisiana, but he made it clear that the representatives were to come from among the state's own loyal citizens, elected by them. Before Christmas the elections were held, and though the voter participation proved barely half of those eligible, still the next February two new Congressmen from the state of Louisiana took their seats in Washington. Lincoln felt absolute delight at the start thus made.[8]

Butler caused unending trouble, however. Charges of corruption in his administration in New Orleans, combined with the hatred he engendered among Southerners all across the Confederacy, forced Lincoln to replace him early in 1863 with an equally practiced politician, Nathaniel Banks. And here, perhaps, is evidence of at least some wisdom in the President's unfortunate policy of giving important commands to politicos turned soldiers. They might not have the skills to win battles, but with the battles won they could be useful instruments in implementing his policy of reestablishing functioning Union governments. Thus the sending of John C. Frémont to Missouri, of Butler and Banks to Louisiana, and of Andrew Johnson to Tennessee. It was a policy of mixed blessings.

A new problem faced Banks when he took over. Besides the garrison at Port Hudson to occupy his attention, he also faced a terrible problem with conciliation of the more influential secessionist elements in New Orleans. Loyal Louisiana quickly divided into two camps, one of those who opposed Butler and favored a more conservative approach to forming a new state government, and the other of those radically in favor of Butler's outspoken anti-slavery ideas. The Emancipation Proclamation was law already, but many Louisiana slaveholders hoped somehow to avoid its economically damaging effects by simply ignoring it, or else maintaining that the state, being now represented in Congress, was no longer in rebellion, and therefore not subject to the provisions of the edict. Banks tried manfully to appease both sides, and uniformly failed. Then came the Port

Hudson campaign, and his efforts at reconstructing the state had to be set aside for a time. On August 5, 1863, Lincoln wrote to the now-victorious Banks and urged him to renew his efforts. He wanted the state to frame a new constitution that recognized and accepted the Emancipation Proclamation. "And while she is at it," he went on, "I think it would not be objectionable for her to adopt some practical system by which the two races could gradually live themselves out of their old relation to each other, and both come out better prepared for the new." Go to work, he told Banks, "and give me a tangible nucleus which the remainder of the state may rally around as fast as it can, and which I can at once recognize and sustain." The reason for the President's sense of urgency is no mystery. He well knew that powerful forces in Congress wished to take the reconstruction matter out of his hands and impose a harsh retribution. He could only thwart them by vetoing their legislation if it passed, and by trying to bring the states back into the Union as quickly as possible lest the Congress override his veto.[9]

While Banks labored in Louisiana, Lincoln faced yet another opportunity for applying his still-evolving views on reconstruction to a Confederate state regained. Arkansas, though turbulent and still militarily volatile, came basically under Federal domination after the defeat at Pea Ridge, or at least enough for the Federals to begin efforts at establishing a government. Support for secession always ran thin among the razorbacks. In the polls of February 1861, the state's voters repudiated secession by a fair majority. They did, however, call for a state convention to decide what should be done in the crisis, and that convention adjourned with still a stand with the Union. But after the secession of Virginia and Tennessee, another convention convened, and this time the conservative element in the state, horrified at the prospect of being called on to fight against fellow "Southrons," finally won out. "Arkansas never seceded by the will of the people," said one Unionist, but only by the fevered choice of this convention.[10]

This became increasingly apparent as Union armies marched into the state. Despite the sporadic guerrilla raids and roadside bushwhackings, most of the citizens met the advancing bluecoats with indifference at worst, and often with open welcome. And of the state's Confederates, not a few held to a tenuous allegiance. Until the fall of Vicksburg, they maintained their support of the Confederacy, but after that thousands simply abandoned the cause. Edward W. Gantt, for instance, had been a congressman, and then colonel of the 12th Arkansas. But when he was turned down in his application for a commission as a brigadier general, he forthwith transferred his loyalty to the Yankees and began denouncing Confederate generals in the state and advising capitulation. One old Confederate lamented that "Most of those who were so willing to shed the last drop of blood in the contest for separate government, are entirely un-

willing to shed the *first*." Worse, with the breakdown of Confederate authority, civil chaos ensued, and any law and order, even Yankee-style,
looked better than anarchy.[11]

By late 1863 the Federal domination of the state approached completion. Little Rock fell to General Frederick Steele on September 10, and
soon thereafter Lincoln was working on the general, his de facto military
governor, to ready the state for elections and a new government. A
shadow Unionist government had in fact existed ever since secession, its
governor John Smith Phelps holding court in a St. Louis hotel room, but
the liberation of Little Rock allowed a real legislature to convene once
more. Like every other state that faced reconstruction, Arkansas would
find itself divided into several rival factions, but Steele's adept and concil-
iatory management lessened the divisiveness to a point that this state's
path back into the Union would be smoother than most.[12]

Tennessee now offered Lincoln yet another chance to put his policy
to the test. The exit of Bragg and his army left almost the entire state securely in Federal hands, though the President began addressing the restoration of the state more than a year before. On March 4, 1862, he appointed Andrew Johnson military governor. Johnson was an interesting
man. He rose from humble beginnings that rivaled Lincoln's, a native of
North Carolina, but an ardent Tennessean all his life. In 1835 he began a
modest political career that thereafter never ceased, rising to governor in
1853, and senator four years later. He was a Democrat, opposed to abolition, and in 1860 he supported Breckinridge for the Presidency. But when
war came he unequivocally proclaimed himself for the Union. That made
him, as a War Democrat and one of only two Southern senators remaining, a man of considerable influence and political usefulness.

At the same time that he made Johnson governor of Tennessee, Lincoln gave him a commission as a brigadier general, though Johnson would
never lead troops in the field. It merely made the case consistent with his
policy of military governors. To Johnson he bestowed all powers necessary
"to enable the loyal people of Tennessee to present such a republican
form of State government, as will entitle the State to the guaranty of the
United States therefor." He wanted Johnson to see that the loyal people
elected congressmen and a legislature. Johnson maintained a good hold
on affairs, and managed to bring about the election late in December
1862. But just before the polls were to open, Forrest raided deep into the
state, and then the battle at Stones River followed. Despite Bragg's retirement from the field, Rosecrans failed to pursue him and drive him out of
the state, and with an enemy army poised in middle Tennessee, the elections could not go on. Worse, eastern Tennessee still lay in the hands of
the Confederates, yet that region housed the great bulk of genuine Union
sympathizers in the state. Clearly nothing could be done until Bragg was
forced out and east Tennessee liberated. Both events, as it happened,
came at the same time that the line on Missionary Ridge collapsed.[13]

When he got word of the victory at Chattanooga, Lincoln hastened to hurry Johnson forward in his work. There must be a new state constitution that included emancipation, and a new state government. Yet Tennessee would prove slow to come around. The convention that was needed lay months in the future. Meanwhile there was a fourth and final Rebel state that the President tried to reconstruct, and indeed here his efforts dated back to the first month after Fort Sumter. Few even at the time realized that there was a Union government for the Old Dominion of Virginia.

After the state seceded, many of its loyal people came to Alexandria as soon as the Confederates were driven out in May 1861. There a chimerical "restored government" of the state came in 1863 after having existed in Wheeling for almost two years. Its governor was Francis Harrison Pierpont, and it elected a "legislature" and sent two senators to Washington. There was tremendous infighting in the western counties to see who should control the largely loyal region, and those who sought to uphold the laws had to do so by breaking them themselves. Anarchy reigned over much of the area, which Pierpont called the new State of Kanawha. By May 1862 the name had been abandoned in favor of West Virginia, and two years later the new state was formally admitted to the Union. But that left Pierpont, who claimed to be governor of Virginia, without a domain, and so he and his followers removed to Alexandria and continued to maintain the pretense of government. They drafted a new constitution that recognized emancipation, and obtained a minimal representation in Congress. It was not much, but the propaganda value of having Virginia "represented" in Washington made Lincoln patient with Pierpont.[14]

Thus, by the end of 1863 the Union looked down upon four once-Confederate states now again on the verge of returning to the mantle of the Constitution: Louisiana, Arkansas, Tennessee, and Virginia, after a fashion. As December 1863 approached, and with it the new session of Congress, Lincoln faced a battle over his whole reconstruction program. Indeed, he had yet to enunciate precisely his policy, which helped fuel his opponents' fire, but what they had seen gave them more than enough to attack. Leading the charge was Charles Sumner, a man in his way just as doctrinaire as Alexander Stephens. Neither could see that the greater good sometimes demanded the compromise of a principle. Proclaiming his doctrine of "State Suicide," he declared that in seceding, the Confederate states had killed themselves as organizations and reverted to territorial status. Clearly he was attacking Lincoln himself, for he and the Radicals greatly feared that the President would successfully reconstruct the states before these zealots in Congress would have their chance at vengeance and social revolution. All of the Confederacy, he argued, was now "under the exclusive jurisdiction of Congress." Lincoln did not defend himself in print or speech, but others did. Yet the growing conflict soon permeated even his cabinet, as Seward stood with the President while Treasury Secretary Salmon P. Chase, motivated by his own ambition for the Executive Mansion, sided with Sumner.[15]

While all this went on, Lincoln viewed with interest the elections in the Confederacy that fall. Anti-Davis men won several governorships and many seats in the Richmond Congress. Indications came from many quarters that Union sentiment—or at least a peace sentiment—was on the rise. This only confirmed his belief that harsh measures would not be needed to bring conquered states back into the Union effectively. Indeed, some of the Rebel press were already calling for an end to the war. Clearly, it was time for Lincoln to announce a policy at last, one on which he could stand and fight his detractors, and one from which he could beckon to that growing element in the Confederacy who just wanted to stop fighting and come home.

Congress convened on December 7, and the next day Lincoln sent his annual message. It began innocently enough. There was peace abroad. Britain had seen its duty and ceased outfitting enemy cruisers. Some South American matters were discussed, as were a number of other foreign and domestic topics. Then he came to the subject of the war. It went well at last. So well, in fact, that they must look now "to the present and future, and with reference to a resumption of the national authority within the States wherein that authority has been suspended." To that end, he presented them with a "Proclamation of Amnesty and Reconstruction."

It was a document delicately calculated to go far, but not too far, to injure the rebellion without hurting the rebels, to achieve much, but not too much too soon. For the reconstruction of the seceded states, he proposed a simple formula. Whenever as many as 10 percent or more of those who cast votes in the 1860 Presidential election should take an oath of allegiance to the Union and organize a state government on republican principles, that government should be recognized as the lawful existing state authority, and such state should thereafter be received into the protection of the national government, including with it the right to send once more representatives to Congress. Further, he would countenance any state constitution recognizing emancipation, even if it in some way recognized the slaves' "present condition as a laboring, landless, and homeless class." He did not propose to confiscate the property of the Rebels to give it to their former blacks.[16]

And here the President addressed another subject as well, and one that went hand in hand with reconstruction, and which promised to foment an equal controversy in his government. Amnesty. From the beginning of the war it was apparent that some kind of policy for dealing individually with former Confederates would be just as necessary as one treating with their states. As far back as the summer of 1862 discussions began that favored a general amnesty, that is, a pardon to all but certain classes of people. From his military governors like Butler, Lincoln received word that many onetime Confederates would willingly resume their allegiance to the Union if they could do so without fear of reprisal, assured that "the past would be forgiven." Indeed, Butler and others urged that the announcement of such a plan of amnesty would strike a severe blow at the Rebellion, for it would encourage many to put down their arms or even desert. Lincoln soon gave all his generals instructions to allow prisoners of war to take an oath of allegiance, yet he delayed announcing any general amnesty plan, and with good reason. Like the Emancipation Proclamation, it must come at the right time, and all during the dreadful year of 1862 and early 1863, with defeat after defeat, such a proclamation would have seemed ludicrous. Yet as 1863 came to a close, with the Union armies marching to victory on most fronts, clearly the time had arrived. Gettysburg, Vicksburg, and Chattanooga all proclaimed the inevitable failure of the Confederacy. Rumors came in increasing abundance of disaffection in the South, and even of some states talking of withdrawing from the Confederacy itself. The iron was hot, and now was the time to strike.[17]

Lincoln hinted at an amnesty during the later months of 1863, but from the first he envisioned it as a part of his overall reconstruction plan. Individuals must first be restored to their rights and privileges before they could band together to restore their states. Late in November he proposed an amnesty program to his cabinet, and the members approved it unanimously. Now he offered it to Congress.

Of course, not every Rebel could be pardoned. Some had committed crimes too grievous to forgive, or had shown a betrayal of public trust that made it inadvisable to include them with the masses. The President decided that six categories of Confederates must be excluded from his measure. All civil and diplomatic officials of the Confederate Government, from Jefferson Davis down to the ministers abroad, would not qualify. Neither would any who had left positions on the legal bench in the United States to join the uprising. Every officer above colonel in the army and lieutenant in the navy should be excluded, and so should all who left seats in the United States Congress or who resigned commissions in the army and navy. And anyone who mistreated white or black prisoners of war could not look to this proclamation for forgiveness.

Besides these exemptions, all others now in the rebellion might be restored to their rights and privileges as citizens unmolested and unafraid of confiscation of property, so long as they swore to a simple oath of allegiance that bound them to "support, protect, and defend" the Constitution and the Union, and to abide by the laws and proclamations passed during the war, including those relating to emancipation. Furthermore, though Lincoln waited another three months to make it explicit, he also envisioned that even those excluded from the general amnesty might individually apply for pardon. Their cases would be judged individually on their own merits, whereas with the great mass of Confederates no questions or qualifications would be asked other than the oath. Indeed, just a few days before Lincoln's message to Congress he had already granted a special pardon to one who would be left out of the amnesty, Colonel Gantt. More than that, when Gantt took the oath and received his pardon, he also received a commission in the Union army! Thus "the merciful disposition of the President" toward even the higher-ranking Confederates made itself known. Certainly some would have to be punished, but only those of demonstrable criminal acts.[18]

The amnesty and pardon program, like the rest of Lincoln's reconstruction scheme, met with mixed reactions, North and South. In the Confederacy it did not become at all well known for some time, and certainly Southern authorities made no effort to publicize what was clearly an invitation to desertion. Some Yankee commanders attempted to circulate handbills announcing the policy to the men in the Confederate ranks, but the clandestine endeavor met with poor results, and only served to arouse the ire of the gray-clad commanders. Longstreet, always contentious whether with friend or foe, chided one Union general, "And now, the most ignoble of all, you propose to degrade the human race by inducing soldiers to dishonor and forswear themselves." In the Confederate press, of course, Lincoln was raked over the coals and his proclamation called a desperate act, his exhortation to desertion a clear revelation that the North was losing the war. Only a few editors saw with the vision of the Savannah *Republican*. It, too, condemned the amnesty offer, but then fathomed that behind it lay a Northern conviction of triumph. "It may be a delusion with them," said the journal, "but they believe in it and it may be death to us." Unless the South aroused itself to the true condition of affairs, the Yankees, believing themselves about to triumph, would redouble their efforts and in the end would do so. That done, said the *Republican*, "we are a doomed people."[19]

Not everyone in the North accepted the amnesty with much more grace. "The Despot's Edict," some called it. The Copperhead and conservative press denounced the measure as autocratic and degrading to the South, while the Radical journals complained that it was too lenient upon those who should be made to howl for their crimes. And at least one segment condemned the measure, and anyone who accepted amnesty under it. Should the South accept the terms, "the degradation they offer will not be half as severe as should be inflicted upon a people who could accept that degradation." Any Confederate who shamed himself by accepting such a pardon "should be compelled to change positions with the slaves." No real American would try to inflict such a humiliation upon his fellow citizens.[20]

Despite the outcry from both sides, the announcements contained in Lincoln's proclamation for amnesty and reconstruction struck a responsive chord with the majority of the people of the Union. They were fair, they were reasonable, and the measures were eminently American, filled with that mix of practicality and compassion which most Americans liked to think characterized their nation. "Nothing," wrote William Cullen Bryant, "could be more magnanimous." Despite the opposition to the principle of Presidential reconstruction, many in Congress approved at first, and one of the President's secretaries even claimed that "I have never seen such an effect produced by a public document." But it did not take long for the Radicals to rise again in opposition. The measure, like so many of Lincoln's, did not go far enough. They wanted the extreme; he always contented himself with traveling to the center.[21]

However, even the Radicals did not argue with one often-overlooked portion of the annual message and proclamation. Lincoln saw more than just Southern states and Southern people that needed reconstruction. The documents also began a program for the "reconstruction" of the freed Southern slaves. Couched within its conditions for the recognition of the Emancipation Proclamation, demanding that the states "recognize and declare their permanent freedom," was a clause that introduced for the first time the expectation that the reconstructed states would "provide for their education" as well. Here, as everywhere in his proclamation, the President tried to look ahead to anticipate the needs that would come with the inevitable peace.[22]

Now it was time to pursue the reconstruction of the states under this plan, or to try. Congress would soon rally itself to fight Lincoln, that he knew. It is no surprise that immediately after he delivered his annual message he began anew to press his military governors to get new constitutions written for Louisiana, Arkansas, and Tennessee, and to elect new governments. Louisiana would be able to report and vote on a constitution by April of the next year. That looked promising. Arkansas looked to March 1864 to convene and vote on a new constitution. In Tennessee it would take longer, perhaps not until the following fall. All he could do was to press his governors as he pressed his generals. "I think the thing should be pushed forward," he said. There was a note of desperation in his exhortations to haste. He knew that he and Congress did not stand together on this subject. They were and would be working at odds. The best he could hope for was that he had foreseen the need for a reconstruction program and provided a reasonable basis for it. If he could hold Congress at bay, he could implement the plan as more and more states fell to his armies. No matter that the plan had its flaws, that it did not cover all possible contingencies. It was magnanimous, as a victor could afford to be magnanimous. If he could bring the South back into the Union as painlessly as possible, perhaps he could prevent the generation of decades of hostility and resentment that might follow. He did not just see his task of ending the war. There was more than that. Perhaps already in his mind he heard a voice calling him to "bind up the nation's wounds." It was a great challenge. It tasked him, and his generals as well, for on their victories rested the future of his reconstruction. They must be swift and decisive if he could hope to live to see the nation reunited as he envisioned. All depended upon his generals, and upon how long Lincoln lived.[23]

CHAPTER 17

"IT HAS PROVED
A FAR BETTER YEAR"

The war seemed to take a life of its own as the winter of 1863 sent the worst cold in decades sweeping across the country. The chilly north wind brought more than Yankee troops to the doorstep of Georgia and Alabama, to Virginia and North Carolina. It brought more hunger, more privation, more discontent. And in the old Union there came a war weariness. This was the third war winter. How many more would there be? "It has proved a far better year for the country than it promised at its birth," wrote a New Yorker. He looked ahead to 1864 with hope for better things to come, wishing a Happy New Year to all but Jefferson Davis and his government. "To them, I wish virtue enough to withstand urgent daily temptations to hang themselves." It was bold talk, and he knew it, for to himself he confided that "only a very bold man can prophesy for a whole year ahead in these times."[1]

He would be bolder yet to make that prediction on the basis of what had happened in the war in the East after Gettysburg, for both Lee and Meade showed something approaching timidity in their campaigns for the balance of the season. It was as if the shock of Gettysburg, both for victor and vanquished, could not be overcome. Lee marched south with an army almost shattered by the battle in Pennsylvania, his command system in a shambles. Too many good officers had been lost or put out of action. Only three of his division commanders had been at their posts for a year or more. Of his thirty-eight infantry brigades, only five now followed men who had been brigadiers as much as a year. Reorganizing as he retreated, Lee found himself with virtually a new high command, much of it untested. As for Meade, he suffered the same problem in a lesser degree. He complained of "the want of active and energetic subordinate officers, men upon whom I can depend and rely upon taking care of themselves and commands." He felt deeply the loss of the dead Reynolds, and of Hancock now out of action with his wounds. "Their places are not to be supplied," he groaned. He hardly lamented the loss of Sickles.[2]

Still Meade could bring himself to conceive of another stroke at Lee, even if he did not vigorously pursue it at first. The Army of Northern Virginia crossed the Potomac back into Virginia on July 14 and moved slowly back up the Shenandoah. Three days later Meade put the Army of the Potomac across as well and started moving south, just east of the Blue Ridge, parallel to Lee's route. And once on the march, the Federals considerably outdistanced the Confederates for a change. Meade kept himself between Lee and Richmond all along the march. As the Confederates came to each of the Blue Ridge gaps by which they might cross to the east, they found Meade there first. He was feeling his strength again gradually. Even after Gettysburg the Federals counted 86,000, and Lee could muster barely more than half that. Though Meade considerably exaggerated Lee's strength, even suggesting that he was being reinforced by Bragg, still the Yankee commander believed that he could pen up the enemy in the Shenandoah if he closed all these gaps, thereby cutting Lee off from Richmond and leaving the Confederate capital isolated and easy prey.

Lee knew what Meade was about, but could not effectively stop him. By July 22 Meade's forward elements reached Manassas Gap, while the Army of Northern Virginia lay spread out in a long thin marching line in the valley below. Meade ordered Major General William Henry French, now commanding Sickles' old III Corps, to attack the next day. If successful, it would undoubtedly shatter Lee's rear and flank. But French was no fighter. For all of his faults, Sickles would have blundered forth from Manassas Gap and launched headlong into the enemy. French did not, and they escaped him. Meade planned a major assault the next day, but when the dawn came the enemy had slipped away. With it went the most glowing opportunity ever afforded a Federal commander in the East, for at no other time of the war would Lee's army be so vulnerable to utter annihilation. Meade was terribly disappointed, as were his commanders, and all of them lost considerable confidence in the timid French. A few days later Lee finally crossed the Blue Ridge and concentrated his army around Culpeper. Meade, content now to await another opportunity, moved to the Rappahannock fifteen miles away. The great battle of Manassas Gap that might well have ended the war in Virginia, and made Meade a hero to rival Grant, died aborning.[3]

The armies rested in August, their first real opportunity since Gettysburg. A depressed Lee, seeing desertions mounting, particularly in his North Carolina regiments, believed that the army had lost confidence in him after the defeat in Pennsylvania. To President Davis he offered his resignation, but the Mississippian would not hear of it. Steadfast as he could be in sustaining an incompetent like Bragg, this President stood even firmer in his confidence in the finest commander in his service. Lee would remain, and probably no single decision Davis ever made did more to lengthen the life of the Confederacy.[4]

Now was the time for a brief shift in policy. Everywhere, it seemed, the South was losing ground: Gettysburg, Vicksburg, Port Hudson. Charleston had not fallen, but the enemy was attacking in increasing numbers. Obviously the only way to reverse the trend was for the South to strike some great blow that would regain for them the initiative. Where? Bragg suggested that he and Johnston join and crush Grant. Others wanted the reverse, that they meet instead and defeat Rosecrans. Lee expressed a feeling that if properly reinforced, he might take the offensive and drive Meade out of Virginia. There were arguments against all, but in the end it was "Old Pete" Longstreet who won out. He, too, wanted a concentration against Rosecrans, but Johnston's troops from Mississippi were not up to it. Instead, he wanted to see Bragg reinforced from the Army of Northern Virginia, and this of course is what happened. Longstreet and two of his divisions left for Tennessee, and their triumph at Chickamauga.[5]

The intelligence that Lee had weakened his army did not stay a secret for long, and when Meade learned of it he determined to renew his offensive. On September 13, just one day after Longstreet himself departed, the Federal cavalry crossed the Rappahannock and began to operate on Lee's flank. Meade crossed his army soon thereafter and began a march calculated to bring on a decisive battle. Lee retired several miles to poise behind the Rapidan, and then came the news of the disaster at Chickamauga. At once Hooker and two of Meade's corps were detached to go west, effectively stalling his offensive. By October 1 Lee learned of the weakening of his opponent, and decided to seize the initiative himself. Meade was not fooled, but decided not to accept a battle now. Thus, while Lee tried to turn his flank and cut him off from Washington, Meade outran him once more in a withdrawal that went more than forty miles back toward Washington, to the old Bull Run battlefield near Centreville. Meade never gave Lee a good opportunity to attack him with a hope of success, something none of his predecessors had managed, and it was only on October 14 that a clash finally came.

Near Bristoe Station, ten miles south of Centreville on the Orange & Alexandria, General A. P. Hill finally came up with Meade's rear guard and attacked. Hill mistook French's III Corps for the only Federals present, and completely missed the II Corps, now led by General Gouverneur Warren. Warren's command lay concealed in wait for the enemy, and when Hill sent his first two brigades forward they were almost destroyed in a cross fire. Confederate losses came to nearly 2,000, while Meade's ran only one fourth that cost. Hill himself felt mortified. He knew that he had not properly reconnoitered the enemy, else how could he have failed to see an entire Union corps, even if they were behind defenses. He took the full responsibility upon himself. Lee understood, though deeply pained. "Well, well, General," he said to Hill, "bury these poor men and let us say no more about it." How he missed his Jackson.[6]

Now it was Lee's turn to run again. The check at Bristoe took all the steam out of his advance. He had outrun his supply lines and faced Meade in a formidable position. He could do nothing but withdraw once more to the Rappahannock and await the return of Longstreet or some Federal folly that might give him another opportunity. He could hardly expect that now, for Lee was discovering that Meade was not like those he had faced before. If less daring, so was the Pennsylvanian less careless. He possessed not the conceit of brag and bluster, but the self-confidence of professionalism. Lee knew that he did not face another McClellan or Pope.

Meade pursued, slowly, as he had to rebuild the Orange & Alexandria as a supply line, and also as he had to fight Washington in his rear. The Radicals clamored for his replacement thanks to his failure to trounce Lee completely after Gettysburg. Even Lincoln ranted occasionally, but admitted, "What can I do with such generals as we have? Who among them is any better than Meade?" Personal relations between President and general improved, and where in the early fall Lincoln feared for Meade to risk another general engagement, now he pressed for it. The two could not agree for a time on a plan of attack, but early in November the Army of the Potomac moved south once more, intent upon forcing Lee back from the Rappahannock and using the excellent fall weather to outmarch and outfight the enemy.[7]

On November 7 the campaign began, and at once it inflicted upon the Confederates a humiliating reverse. Lee had withdrawn his army behind the Rappahannock, but wanted to hold a good crossing place in case an opportunity should present itself for him to strike across the stream at Meade's flank. Accordingly, he placed a strong guard at Kelly's Ford, and then fortified a bridgehead on the north side at Rappahannock Bridge, on the Orange & Alexandria. But when the Federals advanced, they easily pushed their way through Kelly's Ford, and the command at the Rappahannock Bridge, two full brigades, was all but swallowed up without a real fight. "It is absolutely sickening," wrote an officer of the Confederate II Corps. "Oh, how every day is proving the value of General Jackson to us!"[8]

But now the Yankees were across, and forcing Lee to withdraw behind the Rapidan once more. When nothing happened in the two weeks that followed, Lee began the work of preparing for the winter, though ever mindful that Meade might still strike at him before the cold weather came. For his part, Meade was taking his time, rebuilding the railroad for a supply line, and meticulously planning his next move. He remembered too well the nightmare of Fredericksburg, when the Federals attacked across a river against fortified Confederates. He would not try that again on the Rapidan. Instead, he conceived a plan to march downstream unknown to Lee, cross at Germanna and Ely's fords, and then sweep back up the south side of the Rapidan. At that moment, Richard Stoddard Ewell and the II Corps stood along the river itself, while A. P. Hill and the III Corps lay several miles south near Orange Court House. If Meade could drive between them before they discovered his movement and linked, he could destroy both. While the rest of the Army of the Potomac moved in support maneuvers, Meade put the real fighting in the hands of his best corps commander, John Sedgwick, and his worst, French. There was little choice, for they commanded the two largest corps in the army. Meade's plans were precise to the final detail, flawed only by their precision, allowing little for the unexpected. The unexpected was, in fact, one of the few things that a Civil War general could always count on.[9]

On November 23 Meade gave the order. The army would march on the morrow. But then came the first delay. Rain swelled the rivers and mired the roads. He postponed the advance for two days. Almost from the first General French and his leading division commander, Brigadier General Henry Prince, dallied, failing to make their allotted mileage. Worse, a miscalculation resulted in the pontoons brought to erect a bridge being too few. The river was wider than expected. All told, a full day was lost right at the outset before the Army of the Potomac got across the Rapidan, and Lee's outposts discovered the advance even as the first Federals were crossing. He ordered Hill to bring his corps onto the field, and directed Jubal Anderson Early, commanding the II Corps instead of the ailing Ewell, to delay Meade's advance while also establishing a line along the west bank of Mine Run, a creek that flowed north into the Rapidan directly between the two armies. If need be, Lee would stand behind the creek to defend his ground.

Skirmishing became almost constant as Meade advanced toward Mine Run. Soon Warren and the II Corps was in line and ready to attack, but no one knew what had happened to French. "Where the devil is French?" Meade asked. Yet French and Prince, with only four miles to cover that day, were sitting some distance back of the field arguing, sometimes incoherently, about which road to take. It did not help that French was almost reeling drunk. Later in the day Major General Edward "Allegheny Ed" Johnson's Confederate division moved east of the Mine

Run line and struck at Prince and his division. In a deft and daring fight, they stopped Prince from advancing for the rest of the day. In so doing, they also stopped the rest of French's and the II Corps, and in doing that they halted Sedgwick and the VI Corps behind them. Johnson, with only 545 casualties, kept 36,000 men from joining Warren. That gave Hill time to bring his corps into the Mine Run line and erect such defenses as they could.

The next day, November 28, Meade ordered Warren forward to attack, only to find that Lee had pulled his entire army behind Mine Run, and now looked across the stream at the Federals from behind a formidable line of defenses. Meade's whole plan of surprise had come to naught, but he was not yet ready to abandon the campaign. All day he and his corps commanders reconnoitered the enemy lines. Finally they agreed that Warren would march south, attempting to find a way around Lee's right flank, while Sedgwick believed he had spotted a place on the enemy left that offered a good chance of success. All the next day Meade massed his corps on his two wings for the attack. Finally on November 30 the great battle began. Almost at once it fizzled. Warren found that Lee had strongly reinforced his front, and now he told Meade that he could not attack. "The works cannot be taken," he told his commanding general. "I would sooner sacrifice my commission . . . than . . . my men." The men themselves felt considerable relief when the attack was canceled. All through the night they heard the sounds of spade and axe across the creek, as the enemy fortified their high ground. Many of the Federals had spent their last minutes pinning slips of paper on their uniforms, that they might be identified if killed.

At first Meade raged, and flew over to Warren to see for himself. Warren was right, and Meade sustained him entirely in his decision to stop the attack. The rest of the army saw the wisdom of it as well, all but the blustering French. "Where is your young Napoleon?" he complained of Warren. "Why don't we hear the sounds of his guns?" Yet there were others who saw through French's foolishness. "Wherever the fault lies," wrote one officer, "I shall always be astonished at the extraordinary moral courage of General Meade, which enabled him to order a retreat when his knowledge as an engineer and a soldier showed that an attack would be a blunder. The men and guns stood ready; he had only to snap his fingers, and that night would probably have seen ten thousand wretched, mangled creatures lying on those long slopes, exposed to the bitter cold and out of reach of all help."

And retreat is what Meade decided to do. The winter was almost upon him. His supplies were dwindling and, believing that the enemy numbers were greater than they actually were, he saw nothing before him now but another matching of blow for blow with little to gain and much to lose. He ordered the army to withdraw back north of the Rapidan, and just in time, for Lee was ready to take the offensive. When Meade failed to attack on November 30, Lee believed that the Federal initiative was exhausted. Now he saw an opportunity to send Hill and two divisions on a sweeping flank march around Meade's left, just as Jackson had marched around Hooker's right at Chancellorsville. On December 2 Hill struck, but found only the debris of a withdrawn army and the remains of the thousands of campfires that the Federals left behind to fool the Rebels into thinking they were still there. When the Yankees recrossed the river, they found one of their bands playing a popular tune, "Oh, Ain't You Glad to Get Out of the Wilderness!"[10]

And so, at year's end, the situation in Virginia lay as it almost always did, unchanged. The Federals were no closer to Richmond or to defeating Lee decisively than they had been the year before. The Confederates still held their capital and most of their beloved Virginia. The only real success in the East after Gettysburg came at Charleston where, after months of virtual siege, Battery Wagner finally fell to the Federals. Yet still Sumter and Charleston itself defied Lincoln's minions. Only in the West did the course of resolution move ahead, only there was one side winning in the field real victories, the vanquished losing real losses. Lee lost little more than good men at Gettysburg—some of them great men—but in eastern Tennessee Bragg and the Confederates were losing the heartland of the South. Indeed, the very day that Meade's army finally went back into camp north of the Rapidan, after accomplishing nothing and losing nothing, the decisive campaign for Tennessee came to an end in Federal victory.

It ended in the shattered dreams of glory of "Old Pete" Longstreet. Ardently he wanted an independent command, the chance to shine on his own instead of beneath the shadow of Lee. His falling out with Bragg after Chickamauga made it much easier for him to press his hopes, and President Davis readily approved the plan for Longstreet to move with his corps—two divisions really—to try to take Knoxville from the enemy. The plan begged for defeat from the first. Bragg thought the Federals at Knoxville would fall quickly to Longstreet, enabling him to return to face Grant at Chattanooga. But Longstreet would have only 15,000 to face 22,000 or more Federals. All of his support facilities from supply to transportation were broken down or inadequate. And Bragg would give him enough troops to fatally weaken the army at Chattanooga, without being sufficient to defeat the enemy at Knoxville. Faced with the prospect of ensured success at the latter place, or a fair chance at the former, Bragg opted to go halfway on both and hope for the best.

He got far less. Longstreet's campaign to Knoxville would prove to be the most mismanaged Confederate campaign of the war. The expedition began on November 2, but delays prevented any movement at all for several days. It was November 14 before Longstreet had moved his command to a point below Knoxville where he could cross the Tennessee, and there the Federals were ready for him. Ambrose Burnside had been sent from

Virginia with part of the IX Corps back in March, his orders to take Knoxville. But then came demands for the Vicksburg siege and Rosecrans' own movements in the Tullahoma region, so that it was September before Burnside finally occupied the east Tennessee city with elements of the IX and XXIII Corps. From this vantage point he posed a constant threat to southwestern Virginia via Cumberland Gap, which he took from the Confederates on September 9. If Longstreet could drive him out he could open up again the vital East Tennessee Railroad that linked Chattanooga with Virginia via Knoxville, force Grant to dilute his strength facing Bragg, and perhaps win a permanent independent command, maybe even replacing Bragg.

Thus Longstreet decided to try to take Burnside before he retired into the Knoxville defenses. But Burnside himself was intent upon pulling back before doing battle. Thus the two armies engaged in a footrace as the Confederates for three days chased and tried vainly to catch the retiring Yankees. When they did briefly come up with Burnside, the Rebels tried to launch an attack with an artillery barrage, but the ammunition proved so faulty that most shells did not explode at all, and others went off prematurely. Darkness prevented the infantry from heeding "Old Pete's" attack order, and his own generals then fell to feuding among themselves over who had failed first and why. Meanwhile, by late on November 16, Burnside had his army safely inside the Knoxville defenses, and formidable they were. Though hastily erected, the line of works proved powerful indeed, lines of breastworks across the western approaches to the city being anchored at top and bottom on two forts, Sanders and Smith.

When the Confederates came to the outskirts of the city, they hastily reconnoitered the enemy lines, and were dismayed by what they saw. Still, engineers detected what they took to be a weak spot at Fort Sanders that made an infantry assault possible. At once Longstreet began preparations, but that is all he did at once. Somehow he managed to consume the next eleven days in "preparations." There was bickering again among his subordinates. Then he waited for two more brigades to join him from Bragg's army. All this time Burnside worked feverishly to strengthen his position, and then the arrival of Brigadier General Danville Leadbetter in Longstreet's camp gave the Yankees even more time. The oldest engineer in the Confederate service, and a man whose views were much valued by Bragg, Leadbetter now counseled a different point of attack. Once more "Old Pete" put off his attack until the matter could be settled and Leadbetter could make a thorough examination of the enemy works. Dawn came on November 28, 1863, before Longstreet finally felt ready to launch his assault. But then the weather interfered, and he postponed the engagement until the next morning, to follow an artillery barrage. Now Leadbetter stepped in one more time, persuading Longstreet that the attack would be more successful if made by surprise during the dark hours. That meant no barrage. Edward Porter Alexander, Longstreet's chief of artillery, believed that this cost them the battle.

Before dawn on November 29 the Confederates attacked. They became at once confused and intermingled, slowed by entangling telegraph wire strung in front of the Federal works. Then they tried to climb and crawl up the sloping sides of Fort Sanders' parapet, only to find them glazed with frozen dew and rain. In a few minutes thousands of milling Confederates stood scrambling in the ditch at the foot of the parapet while the Yankees above threw all manner of projectiles at them, including artillery shells with lit fuses. It was an utter failure, and soon the men pulled back. Longstreet ordered another attack, but just then came word of the rout at Missionary Ridge. Now "Old Pete" was isolated in east Tennessee, with no choice but to get out as best he could. He stayed in front of Knoxville until December 3, hoping to draw some Yankees away from Bragg, and succeeding. Then he made his way slowly to Russellville, Tennessee, just thirty miles from Virginia, and settled down for the winter. All he finally succeeded in achieving was severe embarrassment to Burnside, who asked to be relieved of his command after censure for not pursuing the Confederates, and the holding of a substantial number of Federals in east Tennessee to guard against a winter attack. It came at the cost of 1,296 casualties, and the harmony within the I Corps' command. In the long winter months that followed, Longstreet began his own campaign against his own generals, eventually preferring charges against three of them when, in fact, virtually all the general officers of the corps bore the responsibility of a bungled campaign. There it ended.[11]

And so ended the turn of war's wheel for 1863. It had been a long fifteen months since Antietam, a long year since the Emancipation Proclamation, and always the wheel moved in circles, yet ever forward toward its as yet unseen destination. It had spun Lee out of Maryland in 1862, to spin him back north again, and out again, in 1863. Its fickle whim gave him victory at Fredericksburg and Chancellorsville, and defeat at Gettysburg, and after all that effort left him no better off than when he began, but much the worse. The wheel grasped Burnside and Hooker and nearly flung them off into oblivion, only to land out West in Tennessee. At Charleston it revolved like the turrets of Dahlgren's monitors, turning uselessly in the futile attempt to reduce Fort Sumter and eliminate the seedbed of the rebellion.

But in the West the ironshod juggernaut moved with a slower turn, yet the more devastating. It elevated men and generals to greatness less rapidly than in the East, and hurled them to ignominy that much slower. Bragg would not have lasted so long in Virginia, nor would Grant's rise have been as slow. Victories and losses out here seemed too distant, too removed from Washington and Richmond for the speedy reaction occasioned by a Chancellorsville. The slow and crushing turn of the tire made campaigns last longer and caused them to be more destructive. The grinding wheel of war was devastating the South. If it lost its war, as it was losing it all through 1863, the defeat would be ghastly. If somehow it should still win its cause, there might be only the shadow of a nation to celebrate the victory.

Much then depended on how the North and the South used this coming winter. It would be a cruelly cold season, one of the most severe within memory in the South. Men of both sides would sit huddled for warmth around pitiful fires in their rude winter huts. In the Confederacy food would be even more scarce than usual. In the Army of Tennessee at Dalton, some Confederates had to scavenge at the horses' feeding places, looking for stray kernels of grain left by the animals. It proved a time of introspection and resolution, of despair and desertion. Two nations grown weary on war hardly looked forward to the coming of the spring.

Yet that season would bring changes, as spring always does, and in that the men and women of Union and Confederacy could find some heart. Some changes came too late, some too soon, and some not at all, but Americans of the time, as of all times, could see hope for something better in another spring. The crops promised to be good in 1864, an especially beneficial prospect for the Confederacy, which had less land now to grow them. No matter how often the war wheel trespassed over the furrowed fields, they always sprang once more to life with a new season. However vicious the fighting and the bitterness of side against side, these men in blue and gray stopped short of sowing salt in enemies' fields. They might kill enemy Americans, but they could not destroy the American land. It was the prudent course, the middle road that even a civil war would follow when fought by Americans.

Round and round the disc had spun. Southerners in 1861 rebelled against the tyranny of an oppressive central government as they saw it. Opposition to it—disloyalty by some standard—ran so high that finally it ceased to be a "loyal opposition." And so came secession. Now, almost three years later, Southerners once again stood at the verge of rebellion against a grasping, oppressive, tyrannical government, this time their own. Secession threatened, plots were fomented, treason practiced its arts. Everything had changed since the South left the Union, yet somehow it all seemed the same. What had not changed was the essential nature of the people themselves. As the war went spiraling onward, many Confederates would have difficulty knowing precisely who the enemy was, Mr. Lincoln and his army, or themselves.

And did it differ much above Mason and Dixon's line? Lincoln began this war a minority President with a minority administration. Only secession left them in the ascendancy. His draft and enlistment calls were resisted in 1861, and so were they now. There would always be enough men, but would he always have enough of them in Congress to sustain him? Only by tampering with elections, it seems, could some states be kept in line. Surely there was oppression, and thousands clamored against it. The coming year would bring another Presidential election. The opposition, the Democrats, however loyal to the Union, were not so loyal to the war or to his prosecution of it. Who would sustain him in 1864, and how well? He felt in his heart that his armies could not lose this war, but it could be lost at the polls. There was talk of other candidates. Of McClellan or Franklin Pierce for the Democrats. Of Frémont for the Republicans. With McClellan or Pierce at their head, the Democrats might end the war without reunion. With Frémont the Republicans might give the war away in pure foolishness. Lincoln sat just as uneasily in his chair now as he did in 1861. Nothing had changed, it seemed.

In the nations that those two Presidents ruled, the turning fortune of the conflict left varied tracks. The people and industry and economy of the South lay in near shambles. There were still men enough to fill the armies, though they were harder to find, and harder still to keep in the ranks. But the problems of 1861 became anew the problems of 1863, and would go on. The war began its spin with too few manufactories, too few skilled workers, too little capital. The surge of patriotic enthusiasm swept the Confederacy into a miniature internal revolution of sorts. By 1862 almost all of Southern industry converted to war production, and at the fullest capacity possible, only to see 1863 come to an end with a plant that lay exhausted, unserviced, in need of parts and replacement and repair that was not to be had. Those shells of Longstreet's that failed to explode properly at Knoxville were Southern-made and standard-issue, and by 1863 they were about the best that Confederate resources and workers and factories could produce. Up and down again with a turn of the wheel had gone the Confederate industrial effort. Their enemies to the north suffered a kinder fate, since they enjoyed a land more blessed with raw materials and fuels and factories which could be made into a war machine. More blessed, too, were they in the people to work that industrial plant. Not just men with skills, now, but women as well, and children in some factories. The lot of the rural woman, North or South, war or no war, was always hard. Yet in some places they were breaking out of their crinolines and homespun. How long they stayed out depended on the war, and whether or not they stayed out permanently would depend on the men when the wheel thrust them home again.

For all the importance of society and economy and industry and morale and loyalty at home, the hub of that wheel remained the armies. So long as they turned and turned about the countryside, so long then would the war go on. Whatever changed and whatever did not change at home, in the field the men of arms still carried the war on their lean and sinewed frames. They too moved in circles, dizzy from the spinning, it sometimes seemed, yet there were changes coming to them as surely as the turn of season. Spring touched everything.

Old faces were going, some of them. No more will Rosecrans cast his queer half-smile over the Army of the Cumberland. "Old Rosey" will go to Missouri for the duration. No more, too, of Theophilus Holmes, an old man who only wants to be left alone. Poor John C. Pemberton has seen his last days of high command, with all its heartache, and so, too, has the ever-scheming John McClernand. It will be back to politics for him in time. Many leave the field not quite whole. Dan Sickles lost his leg at Gettysburg, and with it any further military career, to the great relief of his superiors. And to the eternal dismay of the Confederacy, Thomas Jonathan "Stonewall" Jackson lost an arm and a life, and much of the best hope of his cause.

Others kept their hold on the wheel more firm, hanging on until it spun them to some new place, some new plateau. It seemed for a time that the defeat that crushed Bragg at Missionary Ridge might have crushed John C. Breckinridge as well. His first real corps command had disintegrated shamefully before his eyes. Bragg was campaigning against him again, and Bragg had gone to Richmond where he had the President's ear. The Kentuckian's was a curious trip on the spinning cycle of the war anyhow. He never wanted it, did not believe in it, and doubted from the first that the Confederacy could succeed. Yet he rose high in its military counsels, and commanded considerable political influence should he ever break his vow not to use it. And now this winter the disaster of Chattanooga cast him from the Army of Tennessee. He landed in southwest Virginia, assigned by the President to a graveyard department that had eclipsed eight commanders before him, and almost tarnished even Lee. It would be a favorite raiding ground of Federals, of that he was certain. Yet it might serve as well as a jumping-off place. Just across the line lay Kentucky, and the old dream died hard. It came in 1861, and again in 1862. Might it not come once more in 1864? Only the turnings of fortune could tell what Breckinridge and his department might encounter. The war had seemingly cast him down. Might it raise him again?[12]

Wade Hampton fastened his grip on fortune's spin despite the pain of his Gettysburg wounds. He held on to be promoted to major general the month after the battle, though when he would return to the field, healed, no one could say. He would be Jeb Stuart's second-in-command if again he mounted his giant warhorse with the cavalry of the Army of Northern Virginia. Should Stuart fall, what would Hampton do in his place? Such men did fall, and Stuart liked a fight too much for safety.

What of Kirby-Smith and "Kirby-Smithdom"? There was promotion in the war for him. In February 1864 the President and Congress designated him a full general, though perhaps the title of emperor would have been more fitting. Would the growth in rank help him to sustain the largest territorial command in the Confederacy in utter isolation from the rest of the nation? He had traveled a lot in this war, it seemed, almost as much as Breckinridge. From Virginia to Tennessee to Kentucky to the Trans-Mississippi, the higher he rose in rank the farther he seemed to recede from the active seat of the war. Where on the circle he might next alight no one could say. Indeed, one thing that never changed is that all too many failed to recognize that Kirby-Smith or his department existed at all. Longstreet knew it, however, and resented it. He and Kirby-Smith made lieutenant general on the same day, and "Old Pete" had ranked him in the old army. Now the younger Kirby-Smith was elevated higher on the rolls than he. The Georgian toyed with resignation in protest, but as always before he came around. He was a Confederate first.

Not so Braxton Bragg. He resigned and meant it, though in the passage of a short time he hoped to regain his army and redeem his disgrace. His enemies cost him Chattanooga, not his own folly. Indeed, just weeks after he left the army he felt that "I believe, from what I hear, that I could do more good by returning to my old place than in any other." He will claim that he resigned only to reveal to the world that the clamoring against him in the army came from a few who "were actuated by one of two motives, *Ambition* and *Revenge*." Yet somehow Davis began to see through it all. He still believed in his old friend. The President never abandoned a friend however incompetent. He called him to Richmond to be his chief military adviser. Having failed as a general in the field, Braxton Bragg would now help formulate military policy for the entire nation, as strange and inexplicable a cast of fate as this war would see.[13]

Called to fill his place as the spring approached was another whom the spinning wheel cast alternately up, then down. Many were the generals considered for the Western command. Davis first thought of Pierre G. T. Beauregard, whose own fortunes ebbed low in 1863. But the President despised him. Would not Lee accept the command? He would not. Since the Confederacy had but five full generals, that left but one choice. Bragg was in Richmond, Lee with his army, Kirby-Smith in the Trans-Mississippi, and Beauregard unacceptable. Only Joseph E. Johnston remained, and Davis despised him as much as he loathed Beauregard. But Johnston was unwittingly the favorite of the anti-Davis party in the capital. Appointing him might in some way quiet them, a vain hope at best, but on December 16, 1863, the President offered the troublesome Virginian the command, and he took it. Once more, the general who engineered the first Confederate victory of the war had an army. A year before he had been in near oblivion. Now he lay entrusted with the fate of nearly the entire central Confederacy. His fate, once the spring came, might well be that of his cause.[14]

Johnston would not decide that fate alone in the West. Other men, men in blue, found themselves thrust up by their talents and their fortune. New names emerged from the lists of minor commanders. One of them was Philip Henry Sheridan. He started as a quartermaster in Missouri and Mississippi, then was a cavalryman, a brigadier general at Stones River, and a major general of a division at Chickamauga. He it was who first led his men over the crest at Missionary Ridge. He was a small man, his brow an unyielding frown, his grasp a bulldog's, his mercy barely extant. Such men could win wars, and now he had been noticed. Fortune never stopped rising for "Little Phil."

Better still fared the Rock of Chickamauga. George H. Thomas possessed little personality, little dash, and no flair. Yet he was, as his sobriquet declared, a rock. He stayed steady and cool. If he had scant imagination, still he felt no fear. With the fall of Rosecrans, "Old Pap" rose in his place. He was a Virginian of unquestioned loyalty to the Union, so much so that he and his family lay estranged. Always he fought hard and well. He doubted that he should hold the army command at times, and this war showed often that men who doubted themselves frequently did so with just cause, yet he had deserved it, and he made the Army of the Cumberland into one of the finest fighting machines in the Union service.

The promise of the spring held much for Thomas, but his fortune would depend upon that of another, his old West Point classmate William T. Sherman. Surely fate practiced its mercurial art more upon Sherman in this war than any other. The debacle at Bull Run almost eclipsed his career as it began, and then when reports of insanity surrounded his command in Kentucky, he was relieved of command for a time. He and Grant shared in being surprised at Shiloh, and only their final victory saved him from certain oblivion. In the next year he survived Chickasaw Bluffs and McClernand and a hostile press, and finally emerged from a captured Vicksburg with a secure hold on his position. The capture of Chattanooga only added to his reputation. By February 1864 he was conducting a highly successful campaign to Meridian, Mississippi, to destroy the Confederate communications in the state's interior. When he returns to Nashville in March, he will find himself placed in command of all Union armies west of the Alleghenies and east of the Mississippi. He it was, now, who must face Johnston in Georgia, and yet no one could expect what this Sherman would do to Johnston, the Confederacy, and to war itself.

If there was one, however, who did suspect, then surely it was Sherman's superior, indeed, now everyone's superior, Ulysses S. Grant. Chattanooga had confirmed him as the great hero of the Union. The very same day that Lincoln issued his proclamation of amnesty and reconstruction, he wrote also to Grant. "My profoundest gratitude," he offered, "God bless you all." So felt others in Washington, many of them the self-appointed proponents of Grant's career. In Congress they pushed through a bill to revive the unused rank of lieutenant general, not held—except as an honorary title by Winfield Scott—by any American soldier since Washington. No one deserved the rank more than Grant, and with it would automatically go the status of general-in-chief of all Union armies. The entire military control of the war would be in the hands of a man who had failed as a potato farmer. Surely here was the strangest cast of fate of them all, one that transcended even the unpredictable revolutions of the war. On March 9, 1864, called to Washington by a grateful President, Grant listened quietly to a speech Lincoln had rehearsed with him the day before. The new lieutenant general responded in kind, both of them reading their simple remarks from written notes, uttering brief sentences that schoolboys could have committed to memory. The ceremony was, by Lincoln's calculation, simple and unaffected. Yet the night before, when he and Grant first met at a Presidential reception, there were already signs of a new way of life which the general feared, yet secretly desired. They cheered him, made him stand on a couch for all to see. People applauded him everywhere in the capital. Here, surely, was success at last. This was no potato farm, no tannery, no failing business as a bill collector, no boring frontier duty relieved only by drink. Even his father could not question that at last "Ulys" had found something he could do well. Sherman believed that Grant succeeded because he possesses a "simple faith in success."[15]

Faith might move mountains, but now only Grant would demonstrate whether or not it could move armies on to Richmond and Charleston and Atlanta. Johnston and Kirby-Smith and Lee, above all Lee, awaited Grant's turn at the wheel. The man who had so dominated the war in the West must now face that almost mythical hero who had so ruled the conflict in Virginia. They had met once in Mexico, many years ago. Grant remembered it. He always remembered his brushes with the great, the wealthy, the men of bearing and influence. They seldom remembered him, and Lee for his part had only the faintest recollection of Lieutenant Grant. Memory too, like war, moves in circles. As so many other changes and resurrections would come with the warming sun of the new season, so would Lee's recollection. After next spring, Lee would remember Grant.

DOCUMENTATION BY CHAPTER

INTRODUCTION

1. M. A. De Wolfe Howe, *Home Letters of General Sherman* (New York, 1909), p. 200.

CHAPTER 1

1. J. Stoddard Johnston Diary, August 14, 1862, J. Stoddard Johnston Papers, Filson Club, Louisville, Ky.; U. S. War Department, *War of the Rebellion: Official Records of the Union and Confederate Armies* (Washington, D.C., 1880–1901), Series I, Volume 7, part 2, p. 628, Volume 16, part 2, p. 995 (hereinafter cited as O.R.).

2. Elise Bragg to Braxton Bragg, April 2, 1862, Braxton Bragg Papers, Western Reserve Historical Society, Cleveland, Ohio; Elise Bragg to Bragg, n.d., Elise Bragg Papers, Chicago Historical Society.

3. Robert M. Johnson to John C. Breckinridge, August 10, 29, 1862, H. C. Burnett to Breckinridge, August 5, 1862, Breckinridge Family Papers, Library of Congress.

4. William C. Davis *Breckinridge, Statesman, Soldier, Symbol* (Baton Rouge, La., 1974), p. 326.

5. Grady C. McWhiney, *Braxton Bragg and Confederate Defeat, Field Command* (New York, 1969), pp. 272–74; Thomas L. Connelly, *Army of the Heartland, The Army of Tennessee, 1861–1862* (Baton Rouge, La., 1967), pp. 205–15.

6. McWhiney, *Bragg*, pp. 295–99; O.R., I, 16, part 2, p. 846; Connelly, *Army of the Heartland*, 206.

7. O.R., I, 16, part 2, pp. 996–99; George Brent to Breckinridge, Oc-

tober 12, 1862, Chapter II, Volume 302, Record Group 109, National Archives.

8. Davis, *Breckinridge*, pp. 329–31.

9. E. Porter Thompson, *History of the Orphan Brigade* (Cincinnati, 1898), pp. 201–2, 774; Sallie Lewis to Breckinridge, September 21, 1869, A. Ward to Breckinridge, July 22, 1875, Breckinridge Family Papers.

10. Davis, *Breckinridge*, pp. 335–37; James Lee McDonough, *Stones River, Bloody Winter in Tennessee* (Knoxville, Tenn., 1980), pp. 136–40.

11. McDonough, *Stones River*, pp. 148–49, 150–51; McWhiney, *Bragg*, p. 364.

12. McDonough, *Stones River*, p. 159.

13. Davis, *Breckinridge*, p. 338.

14. Cincinnati, *Commercial*, May 18, 1875; New York, *Turf, Field and Farm*, May 21, 1875; O.R., I, 20, part 1, pp. 785, 790; Theodore O'Hara to Breckinridge, January 16, 1863, John C. Breckinridge Papers, New-York Historical Society.

15. O.R., I, 20, part 1, pp. 786–87; Rice E. Graves, Charges and Specifications, etc., n.d., in John C. Breckinridge Papers, Chicago Historical Society.

16. Luke Blackburn to Breckinridge, January 4, 1863, T. B. Roy to Breckinridge, January 4, 1863, Joseph Wheeler to Breckinridge, January 4, 6, 1863, Wheeler to O'Hara, January 4, 1863, Breckinridge Papers, Chicago; O.R., I, 20, part 1, pp. 682–84, 699.

17. O.R., I, 20, part 1, pp. 665–66, 758–59, 760–61; Bragg to Felix Robertson, February 16, 1863, Breckinridge to Henry Dawson, January 20, 1873, Breckinridge Papers, New-York Historical Society.

18. Davis, *Breckinridge*, p. 353–54.

19. John B. Gordon, *Reminiscences of the Civil War* (New York, 1903), 192–94; Breckinridge to George B. Hodge, March 9, 1863, John C. Breckinridge Compiled Service Record, Record Group 109, National Archives.

20. Davis, *Breckinridge*, pp. 357–59.

21. Brent to Bragg, March 15, 1863, Breckinridge Papers, New-York Historical Society; Graves, Charges and Specifications, Breckinridge Papers, Chicago; O.R., I, 20, part 2, pp. 498–99.

22. Davis, *Breckinridge*, p. 361; Johnston Diary, July 19, 1863.

CHAPTER 2

1. Edward Magdol, *Owen Lovejoy, Abolitionist in Congress* (New Brunswick, N.J., 1967), p. 329.

2. Allan Nevins, *The War for the Union: War Becomes Revolution* (New York, 1959), p. 299.

3. Magdol, *Lovejoy*, pp. 363–66.

4. Hans Trefousse, *The Radical Republicans* (New York, 1969), pp. 255–56; Nevins, *War Becomes Revolution*, p. 301; Leroy H. Fischer, *Lincoln's Gadfly, Adam Gurowski* (Norman, Okla., 1964), p. 100.

5. Nevins, *War Becomes Revolution*, pp. 307–8, 319; Trefousse, *Radical Republicans*, p. 259.

6. David Donald, *Inside Lincoln's Cabinet; The Civil War Diaries of Salmon P. Chase* (New York, 1954), pp. 167–68; G. R. Tredway, *Democratic Opposition to the Lincoln Administration in Indiana* (Indianapolis, 1973), p. 30; Kenneth M. Stampp, *Indiana Politics During the Civil War* (New York, 1949), pp. 152–53.

7. Tredway, *Democratic Opposition*, pp. 108–14, 123–24.

8. Ibid., p. 115; Stampp, *Indiana Politics*, pp. 150–51; Nevins, *War Becomes Revolution*, p. 318.

9. Stampp, *Indiana Politics*, pp. 156–57.

10. Magdol, *Lovejoy*, pp. 368–72; Nevins, *War Becomes Revolution*, p. 320.

11. Nevins, *War Becomes Revolution*, pp. 303–5, 320–21.

12. Roy P. Basler, ed., *The Collected Works of Abraham Lincoln* (New Brunswick, N.J., 1953–55), V, pp. 493–95.

13. Frank L. Klement, *The Limits of Dissent: Clement L. Vallandigham and the Civil War* (Lexington, Ky., 1970), pp. 45–46, 96–97, 100.

CHAPTER 3

1. Basler, *Collected Works*, V, pp. 485–86.

2. Nevins, *War Becomes Revolution*, p. 331.

3. Charles A. Dana, *Recollections of the Civil War* (New York, 1898), p. 138.

4. Warren Hassler, *Commanders of the Army of the Potomac* (Baton Rouge, La., 1962), p. 101.

5. O.R., I, 21, pp. 84, 99–101.

6. Ibid., pp. 101, 105, 773–74, 775.

7. Richmond, *Enquirer*, November 15, 1862; O.R., I, 21, pp. 550–51, 1018–19, 1021–22, 1027–28, 1033.

8. O.R., I, 21, p. 87.

9. Ibid., pp. 88–89, 170.

10. Ibid., pp. 89–91.

11. Ibid., pp. 510–11; Philip Mercer, *The Gallant Pelham* (Kennesaw, Ga., 1958), pp. 134–37.

12. O.R., I, 21, pp. 512–13; Edward J. Nichols, *Towards Gettysburg: A Biography of General John F. Reynolds* (University Park, Pa., 1953), pp. 152–53, 155.

13. Frank E. Vandiver, *Mighty Stonewall* (New York, 1957), pp. 427–31.

14. *O.R.*, I, 21, pp. 94, 219.

15 J. B. Stine, *History of the Army of the Potomac* (Washington, D.C., 1893), p. 291.

16. Stine, *Army of the Potomac*, pp. 289–90.

17. Hassler, *Commanders*, pp. 115–16.

18. Ibid., p. 117.

19. Ibid., pp. 117–18.

20. Stine, *Army of the Potomac*, p. 293.

21. *O.R.*, I, 21, p. 67.

22. Ibid., pp. 941–42, 945, 1011.

23. Stine, *Army of the Potomac*, pp. 296–97.

24. *O.R.*, I, 21, pp. 998–99, 1004–5; T. Harry Williams, *Lincoln and His Generals* (New York, 1952), pp. 205–6.

25. Hassler, *Commanders*, p. 124; Vandiver, *Mighty Stonewall*, p. 432.

CHAPTER 4

1. E. Milby Burton, *The Siege of Charleston, 1861–1865* (Columbia, S.C., 1970), p. 75.

2. Ibid., p. 76.

3. *O.R.*, I, 6, p. 309; Francis Pickens to Milledge Bonham, July 7, 1861, Milledge L. Bonham Papers, South Caroliniana Library, University of South Carolina, Columbia.

4. *O.R.*, I, 6, pp. 350–51; Douglas S. Freeman, *R. E. Lee* (New York, 1934), I, pp. 610–13.

5. Burton, *Charleston*, pp. 81–84; U. S. Navy Department, *Official Records of the Union and Confederate Navies in the War of the Rebellion* (Washington, D.C., 1896), Series I, Volume 12, pp. 207, 416 (hereinafter cited as *O.R.N.*).

6. Burton, *Charleston*, p. 85.

7. *O.R.*, I, 6, p. 42.

8. Ibid., p. 354.

9. Burton, *Charleston*, pp. 88–89.

10. *O.R.*, I, 14, pp. 14, 15, 504, 521; *O.R.N.*, I, 12, pp. 820–22.

11. *O.R.*, I, 14, pp. 556, 566–67.

12. Ibid., pp. 42–43, 46, 51–52.

13. Ibid., pp. 1048–49.

14. Ibid., pp. 43, 47, 51, 90–91; I, 51, pp. 90–91; Johnson Hagood, *Memoirs of the War of Secession* (Columbia, S.C., 1910), p. 96.

15. *O.R.*, I, 51, pp. 642–43.

16. Charleston, *Courier*, January 28, 1863; Maurice Melton, *The Confederate Ironclads* (New York, 1968), p. 155.

17. Samuel Jones, *The Siege of Charleston and the Operations of the*

South Atlantic Coast in the War Among the States (New York, 1911), p. 145; Clement A. Evans, ed., *Confederate Military History* (Atlanta, 1899), XII, p. 69; J. Thomas Scharf, *History of the Confederate States Navy* (New York, 1887), p. 676.

18. O.R., I, 14, pp. 205–7; Melton, *Ironclads*, pp. 159–60; Burton, *Charleston*, pp. 130–31.

19. O.R.N., I, 13, p. 535.

20. Ibid., I, 14, p. 5.

21. Ibid., I, 14, pp. 6–8, 9–10, 21–25.

22. O.R., I, 14, p. 269.

23. Ibid., I, 14, p. 437; O.R.N., I, 14, pp. 45, 52, 58.

24. O.R.N., I, 14, pp. 311–17; John A. B. Dahlgren, Memoranda of Naval Operations off Charleston from July 1863, written October 1868, John W. Draper Papers, Library of Congress.

25. O.R., 28, part 1, p. 71.

26. Daniel Eldredge, *The Third New Hampshire* (Boston, 1893), p. 230.

27. O.R.N., I, 14, pp. 319–20, 325–26.

28. Ibid., I, 14, p. 326; Dahlgren, Memoranda.

29. Dahlgren, Memorandum; O.R., I, 28, part 1, p. 12.

30. Dahlgren, Memorandum; O.R., I, 28, part 1, pp. 15–16; O.R.N., I, 13, pp. 579–84, 593, 620.

31. O.R., I, 28, part 1, p. 16.

CHAPTER 5

1. Chicago, *Daily Tribune*, October 7, 1863; O.R., I, 28, part 2, p. 41.

2. Davis, *Breckinridge*, pp. 52–53.

3. J. Cutler Andrews, *The North Reports the Civil War* (Pittsburgh, 1955), pp. 9–14, 31.

4. J. Cutler Andrews, *The South Reports the Civil War* (Princeton, N.J., 1970), pp. 24–26, 28–32.

5. Andrews, *North Reports*, p. 32; Andrews, *South Reports*, pp. 33–34.

6. Andrews, *North Reports*, pp. 14–18.

7. Ibid., pp. 7, 18; New York, *Herald*, August 14, 1861.

8. New York, *Times*, March 27, 1898.

9. Andrews, *North Reports*, pp. 31–34.

10. New York, *Times*, September 25, 1901.

11. Andrews, *South Reports*, pp. 41–42.

12. Richmond, *Whig*, October 15, 1864.

13. B. Kimball Baker, "The Memphis Appeal," *Civil War Times Illustrated* XVIII (July 1979), pp. 32–39.

14. Andrews, *South Reports*, pp. 41–43; Richmond, *Examiner*, June 1, 1863.

15. Atlanta, *Daily Southern Confederacy*, February 1, 1863.

16. Andrews, *South Reports*, pp. 47–50.

17. John M. Daniel, *The Richmond Examiner During the Civil War* (New York, 1868), p. 232.

18. Gideon Welles, *Diary* (Boston, 1909–11), II, p. 131; Andrews, *North Reports*, p. 55.

19. New York, *Times*, July 24, 1861, May 26, 1862; Andrews, *North Reports*, 267, 552, 595, 648–50.

20. Andrews, *South Reports*, pp. 364, 529; Richmond, *Whig*, March 7, 1865.

21. See the Introduction to *Shadows of the Storm* (New York, 1981), by William C. Davis, for a full account of this, as well as Frederic Ray's "The Photographers of the War" chapter in the same volume.

CHAPTER 6

1. Hassler, *Commanders*, pp. 126–32; John Bigelow, *The Campaign of Chancellorsville* (New Haven, 1910), pp. 6–7; *Harper's Monthly Magazine*, XXXI (1865), pp. 639–45.

2. Basler, *Collected Works*, VI, pp. 78–79.

3. Hassler, *Commanders*, p. 132.

4. O.R., I, 25, part 2, p. 5; U. S. Congress, *Report of the Joint Committee on the Conduct of the War* (Washington, 1863–66), Army of the Potomac, part 2, p. xli (hereinafter cited as CCW).

5. Hassler, *Commanders*, p. 134; CCW, p. xlii.

6. Bigelow, *Chancellorsville*, p. 15; Douglas S. Freeman, *Lee's Lieutenants* (New York, 1944), II, pp. 397ff.

7. Manly Wade Wellman, *Giant in Gray, A Biography of Wade Hampton* (New York, 1949), pp. 104–6.

8. Freeman, *Lee's Lieutenants*, II, pp. 459–63.

9. Ibid., II, pp. 494–95.

10. CCW, p. xlii; Allan Nevins, ed., *Diary of the Civil War 1861–1865* (New York, 1962), p. 312.

11. CCW, p. xliii.

12. Bigelow, *Chancellorsville*, pp. 174–75.

13. O.R., I, 25, part 2, p. 859; 25, part 1, p. 171.

14. Ibid., I, 25, part 1, p. 171; William Swinton, *Campaigns of the Army of the Potomac* (New York, 1882), p. 275.

15. Freeman, *Lee's Lieutenants*, II, p. 526.

16. Hassler, *Commanders*, p. 139.

17. O.R., I, 25, part 1, p. 558; Hassler, *Commanders*, pp. 140–41.

18. Freeman, *Lee's Lieutenants*, II, pp. 532–33, 535–37.

19. Ibid., pp. 539–47.

20. O.R., I, 25, part 1, pp. 231, 386–87, part 2, p. 363; CCW, pp. 4–5.

21. Statement in Thomas T. Munford File, Alumni Files, Virginia Military Institute, Lexington.

22. Freeman, *Lee's Lieutenants*, II, pp. 565–68.

23. Bigelow, *Chancellorsville*, pp. 363–65; O.R., I, 25, part 1, p. 307.

24. Hassler, *Commanders*, pp. 148–49.

25. Bigelow, *Chancellorsville*, pp. 434–35.

26. Freeman, *Lee's Lieutenants*, II, pp. 680–82.

CHAPTER 7

1. Wellman, *Hampton*, pp. 105–6.

2. Andrews, *North Reports*, pp. 370–73; Basler, *Collected Works*, VI, pp. 201, 215, 217–18.

3. Hassler, *Commanders*, pp. 150–51.

4. Wellman, *Hampton*, pp. 106–9.

5. Basler, *Collected Works*, VI, pp. 257–58.

6. Wilbur S. Nye, *Here Come the Rebels* (Baton Rouge, La., 1965), p. 74.

7. Basler, *Collected Works*, VI, pp. 276, 280–82; O.R., I, 27, part 1, pp. 58–60; Hassler, *Commanders*, pp. 154–57.

8. Nichols, *Reynolds*, pp. 182–84; Freeman Cleaves, *Meade of Gettysburg* (Norman, Okla., 1960), pp. 123–24.

9. Cleaves, *Meade*, pp. 128–29.

10. O.R., I, 27, part 2, p. 316; Cleaves, *Meade*, p. 126.

11. Nye, *Here Come the Rebels*, pp. 328–42.

12. Ibid., p. 343.

13. Cleaves, *Meade*, p. 127; Edwin B. Coddington, *The Gettysburg Campaign, A Study in Command* (New York, 1968), pp. 262–64.

14. Cleaves, *Meade*, p. 135.

15. Coddington, *Gettysburg*, pp. 266–68.

16. Ibid., pp. 282–83.

17. James Longstreet, *From Manassas to Appomattox* (Philadelphia, 1896), p. 357.

18. Coddington, *Gettysburg*, pp. 297–98.

19. Ibid., pp. 314–15, 320–21.

20. O.R., I, 27, part 3, p. 466.

21. Cleaves, *Meade*, pp. 138–39, 143–44.

22. Longstreet, *Manassas to Appomattox*, p. 384; Coddington, *Gettysburg*, pp. 361–63.

23. Freeman, *Lee's Lieutenants*, III, p. 120.

24. Cleaves, *Meade*, pp. 146–54; Coddington, *Gettysburg*, pp. 402–3, 414; Frank Haskell, *The Battle of Gettysburg* (Boston, 1958), p. 52.

25. Coddington, *Gettysburg*, pp. 428–37.

26. Cleaves, *Meade*, pp. 155–57.

27. Coddington, *Gettysburg*, pp. 443–47, 454–60.

28. Ibid., pp. 462–63.

29. O.R., I, 51, part 1, p. 1068; George Meade, *With Meade at Gettysburg* (Philadelphia, 1930), pp. 147–50.

30. Coddington, *Gettysburg*, pp. 499–500.

31. Cleaves, *Meade*, pp. 166–69.

32. Hassler, *Commanders*, p. 185.

33. Wellman, *Hampton*, pp. 114–16.

34. Ibid., pp. 120–21.

35. Hassler, *Commanders*, pp. 188–89; Cleaves, *Meade*, p. 185; Basler, *Collected Works*, IX, p. 39.

CHAPTER 8

1. Clement Eaton, *A History of the Old South* (New York, 1949), pp. 372–77.

2. Robert Black, *Railroads of the Confederacy* (Chapel Hill, N.C., 1952), pp. 9–10.

3. J. G. Randall and David Donald, *The Civil War and Reconstruction* (Boston, 1969), pp. 34–35.

4. Frank E. Vandiver, *Ploughshares into Swords; Josiah Gorgas and Confederate Ordnance* (Austin, Tex., 1952), pp. 159, 179; Dunbar Rowland, ed., *Jefferson Davis, Constitutionalist* (Jackson, Miss., 1923), V, p. 413.

5. Frank E. Vandiver, ed., *The Civil War Diary of General Josiah Gorgas* (University, Ala., 1947), pp. 90–91.

6. Emory M. Thomas, *The Confederate Nation, 1861–1865* (New York, 1979), pp. 206–13.

7. Charles B. Dew, *Ironmaker to the Confederacy: Joseph R. Anderson and the Tredegar Iron Works* (New Haven, Conn., 1966), pp. 4, 6, 9, 86–87, 115–20, 128–29, 140–41, 142–43.

8. Thomas, *Confederate Nation*, pp. 206–10; Dew, *Ironmaker*, pp. 111, 130, 166, 221.

9. Nevins, *War Becomes Revolution*, pp. 485–86.

10. Ibid., pp. 490–92.

11. Theodore Collier, "Providence in Civil War Days," *Rhode Island Historical Society Collections*, XXVII (July 1934), p. 82; Nevins, *War Becomes Revolution*, p. 490.

12. Nevins, *War Becomes Revolution*, pp. 492–94, 496–98.

13. Maury Klein, "The War and Economic Expansion," *Civil War Times Illustrated*, VIII (January 1970), pp. 37–42; Harry N. Scheiber, "Economic Change in the Civil War Era; An Analysis of Recent Studies," *Civil War History*, XI (December 1965), pp. 409–11; Thomas C. Cochran, "Did the Civil War Retard Industrialization?" *Mississippi Valley Historical Review*, XLVIII (1961), pp. 197–210.

CHAPTER 9

1. John C. Pemberton, *Pemberton, Defender of Vicksburg*, (Chapel Hill, N.C., 1942), p. 60.

2. John Y. Simon, *The Papers of Ulysses S. Grant* (Carbondale, Ill., 1967–79), VI, p. 243 (hereinafter cited as *Grant Papers*).

3. U. S. Grant, *Personal Memoirs* (New York, 1885), I, pp. 423–24.

4. *Grant Papers*, VI, pp. 344–45, 349.

5. Grant, *Memoirs*, I, pp. 426, 427; *Grant Papers*, VI, pp. 288–89.

6. *Grant Papers*, VI, pp. 371–72, 390, 400–1, VII, pp. 61–62, 69; Grant, *Memoirs*, I, pp. 429–31.

7. *Grant Papers*, VII, pp. 50–56; John Y. Simon, ed., *Personal Memoirs of Julia Dent Grant* (New York, 1975), p. 107.

8. Simon, *Julia Dent Grant*, pp. 107–8; Grant, *Memoirs*, I, pp. 432–35; *Grant Papers*, VII, p. 83.

9. *Grant Papers*, VII, pp. 107–9; Grant, *Memoirs*, I, p. 437; William T. Sherman, *Memoirs of Gen. W. T. Sherman* (New York, 1875), I, pp. 313, 317–21.

10. Sherman, *Memoirs*, I, pp. 322–25; David D. Porter, *Incidents and Anecdotes of the Civil War* (New York, 1886), p. 123.

11. *Grant Papers*, VII, pp. 209–11, 218, 234–35, 264, 274–75; Porter, *Incidents*, pp. 131–32; Grant, *Memoirs*, I, 440–41.

12. Grant, *Memoirs*, I, pp. 443–46.

13. *Grant Papers*, VII, pp. 233, 278–79, 340, 366, 384, 474; Grant, *Memoirs*, I, pp. 446–47.

14. *Grant Papers*, VII, pp. 257–59, 284–85, 390, 399–400; Grant, *Memoirs*, I, p. 448.

15. Grant, *Memoirs*, I, pp. 449–51; *Grant Papers*, VII, pp. 239, 286–87, 289–90, 334–35; Porter, *Incidents*, pp. 143–44.

16. Porter, *Incidents*, pp. 137–38.

17. *Grant Papers*, VII, pp. 409, 422–23, 424–25, 427; Porter, *Incidents*, pp. 145–48; Sherman, *Memoirs*, I, pp. 335–36.

18. Porter, *Incidents*, pp. 162–63; Sherman, *Memoirs*, I, p. 339.

19. Sherman, *Memoirs*, I, pp. 336–39; Porter, *Incidents*, pp. 168–69; Grant, *Memoirs*, I, pp. 454–55.

20. *Grant Papers*, VII, pp. 479–80.

CHAPTER 10

1. Pemberton, *Pemberton*, pp. 60, 173, 181–82.
2. Edward Cunningham, *The Port Hudson Campaign* (Baton Rouge, La., 1963), pp. 6–11, 15.
3. Sherman, *Memoirs*, I, pp. 342–43; *Grant Papers*, VIII, pp. 4, 9.
4. *Grant Papers*, VIII, pp. 10–12; Sherman, *Memoirs*, I, pp. 343–44; Grant, *Memoirs*, I, pp. 456–57.
5. Porter, *Incidents*, pp. 175–77; Grant, *Memoirs*, pp. 463–64; Sherman, *Memoirs*, I, pp. 345–46.
6. *Grant Papers*, VIII, pp. 85, 88–89, 151–52, 155; Grant, *Memoirs*, I, pp. 465, 471–72, 478; Pemberton, *Pemberton*, pp. 107–9; Sherman, *Memoirs*, I, p. 347.
7. Dee Brown, *Grierson's Raid* (Urbana, Ill., 1954), pp. 19, 109–13; *Grant Papers*, VIII, pp. 139, 148.
8. Grant, *Memoirs*, I, 491–93; *Grant Papers*, VIII, pp. 183–84, 189.
9. Grant, *Memoirs*, I, pp. 493–95, 496, 499.
10. Ibid., I, pp. 506–9; Sherman, *Memoirs*, I, pp. 349–50.
11. Pemberton, *Pemberton*, pp. 146–47, 152–53; *Grant Papers*, VIII, pp. 220, 222.
12. *Grant Papers*, VIII, p. 224; Grant, *Memoirs*, I, pp. 512–13, 516–17, 519–20, 521.
13. *Grant Papers*, VIII, p. 228; Grant, *Memoirs*, I, pp. 524–26.
14. Grant, *Memoirs*, I, pp. 526–27; Sherman, *Memoirs*, I, p. 353.
15. *Grant Papers*, VIII, p. 237; Sherman, *Memoirs*, I, p. 353; Grant, *Memoirs*, I, pp. 529–31.
16. Sherman, *Memoirs*, I, pp. 355–56; Grant, *Memoirs*, I, p. 531; *Grant Papers*, VIII, pp. 220, 384–86.
17. *Grant Papers*, VIII, pp. 249, 257; Grant, *Memoirs*, I, pp. 534–35.
18. A. A. Hoehling, *Vicksburg: 47 Days of Siege* (Englewood Cliffs, N.J., 1969), pp. 42–43; W. H. Tunnard, *A Southern Record: The History of the Third Regiment of Louisiana Infantry* (Baton Rouge, La., 1866), p. 239.
19. Tunnard, *Southern Record*, pp. 240–41, 243; Pemberton, *Pemberton*, pp. 188–91, 198–99, 200, 201, 204–5, 207–8, 209.
20. Tunnard, *Southern Record*, pp. 254, 260, 263; Grant, *Memoirs*, I, pp. 552–53.
21. Grant, *Memoirs*, I, pp. 546, 553.
22. Ibid., I, pp. 553–54; O.R., I, 24, part 1, pp. 281–83; Tunnard, *Southern Record*, p. 264.
23. Grant, *Memoirs*, I, pp. 556–63; *Grant Papers*, VIII, p. 455; Tunnard, *Southern Record*, pp. 271, 276–77.

24. Grant, *Memoirs*, I, pp. 555, 566, 569–70; *Grant Papers*, VIII, p. 469; Pemberton, *Pemberton*, p. 241; Archer Jones and Thomas L. Connelly, *The Politics of Command* (Baton Rouge, La., 1973), p. 187.

25. Cunningham, *Port Hudson*, pp. 50, 66–67, 92–93, 99–100, 107–8, 117–19, 120–23.

26. Davis, *Breckinridge*, pp. 365–67; *Grant Papers*, VIII, p. 479; Sherman, *Memoirs*, I, pp. 359–60.

27. Simon, *Julia Dent Grant*, p. 114; Basler, *Collected Works*, VI, p. 326.

CHAPTER 11

1. Nevins, *Diary*, p. 330.

2. Allan Nevins, *The War for the Union: The Organized War, 1863–1864* (New York, 1971), pp. 117–18.

3. Adrian Cook, *The Armies of the Streets: The New York City Draft Riots of 1863* (Lexington, Ky., 1974), pp. 49–50.

4. O.R., III, 2, p. 957; Nevins, *Organized War*, p. 120.

5. *Frank Leslie's Illustrated Newspaper*, March 14, 1863; Cook, *Armies*, p. 51.

6. Cook, *Armies*, p. 52.

7. O.R., III, 3, pp. 1046–49; V, pp. 616–19.

8. Cook, *Armies*, p. 29.

9. Nevins, *Diary*, p. 333; Nevins, *Organized War*, p. 121; Cook, *Armies*, pp. 55–56.

10. Cook, *Armies*, pp. 57–59; Nevins, *Diary*, pp. 335–37; Nevins, *Organized War*, p. 122.

11. Cook, *Armies*, pp. 97, 101, 104–5, 107.

12. Ibid., pp. 116, 118–19.

13. Nevins, *Diary*, p. 337; Nevins, *Organized War*, p. 123; Cook, *Armies*, pp. 140, 154–55, 164.

14. Cook, *Armies*, pp. 176, 178–80, 193–94.

15. Herman Melville, "The House Top."

16. Mary E. Massey, *Bonnet Brigades* (New York, 1966), pp. 5, 8–9, 10–11, 14, 23–24; Cook, *Armies*, pp. 28–29.

17. George A. Sala, *My Diary* (London, 1865), I, p. 359; Massey, *Bonnet Brigades*, pp. 30–31.

18. Robert Bremner, *The Public Good: Philanthropy and Welfare in the Civil War Era* (New York, 1980), pp. 39–40, 44–45, 57–59; Massey, *Bonnet Brigades*, p. 32.

19. New York, *Herald*, April 5, 1864; Massey, *Bonnet Brigades*, pp. 44–45, 49, 62, 64, 85.

20. Massey, *Bonnet Brigades*, pp. 80–82; *Frank Leslie's Illustrated*

Newspaper, March 7, December 28, 1863; Bell I. Wiley, *The Life of Billy Yank* (Indianapolis, 1951), pp. 337–38.

21. Massey, *Bonnet Brigades,* pp. 84–85.

22. Bremner, *Public Good,* pp. 14–15, 19, 20–21.

23. Ibid., pp. 74–75, 81–82, 85.

24. Ibid., pp. 91, 97, 98–110 passim.

25. Frank L. Owsley, *Plain Folk of the Old South* (Baton Rouge, La., 1949), pp. 133–49.

26. Albert Moore, *Conscription and Conflict in the Confederacy* (New York, 1924), pp. 52–53; Thomas, *Confederate Nation,* p. 154.

27. Thomas, *Confederate Nation,* pp. 234–35.

28. Bell I. Wiley, *Southern Negroes 1861–1865* (New York, 1938), pp. 32–43, 63–70.

29. Emory Thomas, *The Confederacy as a Revolutionary Experience* (Englewood Cliffs, N.J., 1971), pp. 125–27.

30. Thomas, *Confederate Nation,* pp. 225–27.

31. Massey, *Bonnet Brigades,* pp. 47–48, 52.

32. Massey, *Bonnet Brigades,* p. 78; Davis, *Breckinridge,* p. 364.

33. Wiley, *Johnny Reb,* p. 334; Sylvia D. Hoffert, "Madame Loretta Velasquez," *Civil War Times Illustrated,* XVII (June 1978), p. 31; O.R., II, 8, p. 936.

34. Bremner, *Public Good,* p. 47; Davis, *Orphan Brigade,* p. 207.

35. Mary Elizabeth Massey, *Refugee Life in the Confederacy* (Baton Rouge, La., 1964), pp. 29–30, 34, 46–47.

36. Ibid., pp. 242–62; Bremner, *Public Good,* p. 76 ff.

37. Thomas, *Confederate Nation,* pp. 228–29; Massey, *Refugee Life,* pp. 40–42.

CHAPTER 12

1. Randall and Donald, *Civil War,* p. 359; Charles F. Adams, Jr., *Charles Francis Adams* (Boston, 1900), p. 146.

2. Randall and Donald, *Civil War,* pp. 361–62; Lynn M. Case and Warren F. Spencer, *The United States and France: Civil War Diplomacy* (Philadelphia, 1970), pp. 190–95.

3. Norman Ferris, *The Trent Affair, A Diplomatic Crisis* (Knoxville, Tenn., 1977), p. 191.

4. Frank Merli, *Great Britain and the Confederate Navy* (Bloomington, Ind., 1970), pp. 15–17.

5. James D. Bulloch, *The Secret Service of the Confederate States in Europe* (London, 1883), I, pp. 68–69; Merli, *Great Britain,* pp. 66–73.

6. O.R.N., II, 2, pp. 148–49.

7. Bulloch, *Secret Service*, I, pp. 227–28; Merli, *Great Britain*, pp. 86–87.

8. Merli, *Great Britain*, p. 89; Bulloch, *Secret Service*, I, pp. 238, 260–62.

9. Bulloch, *Secret Service*, I, pp. 238–39; Merli, *Great Britain*, pp. 92–93; Philip Van Doren Stern, *When the Guns Roared* (New York, 1962), pp. 148–49; William S. Hoole, *Four Years in the Confederate Navy* (Athens, Ga., 1964), p. 56.

10. Merli, *Great Britain*, pp. 107–11.

11. Case and Spencer, *United States and France*, pp. 590–95; Merli, *Great Britain*, pp. 114–16.

12. Bulloch, *Secret Service*, I, pp. 382–83.

13. Ibid., I, pp. 386–90, 396–97.

14. Nevins, *Organized War*, pp. 494–95.

15. Douglas Maynard, "The Forbes-Aspinwall Mission," *Mississippi Valley Historical Review*, XLV (June 1958), pp. 67–89.

16. Samuel B. Thompson, *Confederate Purchasing Operations Abroad* (Chapel Hill, N.C., 1935), pp. 70–75.

17. Stern, *Guns*, p. 179.

18. Bulloch, *Secret Service*, I, pp. 400–1.

19. Ibid., I, pp. 401–3; Merli, *Great Britain*, pp. 161–66.

20. Randall and Donald, *Civil War*, p. 366; Bulloch, *Secret Service*, I, pp. 400–8.

21. Charles Cullop, *Confederate Propaganda in Europe, 1861–1865* (Coral Gables, Fla., 1969), pp. 18–28, 60–62.

22. Caleb Huse, *The Supplies for the Confederacy* (Boston, 1904), pp. 19–20, 24.

23. Frank L. Owsley, *King Cotton Diplomacy* (Chicago, 1959), p. 52; Paul P. du Bellet, *The Diplomacy of the Confederate Cabinet of Richmond and Its Agents Abroad* (Tuscaloosa, Ala., 1963), pp. 38–39, 46–47.

24. Owsley, *King Cotton Diplomacy*, pp. 202, 216–17.

25. Stern, *Guns*, pp. 207–8.

26. Merli, *Great Britain*, pp. 196–97; Stern, *Guns*, p. 209.

27. Nevins, *Organized War*, pp. 496–97; Bulloch, *Secret Service*, I, p. 418; Stern, *Guns*, p. 211.

28. Bulloch, *Secret Service*, I, pp. 418–19, 421; Stern, *Guns*, p. 211; Merli, *Great Britain*, p. 201.

29. Stern, *Guns*, p. 213; Merli, *Great Britain*, pp. 202–3, 207–10; Willson Beckles, *John Slidell and the Confederates in Paris* (New York, 1932), pp. 166–67, 169–70; Owsley, *King Cotton Diplomacy*, pp. 421–22; Bulloch, *Secret Service*, I, pp. 422–26.

30. Bulloch, *Secret Service*, I, p. 432; O.R.N., II, 2, pp. 583–86; Merli, *Great Britain*, p. 212; Nevins, *Organized War*, p. 503.

CHAPTER 13

1. E. Kirby-Smith to John Slidell, September 2, 1863, in Joseph Rubinfine Autograph Catalog ※65, n.d.

2. Martin H. Hall, *Sibley's New Mexico Campaign* (Austin, Tex., 1960), pp. 16–20, 30–31; O.R., I, 4, p. 93.

3. O.R., I, 4, p. 90.

4. Hall, *New Mexico Campaign*, pp. 51, 104–6.

5. Ibid., p. 118; Ovando Hollister, *Boldly They Rode* (Chicago, 1949), pp. 97–100.

6. Hall, *New Mexico Campaign*, p. 167; O.R., I, 9, pp. 510, 665, 1208–9; Clarence C. Clendenin, "The Column from California," *Civil War Times Illustrated*, IX (January 1971), pp. 22–27.

7. Hall, *New Mexico Campaign*, pp. 202–3, 206, 214–15.

8. Albert Castel, *General Price and the Civil War in the West* (Baton Rouge, La., 1968), p. 65.

9. Ibid., pp. 68, 70, 75–76.

10. Ibid., pp. 82–83; Robert L. Kerby, *Kirby-Smith's Confederacy, The Trans-Mississippi South, 1863–1865* (New York, 1972), pp. 31–32.

11. Kerby, *Kirby-Smith's Confederacy*, p. 33; Castel, *Price*, pp. 140–41.

12. Kerby, *Kirby-Smith's Confederacy*, pp. 38–42.

13. W. W. Denison, "Battle of Prairie Grove," *Kansas Historical Collections*, XVI (1915), pp. 586–90.

14. Kerby, *Kirby-Smith's Confederacy*, pp. 17–20.

15. Joseph H. Parks, *General Edmund Kirby-Smith, C.S.A.* (Baton Rouge, La., 1954), pp. 251–53, 256; O.R., I, 22, part 2, pp. 802–3; Kerby, *Kirby-Smith's Confederacy*, p. 30.

16. O.R., I, 22, part 2, pp. 871–73; Parks, *Kirby-Smith*, p. 259; Castel, *Price*, pp. 140–42.

17. O.R., I, 22, part 2, pp. 802–3.

18. Ibid., I, 22, part 1, p. 407, part 2, pp. 834–35, 839–40, volume 15, pp. 386–87; Kerby, *Kirby-Smith's Confederacy*, p. 105.

19. Kerby, *Kirby-Smith's Confederacy*, pp. 111–12; Richard Taylor, *Destruction and Reconstruction* (New York, 1879), pp. 137–38, 170–71; Parks, *Kirby-Smith*, pp. 272–73.

20. Kerby, *Kirby-Smith's Confederacy*, pp. 135–39.

21. O.R., I, 22, part 2, pp. 856–57; Albert Castel, "The Guerilla War," *Civil War Times Illustrated*, XIII (October 1974), pp. 8–9.

22. Castel, "Guerilla War," pp. 18, 20–21, 22–23, 45; Kerby, *Kirby-Smith's Confederacy*, pp. 209–11, 214.

23. O.R., I, 34, part 2, pp. 869–70.

CHAPTER 14

1. John H. Reagan, *Memoirs, with Special Reference to Secession and the Civil War* (New York, 1906), p. 165.

2. Ibid., pp. 124–27, 157–58.

3. Ibid., p. 147; James D. Richardson, comp., *Messages and Papers of the Confederacy* (Nashville, Tenn., 1905), I, p. 277.

4. Reagan, *Memoirs*, p. 147.

5. C. Vann Woodward, ed., *Mary Chesnut's Civil War* (New Haven, Conn., 1981), p. 56; John B. Jones, *A Rebel War Clerk's Diary* (New York, 1957), pp. 57, 103; Thomas, *Confederate Nation*, p. 139; Frank L. Owsley, *State Rights in the Confederacy* (Gloucester, Mass., 1961), pp. 162–63.

6. Reagan, *Memoirs*, pp. 161–62; Wilfred Buck Yearns, *The Confederate Congress* (Atlanta, 1960), pp. 220–21.

7. Yearns, *Congress*, pp. 218–20; E. A. Pollard, *The Lost Cause* (New York, 1867), p. 656.

8. Yearns, *Congress*, pp. 224–25.

9. Alvy L. King, *Louis T. Wigfall, Southern Fire-eater* (Baton Rouge, La., 1970), pp. 139, 187.

10. Thomas, *Confederate Nation*, p. 143.

11. Rosser H. Taylor, ed., "Boyce-Hammond Correspondence," *Journal of Southern History*, III (1937), p. 349.

12. Bell I. Wiley, *The Road to Appomattox* (Memphis, Tenn., 1956), p. 83; Yearns, *Congress*, p. 226; Woodward, *Chesnut*, p. 318.

13. Yearns, *Congress*, pp. 226–27.

14. Robert Toombs to Gustavus W. Smith, March 25, 1865, in David Battan Autograph Catalog ♯19 (Fresno, Calif., 1977), p. 3; William Y. Thompson, *Robert Toombs of Georgia* (Baton Rouge, La., 1966), pp. 210, 217.

15. O.R., I, 51, part 2, pp. 818–20.

16. U. B. Phillips, ed., "The Correspondence of Robert Toombs, Alexander H. Stephens, and Howell Cobb," *Annual Report of the American Historical Association* (Washington, D.C., 1911), II, pp. 633, 639; O.R., IV, 3, pp. 234–35, 278–81; Owsley, *State Rights*, p. 188–89.

17. Phillips, "Correspondence," pp. 639–41.

18. O.R., IV, 3, pp. 735–36; Owsley, *State Rights*, pp. 191–92.

19. Walter L. Fleming, *Civil War and Reconstruction in Alabama* (New York, 1905), pp. 101–2; Georgia L. Tatum, *Disloyalty in the Confederacy* (Chapel Hill, N.C., 1934), p. 20.

20. O.R., I, 32, part 3, pp. 682–83; IV, 3, pp. 806, 809–11.

21. O.R., I, 26, part 2, p. 285; Tatum, *Disloyalty*, pp. 38–40; Philip

Rutherford, "Defying the State of Texas," *Civil War Times Illustrated,* XVIII (April 1979), pp. 17–21.

22. Tatum, *Disloyalty,* pp. 50–52.

23. Frederick H. Dyer, *A Compendium of the War of the Rebellion* (Des Moines, Iowa, 1908), II, pp. 997, 1020, 1212, 1343, 1471, 1636, 1654, volume I, p. 11.

24. Tatum, *Disloyalty,* pp. 59–60, 65–67; O.R., IV, 2, p. 726.

25. Tatum, *Disloyalty,* pp. 71–72, 73–74; O.R., I, 53, p. 319.

26. Tatum, *Disloyalty,* pp. 97–98.

27. Ibid., pp. 116–17; O.R., I, 23, part 2, p. 952.

28. Tatum, *Disloyalty,* p. 159; O.R., IV, 3, pp. 804–16; Davis, *Breckinridge,* p. 461.

29. Yearns, *Congress,* p. 227; Reagan, *Memoirs,* p. 179.

CHAPTER 15

1. John W. Caldwell Diary, February 16, 1862, in possession of I. Beverly Lake.

2. Mary C. Breckinridge to Breckinridge, June 11, 13, 26, 1863, Breckinridge Service Record.

3. Davis, *Breckinridge,* pp. 368–69.

4. Thomas L. Connelly, *Autumn of Glory: The Army of Tennessee, 1862–1865* (Baton Rouge, La., 1971), pp. 170–71.

5. Ibid., pp. 180–85, 188–90.

6. Bragg to "Dear General," December 29, 1863, Murray J. Smith Collection, Archives, U. S. Army Military History Institute, Carlisle Barracks, Pa.; Davis, *Breckinridge,* p. 369; J. W. Ratchford, *Some Reminiscences of Persons and Incidents of the Civil War* (Austin, Tex., 1971), p. 53.

7. Connelly, *Autumn of Glory,* pp. 202–4; Davis, *Breckinridge,* pp. 369–70.

8. Connelly, *Autumn of Glory,* pp. 207–9.

9. O.R., I, 30, part 2, pp. 198, 203, 215, 233; W. M. Polk, *Leonidas Polk, Bishop and General* (New York, 1915), II, p. 256; Connelly, *Autumn of Glory,* p. 215.

10. Davis, *Breckinridge,* pp. 371–72.

11. John B. Hood, *Advance and Retreat* (New Orleans, 1880), p. 62; Breckinridge to W. M. Polk, November 12, 1874, Breckinridge Family Papers.

12. O.R., I, 30, part 2, pp. 108, 204, 206–7.

13. Davis, *Breckinridge,* pp. 375–76.

14. John A. Wyeth, *That Devil Forrest* (New York, 1959), p. 229; Ratchford, *Reminiscences,* p. 35; OR., I, 30, part 2, pp. 144, 200.

15. Davis, *Breckinridge*, pp. 377–78.

16. O.R., I, 30, part 2, pp. 144–45, 200.

17. Ibid., p. 201; John L. McKinnon, *The History of Walton County* (Atlanta, 1911), p. 289; Davis, *Breckinridge*, p. 379; Woodward, *Chesnut*, p. 554.

18. Connelly, *Autumn of Glory*, pp. 231–34.

19. Davis, *Breckinridge*, pp. 380–81.

20. Breckinridge to D. H. Hill, October 15, 16, 1863, Daniel H. Hill Papers, North Carolina Department of Archives and History, Raleigh; Bragg to "Dear General," December 29, 1863, Smith Collection; O.R., I, 31, part 2, p. 650.

21. Woodward, *Chesnut*, pp. 482–83.

22. Connelly, *Autumn of Glory*, pp. 250–51.

23. Ibid., pp. 262–64; O.R., I, 31, part 1, pp. 218, 455; Longstreet, *Manassas to Appomattox*, p. 481.

24. O.R., I, 31, part 2, pp. 717–18; Connelly, *Autumn of Glory*, pp. 270–71.

25. O.R., I, 31, part 2, pp. 673, 676, 721, 739.

26. Davis, *Breckinridge*, pp. 385–86.

27. Ibid., pp. 386–87.

28. O.R., I, 31, part 2, pp. 684, 745; Richmond, *Daily Dispatch*, December 1, 1863.

29. O.R., I, 31, part 2, pp. 741–42; Davis, *Breckinridge*, pp. 389–90.

30. Davis, *Breckinridge*, pp. 391–93.

31. O.R., I, 31, part 3, pp. 767–68, volume 52, part 2, pp. 568, 573, 745–46; Polk, *Polk*, II, pp. 308–13.

32. Bragg to "Dear General," December 14, 29, 1863, Smith Collection; Davis, *Breckinridge*, p. 395.

33. McWhiney, *Bragg*, pp. 161–62, 217; O.R., I, 31, part 2, p. 690, part 3, p. 833.

34. Woodward, *Chesnut*, p. 544.

CHAPTER 16

1. Nevins, *Organized War*, p. 460.

2. Washington, *National Republican*, February 11, 1862.

3. Washington, *Daily National Intelligencer*, March 1, 6, 1862.

4. W. G. Brownlow, *Sketches of the Rise, Progress and Decline of Secession* (Philadelphia, 1862), pp. 289, 413, 438.

5. E. Merton Coulter, *Civil War and Readjustment in Kentucky* (Chapel Hill, N.C., 1926), pp. 142–44, 161–63.

6. Ibid., pp. 171–72.

7. Ibid., pp. 176–77.

8. Joe Gray Taylor, *Louisiana Reconstructed, 1863–1877* (Baton

Rouge, La., 1974), pp. 13–15, 16–17; Basler, *Collected Works*, V, pp. 462–63, 504.

9. Taylor, *Louisiana*, pp. 19–21; Basler, *Collected Works*, VI, pp. 364–65.

10. Michael B. Dougan, *Confederate Arkansas: The People and Policies of a Frontier State in Wartime* (University, Ala., 1976), pp. 45–50, 62–63.

11. Dougan, *Arkansas*, pp. 110–11.

12. Ibid., pp. 119–21.

13. Basler, *Collected Works*, V, p. 469.

14. Randall and Donald, *Civil War*, pp. 240–41.

15. Magdol, *Lovejoy*, p. 399; Nevins, *Organized War*, p. 163.

16. Basler, *Collected Works*, VII, pp. 50, 54–56.

17. O.R., I, 15, pp. 466, 516; Jonathan T. Dorris, *Pardon and Amnesty Under Lincoln and Johnson* (Chapel Hill, N.C., 1953), pp. 30–32.

18. Basler, *Collected Works*, VII, pp. 54–56; Dorris, *Pardon and Amnesty*, p. 35.

19. Frank Moore, comp., *The Rebellion Record* (New York, 1861–68), VIII, pp. 296–97; O.R., IV, 3, pp. 50–54; Dorris, *Pardon and Amnesty*, pp. 41–42.

20. Dorris, *Pardon and Amnesty*, pp. 42–44.

21. Nevins, *Organized War*, pp. 470–71.

22. Basler, *Collected Works*, VII, p. 55.

23. Ibid., VI, p. 365; Randall and Donald, *Civil War*, pp. 557–58.

CHAPTER 17

1. Nevins, *Diary*, pp. 387, 389.

2. Freeman, *Lee's Lieutenants*, III, p. 205; O.R., I, 43, pp. 104–7; George Meade, *The Life and Letters of George Gordon Meade* (New York, 1913), II, p. 136.

3. E. B. Long, "The Battle That Almost Was . . . Manassas Gap," *Civil War Times Illustrated*, XI (December 1972), pp. 20–27.

4. Freeman, *Lee's Lieutenants*, III, pp. 217–18.

5. Ibid., pp. 220–21.

6. Freeman, *Lee*, III, pp. 183, 351.

7. Welles, *Diary*, I, pp. 439–40.

8. Freeman, *Lee's Lieutenants*, III, p. 267.

9. Ibid., p. 267.

10. Jay Luvaas and Wilbur S. Nye, "The Campaign That History Forgot," *Civil War Times Illustrated*, VIII (November 1969), pp. 14–36.

11. Maury Klein, "The Knoxville Campaign," *Civil War Times Illustrated*, X (October 1971), pp. 7–10, 40–42.

12. Davis, *Breckinridge*, pp. 408–9.

13. Bragg to "Dear General," December 14, 1863, Smith Collection.

14. Connelly, *Autumn of Glory*, pp. 281–85.

15. Basler, *Collected Works*, VII, pp. 53, 234; Sherman, *Memoirs*, II, pp. 399–400.

INDEX

Abolitionism, 18, 19, 21, 23, 25, 29, 71, 206, 256, 300, 306
Adams, Charles Francis, x, xviii, 222–23, 225, 227–32, 235, 236–37
Adams, Henry, 224, 238–39
Adams, John, 222
Adams, John Quincy, 222
Africa, 145
Alabama (ship), 226–27, 232, 235, 236
Albuquerque, N.M., 244–45
Aldie, Va., engagement at, 114
Alexander, General Edward Porter, 130, 321
Alexander, Peter, 78
Alexander's Bridge, 283, 285
Alexandra affair, 231–32, 235, 237
Alexandria, La., 253, 254
Alexandria, Va., 307
American Colonization Society, 211
Amite River, 175
Anderson, Joseph R., 140, 141
Anderson, General Richard H., 94, 95
Anderson, William C. "Bloody Bill," 256, 257–58
Andrew, John A., 26
Anthony, Susan Brownell, 206
Antietam, Battle of, ix, xiv–xv, 21, 27, 31, 35, 88, 91, 104, 108, 113, 132, 228, 279, 321
Apache Canyon, skirmish at, 245
Apache Indians, 33, 241
Appeal Battery, 74
Arkansas (ironclad), 1, 57, 168
Arkansas Post expedition, 158–59
Arkansas River, 158, 250
Armistead, General Lewis Addison, 129, 130
Armour, Philip Danforth, 148
Army of New Mexico, 242–43
Army of Northern Virginia, 39, 54, 90–105, 249, 264, 313–19; desertions, 275, 315; invasion of the North, 106–33. *See also* names of battles
Army of Tennessee, 16, 75, 274; Dalton, 296–97, 298, 322; loss of Chattanooga, 278–98
Army of the Cumberland, victory at Chattanooga, 278–98

Army of the Potomac: Burnside's command, 32–48; corps badges, 90; desertions, 89; "Grand Divisions" reorganization, 37, 40; Hooker's command, 86–105, 106, 107, 108, 110, 111–12, 133; Meade's command, 112–33, 313–19. *See also* names of battles
Aspinwall, William Henry, 230, 231
Atlanta, Ga., 3, 50, 126, 139, 279, 291, 327; "refugee" newspapers in, 75; refugee problem, 220
Atlanta *Confederacy*, 77
Aubry, Kan., raid of 1862, 257
Augusta, Ga., 137, 139
Australia, 145
Austria, 238
Azores, 227

Baltimore, Md., 113, 115, 116
Banks, Major General Nathaniel Prentiss, 85, 170, 174, 175, 176, 179, 180, 190, 191–93, 195, 196, 253–54, 255, 266, 273, 304–5
Banks' Ford, 46
Bardstown, Ky., 5
Barnard, George, 83, 84
Baron De Kalb (gunboat), 163
Barton, Clara, 206, 208
Baton Rouge, La., 1, 168, 170, 174, 175
Battery Gregg on Cummings Point, 63
Battery Wagner, 56, 63–67; fall of, 319
Bayou Baxter, 161
Bayou Macon, 161
Bayou Vidal, 170, 172
Beatty, John, 287
Beaufort, S.C., 33
Beauregard, General Pierre Gustave Toutant, xviii, 4, 89, 290, 325; defense of Charleston, 56–57, 60, 62, 63, 65, 66, 67
Beecher, Henry Ward, 22–23
Bell, John, 26
Bell, Joshua, 303
Belmont, Mo., Confederate bushwhackers at, 151
Benham, Brigadier General Henry W., 55, 56
Benjamin, Judah Philip, xviii, 233, 234

Bennett, James Gordon, 70, 72
Benton (ironclad), 145, 171–72
Bergstresser brothers, 83
Berry, General Hiram, 103
Bessemer steel process, 148
Bickerdyke, "Mother" Mary, 208
Big Black River, 176, 177, 178, 179–80, 183, 184
Big Pipe Creek, 116, 121
Big Round Top, 117, 122
Birkenhead, England, 236, 237, 240
Black Hawk (flagship), 158
Black Joke Engine Company Number 33, 201
Blackwell, Elizabeth, 206
Blalock, Keith, 217
Blalock, Mrs. Malinda, 217
Blockade-runners, 50, 53, 59, 138
Blunt, Brigadier General James G., 250, 251, 258
"Bohemian Brigade," 82
Bolton, Miss., 178
Bonham, Tex., 272
Boonville, Battle of, 242
Border Ruffians, 257
Botulism, 146
Bowen, Brigadier General John Stevens, 173, 174, 188–89
Bowery Boys, 200
Boyce, W. W., 266
Boyle, General Jeremiah T., 24, 303
Brady, Mathew, 82–83
Bragg, General Braxton, 1–17, 18, 45, 83, 177, 191, 193, 194, 241, 267, 277, 290–91, 306, 314, 315, 320, 323; accuses Breckinridge of drunkenness, 297–98; army reorganization (after Chickamauga), 291–92; at Chickamauga, 278–86, 289, 296, 319; feud with newspaper correspondents, 81, 82; Kentucky campaign, 1–8, 12, 17, 21, 25, 145, 151, 218, 252, 302; at Missionary Ridge, 293–97, 298, 324; Perryville battle, 5, 6, 8, 11, 16, 17; resignation of, 297, 325; Stones River battle, 9–17, 286, 291, 298
Bragg, Mrs. Elise, 2
Bramlette, Thomas, 303
Brandy Station, Battle of, 108–10, 114, 132
Brandy Station, Va., 106
Brashear City, 253, 255
Bravay and Company, 232, 236, 238
Breckinridge, Clifton, 11
Breckinridge, Major General John Cabell, x, xviii, 1–2, 26, 82, 193–94, 195, 197, 208, 243, 276, 291, 301; accused of drunkenness, 297–98; at Chickamauga, 278, 279, 283–90; flight from Missionary Ridge, 296–98; Kentucky campaign, 1, 2, 3, 5–7, 8, 81, 169; loathing of Bragg, 8, 278; at Lookout Mountain, 292–93, 297–98; at Missionary Ridge, 293–95, 296–97, 298, 324; Presidential candidacy of, 29, 69, 70, 117, 290, 306; at Shiloh, 1, 2, 195; Stones River battle, 9–17, 81, 195, 286, 291, 298
Breckinridge, Margaret, 208
Breckinridge, Mrs. Mary, 6, 7, 11, 217, 278

Bridgeport, Tenn., 292
Bright, Jesse David, 20, 197
Bright, John, 231
Bristoe Station, Va., 315–16
British Admiralty, 226
British Empire, 145
Brock Road, 99
Brooks, Noah, 78–79, 105
Brooks, General W. T. H., 47
Brooks Brothers (clothing store), 203
Brown, Joseph Emerson, 214, 263, 264, 268, 269, 270, 274
Bruinsburg, Miss., 173
Bryant, William Cullen, 70, 311
Buchanan, James, 23, 31, 243
Buckner, Lieutenant General Simon Bolivar, 4, 7, 279, 283, 284, 290, 291, 292
Buell, Major General Don Carlos, 4, 5, 6, 19, 21, 24, 26, 27
Buford, Brigadier General John, 116, 118, 122
Bulloch, Captain James Dunwody, 224–27, 229–32, 233, 234, 238
Bull Run, First Battle of, xiii, xiv, xvi, xviii, 33, 35, 55, 56, 79, 87, 91, 135, 146, 177, 210, 249, 252, 261, 265, 280
Bull Run, Second Battle of, xiv, 21, 30, 35, 80, 88, 113, 261
Burnside, Major General Ambrose Everett, 87, 88, 144; Army of the Potomac command, 32–47, 48; background of, 32–33; Congressional testimony, 47; Fredericksburg battle, 38–45, 46, 47, 48, 81, 85, 89; in Knoxville, 293, 319–20, 321; "Mud March" of (1863), 46–47, 89; North Carolina operations, 33, 34; promoted, 33; relief of Washington (1861), 33; relieved of command, 46, 86
Burnside carbines, 33, 144
Buschbeck, Colonel Adolphus, 101
Butler, Major General Benjamin Franklin, 29, 30, 170, 212, 266, 303–4, 309
Butterfield, General Daniel, 90

Cairo, Ill., 151, 156
Calhoun, John Caldwell, 262
California, 241, 243, 245–46
Canada, 145, 198, 224
Canby, Colonel Edward Richard Sprigg, 243, 244, 245, 246
Canton, Miss., 194
Cape Hatteras, 59
Carleton, Colonel James Henry, 246
Carlisle, Pa., 114, 131
Carnegie, Andrew, 147
Carolina Institute Hall, 52
Carondelet (gunboat), 164, 171
Carte-de-visite, 83, 86
Carthage, Battle of, 242
Cashtown, Pa., 115–16, 119
Catherine Furnace, 99
Catskill (monitor), 59, 64
Cedar Mountain, Battle of, 170, 261
Cemetery Hill, 117, 118, 119, 120, 121, 125
Cemetery Ridge, 117, 122, 123, 124, 126, 128–29
Centreville, Va., 315–16

Chambersburg, Pa., 115
Champion's Hill, 178–79, 181, 194
Chancellorsville, Battle of, 93–105, 106, 107,
    108, 113, 119, 261, 289, 319, 321;
    casualties, 101, 103, 105; cost of victory
    (to the South), 105; end of, 105; Federal
    withdrawal, 104–5; at Hazel Grove, 103;
    Jackson's plan, 99; at Marye's Heights,
    95, 103; Rappahannock River crossings,
    94, 104, 105, 106; reaction to (in the
    North), 106, 198; at Salem Church, 104;
    Tabernacle Church skirmishes, 96; in the
    Wilderness, 94, 96, 98, 99, 105
Chancellorsville, village of, 94, 95, 101
Chandler, Zachariah, 20
Charleston, siege of, 49–67, 83, 261, 315,
    319; abandonment of James Island, 56;
    April 7 attack, 59–62; blockade, 50, 57,
    58–59; Bonham's assault, 55, 56; capture
    of Port Royal, 50–51; Fort Sumter and,
    51, 56, 60, 61, 63, 66, 67; at Fort Wagner,
    63–67, 68; harbor ship sinkings, 52–53;
    July 10 attack, 63–65; at Secessionville,
    55, 56; use of Negro troops, 66
Charleston, S.C., xiii, 70, 139, 327; arrest of
    Yankee reporters, 71–72; fire of 1863,
    51–52; rail link with Savannah, 63
Charleston Courier, 57, 78
Charleston Squadron, 57, 58–59
Chase, Salmon Portland, 23–24, 230, 308
Chattanooga, Tenn., 3, 4, 84, 137;
    Confederate evacuation of, 281; Union
    victory at, 278–98, 299, 307, 309, 324,
    326. See also Chickamauga, Battle of;
    Lookout Mountain; Missionary Ridge
Chattanooga Daily Rebel, 75
Chattanooga Valley, 293
Cheatham, 283, 297
Cherokee Indians, 249–50
Chesnut, Mary, x
Chickamauga, Battle of, 278–90, 291, 315,
    325; advance toward, 278–82; at
    Alexander's Bridge, 283, 285; beginning
    of, 283–84; casualties, 287, 289–90; extent
    of fighting line, 282–83; gap in Federal
    lines, 288; at Glass's Mill, 282, 283; at
    Kelly Field, 286–88; at Lee and Gordon's
    Mills, 282, 283–84, 285; number of
    troops, 282; shift in Confederate
    command, 284–85; Thomas' withdrawal,
    289
Chickamauga Creek, 282, 296, 298
Chickamauga Station, 296, 297
Chickasaw Bayou, 157
Chickasaw Bluffs, Battle of, 157, 162, 326
Chickasaw Indians, 249–50
Chicora (ironclad gunboat), 56, 58
Child, Lydia, 206
Children's Aid Society, 212
Chillicothe (gunboat), 163
Chivington, Major John Milton, 245
Choctaw Indians, 249–50
Cincinnati (gunboat), 164, 165–66
Cincinnati, Oh., 144–45
Cincinnati Enquirer, 69
Cincinnati riots of 1862, 23
Clarksville, Va., 139

Clay, Henry, 2
Cleburne, Major General Patrick Ronayne,
    281, 283, 286, 287, 289, 291, 298
Cleveland, Oh., 148
Clock and watch industry, 142, 147
Clothing industry, 139, 143, 144–45, 147
Coal industry, 139, 142, 143
Cobb, Thomas R. R., 43, 265, 267
Cochrane, General John, 47
Coffee County courthouse, burning of
    (1864), 274
Coldwater River, 162, 163
Colorado volunteers, 245
Colt, Samuel, 143, 147
Columbus, Ga., 139; fall of, 76
Comanche Indians, 241
Committee on the Conduct of the War, 47
Confederate Congress, 7, 14, 17, 35, 138,
    214, 230–31, 242; anti-Davis faction, 264,
    308; censorship doctrine, 81–82; relations
    with Davis, 262, 264, 265, 267, 269, 274,
    276; Tredegar partnership, 141
Confederate Press Association, 81
Confederate States of America: black
    troops in Yankee service, 273; command
    system, 3–4; conspiracy, sabotage, and
    treason, 269–77; elections of 1861 and
    1863, 265; habeas corpus suspension, 265,
    268–69, 270, 276; Indian treaties, 250;
    industry and manufacturing, 134–42, 148;
    newspaper publishing, 73–78, 81–82, 266,
    308; photographers, 82–84; political
    parties, 263; Provisional Government, 265;
    railroads, 135, 136–37; women in, 213–21
Confederate Territory of Arizona, 244
Conscription, 7, 19, 25, 199, 215, 248, 265,
    270, 272, 275, 322; draft riots, 199–205,
    214; exemptions, 201, 214; Lincoln and,
    199; substitutes, 197, 199–200
Conscription Bureau (Confederate War
    Department), 214
Contrabands, 212
Cook, George S., 83
Cooke, Jay, xviii, 208
Cooley, Samuel A., 83, 84
Cooper, Colonel Douglas Hancock, 249,
    250
Copperheads, xvii, 20, 29, 300, 310
Copper industry, 139
Corinth, siege of, 1, 2, 17, 74, 151, 195
Corning, N.Y., 136
Cottage industries, 139
Cotton, 135–36, 137, 143–44, 145, 155, 168,
    241, 253, 270; British textile mills and,
    224; Confederate bonds and, 230–31
Couch, General Darius Nash, 44, 97, 98
Cowardin, James, 71
Creek Indians, 249–50
Crimean War, 82, 208
Crittenden, John Jordan, 9
Crittenden, Major General Thomas
    Leonidas, 9, 10, 11, 280–83, 286, 288
Culpeper, Va., 36, 106, 314
Culp's Hill, 119, 120, 122, 124–25, 126, 127
Cumberland Gap, 3, 320
Cumberland River, xv, 151
Cumberland Valley, 108

Curry, Jabez Lamar Monroe, 274
Curtis, General Samuel Ryan, 247, 248, 249, 250
Custer, General George Armstrong, 132

Dahlgren, Admiral John Adolphus Bernard, 63–65, 66–67, 68, 321
Dalton, Ga., 296–97, 298, 322
Dana, Charles A., 34
Daniel, John M., 71, 78
Dargan, Edmund, 267
Davis, Captain Charles H., 52
Davis, Jefferson, xii, xviii, xix, 2, 3, 5, 7, 29, 51, 54, 108, 177, 191, 193, 202, 214, 219, 278, 293, 297, 309, 313, 315, 325; in Atlanta, 291; Cabinet and government of, 261–62, 263; 1863 message to Congress, 138; election of 1861, 265; foreign diplomacy, 223, 225, 234, 255; inauguration of, 83; military appointments of, 266–67; opposition to, xvi–xvii, 263–69, 270, 275–76; relations with Confederate Congress, 262, 264, 265, 267, 269, 274, 276; relations with the press, 81; suspension of habeas corpus, 265, 268–69, 270, 276; Trans-Mississippi department and, 242, 243, 249, 252, 253, 255, 258; vetoes of, 267
Davis, Mrs. Jefferson, 218
Davis, Theodore, 71
Dayton, Oh., 198
Dayton, William Lewis, 222
Dead Rabbits (association), 200
Deer Creek, 163, 164, 165
De Leon, Edwin, 234
Democratic Party, 88, 143, 197, 198, 201, 263, 306, 323; fall campaigns and elections (1862), 18–31; newspapers, 69; secret societies, 24–25; Southern dominance and, 30–31
Denmark, 238
Department of East Tennessee, 3
Department of the Trans-Mississippi, 240–59, 260, 261, 272; Arizona and New Mexico operations, 242–45, 246; guerrilla warfare, 256–58; Indian regiments, 249–50; siege of Vicksburg and, 253–55, 261; territory of, 241–42, 248. See also names of battles
Devil's Den, 118, 122, 123
Dill, Benjamin F., 74, 75, 76
Diplomacy, 53, 222–39; Alexandra affair, 231–32, 235, 237; Confederate shipbuilding and, 225–27, 229, 231–32, 233, 235, 236–38; Erlanger loan fiasco, 231, 235; European armistice proposal, 228–29; Forbes-Aspinwall mission, 230, 231; privateering and, 224–25, 230, 232; Trent affair, 224, 225, 226
Dispatch No. 10 (Seward), 223
District of Arkansas, 242
District of Texas, 242, 251
Dix, Dorothea, 208
Donne, John, 240
Doubleday, General Abner, 42, 97, 118, 119–20
Douglas, Stephen A., 26, 28, 29

Douglas Democrats, 28, 29, 30
Draft riots, 199–205, 214
Drayton, Brigadier General Thomas, 50
Drewry's Bluff, 62
Du Bellet, Paul Pecquet, 234
Du Pont, Flag Officer Samuel F. I., 50, 51, 56–57, 59–62, 63, 64
Dyer's Ford, 282

Eads, James Buchanan, 145
Early, Brigadier General Jubal Anderson, 38–39, 41, 42, 95, 96, 97, 99, 103–4, 114, 115, 119, 125, 317
East Tennessee Railroad, 320
Edisto Island, 54
Edwards, J. D., 83
Egypt, 232, 236, 238
Election of 1860, xiii, 117, 308
Election of 1862, 32; coalition politics, 19–20, 27; emancipation issue, 19, 24, 27–28; fall campaign, 18–31; Negro question, 23, 25; results of, 26–27; secret societies, 24–25
XI Corps (Hooker's), 292
XI Corps (Howard's), 93, 96, 98, 100, 101, 102, 118, 119, 122, 125
XI Corps (Slocum's), 116, 117
11th New York, 203
El Paso, Tex., 244, 245, 246
Ely's Ford, 317
Emancipation Proclamation, ix, xvii, 19, 24, 27–28, 198, 239, 302, 304, 305, 309, 311, 321
Emmitsburg, Md., 115, 116
England. See Great Britain
Enrica (ship), 227
Erlanger loan fiasco, 231, 235
Essex (armor-clad), 145
Evans, Brigadier General Nathan G. "Shanks," 55–56
Ewell, General Richard S. "Old Baldy," 107, 110, 111, 113–14, 115, 118, 119, 120, 121, 124, 126, 127, 317
Ewing, Brigadier General Thomas, Jr., 257

Falmouth, Va., 37, 38, 46, 93
Farnsworth, John, 26
Farragut, Admiral David Glasgow, xviii, 1, 57, 62, 152, 158, 303
Fayetteville, Ga., 139
Federal 1st Texas Cavalry, 272
Fenton, Roger, 82
Ferrero, General Edward, 47
XV Corps (Sherman's), 173, 177, 180, 181, 194, 292
V Corps (Army of the Potomac), 32
V Corps (Meade's), 93, 96, 98, 102, 113
V Corps (Warren's), 123
54th Massachusetts, 66
Firearms industry, 143, 147
1st Alabama Cavalry, 273
1st Arkansas Cavalry, 272
I Corps (Army of Northern Virginia), 92, 127
I Corps (Army of the Potomac), 116, 119, 122, 124
I Corps (Hardee's), 292

I Corps (Longstreet's), 35–36, 38, 107, 231
I Corps (Reynolds'), 93, 102
1st Kentucky "Orphan" Brigade, 1, 2, 7, 10, 12, 13, 193–94, 217–18, 283, 287, 295
First Manassas. *See* Bull Run, First Battle of
1st Rhode Island Volunteer Infantry, 33
Five Nations, 250
Fleetwood Hill. *See* Brandy Station, Battle of
Florence, Ala., 137
Florida (ship), 226, 235, 236
Fontaine, Félix G. de, 78
Food processing and packing industry, 146
Foote, Henry S., 267
Forbes, Edwin, 71
Forbes, John M., 230, 231
Foreign Office (Great Britain), 235
Forrest, General Nathan Bedford, 153, 156, 283, 292, 306
Forsythe, John, 70
Fort Beauregard, 50
Fort Bisland, 253, 254
Fort Bliss, 244
Fort Craig, 244
Fort Donelson, xv, 4, 9, 13, 28, 151, 189, 235, 248, 261, 283
Fort Fillmore, 243–44
Fort Henry, xv, 28, 151, 248, 261
Fort Hill, 181
Fort Monroe, 33
Fort Moultrie, 60, 62, 67
Fort Pemberton, 163, 164
Fort Pillow, xvi
Fort Pulaski, 62
Fort Sanders, 320, 321
Fort Smith, 320
Fort Sumter, xiii, xviii, 42, 135, 140, 143, 151, 243, 261, 319, 321; bombardment of (1861), 78, 79; fall of, 49; Lee at, 51; siege of Charleston and, 51, 56, 60, 61, 63, 66, 67
Fort Union, 245
Fort Wagner, attack on, 63–67, 68
Fort Walker, 50
XIV Corps (Thomas'), 280
Fox, Gustavus V., 52, 53
France, 53, 255; adventure in Mexico, 234–35, 240, 241; diplomacy toward U.S. and Confederacy, 222, 225, 228–29, 231, 232, 234–35, 236
Frankfort, Ky., 302
Frank Leslie's Illustrated Newspaper, 71, 84
Franklin, Benjamin, xi
Franklin, General William Buel, 37, 40, 41, 42, 43, 44, 45, 47
Fraser, Trenholm & Co., 234
Frederick, Md., 111, 115, 116
Fredericksburg, Battle of, 38–45, 46, 47, 48, 81, 85, 89, 91, 105, 113, 160, 261, 317, 321; army strength, 40; casualties, 43, 44, 45; end of, 44–45; at Marye's Heights, 39, 40, 41, 43, 44; Meade's breakthrough, 42; Pelham's battery, 41–42; Rappahannock River crossing, 39, 40–41, 45

Fredericksburg, Va., 36, 37, 38, 39, 41, 93, 94, 95, 96, 97, 103, 107, 111, 219
Freedmen's Savings Bank, 213
Frémont, Major General John Charles, 85, 304, 323
French, Major General William Henry, 43, 314, 316, 317, 318

Galena (ironclad), 62
Gallery Point Lookout, 84
Galveston, Tex., 251–52, 272
Gantt, Colonel Edward W., 305, 310
Gardner, Alexander, 83, 84
Gardner, Major General Franklin, 192–93
Gardner, James, 83, 84
Garfield, General James Abram, 23
General Order No. 8 (Burnside), 47
General Orders No. 10 (Ewing), 257–58
General Orders No. 11 (Ewing), 257–58
General Orders No. 11 (Grant), 155–56
General Price (gunboat), 166, 171
Georgia (ship), 231
Georgia Relief and Hospital Association, 218
Germanna Ford, 317
Getty, George, 44
Gettysburg, Battle of, 116–33, 134, 146, 149, 188, 195, 196, 199, 201, 205, 235, 261, 262, 273, 309, 313, 314, 315, 316, 319, 324; at Big Round Top, 117, 122; casualties, 118, 124, 130; at Cemetery Hill, 117, 118, 119, 120, 121, 125; at Cemetery Ridge, 117, 122, 123, 124, 126, 128–29; Confederate withdrawal, 130, 131–33; at Culp's Hill, 119, 120, 122, 124–25, 126, 127; at Devil's Den, 118, 122, 123; at Little Round Top, 117, 122, 123, 124; at McPherson's Ridge, 117, 118; at Oak Hill, 117, 118; Pickett's Charge, 128–29; reaction to (in the North), 132, 196; reconnaissance operations, 121, 130; "Schimmelfennig's headquarters," 120, 130; at Seminary Ridge, 117, 118, 120, 121, 122, 127, 128, 129
Gettysburg, Pa., 114, 115, 121; Confederate advance toward, 116–17
Gibbon, Brigadier General John, 42, 124–26, 128, 129, 130
Gibraltar, 225, 226
Gibson brothers, 83
Gideonites, 212
Gillmore, Brigadier General Quincy Adams, 62–64, 65–66, 67, 68, 302
Gladstone, William, 228
Glasgow, Ky., 4
Glass's Mill, 282, 283
Gorgas, Colonel Josiah, 138–39, 141, 252
Gould, Jay, 148
Grand Gulf, 170–71, 173, 174, 175, 176, 180, 188, 195
Grand Junction, 152–53, 156, 169, 170, 171
Granger, General Gordon, 280, 282, 284, 288
Graniteville, S.C., 135–36
Grant, Fred, 174
Grant, Jesse, 156
Grant, Jesse Root, 153, 155, 195, 327
Grant, Mrs. Julia, 153, 156, 167, 170, 176

Grant, Lieutenant General Ulysses S., ix, 19, 26, 27, 74, 87, 254, 261, 271, 315, 321; background of, 150–51; Department of the Tennessee command, 150–67, 320; drinking rumors, 160; first military endeavor, 151; General Orders No. 11, 155–56; meeting with Pemberton, 189–90; Mexican War, 189, 327; at Missionary Ridge, 293, 294–95, 296; overall army command, 292, 327; relations with the press, 80; at Shiloh, xv, 4, 151, 158, 248, 292, 325; tent-cloth factory visit, 216; Vicksburg campaign, xvi, xviii, 1, 3, 17, 86, 108, 168–95, 196, 198, 207, 210, 216, 235, 251, 254, 255
Graves, Chief of Artillery Rice E., 289
Great Britain, xii, 53, 146, 202, 240, 308; diplomatic strains with U.S., 223–39; neutrality policy, 223, 232, 238, 239
Greeley, Horace, xvii, 30, 70, 71, 73, 301
Gregg, William, 135–36
Grenada, Miss., 74, 75, 152, 154, 157
Grierson, Colonel Benjamin Henry, 174–75
Griffin, General Charles, 44
Grimke sisters, 206
Griswoldville, Ala., 137
Groveton, Battle of, 107
Guerrilla warfare, 151, 256–58, 280, 305
Gurowski, Adam, 23

Haas and Peale, 83
Habeas corpus, suspension of (in the South), 265, 268–69, 270, 276
Hagood, Brigadier General Johnson, 56
Halleck, General-in-Chief Henry Wagner "Old Brains," 36, 41, 45, 46, 47, 63, 68, 80, 85, 86, 87, 90, 108, 111–12, 113, 151, 152, 153, 154, 155, 157, 159, 160, 162, 170, 171, 175, 176, 179, 180, 182, 183, 187, 190, 195, 256
Hammond, James, 266
Hampton, Frank, 110
Hampton, Major General Wade, ix, xviii, 91, 106, 108, 109, 110, 131, 132, 324
Hampton Legion, xviii, 91, 126, 132
Hampton Roads, 57
Hancock, Major General Winfield Scott, 43, 117; at Gettysburg, 119–20, 121, 122, 123, 124, 125, 129; wounded, 120, 130, 314
Hanover, Pa., 116, 131
Hanson, Brigadier General Roger, 9, 10, 11, 12, 13, 217
Hardee, Major General William Joseph, 9, 10, 11, 13, 16, 242, 279, 292–96, 297
Hard Times, 173
Harpers Ferry, 35, 90, 107, 110, 111, 115
Harper's Weekly Illustrated Newspaper, 71, 84
Harriet Lane (gunboat), 251
Harrisburg, Pa., 113, 114, 115, 116, 300
Harrison, James, 115
Harrisonburg Rockingham Register, 74
Hawes, Richard, 5, 7
Hawthorne, Nathaniel, 206
Haynes' Bluff, 157, 163, 164, 173; Federal capture of, 181
Hazel Grove, 103

Hébert, General Paul Octave, 272
Helena, Ark., 154, 162, 168, 249, 255
Helm, General Ben Hardin, 283, 287, 289
Henry Clay (transport), 172
Herron, General Francis Jay, 250
Heth, General Henry, 118
Hill, General Ambrose Powell, 41, 92, 102, 106, 111, 114, 115, 116, 118, 119, 120, 121, 126, 127, 315–16, 317, 319
Hill, Lieutenant General Daniel Harvey, 279, 281, 283–86, 288, 289, 291, 292
Hilton Head Island, 51, 54, 55, 68
Hindman, Major General Thomas Carmichael, 248–49, 250–53, 257, 281, 283, 289, 291, 292, 298
Hodgers, Jennie, 210
Hogarth, William, 219
Holden, W. W., 275
Holly Springs, 152, 153–54, 155, 156, 157, 158, 167, 169
Holmes, Major General Theophilus Hunter, 249, 252, 253, 255, 324
Homer, Winslow, 71
Hood, Major General John Bell, 39, 40, 122; at Chickamauga, 283, 286, 288, 289; at Gettysburg, 122–23, 130
Hooker, Major General Joseph "Fighting Joe," 32, 34, 37–38, 47–48, 85, 315, 321; at Antietam, 88; Army of the Potomac command, 86–105, 106, 107, 108, 110, 111–12, 114, 133; arrested, 112; attitude toward Lincoln, 89; background of, 86–87; at Chancellorsville, 93–105, 107, 108, 319; first planned offensive, 92–93; Fredericksburg battle, 40, 41, 43–44, 45; at Lookout Mountain, 292–93, 294, 295, 296, 297–98; loss of courage, 96–97, 101, 105; Mexican War, 87; at Missionary Ridge, 293, 294, 295; resignation of, 112; Second Bull Run, 88, 113; sobriquet, 87–88, 90
"Hookers" (prostitutes), 87, 90
Hotze, Henry, 233, 234
Houghton, George W., 83, 84
Howard, General Oliver Otis, 41, 43, 96, 98, 99, 100, 101, 102, 117, 118, 119, 122, 125
Humphreys, Brigadier General Andrew A., 44
Hunt, General Henry Jackson, 40, 123
Hunter, General Davis, 32, 55, 56, 62, 71
Hunterstown, engagement at, 131–33
Huntington, Collis Potter, 148
Huse, Major Caleb, 233–34

Illinois Central Railroad, 33
Impressment, 214, 215, 265, 270
Independence, Mo., guerrilla capture of, 257
Index (newsaper), 233, 234
Indians, 241, 249–50
Indian Territory, 241, 242, 248, 249
Industrial Revolution, 141
Industry and manufacturing, 134–49, 150; in the Confederacy, 134–42, 148, 323; differences in war effort (between North and South), 147; employment, 139, 141; entrepreneurism, 143, 147–48; laborers'

wages, 198; negative impact (in the
North), 148–49; repudiation of
Confederate debts, 143; slave labor,
215–16; strikes, 198, 205, tariffs, 135, 143,
144, 145, 147; women laborers, 198,
205–6, 216. *See also* names of industries
Ingraham, Commodore Duncan, 57, 58–59
Iron industry, 136, 139–41, 142, 143, 144,
147, 148
Italy, 234, 238
Iuka, Miss., 17, 151

Jackson, Andrew, 28, 249, 262, 270
Jackson, Miss., 75, 216; Confederate
evacuation of, 178; Vicksburg campaign
and, 152, 156, 169, 174, 176, 177, 194
Jackson, Lieutenant General Thomas
Jonathan "Stonewall," 35–36, 38, 91, 92,
107–8, 122, 126, 133, 170, 262, 316; at
Chancellorsville, 95–102, 103, 105, 319;
death of, 105, 107, 324; Fredericksburg
battle, 39–40, 42
James, Frank and Jesse, 257
James Island, 54–55, 63; Federal
abandonment of, 56
James River, xiv, 62
Jamestown Colony, xii
Japan (ship), 231
Jasper, Ga., 274
Jayhawkers, 257
Jefferson, Thomas, 30
Jenkins, Brigadier General Albert Gallatin,
111, 114, 115
Jews, xviii, 155–56
Joan of Arc, 209, 210
John's Island, 54
Johnson, Andrew, 32, 299, 304, 306–7
Johnson, Major General Bushrod Rust, 282,
288
Johnson, Major General Edward "Allegeny
Ed," 125, 317–18
Johnston, General Albert Sidney, xv, xvi, 2,
3, 4, 267
Johnston, General Joseph Eggleston, xviii,
138, 177, 178, 183–86, 188, 190, 191, 193,
194, 252, 264, 266, 278, 291, 315, 325,
326, 327
Johnston, Colonel Josiah Stoddard, 1, 16
Jones County, Miss., pro-Union men and
Confederate deserters in, 274

Kelly Field, 286–88
Kelly's Ford, 92, 94, 110, 316
Kendall, George W., 70
Kentucky campaign, 1–8, 12, 17, 18, 21, 25,
81, 145, 151, 169, 218, 252, 302; army
reorganization, 4; capture of Munfordville
garrison, 4, 5; cavalry feints, 6–7;
Confederate withdrawal to Tennessee,
5–6; desertions, 8; end of, 6; summer
maneuvers, 2–3; use of enforced
conscription, 7
Kentucky Relief Association, 218
Keokuk (monitor), 59, 60–61
Key, Francis Scott, 100
Keystone State (ironclad), 58
Kiowa Indians, 241

Kirby-Smith, Lieutenant General Edmund,
3, 4, 5, 177, 327; military and political
power of, 255–56; at Richmond, Ky., 24;
Trans-Mississippi command, 240–43,
252–59, 260, 261, 272, 324–25
Knights of the Golden Circle, 25
Know-Nothings, 271–72
Knoxville, Tenn., 5, 6, 11, 16, 75, 137, 279,
293; Longstreets' campaign to, 319–21,
323
Knoxville *Daily Register,* 75

Lafeyette (ironclad), 171
Lafayette, Tenn., 282, 286, 287, 288
La Grange, Tenn., 153, 174
Laird, John, 231
Laird brothers (firm), 226, 227, 229–30,
231, 232, 236
Laird rams, 229, 233, 235, 236–39, 241
Lake Providence, La., 160, 161, 162
Lake St. Joseph, 170
Lancaster, Pa., 114
Lawrence, Kan., raid of 1863, 258
Leadbetter, Brigadier General Danville, 320
Leather industry, 145, 147
Lebanon Pike, 9–10
Lee, Brigadier General Fitzhugh, 92, 98
Lee, General Robert Edward, xiv, 17,
35–36, 37, 38, 89, 90, 91, 92–93, 106, 142,
159, 195, 241, 249, 266, 267, 273, 276,
279, 282, 325, 327; at Antietam, 35, 132,
279; army reorganization, 91, 107, 314; at
Bristoe, 315–16; Burnside's "Mud March"
and, 46; at Chancellorsville, 93–105, 289,
321; in Charleston, 51, 53, 54;
Fredericksburg battle, 38–43, 45;
Gettysburg battle, 116–30, 131, 134, 149,
188, 196, 313, 319, 321; "if practicable"
orders of, 120, 124; invasion of the
North, xiv, 21, 34, 35, 106–33, 321;
Meade's pursuit (after Gettysburg),
132–33; Mexican War, 327; use of
Northern newspapers, 80; in the
Wilderness, 316–19; withdrawal from
Gettysburg, 130, 131–33, 313–14
Lee, Mrs. Robert Edward, 218
Lee and Gordon's Mills, 282, 283–84, 285
Lee County, Va., pro-Unionism in, 275
Left Grand Division, 40
Lewis, Colonel Joseph, 287
Lexington, Ky., 4, 5, 69, 219
Lexington, Mo., 242
Lexington *Kentucky Statesman,* 69, 70
Lincoln, Abraham, xi, xiv, xv, xvi, xvii,
xviii, xix, 9, 32, 33, 36, 45–46, 47, 48, 117,
202, 208, 219, 261, 266, 271, 292, 298,
319, 322–23, 326–27; coalition politics,
19–20, 27; and conscription, 199; Cooper
Union speech, 85; election of 1860, xiii,
22; fall campaigns and (1862), 18–31,
198; foreign diplomacy, 222, 223, 224,
228, 229, 230; Hooker's command and,
86, 87, 88–89, 90, 93, 100, 105, 106–7,
108, 110, 111, 112; judgment of men, 47;
and Meade's pursuit of Lee, 132, 133;
reaction to Chancellorsville, 105;
reconstruction program, 299–312;

relations with the press, 78–79, 84–85; siege of Charleston and, 49–50, 52, 53, 62, 67; Vicksburg campaign and, 170, 195; and War in the West, 152, 155, 158, 159, 160, 161; wartime industry and, 148–49
Lincoln, Mrs. Mary Todd, 219
Linn, R. M., 84
Little Rock, Ark., 249, 251, 252, 306
Little Round Top, 117, 122, 123, 124
Liverpool, England, 225, 227, 231, 235, 236
Logan, Brigadier General John Alexander, 28–29, 179
London *Times,* 71, 78
Long, Colonel Armistead L., 98–99
Longstreet, Lieutenant General James "Old Pete," 35–36, 37, 38, 92, 107, 114, 115, 291, 310, 316; campaign to Knoxville, 319–21, 323; at Chickamauga, 279, 282, 284, 286–88, 289, 315, 319; Fredericksburg battle, 38, 39, 41, 42, 43; at Gettysburg, 121–29, 132; Lookout Mountain reconnaissance, 292–93; Mexican War, 127; at Missionary Ridge, 293; promoted, 325
Lookout Mountain, 84, 290, 292–93. *See also* Missionary Ridge
Lookout Mountain, Battle of, 294, 296, 297–98
Loudon, Tenn., 279
Loughborough, Mary, 184, 185
Louisville (gunboat), 164, 171
Louisville *Journal,* 70
Lovejoy, Elijah, 18
Lovejoy, Owen, x, xviii, 18, 19, 21, 22, 25–26, 300
Lowell, Mass., 136
Lumber industry, 142
Lynchburg, Va., 137
Lyon, Brigadier General Nathaniel, 242

McClanahan, Colonel John, 74, 75, 76
McClellan, Major General George Brinton "Little Mac," xvi, 80, 85, 87, 114, 122, 126, 154, 316, 323; Antietam battle, xiv–xv, xvii, 21; campaign failures, xiv, 75; removed from command, xv, 32, 34, 36; in Virginia, 19, 20, 21, 26, 27, 28, 33, 34–35, 36, 75, 177, 218
McClelland, Robert, 205–6
McClernand, Major General John Alexander, 28, 30, 154–60, 161, 170–74, 176, 178–81, 182, 183, 266, 324, 326
McCook, Major General Alexander McDowell, 280–82, 286, 288
McCook, Charles, 280
McCook, Daniel, 280
McCook, Brigadier General Daniel, 280
McCook, Colonel Edwin, 280
McCook, George, 280
McCook, Brigadier General Robert, 280
McCormick, Cyrus, 143
McCulloch, General Ben, 246, 247, 258
McCulloch, General Henry, 258
McDowell, Major General Irvin, 33, 34, 37, 79
McIntyre, A. C., 83
Mackall, General W. W., 14

McLaws, Major General Lafayette, 43, 104
McLemore's Cove, 281, 282
Macon, Ga., 137, 139
McPherson, Major General James Birdseye, 160, 161, 162, 173, 174, 176, 177–82
McPherson and Oliver, 83
McPherson's Ridge, 117, 118
Maffitt, Captain John Newland, 226
Maffitt's Channel, 53
Magoffin, Beriah, 301
Magruder, General John Bankhead, 249, 251, 252–53
Mallory, Stephen Russell, 139, 140, 225, 226, 229, 230, 231
Malvern Hill, Battle of, 104
Manassas. *See* Bull Run, First Battle of; Second Battle of
Manassas Gap, 314–15
Marmaduke, General John Sappington, 251
Marye's Heights, 39, 40, 41, 43, 44, 95, 103
Mason, James Murray, 53, 223–24, 231, 234
Mason and Dixon's line, xii, 136, 322
Maximilian, Archduke, 228
Meade, Major General George Gordon, 34, 86; Army of the Potomac command, 112–33, 313–19; background of, 112; at Bristoe Station, 315–16; at Chancellorsville, 96, 97, 98, 102, 103, 104, 113; Fredericksburg battle, 41, 42, 113, 317; at Gettysburg, 116–30, 134, 149, 188, 313, 314, 316; at Manassas Gap, 314–15; Mexican War, 112; pursuit of Lee (after Gettysburg), 132–33, 313–14; in the Wilderness, 316–19
Meat packing industry, 148
Mechanicsburg, Pa., 114
Meigs, Quartermaster General Montgomery Cunningham, 33, 146
Melville, Herman, 205
Memphis, Tenn., 151, 154, 156, 157, 160; surrender of, 74
Memphis *Appeal,* 74–76, 218
Mercedita (ship), 58
Meridian, Miss., 75, 326
Merrimack (ironclad), 140
Mesilla, N.M., 244
Mesilla Valley, 243
Mexican War, xii, 16, 33, 51, 69, 82, 87, 112, 127, 248, 327
Mexico, French protectorate in, 234–35, 240, 241
Middleburg, Va., 116; engagement at, 114
Milliken's Bend, 157, 159, 170, 171
Mill Springs, Battle of, xvi, 280
Milroy, General Robert Huston, 110
Mine Run, 317–18
Missionary Ridge, 281, 290, 292–98, 306, 321, 324, 325; Confederate retreat from, 296–98; at Tunnel Hill, 293–94, 295. *See also* Lookout Mountain, Battle of
Mississippi Central Railroad, 152, 160, 175
Missouri River, 242
Mobile, Ala., 3, 75, 226, 233
Mobile *Register,* 70
Monitor (ironclad), 57, 59, 62
Monroe Doctrine, 238, 241

Montauk (monitor), 59
Montgomery, Ala., 75, 76, 83, 261, 265
Montgomery County, Va., pro-Unionism in, 276
Mook Lake, 162
Moore, Frank, 72
Morgan, John Hunt, 2, 7
Mormons, 243
Morrill, Justin Smith, 144, 145
Morris Island, 56, 60, 63, 64, 65, 66, 68
Morrisville, Va., 92
Morton, Miss., 195
Morton, Oliver Perry, 23–24, 25
Mott, Lucretia, 206
Mound City (gunboat), 164, 171
Mound City, Ill., 145
"Mud March" of 1863, 46–47, 89
Munford, Colonel Thomas T., 101
Munfordville garrison, 4, 5
Murfreesboro, Tenn., 6, 7, 9, 11, 290. *See also* Stones River, Battle of

Nahant (monitor), 59, 61
Nantucket (monitor), 59, 61
Napoleon III, Emperor, 228, 229, 235, 238, 240, 241
Nashville, Tenn., 70, 220, 290, 326
Nashville Pike, 9
Nassau, 59, 225–26
Natchez, Miss., 161
Nelson, General William, 24
New Bern, N.C., 33
New Carthage, 172–73
New Ironsides (ironclad), 59, 60, 63
New Orleans, xvi, xviii, 83, 90, 136, 137, 151, 170, 174, 211, 219, 220, 303–4
New Orleans *Picayune,* 70
Newspapers, 68–85, 198, 233; arrest of war correspondents, 68; associations, 73, 81; censorship, 80–82; in the Confederacy, 73–78, 81–82, 266, 308; editorials, 69, 79; "extras," 73; growth of, 72; headlines, 73; Lincoln and, 78–79, 84–85; *noms de plume,* 71; pseudonyms, 78; strikes, 76; Sunday editions, 73; War Department (U.S.) and, 79, 80
Newton, General John, 47, 124
Newtonia, Mo., Federal attack at, 250
Newton Station, 174
New York Associated Press, 70, 73
New York *Courier and Enquirer,* 87
New York Draft Riots, 199–205
New York *Evening Post,* 70
New York *Herald,* 70, 72, 78, 208
New York *Illustrated News,* 84
New York *Times,* 70, 73, 80
New York *Tribune,* 70, 71, 73
Niggerheads, 300
Nightingale, Florence, 208, 209
95th Illinois, 210
IX Corps (Army of the Potomac), 44, 320
IX Corps (Department of the Tennessee), 194
Niter and Mining Bureau, 139
North Edisto Island, 59

Oak Hill, 117, 118

O'Brien, Colonel Henry, 203, 204
Oil City, Pa., 146
Oil industry, 143, 146, 148
Old Dominion Nail Works, 136
Orange & Alexandria Railroad, 36, 315, 316
Orange Court House, 317
Orange Turnpike, 96, 98
Orchard Knob, 294
Ord, Major General Edward Otho Cresap, 182
Order of the Heroes of America, 271–72, 275–76
Ordnance Department (Confederate States of America), 138
Oreto (ship), 225–26, 232
Orphanages, 212
Orphan Brigade. *See* 1st Kentucky
Osborn and Durbec, 83, 84
O'Sullivan, Timothy, 83, 84
Owens, Mary, 210
Oxford, Miss., 154, 156
Oyster's Point, 114

Palmerston, Lord, 231
Palmetto State (ironclad), 56, 58, 216
Passaic (monitor), 59, 61
Patapsco (monitor), 59, 61
Patent Office, 206
Peace and Constitutional Society, 271, 272
Peace Democrats, 29, 30
Peace Society, 271, 273–74
Pea Ridge, Ark., 249
Pea Ridge, Battle of, 247–48, 250, 261, 305
Pearson, Frank, 131
Pelham, Major John, 40, 41–42, 91–92
Pemberton, Lieutenant General John Clifford, 54, 56, 152, 154, 157, 158, 160, 161, 253, 254, 291, 324; defense of Vicksburg, 56, 169, 170, 173–91, 193, 255, 273; meeting with Grant, 189–90; retreat to Jackson, 194, 195
Pender, General William Dorsey, 118
Pennsylvania Railroad, 144
Pensacola, Fla., 83
Perryville, Battle of, 18, 27, 28, 31, 48, 261
Petersburg, Va., 137
Phelps, John Smith, 306
Philadelphia Associated Press, 73
Photographers, 82–84
Pickens, Francis W., 51, 54
Pickett, Major General George Edward, 39, 126, 127, 128–29
Pickett's Charge, 128–29
Pierce, Franklin, 29, 31, 323
Pierpont, Francis Harrison, 307
Pigeon Mountain, 281, 282, 296
Pike, Brigadier General Albert, 250
Pillow, General Gideon, 13, 15, 16
Pillsbury, Charles Alfred, 148
Pittsburgh (gunboat), 164, 171
Pittsburgh, Pa., 142, 145
Planter (cotton steamer), 54
Pleasonton, Brigadier General Alfred, 44, 108–10, 114
Pocahontas (ship), 50
Polk, Lieutenant General Leonidas, 5, 9, 10, 11, 279, 281–89, 291, 292

Pollard, Edward A., 71, 265
Pope, General John, xiv, 21, 34, 35, 90, 316
Porter, Admiral David Dixon, 157–66, 167, 171–72, 173, 175, 181–82, 183, 184, 188, 190, 254
Porter, General Fitz-John, 32
Port Gibson, Battle of, 174
Port Hudson, La., 1–2, 151, 152, 161, 169, 170, 174, 175–76, 191–93, 253, 254, 255, 261, 273, 304–5, 315
Port Royal, S.C., 54, 59, 212; capture of, 50–51
Port Royal, Va., 39, 41
Port Royal Sound, 50
Post Office Department (Confederate States of America), 262
Potomac River, 35, 111, 114, 115, 121, 130, 133, 316
Powell, Lazarus W., 301
Prairie Grove, Battle of, xvi, 250–51
Preliminary Emancipation Proclamation, 21–22, 26
Prentice, George D., 70
Preston, Brigadier General William, 7, 9, 12
Price, General Sterling, 17, 151, 242, 246, 247, 248
Prince, Brigadier General Henry, 317, 318
Privateering, 224–25, 230, 232
Privateering Act (U.S.), 230
"Proclamation of Amnesty and Reconstruction" (Lincoln), 308–12, 326
Prostitutes, 87, 90, 211, 212, 217
Providence, R.I., 144
Pulaski County, Va., pro-Unionism in, 276
Pullman, Ill., 136
Putnam, Colonel Haldimand, 66

Quaker City (ironclad), 58
Quaker guns, 251
Quakers, 207
Quantrill, William Clarke, 257–58
Quinby, Brigadier General Isaac Ferdinand, 163, 164, 165

Radical Republicans, 18, 19, 21, 22, 23, 26, 29, 88, 89–90, 106, 300, 311, 316
Railroads, 3, 141, 143, 144, 147, 148, 279; track gauges (in the South), 136–37
Rains, George W., 139
Raleigh Standard, 275
Randolph, Wythe, 264
Rapidan River, 315, 317, 318, 319
Rappahannock Bridge, 316
Rappahannock River, 36, 37, 38, 39, 41, 46, 48, 90, 91, 92, 93, 94, 96, 98, 101, 102, 104, 105, 106, 107, 108, 314, 315, 316
Raymond, Battle of, 177–78
Raymond, Henry, 70
Reagan, John Henninger, xviii, 260, 262, 264, 276
Rebellion Record (Moore), 72
Reconstruction program, 299–312; amnesty question, 308–10; in Arkansas, 305–6, 311; in the border states, 301–3, 304; debate over, 299–301, 307–8, 311; Emancipation Proclamation and, 302, 304, 305, 309, 311; Lincoln's proclamation,

308–12, 326; in Louisiana, 303–5, 311; newspaper reactions, 300, 310; oath of allegiance, 308, 309; Radical Republicans and, 300, 311; in Tennessee, 299, 304, 306–7, 311; in Virginia, 307
Rector, Henry Massey, 272
Red River, 161, 272
Red River expedition, 176, 191, 253–54
Red River Valley, 254
Republican Party, xiv, 197, 198, 323; fall campaigns and elections (1862), 18–31; founded, 18; newspapers, 69; secret societies, 24–25; wartime industry and, 143, 148
Resaca, Ga., 280
Reserve Corps, 281, 283
Reynolds, Major General John Fulton, 42, 86, 102, 103, 112, 113, 116–17, 118
Rhett, Robert Barnwell, xvii, xviii, 266
Rhode Island (ship), 59
Richmond, Fredericksburg, & Potomac Railroad, 39
Richmond, Ky., battle at, 24
Richmond, Va., xiv, 2, 11, 36, 110, 216, 217, 218, 257, 261, 314, 319, 324, 327; food riots, 214; industry and manufacturing, 136, 137, 139–41; newspaper publishing, 70–71, 78, 81; refugee problem, 220
Richmond Dispatch, 70, 71
Richmond Enquirer, 70, 71
Richmond Examiner, 70, 71, 77, 78
Richmond Sentinel, 70
Richmond Whig, 70, 82
Ringgold, Ga., 296
Rio Grande, 241, 244, 245, 246, 251
Ripley, Brigadier General Roswell S., 54
Rives, William Cabell, 267
Roanoke Island, 33
Roanoke Valley Railroad, 137
Robertson, Captain Felix, 12–13, 14, 15, 16
Robinson, James F., 302
Rockefeller, John Davison, 147–48
Rockville, Md., 130–31
Rodes, General Robert Emmett, 114
Roebuck, John, 235, 239
Rolling Fork, 164, 165
Rome, Ga., 281
Rosecrans, Major General William Starke "Old Rosey," 6, 8–13, 16–17, 47, 191, 211, 293, 306, 315, 326; Army of the Cumberland command, 278–90, 323–24; at Chickamauga, 278–81, 282–84, 286, 288, 289, 290; relieved of command in Chattanooga, 292; Stones River battle, 86
Ross, Brigadier General Leonard, 163, 164, 165
Rost, Pierre Adolphe, 234
Roundaway Bayou, 170, 172
Round Forest (or "Hell's Half Acre"), 10
Ruffin, Edmund, x, xviii
Russell, Captain A. J., 83
Russell, Lord John, 223–25, 227–30, 232, 235–39, 240
Russell County, Va., pro-Unionism in, 275
Russellville, Tenn., 321
Russia, 228, 234

Sabine City, 251
Sabine Pass, 251–52
Sabine Pass, Battle of, 251
Sacramento *Union,* 78
Salem Church, 104
Salisbury, N.C., 139
San Antonio, Tex., 243, 246
Santa Fe, N.M., 243, 244, 245
Savannah, Ga., 50, 52, 62, 63
Savannah *Republican,* 310
Schenck, General Robert Cumming, 23, 30
Schimmelfennig, Brigadier General
    Alexander, 120, 130
Schofield, Major General John McAllister,
    250
Schurz, Major General Carl, 27, 87, 118–19,
    125
Scott, General-in-Chief Winfield, 16, 79, 87,
    301, 326
Seabrook Island, 54
Secession, xvii, 20, 52, 71, 91, 214, 242, 261,
    262, 266, 267, 270, 274, 275, 300, 301,
    305, 306, 322
Secessionville, 55, 56
II Corps (Army of Northern Virginia), 95,
    97, 100, 102, 106, 316, 317
II Corps (Breckinridge's), 292
II Corps (Couch's), 98
II Corps (Hancock's), 122, 124, 125 26
II Corps (Jackson's), 35, 92, 106, 107
II Corps (Warren's), 316, 317, 318
Second Manassas. *See* Bull Run, Second
    Battle of
2nd Michigan Infantry, 210
Second Street Armory (New York City),
    202
Seddon James A., 253, 264, 266
Sedgwick, Major General John, 93, 94, 95,
    96–97, 98, 99, 100, 103, 104, 113, 121,
    127, 317, 318
Seelye, Sarah, 210
Selma, Ala., 137, 139
Seminary Ridge, 117, 118, 120, 121, 122,
    127, 128, 129
Seminole Indians, 249–50
Seminole War, 243
Semmes, Captain Raphael, 225, 226, 227
Seven Days battles, xiv, 33, 210, 249, 261
XVII Corps (McPherson's), 160, 161, 173
XVII Corps (Sherman's), 292
7th Michigan, 40
7th New York, 204
Seward, William Henry, 20, 22, 53, 223,
    230, 235, 236–37, 300, 307
Seymour, Horatio, 26, 203
Seymour, Brigadier General Truman, 65, 66
Shaw, Colonel Robert G., 66
Seymour, Brigadier General Truman, 65, 66
Shaw, Colonel Robert G., 66
Shenandoah Valley, 35, 90, 97, 107, 108,
    110, 111, 115, 170, 314
Shepley, George F., 304
Sheridan, Major General Philip Henry,
    325–26
Sherman, Brigadier General Thomas W.,
    50–51
Sherman, Major General William

Tecumseh, xiii, 87, 257, 292, 326, 327;
    Arkansas Post expedition, 158–59; at
    Chickasaw Bluffs, 157, 162, 326;
    Department of the Tennessee operations,
    154–59, 160, 162, 164–65, 166; at Jackson,
    Miss., 194–95; loathing of the press, 80;
    at Missionary Ridge, 293, 295; tent-cloth
    factory visit, 216; Vicksburg campaign,
    171–74, 176, 178, 180–81, 182, 183,
    194–95, 196, 216
Shiloh, Battle of, xv, 1, 2, 4, 74, 80, 151,
    158, 195, 210, 235, 248, 261, 292, 325
Shoe business, 139, 145, 147
Shreveport, La., 240, 252
Sibley, Brigadier General Henry Hopkins,
    243–46, 247, 251
Sickles, Major General Daniel Edgar, 96,
    100, 102–3, 119, 120, 122–25, 126, 314,
    324
Sigel, Major General Franz, 266
Singer, Isaac, 143
VI Corps (Army of the Potomac), 93, 318
VI Corps (Sedgwick's), 121
6th Kentucky Brigade, 8
65th New York, 204
Skinker's Neck, 38–39, 40, 94
Slavery, xii, xiii, xiv, xviii, 19, 21, 24, 30,
    135, 206, 215–16, 241, 256, 270
Slidell, John, 53, 224, 232, 234 35, 238, 240,
    241, 255
Slocum, Major General Henry, 96, 98, 103,
    113, 117, 119, 120, 122, 124, 126, 127
Smalls, Robert, 54
Smith, Major General Andrew Jackson, 189
Smith, General Gustavus Woodson, 249,
    252, 253, 254, 255, 264
Smith, General William F., 47
Snodgrass Hill, 282, 285, 286
South America, 145, 308
Southern Associated Press, 73
Southern Illustrated News, 71
Spain, 228
Sporting Hill, Battle of, 115
Stafford Heights, 39, 40, 95
Standard Oil Company of Ohio, 148
Stanton, Edwin M., 45, 46, 86, 89, 100, 112
Steele, General Frederick, 306
Steele's Bayou, 163, 164, 170
Steel industry, 143, 147, 148
Stephens, Alexander Hamilton, xviii,
    263–65, 267, 268–69, 276, 307
Stephens, Linton, 268
Stevens, General Isaac I., 55
Stevens, Thaddeus, 23, 300, 301
Stevenson, Major General Carter Littlepage,
    184
Stewart, Alexander Peter, 292
Stone Fleet, 52
Stoneman, General George, 89, 93, 94, 98
Stones River, Battle of, 9–17, 28, 31, 47, 81,
    195, 217, 261, 286, 291, 298, 306, 325;
    casualties, 12, 14, 15; at "Hell's Half
    Acre," 10; January 2 attack order, 12–13,
    14, 15; Lebanon Road problem, 9, 10;
    report to Richmond, 13–17; results of,
    16–17; Wayne's Hill front, 9, 10, 11
Stono Inlet, 54

Stowe, Harriet Beecher, 206
Streight, Colonel Abel D., 273–74
Strong, Brigadier General George C., 64, 66
Strong, George Templeton, 204, 207
Strother, Colonel David H., 71
Stuart, General James Ewell Brown "Jeb,"
   35, 38, 91–92, 106, 174, 324; Aldie,
   Middleburg, and Upperville engagements,
   114; Brandy Station battle, 108–10, 114,
   132; at Chancellorsville, 94, 98, 101, 102,
   103; First Manassas, 91; Fredericksburg
   battle, 40, 41, 42; invasion of the North
   and, 114, 115, 116, 119, 120, 122, 126,
   130–32; Rockville, Md., expedition,
   130–31
Sturgis, General Samuel D., 47
Sugar Creek, 247
Sullivan's Island, 60, 66
Sumner, Charles, xvii, 22, 300, 301, 307,
   308
Sumner, General Edwin Voss, 37, 38, 40,
   41, 43, 44, 45, 47
Sumter (commerce raider), 225, 226
Sunflower River, 163–64, 165
Susquehanna River, 113, 114, 115

Tabernacle Church, 96, 97
Tallahatchie River, 162, 163
Taneytown, Md., 121
Taylor, Major General Richard, 252–53,
   254–55
Taylor, Zachary, 252–53
Tennessee River, xv, 151, 279, 292, 294
Tennessee Valley, 84
Tensas River, 161
Texas Rangers, 241
Textile industry, 135, 142, 143–44, 253
III Corps (Army of Northern Virginia), 95,
   317
III Corps (Army of the Potomac), 32, 93,
   96, 116
III Corps (French's), 314, 316
III Corps (Hill's), 107
III Corps (Longstreet's), 292
III Corps (Sickles'), 100, 102–3, 122, 123,
   124, 125, 314
III Corps (Slocum's), 117, 120, 124
3rd Louisiana, 185, 187
XIII Corps (McClernand's), 159, 177, 182,
   194
Thomas, Major General George Henry
   "Rock of Chickamauga," xv–xvi, 280–83,
   286, 287–89, 292, 293, 294, 295, 296, 326
Tigress (headquarters boat), 158
Titusville, Pa., 146
Tobacco industry, 136
Todd, Elodie, 219
Todd, George, 256
Toledo, Oh., riots of 1862, 23
Tompkins, Sally, 217
Toombs, Robert Augustus, 263–64, 267,
   268, 269, 277
Trans-Mississippi District, 246
Tredegar Iron Works, 136, 139–41, 142,
   144; pig iron production (1863), 142;
   War Department partnership, 141
Trenholm, George A., 234

Trent affair, 224, 225, 226
Truth, Sojourner, 206
Tubman, Harriet, 206
Tucson, Ariz., 243, 246
Tullahoma, 6, 13, 14, 16, 320
Tunnard, Sergeant Willie, 185, 187, 188, 190
Tunnel Hill, 293–94, 295
Tupelo, Miss., 2, 3
Turkey, 238
12th Arkansas, 305
XII Corps (Army of the Potomac), 122
XII Corps (Hooker's), 292
XII Corps (Slocum's), 93, 96, 98
XX Corps (Crittenden's), 280, 282
XX Corps (McCook's), 280
21st Illinois, 151
26th North Carolina, 217
XXIII Corps (Army of the Cumberland),
   320
290 (or C.S.S. Alabama). See Alabama
   (ship)
Tyner's Station, 279

Uncle Tom's Cabin (Stowe), 206
Union Church, Miss., 175
Union Loyal League, 272
Union Steam Works, 203
United States Christian Commission,
   207–8, 211
U.S. Constitution, xv, 20, 30, 270, 309
United States Sanitary Commission, 207–8,
   211, 218
Upperville, Va., engagement at, 114
Utah, 243

Vallandigham, Clement Laird, 20, 29–30,
   198
Valverde, Battle of, 244, 246
Van Buren, Ark., 248
Vance, Zebulon Baird, 268, 275
Vanderbilt, Cornelius, 148
Van Dorn, Major General Earl, 1, 3, 5, 6,
   17, 82, 151, 152, 156, 157, 168, 169, 242,
   246–48
Vatican, 234
Velazquez, Loretta (Captain Harry
   Buford), 217
Vick, Reverend Newitt, 168
Vicksburg, Miss., 167
Vicksburg, siege of, xvi, 1, 3, 17, 56, 57, 75,
   86, 108, 168–95, 198, 199, 201, 207, 210,
   216, 235, 240, 241, 252, 253, 261, 262,
   273, 278, 279, 305, 309, 315, 320, 321,
   326; capture of Port Gibson, 174, 191–93;
   casualties, 175, 179, 186; Champion's Hill
   position, 178–79; conditions in the city,
   184–85, 187; Confederate morale, 186;
   food shortages, 185–86, 187; at Grand
   Gulf, 170–71, 173, 174, 175, 176, 180,
   188, 195; Grant's expedition toward,
   150–67; Grierson's raids and, 174–75;
   gunboat bombardments, 182, 184, 185,
   187; at Jackson, Miss., 194–95;
   reconnaissances, 176; shellings, 184–85,
   186; surrender of the city, 190, 192, 194;
   terms of surrender, 189–90;

Trans-Mississippi department and, 253–55, 261; truce, 185, 188–89
Vicksburg & Jackson Railroad, 177, 194
Vicksburg *Citizen,* 186
Victoria, Queen, 223, 239
Virginia (ironclad), 57, 140, 229
Virginia (ship), 231
Virginia Military Institute, 101

Wade, Benjamin, 20, 23
Wadsworth, General James S., 26, 118
Walker, General William Henry Talbot, 281–84, 286–88, 289, 292
Wall's Bridge, Battle of, 175
War Democrats, 19, 20, 24, 26, 30, 100, 306
War Department (Confederate States of America), 4, 6, 14, 17, 51, 138, 139, 140, 141, 190–91, 214, 248, 253, 291
War Department (U.S.), 34, 37, 79, 80, 83, 144, 147, 151, 159–60
Warren, General Gouverneur Kemble, 123, 125, 129, 316, 317, 318
Warrenton, Va., 35
Wartmann, John, 74
Washburne, Elihu, 26
Washington, George, 262
Washington Arsenal, 147
Washington County, Va., pro-Unionism in, 276
Washita River, 161
Watie, Brigadier General Stand, 250
Waud, Alfred R., 71
Wayne's Hill, 9, 10, 11
Weehawken (monitor), 59, 60
Welles, Gideon, 52, 53, 59, 62, 79, 230
Western & Atlantic Railroad, 279
Western Associated Press, 73
West Virginia, 270, 307
Whaling industry, 146
Wheeler, Major General Joseph, 279, 280
Wheeling, West Va., 307
Whig *Observer & Reporter,* 69
Whig Party, 69, 143, 263
Widow Glenn's, 286
Wigfall, Louis T., 264, 266, 267
Wilcox, Brigadier General Cadmus, 104

Wilder, Colonel John Thomas, 4
Wilderness, the, 94, 96, 98, 99, 105, 316–19
Wilderness Tavern, 99
Wilkes, Commander Charles, 224
Williams, General Robert, 55
Williams, General Thomas, 160
Williams' Bridge, 175
Wilmington, N.C., 50
Wilson, Fanny, 210
Wilson, Lieutenant Colonel James Harrison, 162–63
Wilson's Creek, Battle of, 242, 250, 261
Winchester, Battle of, 110, 113
Wise County, Va., pro-Unionism in, 275
Women, 196–221; abolitionists, 206; aid and relief societies, 207–8, 211–12, 218; in the army, 208–11, 217; attitude toward Yankees, 220; class barriers and, 220–21; in education, 212–13; in employment, 198, 205–6, 216; food riots, 214; as nurses, 208, 209, 210, 216–17; orphanage work, 212; prostitutes, 211, 212, 217; as refugees, 218–20; in the South, 213–21; *vivandières,* 209
Woodbury, Brigadier General Daniel Phineas, 40, 41
Wool industry, 144, 145
Wright, Major General Horatio Gouverneur, 55, 302
Wrightsville, Pa., 114

Yalobusha River, 154
Yancey, William Lowndes, xvii, xviii, 262, 267, 274
Yazoo Bluffs, 173
Yazoo Pass, 162, 163, 165
Yazoo River, 157, 163, 164, 166, 168, 169, 170, 171, 181, 255
Yellow fever, 169, 211
York, Pa., 114, 115, 116, 119
York River, xiv
Yorktown, siege at, xiv
Younger, Cole, 257
Young Men's Christian Associations, 211, 218